Five Parishes
Their People and Places

A History of the Villages of Castor, Ailsworth, Marholm with Milton, Upton and Sutton

By the CAMUS Project

Published by the CAMUS Project, The Rectory, Castor, Peterborough, PE5 7AU, United Kingdom

All sales and distribution inquiries to The Rectory, Castor, Peterborough, PE5 7AU, United Kingdom

Printed by Stylaprint, Ailsworth, Peterborough.

ISBN 0-9547881-0-9 (Hardback)
ISBN 0-9547881-1-7 (Paperback)

This book has been produced with assistance from the Heritage Lottery Fund.

Cover design by Bev Rigby, using a map of 1828 by ET Artis as the background.

Ordnance Survey map reproduced by kind permission Crown Copyright

THE CAMUS PROJECT

Local Heritage *initiative*

Heritage Lottery Fund   Nationwide   The Countryside Agency

FOREWORD
– Sir Stephen Hastings

The CAMUS Project is a collection of personal reminiscence, record and research about a group of five English villages on the borders of Northamptonshire and Cambridgeshire. It may be unique: for it is compiled not from external research by questing academics or historians but, in their own words, by the people of these rural communities themselves. Several of them farm the same land their grandfathers did; some may trace their presence back to the Domesday Book. It tells of their history, their architecture, their way of living and their means of livelihood from the coming of the Romans until the edge of living memory.

Tenant farmers many were, and still are: first of the Abbey of Medehamsted (now Peterborough); later of the Fitzwilliam family, whose progenitor, Sir William, stapler of Calais and client of Cardinal Wolsey, purchased the estate of Milton in 1502. Milton has remained in the ownership of this family ever since and their benign influence still forms much of the background of life in these Parishes. As with many great rural estates, the story of Milton would be incomplete without a note on the Fitzwilliam Foxhounds, one of only four private Packs still left in the country. Kennelled at Milton, an account of their Masterships, Huntsmen and coverts provides a vivid impression of how from the early 18th century until the present day, hunting has been woven into the fabric of country life. The church bells are rung by willing hands, today, when hounds meet on Castor village green.

Through these pages we trace the changes in shape and method of farming, from the excavation of a Roman holding through the open field system of ridge and furrow, to the Enclosures of the late 19th century and on to the age of the combine harvester. Here are recalled the very names of the last teams of working horses; splendid Percherons and Shires, and of the fields they ploughed. The rattle of the milk pails in the early morning was still greeted in these villages as late as the 1950s.

The section on the Parish records makes compelling reading. Not simply for the pattern and identity of birth, death and marriage, historically significant though some were, but as a social study. The Parish system was used 'to administer nearly all local matters' including the Muster rolls, Tithe rolls and the Poor Law. 'Bastardy' for instance, and the care of illegitimate children, was a matter for the Parish. It seems to have been dealt with fairly, practically and with humanity – the fathers' responsibility generally established and admitted – be he married parishioner, village doctor, or even Abbot! A useful example perhaps for those responsible for these matters in our cities today.

We learn the names of those villagers called to the service of their country, from the indentured archers and billhook men on the Muster rolls of the parishes in Henry VIII's reign, to the long rolls of honour from the two great wars of the 20th century.

Thus, from their Celtic ancestors to the coming of Rome; from the earliest Anglo Saxon settlements through the ferocious Danish raids; from the establishment of Ecclesiastical administration and the power of the Great Abbey, to the Dissolution and the arrival of the Tudor dynasties; from the depredation of Cromwell's puritans to the Restoration; here is the testimony of Peer, Parson, Ploughman and Poacher. It is the veritable story of the centuries in a corner of the heart of England.

But for all their sense of history and heredity, there is no static nostalgia here. The authors of these essays and the population of these villages represent a vital and energetic community. The integrity of life has held against the assaults of time and the King's enemies. In the age of television and computer, Sunday worship is still normal and the bonds which have linked folk for generations remain. People look after each other in these villages and respect their monuments and their institutions. Here is the evidence to prove it.

Apart from its great intrinsic interest the CAMUS Project is of public importance and deserves to be widely read. The authors are too numerous to mention here but they deserve our profound thanks and congratulations. Finally, no praise is too high for the Editor, The Rev William Burke, Rector of these Parishes, who promoted and organised the whole enterprise, as well as contributing four fascinating chapters himself.

Stephen Hastings

CONTENTS

GENERAL MAPS
1xA3 1:25000, Whole of Benefice (Map in colour section)
5xA4 1:10000, Village Centres in Village History Chapters
Roman Roads, 1:50000 Map in Chapter 2

THE CAMUS PROJECT

The CAMUS Project (named after Castor, Ailsworth, Marholm, Milton, Upton and Sutton) grew out of the Castor Parish Church Archive Group, which was concerned with researching, collecting and indexing material about the history of the five villages and Milton estate. In 2002 a group from the villages agreed to write a book and to put all the archives and material collected, including the parish registers, on to a web-site, to make the information more widely available and ensure its survival. The project was awarded a Local Heritage Initiative Grant by the Heritage Lottery Fund. The web-site has now been established (www.thearchive.org.uk) and the lengthy process of transferring material onto the web has started. This is a process that will be continuous as more information is collected. Meanwhile, the first fruits of the project are the chapters in this book.

Why these Five Villages and this Park? Quite simply, because there have always been close historical, ecclesiastical and personal ties between them. It would be very difficult to write a history of one without much reference to the others. They have always been in the same Hundred (the Upton, later to become the Double Hundred of Nassaburgh). All five villages and Milton Park were part of the Abbey Lands, with the Abbot of Peterborough as their feudal overlord. Castor, Ailsworth, Belsize, Sutton, Upton and Milton were in the same parish from the earliest days of Christianity until 1851 (Ailsworth, Belsize and Milton are still in Castor Parish.) Marholm, while being a separate parish since 1217, was originally probably part of the same parish, and for much of its history has shared the same parish priest as the others since then.

Today these parishes share the same rector. Many of the farming families, such as the Darbys, Jarvises, Longfoots and Harrises extend across the parishes, as do Milton's lands and interests. Today the villages share the same school. They still support each other in many ways.

An old navigational epithet states that *"You cannot know where you are going, unless you know where you are, and you cannot know where you are, unless you know from whence you came."* The same may be said of communities. There is something metaphysical in talking and writing about communities. There is a sense of seeking for that essence which is larger than us as individuals, something greater than us, but of which we are part. By being members of a community we become part of, and contribute, to history. This book is an attempt to distil something of the history which has brought us to the beginning of the Third Millennium.

The authors of the chapters are not professional writers, but are members of the communities about which they have written - many of them born in the villages. The contributions are in many respects highly personal. Foot-notes and appendices have been included, where appropriate, in an attempt to assist anyone who wishes to follow up a subject for further research.

There are many people who have not written articles but without whom the project could not have been completed. Among other people, we owe thanks to Steve Walker, co-ordinator of the CAMUS Project, and Nigel Blanchford our Treasurer, and to the Heritage Lottery Fund who with Nationwide and the Countryside Agency funded the writing of the book. Others have contributed behind the scenes: Jim Tovey, Stuart Weston and Edmund Burke helped with and produced much of the art work and graphics; Jim Tovey and Tracey Blackmore took many of the photographs; Millie Weston maintained the Data-Base, set out many of the appendices and typed articles for people; Helen Tovey, Gill Slidel and Sally Leeds proof-read texts. Ben Robinson, Curator of Peterborough Museum, acted as our archaeological advisor. The Nene Valley Archaeological Trust allowed us to reproduce their material, as did the Northamptonshire Record Society and the Victoria County History Society. The Northamptonshire County Record Office and Richard Hillier of the Local Studies Section of Peterborough Library have been invaluable resources. We had no publisher and have consequently imposed hugely on our village printer, Andy Vernum of Styalprint in Ailsworth - many thanks to him for his advice, guidance and forbearance.

Lastly, many in the villages provided us with information, photographs and valuable advice and encouragement. It is just not possible to include all the material we have collected – over 2000 documents – in one book. All the material has been kept, recorded and placed in the Parish Archives in the Cedar Centre at Castor, and will find its way onto the Archive Web-Site, the second stage of the CAMUS Project.

William Burke
The Rectory, Castor
The Summer Festival of St Kyneburgha of Castor 2004

Subscribers

We are grateful to the Heritage Lottery Fund, the Countryside Agency and the Nationwide Building Society for the Local Heritage Initiative grant that made this project possible. We would also like to thank the following subscribers for additional financial support:

Mr Richard and Mrs Karen Anker (nee Conkey)
Jon and Ann Ardron
Roy and Diane Armitage
Jack and Delsia Bailey
Val and Bob Bailey
Ian and Donna Balfour
Clyde and Beverley Banks
David Banks
James Barclay
Liz Berryman and Steve Barker
Rev John A H and Mrs D E Barley
Graham and Pauline Barnes
Geoffrey and Heather Barton
Ian and Fiona Baugh
Mrs Joan Baxter
William and Anne Baxter
Mr and Mrs E A Beale
Lyn and Michael Bell
The Bennett Family
Mrs Gwendoline Berridge
Margaret Berridge and Judith
Mick and Evelyn Biddle
Tracey and Justin Blackmore
John and Christine Bladon
Lynette, Nigel, Claire, Tom and Alastair Blanchford
Graham and Carol Boyall
David and Gill Boyman
Stephanie and Martin Bradshaw
Vincent and Rosalind Brierley
Helen and Michael Brocksom
Chris and Alison Brown
Colin Brown
Colin and Margaret Brown
Air Vice-Marshal and Mrs M J D Brown
N S Brown
Simon and Christopher Brown
Ken and Christine Bryan
Margot and Norman Burden
A Burgess
Mr E W D Burke
Diana Burke
William Burke
Jerry and Diane Caesar
Michael and Delia Caskey
David, Carol, Alice, Benjamin and Samuel Castle
Castor Church of England School
June Cawsey
Gordon and Sue Chambers
The Chillcott Family
Arthur and Jeanne Chilvers
Evelyn and Peter Chitty
Albert and Moira Clark
Charles and Joyce Clarke
Janet Codd
Mr Kevin and Mrs Deborah Conkey
Mrs Margaret Conkey
Mr Martin George and Mrs Deborah Conkey
Jonathan and Jackie Cook
Pam Cooper
Mr and Mrs J H W Costin
William and Bella Craven
Jonathan and Corinne Craymer
Neil Cunningham
Richard and Susan Custance (Sutton)
Helen and Kevin Daly
Leonard and Erika Danks
Noel and Joan Darby
Adrian and Kerry Davies
Robert Dickens and Judith Dickens
Joy and Harold Dillistone
Carlos and Wendy Dominguez
Mrs Rebecca Dudgeon
Betty Dunham
Norma and Clive Dunn
Mr and Mrs T P J Dyke
In memory of John and Ann Eades
Tony and Rosemary Evans
Mr and Mrs J A Fell
John, Emily and William Finnie
Mr Andrew and Mrs Victoria Fisher
Judy and Roy Fisher
Lorna and Leonard Fisher
Mr William Forman
David Frankland and Judith Arrowsmith

John and Helen Franks
M Gailer
Clive and Marilyn Gardner
Mr & Mrs Keith Garrett
Freddie and Grace Gibbs
Brian and Alison Gibson
Chloe Gibson
Hannah Gibson
Joyce and Wallace Giddings
Bryan and Pauline Golding
Bridget and Brian Goode
John and Susan Gowler
Barbara and Malcolm Groves
Vic and Sandra Griffin
Amber Grys
Cara Grys
Nadia Grys
Shelley Grys
Stephen Grys
Valerie Grys
Colin and Claire Hailey
Mr and Mrs P Hammond
Peter and Claire Harris
Joyce Harris Kendal
Sir Stephen Hastings
Stephen and Melanie Hawkins
Gwen Heighton
Kath and David Henderson
Charlotte and Dominic Hensman
Meena and Theo Hensman
Allen and Joyce Herbert
Richard and Sian Higgins
John and Gina Hill
Melvyn and Miriam Hill
John and Sue Hodder
Eleanor Hoggart
Mike and Jean Hooper
Anna, Barry and Trevor Hornsby
Mr and Mrs P Huckle
Michael and Angela Hudson-Peacock
Colin and Carole Humphries
Chris Hunt
Mollie and Wilf Hutchinson
Mr and Mrs G H Ingle
Richard, Caroline, Amy and Simon Ingram
Mandy Ireland (Whizz)
Andrew and Helen Jarvis
Stanley and Fay Jarvis
Eric and Margaret Jinks
Melvyn and Enid Johnson
John and Margaret Kennedy, Australia
Mr and Mrs K Kimber
Reg Lambert
Rachel Lay
Peter and Janet Lee
The Leeds Family
David and Maureen Lewis
Dinah Lewis and David Sillett
Chris and Bob Little
Mr and Mrs B W Long
Michael and David Longfoot
Professor and Mrs R Lyman
Mr and Mrs Andrew Lytwynchuk
The MacDonald Family
Richard and Jennie Manning
Geoff Marriott
Joan M Marriott
Andy, Jenny, Annabel and James Martin
Margaret and Derek Mathieson
Mrs Jill McGarry
Sue and Bill McKenzie
Joyce McMillan
Nigel, Jackie and Niki Mercy
Milton (Peterborough) Estate
David and Berenice Moll
Avril M Morris
Andrew and Sue Nash
Elizabeth Nash
Thomas Nash
Sir Philip Naylor-Leyland Bt.
David and Noreen Newton
Iris Beryl Florence Newton
Hugh and Jan Nicholls
David Nobbs

Heather Nobbs
David and Maggie Noble
Mick and Elaine O'Boyle
Des O'Connell
Keith and Lindsay Oliver
Ron and Roz Pearson
Mr W and Mrs J M Pearson
In memory of Annetta Peel (nee Bass)
Michael and Lois Peters
Jane M Pickett
Joan and James Pickett
Jack and Joyce Pitts
Mr James and Mrs Monica Pollard
Ben and Rosie Pounsett
Chris and Antonia Pounsett
Dr and Dr (Mrs) N Rajagopalan
Mrs Eileen Rattenbury
Mr and Mrs George Read
Robbie, Jane and Lisa Reid
Mrs Leslie Rigby
Quentin & Beverley Rigby, Benjamin, Alastair, & Robyn
Roz, Joanna and Fiona Roden
Ian and Marilyn Rogers
Michael and Glenis Rose
Jennie Russell (nee Bass)
Keith and Brenda Salter
Mr David and Mrs Angela Scott
The Shannon Family
Mrs Margaret Sharpe
Dianne and David Shaw
Ian and Ginny Sheldon
Freda Shimmin
Charles and Gill Slidel
Mark, Denise, Kevin and Reece Smith
John and Brenda South
Mary Speechley
Mr Graham and Mrs Gaynor Spence
Mrs Susan Spence
Reg and Monica Spooncer
Jane and Robert Steward
Mrs Lesley (Daffodil) and Mr Paul Stubbs
Miss Danica Summerlin
Paul, Susan, Jennifer and Rebecca Sykes
John and Julie Taylor
Jill Tebbutt
Mr and Mrs R J Tedcastle
Mr and Mrs Derek Terrill
Ted and Lynne Thain
The Church of St John the Baptist, Upton
The Church of St Kyneburgha of Castor
The Church of St Mary the Virgin, Marholm
The Church of St Michael & All Angels, Sutton
The Royal Oak, Castor
Jim and Tess Thompson-Bell
Marian and Peter Tomkin
Amelia Tovey
James and Helen Tovey
Poppy Tovey
Helen and Len Trundle
Nick and Bridget Vergette
Duncan, Gill, George, Claudia and Molly Vessey
Steve and Jo Walker
Sophie, Ben and Emily Walker
Norman and Jean Warnes
Mrs Mildred Watt (former resident of Ailsworth)
Valerie and James Webb
Sue Welch
Norman, Rachel, Simon and Hannah Westcott
Millie Weston
Stephen and Sharon Weston
Stuart Weston
Jim and Margaret White (nee Ward)
Mr and Mrs Maurice Wickham
Mr and Mrs Ben Winfrey
Claire and Ian Winfrey
Drs Peter and Rebecca Winfrey
Jay Winfrey and Family
Jim and Patsy Wood and Family
Stewart and Sarah Wood
Mr and Mrs John Wylde
Rodney and Hazel Yates
Daryl and Philip Yea

THE HISTORICAL BACKGROUND

The Villages, the Park and the Soke of Peterborough

Welcome to the story of our villages as told by the villagers. The book will take you through the life, work, worship, joy and pain of our history from the time of the Roman Empire to the present day. Whilst Castor itself has a much longer history, the history of the Benefice (of Castor-cum Ailsworth with Sutton and Upton with Marholm) really starts with the grant of lands to the Monastery of Medeshamstead – the old name for Peterborough - by Wulfhere, King of Mercia, in AD664. The grant to the monastery included among others *'Eylesworthe, Castre, Sutton, Milton and Marham.'* The monastery was subsequently sacked by the Vikings, but a further grant was made by Edgar, King of England, in AD972 for the re-founding of the monastery at Medeshamstead. These two charters included the Hundred of Upton, later with Burgh to become Double Hundred of Nassaburgh, otherwise known as the Soke or Liberty of Peterborough as we know it today. These early charters were confirmed by subsequent kings, such as William I in 1070, King John on 29 December 1215 and others.

Topography

The villages are grouped on the North bank of the Nene between Peterborough and Wansford and extend across the higher land to the North which forms part of the watershed between the rivers Nene and Welland. They are part of the Ness of Burgh. The Ness (literally the "nose-shaped" piece of land) of Burgh (an old name for Peterborough) is shown on Mordern's map of 1695. It is very roughly triangular, bounded by the River Welland to the North and the River Nene to the South, with its apex where the two rivers used to meet under Croyland's ancient three-arched triangular bridge. The third side runs roughly North-West/South-East and forms the administrative boundary with the Willowbrook Hundred to the West. The river banks were alluvial gravels and water-meadows. Further inland lay the arable land between 20-30 feet Above Mean Sea Level (AMSL), with virtually unoccupied forested uplands (hanglands) at the watershed of the two rivers, about 100 feet AMSL, which were used for timber and hunting. Castor and Ailsworth sit on the spring line of the upland edge and face Southwards.

In 1849, the managed acreage of the benefice was 8810 acres, which would not have been greatly different from that in the 12th century. The Domesday acreage of the whole Soke of Peterborough was given as 70 hides and three-and-a-half virgates.

History

Most of the Soke of Peterborough was originally a woody swamp, but Abbot Adulph (972-992) cleared it by degrees and built manor houses and granges. Indeed the place names indicate the Westward spread of settlements by the Abbey. The word *ton* is Old English for a settlement or farmstead, so we have Netherton (nether=lower), Orton (originally Overton), Milton (Middleton), Upton (Upper Settlement)

Fig 1. Mordern's map of 1695, showing the Nassaburgh or Upton Hundred

and Sutton (South of Upton). In the time of Abbot Ernwulf (1107-1114), revenues were set aside for parochial minsters and from this stems the rebuilding of Castor's magnificent minster church.

The special privileges granted to the Abbey were freedom from the jurisdiction of King, Bishop and Sheriff *'with Soc (Soke) & Sac, Toll & Team, Ingfangethef & Outfangenthef,'* that is: to receive revenues and services from manorial and hundred courts, and to hold judicial courts. In 1361, quarter and petty sessions were established throughout England, but the abbot retained control in the Soke, setting up his own sessions and nominating justices. The original meeting places for the Upton or Nassaburgh Hundred were the sites of Sutton Cross and the Langdyke Bush, (so-called after the old name for King Street, 'the Langdyke'-long dyke) where the Roman road crosses the Northern parish boundary of Upton. The Court Baron for the whole Liberty (Barony or Soke) of Peterborough was for much of its time based at Castor.

At the dissolution of the monasteries, in 1541, these rights reverted to the crown, but, on the formation of the Diocese of Peterborough, were granted to Bishop John Chambers (the last abbot), while the lordship of the manors with *'all other manner of portions, tithes and pensions in the parishes of Castor etc ...meadows, woods, rents, waters, fisheries etc of Castor, Ailsworth, Sutton, Upton, Belsize, Marholm,'* were granted to the Dean and Chapter.

Canon Symon Gunton in the 17th century writes *'Here I must acknowledge myself at a stand, as not able to give a perfect account of all Mannors, Lands, and Tenements belonging to the Monastery of Peterborough at the time of the Dissolution; for it had Lands, or Tenements in...Upton...Marholm...etc. Which, how or when they were alienated from this Monastery, whether by the King, or by the Monastery itself before, I cannot say; But of such lands as the Abby was at this time in full tenure and possession of, King Henry made a tripartite kind of division, assuming a third to himself, confirming another third upon the Bishop, and the rest upon the Dean and Chapter.'*

Bishop Scamler returned his privileges to Queen Elizabeth I, who granted them and the title *'Lord Paramount of the Soke of Peterborough and Custos Rotularum'* (Keeper of the Rolls) to William Cecil, Lord Burghley, ancestor to later Marquises of Exeter.

The church initially owned most of the land in the parishes until the beginning of the 17th century, when the Lord of the Manor of Upton was Bishop Dove in his own right, (he also happened to be Rector of Castor.) The Dove family sold their land and interests to the Fitzwilliams in the 18th century. Meanwhile the Fitzwilliams, having been feudal vassals of the Abbey and then the Dean and Chapter, came to hold much of their land freehold, although it was not until after 1836, that they finally bought Belsize from the church. In the case of Sutton, the church remained the Lord of the Manor until the 1898 when the Hopkinson family bought the Manor of Sutton from the Church. The Lord of the Manors of Ailsworth and Castor today is still the Church Commissioners, although most of their land has been sold, either to Milton, or compulsorily purchased by the Peterborough Development Corporation. When talking of church-owned land, note the distinction between land owned by the Bishop, the manors owned by the Dean and Chapter, and glebe land, that which was owned by the local parish church. This latter land - the Glebe - was previously used to fund the local church and its ministry until it was removed from rural parishes by Act of Parliament in the 1970s. Its ownership and control was centralized under the Church Commissioners, but the effect was to remove from rural parishes the historic resources used by the local church.

In 1888, most local administration passed to county councils, but the third Marquis of Exeter, as Lord Paramount, ensured that the Soke became an administrative county separate from the County of Northampton, with full powers retained. In 1964 the Soke became part of the County of Huntingdon, and the Liberty of Peterborough Quarter Sessions were absorbed into the Huntingdon and Peterborough Sessions. In 1972 Huntingdonshire became part of the new greater County of Cambridgeshire. In 1998 the City of Peterborough, including our villages, became a unitary authority.

Keith Garrett and William Burke

Fig 2. Prospect of Castor by Stukeley 1724; interesting but not especially accurate.

Fig 3. Tithe map of 1847, 50 years before the Enclosures. Each strip in the Open Fields is numbered – the dark black mark on each strip is its number; the map has been reduced in size to fit, in fact the original map is some 10ft by 10ft. North is at the top.

A Chronology of our Parishes

This chronology is intended to help the reader to find his bearings in the lengthy period considered. The dates given are not all concerned with the events of our parishes; some refer to matters of wider significance including a selection of landmarks in national history. Local events are in **bold.**

AD

43	Roman invasion of Britain
47	Roman legions reach River Trent

Area under Roman occupation; building of Roman villas in the parishes commences

122	Building of Hadrian's Wall (Tyne – Solway) commenced
c250	**Praetorium built at Castor**
312	Constantine the Great proclaimed Emperor at York
314	Council of Arles (Gaul) **attended by Bishop of Lincoln**
367	Attacks on Britain by Picts, Scots and Saxons
406	Constantine III withdraws forces from Britain: probable end of Roman military occupation
418	Romans bury, by order, gold hoards – or move them to Gaul

Burial of Water Newton treasure?

432	St Patrick begins mission to Ireland.
448	Barbarian invasions of Britain – appeal to Rome for help

Saxons arrive in East Anglia

515	'King' Arthur killed at battle of Camlann
563	Columba at Iona
582	Penda – son of king of Mercia - born
597	St Augustine arrives in Kent
627	Edwin – King of Northumbria - baptised
632	Penda – **father of Kyneburgha** – becomes King of Mercia
634	Oswald becomes King of Northumbria
641	Penda kills Oswald
655	Penda killed. Succeeded by Peada and Wulfhere

Peterborough Abbey - 'the Abbey of St. Peter' - built

664	Synod of Whitby **(attended by Kyneburgha?)**

Castor Convent built

c710	**Death of Kyneburgha. Her sister, Kyneswitha, takes over as Abbess.**
735	Death of Venerable Bede

787	First Viking raids
827	Egbert – King of Wessex – becomes King of all England
856	King Alfred recaptures London from the Danes
870	**Castor Convent attacked by Danes; subsequently functions as a minster church with chapels-of-ease in neighbouring villages**
899	Death of Alfred the Great
937	West Saxon Kings become masters of England
1012	**Castor Church in ruins from Viking raids. 7th March – Bodies of Kyneburgha and Kyneswitha translated to Peterborough Abbey by Elsinus**
1016	Canute becomes King of England: builds short-lived Danish 'empire'
1066	Norman Conquest of England under William the Conqueror
1070	**Hereward the Wake (Saxon) seeks to retrieve 'his' land from Abbot of Peterborough**
1086	Compilation of Domesday Book: probably to enable William to maximise taxation prospects
1124	**Castor Church rebuilt and rededicated (17th April)**
1126	Jury system established in England
1214	**Belsize Farm founded as an assart**
1215	Authority of Medieval Church & Papacy at height. Barons extort Magna Carta from King John
1217	**Marholm becomes a separate parish**
1304	**Milton receives Charter for market**
1338	Beginning of Hundred Years' War between England and France
1340	**Castor receives Charter for market and fair**
1348	Black Death reaches Europe (England 1349 – Scotland 1350)
1362	English becomes official language of Parliament and Courts
1415	Battle of Agincourt: great success of Henry V of England in France
1455	Beginning of Wars of the Roses: Yorkists v Lancastrians
1476	William Caxton sets up his printing press at Westminster
1485	Henry (VII) Tudor victorious at Bosworth Field: beginning of Tudor period. Leonardo da Vinci
1492	Christopher Columbus reaches the New World
1502	**Fitzwilliams buy Milton**
1509	Henry VIII - King of England (1509-47). Michelangelo: Sistine chapel ceiling
1515	Thomas Wolsey becomes Lord Chancellor of England and Cardinal
1534	Act of Supremacy: Henry VIII asserts control over English Church. Start of English Reformation
1536	Dissolution of smaller monasteries (remainder dissolved 1539). Execution of Ann Boleyn

1541	**Reformation – Peterborough Abbey becomes Peterborough Cathedral**
1553	Mary Tudor - Queen of England (1553-8); persecution of Protestants
1558	Elizabeth I - Queen of England (1558-1603)
1587	Mary Queen of Scots executed
1588	Spanish Armada defeated. **Wilbores, Darbeys, Tebbotts were among those mustered from this parish for the defence of London.**
1603	James VI of Scotland becomes James I of England (1603-25)
1604	Gunpowder Plot
1611	Authorised Version of the Bible in English
1613	**Thomas Dove – Bishop and Rector of Castor**
1616	Death of William Shakespeare
1625	Charles I - King of England (1625-49)
1642	English Civil War begins (1642-9): Roundheads v Cavaliers
1645	Battle of Naseby. **Anglican priest killed at Woodcroft by Puritans**
1646	**Rector of Castor imprisoned by Cromwell in Tower of London: dies there in 1648**
1649	Charles I executed. England governed as Commonwealth. Oliver Cromwell - 'Protector' (1653-8)
	All church property in Castor, Ailsworth, and Sutton stolen and sold
1660	Restoration of Charles II (1660-85). **Church property restored in parishes**
1665	Great Plague of London
1666	Fire of London. Newton's discovery of laws of gravity
1684	**Great fire of Sutton**
1685	James II - King of England, Scotland, and Ireland (1685-8)
1688	William (1689-1702) and Mary (1689-94) reign
1707	Act of Union between England and Scotland
1750	**Dove family sell Upton Manor to Fitzwilliams**
1776	Declaration of Independence by 'The Thirteen Colonies': American War of Independence
1793	Start of the Long Wars (Revolutionary and Napoleonic)
1795	**White family buys Castor House from the Church**
1797	Norman Cross Depot receives its first French prisoners-of-war
1805	Battle of Trafalgar
1815	Battle of Waterloo (end of Long Wars)
1829	**Castor Fitzwilliam School founded**

1831	Great Reform Act: greatly improves arrangments for electing Members of Parliament
1837	Accession of Queen Victoria
1843	Upton fields enclosed
1845	**Peterborough's first (limited) railway connection – through Northampton to Blisworth**
1851	**Sutton and Upton become separate parishes. Bishops no longer rectors at Castor**
1861	**Castor Infant School founded**
1868	**Restoration of Marholm Church – side aisles rebuilt**
1870	The "Forster" Act : moves towards the principle of compulsory education
1875	First intelligible telephonic transmission (Alexander Graham Bell)
1896	Motoring made legal – London to Brighton motor car 'run'. First (silent) cinema film in England
1898	**William Hopkinson buys Lordship of Sutton Manor off Cathdral Dean and Chapter Enclosures at Castor and Ailsworth**
1903	**Enclosures at Sutton**
1908	Old Age Pensions introduced - for those of seventy years and over - at five shillings a week
1914	World War I (1914-18)
1918	Votes for women aged thirty years and over. (1928 – for women aged over twenty-one years)
1922	BBC starts broadcasting regular programmes on the 'wireless'. BBC TV (1930); ITA (1955)
1936	January: Accession of Edward VIII. December: Accession of George VI
1939	Outbreak of World War II (1939-45)
1944	Education Act: leads to sweeping changes especially as regards post-primary education
1948	Welfare State legislation based on ideas of Sir William Beveridge **Last recorded use of horses for ploughing in the benefice (Fred Hornsby)**
1952	Accession of Elizabeth II
1963	USA President John Kennedy assassinated. Beeching Report axed railways
1971	UK decimal coinage introduced. Divorce Reform Act in force. End of free school milk
1973	UK, Ireland and Denmark join European Economic Community. VAT introduced in UK
1977	**New Township – 'Battle of Castor'. Nene Valley Railway started**
1979	Margaret Thatcher first woman Prime Minister
1989	Berlin Wall comes down. Church of England Synod votes in favour of ordination of women
2000	Global celebrations mark the advent of the new millennium. **Celebrations throughout the parishes; bulb planting; opening of the Cedar Centre; two new bells and new vestments at Castor Church**

Gill Slidel

Gill Slidel is a former headteacher who was born in Hampshire but has lived in Castor – at first in Stocks Hill and subsequently in High Street - with her husband and family since the early 1970s.

Roman 'herring-bone' masonry: foundations of the Roman Praetorium on Stocks Hill Castor.

Poplar Farmhouse, Marholm.

Sutton Cross, an ancient meeting place beside another Roman road, Ermine Street.

Jack Wood who lived at The Elms Castor in the 1920s.

The site of Salter's Tree on the Castor-Marholm road. The stump of an old elm could be seen until recently. This is thought to be the site of an old gibbet.

Milton Temple as rebuilt in 1986, having originally been built before 1775. It had collapsed before 1884. The bust in the niche of the Temple is of the 4th Earl Fitzwilliam.

The barns and old farmyard at ' The Cedars' Castor.

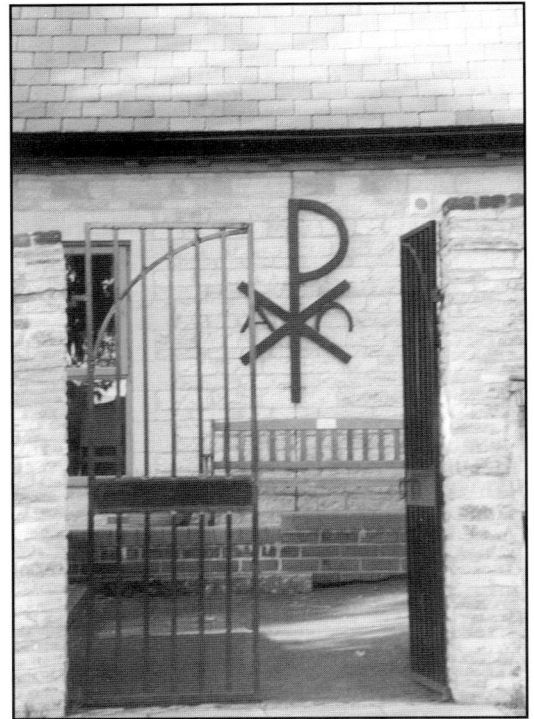

The newest meeting place - The Cedar Centre, 2000AD

Castor Infants School 1929 can you work out who still lives in the villages?
Back (l-r): Miss Hales, unknown, unknown, Alec Jakes, Walter Pendred, unknown, Harry Hill, Kenny Baker.
2nd Row from back: Doris Ward, Mona Wodward, Maisie Hill, Joan Nix, Olive Afford, Margaret Ward, Joan Brown, Joyce Milford, Hilda Parker. 3rd row: Don Harman, Sheila Catmull, Horace Ward, Ewart Hill, Barbara Sharpe, Betty Taylor, June Milford. Front: Ernest Hornsby, Geoff Ward, Peter Dudley, Billy Pearson, Clem Rylott (Upton).

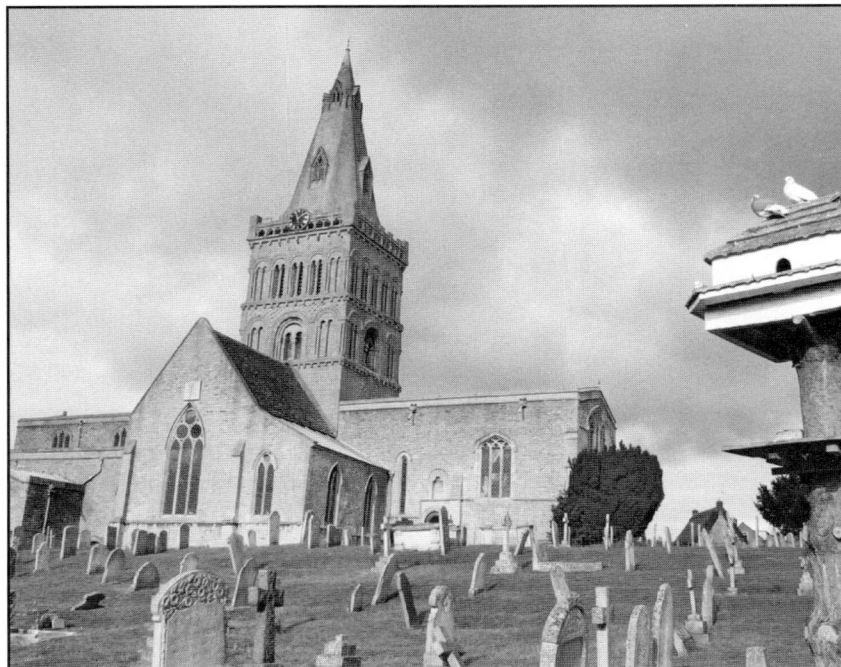

Castor Church the oldest building is still used for its original purpose. The Church is built of stone from the oolitic limestone outcrop known as 'Barnack Rag', distinguished by its 'shelly' content. This stone has not been quarried since the 16th century.
(Photo: J Tovey)

Colour Plates

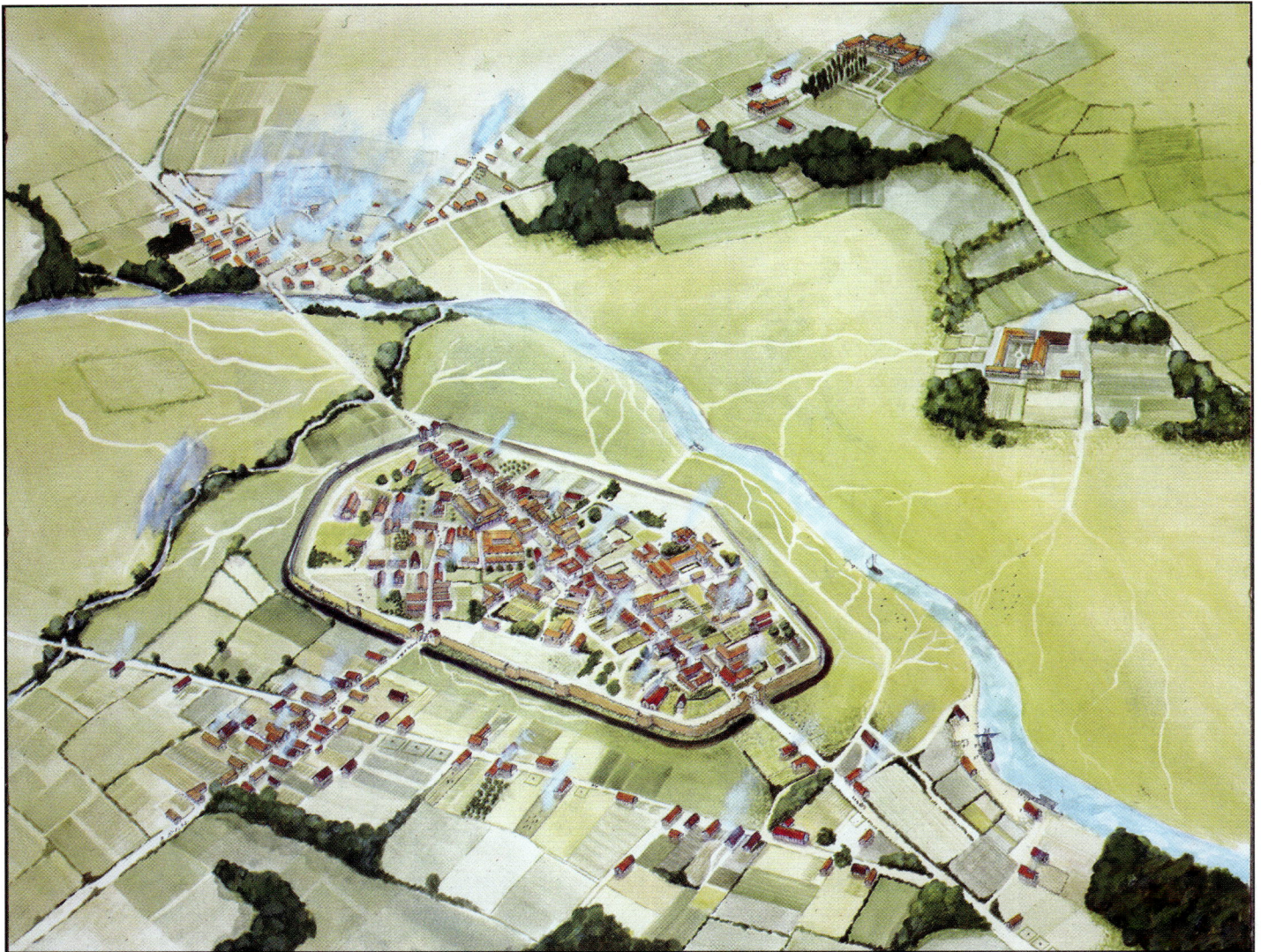

Plate 1. *An artist's impression of the town of Durobrivae as it would have appeared in the 4th century AD. The major Roman road - Ermine Street, passes through the town and continues through the industrial suburb to the North-east. The large 'palace' due North of the town is situated on what is now Church Hill in Castor. . (Peterborough Museum)*

Plate 2a & 2b. *Two examples of the high-quality pottery produced in the kilns near Durobrivae which was traded across Britain. Left- a drinking vessel or 'Hunt Cup' named after the chase scene depicted, a hare running from two hounds   Right - a small decorated vessel probably used for cooking or food storage, known as a 'Castor Box'. (Peterborough Museum)*

Plate 3. *Part of the collection of late Roman silver that forms the Water Newton treasure. Many of the items bear Christian symbols and almost certainly comprise the oldest collection of Christian church plate found anywhere in the Roman world. From left to right: jug, bowl dedicated to Publianus, two-handed cup and wine -strainer. In front: plaques and gold disc with Chi-Rho motifs. (Peterborough Museum)*

Plate 4. A Roman mosaic floor excavated from a Roman building on the site of the Cedars in Castor by E.T. Artis in 1821 and recorded in his volume 'Durobrivae'. It is now located in the dairy at Milton Hall. (from Artis's Durobrivae 1828)

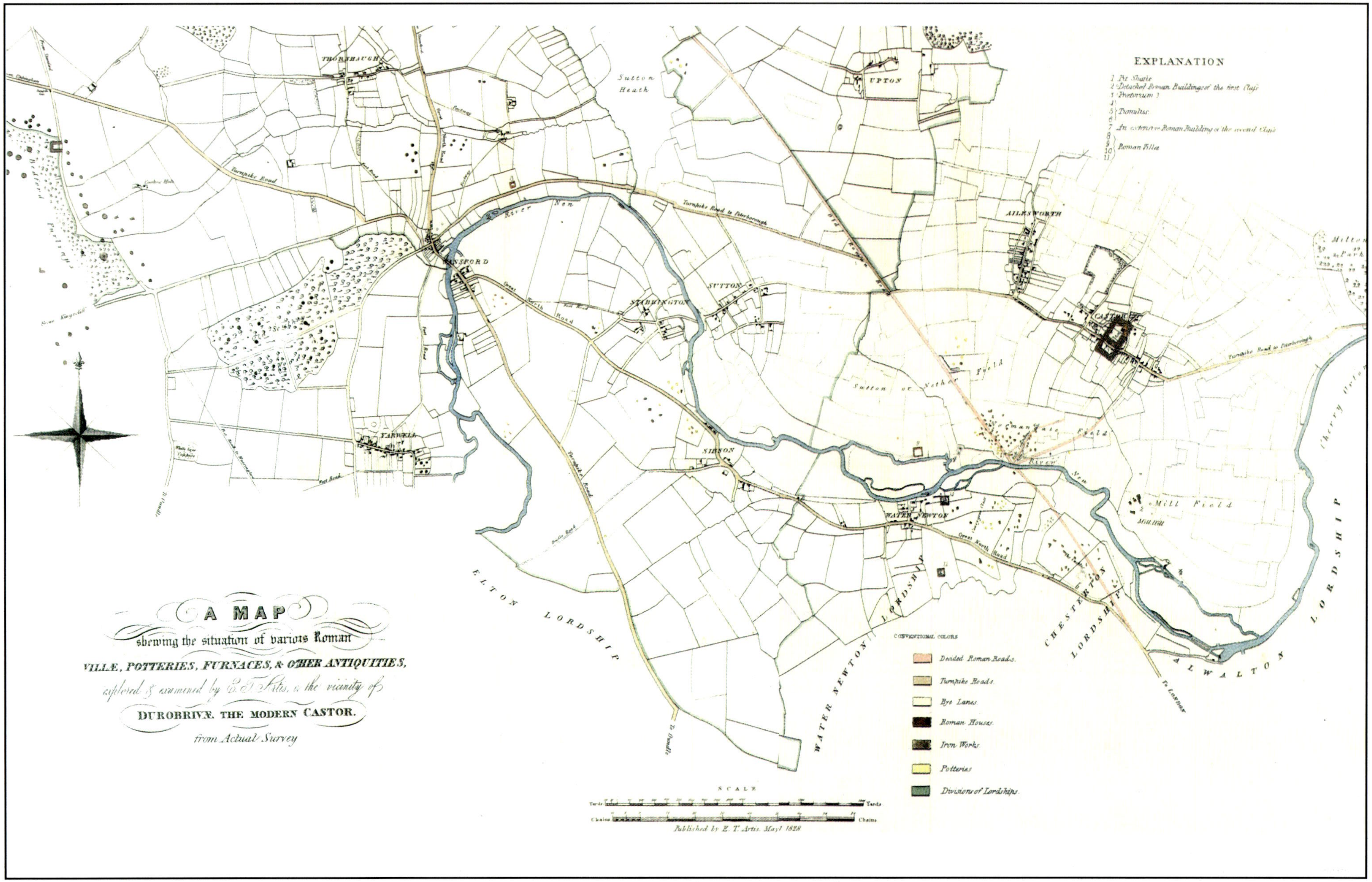

Plate 5. " A Map Shewing the situation of various Roman Villae, Potteries, Furnaces, & Other Antiquities from The Durobrivae of Antoninus, Identified and Illustrated by E.T. Artis, 1828 ".

Plate 6. Medieval pond at Castor Hanglands. (Photo: Paul Glendell, English Nature)

Plate 7. Flowers found in the meadows beside the River Nene at Castor. A watercolour by Roger Banks, 1985. (Photo: J Tovey)

Plate 8. Castor Hanglands National Nature Reserve. Surviving historic meadow at Ailsworth Heath, showing common spotted orchids. (Photo: Paul Glendell, English Nature)

Plate 9. Ailsworth village sign, donated by the W.I. To celebrate their centenary, 1981.

Plate 10. Ailsworth Methodist Chapel.

Plate 11. Castor Green. At the base of the tree on the right the stump of the old village cross can be seen.

Plate 12. Barns adjacent to Castor Village. Picture taken 2004.
(Photo: by T.Blackmore)

Plate 13. Castor House, 1976, showing the old farmyard that is now Poll's Yard at the bottom left corner.

Plate 14. Roman masonry in the wall of the Old Rectory,
Stocks Hill, Castor.

Plate 15. Patronal Festival, the year of the Queen's Jubilee, 2002.

Plate 16. The Choir 2002 Back (l to r): Theo Hensman, Brian Goode, Bridget Good, Pam Tedcastle, Leslie Rigby, Sue Hodder, Jen Poling, Will Craven, Joan Pickett, Geke Kooistra, Douglas Gillam, Eric Jinks. Middle: Alex Elliot, Heather Hunt, Alice Scott, Alistair Dutton, Lauren O'Boyle, Ellen Couchsmith, Nadia Grys, Amy O'Boyle, Stuart Baugh. Front: Clare Atkinson, Becci Stevens, Brooke Poling, Yllana Hunt, Jennifer Sykes, Alice Castle, Ben Dutton.

Plate 17. Banners dressed for the Patronal Festival at Castor, 2002.

Plate 18. Castor Church: Early English Chancel AD 1220 and Sanctuary Party Candlemas 2004. Churchwardens: right Theo Hensman, left Brian Goode, Crucifer Eric Jinks, Acolytes Alice Castle (left) Yllana Hunt (right), Thurifer Edmund Burke, Boatboys Millie Tovey (left) and Jack Howard (right), Servers Ben Dutton (left) Steffie Elliott (right) Bridget Goode (Pastoral assistant). The children have many relations in the village in addition to their parents. Millie's grandparents live in the village. Jack has two grandmothers as well as a grandfather and great-grandfather living in the village. Steffi has grand-parents and many other relations in the village.

Plate 19. Castor Church: Chapel looking South as reordered in 2002, the medieval 'mensa' altar re-consecrated Eve of Lady Day 2004. (Photo: J Tovey)

Plate 20. Castor Church arcade (AD1210) with roof angels and figures (AD1450). (Photo: J Tovey)

UFFORD CP

SOUTHORPE CP

OKE FELDE

CASTOR HANGLANDS NNR

MYLL FELDE

UPTON CP

OLDFIELD

DOLE FELDE

SUTTON CP

AILSWORTH CP

CASTOR CP

NORTH FIELD

UPTON FIELD

WOOD FIELD

MILTON FIELD

DOLES FIELD

MIDDLE FIELD

LITTLE FIELD

MEADOW FIELD

NETHER FIELD

LAMMAS CLOSES

THORN FIELD

NORMANGATE FIELD

MILLFIELD

SIBSON CUM STIBBINGTON CP

CASTOR FLOOD MEADOWS SSSI

SUTTON HEATH & BOG SSSI

AL WALTON

Southorpe Terrace
Newport Farm
Lambpits Spinney
Middle Farm
Quarry (dis)
Southorpe
Bottom Farm
Fox Covert
Long Spinney
High Farm
Merryshaws Spinney
Tom's Wood
Boar's Hill Planting
Bushey Wood
Dearden Wood
Gazley Lodge
Lady Wood
Blackthorn Spinney
G Spinney
Windmill Hill Plantation
The Severalls
New Close Wood
Southey Wood
Ufford Heath Farm
Southey Lodge
Langdyke Bush
Observation Tower
Hayeswood Spinney
Ailsworth Heath
Castor Hanglands
Fire Tower
Lady Wood
Wildboar Coppice
Moore Wood
Upton Wood
Woolpits
Wall Spinney
Crow Spinney
Quarry (dis)
Sutton Wood
Jubilee Spinney
Beech Spinney
Top Lodge Farm
Model Farm
Upton
Manor House
Hell Corner
Top Field Spinney
Blind Lane (Track)
Heath House
Deep Springs
Sutton
Manor Farm
The Grange
Stibbington
Field Studies Centre
Roman Road
Lower Lodge Farm
Roman Camp (site of)
Sutton Crossways (Track)
Sutton Cross (remains of)
Ailsworth
Castor
Lowe's Hill
Moat
Grn Gd
Normangate Field
Roman Villa
Roman Pottery Kilns (sites of)
Tumulus
Wansford Station
Nene Valley Railway
Sibson
Manor Farm
Manor House
Water Newton
Sibson Hollow
Water Newton Gorse
Water Newton Bridge
Roman Pottery Kilns (sites of)
Roman Villa
The Castles DUROBRIVAE ROMAN TOWN
Hereward Way
Nene Way
Mill Road
Landy Green Way
Mill Hill
Roman Villa (site of)
Castor Mills
Back Dike
East Holmes
Sibson Aerodrome
Brookfield Spinney
Hostel Farm
High Leys Farm
Holborn Spinney
High Holborn Lodge
Horse Close Spinney
Camp Site (dis)
Woodcroft Lodge
Pellett Hall
Oxey Wood
Helpston Quarry (disused)
Scotts Cottage
Scotsmans Lodge
Simon's Wood
Ramsall Cottages
Hayes Wood
Foster's Coppice
Bushy Wood
Blackthorn Spinney
Brakes Wood
White's Spinney
Popple's Coppice
Belsize Farm
Belsize Wood
Oldfield Pond
Salter's Tree
Cow Lane (Track)
Stamford Road
Ermine Street
Roman Road
Jurassic Way
King Street
Main Street
Walcot Road

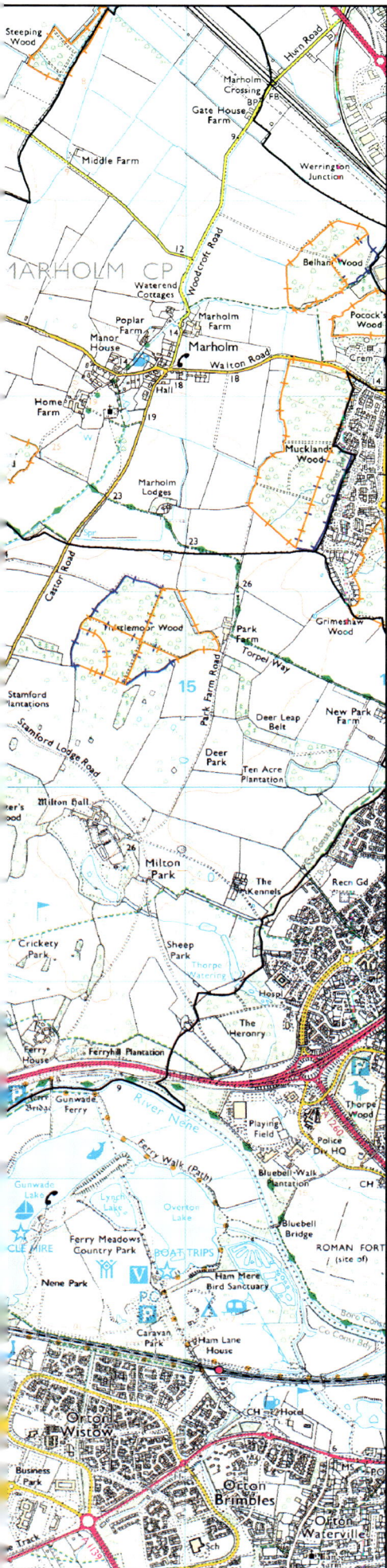

Key

—— **Parish Boundaries**

Medieval Open Field Names *NORMANGATE FIELD* **(See chapter 18)**

Moat *Moat* **(See chapter 5)**

Natural History Sites *CASTOR FLOOD MEADOWS SSSI* **(See chapter 25)**

Castor Hanglands NNR (Public Access)
Local SSSIs (Private Land)
Ancient Woodland (Semi-Natural)
Ancient Woodland (Replanted)

Map Backdrop

Copyright eMAPSite and Suppliers 15/01/04

Designated Sites, Woodland & Parish Boundaries

Copyright English Nature 24/03/04

Plate 21. St Kyneburgha's pageant, 1974, celebrating the 850th anniversary of the re-founding of Castor Church.

Plate 22. Cedar Centre opening and Dedication July 2000. left to right: William Burke (Rector), Brian Goode (Churchwarden), Jay Winfrey (holding mic'), Florence Jackson (oldest member of the congregation), Theo Hensman (Churchwarden), Becci Dudgeon (the Cedars), Fr Ron Amis (Assistant Priest), Ven David Painter (Archdeacon).

Plate 23. Castor and Ailsworth Millennium Street Party Whit Monday June 2000. (Photo: M Smith)

Plate 24. Terrier racing, 2002 at the St Kyneburgha's annual Summer Festival.

Plate 25. Betty Andrews unveiling the Marholm Village Millennium Sign which she designed.

Plate 26. This team of Marholm ladies made the Patronal Banner of Our Lady for the Millennium. Left to right, Enid Johnson, Bernice Moll, Di Armitage, Gill Atkinson, Fay Jarvis, Gina Hill, Marie Stevens. (photo 2000)

Plate 27. Home Farm, Marholm, view from the South-east. This old courtyard farm has barely changed for 200 years. (photo 2004)

Plate 28. Marholm Flower Festival 2001 The Chancel (Arr. by Monica Agnes, Janet Dykes, Enid Johnson, Heather Vigar and Gill Young).

Plate 29. Marholm Flower Festival 2001. The Knight's Tomb (Arr. By Fay Jarvis and Marie Stevens).

Plate 30. Manor Farm, Sutton, showing the old duck pond. Water colour by H.B.Gathercole, 1958.

Plate 31 The Sutton Stone, a parish boundary marker –note the letter "S"

Plate 32. There are more animals than people in Upton Parish. Fergus the Bull from Top Lodge Farm is the largest inhabitant. 2004

Plate 33. Upton Church from the South.

Plate 34. Upton inhabitants having tea at Mick and Lyn Bell's "Open Garden", 2002, in aid of Upton Church (Left to right - Ron Baldwin, Ann Cunnington, Liz Goulding, Robin Goulding.

Plate 35. The Langdyke Bush. This mound in Upton Parish beside King Street the old Roman road, was the meeting place for the Upton Nassaburgh Hundred from Saxon times (photo 2004)

Plate 36. A modern combine harvester working in Normangate Field. Left to right David Longfoot and Michael Longfoot of Model Farm Upton. (photo 2002)

Plate 37. Belsize Bank. Belsize has been a farm since 1214, starting as a grange for the Abbey. The earth work in front is the "Roman Bank". (photo 2004)

Plate 38. *Fitzwilliam Hounds (Milton) meet Castor Green on Christmas Eve 2002.*

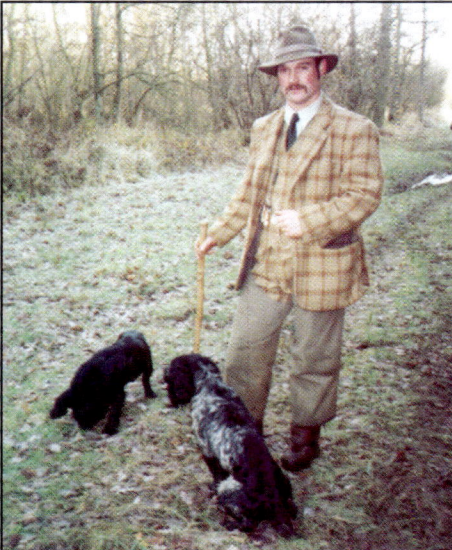

Plate 39. *David Webster, the last game-keeper, in 'Milton Tweed' 2003. (Photo: M Smith)*

Plate 40. *Hanglands Day Shoot c1992 Standing (l-r) Stuart Weston, Nick Kirby, ?, Stephen Goodson, Wilf Hutchinson, Paul Goodson, Roger Smith, Nigel Goodson, Dave Todd, ?, Stephen Weston, Peter Blatch, Keith Dickinson, Pete Hibbert, Chris Goodson, Ron Heron, Tony Cunnington, Colin Goodson, Aubrey Weston, Stan Cunnington, Jed Aspitall. Front kneeling: Paul Sayer, J Yarman, D Carrington, Andrew Jarvis, Kevin Conkey, David Dearman, Nigel Tee.*

Plate 41. *Beaters and Keepers Day, Jan 2003 in front of Breaks Wood: (l-r) Andy Olik, Matthew Hill, Roy Sansby, keeper David Webster, Tim Sansby, Mark Smith, Nigel Tee. (Photo: Pat Olik)*

Plate 42. Alice and Charlie Brown dance on the bar at the Summer Fete Barbeque, 2002 . Ian Sheldon grumpily walks away while Steve Grys patiently waits for them to return to pulling pints.

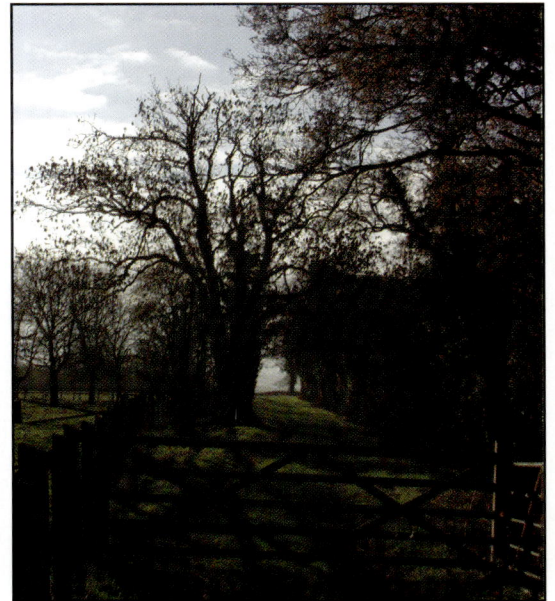

Plate 43. Ermine Street, the old Roman Road, formerly known as the "Forty Foot Way as it runs through Upton. (Photo: J Tovey)

Plate 44. The Dovecote at Village Farm, Castor.

Plate 45. Old Bake House, converted for use as a modern kitchen, now the home of Andrew and Helen Jarvis.

Plate 46. The Summer Fete Tug of War 2002. The Royal Oak pulls against The Prince of Wales Feathers. Brian Gibson shouts his team to victory.

Plate 47. Red Valerian growing on the North wall of Church Hill Castor. This plant, used by the Romans for herbal remedies is thought to have been introduced to Britain by the Romans. They also used to lay Red Valerian on their altars. It grows profusely in the village today.

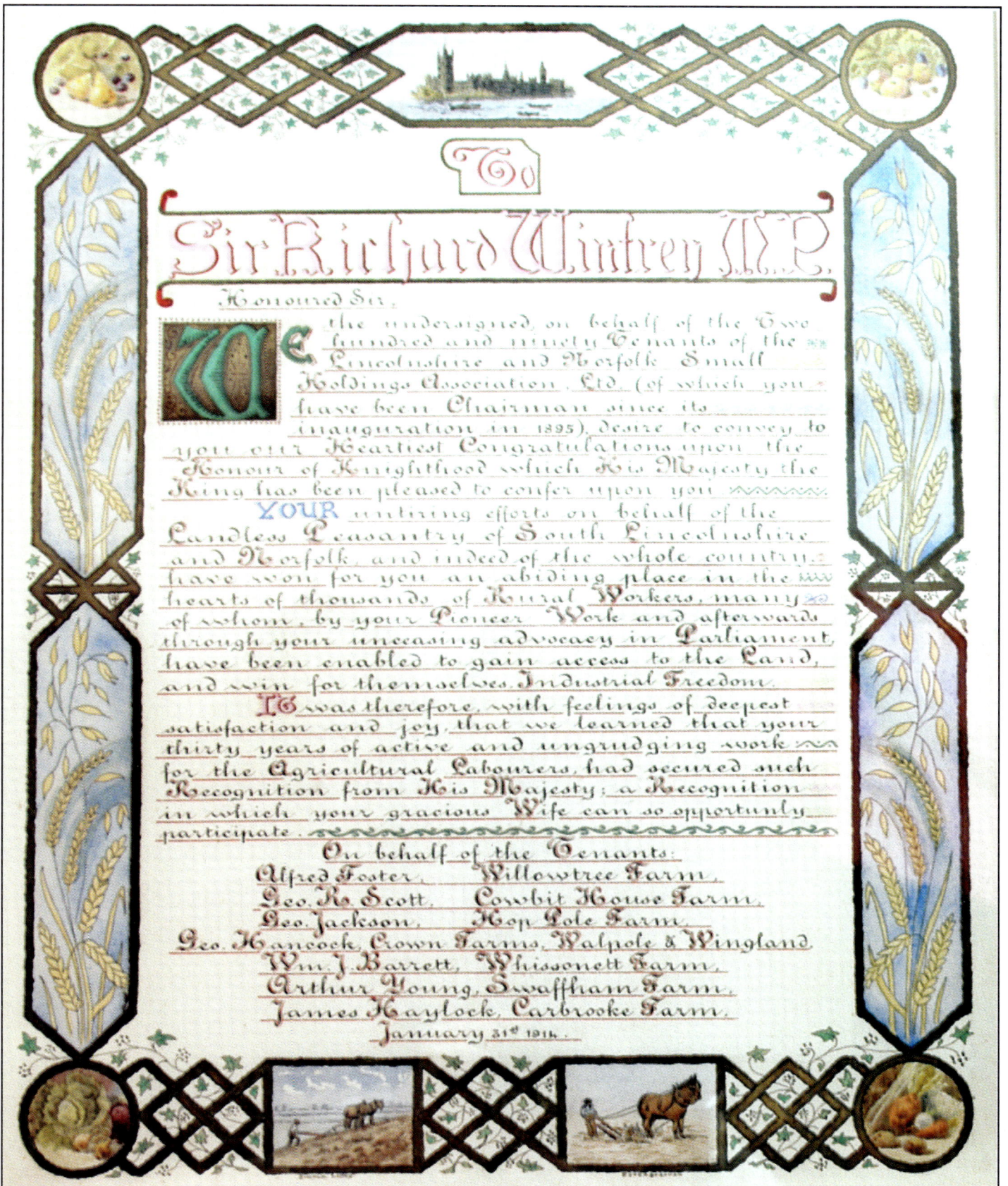

To

Sir Richard Winfrey M.P.

Honoured Sir,

WE the undersigned, on behalf of the Two Hundred and ninety Tenants of the Lincolnshire and Norfolk Small Holdings Association, Ltd. (of which you have been Chairman since its inauguration in 1895), desire to convey to you our Heartiest Congratulations upon the Honour of Knighthood which His Majesty the King has been pleased to confer upon you. YOUR untiring efforts on behalf of the Landless Peasantry of South Lincolnshire and Norfolk, and indeed of the whole country, have won for you an abiding place in the hearts of thousands of Rural Workers, many of whom, by your Pioneer Work and afterwards through your unceasing advocacy in Parliament, have been enabled to gain access to the Land, and win for themselves Industrial Freedom.

IT was therefore, with feelings of deepest satisfaction and joy, that we learned that your thirty years of active and ungrudging work for the Agricultural Labourers, had secured such Recognition from His Majesty; a Recognition in which your gracious Wife can so opportunly participate.

On behalf of the Tenants:

Alfred Foster, Willowtree Farm,
Geo. Rt. Scott, Cowbit House Farm,
Geo. Jackson, Hop Pole Farm,
Geo. Hancock, Crown Farms, Walpole & Wingland,
Wm. J. Barrett, Whissonett Farm,
Arthur Young, Swaffham Farm,
James Haylock, Carbrooke Farm,

January 31st 1914.

Plate 48. Illustrated scroll given to Sir Richard Winfrey by the Tenants of Lincolnshire and Norfolk Small Holders Association for his work on their behalf in 1914.

Chapter 1
The Nene Valley in Prehistoric and Roman Times

Introduction - The Early Archaeologists

To understand the beginnings of human settlement around our villages we must look beyond the five parishes to the wider landscape of the Nene river valley, from the woodlands West of Wansford to where the river joins the edge of the fens East of present-day Peterborough, and from the limestone hills to the North between Upton and Marholm to the lower ground South of the river in the parishes of Water Newton and Chesterton.

This stretch of the lower Nene valley has long been known for its ancient history. Antiquarians such as Camden in the 16th century and Stukeley in the 18th, described Roman remains in the area and were aware of the existence of a Roman town South of the Nene and a Roman settlement under Castor village itself. However it is the local figure, Edmund Tyrell Artis (1789-1847), who has emerged as one of the leading early British archaeologists and who first made a comprehensive study of the landscape around Castor, revealing its true importance. Artis was a talented individual, interested in natural history and geology, an accomplished artist as well as an antiquarian, but his true passion was archaeology. He was steward to Earl Fitzwilliam at Milton and between 1820 and 1828 was able to excavate sites extensively and systematically within Castor and the surrounding area. Unlike many of his contemporaries, whose main interest was in searching for ancient treasures for private collections, he measured and recorded his discoveries carefully. Artis also attempted to place this information within the wider landscape, observing how the various elements, settlements, roads, industry and temples may have related to each other, thus attempting to understand Roman society as a whole.

Artis's major work was *The Durobrivae of Antoninus* (1828) [1], a volume of beautifully engraved plates of his excavations, illustrating the buildings, mosaic floors and many other artefacts he had discovered.

Fig 1a. A plate from 'The Durobrivae of Antoninus' showing ET Artis supervising his labourers excavating a Roman kiln in 'Normanton Field Castor'

Unfortunately there is no text because Artis died in 1847 before the proposed accompanying volume could appear, and his notebooks did not survive. To this day *'Durobrivae'* remains an important starting point for any local historian. Artis is buried in Castor churchyard, close to the 'antiquities' he worked so hard to uncover.

Our understanding of the Roman period has continued to develop through the work of many archaeologists. In the early 1970s there was much concern that Castor and its environs, including many unrecorded historical sites, would be swallowed up by the development of one of Peterborough's new townships. The planned township was not built, but the Nene Valley Research Committee was responsible for much useful work at this time, published in its journal *Durobrivae*. There have since been a number of investigations in Castor and beyond, mainly as a result of small scale developments, resulting in some important new finds and very interesting published work, all of which have added to our knowledge. For example, in advance of proposed building work, archaeological investigations involving an electric resistance survey and test pitting, located a hitherto unknown Roman building range beneath Castor School playing fields in 2000 [2]. New and developing techniques, such as geophysical surveys, and well established techniques, such as aerial photography, have revealed new sites and settlements but it is sobering to reflect how little we still know about these early periods of our history and how threatened is much of the remaining evidence by modern agricultural methods and continuing rural and urban development.

Before the Romans

There is considerable evidence of early human occupation in the valley from the flint artefacts of the Neolithic period (c.4000 BC to 2200BC) to the Bronze Age (c.2500BC to 700BC) weapons and tools found at Upton and the important Bronze Age site at Flag Fen. This site of national importance has been reconstructed to give an insight into life in the Bronze Age. A significant Bronze Age 'Beaker' burial at Barnack included rich grave goods and there have been many finds of early pottery.

The introduction of iron, a stronger and more hard-wearing material than the the copper alloys used in the Bronze Age, brought radical changes. Iron Age people (800 BC to AD43) were able to work the land more intensively because their ploughs could cope with heavier soils. Their settlements were larger and more numerous. Aerial photography shows there were many settlements of timber-built thatched round dwellings all over this area.

Fig 1b. A modern reconstruction of a Bronze or Iron Age roundhouse from Flag Fen typical of many that must have stood in the Nene Valley (Peterborough Museum)

They were surrounded by small fields and paddocks, often protected by ditches. Such open settlements used mixed farming methods, relying heavily on livestock such as cows and sheep. The gravel terraces of the lower valley provided fertile soils for arable farming. Surplus grain could be stored in large jars or pits for winter consumption or for trade. Such houses and field systems have been excavated at Lynch Farm at Orton [3], but there is further evidence of these round house enclosures in all our parishes, including areas later developed in the Roman period. There are fewer settlements enclosed by protective earthworks, although a large, near-circular, earthwork and two ditch circuits and banks survive at Borough Fen. Notwithstanding this, most local sites seem to have been undefended. The Lynch Farm site sits within a meander of the river on three sides and is protected by a series of straight deep ditches on the other. The major threat may well have been cattle rustling rather than full-scale tribal warfare.

Britain in the late Iron Age was divided into distinct tribal areas or kingdoms. Peterborough lay on the borders of the areas governed by the Catuvellauni to the South, (present day Northamptonshire, Bedfordshire and Cambridgeshire) the Corieltauvi to the North and West (Lincolnshire) and the Iceni to the East (present day East Anglia). There is no evidence of who controlled our immediate area before the Roman invasion but the evidence suggests it formed part of a prosperous and relatively peaceful agricultural landscape.

Roman Invasion and Settlement

The coming of the Romans to Britain spelled the end of a dominant native British culture which had lasted for hundreds of years. The four hundred years of Roman rule which followed were not static and the land and its people changed significantly throughout that period. To understand the beginning of the Roman settlement of our area we must understand how the site near Water Newton, just South of the Nene, became the site of a Roman town, later developing important suburbs on both sides of the river.

Julius Caesar first landed in 55 BC on the South coast but did not stay or consolidate his conquest. It was another 98 years before the main Roman invasion of Britain was ordered by the Emperor Claudius in AD 43. He assembled a formidable fighting force of some 40,000 men. The island may have been seen as a rich prize ready to be taken and as an opportunity for Claudius to boost his popularity and prestige by enlarging the Roman Empire. Britain was not unknown to the Romans, who had already established trading links with the Southeast and political links with some of the tribal kingdoms. Thus the Romans could exploit inter-tribal rivalries, so that some tribes accepted the appearance of the conquerors quite readily, while others were bitterly opposed to them. Following a landing on the Kent coast and a major victory over the Britons near the river Medway, the army advanced over the Thames, creating Londinium, and pushed on through present day Essex to Camulodonum, now Colchester, the capital of the Catuvellauni, the dominant tribe of central Southern Britain. Once control had been established the four legions were sent off on divergent paths to conquer the rest of the island. It was Legion IX, named *Hispana*, which pushed Northwards towards present day Lincoln and York, laying down roads and establishing fortified camps as it did so. The main North to South route of Eastern Britain became the Roman road, Ermine Street, and a small fort covering five acres was established on it, South of the River Nene at Water Newton, fortified by a double ditch to defend this important river crossing.

In the early years of the invasion the limits of Roman expansion stretched from the Bristol Channel in the West to the Humber River in the East. Between 1967 and 1971 S Frere and J K St. Joseph excavated the site of a much larger fort covering 27 acres at Longthorpe, now under the golf course [4]. It partly overlaid an earlier native farmstead and included an area outside the defences used for pottery manufacture, presumably to meet the domestic needs of the troops.

The fort itself dated from the early years of the invasion (AD 43-65). Evidence of the

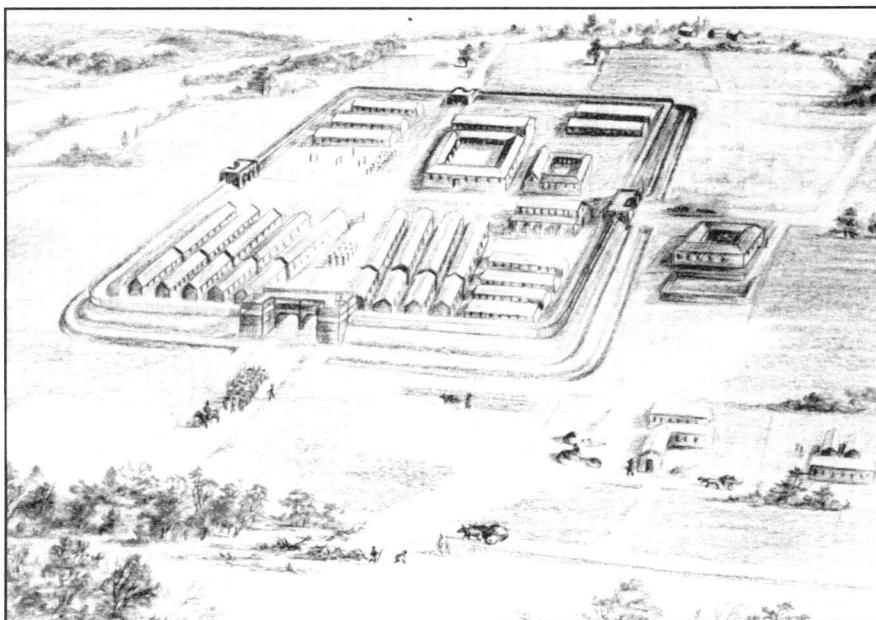

Fig 1c. An artist's interpretation of the Roman fortress at Longthorpe, built about AD43 but abandoned about 20 years later (Peterborough Museum)

necessary ditched fortifications, headquarters, barrack buildings and store houses was found. The fort was almost certainly intended to house a substantial garrison, probably four infantry cohorts or half a legion, brigaded with other auxiliary troops, amounting to perhaps two to three thousand men. Their task was to keep watch on the local population and be prepared to move rapidly to quell any trouble that might occur, as it did from the Iceni in the East in AD 48. Tacitus, the Roman historian, describes the major revolt by the Iceni under Queen Boudicca in AD 60 which mounted an enormous challenge to Roman rule. As she besieged Colchester elements of Legion IX advanced Southwards at high speed from their base to relieve the town but were heavily defeated by the Britons, the infantry being slaughtered while the surviving cavalry escaped to their fortified camp. Longthorpe is the most likely site for this camp as it is far closer than the other possible alternatives of Leicester or Lincoln. Evidence from the excavated fort also shows that at some period the perimeter of the fort was substantially reduced. One explanation could be that following his defeat, the commanding officer was taking emergency steps to defend the fort, with a much reduced garrison, against threatened attack. The Iceni rebellion was eventually decisively defeated after a pitched battle in the Midlands. Roman rule was re-established in the region and the fort at Longthorpe seems to have become disused by about AD 65. Its military function was no longer required as the invasion frontier moved North and West.

The Road and River Network

The site of the river crossing near Water Newton continued to grow however, and eventually became the substantial Roman town of *Durobrivae*. The low mounds that cover the remains of its walls can still be seen, South of the Nene, in a field alongside the busy A1 road. It held a significant strategic position at the junction of Ermine Street and the important route to the Southwest towards Northampton. There may also have been a link with the Fen Causeway, a system of roads, causeways and canals running across the wetlands to the East. Originally this would have had a military purpose, changing over time to a communication and trade route as the fens became an important area for agriculture as well as the extraction of salt. The road network would have been built by the army and then maintained by local officials. Sections across Ermine Street to the South of Ailsworth have shown that it was re-surfaced many times.

A good communication system was essential for economic growth, enabling goods, information and people to travel swiftly by horsedrawn cart or on horseback to and from London, Leicester (then called *Ratae Corieltavorum),* or Lincoln (*Lindum Colonia*). At the river crossing at Durobrivae a bridge was built, with stone piers but with timber upper works. The piers survived until the river was dredged in 1925. For a fuller description of the Roman road transport system see Chapter 2.

River transport was also of great importance. It was far cheaper to move heavy freight by river than by road and the

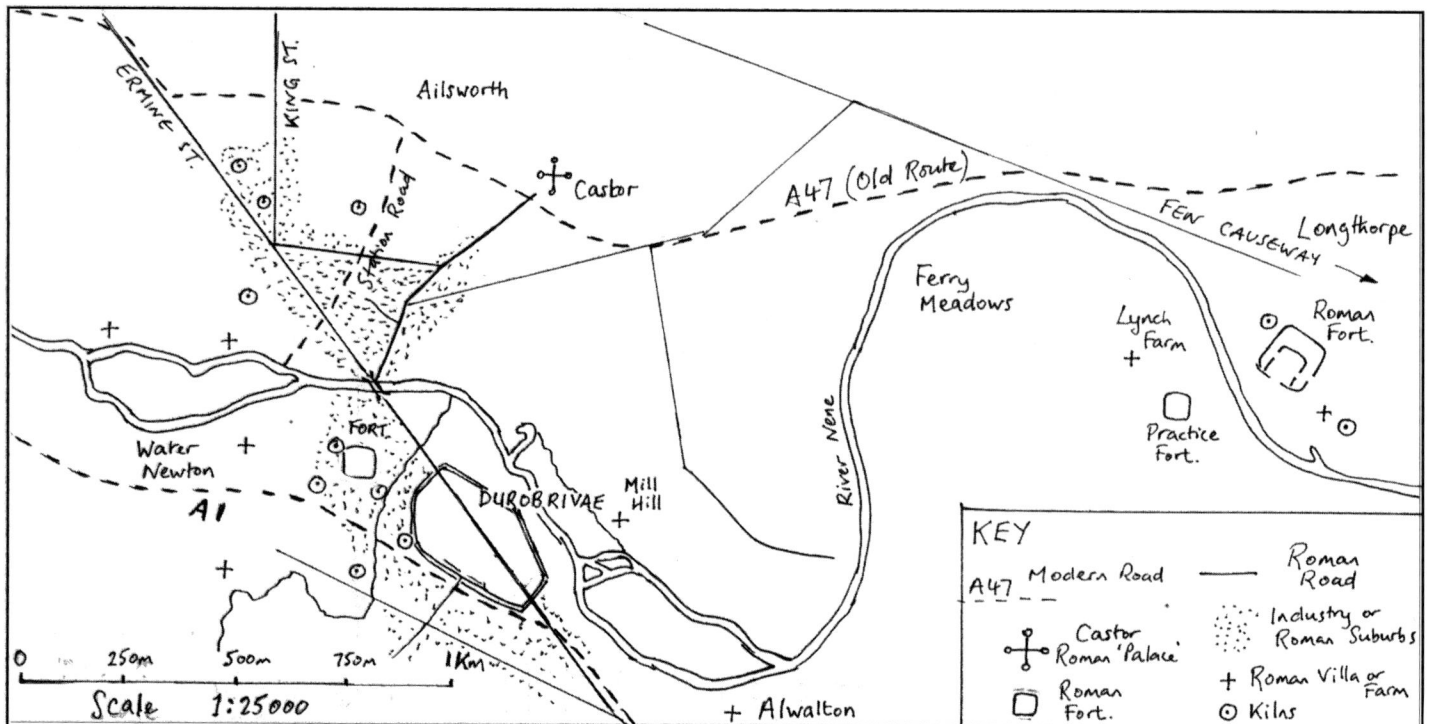

Fig 1d. A map of the Nene Valley showing the major Roman sites that have been identified.

Nene and other waterways provided important links with the Wash and the East coast. The river would have been used to bring agricultural produce from the fenlands in addition to raw materials, such as iron ore and wood for fuel, to the town. Water transport would also be the principal means of exporting pottery and other manufactured products. The Car Dyke, an artificial waterway to the East of Peterborough, was constructed along the edge of the fenlands, although its exact purpose is still disputed. It may have carried freight, but the primary characteristic of a canal is that it should have a level bed and be continuous, whilst the Car Dyke is neither of these. It may, more possibly, have been intended to drain the low lying fenland and increase the amount of land available for agriculture. A more detailed account of the important role of the River Nene in our history is given in Chapter 24.

The Town of Durobrivae

Two classical texts, the *Antonine Itinerary* and the *Ravenna Cosmography*, list the towns and cities of the Roman province. Among them is Durobrivae, literally meaning 'fort by the bridge'. Its identity has been confirmed by the evidence of two pieces of pottery found in this area, a fragment of *mortarium* or mixing bowl stamped with the words *Cunoarus fecit/Vico Durorivis* (made by Cunoarus at the Vicus of Durobrivae) and another signed *Sennianus DurobrivaeVrit* (Sennianus fired this at Durobrivae) thus also naming two of the town's inhabitants. As the army garrisons were withdrawn to the North and West to continue the conquest of more troublesome areas and tribes, so the settlement outside the fort next to the river crossing grew. A settlement associated with a military fort is called a *vicus* and would usually have sprung up initially to meet the needs of the garrison. It is generally agreed that many of the local British found Roman ways to their liking and readily adopted a Roman lifestyle, which influenced the clothes they wore, the food they ate, the goods they produced and, of course, the language they spoke. Camp followers, commercial traders, shop keepers and craftsmen of all kinds will have been drawn to the area, with shops and houses spreading along Ermine Street and a network of side streets. A civil authority replaced the military and the administration of the town would have been handed over to the new, self-governing community.

The town developed on the slightly higher ground close to the fort and bridge, but away from the immediate floodplain of the river. Because of the work of Don Mackreth of the Nene Valley Research Committee [5] in compiling a plan based on a remarkable collection of aerial photographs of crop-markings, a considerable amount is known about the

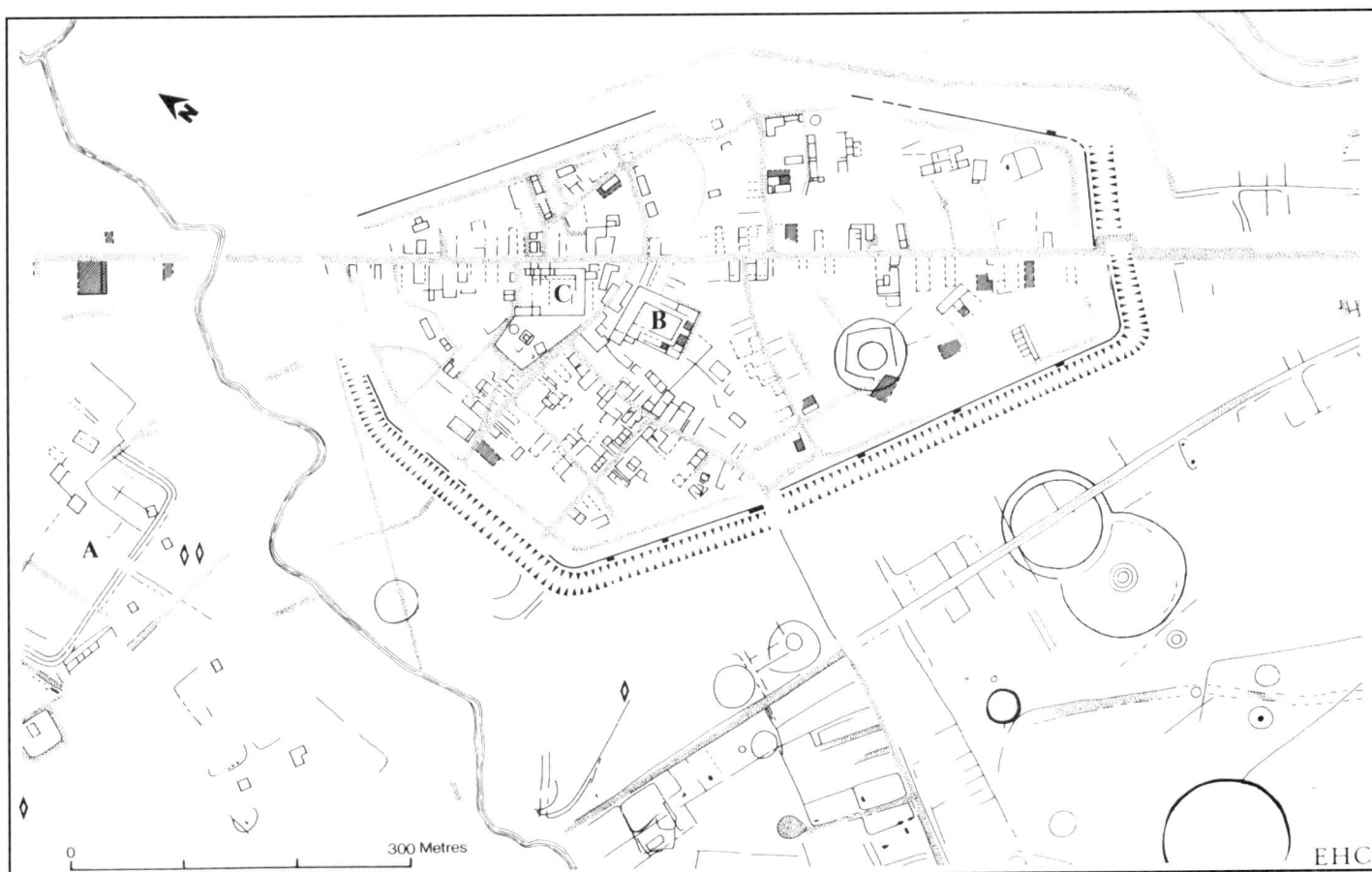

Fig 1e. A plan of the town of Durobrivae based on the evidence of aerial photography. A marks the site of the early fort by the river crossing, B the site of a possible 'mansio' or government staging-post and C another large building with a precinct possibly with a group of temples (after Mackreth 1984).

plan of the town and its surrounding area but very little has actually been excavated in modern times, apart from certain small areas outside the town walls and in the industrial area North of the river. The long line of shops and workshops, many having frontages onto Ermine Street, developed in an unplanned way and indeed Durobrivae is often cited as an example of this sort of unplanned growth.

Some time in the 4th century defensive walls were erected around the town centre, backed by a clay bank and protected by a ditch. The enclosed area is roughly hexagonal in shape due to the need to enclose an area that was already developed and covers about 44 acres in total. Three gates can be seen, two on Ermine Street and a third on a road leading towards Northampton to the Southwest. The defences were strengthened by square towers or bastions on at least two sides of the town, possibly added at a later date. A flood bank on the Northeast side, near the river, may have been a bypass road. There will also have been wharves and warehouses fronting the river itself. Inside the walls Ermine Street forms the main axis but narrow lanes leading from it divide the walled area into irregular plots of land. These plots or *insulae* may have contained a complex pattern of closely-packed stone and timbered buildings. Many of these were on narrow frontages with shop fronts on the road and workshops and living quarters behind for the craftsmen and their families. There is evidence of regular rebuilding of these structures, indicating that the town was a thriving community over a considerable period. Inside the town there is evidence of a number of courtyard buildings which are likely to have had specialized functions. A large courtyard building lay at an angle to the main street, its layout suggesting that it was a *mansio*, a government staging post or inn for travelling officials and couriers. The other large building that fronts Ermine Street has a precinct or yard, containing what may be three temple structures. If so, the building may have served these roadside shrines or have been the headquarters for a local religious cult. Within the town few of the individual buildings had garden plots behind indicating their occupants were dependent on specialized trades or farmed lands elsewhere. Craftsmen such as bronze, gold and silver smiths, carpenters and joiners, shoemakers and leather workers, and many others will have lived in Durobrivae. None of these trades leave much evidence of their existence unlike the heavy industries of pottery and iron-working outside the town. In the Southeastern corner of the town there are signs of larger and more substantial dwellings at the end of short side lanes. These are likely to have been the houses of the town's wealthier inhabitants. Artis did some excavation here, noting some dwellings with Alwalton 'marble' (a polished limestone) on their walls.

Determining the actual status of the town has always been problematic. It obviously enjoyed some degree of self government but the sheer size of the town, together with its extensive suburbs and industrial area, sets it apart from many of the other 'small towns' of Roman Britain [6]. A milestone was found nearby in 1785, originally erected in AD276 and stating that it stood one mile from its original point of measurement. It is usually accepted that such milestones were measured from *Civitas* capitals, towns serving as centres of regional tribal government, suggesting the town had been promoted to this rank towards the end of the 3rd century. This may reflect the town's growing size and commercial importance and fits with the apparent evidence of some high status buildings and private dwellings within the walls. If it was a *civitas* it would have governed a surrounding area, possibly extending as far Southwards as Sawtry and Southwest to Thrapston.

Industry and the Suburbs

The characteristic which sets Durobrivae apart from other Roman towns is the sheer scale of the industrial area which surrounds it, both to the West and South, and North over the bridge along Ermine Street in what has been traditionally known as the Normangate Field. This area now sits on either side of the fields bordering Station Road in Ailsworth, separated from the site of the enclosed part of Durobrivae by the Nene Valley Railway. Despite its current appearance as peaceful farmland, this was once one of the largest known industrial areas in the whole of Roman Britain (see colour plate section). The suburbs seem to have developed extensively prior to the building of the town walls. Early occupation appears to have been concentrated along Ermine Street and other side roads, suggesting a haphazard, 'ribbon development'. However the presence of some very regular plots at the North end of Normangate Field, which have been dated to the early 2nd century, along with similar plots to the South of the town, suggests that land distribution was regulated and under official control. Those plots on prime sites close to Ermine Street show the clearest evidence of industrial use, with buildings, workshops, kilns and furnaces becoming more densely crowded as time went on. The suburbs continued to flourish, reaching furthest in the 4th century when they covered at least 250 acres.

It is clear that the pottery industry was a major factor in this expansion. In the Roman world pottery vessels were widely used for food storage and preparation as well as tableware. At first the Roman garrisons would have used locally-produced wares, in the form of calcite-gritted pots and storage jars, along with much finer continental imports. However the excavations of the Longthorpe fort suggest the garrison soon began to manufacture its own tableware and cooking pots of a much better quality, fired in a battery of kilns to the Southeast of the fort. These kilns were in use around AD 50-65 and were probably operated by potters brought specially from the Rhineland. After they fell into disuse it is only in the second quarter of the 2nd century that a new style of local pottery started to appear, fired in kilns to the West of Durobrivae, over two miles from Longthorpe. In places these overlay the old fort next to the river, indicating that it was now disused.

This new pottery was the colour-coated ware which was later found in such quantities locally that Artis called it *Castorware*. It is now more usually known as *Nene Valley ware* and is one of the best known types of Romano-

Fig 1f. Another engraving from Artis's 'Durobrivae' showing the construction of a kiln he had excavated.

British pottery. The skills to make it may again have been imported from the Continent but were quickly mastered by local craftsmen. Numerous kilns have also been found in Normangate Field itself. Several local designs became famous, including 'Hunt cups' which were beakers depicting hunting scenes, and others with a scroll design. A wide range of different vessels were produced including dishes, jars, bowls, flagons and jugs. This high-quality tableware has been found throughout the country and was exported further afield to other parts of the Roman Empire [7](see colour plate section). For more local markets, including the fenland area, a coarser *greyware* was developed, producing cheaper utensils. The industry grew rapidly to meet increasing demand and in the 3rd century the potters introduced an imitation of the high quality Samian ware whose import had ceased. The quality of the local product is, however, very noticeably inferior to the original.

The industry was partially dependent on river transport to bring in the raw materials and fuel (probably charcoal) for the kilns, and to distribute the finished products. Middlemen, known as *negotiatores,* would have purchased in bulk and taken the wares to more distant markets. In the 3rd century, potteries were also established at Stanground, Sibson and Stibbington, possibly more conveniently located with respect to the markets and raw materials; certainly the number of working kilns in the Normangate area seems to have declined around this time.

It was not only pots that were needed however. Artis discovered evidence of iron ore and iron smelting in the Bedford Purlieus and Old Sulehay forest to the West of Wansford, and there is more recent evidence of intensive metalworking at Sacrewell. In 1969 a large aisled building containing over twenty furnaces was excavated in Normangate Field. The furnaces resembled others found at nearby sites, such as Lady Lodge farm at Orton Longueville, and can be identified as smithing furnaces. The lack of metalworking debris suggests the iron ore was first roasted, then iron was smelted in Bedford Purlieus and Old Sulehay forest and the iron *blooms* transported to the workshops at Normangate and elsewhere to be forged into the finished tools and implements. Smaller furnaces have been found on the sites of several local farms, suggesting that farm implements and other articles were repaired, and perhaps even manufactured, on site.

Neither was iron the only metal worked. A single crucible with an attached droplet of bronze discovered in Normangate Field indicates the presence of a small bronze industry, and other finds such as a goldsmith's weighing scales show the precious metals trade may also have been present. One find made by Artis was a coin mould obviously used by a forger, indicating that not all trade was legitimate, even in Roman Britain! It has also been argued, largely on stylistic grounds, that a group of artist-artisans making mosaics was established within the town itself in the latter part of the 4th century. Artis claimed to have found a possible workshop for the mosaicists. Certain common mosaic designs have been found across the wider region. but the only buildings in the immediate locality with mosaic floors of similar design are the high status villa on Mill Hill and the *praetorium* on Church Hill (see colour plate section).

Agriculture

Despite the existence of a thriving market town with its industrial outskirts, the majority of the population will have lived off the land, and the prosperity of the town will have depended on that of the farming community around it. The pattern of agriculture in the Iron Age will still have been common in the early years of Roman rule since the outlines of many small farms and settlements, with ditched fields, farm yards and enclosures for stock can be seen on aerial photographs of much of the Nene valley. The towns drew on the produce of farms from a wide area to feed their populations. Mixed arable and livestock farming would have been needed to supply the demand for meat, dairy products and cereals, as well as hides and wool.

These native-type settlements are much more common in the Welland valley than in that of the Nene, where it is possible that the Roman garrisons may have taken over the land to produce food for themselves, or that large villa estates were established at an early date, replacing the smaller farms. Another theory is that local native farmers could have been evicted from the area and encouraged to settle newly drained land at the fen edge, in which case we might well have expected to see the cropmarks of their abandoned settlements. The possibility cannot be excluded that the more prosperous local tribesmen may themselves have adopted Roman villa building styles and farming practices at an early date. What is certain is that a network of substantial Roman-style stone villas with courtyards and outlying farm buildings was established close to Durobrivae.

There is evidence of five villa locations within two miles of Durobrivae. Artis identified the site of a large courtyard villa on Mill Hill with signs of a tesselated floor and painted walls, both indications of substantial wealth. There are two in Ailsworth parish on the banks of the Nene only 600 metres apart, the more Easterly of which shows evidence of large enclosures which could have been vegetable gardens or stock enclosures. Both of these buildings would have enjoyed fine river frontages and had water meadows. The estates belonging to these villas are likely to have stretched Northwards towards the higher ground above Ailsworth and Sutton where the clay uplands may have been used for pasture. Roman agricultural methods were sophisticated and local farmers would have exploited the natural resources to the full. They are likely to have farmed cattle, sheep and pigs as well as wheat and barley, rotating their crops with beet to enrich the soil. A stone structure excavated at Hall Farm in Orton Longueville has been shown to be a corn dryer. Grain was roasted on a stone floor, heated from below, so that it could be stored and preserved. At the Lynch Farm site

Fig 1g. Artis's plate showing the remains of a substantial villa at Mill Hill Castor. The engraving shows a view towards the Nene, Durobrivae and Sutton and Normangate fields.

in what is now Ferry Meadows, evidence of fish farming has been found. There are similar villa sites to the West and South of the town, some on the other side of the present A1 road as well as evidence of other Roman sites at Marholm, near Burmer Wood, and at Top Lodge Farm, Upton. More such sites might have been expected, but it is possible that land to the Northwest of the town, around Ailsworth, could have been managed woodland, providing fuel for the town and for the kilns and furnaces on Normangate Field.

The town may also have been supplied with produce from a much wider area. It is known that farmers started to colonize the rich silt soils of the fens in the 1st century and finds of Durobrivae pottery in that area indicate the fenlands were also a market for the town. Boats carrying the pottery downstream could easily have returned laden with agricultural produce. There have been few possible sites of villas found within the fens, despite the area's obvious importance for food production. One explanation is that the fens were a large imperial estate with small communities of local tenants, but without a wealthy landowning class who would have benefited from the profits from the markets further inland. Extensive settlements and field systems were constructed on the numerous low islands, many perched on the exposed banks of prehistoric rivers no longer existing today. Salt was extracted from the tidal rivers which still ran far inland. The Car Dyke might then also have served as a distinct boundary to this productive area. Durobrivae is the closest substantial Roman town to the edge of the fens, with good road and river links to the East. The town may well have been the economic centre for the fens, providing the necessary administration as well as acting as a depot from which produce could be sent further afield. If the town did serve such a purpose it might explain the anomaly between its size and apparent status, as well as providing a possible explanation for the impressive *praetorium* building in Castor village as the residence of a local imperial official [8].

Religion

Roman official religious policy, especially before Christianity became the state religion of the Empire, was one of complete tolerance of personal religious belief and practice, subject only to an individual willingness to undertake additionally the formal observances addressed to the state gods representing the guardianship and spirit of the Empire. Any individual could address a particular chosen deity, who might be the guardian of the house or family, the spirit of a particular place, or have certain powers or characteristics needed by the supplicant, or might even simply be favoured by that person. Only Jews, and later Christians, insisted there was only one true god and that all others were false. The classical Roman gods were naturally popular, as was the worship of deceased emperors. However, many gods were rooted in local native traditions, often connected with features such as springs, rivers or lakes, themselves thought to be sacred. Many of these divinities were Celtic in origin and pre-dated the Roman period. It had been the custom in Bronze and Iron Age Britain to make votive offerings to these gods by depositing weapons or jewellery in the water at such places. Evidence of this practice has been found at the site of the Fengate power station and the old river bed at Orton Longueville. Sometimes the names of local deities became linked with Roman ones, suggesting they had common characteristics. The native god, *Camulos*, for example, is often paired with Mars the Roman god of war, whilst the surviving temple at the hot springs at Bath was dedicated to *Sulis-Minerva*, a composite of *Sulis*, a native deity, and Minerva, the classical patron goddess of arts and handicrafts. The capacity of Roman religious beliefs to accommodate existing gods may have been one reason for the acceptance of Roman ways by so many of the native population.

There was a variety of places of worship for these many divinities, sometimes in large temples, often in roadside shrines, in temples within certain precincts within towns, or within private houses and villas in the countryside. The typical Romano-British temple contained a small central shrine or *cella* surrounded by an *ambulatory* or walk-way and often facing East or Southeast. There might have been an apse that would contain a statue of the god or goddess, or an altar suggesting offerings or sacrifice. There are local examples of several of these. The excavation at Lynch Farm uncovered what was thought to be a small Romano-Celtic temple within the farm itself [9]. In Normangate Field a potter's workshop within the industrial area seems to have been converted to religious use with an apse added for a religious statue. Within Durobrivae there seems to have been a precinct attached to one of the major buildings that contains the outline of three possible shrines, one at least having an *ambulatory* around it. During excavation of a gas pipeline in 1998, two small temples or shrines were found on either side of Ermine Street Southwest of Ailsworth at what must have been the edge of the industrial suburbs. We can easily imagine travellers making offerings as they started a long journey, or giving thanks for the completion of their journey as they approached the town. Artis also records the discovery of two statues in a stone quarry at Sibson, one of Minerva, and the other of Hercules. There is thus ample evidence that a wide range of pagan divinities were worshipped in the locality.

The most remarkable find of religious significance near Durobrivae is neither Celtic nor classical but Christian. It is established that Christianity took root in Britain, probably some time in the 3rd century, even before the emperor

Constantine I made it the official religion of the Empire, in around AD 312. Christians had been persecuted intermittently since the 1st century and the martyrdom of St Alban in the 3rd century in Britain is evidence of the conflict and struggle between the pagan adherents of the old gods and the followers of the new religion. It is not surprising that those who upheld the polytheism of the old ways should have felt threatened by Christianity's rejection of all other gods and its allegiance to a single ultimate divine authority. The Church must have prospered however, at least in some places and for some sections of society, because it is recorded that Christian delegations from the four provinces of Britain, three of them led by bishops, attended the Council of Arles in AD 314.

There is evidence of Christian communities in Colchester, London and York and they must also have existed elsewhere. Mosaics and wall-paintings depicting Christian symbols and figures have been found at several villa sites in Southern Britain. A large lead tank, almost certainly used for baptisms and decorated with Christian symbols, was found at Ashton near Oundle. Few people could have anticipated, however, that a relatively insignificant provincial centre like Durobrivae would be the location for the discovery of a Christian treasure of great value. In 1975 a local metal detectorist produced a pottery vessel said to have been found near the banks of the Nene, close to the Durobrivae site. When unpacked it was found to contain a collection of Roman silverware, nearly thirty items, including a dish, cup, bowl, jug, strainer and a number of triangular plaques (see colour plate section). What made the finds so remarkable was not simply their design or age, but the number and nature of symbols engraved upon the various items, including the Greek Chi-Rho as well as the letters Alpha and Omega. These are undoubtedly Christian symbols, widely used in the early Church before the cross was adopted as the universal Christian emblem. The items could clearly have been used as part of the Christian liturgy, possibly for the mass or baptism. This collection has come to be known as the Water Newton Treasure and its discovery attracted enormous attention. The style of the pieces is Byzantine and they have been dated to the late 3rd or early 4th century [10]. The historian, Guy de Bedoyere, describes them as having *'the most overtly religious tone of any of the major treasures of Roman Britain'* [11]. An inscription on one of the bowls confirms this interpretation. The bowl bears the name Publianus and the words '*Sanctum altare tuum Domine subnixus honoro*' meaning 'I honour your holy altar, O Lord in the name of Christ'. One of the cups is inscribed with the names *Innocentia et Viventia*, as well as Christian symbols. Possibly these were all members of a Christian community. Yet although the pieces are undoubtedly Christian, some aspects of their design suggest links with a pagan past. Known pagan rituals sometimes involved the use of a wine strainer similar to that in the collection. The triangular plaques also show echoes of pagan origins, despite their Christian inscriptions, as such plaques were often nailed to the outside of temples as dedications or offerings to a particular god or to fulfil a vow. One plaque bears the words '*Iaemcilla votum quod promisit complevit*', meaning 'Iamcila fulfilled the vow she promised'. The treasure may thus indicate some memory and continuation of elements of earlier religious traditions, or the deliberate adoption of some elements of pagan worship which were later to be assimilated into Christian practice.

It is likely the items came from a church of some kind nearby. The word *altare* can mean 'sanctuary' as well as our understanding of the word 'altar', but both meanings imply some sort of building which contained a sanctified area. This could have been a building within the town itself or possibly a sanctified area within the large Roman *praetorium* building at the top of Church Hill in Castor which lies partly under the foundations of St Kyneburgha's Church. *Publianus, Innocentia* and *Viventia* appear to be the earliest recorded names of members of a Christian congregation in England, and that congregation might even have worshipped on the site of the existing church. As to why the treasure was buried, there are a number of possible explanations. It was obviously hidden for safe keeping, possibly by a thief to collect later, or by a group of marauding Saxons who looted it in the 5th century from a church site. The most likely explanation, however, is that it was buried by a priest or by members of a Christian church during the turbulent times towards the end of Roman rule, or during a period of conflict between pagan and Christian communities. Yet despite all that is unknown about its origin or significance, there can be no doubt that the Water Newton silver is of great historical and religious value, the earliest known collection of Christian church silver from the whole Roman Empire and a source of great pride for our local community.

Castor

Less than a mile to the Northeast of Normangate Field lies the village of Castor itself. Fragments of Roman pottery, brick and tile have been found around many of its buildings and there are large quantities of Roman building material in the walls of St Kyneburgha's church. Once again it was Artis who, over a period of several years in the 1820s, uncovered several Roman buildings around the top of Church Hill and Stocks Hill and immediately below the hill, on the Peterborough Road.

Substantial mortared 'herringbone' coursed limestone foundations of Roman buildings can still be seen protruding from the walls on Stocks Hill and Church Hill. These were not humble dwellings, many of the structures having mosaics and tessellated floors, painted wall plaster and heating systems, indicating substantial wealth. One of Artis's illustrations shows a bath house with a hypocaust, or under-floor heating, under the lane leading up to the church, beside the present day school field. This was a high status building, with its changing room, cold bath, and various heated chambers. Excavations in the lower churchyard by Charles Green and others in the 1980s [12] revealed another bath house building with a hypocaust a little Westward of the gate leading to Castor School playground. This may have been demolished however prior to the erection of the complex already mentioned.

It is the later structures around the crest of Church Hill, however, that are of the greatest interest. Whilst it was first thought they were separate buildings, more recent work by J P Wild [13] and Donald Mackreth [14] has suggested they were a series of rooms or chambers belonging to one large structure, an imposing building with large rooms and an open courtyard flanked by wings projecting down the slope to the Southwest. The view from the top of this prominent location must have been magnificent, a panorama of the valley below with its green fields, the river, the potteries in the busy suburbs and the town itself. Careful measurement of the levels of the various rooms proved that the building was terraced in relation to the sloping ground and was truly palatial in size. The overall site measures 902ft by 400ft, the left wing having

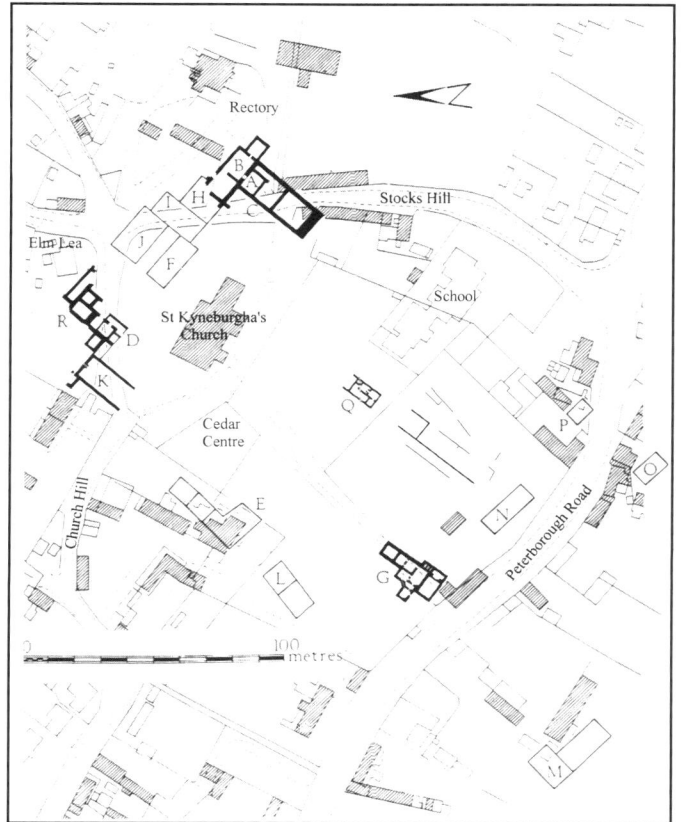

Fig 1h. Plan of Castor village showing the remains of Roman buildings around the church. The structures A-H are those so lettered by Artis in 'Durobrivae'. Foundations confirmed by modern excavation are outlined in solid black (after Mackreth 1995)

Fig 1i. The bath house excavated by Artis that lies beneath the lane leading up to the church. This building is marked 'G' in Fig 1h.

27

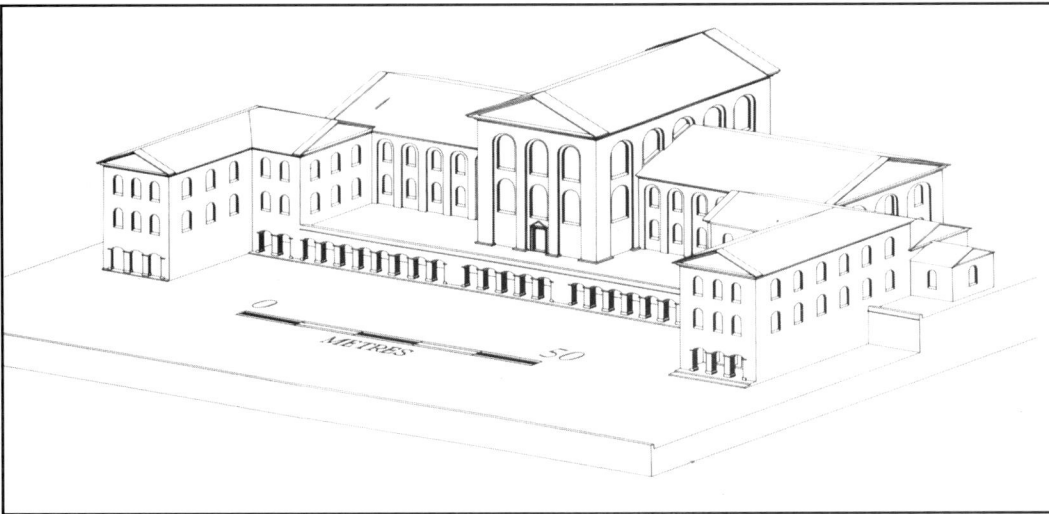

Fig 1j. A possible reconstruction of the great Roman Building on top of Church Hill and Stocks Hill in Castor (after Mackreth 1984)

a single room no less than 79ft long and 30ft wide. The building could have stood as much as 63ft high, including the gable and the terrace it stood on. The main chamber on the central terrace cannot have been much smaller. The complex has been dated to around AD 250 and is clearly far more substantial than an ordinary villa. It has been interpreted as being a *palatium* or *praetorium*, the official residence of a Roman dignitary, as yet unidentified. We can only speculate who this may have been. Possibly this may have been the headquarters of a senior military figure, or perhaps a senior civilian official involved with the administration of the town or of an imperial estate on the fens. Small-scale excavations in 1989 by Ian Meadows [15] in the playing fields of the Woodland Leisure Centre uncovered evidence of further high quality buildings flanking the approach to Castor from the South. It is not hard to imagine an avenue of buildings lining a road leading up to the impressive structure on the hill. Once again we are faced with a tantalising set of unanswered questions about an important aspect of our local history.

The End of Roman Britain

A traveller from London to York in the 4th century would have passed through a succession of prosperous small towns on his journey, set in flourishing countryside. This tranquillity may have masked the increasing political instability within the Roman Empire and increasing threats to it from outside. A number of rebellions saw political leaders, supported by the army in Britain and Gaul, set themselves up as rival emperors, leading to civil war with the forces of Rome itself. There were also increasing threats from Saxon pirates on the East and Southern coasts of Britain which led to the building of a number of forts and the reorganisation of defences under an official entitled 'Count of the Saxon Shore'. It is hard to say how these factors affected local communities. There is evidence of a real decline in the pottery industry in

Fig 1k. A view from what is now the Old Rectory of the Roman remains excavated by Artis which formed the North-eastern range of the large Roman building on Stocks Hill Castor, marked 'B' in Fig 1h.

the later 4th century, but this may not have been a sign of an overall economic decline. The town walls of Durobrivae were strengthened by the building of bastions to carry artillery, probably around AD 370, but the extent of the threat from raiders at that time is uncertain.

There is more certainty about the political changes. No new Roman coins were minted in Britain after AD 407 which would have progressively paralysed the trading economy. The town councils of Britain were told in about AD 408 that they could no longer rely on the Roman army for their defence. The central administration and the few imperial troops remaining in Britain were withdrawn by AD 410, and Rome itself was sacked that same year. There is much debate about the impact of the political break with Rome. Some have suggested there was a sudden descent into chaos and anarchy as society broke down with the end of centralised authority and waves of invasions by Angles, Jutes and Saxons. It is more likely, however, that Roman ways persisted for some time and that there were gradual changes in British society as it adapted to a more local structure and the influence of incomers from across the North Sea. With the withdrawal of the central administration and the army there would have been nobody to maintain law and order for the protection of travellers and neither the finances nor the specialist manpower to maintain the roads and bridges, so that travel would have become progressively more difficult and dangerous. The consequential impact on trade and the economy generally is illustrated by the complete absence of evidence that the industrial production of pottery continued into the early 5th century. In addition the growing scarcity of coinage would inhibit trade, even between adjacent towns.

There is some evidence that farming continued and that a simple local economy was maintained. At Hall Farm, Longthorpe [16], Saxon pottery has been found as well as Roman, indicating that the farm remained occupied during troubled times. Similar finds of early brooches from Woodston and Peterborough suggest that Anglo Saxon settlements may have begun in the Nene valley before AD 500. Durobrivae itself and the *praetorium* on Castor Hill were most likely abandoned, the buildings left to decay or robbed for their stone, There is evidence however that some structures were re-used, the archaeological investigation ahead of the building of the Cedar Centre showing that the shells of some of the Roman buildings on the site were occupied in the Saxon period [17].

The first recorded historical event of the new era was the arrival of St Kyneburgha soon after AD 654, to found a monastery among the ruined buildings. Even the remains of the Roman structures must have been impressive as the new inhabitants called their settlement *Ceaster*, an Old English word meaning 'fortified place', from which the modern name of Castor is derived. In time, the memory of what had gone before faded as new kingdoms and a new social structure emerged. Today there are few obvious signs of the importance of our locality in Roman times, the town of Durobrivae with its industries and

Fig 1l. A view looking down Church Hill Castor with the Churchyard wall on the left, of the foundations of part of the Western wing of the Roman building, marked 'D' in Fig 1h.

the great house on Church Hill have all vanished. The Water Newton treasure is safely preserved in the British Museum. We have sought, though, to retain a sense of continuity with our past, for on the walls of the Cedar Centre is mounted the Chi-Rho and the Greek letters Alpha and Omega, the chief emblems of Christianity in Roman Britain.

Fig 1m. The Chi-Rho

Andrew Nash

Andrew has lived in Ailsworth with his family for over 25 years. After receiving his MA in English literature from Cambridge University he came to the Peterborough area to pursue his career as a social worker. He now works for Peterborough City Council, developing new services for people with learning disabilities. His interest in history and archaeology has grown over the years and he completed a course in archaeology at Peterborough College of Adult Education in 2000. He hopes to do further research into the history of this area and to produce an account of its Roman past that everyone can read and enjoy.

I would like to acknowledge the assistance I have received from the following archaeologists in writing this chapter - Ben Robinson of Peterborough museum for his considerable help in finding source materials, selecting illustrations and for generously giving help and advice whenever asked, Ian Meadows for providing the original inspiration to study local Roman history in his role as course tutor at Peterborough College of Adult Education and for sharing the results of his excavations at Castor School and the Woodlands site, and Donald Mackreth for allowing me to quote from his valuable written work on *Durobrivae* and the Castor *Praetorium*.

Notes

1. E.T Artis, *The Durobrivae of Antoninus Identified and Illustrated,* London 1828.
2. A.Hatton and P.Spoerry, *Later Roman Building Remains at Castor Primary School,* Cambs CC. 2000.
3. R. Jones, *The Romano-British Farmstead and its Cemetary at Lynch Farm near Peterborough.*
4. S.S.Frere and J.K. St.Joseph, *The Roman Fortress at Longthorpe* Britannia Vol.5 1974.
5. D.F..Mackreth, *Durobrivae* in Durobrivae –A Review of Nene Valley Archaeology Vol 7 1979.
6. B.C.Burnham and J.Wacher, *Water Newton* in *The Small Towns of Roman Britain* 1990.
7. M.Howe, *Roman pottery from the Nene Valley: A Guide* Peterborough City Museum 1980.
8. D.F.Mackreth, *Durobrivae, Chesterton, Cambridgeshire* from conference report *Small Towns in Roman Britiain.*
9. R.Jones, *ibid.*
10. K.Painter, *The Waternewton Silver Treasure* in Durobrivae – A Review of Nene Valley Archaeology Vol 4, 1976.
11. G. de la Bedoyere, *The Golden Age of Roman Britain,* Tempus 1999 p.68.
12. C & I. Green and C.Dallas, *Excavations at Castor,Cambridgeshire, in 1957-8 and 1973* Northamptonshire Archaeology 21, 1987.
13. J.P.Wild, *New light on origins of Castor* Castor Parish Archives ref D/R 1010.
14. D.F.Mackreth, *Castor* in Durobrivae – A Review of Nene Valley Archaeology, Vol 9, 1984.
15. I.Meadows, *Splash Lane, Castor* from Nene Valley Research Committee Annual Report 1989-1990 para 3.3.4.
16. D F Mackreth, *Orton Hall Farm – A Roman and Early Anglo-Saxon Farmstead* East Anglian Archaeology, 1996.
17. G.Lucas, *From Roman Villa to Saxo-Norman Village –An Archaeological Evaluation of the Cedar Centre Castor.* Cambridgeshire Archaeological Unit, May 1998.

Chapter 2
Survey of the Roman Roads

Introduction

One of the obstacles to a better understanding of the past occupation and economic utilisation of our landscape is the lack of a fully representative sample of archaeological sites for investigation. The Roman sites that are known are often discovered almost by chance, or when modern building developments are under consideration. There are exceptions, of course, such as the major roads or forts whose pronounced embankments and walls are clearly apparent, but lesser sites are frequently invisible to casual observation. Thus we are in danger of making false deductions based upon an incomplete and unrepresentative knowledge of the true pattern of past land settlement.

Sites of significant human activity, in communities functioning at any level above that of a peasant subsistence economy, are almost always located adjacent to roads or tracks, since the occupants would need to transport their produce and goods to and from market. Thus a study of the Roman roads can provide valuable clues to the location of hitherto unknown occupation sites.

The present author has spent many years developing a method for identifying the possible existence and routes of unrecorded Roman roads. The motive for these studies has been the hope of assisting the discovery of occupation sites through well-directed search rather than by chance. The present chapter reports a survey of the Roman roads of the local area utilising this method. In brief, it appears that there exists a network of both local and through roads much more extensive than is presently recorded. The complete network of roads, both known and newly identified, is illustrated at Fig 2a and is described more fully later in this chapter. Background information is also included to assist any readers who would like to make their own researches, for there is surely much more to be discovered.

Roman Roads in General

A Brief History
The Roman roads have left an indelible impression on the English countryside, particularly in our local area, where no less than five [1] of the known main roads converge towards Castor and the River Nene between Ailsworth and Water Newton. According to the official definitive map [2] of Roman Britain such a high degree of connectivity is exceeded only by Manchester, and matched only by major centres such as London and York.

Initially constructed for purely military needs in the early years of the Roman occupation after AD43, the national road network was progressively developed during the following three centuries to serve the needs of an expanding and diversifying cash-based trading economy. At district and local level a network of minor roads appeared through local and private initiatives, linking villages and individual land holdings with nearby main roads and providing convenient shortcuts and access to local facilities. The Romans also made much use of water transport; building dams, locks and wharves for efficient navigation of rivers far inland. Throughout the period the regular legionary troops of the Roman Army provided the core skills for planning and implementing the whole range of Government-sponsored building projects, from main roads and official buildings to public forums and theatres, etc. Even for quite minor projects undertaken at local government level, legionary surveyors and draughtsmen would provide design guidance and on-site supervision.

From about AD350 the resident garrison of the Roman army in Britain was greatly reduced to provide reinforcements for the threatened central European frontier of the Empire, and the increasing number of seaborne raids against Britain from Scandinavia and Northwest Germany led to a final phase of improvised forts and road construction to speed the available troops to areas of the East coast coming under attack.

After the formal withdrawal of Roman government in AD410 it was no longer possible to maintain the network of main roads in Britain, since neither the tax revenues nor the specialist engineering skills of the legionary troops were any longer available for construction projects. From then until well after the Norman Conquest the network of Roman roads remained in use, though many sections progressively deteriorated or became impassable as bridges collapsed and road

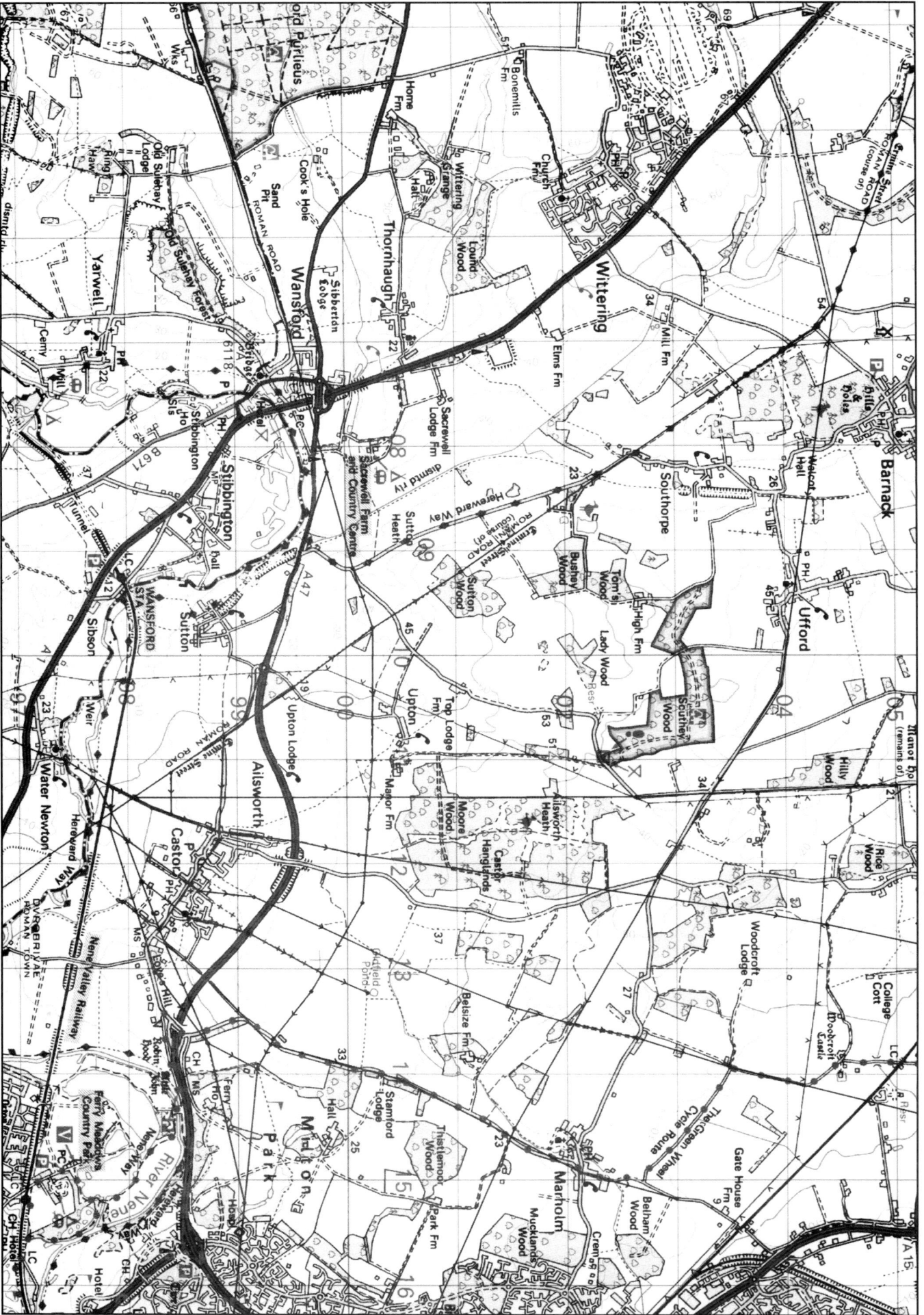

Fig 2a. Map of the local area with the known and conjectured Roman roads. Reproduced from Ordnance Survey mapping on behalf of The Controller of Her Majesty's Stationery Office © Crown Copyright 100042620 2004

surfaces disintegrated through lack of repair. Not until the major programme of turnpike road-building in the 18th century was a co-ordinated effort made to put the roads of England and Wales into better order.

The Roads and their Users

The fundamental purpose of a road is to enable heavier loads to travel further and faster and with less fatigue and discomfort for the traveller than would be the case with a natural surface. Roads therefore require strong foundations in contact with bedrock or fully-compacted subsoil in order to carry the gross weight of the heaviest individual item of traffic envisaged. A hard surface for the road must be provided to resist traffic damage and to sustain high contact pressures, thus allowing the use of narrow wheels on vehicles for reduced contact area and friction drag. The surface must also be as smooth as possible to reduce rolling friction and allow higher speeds without excessive jolting.

Road-building is always a laborious process, involving the use of skilled manpower, much manual labour, and the movement of large quantities of materials. Roads are therefore built to the lightest construction standards that will meet the purpose at hand. Examination of the known Roman roads in Britain and elsewhere in the Empire clearly indicates different classes of road construction, ranging from strategic military routes for rapid deployment of complete units or detachments; roads for use by civilian goods vehicles; and minor roads or footpaths suitable for pack animals or pedestrians [3][4]. A gravelled path three feet or so in width easily meets the needs of pedestrians and pack animals, whilst a main military road would need to accommodate troops marching four-abreast, followed by a baggage train of mules for their tents and camp supplies and carts carrying heavy equipment and spare weapons. Allowing sufficient elbow room, the military road would need to be some 20 feet in width.

School lessons commonly describe the construction of Roman roads in terms of foundations dug to a depth of three feet or so, filled with heavy stones at the base progressively reducing in size nearer the surface, topped with close-fitting stone slabs, and edged with paved kerbs and drainage ditches. Every mile of such a construction requires in excess of 20,000 tons of stone, and in many places stone is simply unobtainable. Of some 10,000 miles of identified Roman roads in Britain only three miles of such paved roads have been recovered. In South east England including East Anglia the most common method of construction was a mixture of small stones and gravel carefully mixed with clay as a binder; much as stone chippings and bitumen are used on modern roads. A good example of a Roman clay and gravel road surface can be seen in the exposed section of the road known as the Fen Causeway at the Flag Fen archaeological site (TL 226 989) East of Peterborough. Similar construction is still used today, such as the network of roads used for extracting felled timber from Southey Wood (TF 110 023) shown in Figs 2b and 2c and routinely used by modern 32-ton trucks without any apparent damage to the road surfaces.

Fig 2b. Modern forestry road of similar construction to many Roman roads

A road surface subject to surface water retention deteriorates quite rapidly under traffic loads, so it is important to ensure good drainage. Roman engineers would therefore take advantage of natural ridges in the landscape to carry their roads above ground subject to waterlogging or flooding; the route of Ermine Street across Normangate Field (TL 115 979) to the South of Ailsworth follows just such a natural ridge. Where this was not possible they would construct an embankment, or *agger*, to ensure drainage. A fine example of an agger some three feet high, shown at Fig 2d, can be seen at Sutton Cross (TL 108 989) where the modern local road leading Westward from Ailsworth to the A47 makes use of the old Ermine Street alignment for a few hundred yards. Aggers are so common a feature of Roman roads at sites with excellent natural drainage that they are often thought to be a component of their construction decreed

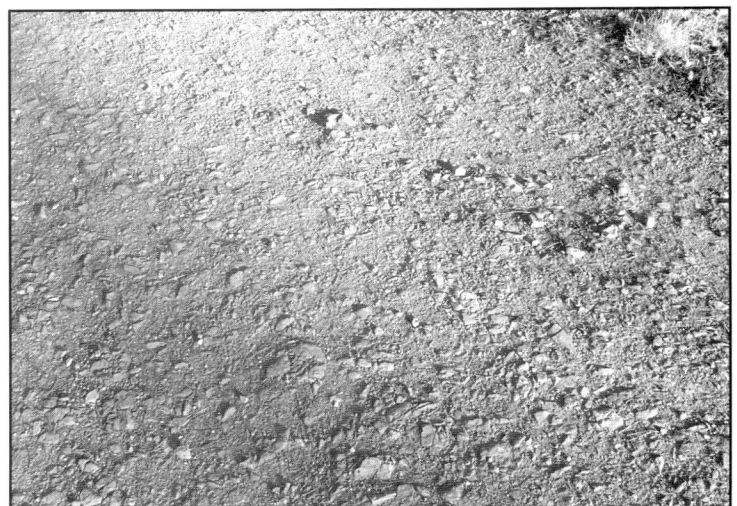

Fig 2c. Close view of a clay-bonded gravel road surface

Fig 2d. The Ermine Street agger looking South from Sutton Cross

by policy, but the numerous exceptions to any such rule and the commonsense avoidance of needless effort makes it much more likely that aggers frequently resulted just from the accumulation of surfacing materials over the course of many years of road maintenance.

The Romans were highly accomplished engineers capable of building masonry arches of considerable span, but to carry their roads across rivers they generally preferred flat beam bridges with wooden superstructures supported on stone piers or wooden trestles. Causeways to carry roads across river flood plains usually consisted of timber decking surfaced with gravel, and carried on open trestles so as not to impede the rapid dispersal of floodwaters.

Largely for reasons of economy Roman roads tended to proceed across country as a series of straight sections, ignoring all but the very steepest of gradients. Gradients were simply of no great consequence to the Roman army who always had plenty of men who could attach ropes to their carts to assist their horses or oxen to climb the steepest hills. Such assistance would not be generally available for civilian traffic but, as we shall see below, most commercial cargoes went by water except for the shortest of distances. Roman surveyors worked by establishing straight lines of sight, extended across country from the highest point of one natural ridge line to the next; thus their roads normally only changed direction at such summit points to effect an intended route change or to correct any unplanned divergence from the desired straight line. When testing a conjectured route for an unknown Roman road the occurrence of evident turning points mainly at such ridge lines provides strong evidence that the investigation is on the right scent.

The best general guidebook [5] to the Roman roads of Britain by Ivan Margary is sadly long out of print but can be consulted or obtained on loan from public libraries.

The Importance of Water Transport

Until very recently it was received wisdom that the Roman roads carried almost all of the inland heavy commercial traffic in goods and supplies. The basis for such a belief was the general opinion that river locks were not invented until the early 14th century, and thus it was held that the Romans would not have been able to regulate the depths of water in rivers to allow navigation by craft of any useful size. It is now clearly established that such a belief was unfounded; Raymond Selkirk discovered [6] the remains of a lifting-gate lock (such as the modern ones used on the River Nene) at Piercebridge in County Durham in 1979, confirming the application in Britain of river engineering principles well-attested elsewhere in the Roman Empire. The advantages of water transport over ox-wagons is overwhelming; the standard Roman *codicaria* (river barge) crewed by five men, and needing little more than a three feet depth of water, could carry a load of 10 tons 15 to 20 miles per day [7]. A similar load carried by road would require a convoy of 15 wagons, between 30 and 120 oxen, 30 men, and travel less than 8 miles a day. Thus we find that virtually every known site of any significant size in Roman Britain is accessible by such river traffic. The convergence of the known roads at their Ailsworth and Water Newton crossings of the River Nene is clearly of immense significance for the adjacent establishment of the large-scale pottery industry at Normangate Field and the choice of Castor as the location of the huge *praetorium* building described in Chapter 1.

The Survey Study Method

The quest for unknown roads begins by marking known Roman sites, roads, and river crossings on the Ordnance Survey map of the area [8] paying careful attention to centres of industry and mineral extraction. In the Castor area this step is particularly easy with the five known major roads, the Ermine Street crossing of the River Nene, the pottery-making sites at Normangate Field, and the town of Durobrivae itself. Next we mark any sharp turns on the known roads as these are possible locations for junctions with the unknown roads that we seek. Then comes the time-consuming part where we draw tentative routes for unknown roads, based on making convenient connections between significant places and the known roads. Experience is a major factor at this stage since we are looking for alignments of apparently unrelated segments of present-day roads, footpaths, edges of woodlands and field boundaries, etc. Some of these features often overlay Roman roads that had become disused by the medieval period because the accumulation of compacted roadstone made them too hard to be removed with the rather feeble farm implements used in the Middle

Ages. As it is easy to be led astray by map alignments that are actually chance occurrences it is important to look for any supporting evidence, including suggestive place names containing elements like gate, stone, or way or obvious Latin-derived words. A larger scale map can be helpful at this stage [9].

After the theorising comes the fieldwork. At this stage we visit as much of the tentatively identified Roman road network as possible, looking for such signs as abandoned quarries where road-building materials were extracted and land terracing or cuts through the lips of ridge lines. Water crossing points merit particular scrutiny for signs of bridge abutments, culverts, or improvements to the beds of streams as fords. It has been extremely helpful to our investigations that the local area is very well provided with public footpaths and bridleways, and we take this opportunity to pay tribute to the careful maintenance work done by the landowners and occupiers, so that nowhere has access to the points we wished to examine been impeded.

Wherever the line of a conjectured road crosses a footpath at the edge of a recently-ploughed field it is worth looking very carefully for broken pottery lying on the surface. The Romans seem to have been prodigious breakers of crockery, and it is rare indeed to find any area travelled or occupied by them lacking a goodly quantity of fragments. Pottery has been especially important in the present study because archaeological excavation in the local area is heavily regulated and effectively prohibited to an individual investigator. Cattle trampling the river banks where they go down to drink often expose fresh soil layers, and rabbits extending their warrens are unaware of the regulations when they throw out bits of buried pottery with the other unwanted debris; such opportunities for archaeological excavation by proxy should never be overlooked. It has been particularly helpful to the present study that the abundant fragments lying on the Normangate Field provided a good reference sample of attested Roman pottery for comparison with finds from elsewhere in the local area. Fig 2e, illustrative of one of our local familiarisation periods early in the study, shows how easy it is to scan the ground without intruding on the cultivated farmland.

Fig 2e. Looking for Roman pottery at the edge of Normangate Field

Description of the Roman Roads in the Castor Area

Scope of the Survey

The area of principal concern to the study for the Parish Book Project is, of course, the five parishes of Castor, Ailsworth, Marholm, Upton, and Sutton. To establish a linkage with the main road network of Roman Britain we have also looked more widely where necessary, and reference to a present-day road atlas will prove helpful in understanding the larger picture.

Interpretation of Results

As will be seen below, there appears to be a significant amount of duplication and perhaps illogicality in the location and routes of the hitherto unknown Roman roads that have emerged from the study. It must always be remembered, however, that the period of formal Roman governance of the East Midlands area lasted from soon after AD43 until AD410; a span of time very nearly as long as that which separates us today from the reign of Queen Elizabeth I. During that long period there were immense changes in land occupation and utilisation stemming from the growth of manufacturing industries and of agricultural production for cash sale, and the emergence of service industries such as transport, etc. New roads would be constructed as important new centres emerged, whilst roads no longer significant were either abandoned completely or were downgraded to local status. Such confusion seems to have particularly affected the roads leading Northeast from Castor. At Castor itself the construction of the praetorium building and its surrounding outbuildings and demesne seems to have required the diversion of existing roads. We make some attempt to give a chronological explanation of the development of the local road network but there is a good deal of uncertainty in this regard. Further research is required, but is beyond the scope of the strictly non-invasive methods available to the present study.

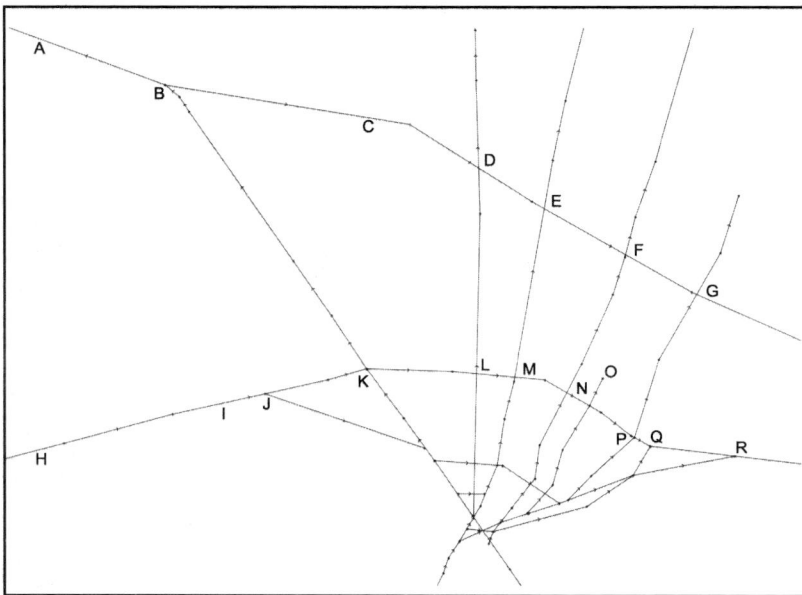

Fig 2f. General key to the points of interest on the local area map

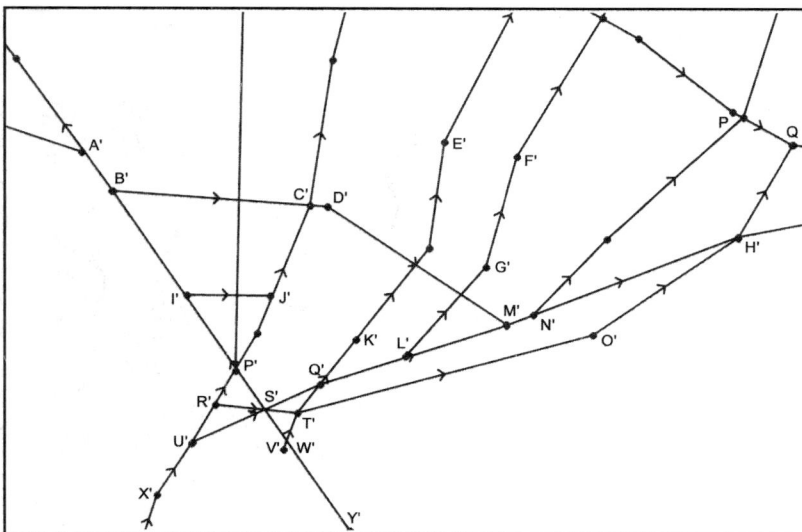

Fig 2g. Key to the map points of interest close to Castor

Any road alignments marked on the map at Figure 2a but not described below should be regarded as currently without logical explanation or lacking confirmatory evidence. They are included for interest and as agenda items for further investigation.

To assist in describing the Roman roads, both known and tentatively located in the study, Figs 2f and 2g assign letter identifiers to significant points on the main map shown at the beginning of this chapter. Plain letters will be found on Fig 2f, whilst apostrophised letters are located on Fig 2g which covers more plainly the area close to Castor village.

The Roman Main Roads and their Possible Extensions

Historical Sources
No contemporary written records of the Roman conquest and occupation of Britain survive; we have only a couple of pages in the fragmentary 3rd century writings of Cassius Dio recounting the events of the first few weeks of the invasion campaign. We therefore have to rely heavily on the archaeological evidence of the network of forts established by the Roman army as they advanced Northwards and consolidated their control of the conquered area [10].

The Castor Area
The future importance of the Castor area was determined by about AD45 with the establishment of a Roman lateral support road across the front of the occupied area, from Peterborough to Wimbourne in Dorset. In its Northern sector the main supply line for the army ran from the London bridgehead to the Water Newton area via Waltham Abbey, Braughing and Godmanchester; thus defining the Southern section of the future Ermine Street. The lateral road itself ran through Towcester and Irchester, passing Thrapston to arrive at the South bank of the River Nene also at Water Newton. A temporary legionary fortress was established at Longthorpe. Almost 50 miles to the Northeast, near Skegness, a fort at Burgh-le-Marsh was left apparently supported only by a water route across the Wash, of which more later. In the subsequent advance of the conquest zone King Street carried the main supply line Northwards to Lincoln via Bourne and Ancaster. The ensuing development of these military roads as part of the permanent strategic network, together with the engineering of the River Nene for safe and easy navigation, endowed the local area with great economic advantages for the future pottery and iron-founding industries established in the 2nd century [11].

Ermine Street
Leaving the Northwest gate of Durobrivae at Y' the low agger of Ermine Street is only visible for a short distance before the line enters the Southern flood plain of the River Nene. As already mentioned, it is likely that the road would be carried forward on a trestled viaduct to the river bank to avoid impeding any flood waters. Margary remarks [5] that the remains of a bridge were formerly seen in the river, but there is nothing visible now. The general lie of the land, however, suggests that the bridge crossed the river at an angle, in the direct line of the road, landing some distance up the quite steep slope above the North bank of the river at W'. A little way to the West of the conjectured landing point, at the edge of the field bounded by the pollarded trees visible in Fig 2h, a slight agger runs from V' straight up the slope to meet the Ermine Street line at the edge of the present Nene Valley Railway line.

At the river edge between V' and W' we found a considerable quantity of pottery fragments as illustrated at Fig 2i, representing a range of painted and patterned vessels of more diverse types than finds associated with the local potteries in Normangate Field.

The finds included the iron arrow head shown at the bottom left of the picture, which has flat edges and has quite clearly never been sharpened. We identify the collection as representing damaged or mislaid trade goods being handled at a riverside wharf. Supporting indications for such a conjecture are given by an untypical concentration of large stones embedded in the river bank and lying on the river bed adjacent which we interpret as the backfill of a wooden-fronted wharf. At the top of the slope, just South of the railway line, rabbits extending their warrens had thrown out more Roman pottery as illustrated at Figure 2j. This material is distinctly domestic in character and clearly of lower status than the trade goods at the riverside site so we identify the area as residential, perhaps of people acting as dockers or security guards at the wharf. Supporting evidence for this assessment is provided by the fragment of animal bone at top left of the picture which has several cut marks caused by butchery.

Continuing across Normangate Field, the Ermine Street line intersects the Thrapston road at P' and thence continues to Sutton Cross at B' where it becomes the modern road for about 300 yards and thence to B, Southwest of Barnack, where it makes a quite sharp turn Westwards and out of our area.

King Street

Though there are no visible clues to its existence, the obvious line of King Street runs Northward from the junction of Ermine Street and the Thrapston Road at P' along the Western edge of Moore Wood and Ailsworth Heath. North of Point D on the Marholm to Ufford road, King Street is duly attested on the Ordnance Survey maps and runs very nearly due North to Bourne along the route used by its modern successor. King Street continues Northwards from Bourne until it unites with the Ermine Street route just South of Ancaster. The main problem with the duplicated route to Ancaster is that Ermine Street, which Margary supposed [5] superseded King Street, offers no advantage in terms of easier gradients or lesser exposure to adverse weather to offset its greater distance. We might therefore conjecture that the Ermine Street loop is actually the beginning of

Fig 2h. View of the River Nene at the Ermine Street crossing

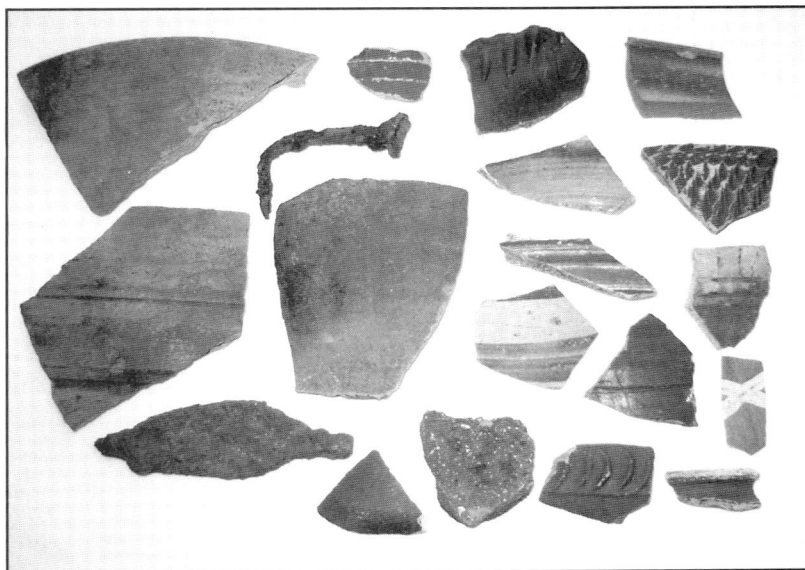

Fig 2i. Roman pottery, arrow head, and nail from the conjectured wharf

Fig 2j. Roman domestic pottery and bone fragment from living area near wharf

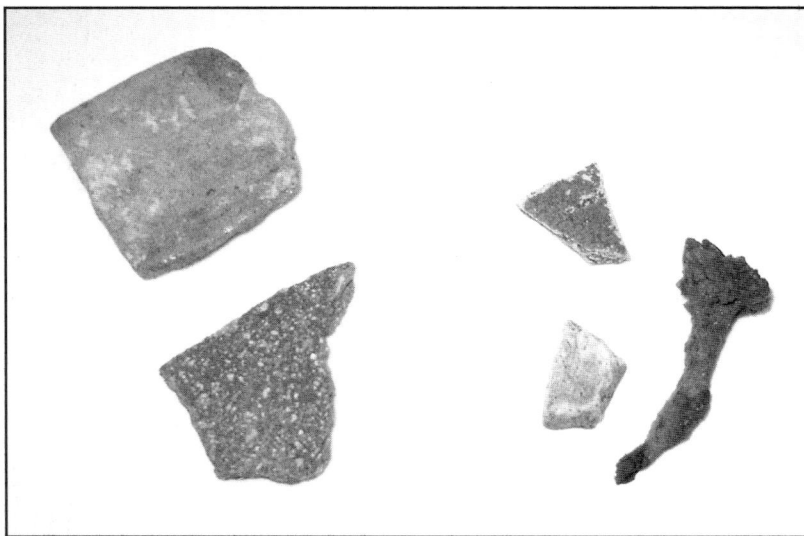

Fig 2k. Roman pottery from Alwalton Lock (left) and Water Newton ford (right)

an undiscovered Roman road running from the vicinity of Greetham just off the modern A1 North-westwards towards Nottingham.

Thrapston Road

The known Roman road passing Thrapston is part of the military lateral road of AD45. It is duly attested on the Ordnance Survey maps as far as Warmington, but its probable route onwards is easily traceable via Elton Park to Water Newton village. Crossing the main branch of the River Nene by the mill and lock we pass over a wide ditch which looks very similar to the Roman lock bypass canal discovered by Selkirk at Piercebridge [6]. Across the small island a very faint cropmark leads toward a ford in the shallow Northern channel of the river. Clear signs of a gravelled road surface are visible where the ford emerges on the North bank close to the extended line of Station Road, Ailsworth at U'. The ford lies about five yards West of the exact line of the road, prompting the speculation that it may have replaced a ruinous Roman bridge in medieval times. We expected no obvious signs of Roman activity at the ford, since the route between Water Newton Mill and Ailsworth would be have been in constant use from medieval times until at least the coming of the railway. Thus it was a pleasant surprise to find the fragments of Roman pottery and an iron nail possibly of that period, shown at the right hand side of Figure 2k, at the exposed edge of the gravel layer. The picture also includes at left two pieces of probable Roman domestic pottery that we found adjacent to Alwalton Lock across the field from Mill Lane, Castor.

The King Street route already described could have served to carry the Thrapston Road Northwards from the Water Newton river crossing, but there other intriguing possibilities that fit well with what little is known of the Roman conquest period. From its intersection with Ermine Street at P', there is an obvious direct extension of the Thrapston Road along Station Road entering Ailsworth at Point C', and thence towards Market Deeping through Points M and E, on a line that coincides with some 600 yards of the path through Castor Hanglands and a kink in the lane West of Woodcroft Castle. It seems very probable that the AD45 military zone would have included an outpost fort in the vicinity of Market Deeping, but confirmation of our conjectured road was clearly desirable. Where the line shown on the map crosses a footpath to the West of Woodcroft Lodge (TF 125 037), the discovery of the Roman domestic pottery shown at Fig 2l at the edge of the ploughed field provided the supporting evidence we needed.

Another credible extension of the Thrapston Road departs from the edge of the ford at U', passing across the Normangate field via Q', N' and P and thence past Marholm, in a direct straight line with the railway line leading

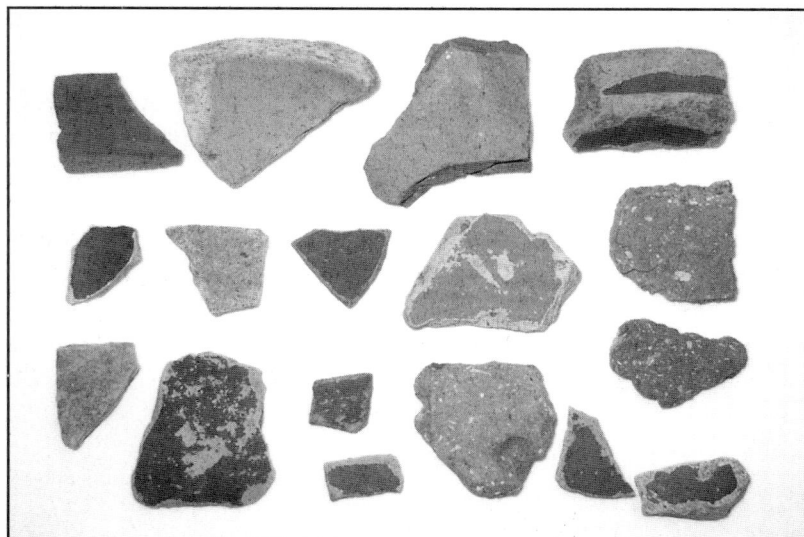

Fig 2l. Pottery fragments from the conjectured Thrapston Road route to Market Deeping

Northeast from Werrington towards Spalding. From Spalding the dismantled railway route is now utilised by the improved A16 road to Boston. From Boston the railway route leads almost directly to the conquest period Roman fort at Burgh-le-Marsh, already mentioned as apparently only supported by a water route across the Wash. Though we have discovered no reports of the existence of a Roman road underlying the railway line, there are apparently other instances in Britain of 19th century railway builders taking advantage of the firm foundations offered by Roman roads, and the extension of the Thrapston road hypothesised here does offer a solution to the otherwise highly unusual deviation from the standard Roman military doctrine of mutual lateral support between forts.

Kingscliffe Road

The known road from Kingscliffe to Wansford leads from nowhere to nowhere in Roman terms, so we must rely on extending its line if we are to discover its purpose. Just two miles West of Kingscliffe up the Willow Brook valley we reach the A43 road, where in Roman times there was a large number of iron-smelting furnaces, whose slag can even be seen lying on the surface today. We can therefore extend the known road with some confidence beyond Kingscliffe, at least as far as an intersection with the present A43 just North of the lodge gateway to Laxton Hall (SP 969 975). Westwards from the A43 at that point, a very clear agger points in a direction to intercept the major Roman road between Leicester and Corby Southeast of Medbourne, and thence to Market Harborough. To the East of Wansford we can extend the Kingscliffe Road to Point K where it meets Ermine Street, and onwards to Point L on King Street and M on our conjectured extension of the Thrapston Road to Market Deeping.

Fen Causeway

East of Peterborough the Fen Causeway can be traced through Whittlesey as far as the Flag Fen site. On the basis of the widely-held belief that the Castor praetorium served as the administrative centre for an agricultural estate in East Anglia it seems reasonable to extend Fen Causeway Westwards towards the Castor area. The process of looking for alignments of segments of modern road, footpaths and field boundaries, etc, suggests a line passing directly underneath Peterborough Cathedral, and thence somewhat speculatively to Point R in Milton Park. Here the Roman road appears to divide, one branch passing via H' and N', through the junction of Castor Main Street and Splash Lane at M' and thence onwards to the junction with Ermine Street at S' and the Water Newton ford at U'. The other branch passes through the Western edge of Milton Park at Point Q and thence via P and N to join the extension of the Kingscliffe Road described above. Yet another branch of the Fen Causeway, originating at Boongate (TL 210 988) in Eastern Peterborough, traverses a very convincing route via Points G to C to join Ermine Street at B where the latter makes a quite sharp turn Westwards.

The Local Roads

Castor Main Street as far as the junction with Splash Lane at M', represents a very credible Roman road in part passing along, as it were, the front garden wall of the Castor praetorium. In his 1935 study [12] of the road system near Durobrivae, Margary identified the line T'Q'L'M' as his Road 1, noting that the agger was particularly clear between Q' and L'. We extend that line to provide a direct link from the Water Newton ford at U' to the Southern branch of the Fen Causeway extension previously described. From Q' we suppose the modern footpath to link with the line of the known Roman local road lying parallel to Port Lane from K' to Castor Main Street and thence up Clay Lane.

At Point L' we can readily imagine a formal entrance drive leading to the front courtyard of the praetorium at G'. From the rear of the building we have a domestic access road to the complex, leading Northeast up Cow Lane to meet the conjectured link between the Kingscliffe Road and Fen Causeway, and onwards to Oldfield Pond at Point O. In an unreported study we have previously identified Oldfield Pond as the site of artesian springs supplying the praetorium by means of an aqueduct following the Cow Lane route. The existence of artesian springs under the pond has been confirmed [13] by observation when it was drained around 1980, and the suggested aqueduct route investigated by the present author by dowsing, and checked against the aqueduct engineering principles known to have been used by the Romans [14]. It therefore appears that we can delineate the praetorium private demesne by the road segment NP, the roads running Southwest from N and P, and the frontage on Castor Main Street. It may be significant also that the Southern branch of the extended Fen Causeway from R points almost exactly at Point P', the intersection of Ermine Street, Thrapston Road and King Street, passing within a hundred yards or so of the praetorium building itself. Unless merely coincidental, this alignment strongly suggest the diversion of pre-existing roads to accommodate the praetorium and its demesne.

The road R'S'T'O'H'Q is difficult to understand, as it appears merely to duplicate the sensible link road route between the Water Newton ford and H' on the Fen Causeway extension. On the ground it appears as a substantial ridge suggestive of an agger from the top of Love's Hill at O' towards H', but too irregular in height, width, and straightness to be convincing. Moreover, members of the Middle Nene Archaeology Group recall [15] a section being cut through it some years ago with nothing found. Were it not for the fact that its line shows as a very definite cropmark on one of the aerial photographs included in Margary's 1935 study report [12] we would have assessed it as merely a low natural ridge in the landscape.

Michael J D Brown

Served in the Royal Air Force 1953-1991, retiring in the rank of Air Vice-Marshal as Director-General Strategic Electronic Systems. Educated Trinity Hall Cambridge (Mechanical Sciences Tripos 1957, MA 1961). Qualified as RAF pilot 1959. Graduate of RAF Staff College 1970 and United States Air War College 1976. Commanded RAF North Luffenham, Rutland 1978-80. Member of the Royal College of Defence Studies 1981. Has studied the Roman roads of Britain for over 50 years. He and his wife Ruth (who finds most of the pottery) now reside in Bretton,

Notes

1. Ermine Street, King Street, an unnamed road from Kingscliffe, an unnamed road from Thrapston, and the Fen Causeway. The route of the Fen Causeway to the West of Peterborough is not officially acknowledged, but the present study clearly identifies it passing North of Castor on its way to joining with Ermine Street to the West of Barnack.
2. Ordnance Survey, *Roman Britain Historical Map and Guide,* 4th Ed, 1978 revised 1991.
3. N H H Sitwell, *Roman Roads of Europe,* Cassell, London, 1981.
4. Derek Williams, *The Reach of Rome – A History of the Roman Imperial Frontier 1st – 5th Centuries AD,* Constable, London, 1996.
5. Ivan D Margary, *Roman Roads in Britain,* John Baker, London, 3rd Ed, 1973.
6. Raymond Selkirk, *The Piercebridge Formula,* Anglia Publishing, Ipswich, 1983.
7. Raymond Selkirk, *On the Trail of the Legions,* Anglia Publishing, Ipswich, 1995.
8. Ordnance Survey, Landranger Series (1:50,000 scale), Sheets 141 (Kettering & Corby) and 142 (Peterborough).
9. Ordnance Survey, Explorer Series (1:25,000 scale), Sheets 227 (Peterborough) and 235 (Wisbech & Peterborough North).
10. Graham Webster, *The Roman Invasion of Britain,* Batsford Academic & Educational, London, 1980.
11. Barri Jones & David Mattingley, *An Atlas of Roman Britain,* Guild Publishing, London, 1990.
12. Ivan D Margary, *Roman Roads near Durobrivae (Castor, Northants),* The Antiquaries Journal - 15(2), 1935, pp 113-118.
13. Theo Hensman, Churchwarden of St Kyneburgha's Church Castor, personal communication.
14. A Trevor Hodge, *Roman Aqueducts & Water Supply,* Gerald Duckworth & Co, London, 2nd Edition, 2002.
15. J A Hadman, Chairman 2003 The Middle Nene Archaeological Group, personal communication.

Chapter 3
The Early Anglo-Saxon Period:
The Beginning of Our Villages

Introduction: A Misty Period

The Roman Empire retreated from this area in the early 5th century, their exodus from Britain the result of bloody conflicts between the Romano-British and Anglo-Saxon invaders intent on taking this island as their own. The cultural impact of these usurpers can be felt far down the centuries in manifold forms. One of the most long-standing contributions of Anglo-Saxons is found in the way we speak. Old English, the tongue of these newcomers, would eventually evolve into the English language we know today. The names of our five villages; Castor, Ailesworth Sutton, Marholm and Upton all have their roots in the Anglo-Saxon language preserving from time immemorial their original identity as old Anglo-Saxon settlements. Both Castor and Ailsworth are mentioned in early church manuscripts dating from the 8th and 9th Centuries. Castor is referred to as '*Kyneburga castrium*' [1], a memorial to St Kyneburgha, while Ailsworth is mentioned as the home of a curious 9th century woman who was convicted of witchcraft and drowned at London [2]. These scant references in medieval monastic records demonstrate that we are dealing with settlements that were established long before these records were written. Yet the world in which these villages have their origin is shrouded in historical mystery. Historians so often despair at this early period of English history because from the 5th to the 7th century the English landscape is difficult to discuss in detail. Contemporary historical accounts are few and far between while archaeology is difficult to interpret. When we narrow the eye to our own landscape the task becomes all the more the difficult to speak of a "local history", but the present writer is willing to do his best to tell such a story drawing upon all that our ancestors have left behind.

The First Anglo-Saxons

Historical tradition has it that in the early 5th a British king called Vortigen invited a group of Germanic armies to Britain to aid the Romano-British against growing conflict between themselves and the Picts, a wild warrior people who lived in present-day Scotland. Little did Vortigen know that as post-Roman Britain became unstable the number of these Germanic warriors would increase. Eventually the visiting tribes began making open war with the British, raiding Romano-Celtic controlled areas and defying British war-chiefs [3]. The Celts fought valiantly yet eventually they were driven back by the mighty sway of the Saxon armies. The impact of these Saxon incursions can be seen very early on in these parts. Signs of Anglo-Saxon tenancy have been found at Woodston and Nassington coupled with the discovery of several brooches, suggesting that the Anglo-Saxons had settled in the Nene valley before the 5th century [4].

This process of foreign occupation did by no means happen overnight, it was a slow and chaotic process. During the classical period Britain had been a well-oiled social machine, kept in check by an organised Roman government, able to control trade routes and maintain law and order as well as provide protection for every citizen who lived in accordance with the state. Roman Britain was as much a place of classical culture as any other Roman province, brimming with the cultural traditions of high antiquity imported from the Mediterranean. Even under early Roman rule many Britons adopted the Roman way of life, their language, manner of dress and cultural pursuits with a great deal of enthusiasm. In 500 years of Roman rule the Britons learned to be proud of the Roman traditions which they took as their own. When the Romans abandoned East Anglia in the early 5th century this Roman culture was maintained by the remaining native population in some parts of this region. In our locality archaeology from Lynch and Orton Hall Farm [5] both attest to the fact that as late as the early 5th century Romano-British rather than Anglo-Saxon techniques of farming were being used on the land. This latter-day use of British agricultural methods seems to show that there was not some violent Saxon take-over in this area; rather the evidence seems to suggest that the Anglo-Saxons slowly integrated into a long established native local culture.

In and around Castor village we can see a similar pattern emerge. Researchers have found that the name from which our settlement derives have both classical and Anglo-Saxons. Some early historians connected the name with the Latin '*Castorium*', meaning "camp" while other more recent study has found that the name is derived from the name '*Caester*', the old English word meaning '*walled town*', referring to the village site and not another walled town nearby, that of Durobrivae [6]. The name's survival and its obvious antiquity are suggestive that there was a smooth transition between Roman settlement and Anglo-Saxon occupation. An examination of remaining Roman buildings excavated in Castor also shows that there was little destruction of Roman walls and similar features; but rather their incorporation into early Saxon dwellings, mostly huts which have been found on the site of the present Cedar Centre near St Kyneburgha's Church [7]. It is likely that when the English first came to the Romano-British settlement, they merely reused the Roman buildings, while adding Anglo-Saxon elements to reinforce those structures which had fallen into disrepair. This practice of salvage is so obvious in the archaeological record that it was remarked upon, even by early historians who lacked the techniques which archaeologists take for granted today. For instance, the Rev Kennet Gibson, the curate at Castor in the 18th century observed;

'Next to the evidence of the antiquities of Castor, of the proofs of Romans having been here, those of the Saxon type may deserve some notice; because it is a very general and just observation, that the Saxons usually built on Roman foundations; and here at Castor we are sure was a Saxon city' [8] .Although the use of the word *'city'* may be rather too grand to describe Anglo-Saxon Castor, this comment by Gibson expresses the notion of stability between eras.

We know nothing of the native population after the 5th century. Were there still Romano-British people living in Castor when these early Saxon dwellings were being constructed? We will never know, but the lack of obvious destruction seems to suggest either abandonment by the Britons or a slow infiltration of Saxons into the Romano-British community. Based on previous agricultural evidence the latter theory seems to be the most likely one.

The Tyrant in the Praetorium

'They (tyrants) often plunder and terrorise the innocent; they protect and defend the guilty and thieving.........they wage wars civil and unjust, they chase thieves energetically all over the country, but love and even reward thieves that sit with them at table' [9].

One of the best examples of Saxon reuse in the Castor area is that of the *praetorium* building, part of which extends into the present parish churchyard. Recent archaeology has found evidence of Saxon rubbish pits on the site [10], suggesting that it was occupied in the early 5th century, but by whom it is difficult to know. One possibility is that the Anglo-Saxons, seeing the grandness of the surviving complex, adopted it as a site of early administration from which a local ruler or warlord controlled the territory. The *praetorium's* size and superior construction would have been ideal for occupants who felt themselves elite enough to forgo the dwellings of ordinary Saxons, like a local war-chief. Secondly such individuals could not have failed to recognise its imperial allure and what it represented, a link to the legitimacy of the previous Roman residents. It would therefore seem a logical step for a Saxon with ambition to take it as his own. Such local monarchy seems to have been common in the early 500s in the form of petty rulers. A Welsh monk called Gildas who was writing in Wales around 530 AD attests to this fact, when he describes a Britain full of evil tyrants who lie, cheat and plunder to gain riches [11]. One such tyrant may have once occupied the *praetorium*, which he used as a base to raid the surrounding countryside. Although this is merely conjecture the rubbish pit remains certainly echo an early date for the *praetorium's* reuse whoever lived there, be it a tyrant or a simple squatter. The remains certainly pre-date by at least 150 years any suggestion of a monastic presence which local tradition connects with St Kyneburgha's House of nuns and monks. These archaeological remnants represent the first Saxons to use the ruins after the Roman exodus in the late 4th century.

The Feast Hall of Caester

'Then there were again as at first strong words spoken in the hall, the people in gladness, the sound of a victorious folk, until, in a little while, the son of Healfdene wished to seek his evening rest'- From Beowulf

In AD 600 the Saxon king Ethelfrith defeated the native Britons at Chester. Unfortunately for the Britons this was the way of the future. Saxon society was expanding rapidly, replacing Romano-British culture with its own. The Saxons were beginning to live together in large rural communities based on agriculture and trade. Local artefacts ranging from pots, a cauldron and brooches suggest that by the 6th century our Saxon communities were established and thriving. It is certain that by at least 600 these obvious signs of organisation had fostered political and social bonds and it is at this time that we can trace the beginnings of the kingdom of East Anglia, ruled by a royal dynasty called the Wuffingas.

A 6th century Saxon hanging-bowl unearthed in Castor Parish in 1990 offers us a tantalising glimpse into this period. Although the bowl's significance has been subject to various interpretations there are several inferences, which can be drawn from it. The first is that the bowl was probably a burial object. Although no human remains were found on the site, bowls of a similar type to that found at Castor have been part of Anglo-Saxon pagan burials, the most famous of which was found at Sutton Hoo. Secondly, we can infer from bowl's decorative design that the vessel belonged to a person of high social status, perhaps an Anglo-Saxon Lord who became prominent in the Castor settlement around this period. What it was used for before it was buried is also subject to some debate, but one likely theory is that the bowl was used as a vessel to hold food at high-feasts. From surviving Anglo-Saxon literature [12] we know that the feast was a pillar of Germanic society. It provided an opportunity for a nobleman to celebrate his military victories and mourn his heroic defeats, recite poetry, play the harp and demonstrate his intellectual skill by speaking in rhymes and riddles, a favourite pastime among the Saxons. Usually at the centre of the hall was a large open fire and set nearest to it, the high table, where the lord of the hall and other highborn Saxons assembled for merry-making. The Castor bowl would probably have sat on the lord's table, a sign of his wealth and power, commissioned by him for feasts or given to him by another nobleman, a token of loyalty.

Fig 3a. The Castor Hanging Bowl, dated AD 620, found in 1990, Peterborough Museum

Since the Anglo-Saxons made their halls from wood, there is little in the way of surviving evidence that this feast-hall existed. Yet, in recent years extensive archaeology has found the presence of post-holes on the Cedar Centre site, which suggests that a wooden structure of early Saxon date was once built there, perhaps the hall which once contained the Castor bowl, and later buried with its owner. While it is difficult surmise what this object tells us about Anglo-Saxon Castor society as a whole, it does suggest that Castor, for some at least was a prospering settlement and in the process confirms the fact that by the 6th century the Anglo-Saxon culture had eclipsed that of the Romano-British. The Age of the Anglo-Saxons had finally begun in earnest.

Christian Missionaries and Saints

As well as a period of rapid social growth the 6th century can also be seen as a period of swift consolidation for the Christian church. Before they came in contact with the Christian faith the Saxons had practiced a complex pagan religion which personified the very forces of nature, Freya, goddess of fertility, Wooden, god of thunder and rain, Balder god of the sun. It was a simple pantheistic spirituality, contrasted by the seemingly transcendental and less earthy God of the Gospel. Yet, despite its perceived otherworldliness, Christianity was a force to be reckoned with. Mercia, the Saxon kingdom in which our villages once resided was alive with missionary activity. Both the Irish and Roman churches were immensely proactive, spreading the new religion to the population at large by gaining influence in the highest ranks of Anglo-Saxon society thus evoking little antagonism from the status quo. In this Age of Saints charismatic figures emerge, St Aidan, St Cuthbert, St Chad to name a few. And in this maelstrom of miracle-workers and Christian wonderers a holy woman walks forth from the mists of our history books, her name Kyneburgha, daughter of King Penda of Mercia. Shrouded in legend and mystery, Kyneburgha lived in an era of troubled politics, social fragmentation and faith, yet spent the last years of her royal life, not as a princess of Mercia but as an abbess of a monastic community built on a site which is now devoted to her name-sake, the church of Castor Parish. Behind the name lies a story, which Avril Morris tells in Chapter 4.

Benjamin Wood
I have lived in Castor Parish since birth and have spent many happy years at Hollies Farm. This village holds a special place in my affections and always will. I have always been fascinated by its past and stirred by the stories that I have heard in part my inspiration for writing this chapter. At present I am in my final year of A-Levels and hope to read Philosophy, Theology and Religion at Leeds University in October 2004.

Acknowledgements

First I would like to thank Liz Heesom for her instruction and support in the past, without which the arts of reading and writing would have remained a problematic and eternal mystery to me. I would also like to thank Avril Morris and William Burke for their kindness and patience in helping a young man achieve his dream of getting his work into print. Thanks also to Andrew Nash for the materials he lent to me during this project. Finally I would like to thank my friends and family for their support and encouragement in writing this chapter, I could not have done it without you.

Notes

1. CG Dallas, *Durobrivae, A Review of Nene Valley Archaeology: 1*, 1973.
2. D Hill, *Durobrivae, A Review of Nene Valley Archaeology: 4*, 1976.
3. Anglo-Saxon Chronicle, Bede, *Ecclesiastical History of The English People*.
4. J.P Wild, *The Romans In The Nene Valley*.
5. D.F Mackreth, *Orton Hall Farm: A Roman and Early Anglo-Saxon Farmstead*, 1996.
6. Rev K Gibson, *The Fifth Journey Of Antoninus Through Britain*, 1772, in which he discusses the various linguistic origins of the name Castor.
7. C Green, I Green, C Dallas, JP Wild, *Excavations at Castor, Cambridgeshire*, 1957-8 and 1973.
8. *Fifth Journey of Antoninus Through Britain*.
9. Gildas, *On The Ruin of Britain*, 5th century Welsh text. This work is one of the few written sources we can draw on at this early period.
10. G Lucas, *From Roman Villa to Saxo-Norman Village, An Archaeological Evaluation at the Cedars, Castor*, 1998.
11. See C A Synder, *The Age of Tyrants: Britain and the Britons AD400-600*, for a further discussion of the 'Tyrant' in 5th century Britain.
12. Remaining Northern European literature, such as the Norse poem 'The Poetic Edda' and the Anglo-Saxon epic 'Beowulf', allows historians to reconstruct the old English feast-hall.

Thanks to Ben Robinson of Peterborough Museum who brought the feast-hall hypothesis to my attention.

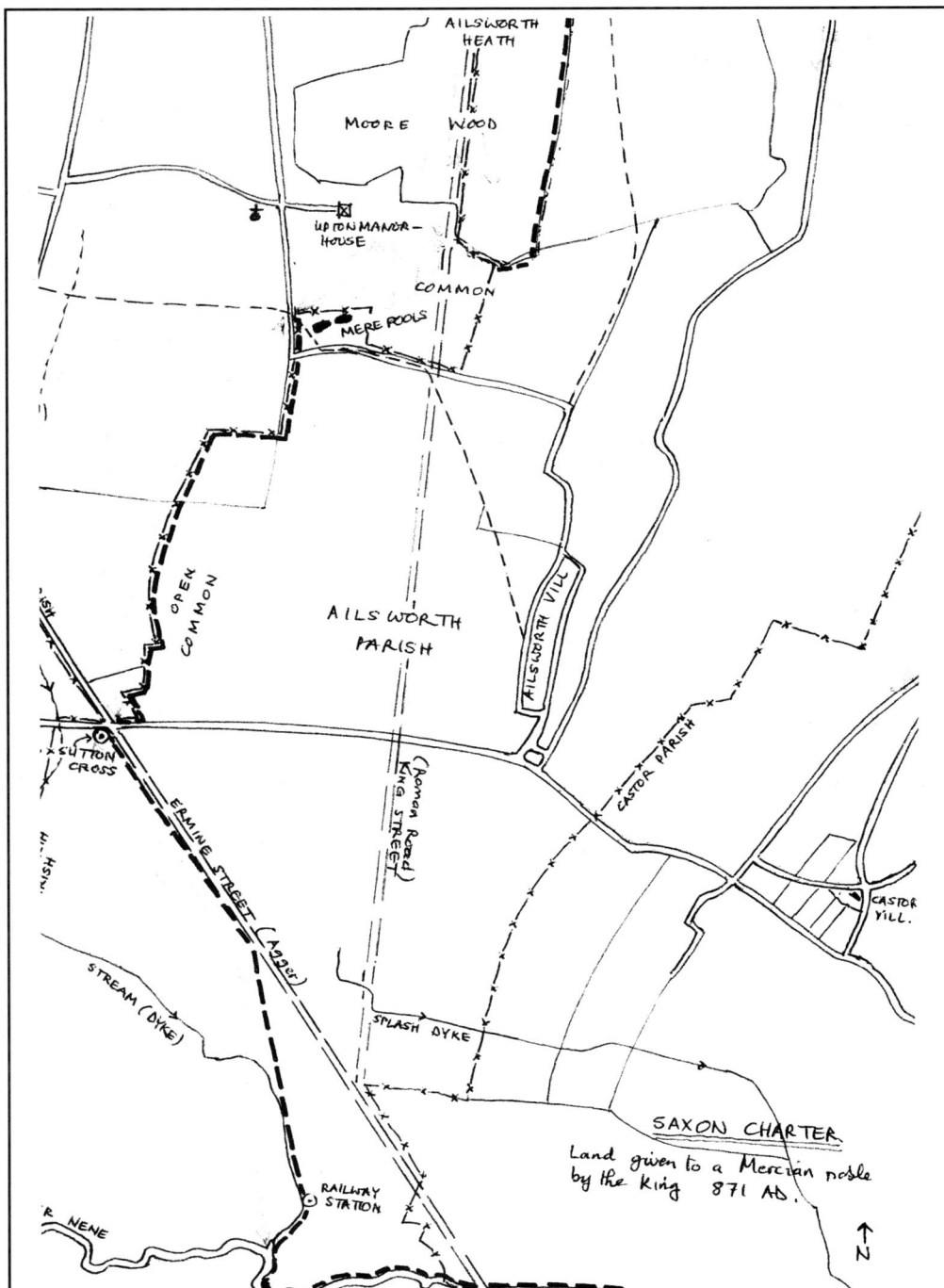

Fig 3b. Sketch map by Richard Harbord showing the boundary of the Saxon Manor of Ailsworth as granted to a Saxon nobleman in AD871.

Chapter 4
The Anglian Period:
The Royal Ladies of Castor [1]

St. Kyneburgha of Castor: from Mercian princess to Northumbrian queen

Castor Parish Church stands upon an escarpment, which has been occupied from at least the Roman period. It bears a unique dedication to the seventh-century saint, Kyneburgha or Cyneburh, a Mercian princess and erstwhile queen of Northumbria who, according to local tradition, retired from court in order to establish a nunnery on the site of an abandoned early fourth-century villa.

Reliable, near-contemporary information relating to Kyneburgha is limited to a single reference in Venerable Bede's *Historia Ecclesiastica* (*c.* 731), in which she was described as the sister of Peada, King of the Middle Angles, and the wife of Alhfrith, a Christian prince of Northumbria [2]. From this statement we may deduce that she was also the daughter of the unrepentant heathen king, Penda of Mercia (*c.* 626-*c.* 655), and his consort, Cynewise, whose stronghold was in the Tamworth area of the Trent Valley [3]. All subsequent references to Kyneburgha are either of post-Conquest date or survive only in the form of twelfth-century copies and, consequently, are much less trustworthy [4]. Nor are there any archaeological finds to substantiate Kyneburgha's relationship with the Castor site. However, by examining *all* of the available sources, in conjunction with place-name and sculptural evidence, it may be possible to gain an insight into the life and times of this remarkable lady.

Kyneburgha was born during an era when England was ruled by a few aristocratic families, both Christian and pagan, who intermarried in attempts to form alliances and to found dynasties in rival provinces. At the same time, they fought and killed one another in their struggle to become rulers of the most dominant Anglo-Saxon kingdom. Bede recorded that, by 650, Mercia was surrounded by territories whose overlords professed to embrace Christianity. They were attracted to the power of the monothesistic God, the King of Kings, through whom they could expect obedience from their subjects during their lifetimes and the promise of prayers for their souls and eternal salvation after death. In the South, Kent was controlled by the pious Eorconberht (640-664) [5], while Anna (633-654), '*a very religious man*', reigned over the East Angles [6]. Even the barbaric Cædwalla of Gwynedd, who had helped his ally, Penda, to kill the convert king, Edwin of Northumbria, in the Battle of *Hæthfelth* in 633, claimed to be a follower of Christ [7]. Although the Northumbrians briefly lapsed into paganism following the death of Edwin, his successor, Oswald (634-642), ensured that their faith was re-affirmed by Aidan, an Irish-trained priest from Iona [8]. Therefore, it was only matter of when and by whom the conversion of Mercia might be achieved.

It was in this climate *c.*654, presumably during a brief *entente* between two usually hostile provinces, that Kyneburgha of Mercia was given in marriage to Alhfrith, sub-ruler of Deira, the Southern province of Northumbria, and son of Penda's arch-enemy, Oswiu, King of Northumbria [9]. By 654, a second marriage was being negotiated between Penda's son, Peada, and Alhflæd, daughter of Oswiu. However, Oswiu stipulated that before the nuptuals could take place, Peada first must adopt Christianity. This, Bede explained, he was ready to do regardless of the outcome of his suit. After receiving religious instruction and additional encouragement from his friend and brother-in-law, Alhfrith, Peada was baptized by Finan, the Irish Bishop of Lindisfarne, at a place called *Ad Murum* [10]. He then returned to Mercia '*rejoycing more in the eternal Salvation than in the virgin he had gotten in Northumberland*' [11].

Peada already had been appointed by his father as sub-king of a people known as the Middle Angles, whose territory probably covered the later counties of Leicestershire and Northamptonshire [12]. We do not know where Peada and his bride established their *villa regalis*. However, the site of the derelict Roman villa on the escarpment at Castor (centred at TL 1251 9854) would have been an obvious choice, a location as relevant in the Anglo-Saxon period as it had been in the early fourth century, when the building had first been constructed [13]. First, Castor was situated in close proximity to an extensive network of Roman roads, including the Fen Causeway, which led from the Midlands into the heart of East Anglia, and King Street, which linked with Ermine Street, the Roman legions' main route from London to York [14]. Secondly, the River Nene was, arguably, still a navigable waterway and the Roman wharf (centred at TL 138- 986-) may have been operational as late as the seventh century [15]. Thirdly, situated on the 'Nass' or headland, the site commanded a spectacular view of the Nene Valley and, consequently, of friends and foes alike approaching from all directions. Finally, Castor was near to the border with another rival kingdom, East Anglia. Thus, the site would have enabled Penda to maintain a presence in a strategic position formerly associated with Roman authority.

Peada and Alhflæd returned to the Kingdom of the Middle Angles with a company of four Irish-trained priests, Adda, Betti, Cedd and Diuma, whose mission it was to evangelize the whole of Mercia. According to Bede, they accomplished this feat with considerable success [16]. Apparently, Penda showed tolerance towards Christians, provided that they were sincere in their faith. However, it is unlikely that he would have allowed the establishment of any churches or monasteries within his own kingdom during his lifetime [17]. This, probably, did not happen until Oswiu and Alhfrith, Kyneburgha's husband, had defeated and killed Penda in the Battle of *Winwaed*, c.655. Magnanimous in victory, Oswiu appointed his son-in-law, Peada, who appears to have been absent from the conflict, as 'client-king' of the South Mercians [18].

We only have the word of *Relatio Hedde Abbatis*, a twelfth-century copy of an early history of Peterborough Abbey, written four hundred and fifty years after the event allegedly took place, that Oswiu and Peada, as a possible gesture of thanksgiving founded *Medeshamstede* [Peterborough], within the territory of the Middle Angles [19]. The story was repeated in Manuscript 'E' of *The Anglo-Saxon Chronicle* and was later elaborated upon by Hugh Candidus in his own house-history, both of which were known to have been compiled in Peterborough [20]. Bede, a more reliable 7th century source maintained that *Medeshamstede* was founded by its first abbot, Seaxwulf, some time before *c.* 673 [21]. However, according to Bede, Oswiu *did* establish twelve monasteries within his own kingdom, after his victory at *Winwæd*. Therefore, it is quite feasible to suggest that he also was involved in *Medeshamstede*'s foundation, at some point between 655 and 670, the year of Oswiu's death [22]. Unfortunately, Peada did not live to see his plans come into fruition. At Easter in 656, he was murdered by his wife, Alhflæd, or so it was said, a deed that resulted in Oswiu's absorption of Southern Mercia under Northumbrian rule [23].

In contrast, Bede, writing over half a century later and over two-hundred miles away in Jarrow, was tantalizingly brief in his account of Peada's demise and even hinted that Alhflæd may not have been the real culprit. Three years later, the Mercian noblemen, Immin, Eafa and Eadberht rebelled against their Northumbrian oppressors and expelled them from the province, installing Wulfhere, Peada's youthful brother as their king [24].

Meanwhile, Kyneburgha appeared to have remained in the North, probably residing within in her husband's sub-kingdom of Deira [25]. Presumably, like her brother, Peada, she was introduced to Christianity by Bishop Finan of Lindisfarne and also by her husband, Alhfrith, whose friends included some of the most ambitious and learned young clerics of the age, such as Wilfrid (634-709), later Bishop of York and founder of Hexham and Ripon (672-678), [26] and Benedict Biscop (628-690), who established Bede's monastery of Wearmouth (674) and Jarrow (681) [27].

Both Wilfrid and Biscop subscribed to the Roman form of Christianity, as opposed to the more ascetic Celtic or Irish version favoured by Oswiu, and made regular pilgrimages to Rome, returning with exquisite artefacts and relics of saints with which they adorned their churches [28]. Alhfrith had been invited to accompany them, in 653, but Oswiu had thwarted his plans [29] However, it appeared that, undeterred, Alhfrith stalwartly supported Wilfrid against his father at the Synod of Whitby of 664, at which the Roman form of Christianity became the official state religion instead of the Irish version [30]. Alhfrith's final recorded act was to dispatch Wilfrid, as the newly appointed Bishop of York, to Gaul to receive consecration as prescribed by the Church of Rome [31]. After 664, Alhfrith vanishes from all records and it is generally assumed that his disappearance was due to an unsuccessful attempt to oust his own father from the Northumbrian throne [32]. This was not the first time that Ahlfrith had embarked upon such a plot. In 643, he had fought alongside Penda against Oswiu, and it is possible that it was during this campaign that his friendship with Peada had developed [33]. Tradition has dictated that an early eighth-century, carved cross at Bewcastle (Cumbria) was erected in Alhfrith's honour, near the spot where he either died or was buried. Unfortunately, the monument is now so badly weathered that it is impossible to read the runic writing, which is said to have born the name '*Cyneburug*' [34]. Furthermore, Douglas MacLean has suggested that the inscription, interpreted by early twentieth-century antiquarians as a dedication to Alhfrith, may possibly have been the work of nineteenth-century forgers [35].

The monastery of *Kyneburge cæstre*

After her husband's death, it is unlikely that Kynebugha remained in Northumbria for long. Perhaps, she was expelled by her father-in-law or, alternatively, she may have decided that it would be prudent to return to her own kingdom. By 664 Mercia, superficially at least, was a Christian kingdom, though vestiges of paganism may still have lingered.

According to Bede, Wulfhere, Kyneburgha's Christian brother, had acceded to the throne upon the expulsion of the Northumbrians from the kingdom, *c.* 658 [36]. Mercia was now a powerful and independent state, but Kyneburgha's presence may have been viewed as somewhat of an embarrassment to Wulfhere. Furthermore, she may have found life in a nunnery more appealing than remarriage. At this time, no known convent existed in the province to which she could retire. Therefore, perhaps, Wulfhere seized the opportunity to establish one, on Kyneburgha's behalf, as a complementary house for nuns *and* monks to *Medeshamstede* (Peterborough), as later medieval chroniclers have suggested [37].

Nevertheless, it is more plausible that it was at Kyneburgha's own instigation that the monastery at Castor was founded. Her husband's friend and mentor, Bishop Wilfrid, later proved to be very efficient at luring Northumbrian queens into convents with the promises of eternal life. He was instrumental in persuading Æthelthryth (Etheldreda) of East Anglia to abandon her husband, Ecgfrith, another of Oswiu's sons, in order to take the veil. She later founded the Abbey of Ely [38]. The example of Æthelthryth may lead us to suggest that the ambitious Wilfrid may have influenced Kyneburgha into taking her vows, thus ensuring that he had a useful ally in Mercia.

Wulfhere, who was also a friend and patron of Wilfrid, may have placed the site of the Roman villa at Castor at Kyneburgha's disposal [39]. Its association with Roman authority and its close proximity to the River Nene and the Roman road system could have had a certain appeal to both the Mercian king, whose power base was at *Tomtun* (Tamworth), and to his sister, who may have wished to have revive what she may have perceived to be a nucleus of Romano-British Christianity [40].

Archaeological evidence

Although local tradition dictates that a convent was founded by St. Kyneburgha during the late seventh century in the courtyard of the massive Roman villa/*prætorium* (centred at TL 1251 9854), no decisive archaeological evidence survives to substantiate its existence [41]. However, there are strong indications of Anglo-Saxon activity in the area, as revealed by the discovery, in 1990, of a bronze hanging-bowl dated *c.* 625 closely resembling those of the Sutton Hoo Hoard [42]. This would imply an aristocratic presence in the vicinity, only a generation before the conjectural foundation of St. Kyneburgha's nunnery. More recently, in 1998, during the installation of the Peterborough to Lutton gas pipeline, three sixth-century pagan inhumations were unearthed (at TL 1134 9929) spanning the former Roman thoroughfare to Lincoln, now known as King Street [43].

The site of the Roman villa/*prætorium*, was first excavated by Edmund Artis (1789-1847) in 1828. He discovered a conglomeration of buildings, including a bath-house and a substantial courtyard edifice, which he interpreted as either a significant residence or a *prætorium* (government offices). Although he meticulously recorded his discoveries in his masterwork, *The Durobrivæ of Antoninus*, he mistakenly identified the complex as the Roman *vicus* of *Durobrivæ*, now known to be on the South bank of the River Nene at Chesterton (TL 1168 9717) [44]. Artis recorded no Anglo-Saxon finds in the vicinity, although they may have been overlooked or even destroyed in his enthusiastic search for Roman remains.

Between 1955 and 1958, further exploratory work was conducted on the site by C & J Green, JP Wild and C Dallas. Not only did they identify the early fourth-century structures revealed by Artis, but they also uncovered, in the garden of 'Elmlea' (centred at TL 1242 9851), two sunken-floored buildings, which over-laid Roman paving, and a cess-pit containing sherds of pottery, dating from *c.*700-*c.*900. Other finds included a pair of shears, a bronze wrist-clasp, a spindle whorl and a decorated bone comb, all artifacts which are associated with women [45].

The most recent archaeological investigation of the villa site took place in 1997/8 in the orchard or rear garden of 'The Cedars' (centred at TL 1239 9853). The work consisted of a geophysical survey by Adrian Challands [46] and a desk-based evaluation of the previous excavations in the area by Gavin Lucas [47], prior to the construction of the Cedars Benefice Centre in the churchyard. Both archaeologists reached the conclusion that the Roman villa/*prætorium* extended further than they had originally believed. Furthermore, they deduced that it had been re-occupied rather than destroyed during the early Anglo-Saxon period, with a timber-post structure having been erected within the shell of its predecessor [48]. Lucas suggested that the earliest identifiable occupation of the Castor complex was by the Romans or Romano-British and that the site continued to be inhabited by early Anglo-Saxon settlers in the region. Moreover, stone appears to have been robbed from the villa at some time between 650 and 870, perhaps, for the construction of a church. However, there is no physical evidence to determine that a seventh-century religious house was present on the site [49].

Documentary evidence

Written evidence pertaining to the foundation of a convent at Castor is also sparse. Although Bede acknowledged Kyneburgha's lineage, he makes no reference to either her sister, Kyneswitha, or her nunnery [50]. Unfortunately, since there was no Mercian equivalent of Bede to record the history of the kingdom, trustworthy records are unavailable [51]. The earliest dependable reference relating to St Kyneburgha's establishment appeared in a twelfth-century copy of an authentic charter, dated 948, in which the bounds of *Ægelswurð* [Ailesworth] were described as being contiguous with those of *Kyneburge cæstre* [52]. However, this document merely implied that a lady of substance by the name of Kyneburgha had owned property in the settlement and, possibly, had resided there herself and makes no reference to a nunnery.

The earliest reliable citation of an actual monastic foundation at Castor is preserved in a version of *The Mildrith Legend*, written at St Augustine's Abbey, in Canterbury, *c.*1100 [53]. Both Kyneburgha and Kyneswitha are mentioned in this '*Vita*' or '*Life of Mildrith*', who was the daughter of Penda's son, Merewahl, and his Kentish wife, Domne Eafe (See Genealogy). It appears that Kyneburgha's reputation reached beyond her own kingdom, since Mildrith's hagiographer declared that she, '*Queen Kyneburgha left behind an illustrious sign of her virtue, more correctly, her own name, at Castor*' [54].

A copy of an early twelfth-century forgery, which claimed to be Wulfhere's foundation charter of AD 664, granting estates and privileges to the Abbey of *Medeshamstede* (Peterborough), was a little more precise in its biography of Kyneburgha, stating that she was '*a former queen, who had exchanged her royal power to become a hand-maiden in Christ, presiding over a monastery which is graced with her name, the mother of many saintly virgins*' [55]. Although this document is spurious, the tradition that Kyneburgha had founded a nunnery at Castor appears to have endured at Peterborough over three centuries after her death. It also is tempting to conjecture that the convent was consecrated in the honour of the Virgin Mary, as a declaration of their celibacy [56]. It would not have been appropriate for Kyneburgha to dedicate a nunnery to herself and it may be assumed that her name was adopted through her association with the site.

This spurious post-Conquest charter probably was used in its 'original' form as a source by the first scribe of Manuscript 'E' of *The Anglo-Saxon Chronicle*, which was compiled in Old English at Peterborough, *c.*1121 [57], and by Hugh Candidus, who commenced his own *Peterborough Chronicle*, *c.*1155 [58]. Both *Chronicles* claim that Kyneburgha and Kyneswitha were involved in the completion of *Medeshamstede*, a role that placed them on a par with their brothers, Æthelred and Merewalh. Furthermore, it reveals that the twelfth-century forger believed that the sisters had a significant role in the promotion of Christianity in the region [59].

The princesses were also linked with Castor in a later appendix of John (Florence) of Worcester's *Chronicle*, written *c.*1295 [60]. Nevertheless, it was not until the fourteenth century that John of Tynemouth, a monk of St. Albans (*c.*1346), began his definitive biography of English saints. In his quest for knowledge, he appears to have studied all the hitherto available data before placing the nunnery, which he named *Dormundescæstre*, '*not far from the River Nene and is called by those living there, Kyneburge castrum*' [61]. It is upon this account that subsequent hagiographies have been based [62].

Therefore, despite the dearth of reliable archaeological evidence, documentary sources suggest that, from 948, at least, it was believed that a monastery had been established at Castor. There may also have been a resident priest, whose duties would have been to deliver pastoral care to the local community and celebrating masses for the souls of the Kyneburgha's relatives [63].

Despite the abundance of dressed stone in the vicinity, it is unlikely that this commodity was immediately put to use at the proposed monastic site at Castor. The Middle Angles may not yet have had the technology in Kyneburgha's day. Both Bede and Stephen of Ripon related how Bishop Wilfrid and Benedict Biscop were obliged to import masons from Gaul and Francia in order to create Ripon and Hexham, Wearmouth and Jarrow some twenty years later [64]. Therefore, one may conclude that the first church and conventual buildings on the site were constructed from timber and thatched with reed, materials readily available in the vicinity.

The monastic lifestyle

Among Kyneburgha's followers was her sister, Kyneswitha, who had been married to King Offa of the East Angles (c.674-709). Inspired by a vision of the Virgin Mary, she apparently managed to extricate herself from the relationship in order to take the veil, adding weight to my theory that the convent may have been dedicated to the Virgin [65]. According to tradition, Kyneswitha succeeded Kyneburgha as abbess after her death, c.680 [66]. It is likely that the sisters' companions were also of noble birth. Anglo-Saxon convents were not refuges for the poor but places to settle devout gentlewomen, widowed aristocrats and unmarriageable daughters, all of whom brought with them a substantial dowry. Therefore, it is possible that their life at Castor was little different from that at court. Bede described the indignation of the ascetic Irishman, Adamnan, a monk of the double monastery of Coldingham, in Northumbria, at the behaviour of his fellow residents, who preferred to slumber instead of attending the night offices. Moreover, Bede related that the nuns at Coldingham spent their waking hours, not in prayer and quiet contemplation, but weaving fine cloths 'to adorn themselves like brides' and in eating, drinking, gossiping and indulging 'in other delights' in their cells [67]. In contrast, at Ely, Abbess Æthelthryth, who, coincidentally, had received her veil and habit from Bishop Wilfrid at Coldingham, adhered to a much stricter regime, fasting instead of feasting and taking a hot bath only at Easter, Pentecost and Epiphany, and then only after the other nuns had washed first [68]. Obviously, Æthelthryth did not consider that cleanliness came next to Godliness.

According to the early twelfth-century forgery of King Wulfhere's Charter (AD 664), which may, as previously stated, contain certain elements of truth, Kyneburgha and Kyneswitha were not incarcerated in their monastery. Indeed, the author suggests that the princesses acted with their brothers, Æthelred and Merewahl, in an advisory capacity to Wulfhere over the completion of the Abbey of *Medeshamstede* after Peada's untimely assassination [69]. Moreover, the two nuns were 'testators' to the forged charter, implying that the author considered them eminent enough to be present at the dedication ceremony. The forger also claimed that Alhfrith's comrade, Wilfrid, and even more astonishingly, Kyneburgha's father-in-law, Oswiu, the Abbey's co-founder, attended and signed the document [70]. However, Alhfrith is conspicuous by his absence from the list of witnesses, prompting speculation that the author of the document believed that the sub-king had already been removed by 664, thus, conveniently freeing Kyneburgha to take her religious vows.

The spurious charter suggests that Wulfhere valued his sister's opinion and that she had been sufficiently astute to escape the wrath of Oswiu after her husband had fallen from grace and that the twelfth-century forger of the charter clearly believed that she was either a consummate diplomat or a force to be reckoned with. Indeed, she was the formidable Penda's daughter!

Kyneburgha's lot cannot have been easy, living with Alhfrith and his machinations, not to mention the possibly strained relationship with her father-in-law, Oswiu whom, it must be remembered, was responsible for the death of her own father [71]. She must certainly have had strength of character and faith in her new religion in order to survive. It is tempting to draw parallels with other indomitable seventh-century ladies, such as Æthelthryth of Ely [72], Abbess Hild, who hosted the Synod of Whitby [73] and Oswiu's queen, Eanflaed, who was instrumental in persuading her husband to adopt the Roman stance at the Council, despite the fact that he had spent his formative years at the Irish monastery of Iona [74].

Castor: a centre of pilgrimage?

After their deaths, the royal sisters were probably laid to rest either in the graveyard or in the monastery church at Castor. In the late-eighth or early-ninth century, a workshop of master sculptors was established at *Medeshamstede*, described by archaeologists as the 'Peterborough Group' [75]. An elaborate sarcophagus depicting a series of saints standing on tiptoe beneath a foliated arcade may have been constructed to house the princesses' mortal remains (Fig 4a). In 1924, a surviving fragment, depicting a single nimbed or

Fig 4a. The 'Castor Slab'.

Fig 4b. The blocked doorway in East wall of the North transept.

haloed figure and part of a second, was discovered, lying face-downwards beneath a paving stone in the twelfth-century chancel when the altar rails were moved [76]. The carving bears a remarkable resemblance to the figures featured on the solid grave-marker of similar date in Peterborough Cathedral, known as the 'Hedda Stone' (Figs 4d.1&2). [77]. The 'Castor Slab' has recently been re-positioned in the Eastern wall of the North aisle, which is believed to have been the site of the sisters' reliquary [78]. A blocked, thirteenth-century doorway, in the Eastern wall of the North transept, contains recycled Anglo-Saxon long-and-short quoins, which may have been deliberately salvaged from an entrance to an earlier shrine in order to maintain a link with the church's pre-Conquest past (Fig 4b). [79].

Surviving sculptural and architectural evidence implies that Castor may have been a centre of pilgrimage during the early ninth century and, perhaps, even as late as the Reformation. Thus, the foundation would have been provided with a lucrative source of income. The layout of the church would suggest that wealthy visitors may have been ushered through a North door, past the saints' painted sepulchre, which may have been glimpsed through a grill, and out via an Eastern door in the North transept, hopefully emerging spiritually refreshed by their experience. This arrangement, reminiscent of Reculver, in Kent, would ensure that the interruption of church services was kept to a minimum [80].

Dr. Miriam Gill has proposed that, during the early fourteenth century, the Eastern section of the North aisle was decorated with scenes from Kyneburgha's life, corresponding with those depicting the passion of St. Catherine at the West end [81]. This would suggest that fragments of the saints' relics had remained at Castor after their bodies had been translated to Peterborough, c.1013 [82]. Since there is no record of a post-Conquest religious community operating at Castor, it can be assumed that by that time St. Kyneburgha's was functioning as purely as a parish church [83]. Therefore, the wall paintings would have served as a visual aid for the education of a mainly illiterate congregation, thus perpetuating the memory of the saint until the Reformation over two centuries later.

Fig 4c. The demi-figure of Christ in the gable of the South porch.

A second fragment of sculpture, which has been associated with the religious community, once stood in the churchyard, implying that it could have been the grave-marker of an Anglo-Saxon dignitary or even an indicator of a place of pilgrimage (Fig 4e). [84]. Its shape and size suggest that it was once a Roman altar, which was reworked during the late eighth or early ninth century, with winged dragons whose tails intertwine, echoing the patterns of 'Mercian beasts' on the roof of the 'Hedda Stone' (Figs 4d.1&2). [85]. Dr. Plunkett's theory, that the stone may have once have functioned as a shrine support, seems improbable on the grounds that there is little evidence of a socket in the upper surface [86]. The absence of this feature would also rule out the likelihood that the altar was converted into a cross-shaft. Nor is there any suggestion of a drainage hole, which would have indicated its use as a piscina or font. It is possible that the Roman altar was pressed into service as a holy water stoup, which was removed from the church upon the Reformation [87].

The enshrinement of the Castor saints may have coincided with the reconstruction of the church in stone c.825-850 [88]. It would appear that the monastery continued to flourish, since a carved tympanum of pre-Conquest date, portraying a demi-figure of Christ in Majesty beneath a sun and moon, survived to be re-sited in the gable of the early thirteenth-century South porch (Fig 4c). The long, lean fingers held in a Benedictine blessing to welcome pilgrims and worshippers alike, would suggest a late tenth or eleventh-century date [89]. The presence of the carving would indicate that the church continued to be of considerable importance, possibly enjoying minster or 'mother church' status during this period, with chapelries at Ailesworth, Milton, Sutton and Upton [90].

The decline of the monastery

Disaster must have befallen the community during the rule of Abbot Ælfsige of Peterborough (1006-1041), possibly at the hands of the Danes, c.1013, for Hugh Candidus recorded that the church at *Cyneburch-caster* [Castor] as being then in a 'much ruined' state [91]. Furthermore, in his twelfth-century history, he stated that the enterprizing monks of Ramsey were preparing to purloin the princesses' relics and to carry them off to their own

Fig 4d.1. The 'Hedda Stone' Peterborough Cathedral. Saints arranged beneath a foliated arcade.

Fig 4d.2. The two central figures depict the Virgin and Christ holding a Gospel. The second saint from the left bears a remarkable resemblance to that on the 'Castor Slab'. Compare the carvings on the roof of the sculpture with those on the Castor cross base. (Fig 4e).

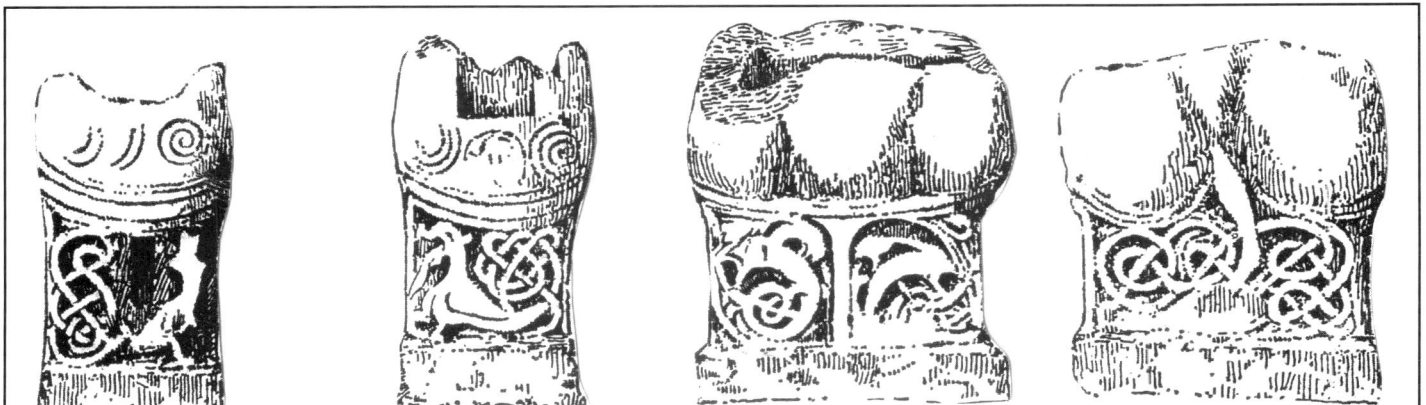

Fig 4e. The Castor cross base reflects the intertwining dragons' tails on the 'Hedda Stone'. (Figs 4d.1 and 2). (Courtesy Victoria County History Society Northamptonshire, Volume 2).

establishment. Fortunately, Leofwin, a monk of the restored foundation of *Burch* [Peterborough], had, through the medium of prayer, invited the saintly sisters to join the rapidly increasing collection of relics at his monastery. Apparently, his request was granted and Kyneburgha and Kyneswitha, together with their kinswoman, St Tibba of Ryhall, were translated without delay [92]. Sadly, the mortal remains of the aristocratic trio were either destroyed in the Nine Days' Fire of 1116 [93] or vanished during the Reformation, although a chapel in Peterborough Cathedral remains dedicated in their honour. Nevertheless, as late as 1532, Castor Church was consecrated to a trinity of royal saints, namely Kyneburgha, Kyneswitha and Tibba [94].

The St. Tibba connection

The life of St Tibba is shrouded in obscurity. Furthermore, there is neither archaeological nor documentary evidence to prove that she was ever interred at Castor or to substantiate the existence of a shrine dedicated to her at Ryhall. Moreover, her final resting place is excluded from an eleventh-century list of saints' burial places, implying that she may have been dismissed as being of minor importance when the work was compiled *c.*1031 if, indeed, her sainthood was recognized beyond her own province [95].

According to the twelfth-century chronicler, Hugh Candidus, Tibba was a pious virgin, who had posthumously requested that she should be buried with '*her saintly friends*', Kyneburgha and Kyneswitha [96]. Both the author of *The Mildrith Legend* [97] and John of Tynemouth, writing *c.* 1346, described Tibba as their blood relative [98], '*who, living in great sanctity and solitude for many years, commended her soul to God*' [99]. Thus, the possibility of relationship between the Mercian princesses and the anchoress of Ryhall should not be entirely disregarded. Retirement from secular life, whether to a convent or to a hermit's cell, was the prerogative of aristocrats, such as Æthelthryth of Ely [100], Hild of Whitby [101] and Mildrith of Minster-in-Thanet [102]. Therefore, Tibba may have been a cousin, perhaps distant, of Kyneburgha and Kyneswitha, and was certainly locally important enough to warrant a shared interment in a chapel at Peterborough.

It is possible that both Tibba's cell and shrine may have fallen into decay by the early eleventh-century, prompting the elevation of her relics to Peterborough. Alternatively, she could have been translated to Castor upon her death. Nevertheless, it must be considered that, if she became a recluse, as John of Tynemouth claimed, then from which religious foundation did she retire? It appears that seventh-century, eremetic saints were initially required to complete their spiritual training and take their vows at a conventional monastery before withdrawing to a life of seclusion [103]. During the late seventh century, the nearest convent to St. Tibba's cell, at Ryhall, was probably at Castor. Therefore, since seventh century nunneries were often family affairs, it is reasonable to speculate that Tibba may have served her noviciate under Kyneburgha and Kyneswitha, suggesting an even closer relationship with the daughters of Penda [104]. After receiving the veil, she may have withdrawn to her sanctuary at Ryhall as part of a spiritual progression, only to be reunited with her relatives either at Castor, upon her death, or three centuries later, at Peterborough. This sequence of events would provide an explanation for their shared interment at Peterborough and triple dedication at Castor.

Myths and legends

Remarkably, over thirteen centuries after its foundation, Kyneburgha's name is perpetuated in her church at Castor. Her saint's day is still celebrated here, each year on 6 March, the anniversary of her translation to Peterborough [105]. She is also commemorated in the Roman track known as Lady Conyburrow's Way, which once led from Castor Field to *Durobrivæ* [106]. There is a charming legend, which relates that a pathway miraculously appeared when Kyneburgha, while on a mission of mercy, was pursued by three villains intent on compromising her. A chasm opened up behind her and engulfed her assailants, whilst a carpet of flowers sprang from the contents of her spilled basket. Thus, her honour was preserved [107]. An early twelfth-century capital of one of the pillars beneath the tower depicts two men locked in armed combat, while a tearful maiden turns her back on the scene (Fig 4f.). Is this folk-lore preserved in stone or an allegory representing Penda, her father, and Oswui, her father-in-law, or Alhfrith, her husband, all of whom may be perceived as preventing Kyneburgha from following her true vocation? Penda, Oswiu and Alhfrith may be interpreted as the three 'ruffians', all of whom were capable of committing the foulest of deeds in order to fulfil their ambitions [108]. The carpet of flowers was, perhaps, intended to symbolize Kyneburgha's virtue and the blossoming of her church.

According to popular tradition, Kyneburgha and Alhfrith were the parents of the child protégé, St Rumwold (Rumbold) [109]. The infant was born at King's Sutton, Northamptonshire, the child of the Christian daughter of King Penda and the heathen son of a Northumbrian king. Rumwold entered the world proclaiming, '*I am a Christian*' and, at three days' old, preached a sermon on the Trinity, announced his impending death and his desire to be interred first at King's Sutton for a year, then at Brackley for two years and, finally, at Buckingham [110]. However, it is more likely that the precocious Rumwold, if indeed he existed, was born to Œthelwald, the son of Oswald, who had allied with Penda and Ahlfrith against his uncle, Oswiu, *c*. 643, and may have married another daughter of Penda, whose name is unknown [111]. During the early decades of the eighteenth century, anecdotes concerning Kyneburgha abounded. The antiquarian, William Stukeley recorded in his diary that, during a visit to Castor in September 1737, he learnt about a saint, '*whom the vulgar call Lady Ketilborough, and of her coming in a coach and six, riding over the field along the Roman road, some nights before Michaelmas*' [112]. Although these stories may be dismissed as figments of a fertile imagination, it may be deduced that a fascination for Kyneburgha had been maintained over the centuries and doubtlessly tales of her life were duly fabricated or adapted from popular myths and contemporary ghost stories.

Fig 4f. A possible carving of St Kyneburgha and two of the three ruffians.

Conclusion

St. Kyneburgha's name has endured at Castor since at least AD 948. She is mentioned by Venerable Bede in his *Ecclesiastical History*, completed a couple of generations after her death. She also appears the tenth-century *The Mildrith Legend* as well as in, Manuscript 'E' of *The Anglo-Saxon Chronicle*, and in the *Peterborough Chronicle of Hugh Candidus*. However, the latter two works although written, in Peterborough, were compiled almost five hundred years after Kyneburgha had allegedly founded her convent and, therefore, may be much less dependable. Two other twelfth-century historians, William of Malmesbury [113] and John (Florence) of Worcester [114], also refer to her in passing. Nevertheless, it is not until the fourteenth century that John of Tynemouth, a monk of St. Albans (*c*.1325-48), began to carefully research her life and that of her sister, Kyneswitha, for his hagiography of English saints, concluding that her monastery was situated not far from the River Nene, '*and is called by those who live there, Kyneburge castrum*' [115]. Although his work was written over six centuries after Kyneburgha's death, John of Tynemouth's hagiography formed the basis for all subsequent accounts of her life [116].

Unfortunately, no archaeological finds have been discovered to corroborate the existence of a nunnery at Castor, during the latter half of the seventh century. Nevertheless, documentary, sculptural and place-name evidence and the unique church dedication all indicate that Kyneburgha, confirmed by Bede as the daughter of King Penda of Mercia, was closely associated with the site [117]. Despite the unreliability of post-Conquest literature, Kyneburgha must have been a truly fascinating, courageous and, probably, formidable character in order to generate so much interest and speculation, over thirteen hundred years after she allegedly founded her 'double monastery' on the escarpment, where Castor Parish Church stands today.

Avril Morris

Avril's interest in Anglo-Saxon ecclesiastical history developed during her childhood in Ryhope Village, three miles South of Sunderland and equidistant from the seventh-century churches of Wearmouth and Seaham. After taking up a teaching appointment at Newark Hill School, Peterborough, in 1970, she transferred her attention from Northumbrian to Mercian studies. The Monasteries of *Medeshamstede* and Castor formed an integral part of her MA thesis. Now retired, she is currently researching for her doctorate at the University of Leicester and is a communicant at St. Kyneburgha's Church.

Genealogy of the Ruling Family of Mercia
(Based on Searle, *Anglo-Saxon Bishops, Kings and Nobles*, 1899)

Penda m. Cynewise
632-654

Peada	Wulfhere	Æthelred	Merewalh (?)	Cyneburh	Cyneswith	Wilburh
Sub-king of Mercia 654-656	King of Mercia 657-675	King of Mercia 675-704	King of the Magonsæte	Later Abbess of Castor	Later Abbess of Castor	
m.	m.	m.	m.	m.	m. (?)	m.
Alhflæd of Northumbria	Eorminhild of Kent	Osthryth of Northumbria	Domne Eafe of Kent	**Alhfrith** of Northumbria	**Offa** of East Anglia	Frithuwold Sub-king of Surrey
│	│	│	│			│
Cenred	St. Werburh	Ceolred	St. Mildrith			St. Osyth
King of Mercia 704-709	Abbess of Ely Died *c.* 700	King of Mercia 709-716	Abbess of Minster Thanet			Died *c.*675

Notes

1. The author would like to thank Dr. Joanna Story of the Department of History, Leicester University, for her helpful advice and comments regarding this chapter.
2. Bede, *Historia Ecclesiastica Gentis Anglorum* [HE.], eds. & trans. B Colgrave & R A B Mynors, Oxford, 1969, iii. 21
3. C Hart, *Early Charters of Eastern England*, Leicester, 1966, 99. See also M Gelling, 'The early history of Western Mercia', In: *The Origins of the Anglo-Saxon Kingdoms*, Leicester, 1989, 191-2.
4. S Foot, *Veiled Women*, Vol. II, Aldershot, 2000, 53-5.
5. HE., iii. 8.
6. *Ibid.*, iv. 19 [17]
7. *Ibid.*, ii. 20
8. *Ibid.*, iii. 3
9. *Ibid.*, iii. 21. Penda had already killed in battle two Northumbrian kings, Edwin (616-633) at *Hæthfelth* [Hatfield Chase] (HE., ii. 20) and Oswald, (634-642), Oswiu's brother, at *Maserfelth* [Oswestry] (*Ibid.*, iii. 9).
10. HE., iii. 21
11. S Gunton, *The History of the Church of Peterburgh* (*sic.*), London, 1686: facsimile edn., Peterborough, & Stamford, 1990, 228
12. HE., iii. 21
13. D Mackreth, 'Castor', In: *Durobrivæ*, Vol. IX, 22-4
14. ID Margary, *Roman Roads in Britain*, Vol. I, London, 1957, 198 (map). 202-5
15. A spoon-shaped depression is visible at TL-138- 986- (PCC., SMR., Rec., No. 08284). See also Margary, *Roman Roads*, Vol. I, 202, & RCHM., *Peterborough New Town*, London, 1969, 22, 39.
16. The missionaries' initials, 'A', 'B', 'C' and 'D', perhaps, represented new beginnings for the Middle Angles (HE., iii. 21).
17. *Ibid.*, iii. 21
18. *Ibid.*, iii. 24
19. London: Society of Antiquaries {Soc. Ant.], MS. 60, ff. 58v-59r
20. *The Anglo-Saxon Chronicle* [ASC (E.).], AD 654. See M. Swanton, *The Anglo-Saxon Chronicles*, London, 2000. *The Peterborough Chronicle of Hugh Candidus* [HC.], ed. W. T. Mellows, Oxford, 1949, 7
21. HE., iv. 6
22. *Ibid.*, v. 24
23. *Ibid.*, iii. 24
24. *Ibid.*, iii. 24
25. South Durham and Yorkshire, North of the River Humber. The River Wear was possibly the demarcation line between the two provinces of Northumbria, Bernicia and Deira.
26. HE., v. 19; *The Life of Bishop Wilfrid by Eddius Stephanus* [Stephen of Ripon], ed. & trans. B Colgrave, Cambridge, 1927, chap. XXII.
27. Biscop established Wearmouth [Monkwearmouth, Sunderland] in 674 and Jarrow in 681(HE., iv. 18 [16]; Bede, 'The lives of the Abbots of Wearmouth and Jarrow', trans. D Farmer, Harmonsworth, 1998, chap.4-5, 7).
28. D Farmer, trans., 'Bede's Lives of the Abbots', In: *The Age of Bede*, ed. J F Webb, London, 1998, chap. 6

29. *Ibid.*, chap. 2. Oswiu who, like his brother, Oswald, was converted to the Irish form of Christianity on Iona, had little time for Wilfrid (HE., iii. 3; iii. 25). However, Wilfrid enjoyed the patronage of Oswiu's wife, Eanflæd, daughter of Edwin of Northumbria, who had received her religious instruction from Paulinus, a disciple of the Roman cause (*Ibid.*, ii. 9; iii. 25; v. 19).

30. HE., iii. 25, v. 19. It is likely that Kyneburgha attended the Synod of Whitby as Alhfrith's consort.

31. *Ibid.*, iii. 28

32. *Ibid.*, iii. 14; DP Kirby, *The Earliest English Kings*, London, 1991, 103

33. *Ibid.*, iii. 14

34. G Baldwin Brown, *The Arts in Early England*, Vol. V, London, 1921, 314, 201-2, inserts between pages 244 & 245.

35. MacLean, 'The date of the Cross', In: *The Ruthwell Cross*, ed. B Cassidy, Princetown, 1990, 57-9). See also F. Orton, 'Northumbrian Sculpture (The Ruthwell and Bewcastle monuments)', In: *Northumbria's Golden Age*, eds. J Hawkes & S Mills, Oxford, 1999, 219.

36. HE., iii. 24

37. John [Florence] of Worcester claimed that Wulfhere and his brother, Æthelred, founded Castor (*The Chronicle of Florence of Worcester*, ed. T. Forrester, London, 1954, 448). See also Barbara Mitchell, 'Anglo-Saxon double monasteries', In: *History Today*, Vol. XLV, No. 10, 1995, 33, 38.

38. HE., iv. 19 [17]

39. B Colgrave, ed. & trans., *Life of Wilfrid by Eddius Stephanus*, Cambridge, 1927, chap XIV

40. The hoard was discovered beneath the Roman town of *Durobrivæ*, centred at TL 1168 9717. It consisted of several liturgical instruments which bear the *chi-rho* motif, suggesting that Christianity was being practised in the Castor area in the early fourth century (K Painter, 'The Water Newton Silver Treasure', In: *Durobrivæ*, IV, 1976, 7-9). The Water Newton Treasure is currently preserved in the British Museum. Facsimiles of the items are displayed in Peterborough Museum. Alternatively, since Castor is in close proximity to a network of Roman roads, the treasure may have been buried by a traveller.

41. G Lucas, *From Roman Villa to Saxo-Norman Village: The Archaeological Evaluation of the Cedars at Castor*, Cambridge Archaeological Unit Report No. 260, 1998, 17

42. The hanging-bowl, now restored and displayed at Peterborough Museum, was discovered, at TL 1387 9946, during the construction of the A 47 Castor by-pass. A nose-piece from a helmet of similar date was discovered at the site. (Peterborough City Council [PCC.] Record No. 8254). As at Sutton Hoo, also *c.* 625, no human remains were found.

43. Network Archaeology, *The Peterborough to Lutton Gas Pipeline*, Vol. I, Report No. 135, April 1998, 32-36. King Street also led to the Anglo-Saxon Hundred Court of the Nassaburgh or Upton Hundred, known as the Langdyke Bush, in the Parish of Ailesworth, at TF 1136 0264 (SAM No. 243).

44. E Artis, *The Durobrivæ of Antoninus*, London, 1928

45. J Green, *et al.*, 'Excavations at Castor, Cambridgeshire', In: *Northamptonshire Archaeology*, Vol. XXI, 1967, 144-5; C Dallas, 'The nunnery of St. Kyneburgha, at Castor', In: *Durobrivæ*, Vol. I, 1973, 16-7; PCC., Rec. No. 00646

46. A Challands, *Report on the Geophysical Survey in Part of the Garden of the Cedars, Castor, Cambridgeshire*, Helpston, 1997.

47. G Lucas, *From Roman Villa to Saxo-Norman Village*, Cambridge, 1998

48. *Ibid.*, 6-7, 16-7

49. *Ibid.*, 17-8

50. HE., iii. 21

51. Felix, St Guthlac of Crowland's hagiographer, although giving graphic descriptions of the fenland landscape and its inhabitants, remained silent on events in the Peterborough area (B. Colgrave, *Felix's Life of St. Guthlac*, Cambridge, 1956).

52. 'Grant of land by King Eadred to his thegn, Ælfsige, three hides at *Ægelswurð*' (Soc. Ant. MS. 60, f. 30v).

53. BL., MS. Cotton Vespasian Bxx, ff. 143r-63v. Published in *The Mildrith Legend: A Study of Early-Medieval Hagiography in England*, ed. DW Rollason, Leicester, 1982

54. Author's translation ['*Cineburga regina sui nominis castrum immo preclariora uirtutum insignia dereliquit*'] (Rollason, *The Mildrith Legend*, 77, 115).

55. Soc. Ant., MS 60, ff. 59v-64r, 'King Wulfhere of Mercia, grant of lands and privileges'). Author's translation ['*Kyneburga . . . quarii prior mutauit impii in xpi ancillarii, presidens monasterio kynebergensi ad suo nomine decoratur mater sacrarii uirginii.*'] (MS. 60, f. 59v). See also F Sawyer, ed., *Anglo-Saxon Charters*, London, 1968, No. 68

56. It was not uncommon for seventh-century nunneries to be dedicated to the virgin (M Clayton, *The Cult of the Virgin Mary in Anglo-Saxon England*, Cambridge, 1990, 130).

57. Soc. Ant., MS. 60, f. 59v-64v. A facsimile edition of Manuscript 'E' has been produced by Dorothy Whitelock and Cecily Clark (*Early English Manuscripts in Facsimile*, Vol. IV: *The Peterborough Chronicle*, Copenhagen, 1954). *The Anglo-Saxon* Chronicles, ed. & trans. M Swanton, London, 2000 [*ASC.*], offers a comprehensive translation of all the recensions of the *Chronicles*.

58. *The Peterborough Chronicle of Hugh Candidus* [HC.], ed. WT Mellows, Oxford, 1949, 10-4

59. Soc. Ant. MS. 60, ff. 59v-60r; *ASC.*, AD 656; HC., 9, 13

60. Forrester, *Florence of Worcester*, 448; Dallas, 'The nunnery of St. Kyneburgha', 17

61. Author's translation ['*non procul ab amne nomine Ven . . . a quo locus ille trahens Kyneburge castrum vocabatur*']. Published in *Nova Legenda Anglie as collected by John of Tynemouth, John Capgrave et al.*, ed. C Horstman, Vol. II, Oxford, 1891, 130

62. Dallas, 'The nunnery of St. Kyneburgha', 17

63. Levison, *England & the Continent*, 22-3; Mitchell, 'Anglo-Saxon double monasteries', 33

64. Bede, *Lives of the Abbots*, chap. 5: Colgrave, *Life of Wilfrid*, cap. XXII

65. Rollason, *Mildrith Legend*, 115; Horstman, *Nova Legenda Anglie*, 131; D Preest, ed. & trans., *The Deeds of the Bishops*, Woodbridge, 2002, chap. 180

66. D Farmer, *The Oxford Dictionary of Saints*, Oxford, 1987, 107

67. HE., iv. 25

68. *Ibid.*, iv. 19

69. Soc. Ant., MS. 60, ff. 59v-64r

70. Soc. Ant., MS. 60, f. 63v

71. *Ibid.*, iii. 24

72. Æthelthryth fled from her husband, King Ecgfrith of Northumbria, in order to become a nun, having refused to consummate the marriage (*Ibid.*, iv. 19).

73. *Ibid.*, iii. 25

74. *Ibid.*, iii. 25. Oswiu had complained that he celebrated Easter at a different time from his wife and her retinue (*Ibid.*, iii. 25).

75. R Cramp, 'Schools of Mercian Sculpture', In: *Mercian Studies*, ed. A Dornier, Leicester, 1977, 192.
    See also AM Morris, 'A Study In Stone: the Peterborough Group of Sculptors', In: *Friends of Peterborough Cathedral Journal*, 2003, 40-2

76. *Peterborough Advertiser*, 2 May 1924. The fragment, measuring 49 X 28.5cm, was either smashed by the Danes, *c.* 1013, searching for treasure, or during the iconoclasm following the Reformation, after which a piece may have been rescued and hidden for safe-keeping.

77. Richard Bailey and Rosemary Cramp have dated the Hedda Stone as late eighth- or early ninth-century, respectively (Bailey, *The Meaning of Mercian Sculpture*, Leicester, 1990, 8; Cramp, 'Schools of Mercian Sculpture', 192, 211). *Medeshamstede* appears to have been the only Mercian monastery in existence at the time of Peada's death. Therefore, it is reasonable to suggest that he was interred there.

78. Dr. G Jones, Centre for Local History, University of Leicester, pers. com., July 2001. The sisters' original shrine may have been situated in a *porticus* built into the North wall of the nave, on the site of the North transept. The North aisle, at Castor, was dedicated to St Kyneswitha in 1960 (Rev. William Burke, pers. com., September, 2003).

79. Dr. Phillip Lindley, Department of History of Art, University of Leicester, pers. com., October, 2001

80. Taylor & Taylor, *Anglo-Saxon Architecture*, Vol. II, 506; Dr. Graham Jones, Centre for Local History, University of Leicester, pers. com., July, 2001; Lindley, pers. com., October 2001)

81. Dr. Miriam Gill, Department of the History of Art, University of Leicester, pers. com., July, 2001

82. See below.

83. D Knowles & RN Hadcock, *Medieval Houses in England and Wales, 940-1216*, Cambridge, 1972

84. PCC., SMR., Rec. No. 0891a. The sculpture was moved into church in 1936 and is currently standing in front of the North door (Rev. William Burke, pers. com., September, 2003).

85. Cramp has suggested that the re-used Roman altar was also a product of the 'Peterborough Group' ('Schools of Mercian Sculpture', 211).

86. I. Henderson, 'Anglo-Saxon Sculpture in Cambridgeshire', In: *Cambridgeshire Churches*, Stamford, 1997, 223-4; T. Eaton, *Plundering the Past: Roman Stonework in Medieval Britain*, Stroud, 2002, 73

87. Recycled Roman altars are known to have been used as stoups at St Andrew's Church, Corbridge, [Northumberland], Michaelchurch [Hertfordshire] and St. Andrew Auckland [Co. Durham] (Eaton, *Plundering the Past*, 67-71). The Auckland stoup was recovered from a farmyard (*Ibid.*, 72).

88. Lucas has concluded that the Roman villa was robbed at some time during the mid seventh to mid ninth century (*From Roman to Saxo-Norman Village*, 8, 17-8).

89. Henderson, 'Anglo-Saxon sculpture', 224

90. J Blair, 'Debate: ecclesiastical organization and pastoral care in Anglo-Saxon Europe', In: *Early Medieval Europe*, IV, No. 2, 1995, 195, 199-203. The settlements of Ailesworth, Milton, Sutton and Upton were listed with '*uillam de Castre*' in the thirteenth-century copy of pseudo-Wulfhere's charter preserved as BL., MS. Cotton Augustus II. 5.

91. '*ecclesia Kyneburgensis castri ualde destructa.*' (HC., 50).

92. HC., 50-1. Peterborough had been restored by Æthelwold, the reforming Bishop of Winchester, *c.* 963 (ASC [E], AD 963: HC., 27). SS. Kyneburgha and Kyneswitha's interments are recorded in *Secgan be þam Godes Sanctum þe on Engla lande ærost reston*, (BL., MS. Stowe 944, f. 38r. Published in RW Rollason, 'List of resting places in Anglo-Saxon England', In: *Anglo-Saxon England*, Vol. VII, 1978, 90).

93. ASC (E)., AD 1116: HC., 97

94. E Serjeantson & H Isham Longden, 'The parishes and religious houses of Northamptonshire: Their dedications, altars and lights', In: *Report from the Archaeological Journal*, Vol. LXX, 1919, 295

95. *Secgan be þam Godes Sanctum þe on Engla lande ærost reston* (BL., MS. Stowe 944, f. 38r). See Rollason, 'List of resting places', 68, 90.

96. '*se cum sacris amicis*' (HC., 51)

97. '*consanguinitate*' (Rollason, *The Mildryth Legend*, 115)

98. *Erat autem beata Tibba sanctarum uirginum predictarum consanginea*' (Horstman, *Nova Legend Anglie*, Vol. II, 131)

99. Author's translation ['*que multis annis in magna sanctitate soltarieire uiuens deo spritum ommendauit*'] (*Ibid.*, 131).

100. HE., iv. 19

101. *Ibid.*, iii. 25, iv. 23

102. Rollason, *The Mildrith Legend*, 77-9, 94-102

103. St Cuthbert progressed from becoming a monk at Melrose to being elevated to the bishopric of Lindisfarne, before he sought solitude on Farne (HE., iv. 27 [25], iv. 28 [26]), while Guthlac received the tonsure at Repton, a possible satellite of *Medeshamstede*, before retreating to Crowland (Colgrave, *Life of Guthlac*, chap. XIX-XX; XXIV-V).

104. King Oswiu of Northumbria, dedicated his infant daughter, Ælfflæd, to the nunnery of his distant cousin, Hild, at Whitby, where she eventually succeeded the saint as abbess, in 680, and was joined by her own mother, Eanflaed upon her widowhood (HE., iii. 24; iv. 26 [24]). Domne Eafe, wife of Merewalh, a possible son of Penda, and her daughter, Mildrith, both presided over Minster-in-Thanet in the late seventh-century (Rollason, *The Mildrith Legend*, 78, 96-8, 102). Aethelthryth, the foundress of Ely, was succeeded by her sister, Seaxburh, after her death in 679 (HE., iv. 19). Upon her demise, Seaxburh's daughter, Eorminhild, widow of King Wulfhere, and *her* daughter, Werburh, both became abbesses of Ely in their turn (*Liber Eliensis*, ed. EO Blake, London, 1962, Book I, chap. XXV, XXXVI, XXXVII; Farmer, 1987, 145; 434).

105. St Kyneswitha's feast day is celebrated on 3 January and St Tibba's on 13 December (*AS.*, Vol. VII, 444).

106. J Morton, *The Natural History of Northamptonshire*, London, 1712, 511; J Gough, 'Castor, Caistre or Castre', In: *Bibliotheca Topographica Britannica*, Vol. X, 1819, 99.

107. Morton, *Natural History of Northamptonshire*, 511

108. Penda had killed the Christian Kings Edwin and Oswald of Northumbria in battle (HE., ii. 20, iii. 9). Oswiu had orchestrated the murder of his own cousin, Oswine, in a power struggle over Deira (Ibid., iii. 14). In 643, Alhfrith had fought alongside the heathen Penda against his own father, Oswiu (*Ibid.*, iii. 14, iii. 24).

109. *Acta Sanctorum [AS.]*, ed. J Bollandus *et al.*, Vol. VII, Paris & Rome 1865, 441. St Rumwold's *Life* in *AS.* was based upon John of Tynemouth's hagiography. Therefore Rumwold's parents were not named (*Ibid.*, Vol. LXII, 1887, 685-6). See A Thacker, 'Kings, saints and monasteries in pre-Viking England, In: *Midland History*, X, 1985, 6-7 & RP Hagerty, 'The Buckinghamshire Saints reconsidered. 3. St Rumwold [Rumbold] of Buckingham', In: *Archaeological Society of the County of Buckingham Journal*, Vol. XXX, 1988, 103-9)

110. '*Vita Sancti Rumwoldi*', In: *Three Eleventh-century Anglo-Latin Saints*, ed. & trans. R Love, Oxford, 1996, chap. I-XXII)

111. HE., iii. 14; Hagerty, 'The Buckinghamshire Saints', 106-8

112. *The Family Memoirs of William Stukeley*, Vol. III, Durham, 1887, 56

113. Preest, *Deeds of the Bishops.*, chap. 180. William of Malmesbury mistakenly referred to Kyneburgha as '*Cynesthryth*'.

114. Forester, *Florence of Worcester*, 448

115. Horstman, *Nova Legenda Anglie*, 132

116. Dallas, 'The nunnery of St Kyneburgha', 17

117. HE. iii. 21

Chapter 5
Castor Village – Overview 1066 to 2000

Introduction

One of the earliest recorded descriptions of Castor as a village is by a travelling historian, William Camden who, in 1612, wrote:

'The Avon or Nen river, running under a beautiful bridge at Walmesford (Wansford), passes by Durobrivae, a very ancient city, called in Saxon Dormancaster, took up a great deal of ground on each side of the river in both counties. For the little village of Castor which stands one mile from the river, seems to have been part of it, by the inlaid chequered pavements found there. And doubtless it was a place of more than ordinary note; in the adjoining fields (which instead of Dormanton they call Normangate) such quantities of Roman coins are thrown up you would think they had been sewn. Ermine Street, known as the forty foot way or The Way of St Kyneburgha, now known as Lady Connyburrow's Way must have been up towards Water Newton, if one may judge from, it seems to have been paved with a sort of cubical bricks and tiles.' [1]

By Camden's time, Castor was a village made up of a collection of tenant farms and cottages, remaining much the same until the time of the Second World War. The village had developed out of the late Saxon village of the time of the Domesday Book, that village having itself grown up among the ruins of the extensive Roman villa and estate that preceded it. The pre-conquest (1066) settlement of Castor is described in earlier chapters. The purpose of this chapter is to give a general overview of the history of Castor's development between 1066 to date, in order to set the context for the later chapters. In some cases the statistics used include Ailsworth and the other villages, as they were all in Castor Parish.

Most of the land for much of the village's history was owned by two great landlords, the Church and the Fitzwilliams of Milton. Castor had probably been relatively a more important place in the early medieval period, with its impressive church, four daughter 'chapelries' at Ailsworth, Sutton, Upton and Milton, and the important baronial court as well as the manor courts [2]. The church, as the landowner, was granted a charter to hold a market and summer fair in 1340, [3] the lineal descendant of which is the Church Summer Festival and Fete. It never developed into a late medieval market town, like Oundle or Uppingham, for which it had the potential in the early Middle Ages – possibly because it was too close to a larger rival, Peterborough.

The Original Saxon and Medieval Village Nucleus

The village of Castor developed around two core areas; firstly, the church with the cluster of buildings surrounding it, including the original rectory – now Vine House, and the Glebe Farm - now the Old Rectory, and secondly the farms around the area of the Green. From the plan in Fig 5b, which shows the cluster of old farms huddled cheek-by-jowl, with the fields surrounding them, the early village nucleus is readily identifiable. The original Saxon and medieval green, around which the farms clustered, was probably much larger, being rectangular in shape and incorporating all the land between the present Green and The Cedars. The dotted lines on the plan show the probable original extent of both the Green and the churchyard, for there are no pre-18th century buildings in that rectangle, whereas the farm buildings surrounding it are earlier in origin. The Elms and Duro Lodge were, it seems, built in the 18th century on what was the central part of the

Fig 5a. Castor Green: view looking North towards Clay Lane before nos 4 & 5 The Green were built (pre 1914).

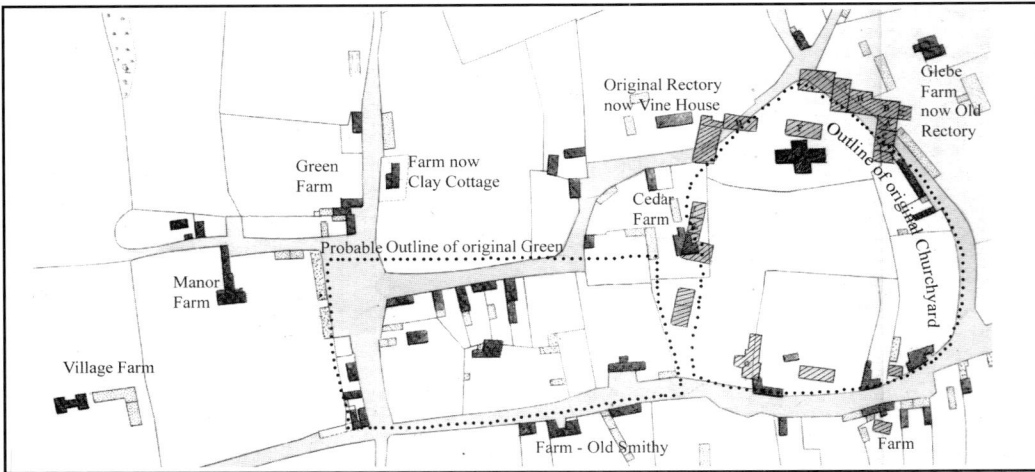

Fig 5b. Castor Historic Centre: This map is an extract from ET Artis' map; super-imposed dotted lines show probable outline of the original Green and Churchyard. The hatched buildings in the area of the churchyard are the Roman buildings Artis excavated. Note the pre-18th century farms round the Green.

Fig 5c. Castor: Church Hill looking East towards The Cedars; the Old Chapel on the right is now Bothamley and Ellington Engineers' Office.

Fig 5d. Village Farm House, photo 1920s. The house dates from 14/15th century.

former Green, as were the smaller cottages and outbuildings surrounding them.

The Village Cross was also on the Green. We know from old photographs that it was at one stage beside the shop on the North East corner of the Green. Its socket and stump are still to be seen on the Green today. The stump of another old cross on Love Hill, beside the wall of Castor House, was dug up and stolen in the early 1990s. We also know from an old map that the village stocks were on the corner of Stock's Hill (hence its name) and the Peterborough Road, near the Royal Oak. The stocks were still being used in the 1830s for we read that on 30th January 1830 'a sharp, frosty night, Thomas Glithero, John Spendlove and William Chamberlain, came home from Peterborough very fresh. Wm Chamberlain was afterwards found set in the stocks' [4].

The Abbey Lands

The village that Camden visited was still very much a product of the feudal system, under which the King, in essence, owned all the land, and granted it to about 150 Tenants-in-Chief, one of which was the Abbot of Peterborough. The Abbot in turn sub-let some of his land to others, knights and so on, and kept some for his personal use. The Abbot's land was the 'honour' or 'barony' of Peterborough, but the 'court baron' for the whole of the barony during much of this period was based at Castor, not in Peterborough. This estate, held by the Abbot, comprised the whole of the present Benefice of Castor and

Ailsworth with Sutton and Upton with Marholm, including Milton. It was divided into a number of manors each with its own manor court. Castor itself, in addition to the baronial court, consisted of two major manors, with a fledgling manor in the parish at Belsize, and a further manor at Milton. The feudal lord of all the manors in the early days was the Abbot, some of these being 'in demesne' (kept for his personal use), other manors being leased to feudal sub-ordinates. King Edgar's charter gave Castor to the Abbot in AD972 [5] and the grant was renewed in many subsequent charters by later monarchs.

The Manors in Castor

Castor or Berrystead Manor

By the time of the Domesday Book [6] in 1086, the abbot held one manor in Castor 'in demesne', later known as the Castor or the Berrystead Manor. In 1146, a Bull by Pope Eugenius III confirmed that Castor and all its appurtenances belonged to the abbey [7]. Abbot Alexander of Holderness (1222-1226) [8] built a hall for his manor at Castor. The site of this hall may be the moat South West of Village Farm at Grid 119985 - now a Scheduled Monument in the 'Empties'. It seems possible that the site of the manor farm was the farmstead now called Village Farm or perhaps Manor Farm. When Abbot Godfrey died in 1321, part of his property 'in demesne' included a manor-house with garden, dovecote, woodland and fisheries in the Nene. This remained a church manor until the 20th century.

Thorold's or Butler's Manor

In addition, the abbot also had a further secular manor in Castor sub-let to five knights, later to be known as Thorold's or Butler's Manor. Part of this eventually descended to the Fitzwilliams. By the time of Richard I [9] in 1189, this manor was in the hands of one Thorold, the Abbot still being the Tenant-in-Chief. It was partitioned by his sons after a court case for which we still have transcripts [10]. Thorold's elder son Richard, the priest of Castor, gave his share to the Abbot as part of his dowry for becoming a monk. This included the advowson of the church at Castor. The rest of the manor descended to the younger son Geoffrey, and this family remained Lords of the Manor for some generations. In 1460 Sir Guy Wolston held the manor, now also described 'as the Manor of Castor, otherwise called the Manor of Butler's and Thorold's'. This manor passed to his son-in-law Thomas Empson, then in 1515 to Richard Fitzwilliam. In 1534 William Fitzwilliam died, holding this manor from the Abbot. It is still held by Milton today.

Milton Manor

The manor of Milton, in the parish of Castor is described in the Domesday Book as being 'of the fee of the Abbey and held by Roger'. By the 12th century, Thorold held it from the abbot and it was then held successively by different families until 1391 when John de Wittlebury leased it. The manor remained with his descendants until Robert Wittlebury and his wife Anne granted it to William Fitzwilliam. Milton Manor seems, in practice, since the time of the Domesday Book, to have included Marholm as well. Milton was clearly a small village at one stage, and was granted a charter for a market in 1304. The villagers probably moved to Marholm when Milton was 'emparked'. The later history of Milton is described in Chapter 22.

Belsize

It would seem that there was also a sizeable hamlet at Belsize, growing up around the grange farm. In 1214 Abbot Robert built houses here and drained the land. The farm was run by the Abbey cellarer. Belsize seemed, at one stage, to have had some of the characteristics of a manor. At the Dissolution of the Abbey the grange farm was granted to the Dean and Chapter, who sold it to Milton in 1836. Although it is in Castor parish, the inhabitants have always looked to Marholm, being that much closer, and its further history is therefore in Chapter 16.

Fig 5e. Castor: the old barn of Manor Farm. All that is left now is the lower part of its East wall used as a garden wall for houses in Manor Farm Lane. The boys are Timothy Ennis and Miles Sheppardson (with bicycle).

The Manors and the Dissolution of the Abbey

Both 'Castor or Berrystead Manor', and 'Butler's or Thorold's' Manor passed to the Dean and Chapter, successors to the Abbot, on the Dissolution of the Abbey in 1537. In the reign of

Fig 5f. Castor: Hay wagon on Walter Longfoot's farm. Phyllis Brawn (mother of Margaret Brown nee Hill) is on top of the cart, Doug Oliver at the rear of the horse, Wally Longfoot at its head.

Queen Mary, the Dean and Chapter sub-let their manor in Castor (The Castor or Berrystead Manor) to Robert Wingfield for 99 years, who was also the Dean and Chapter's bailiff [11]. By the time of James I, Sir William Fitzwilliam held Butler's or Thorold's Manor, by fealty and an annual rent, from the Dean and Chapter and was also renting Belsize from them [12]. The arms of the Fitzwilliam and Wingfield families, above the chancel arch of Castor Church, were probably painted there during this period. Not only did the abbots have a residence in Castor, but also the bishops who succeeded them. We know that Bishop Howland died in Castor in 1599 [13] and it seems possible that Castor House was the bishops' country retreat until 1795, when the church sold the house to the White family. The further history of Castor House is in Chapter 8.

The Civil War and its Aftermath

Much was to change during the Civil War. In 1646, the Bishop and his curates at Castor were *'ejected'* by the Puritans and in 1649 Cromwell's Parliament passed a law stripping the church of its property. The church was ransacked and the manor of Castor and its properties were taken from the church and sold to Thomas Matthew and Thomas Allen, grocers from London. It seems, from the local records, that the villages in this area, including Castor, remained royalist. The pub name *Royal Oak* is an indication of royalist sympathies. In the survey of the 'Manor of Castor or Berrystead', carried out by the Parliamentary Commissioners in 1649 [14] is a description of the Manor Farmhouse; is this Manor Farmhouse or Village Farmhouse? The Manor Farmstead was described as *'consisting of one Hall, one Parlour wainscoted, one Kitchen, one Buttery with a little parlour adjoining, one Larder, one dairy, one Chamber over the Parlour, three other chambers,, one little Chamber over the Porch, one gate entering into the Courtyard Chamber over, one Stable with Outhouses with eight small bays, one Great barn of six bays besides the Berrystead, all built of stone and slated, one Kiln House, the yard and garden being three acres'* – a substantial farmstead for the period. The manor also included fields and other tenants' properties. This almost certainly included the 18 further farmsteads and cottages, as enumerated in Landen's 1765 survey of the manor. Copies of these surveys are held in the Parish Archives.

At the Restoration of King Charles II in 1660, the escheated land was returned to the church. The feudal system was by then gradually disappearing anyway. The village of Castor and the surrounding hamlets, however, remained solidly Anglican in their church life, but this may of course have been simply because the church was the major landlord. In the Compton Census [15] for 1676, the population of Castor consisted of 340 Anglican families and only two Non-conformists. The Congregational Chapel was not built until 1848.

Later Years

The wider world would always impinge on village life. In 1536 Castor [16] had to provide two archers, four billmen, and a horse and harness for military service. In 1762, the Militia List, [17] naming all able-bodied men between 18 and 45, shows 66 men available for duty: one surgeon, six farmers, (including the Serjeants, Wrights and Bates families) one miller, one blacksmith, three bakers, three shoemakers, three carpenters, one tailor and one wheelwright. The rest were all farm labourers, shepherds etc, (and a village constable), which indicates the nature of the community then. This was out of a total population of 475, of which 251 were male and 224 female. In later years, 16 of the men called up for military service were killed in World War I, and a further five in World War II. People did not travel much; abroad literally was bloody – one only went there to fight the King's enemies.

The impression gained of Castor throughout the 18th and 19th centuries is of a quiet farming village, its life dominated by the farming seasons, and its two great landlords, Milton and the Church. Many of the stone houses in the village that still exist today were built in the 18th century, as farming became more prosperous. Even so, the agrarian unrest affecting the countryside throughout England also affected Castor. In the 1830s, land-workers were poorer than they had been in the previous century. The country-wide decade of "rick-burning" affected our parishes. By 30 November 1830, *'through so many incendiary fires ...it was thought proper to swear in special constables at a meeting at the Wheatsheaf in Ailsworth'*. The number of sudden deaths due to accidents, falls from horses, drownings in backwaters after leaving the pub late, accidents at work and suicides would be remarkable to us (over 20 between 1830 and 1846) [18].

Fig 5g. Castor: Hay cart beside the George & Dragon. The Pells were the last landlords here; the house was bought by the Winfreys; Charles and Jay Winfrey lived at Dragon House when they first married.

Population and Employment

The population [19] of Castor grew slowly, being 475 in 1801, reaching a peak of 772 in 1851, and declining gradually to 547 in 1931. It was not until the late 1960s that the population started to rise again.

In 1801, the priest, Revd Christopher Hodgson (Rector of Marholm and Curate of Castor) had to return a questionnaire to the central Government responding to *An Act for taking an Account of the Population of Great Britain* [20]. From this we learn that in 1700, there were 14 baptisms (5 males, 9 females) and 18 burials (9 males, 9 females). Fifty years later the figures for 1750 were 13 baptisms (8 males, 5 females) and 20 burials (6 males, 14 females). Between 1754 and 1801 marriages averaged about five or so a year, the most being ten. By comparison, in the year 2000, there were 19 baptisms at Castor, 10 funerals and 11 weddings – not much difference. In 1849 there were 24 farmers in the benefice, to which may be added a fair number of cottagers. These were people who worked their own small-holdings with some stock, and usually also worked on other farms. Their excess produce would be taken to market for sale.

In 1849 the licensed premises in the parish included the *Fitzwilliam Arms*, the *Royal Oak*, the *Wheat Sheaf*, and the *George & Dragon* (two of the licensees being women). By 1874 the licensees included George Hobbs at the *Barley Mow*, Samuel Popple at the *Fitzwilliam Arms*, Thomas Smith at the *Wheat Sheaf*, and John Upchurch at the *George & Dragon*. Even in 1881, the census shows that most people were still in traditional rural occupations, living in a remarkably static society.

It is notable how many women were in business on their own account in the 19th century. In addition to licensees, we see them as tenant farmers; for example in 1874 there were six women farmers. Women are also listed in the Trade Directories as a coal merchant, a grocer and baker, two shoemakers, a butcher, a shopkeeper and baker, and another shopkeeper. Businesses and trades, run by men, included six male shopkeepers, four cottagers, three blacksmiths, two carpenters, two male shoemakers, two tailors, a wheelwright, a miller, a machine contractor, a builder, a gamekeeper, and a butcher. If we add to those people the number of people in service, apprentices, assistants, gardeners and labourers and so on, we can get an idea of the sheer amount of activity within the village even up to the time of the Second World War. It was definitely not a dormitory or an idyllic retirement place, but a highly active, hardworking, busy and largely self-sufficient community.

Fig 5h. Milton Ferry in 1930s: the Toll Bridge was built in 1716. The Gate-Lodge House (on the right) was moved up the hill to make way for the new A47 by-pass and The Ferry House was burnt out in a disastrous fire on New Years Day 2003.

Fig 5i. Castor: The Long Row. These houses were demolished in 1967. Carlton Court was built on the site.

Fig 5j. George Bell (father of Michael Bell of Upton) outside his house No 1 The Long Row in the 1920s.

Miscellanea

Milton Ferry

The present bridge at Milton (or Gunwade) Ferry was built in 1716 by the then Lord Fitzwilliam. It was, however, the site of a much older toll. The two standing stones nearby, known as Robin Hood and Little John, were, some say, placed to commemorate the free passage of Barnack stone to St Edmundsbury, for the building of the abbey there. It seems more likely that their origin is pre-historic, but who can tell? Daniel Defoe, in his journal, records how outraged he was by the toll. Curiously, Mrs Millie Weston, the last Toll Keeper, writes that in 1964 the charge levied for a car was the same as for a coach in Defoe's day [21]. The Nene Park Trust, which includes Ferry Bridge and Meadows, and the meadowland beside the River Nene in Castor Parish, was established as public park land, as part of the development of Peterborough New Town. This originally included plans for the expansion of Castor. The Nene Park Trust lands are now an important recreational facility.

The Northey & Wright Charity

In 1736, Robert Wright (a Castor farmer) left in his will 'profits of certain lands... £2.12s a year for ever, to give and distribute to the twelve poorest people of Castor and Ailsworth...1d loaf apiece.' [22] Until the 1960s, twelve loaves were placed on a shelf (commemorated by a board) by the entrance to the Lady Chapel in Castor Church. In 1900, Mary Ann Northey bequeathed 'the sum of £300 upon trust to...apply the income arising from such investment for the benefit of the widows, widowers and deserving poor of the Parish of Castor at each new year for the purchase of red flannel and coal' [23]. In 1980 the Charity Commissioners amalgamated the two charities to make better use of the resources, for the relief of those in need. The charity still quietly helps people today.

Dress in the 19th Century

What is interesting about the quote above is the reference to red flannel. Mr Hales elsewhere [24] writes of Castor that, 'the younger women wore the red or scarlet cloak as their principal or outer garment'. The use of red flannel for skirts and cloaks was common in many country areas; for example the national costume of Wales still, and the country women of the West of Ireland were also known for their red flannel skirts. Mr Hales also describes the dress of men in the 1830s: 'not one man in fifty wearing trousers, but small clothes (and most of them leather). No braces but *a leather belt, and either gaiters, leggings, or top boots. I have seen more than one clergyman in the pulpit with boots and spurs. The dog hair hat was the principal hat.'*

Recent Developments

Until the 1950s most people still drew their water from a well or a pump, used an outside privy, and had no electricity. Gwen Heighton, who lived at The Grove on Church Hill with her parents, recalls drinking water being collected in pails from a spring-fed pump at 'Salmon's Corner' on Church Hill, beside the school-master's house. The school-master was then Mr Salmon, head of the Fitzwilliam School. It was not until the 1950s that they first 'had taps' connected to the mains.

The former council houses were built on Stocks Hill in 1927. In 1933, Milton sold off seven 5-acre plots in the Thorn Field alongside Love Hill. The first house to be built there was The Hill House in 1935; the land was bought by Herbert Kirman and the architect was Guy Warwick. This is now the home of William Baxter and his family. Another seven large houses followed, the second one being Kentmere House, built some months later for Sir Edmund Henry Gilpin. The house is now owned by David and Marcia Gibbs. These houses, built for successful Peterborough businessmen, were the first houses for residential use by people who did not work in the village.

The first house built in Castor after World War Two was 12 Peterborough Road. Phillip Meadows bought the plot of land at Castor for £250 from the Church Commissioners in 1948. George and Trudie Meadows now live there. The next developments were the group of houses built on Thorold's Way in 1953 and Silvester Road in the 1960s. The land on which 20 High Street stands was bought from the Church Commissioners in 1957 by Ken Trevitt and others for £200. Charles and Gill Slidel now live there. Evergreen House, another imposing house, was built on Peterborough Road, very much in a traditional style, by Tom Dickens in 1969 – it is now lived in by his son Robert and wife Judith. Samworth Close was built in the 1970s, Kyneburgha Close in 1983 (built by Ted Fairchild who lives in Castor), and Carlton

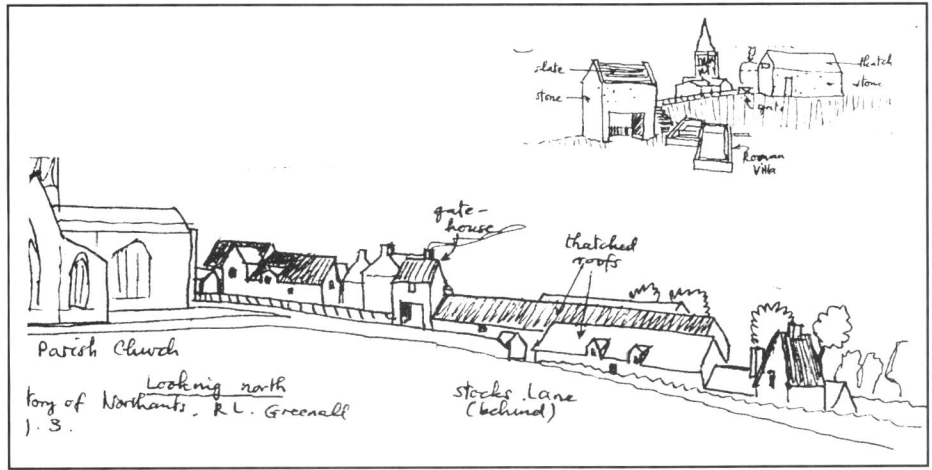

Fig 5k. A reconstruction (drawn by Richard Harbord, nephew of the Rev Tom Adler) of the extensive farm buildings and cottages that used to be alongside Stocks Hill, based on a drawing by ET Artis, and the ground plan from old maps. The farm buildings were probably destroyed in 1851 when the Glebe Farm House became the new rectory (now the Old Rectory!)

Fig 5l. Stocks Hill – the thatched cottages were burnt out in a fire in 1912 Charlie Bell, father of Margaret Sharpe was 16 at the time.

Fig 5m. Robina Gibbons (née Wade) and her sister Lorna (now Sheppardson) playing outside Village Farm in the 1930s. Where were the foxes?

Fig 5n. Sheep in Peterborough Road Castor c1910. In 1934 the Winfrey Homes were built on the right where the cattle are standing. To the right alongside Stock's Hill is 1 Stock's Hill (a Milton house lived in by Mick Westlake, a Milton forester). Further right, in front of the church, the cottages burnt down 1912 can be seen (see 5l).

Court in 1989. The development on the site of the yard of Manor Farm and Village Farm started in 1984. The old threshing barn at Manor Farm and other outbuildings were demolished amid some controversy from 1967 onwards, and the houses in Manor Farm Lane were built on the site in the 1980s.

There was, of course, to follow much greater controversy over the proposed plans for Castor New Town, details of which may be found in Chapter 29. Although the project for the New Town failed, small developments on "in-fill" sites have continued. Despite all this, the housing stock has not increased as much as one would expect. This is because a many of the older cottages were originally two, three or even four separate dwellings, which have been converted into one home. For example, when Jenny Hammond's parents lived at 3 High Street Castor, this was a row of four cottages, end on to the road. This is now one cottage and the Shadbolt family live there. Castor is changing, but more slowly than the planners had originally envisaged in the 1970s. It is, however, becoming a place where people live but work elsewhere, rather than a place where people both live and work.

William Burke

William Burke has been the Rector of the parishes of Castor with Sutton and Upton with Marholm for eight years. He trained for the priesthood at Ripon College Cuddesdon Oxford, having been a soldier prior to that.

Fig 5o. The old threshing barn, probably medieval, of Village Farm. The barn was demolished in 1976. Nos 1 & 2 Village Farm Close were built on the site. The thatched roof was replaced with a corrugated iron one as seen here after a fire in 1947.

Fig 5p. Looking up Church Hill towards the old York Cottage. The shop on the right is now Vic Griffin's coal and fuel merchant's shop.

Fig 5q. Gibbons' Yard Castor 1950: Village Hall on right, Fitzwilliam Arms in background.

Fig 5s. The threshing at the big barn at Manor Farm Castor (W Carter) in 1902. All that is left of this barn is the East wall alongside Castor Green (driver Tom Gibbons, water-boy W Hornsby).

Fig 5r. The yard at The Limes Farm Castor (Dick Longfoot) in the 1950s, with a Gibbon's threshing machine .

Fig 5t Manor Farmhouse - was this the house described in the Parliamentary Survey of 1649? The present occupants are Doctors Peter and Rebecca Winfrey.

Notes

(Copies of all refs in Parish Archives)

1. Camden *Magnam Historiam* 1612.
2. Court Baron, Hugh Candidus, *The Peterborough Chronicle*, Ed WT Mellows,1997, p 45 & n.1.
    See also the many refs to the Court Baron at Castor in *The White Book of Peterborough* Ed Sandra Raban, Northants Record Soc 2001.
3. RL Greenall, *History of Northants and the Soke of Peterborough*, Phillimore, 1979, p 30.
4. John Hales' Diary 1830, Castor Parish Archives Copy. John Hales was a stonemason and Parish Clerk in Castor, and an important recorder of village life in the 19th century.
5. King Edgar's Charter, Hugh Candidus, *The Peterborough Chronicle*, Ed WT Mellows,1997, p 16.
6. Domesday Book 1086 – see Appx One.
7. Hugh Candidus, *The Peterborough Chronicle* Ed WT Mellows, Peterborough Museum Society 1997, p 51
    In time of Abbot Martin. AD1146, '*Papal Bull of Pope Eugenius III…decreeing that whatsoever goods and possessions…Castor with the church and the chapels adjoining the same church with the mills and all its appurtenances*'.
8. Symon Gunton, *History of the Church in Peterborough*,1686, Ed J Higham 1990, p 29.
9. re Manor Histories, *Victoria County History - Northants*, (VCH) 1901, p 473ff.
10. Symon Gunton, *History of the Church in Peterborough*, 1686, Ed J Higham 1990, pp 277-278.
11. re R Wingfield: Founding of Peterborough Cathedral, ed WT Mellows. NRS 1941, p lxviii, and VCH p 474.
    '*Queen Mary sublet their other manor in Castor to Robert Wingfield for 99 years*'.
12. VCH p 475
13. Bp Howland, Symon Gunton, *History of the Church in Peterborough*,1686, Ed J Higham 1990, p 81.
    '*Richard Howland, …Bishop 1584… supervised funeral arrangements of Mary Queen of Scots (and much more about the death and funeral including the Fitzwilliam involvement)…Howland having been Bishop here the space of 15 years, died at Castor, and was buried in his own Cathedral…*' He also wrote a letter from Castor.
14. A Survey of Manor of Castor or Berrystead 1649, NCRO.
15. Compton Census 1676 – see Appx Seven.
16. Muster Roll 1536 – see Appx Eight.
17. Militia List 1762 – see Appx Ten.
18. John Hales' Diary 1830-1846, re incendiaries and accidents: Castor Parish Archives Copy.
19. Population Increase – see Appx Fourteen.
20. 1801 Population Return – see Appx Fifteen.
21. Symon Gunton, *History of the Church in Peterborough*, 1686, Ed J Higham 1990, p 5.
    Robin Hood and Little John – Stones: ' *Nor did the Abbot of Peterborough from these Pitts (Barnack stone pits) furnish only that, but other Abbies also, as that of S Edmunds-Bury: In memory whereof, there are two long stones yet standing upon a balk in Castor-field, near unto Gunwade Ferry.*' Mrs Weston writes: '*In 1964…Anyone using the gate regularly was able to purchase a key, and farm workers were supplied with their own key, otherwise it was 2/6 for a car, 2/- for a motor-cycle and 1/- for cyclists or walkers.*' DBR: T 1004
22. Robert Wright, *Will*, Castor Parish Archives Copy.
23. Mary Ann Northey, *Will*, Castor Parish Archives Copy.
24. re Mr Hales – see Appx Eighteen.

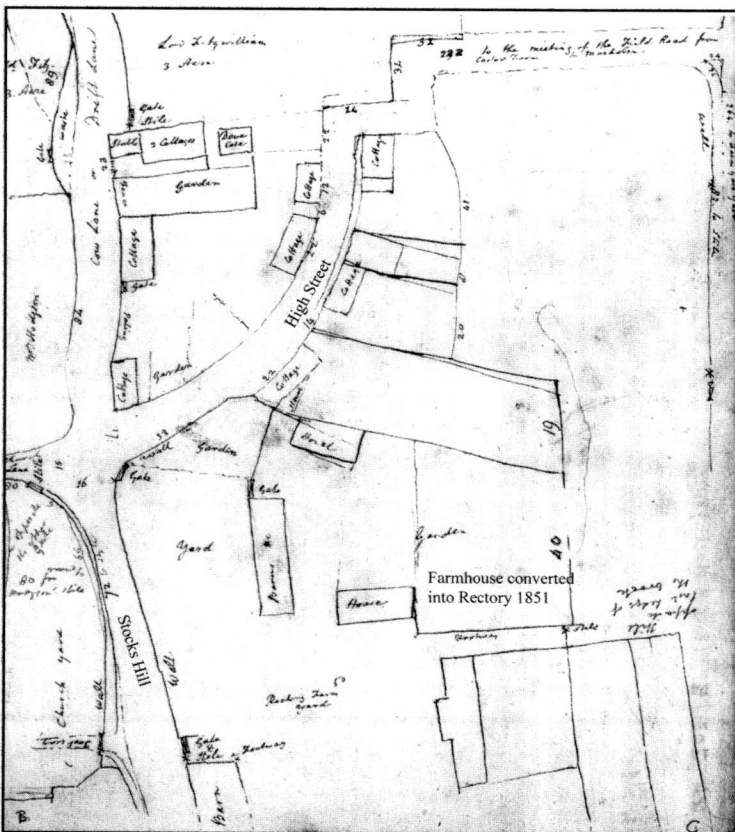

Fig 5u. Sketch map of the Rectory Farmyard, Stocks Hill and High Street Castor drawn in 1820s. The barn and other outbuildings were pulled down in the 1850s, when the Glebe farmhouse was converted into the Rectory.

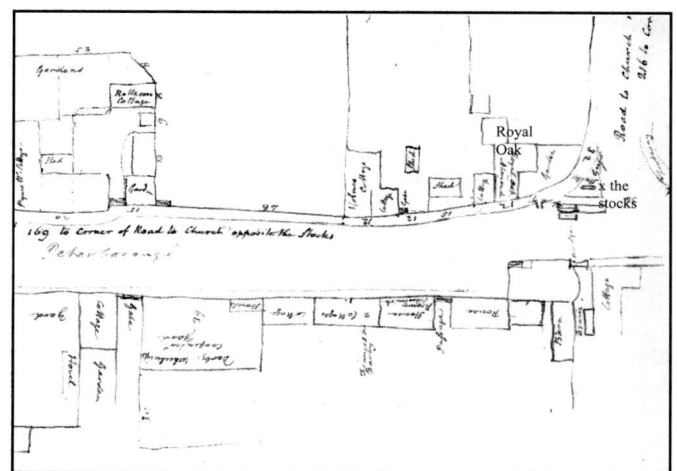

Fig 5v. Sketch map of the junction of Peterborough Road Castor and Stocks Hill drawn in the 1820s. Although the details do not reproduce well, the map is of interest as it shows the location of the stocks on the left side of the junction, and the old cottages which used to be in the Southern portion of the churchyard, now the School Field.

Chapter 6
Castor Church

Castor and Early Christianity in the Area

For one of the important Norman parish churches of England, Castor Church hugs the mysteries of its origins and early significance to itself. Only serious archaeological investigation, and maybe not even that, will reveal some of these secrets, as the written records are scant. Simon Jenkins, in his book *England's Thousand Best Churches,* [1] places Castor in the top one hundred of the 15,000 or so churches in England. The most obvious mystery is why a church in a small village (which even in the *Domesday Book* had only about 40 adult males) should have the most magnificent Norman parish church tower in the country. Some say that Tewkesbury is more impressive still, but it is not an appropriate comparison, as Tewkesbury was built as an important abbey, in a large town, only becoming a parish church after the Dissolution of the Monasteries. And in addition, its tower is merely larger, but not nearly as impressive in terms of the workmanship. The tower at Castor may just be due to the availability of craftsmen; nearby Peterborough Abbey was being re-built at the same time in the 12th century, but then perhaps one would expect the abbey to have an equally important tower, (which it does not) for the tower at Castor is one that many cathedrals would be proud to have grace their roof-line.

Fig 6a. Castor Church – Tower drawn by P Taylor 1912.

The tower may just be due to the ambition of a local landlord or priest, or to the availability of worked stone from the ruined Roman *Praetorium*, in whose courtyard the church was built. But it may allude to the ecclesiastical importance of Castor in its earlier Christian history, to which there are some tantalizing pointers but few established facts. As the village was originally named *'Kyneburghacastre'* after St Kyneburgha, so is the church, the place of her burial, unique in being dedicated to her.

Records and remains of Christianity in the late Roman period (the 4th century) are scarce, but there is no doubt that it was the predominant religion during that time. We know, for example, that in AD314, Bishop Adelphius of Lincoln attended the Council of Arles in France, along with other Romano-British bishops [2]. The area around Castor has produced enough nationally important Christian artefacts from this period to show that Christianity was thriving hereabouts in the latter part of the Roman period. In particular the Water Newton Treasure, found near the South bank of the River Nene, just beyond Castor's present parish boundary, indicates a thriving local church. This treasure comprises the oldest-known Christian liturgical plate anywhere, consisting of cups, dishes and votive plaques.

Dr K Painter, one of the foremost experts on the subject, has surmised [3] that the Water Newton Treasure almost certainly

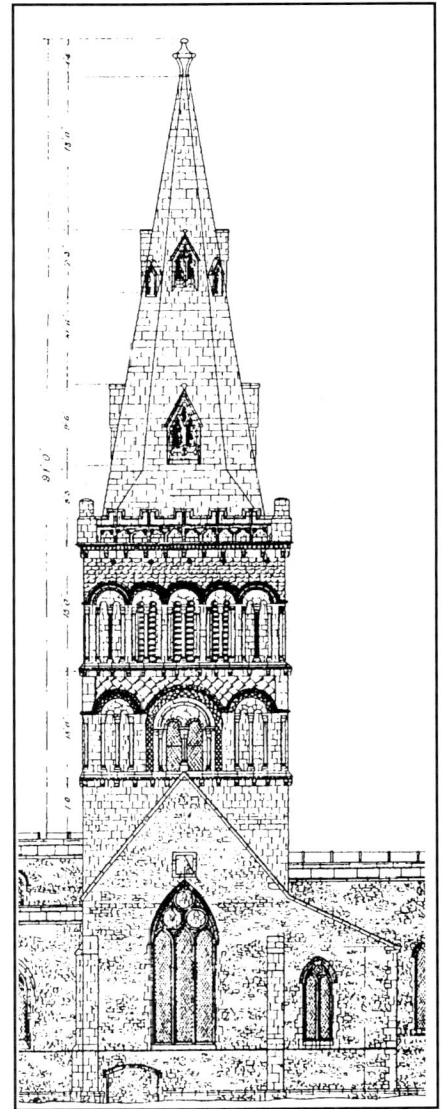

Fig 6b. Castor Church – View from South East on a winter's afternoon: Theo Hensman with sheep grazing in the churchyard, dovecot made by Keith Dickinson of Upton. The young dove in the cage is recovering from a hawk attack.

Fig 6c. Castor Church – West end – note large quoin stones on original nave wall, possibly Roman stone-work reused by the Saxons. (Photo: J Tovey)

originated from the Roman *Praetorium* at Castor, the site of the present church, and that the treasure was removed and hidden deliberately at some stage during the troubled times of the collapse of the Roman Empire. One of the pieces of silver refers to an altar or sanctuary [4] at which gifts were offered. If Dr Painter is correct, then it is highly likely that this Romano-British place of Christian worship was in or near the *Praetorium* at Castor. Even more fascinating, if this is so, is that we may know the names of the earliest members of the Christian congregation at Castor, because some of the pieces of the treasure have the names of their donors inscribed. Another leading authority on the late Roman period in Britain, Dr Ken Dark, has proposed [5] that Saxon minster churches built on the sites of Roman villas may imply a continuity of worship from the Roman period, through Saxon times, to the present day. He states that many late Roman villas in Britain became monasteries in the 4th century; that worship continued in those places; and that, once evangelized, the Saxons established their minster churches at these sites. He thinks that this is especially likely to be the case where Early Saxon pagan burials are rare, the implication being that in those areas the native Romano-Britons were left to get on with their lives (including their religion). The site at Castor meets these criteria.

Whatever preceded it, in the Middle Saxon period around AD650, St Kyneburgha and her sister founded their double convent at Castor in the Celtic tradition with both monks and nuns. Convent rule by a powerful royal princess-abbess was a common feature of Saxon foundations [6]. Castor clearly became an important Minster Church with chapels-of-ease at Sutton, Upton, Ailsworth and Milton. The chapels of Sutton and Upton remained as such until the 19th century when they became independent parishes, although of course they are now in the same benefice as Castor. The chapel-of-ease at Milton is a mystery. There are few references [7] to it, the last one being in the reign of Edward III (c.1330) and it had certainly disappeared before the Reformation, even before 1502. Did Marholm Church take over its role, for when the Fitzwilliams moved into Milton in 1502, they used Marholm as their church? Looking at the parish boundaries, and Marholm's relationship with Milton (Milton is still in Castor parish), it seems likely that Marholm parish was carved out of the area for which the minster church at Castor was responsible. Marholm had certainly become an independent parish by 1217 when its first known rector had been appointed. Surprisingly, Marholm is not mentioned in the *Domesday Book*, but that may be because it was included in the Milton entry.

There is some mystery too about the chapel-of-ease at Ailsworth. A certain Mr Hales records that its remains were demolished in 1854, it then being used as a granary [8]. We do not know when it ceased to function as a chapel, although it seems to have become disused before the Reformation and is not mentioned thereafter. There are, however, folk memories of its existence. From Mr Hales' description, it seems to have been in the back yard of Manor Farm Ailsworth (a church farm) alongside the Helpston Road. The hill at the top of Helpston Road was until recently known as Chapel Hill. A resident of the village, Theo Hensman, (born here and now a churchwarden) recalls playing near some stones beside the Helpston Road known as 'Chapel Steps'.

In summary then, the early church of Castor and its area suggests the following sequence: a flourishing Romano-British 4th century church; the fascinating possibility of continuity in the post-Roman period; the foundation of a Saxon Convent by St Kyneburgha on the site of the Roman *Praetorium*; its destruction by the Danes; and, ceasing to be a convent, becoming a Saxon minster church responsible for the well-being of daughter churches at Sutton, Upton, Milton, and Ailsworth. At some date before 1217 an independent parish church was established at Marholm, though it has shared the same rector as Castor for some hundreds of years, and still now does. These other churches are all dealt with in their own chapters, as is St Kyneburgha herself and the Saxon Church as an institution.

There is yet a further mystery about Castor Church; the extent to which the Norman builders incorporated the stonework of the Saxon church on the site. In many cases the Normans enlarged existing Saxon churches, but incorporated some or much of the Saxon church within the new building. Examples of this are at Corbridge in Northumberland, and at Turvey in Bedfordshire where the Saxon nave, in the rebuilt Norman church, is only readily identifiable because of the survival of Saxon windows. Reculver in Kent provides another example, this time of a Saxon minster church built on the site of a Roman fort, and incorporated in the Norman church. At Castor, Smith *et al* believe that a substantial amount of Saxon work was incorporated in the church by the Normans: *'if you look closely at the stone-coursing of walls and tower you see old Saxon work in the former, and fine late Norman jointing (with thin lines of mortar) in the latter.'* [9] Arthur Mee refers to the Saxon 'long-and-short' work of the blocked-up door in the East wall of the North transept [10]. Was this Saxon stonework reused by the Normans, or is it part of the Saxon North *porticus*? Canon Jack Higham believes that it is possible that the huge quoin stones, still visible in the West end of Castor church may be Saxon work reusing Roman material [11]. If these people are correct then it is possible part of

Fig 6d. Castor Church – Dedication Inscription AD 1124. (Photo: P White)

the Saxon nave was incorporated in the Norman church, as at St Mildred's Church Canterbury [12]. The Late Saxon church at Castor would thus possibly have consisted of a tall narrow nave, and a presbytery, flanked by *portici* on the North and South side, with an apsidal (round) East end. There are other positively identified Saxon sculptures which will be described later.

The Development of the Architecture of Castor Church

The Norman Church – AD1124 – the Cruciform Church and Tower

Turning now from speculation to facts, we know that in 1012 Castor church was in a ruinous condition, [13] as a result of Viking raids. The Normans rebuilt the church, with its unique tower, the church being dedicated on 17 April 1124 by the Bishop of Lincoln [14]. We have a record of this not only in contemporary documents, but also in the rare dedication inscription, in Latin abbreviations, above the priest's door in the external South wall of the chancel, which translates as follows: *'The dedication of this Church was on the 17th April AD 1124'*.

It is possible to reconstruct quite accurately how the Norman church would have looked, because of the existing and fragmentary Norman windows. For example, in the North wall of the North transept are remains of a Norman window, and also on the West face of the South transept above the arch to what is now the Lady Chapel. There is also a Norman window still in use above the decorated window in the West wall of the nave. In addition there is of course the tower. We do not know what the Norman chancel was like, although St Remigius' Church at Water Newton contains re-set Norman 'zigzag' ornamentation taken from the chancel of Castor church [15]. It is assumed the chancel at Castor was apsidal, as was common with most Norman churches. No archaeological survey has taken place and the outline of the Norman chancel could only be confirmed by lifting the present chancel floor to look for the Norman foundations. We know, however, as became apparent during repairs to the East end window in 2000, that there are large masonry foundations underneath the sanctuary. *See Fig 6e.*

Fig 6e. Castor Church – Reconstruction of Norman Church AD 1120-1124. Note East end apse and West end door. (Sketch: J Tovey)

The Norman Tower - External

The tower is built in three external stages: the lowest in plain masonry with internal openings up to the first corbel table; then a stage with three sub-divided round arches on each face (the central arch containing two lights), surmounted with lozenge-shaped stones; and then in the final stage above a second corbel table, five sub-divided round arches on each face (the central three arches containing the bell-chamber louvres). These latter arches are surmounted with fish-scale pattern stones - magnificent work nearly a thousand years old. Note too the strange carvings on the corbels.

One writer describes the tower as follows: *'This thrusting image embodies in the weather-resisting Barnack limestone of the district many characteristics of Norman church-building. The tower is the central feature of a true cruciform design... and combines mass with rich ornament. The whole surface of the structure above the roof-line corbel-table is covered with scale patterns and varieties of rhythmic arcading. It is typical that the central three-light window of the lower stage should be more deeply recessed and more elaborately moulded than the blind flanking arches (though with the same billet motif), and that the three bell-openings should be flanked by blank arcades'* [16].

The unusual open parapet and somewhat squat broach spire, with its uneven octagonal sides and two tiers of *lucarnes* were added in the 14th century, bringing the total height of spire and tower to 128 feet. Standing in the bell-chamber, looking upwards is rather like being enclosed in an enormous stone traffic cone. The internal rib-vaulting above the choir stalls was added at the same time.

The Tower - Internal

The tower capital carvings are a fascinating mixture of scenes from daily life, religious themes, and mythological beasts. They include the following scenes: North-East capitals - Sampson and the Lion, a boar hunt (note man with spear, and one hound sliced in half by the boar) and a man harvesting with a sickle; North-West capitals – 'Green Men' with foliage, an elephant (with cloven feet) and palm tree, a pelican (symbol of the Mass); South-West capitals – two men with 'kite' shields fighting over a woman (St Kyneburgha?);

Fig 6f. Castor Church - Carvings of Green Man on Tower Capital. (Photo: J Tovey)

South-East capitals – two dragons fighting and a man with a basket picking grapes. There are two painted heraldic shields, one either side of the West arch of the tower. The shield on the right contains the arms of the Wingfield family, former Lords of the Manor of Upton and bailiffs of Castor Manor. We know from an old photograph that the shield on the left contained the arms of the Fitzwilliam family of Milton. Both paintings probably date from between 1540 and 1600.

The Early English Period – 13th century, AD1220-1230 – The Chancel Extension and the South Aisle

The church was enlarged between 1220 and 1230 by the extension of the chancel to its present square-ended shape and by the addition of the South aisle, made by piercing three bays, still with round-top arches, on circular columns in the South nave wall. The line of the original lean-to roof of the South aisle is still visible above the entrance arch to the Lady Chapel. The chancel originally had six Early English lancet windows (three on each side) on the North and South walls, the three in the North chancel wall still existing. Two Early English windows on the South side have been replaced, one as a result of a further extension to the South transept, although part of its outline can be seen above the arch between the chancel and the South transept. The side mullions of the Early English lancet windows (probably three) in the East end can still be seen, although the windows themselves were replaced in the 15th century by the present window. When the East end window was repaired in 2001 fragments of the Early English mullions were found, having been used as in-fill in previous alterations. The double round-arched *sedilia* (seats) and the double *piscina* (for ritual washing) with its Alwalton marble columns and dog-tooth moulding on arches were installed at the same time in the sanctuary. It seems strange that these fittings, installed at the same time, should be so different in style, but one of them can hardly be earlier.

Fig 6g.Castor Church Sanctuary AD1220. (Photo: J Tovey)

At some stage, it seems that the Norman West door was blocked-up and eventually replaced by a Decorated Period window, the difference in the stonework on the external West wall showing its location. The impressive Norman South doorway, with its carvings including two 'Green Men', became the inner porch door in the new South aisle. Was the whole of the Norman door moved and rebuilt in its present location? Perhaps there was already a Norman porch, of which the present Norman doorway was the entrance,

Fig 6h. Castor Church - Drawing of 13th century Sedilia and Piscina in Chancel. (drawn in 1870).

which became incorporated in the new South aisle as the inner porch doorway, which it now is. We are unlikely to know the answer, but it does seem strange to go to the trouble of taking down and rebuilding the Norman porch. *See Fig 6i.*

The Early English Period – 13th century, AD1260-1270 – Extension to the South Transept

Further extensions were carried out between 1260 and 1270, when the South transept was enlarged. What is extraordinary is the fact that the style employed is still very much Romanesque (Norman with round arches). Maybe the builder was reluctant to follow the latest fashion. At any rate, the beautiful and airy South transept was also extended to double its previous width, the new South wall being built level with the South porch. It was also extended Eastwards, thus blocking one of the Early English lancet windows in the South wall of the chancel, the window being replaced with an arch allowing a view from the South transept into the chancel. The modification included the elegant clustered column in the middle of the South transept, and the almost Romanesque-style double arch. We do not know the purpose of this extension; it may have been to provide two side chapels, but there is no evidence of a *piscina* in the South transept wall. When the plaster fell off and was replaced in 2001 there was no sign of one. (There is however a *piscina* in Clay Cottage, a building owned by the church until very recently). At the same time cracks in the South wall, probably evidence of a famous lightning strike in 1795 during which bell-ringers narrowly escaped being killed, [17] were uncovered. *See Fig 6k.*

As Castor was a minster church, and the lordship of the manors belonged to the church, the extension may have been to provide facilities for a chapter house function, or meetings for the abbey baronial court and the like. After the Reformation this space was used as the Vestry School, until it was turned into a Lady Chapel, 1924-1928.

The Decorated Period – 14th century, AD1310-1330 – The North Aisle and Spire

Another extension was made to the church between 1310 and 1330 when the North aisle was added. This involved knocking out the lower level of the old North wall and inserting three arches on octagonal columns. At some time a new window was inserted in order to provide better light for the altar. These were the last major additions to the church, apart from the insertion of a stone screen at the East end of the North aisle, and the insertion of a vice (a stairwell) to give access to the Tower thus blocking part of the arch to the North transept. *See Fig 6m.*

The Perpendicular Period - 15th century – The Roof and East Window

The only other major modifications to the fabric were 15th century changes to the roof-line, when the old steeply-pitched roofs of the nave, chancel and North transept were lowered in about 1450 and replaced by an almost flat, lead-covered roof with a priest's room being added over the North transept. The beams of the new roof were carved with a host of angels and other figures. There are 12 winged angels in the central Nave roof, and a further 54 figures, including two angels and two bishops in the porch, and two angels whose wings have been broken off in the upper Priest's Room. These illustrate the theology of the central part of the Mass, when the priest precedes the singing of the Sanctus (Holy, holy, holy) by saying *'Therefore with angels, and archangels and the whole company of heaven we laud and magnify thy holy name, evermore*

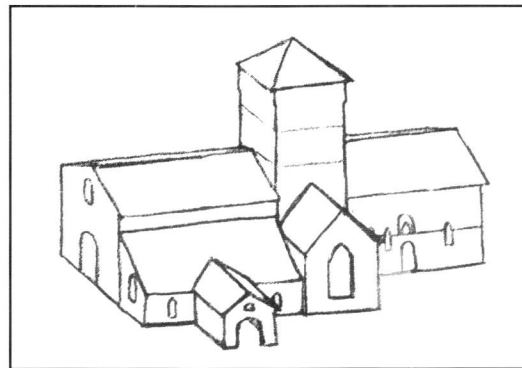

Fig 6i. Castor Church – Reconstruction of the Church 13th century, AD 1220-1230. Note square East end, and South aisle added. (Sketch: J Tovey)

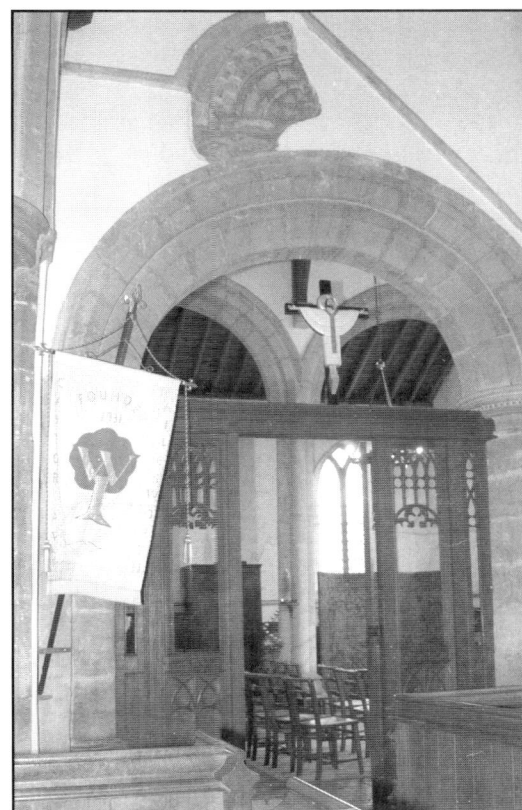

Fig 6j. Castor Church View looking East into Lady Chapel and South Transept 1260 – Note the remains of the external Norman window and old South Aisle roof-line above the entry arch. (Photo: J Tovey)

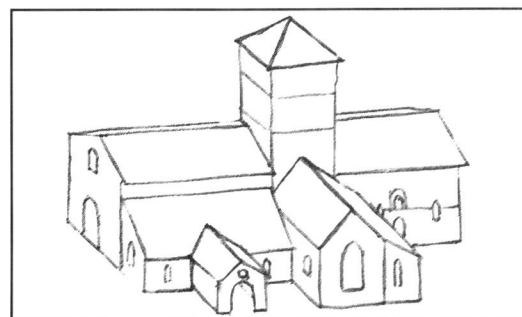

Fig 6k. Castor Church – Reconstruction of the Church 13th century, AD1260-1270. Note the South transept has been extended by the addition of a 'lean-to'. (Sketch: J Tovey)

Fig 6l. Castor Church – North Aisle 14th century screen drawn by P Taylor 1912.

Fig 6m. Castor Church – Reconstruction of the Church 14th century, AD1310-1330. Note addition of North aisle, West door now blocked up, and the spire. The only change after this was the flatter 'Angel' roof in 1450. (Sketch: J Tovey)

Fig 6n. Angel on nave roof. (Sketch: J Tovey)

praising thee and saying' – words still used today. The lines of the former gables can be seen on the external tower walls. At about the same time, the large window in the East end in Perpendicular style replaced the Early English lancets. We know from old prints that the new roof eaves were castellated until about 1850.

The Nave angels were re-gilded and painted in 1973. This work was commissioned for £300 in memory of Hilda Frances Powell formerly of Andrews Close, by her sons David and Jim Powell. The re-gilding of the side-aisle figures was commissioned by Len Sharpe, churchwarden, and his son-in-law Len Pell later a churchwarden.

There have been few changes to the structure of the church since 1450; Castor Church even escaping the addition of a Victorian vestry. This is most unusual and may perhaps be explained by the fact that there was for many years an absentee rector. From 1614, the Bishop of Peterborough held Castor *'in commendam'*, in order to supplement his perceived low income, the bishop's right to the rectorial dues being confirmed by Archbishop William Laud in 1634 [18]. The Bishop, as rector, would have appointed a curate to look after the parish on his behalf and would have taken little interest in the fabric of the church. The result is that there are few records from this period, until 1851, when the Bishop gave up the post of Rector of Castor and George Andrews, formerly the curate, was appointed as resident rector. For much of the absentee period the Rector of Marholm also served as the Curate of Castor, as a result of an agreement between the Earls Fitzwilliam and the Bishop. Sometimes he would live in Marholm, sometimes at Castor, but appointing an assistant curate living in one of the villages to help out [19].

Later History

We do not know how quickly the church here adapted to the changes brought by the turmoil of the 16th century, but we can make some deductions based on a general knowledge of the history of the time. King Henry VIII divided the assets of Peterborough Abbey, including Castor church, between the Dean and Chapter and the Bishop, granting the advowson to the Bishop and the manors to the Dean and Chapter [20]. Under Henry VIII, England had a nationalised, albeit still catholic, church. Under his son Edward VI and especially under Protector Somerset, the regent during the king's minority, the English Church moved in a more puritanical direction. Under Queen Mary, the Church was reconciled with Rome, and became Roman Catholic again. Under Queen Elizabeth I, there was yet another breach with Rome, even though in her search for a compromise she had given orders (largely ignored) that church fittings should remain 'as found' on her accession, nothing to be added or removed. During the reign of the early Stuarts, especially under Archbishop Laud, worship became more traditional and catholic in style again. Altars were railed in at the East end in the chancel for the first time in order to prevent the farmers' dogs from fouling the altar cloths, so clearly dogs accompanied their masters to church. Such altar rails are an English phenomenon, rarely seen on the Continent, the balusters of the rails having to be close enough together to prevent dogs getting through.

High Box Pews and the Village Band

Mr Hales tells [21] us that at some stage high box pews and a West gallery were inserted; they had been removed by the time of his lecture in 1883, probably at the restoration of the church interior in 1851, under the influence of the Tractarian Movement. Other small changes were made according to the whims of those who governed us. We have a list of the property [22] of the church at Castor from 1558, which included a censer and many vestments. Although the list of items then is similar to those owned by the church today, none of those actually mentioned on the list survived the depredations of the Puritans and Oliver Cromwell. Under Cromwell, many Anglican parish priests were ejected, the Prayer Book banned, and the bishops and clergy went into hiding. Our own rector at Castor was deprived [23] of his living, as was the curate, during Cromwell's regime. We still have a copy in the parish archives of the document which abolished the bishop's rights, and a list of the church lands and property in Castor Parish which were forfeited and sold off. The land, and the bishops and priests were re-instated at the Restoration of Charles II but, apart from the chalice and paten of 1632, not many furnishings survived. One sad loss was more recent; a mid 19th century letter from an 'Old Villager' reports that workmen used an old plough, kept in the church, as kindling to dry some plaster [24]. This was almost certainly the last of the old-style ritual ploughs (used on Plough Monday) then remaining in England, reported as still being in the belfry in the 1840s [25]. The same 'Old Villager' describes the old high-backed pews in the 1830s, and the gallery, which he occupied '*in the days of old, when we had all the instruments, great fiddle, little ditto, bassoon, clarinet and flute*'. The village band was replaced by a harmonium in the 1850s, this in turn replaced by an organ and new choir stalls in 1873 [26].

Fig 6o. P Tillemans drawing of Castor Church in 1719.

Fittings Furnishings and Alterations

External

Saxon Carving of Christ-in-Majesty – Gable of South Porch
During a recent trip, a visitor to the church asked why we had a carving of a 'juggler' above the porch. It is in fact a carving of Christ-in-Majesty holding up his hands in blessing, surrounded by the sun and the moon, as High King of Heaven. It must have been moved from elsewhere in the church during one of the Norman or medieval extension works. It is probably Saxon, for the style and subject is very much Celtic-Saxon. (*See Illustration, Chapter 4.*)

The Dedication Inscription – Priest's Door in Chancel
It is likely that the dedication inscription already mentioned was moved from elsewhere in the church when the chancel was extended in 1220. Don Mackreth suggests that it may have been originally in the Norman apse. Certainly the door is Early English not Norman, despite the round arch (the mouldings round the door are the clue). It seems the Roman numeral XXIV was inscribed later, although the year is probably correct [14].

Nave

Saxon Cross Base – North Door Inside
Apart from re-used Roman stonework (known as *spoila*) in the building of the church, the oldest fitting would seem to be the base of the Saxon cross. This was removed from outside, just beyond the East end of the Chancel in the 1930s, first to the East end of the North aisle, and then moved again in 1962 to its present location inside in front of the North door. The cross base is thought to be a re-used Roman pagan altar, its top (or *focus*) having been cut out to make a socket for the Saxon churchyard cross. The carvings of dragons on the base are Saxon. (*See Illustration, Chapter 4*)

Fig 6p. Saxon Cross in the graveyard beyond the East end before being moved inside c1935. It is now in front of the North door.

Saxon Sculpture 8th Century – Beside North Aisle Altar
During alterations to the sanctuary in 1924 an 8th century Saxon carving, thought to be of St Mark, was discovered when

the altar rails were moved [27]. It was found, lying face down in sand, under the old location of the altar rails on the South side. This important discovery, carved in the style of the 'Peterborough' school with limbs visible under the folds of clothes and standing on tip-toe, gives us an idea of the high standard of workmanship that would have been in the Saxon church at Castor. The carving is probably from the original shrine of St Kyneburgha, which we know was destroyed by the Danes. It was, in 1924, placed in the South wall of the sanctuary some six feet above floor level. In recent times, after discussions with English Heritage and the Diocesan Advisory Committee, it was decided that the carving should be better presented, protected, and secured. In 2002 it was moved accordingly from the sanctuary and placed in the East wall of the North aisle, to the right of the altar there, thus bringing it closer to the presumed location of the shrine of St Kyneburgha. At the same time, it was set in a frame of Clipsham Stone by David Carrington, the conservationist from Skillington Workshops. (*See Illustration Chapter 4)*

Font

The rather battered, old 12th century font, which had been lying in the churchyard, probably since the Civil War, was restored in 1928 and placed on a new plinth. The whereabouts of the font it replaced is unknown; old photographs show it standing in front of the blocked-up North door.

The Porch Door

The magnificent oak door is 14th century, its edging closely fitting the stonework of the jambs. It is inscribed round the top and right external sides *'Ricardus Beby Rector Ecclesie de Castre Fec'*, translated 'Richard Beby Rector of Castor Church made [it]'. This probably refers to Richard of Leicester, rector in 1372. The original key, stapled to the door for centuries, was stolen in the 1980s.

North Aisle Screen and Altar

The stone screen, with its five ogee arches, almost certainly held a seated statue of Our Lady, Mary, on the castellated plinth, with saints in the niches either side. The new altar to St Kyneswitha with its slate roundel of two loaves and five small fishes, recalling the Feeding of the Five Thousand, was dedicated in memory of the Hon Mrs Pelham in 1962. At the same time the two aumbry cupboards on the left of the altar were given new oak doors. The bracket for the white lamp indicating the presence of the Blessed Sacrament was made of Victorian nails in memory of Fred Green by Theo Hensman. The statue of St Kyneburgha was carved in ash-wood from Milton by Kevin Daley of Castor and dedicated at the Patronal Festival Mass in 2001.

North Aisle – Wall Painting of the Martyrdom of St Catherine

The wall-painting, dating from the 14th century, contains three scenes from the martyrdom of St Catherine. The top painting shows Catherine in 'Dispute with the Philosophers'; the middle ones the 'Execution of the Philosophers', and the lower one the 'Catherine Wheel' (broken by a knife-wielding angel), preceding Catherine's death. The cult of St Catherine was very popular in the Late Middle Ages. She is supposed to have been the niece of the Emperor Maximus who, on discovering she was a Christian, ordered his philosophers to convert her. However, she succeeded in converting them, and Maximus duly had them strangled. He then ordered her to be broken on a wheel – the origin of the Catherine Wheel. The painting at Castor was uncovered in 1842, and restored in 1986 by Liz Hirst.

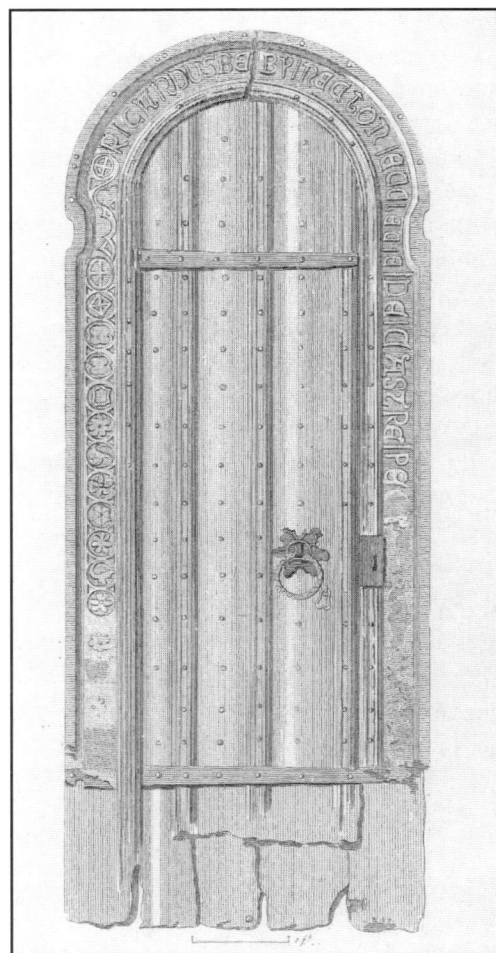

Fig 6q. Castor Church – Oak South Door 14th century (drawn 1769). Note the repairs since then.

Fig 6r. Castor Church – North Aisle Screen and Statue of St Kyneburgha. (Photo J Tovey)

Peter's Pence Box

The medieval solid oak chest, with three locks and three compartments was brought down from the tower in 1928, where it had lain for many years. Two groats from the reign of Henry VII were found lodged in it at the same time.

Old Contemptibles' Standard

The standard of the former Peterborough Branch of the 'Old Contemptibles' now hanging above the old North door, was laid up here at a special service on 9th July 1967 in the presence of the HRH Princess Alice, Duchess of Gloucester. It commemorates the British Regular Army that went to France at the outbreak of the First World War in 1914.

Sanctuary and High Altar

In Canon Morse's day, in 1924, during a restoration to celebrate the 800th anniversary of the re-dedication of the church, the first stage in restoring the chancel took place. Hitherto, two steps had led up to the altar with the altar rails on the upper step. This was apparently very uncomfortable. The altar rails were moved and lowered to their present height of two feet by Mr W T Cooke [28]. New oak riddell-posts were given by Mr Jellings, grandfather of Robert Dickens of Evergreen Hill Castor.

Fig 6s. Castor Church – North Aisle – 14th century Wall Painting of St Catherine (drawn in 1842).

Further work was done in 1928 under Canon Carleton. The chancel roof was restored and a stone cross put above the gable end. The riddell-posts were shortened and the two gilt metal angels put atop the posts. A new altar was given by Rev Francis Hulbert in memory of his parents, the Rev Canon Hulbert (a former rector) and his wife Lady Julia (daughter of the Duke of Somerset) [29]. The standard candlesticks are in memory of Cyril Kingston killed in the Second World War. The sanctuary light above the altar was given in memory of the Hon Lady Hastings of Milton in 1997, (in 1544 Robert Curteys also left a lamp and money to fund its maintenance to Castor Church) [30].

In addition to the *piscina* and *sedilia* already described there are three other recesses in the chancel walls. There seems to be another *piscina*, in the North wall with a flue. There can hardly have been an altar here, and it seems unlikely to have been re-located from elsewhere, although the style matches that of the North aisle screen. It has been suggested that it contained an image, and the flue was for smoke from an oil lamp. The two further recesses are in the walls either side of the high altar. The one in the North wall is probably the remains of an Easter Sepulchre. The purpose of one in the South wall is not clear. It will not have been a *piscina*, as there is one adjacent. On its surface is part of 14th century grave slab with a foliated cross pattern.

South Transept and Lady Chapel

The Vestry School

The South transept was used for many years as the Vestry School. Mr Hales had his early education there in the mid 1800s. He describes the vestry, including the boards inscribed with the Creed, the Lord's Prayer, and the Ten Commandments. These

Fig 6t. Chancel Arch in 1890 with text from Isaiah 45:22.

Fig 6u. Castor Church – South Transept Lady Chapel from 1928-2000 before re-ordering. For the Lady Chapel today (see colour plate section)

boards were removed in 1928 for safe-keeping [31] when the area was being re-ordered as a Lady Chapel, and have never been seen since. Are they stored in a barn somewhere, or have they since been destroyed? In 1920 the War Memorial was erected, and in 1922 the oak-screen was placed between the transept, nave and choir-stalls.

The Lady Chapel

We know that there was an altar dedicated to the Blessed Virgin Mary at Castor in ancient times, for in 1499 Robert Mayden left his *'croft on the hill and all its belongings to the Guild of Our Lady'* at Castor [32].

In 1928 a temporary wooden altar (which remained there until 2003!) was placed in the South transept under the inner two-light East window, and chairs were given in memory of ladies in the parish. Two silver candelabra were hung on chains above the altar. There was no altar rail, but instead six basketwork kneelers. During this time, the 13th century recumbent effigy of a priest, thought to be Virgilius (appointed as rector in 1228), was removed from the South transept to the South side of the chancel [33] where it now lies. Its original location in the South transept is not known. In the North-east corner of the South transept there is the site of a brass of a bishop or an abbot. The brass has been removed, probably during the Civil War, but its impression is still there in the stone. The head and the crozier in the bishop's right hand can be seen, as also can the brass studs used to secure it in the floor. We do not know whom it commemorated. Separating the South transept from the chancel is a plain stone screen about six feet high, above which are iron hooks under the Early English arch. It would appear that the hooks once supported wooden shutters screening the transept from the chancel, presumably while the transept was used as a school-room. The post-medieval doorway, now blocked up, in the East wall of the transept provided external access to the school.

The Lady Chapel today

In 2000 a large stone which then lay in the path outside the priest's door to the Chancel was identified as a pre Reformation medieval *mensa* (stone altar slab). Although much worn and weathered from being outside for hundreds of years and broken into three parts, its location, together with its dimensions (6½ feet by 3 feet) and the fact that it was bevelled on three sides and square cut on one long side, indicate it was very probably the old high altar stone originally set flush against the chancel East wall. It was then brought into the church and laid in the chancel to preserve it from further deterioration. After discussions with our architect, Julian Limentani, and the diocese it was decided to re-install it in the church, this time in the Lady Chapel. Consequently the Lady Chapel was re-ordered to face South to accommodate it. In 2003 the old *mensa* was repaired and set up on six bluestone columns by Fairhavens of Anglesey Abbey, the conservationist workshops, in a style appropriate for its origins, under the three-light Early English window in the South transept. (see colour plate section)

New altar rails were made by Theo Hensman, using wrought iron from the churchyard and old pew tops. The pattern in the wrought iron recalls the fishes and loaves of the Feeding of the Five Thousand. A new blue carpet was laid, and on Rogation Sunday 2003 the rails and carpet were dedicated in memory of Brian Sharpe, member of an old farming family in the village. New cupboards were made for the choir and vestments and placed in the Northeast corner of the transept. The wooden chairs, the parish chest, and other fittings were refurbished by Monica (née Darby) and Jim Pollard. The statue of Our Lady and Child, on the central column, was given to the church by the Mothers' Union to celebrate our Branch Centenary in 1997. The copy of a *della Robbia* ceramic of the kneeling Mary and the infant Jesus in the straw, on the South wall to the right of the altar, was given in memory of Rex Whittome in 2003.

A Walk Round the Outside

People sometimes ask why the stone work of the walls, known as rubble coursing, looks so unfinished when compared with the tower. Quite simply, the answer is that it did not matter what the external stonework looked like, because until the Reformation most parish churches were covered outside in a white-lime and plaster finish (as they still are inside today). This was not just for appearances, for it also helped weather-proof the pointing. From the outside then, the church would probably have been all-white apart from the quoins and the tower. In some cases this external white-lime lasted until the Victorian period when it would have been scraped off, but we do not know when this happened at Castor. But without it, we can see how the builders of the medieval church used large quantities of Roman material - the hundreds of *tegulae* (red-tiles from the roof) and *pilae* (hypocaust bricks) from the Roman building. Pevsner [34] also states that the round stones in the external North wall of the chancel are Roman columns sliced up and reused, although others (including Don Mackreth) have suggested that they are parts of columns from the arcading in the Norman chancel.

Fig 6v. Castor Church – Graveyard before extension looking North (c1920).

In the external South walls of the nave and the Lady Chapel there are two arches about six feet long and four feet long respectively. These are sepulchral arches, burial places for important people, but any evidence of who they might have been has long since disappeared. Beside the arch in the external wall of the South aisle there is an empty 14th century stone coffin and lid. Under the eaves of the Lady Chapel are corbel carvings of faces, ox heads, and so on. Note the sundial on the South external wall of the Lady Chapel. Further East, past the famous priest's door and inscription previously described, there is a carved ram's head high up on the wall. Notice also the huge stone gargoyles spaced out along the roof-line, their gaping mouths used for discharging rainwater well clear of the walls. There are a large number of pink stones (not to be mistaken for Roman tiles) scattered throughout the length of the walls. These are stones that have been burnt by intense heat and then re-used. It is possible that they may be re-used stones from the Saxon church, which we know was badly burnt in a Viking raid [13]. Note too, the Saxon 'long-and-short' work in the blocked-up door in the East wall of the North transept, and the outline of part of a Norman window with its billet moulding in the North wall of the North transept.

The Churchyard

The original churchyard enclosed the whole of the area of the school and cottages that surround the church, as well as part of the grounds of The Cedars, forming the classic Saxon 'tear-drop' shape. The Churchyard wall is probably 18th century, although of course burials in the cemetery go back to the earliest days of the church here. The graveyard has been extended several times. There are a number of medieval body-stones, some left *in situ*, and some that have been re-used as capstones on the wall, notably some fine examples atop the wall on the right side of the Church Hill entrance to the churchyard. Apart from the medieval body-stones, the oldest monuments are those immediately either side of the path South of the church, running from Stocks Hill to Church Hill. The wall running alongside Church Walk, separating it from the School Field, was built in 1949 in memory of a former churchwarden, Major Pelham of The Cedars. The fine church notice-board was made by Michael Glendinning and given in memory of Len Pell by his family in 2000.

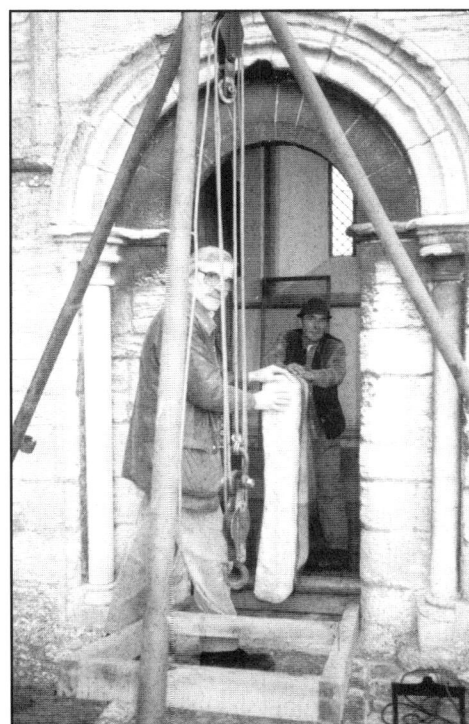

Fig 6w. Castor Church – Churchwardens Brian Goode and Theo Hensman man-handling the 'mensa' through the priest's door.

Fig 6x. Gargoyle. (Photo: J Tovey)

Fig 6y. North transept window. Note billet moulding on left indicating site of previous Norman window. (Photo: J Tovey)

Miscellanea

Plate and Vestments

These include a silver-gilt Communion Cup with Cover Paten 1632; two silver-gilt Breadholders 1673; a silver-gilt flagon 1774; and other items. Major Pelham presented the Churchwardens' wands in 1924. Among the many vestments is a green baize chasuble. The material came from Tobruk, and was given to a previous rector, Tom Adler, to lay over the front of his jeep for services, while he was serving as a chaplain in North Africa during the Second World War. A complete set of new vestments and hangings in green, the pattern again recalling the Feeding of the Five Thousand, was designed by Vanessa Collison and made by ladies from the village under the direction of Diana Burke to celebrate the Millennium.

The Patronage

The advowson, the right to nominate the parish priest at Castor, was in the gift of the Abbot of Peterborough until 1541, when it was assumed by the Bishop of Peterborough. Meanwhile the Earls Fitzwilliam retained the advowson of Marholm, and the Hopkinsons acquired that of Sutton when they bought the manor in 1890 from the Dean and Chapter. When the parishes were re-united into one benefice in 1995 it was decided that the patronage should be shared between the descendants of the last Earl Fitzwilliam (now represented by Sir Philip Naylor-Leyland Bt of Milton), and Mrs V Gunnery, a descendant of the Hopkinsons.

The Cedar Centre – Our New Church Hall

Originally designed by Peter McFarland and completed by Peter Slinger, the Cedar Centre was built to commemorate the Millennium. The total cost, including the land, was £167,000, of which £30,000 came from a Millennium Commission grant. The rest was found after heroic fund-raising by Julie Taylor (nee Speechley) and her team, hard work by the village; and the generosity of Mr and Mrs Charles Winfrey and some private donors. The builders were David Holmes (who lives in Castor) and Granville Builders. On 9th July 2000, after the Patronal Mass, The Cedar Centre was dedicated and blessed by David Painter, the Archdeacon of Oakham, and formally opened jointly by Mrs Jay Winfrey, wife of the late Charles Winfrey, Mrs Becci Dudgeon of The Cedars, and Mrs Florence Jackson, the oldest

Fig 6z. Choir at Candlemas 2004; adults (l-r:)Brian Goode, Eric Jinks (cross), Leslie Rigby, Bridget Goode, Rector, Sue Mackenzie, Will Craven (organist), Joan Pickett, Pam Tedcastle, Carol Castle, Elizabeth Brown, Sue Sykes, Theo Hensman; children: Alistair Dutton, Jennifer Sykes, Alex Elliott, Jack Stalley, Heather Hunt (behind), Yllana Hunt, Ben Dutton (behind), Samantha Dunham, Amber Grys, Lauren O'Boyle, Ross Elliott (front left), Alice Castle, Cara Grys, Tasmin Brown, Rebecca Sykes, Annabel Martin, Poppy Tovey (front). For Sanctuary Party (see colour plate section).

member of our congregation. The ChiRho with Alpha & Omega symbols (as found on the Water Newton Treasure) was sculpted from iron scrap by Theo Hensman, churchwarden and farmer.

St Kyneburgha Historic Building Preservation Trust

In 2000, the St Kyneburgha Historic Building Preservation Trust, known as 'The Friends', was formed to help the parish maintain and promote the building. Lady Isabella Naylor-Leyland of Milton took office as its first President, and Mrs Jonathan (Jackie) Cook of the Old Rectory Castor as first Chairman. The Trust has already helped with the repairs to the East end; the relocation of the Saxon sculpture of St Mark; rewiring; re-liming the nave; and resetting the *mensa* in the Lady Chapel.

Summary

The purpose of this chapter has been an attempt to explain the history of the development of the Church of St Kyneburgha of Castor. For those who want detailed architectural descriptions, the best references are Pevsner's *Buildings of England Series, Bedfordshire, Huntingdon and Peterborough*, (Penguin 1968), and *The Victoria County History Series, Northamptonshire* (1901). The purpose of the church building itself is, of course, different. It stands, not as a museum, but as a witness. It exists to tell the story of God's Incarnation in the person of Jesus; to help all who wish to understand the implications of that revelation in the life of the world; to be there to help the community and its people celebrate their joys; and to comfort them in their sorrows. The fact that this building still stands to tell its story is a tribute, not to great men, but to the churchwardens and people of the village who have cherished it over the centuries. Both the current churchwardens, Brian Goode and Theo Hensman, were born in Castor.

Almighty God, to whose glory this Church of ours was built,
We praise thee for the skill of its craftsmen builders,
And the inspiration of those who set this work in hand,
Grant that here we may find vision,
Grant that here we may find peace,
And grant that from this house we may go out in the fellowship
Of Our Lady, St Kyneburgha, and all thy saints,
To serve thy purposes in the world
Through Jesus Christ our Lord. Amen.

William Burke

Fig6aa. The MU banner dressed for the Summer Patronal Mass Procession 1997. l-r: Eileen Rattenbury, Tess Thompson-Bell, Vera Pell (banner), Win Smith, Joyce Clarke.

Fig 6bb. The two new bells dressed ready for their baptism at the Patronal Mass 1999.

Fig 6cc. Porch doorway. (Photo: P White)

Notes

1. Simon Jenkins, *England's Thousand Best Churches*, Penguin Press, 1999, p.xxxvii.
2. Castor was in the Diocese of Lincoln until 1542, when the new See of Peterborough was established.
3. Dr K Painter FSA, *The Water Newton Treasure*, Lecture, Great Northern Hotel Peterborough, 12 March 1999.
4. Water Newton Treasure, British Museum. An inscription on the bottom of a small silver bowl reads: *"Publianus"* and *"Sanctum altare tuum, D (XP) omine, sub nixus, honoro."* Transl: *"* I honour your holy altar, O Lord, (in the name of Christ)".
5. Dr Ken Dark, *Britain and the End of the Roman Empire*, Tempus, 2000, pp 103-104, pp 115-117, Burial Map p98.
6. *History Today*, October 1995 pp 33-37 (Map showing Castor p 37).
7. Victoria County History, Northamptonshires 1901, p 475 and note 2.
8. John Hales, Extract from *Northamptonshire Notes and Queries* 1888-1889, p 212. *'There is a road running backway from Ailsworth to Helpstone – passing the house of Mr W Briggs on the left, and that of Mr W Carter on the right - called Chapel Lane. It may be interesting to some to know that this name is not without its meaning, as up to the year 1854, there was a building in Mr Carter's yard, at the left of ecclesiastical appearance, used as a granary, etc., which was evidently a chapel of ease, as it had two square-headed windows, one on the North and one on the South side, filled in with early English tracery similar to those at Northborough castle. It was demolished at the above date and the materials used in the erection of agricultural buildings.'*
9. Smith, Hutton and Cook, *English Parish Churches*, 1997, T&H, p 43. *'Another set of contrasts can be seen in the central tower of the cruciform Norman church at Castor, Northamptonshire: a typical piece of Continental Romanesque work, massive, with elaborately carved and coursed stone panels and lights, rich groundwork of chevron-like panelling above the lower arcade, and fish-scale ornaments above. This is capped with an abnormally stocky Early English octagonal spire rising from a fretted stone parapet of later date; but if you look closely at the stone-coursing of walls and tower you see old Saxon work in the former, and fine late Norman jointing (with thin lines of mortar) in the latter. Nor are Castor and New Shoreham singular in portraying so clearly this great transition and transformation of the English people and their churches between the tenth and thirteenth centuries. The story of that great change – as great as that from ancient rural England to modern industrial urban England – is writ large in parish churches.'*
10. Arthur Mee, *King's England, Northamptonshire*, Hodder & Stoughton, 1945, p 68.
11. Canon Jack Higham, recently retired Canon Librarian Peterborough Cathedral. Personal communication.
12. N Pevsner *Buildings of England Series, North East & East Kent*, Penguin, 1983 p 242.
13. Hugh Candidus, *The Peterborough Chronicle*, Ed by W T Mellows, Peterborough Museum Society, 1997 p 23 and his Note 1.
    'There was in his (Abbot Aelfsy) days a much ruined church at Cyneburch-caster (Castor) 1, where reposed S.Cyneburh and her sister S.Cynesswith, the daughters of King Penda.' His Note 1:*A.S.C. 963. It is difficult to reconcile the account of the removal of the bodies of SS. Cyneburh and Cyneswith with the statement in Chron.Abb.John, p. 18, where the author of the latter tells his story of the destruction of the monastery by the Danes in 870 adding: 'Altaria omnia suffosa sanctarum Kyneburge, Kyneswite ac Tibbe preciosa pignora pedibus conculcata…ipsa ecclesia cum omnibus ceteris edificilis concremata.'* Transl: "All the overthrown altars of the holy virgins Kyneburge, Kyneswite and Tibba (with their) valuable pledges (in the form of gifts) trampled under foot…own church with all the rest of the edifice burnt."
14. Rev W D Sweeting, *The Parish Churches round Peterborough*, 1868 p 16, Brit Mus Add MSS 6750. *'1124. Hoc anno Ecclie de Caster solenniter ab Epo. Linc consecrate est.'* Trans: 'this year the church of Castor was solemnly dedicated by the Bishop of Lincoln'. Gunton, records the date inscription as it now is. *(History of the Church in Peterborough*, written in the 17 century, ed J Higham). However some experts have suggested that Castor Church was actually dedicated on 17 April 1104. In some respects this would make more sense; in AD1104, 17 April fell on Easter Day, a popular date for the dedication of churches, and it would also make more sense architecturally. However that would imply that the letters XXIV on the inscription were incorrect (which is possible as they were added later), and that the Bishop of Lincoln's records were also wrong (also possible).
15. N Pevsner *Buildings of England Series, Bedfordshire, Huntingdon and Peterborough*, Penguin, 1968, p364.
16. Smith, Hutton and Cook, *English Parish Churches*, 1997, T&H, p 44, n 19.
17. Revd Kennet Gibson, *The Antonine Itinerary*, written 1769, published 1800, p 179.
18. NCRO Document Hatton-Finch Papers 3130A. Grant by William *(Laud)* Archbishop of Canterbury to Francis Dee. From 1614, the Bishop of Peterborough held Castor *in commendam*, in order to supplement his perceived low income, and the Bishop's rights to the Rectorial dues were confirmed by Arch Bishop William Laud in 6 May 1634.
19. Revd Kennet Gibson, *The Antonine Itinerary*, written 1769, published 1800 p 171. *'At Marholm and Castor, the former being in the gift of Earl Fitwilliam, who generally compliments the Bishop with it for his curate of Castor.'* Gibson (simultaneously Rector of Marholm and Curate of Castor) wrote in 1786 an important history of the villages and churches in the benefice of Castor, Ailsworth, Sutton, Upton and Maholm.
20. *Founding Of Peterborough Cathedral*, ed WT Mellows, NRS, 1941 p lxviii and pp 14-20. *'The Advowson, gift, presentation and rights of patronage of all singularity of the rectors of Castor (and others) granted to Bishop by King Henry viii 4th Sept 1541'* (See also Gunton p 67).
21. John Hales, *Lecture*, Castor, 28th April 1883 – see Appx 18.
22. Church Inventory 1558: Rev WD Sweeting, *The Parish Churches round Peterborough*, 1868 p 13 – See Appx 5.
23. Bp John Towers as rector ejected 1646 (died in the Tower). See Appx 2.
24. Old Plough: An Old Villager, *Parish News*, March 1999, p 14.
25. R Hutton, *The Stations of the Sun*, OUP, 1996, p 126 and n 16. The plough was described as *'an old town plough, roughly made, decayed and worm-eaten… about three times as large as an ordinary plough.'* Also T Davidson, Plough Rituals in England and Scotland, *Agricultural History Review*, 7, (1959).
26. John Hales' Diary 1830-1881 (Copy Castor Parish Archives) and *Peterborough Advertiser*, 2 May 1924.
27. Saxon sculpture found: *Peterborough Advertiser* 2 May 1924 – DBR C/C 1095.
28. Ibid.
29. New Altar etc, *Peterborough & Hunts Standard*, 1928, DBR C/C 1042.
30. Rev WD Sweeting, *The Parish Churches round Peterborough*, 1868, p 14. In 1544 Robert Curteys also left a lamp and money to fund its maintenance to Castor Church He leaves his body to be buried in the North Aisle, and *'to thighe aulter iiis iiiid to the sepulchre light iiis iiiid to the bells xiid…Item I bequeath to Robert Curteys my son vis viiid for to fynde a certen lampe in the church so that yt may at the yeeres ende be made as good by the occupaycon thereof as yt was in the begynninge soo longe as he lyst to kepe itt or else to lett some other have ytt that will occupy ytt of the same manner soo that I wyll nott ytt shulde dekay or peryshe.'*
31. *Peterborough & Hunts Standard* 1928 DBR C/C 1042. See also note 21. These boards were removed in 1928 for safe-keeping, when the area was being re-ordered.
32. Rev WD Sweeting, *The Parish Churches round Peterborough*, 1868, p 14, Robert Mayden left his *'croft on the hill and all its belongings to the Guild of Our Lady'* at Castor.
33. Effigy of Virgilius (Rector in 1238) moved from South transept to the South Chancel. *Peterborough & Hunts Standard 1928*, DBR C/C 1042.
34. N Pevsner *Buildings of England Series, Bedfordshire, Huntingdon and Peterborough*, Penguin, 1968, p 227ff.

Annex A The Bells Of St Kyneburgha's Church Castor

The earliest reference to bells at St. Kyneburgha's appear in North's 'Church bells of Northamptonshire' 1878, where it is stated that in 1552, Castor possessed: 'Furst in o steple iiij grete bellys. Itm in the same a sanctus bell. Itm two hand belles.' These were replaced in 1700 by a new ring of six, cast and installed by Henry Bagley of Ecton, near Wellingborough. North goes on to explain the customs practised at Castor at the time: *'At the Death-knell twice three tolls are given before, and three tolls after the knell for a man; twice two tolls before, and two after for a woman, in both cases on the tenor bell. The same mode is followed in the case of children, but the 4th bell is then used'*. The bells would have been mounted in a large, heavy oak frame supported on oak beams. In 1900 the bells were re-hung in iron frames with steel girders by Taylor's of Loughborough, and the opportunity was taken to 'turn' the bells, (to present an unindented surface to where the clapper strikes the sound-bow). The cannons on top of the bells, used to secure the bells to the old wooden headstocks, would have been removed at this time, together with their crown staples, (loops of iron cast into the top of each bell from which the clapper was suspended) and new clappers fitted. The autumn of 1969 saw the bells being taken down yet again by Taylor's for re-hanging and fitting ball bearings. Apart from re-tuning and removing the cannons, the bells are as cast by Henry Bagley 300 years ago. Towards the end of 1999, under the leadership of our Tower Captain Tony Evans, the Bagley six were augmented to an eight by the addition of two new trebles, cast by Taylor's and hung in an extended framewhich was supplied and fitted along with all the other bell fittings by Hayward Mills. The new bells were baptized at the Patronal Mass 1999 and dedicated on 17 October 1999.

Details of the Bells

Bell	Weight in Cwt-qr-lb	Dia. inches	Note
Inscription.	- Symbol -O- indicates Coin set in Inscription Band		
Treble	4-0-16	25 ½	G
OMNIA FIANT AD GLORIAM DEI (Let all be done to the Glory of God) **XP 2000 AD AΩ** (Christ - 2000 Year of our Lord – Beginning and End) **Rector William Burke. Ringers, William Baxter, Edward Baxter Diana Burke, Tony Evans Capt. Lis Freeman, Yvette Halewood MANTON & DAVID BAXTER, SPEECHLEY FAMILY CHARLES WINFREY & FAMILY**			
No.2	4-0-22	26	F#
UNTOUCHED I AM A SILENT THING, BUT STRIKE ME AND I SWEETLY SING Church Wardens Brian Goode & Theo Hensman. Ringers, Maggie Noble, Anna Reed, Stephen Reed, Beverley Rigby, Virginia Sheldon, Trevor Vercoe **COOK FAMILY, CARLY & BOBBY FREEMAN, GRIFFIN FAMILY, RP & NM WINFREY**			
No.3	4-0-17	27 ¼	E
HENRICVS BAGLEY -O- NOS -O- FECIT –O- 1700 -O-			
No.4	4-0-21	28 ¼	D
HENRICVS BAGLEY -O- NOS -O- FECIT -O- 1700 -O-			
No.5	4-3-14	30 ½	C
HENRY BAGLEY OF ECTON MADE ME 1700			
No.6	6-0-16	32 5/8	B
HENRY BAGLEY OF ECTON MADE ME 1700			
No. 7	7-0-19	35 7/8	A
CANTATE DOMINO CANTICTVM NOVVM (Sing unto the Lord a new song) **HENRICVS BAGLEY DE ECTON NOS FECIT. 1700**			
Tenor	10-0-9	39	G
I TO THE CHVRCH THE LIVING CALL AND TO THE GRAVE DO SVMMON ALL. HENRY BAGLEY MADE ME 1700			

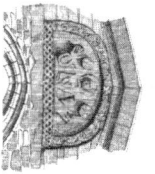

Henry VII (1485 AD).

1 – Porch – a late Saxon carving of 'Christ in Majesty' in the gable above (pictured left),

2 – The Door – leading into the church dates from 1372.

3 – Peter's Pence Box – oak alms chest – pre

4 – The Roof in the Nave – angels with instruments – 15th century oak.

5 – Wall Painting – showing scenes from the life of St Catherine – note wheel – 14th century.

6 – Base of a Saxon cross.

7 – The altar of St Kyneswitha – she was a sister of St Kyneburgha. They were both buried here until their bodies were moved to Peterborough in the 11th century. The screen dates from 1330 AD.

8 – Next to Kyneswithas' Altar – a Saxon carving of an Apostle, this was part of the shrine of St Kyneburgha – 8th century.

9 – Tower Capitals – the carvings show a 'green man', hunting scenes, a man fighting a lion and St Kyneburgha being chased by ruffian soldiers (pictured left), 1120 – 1124 AD.

10 – Priest's Door – on a semi-circular frame of stone, over the Priest's Door in the south wall of the Chancel, is the following inscription: —

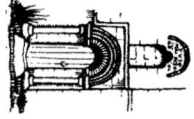

XV. KL.

MAI   DEDICA
TIO   HVI   ECCL'E
A.D.   MCXXIIII

In full this reads:

Quinto decimo Kalendas

Maias Ecclesiae
Anno Domino   MCXXIIII

Or

The dedication of this Church was on the

17th April 1124.

11 – The Chancel – note the tomb of Virgilius, an early Rector – c. 1228 AD

12 – The Lady Chapel – this was rebuilt in c. 1260 AD, and is dedicated to Our Lady Mary, the Mother of Jesus

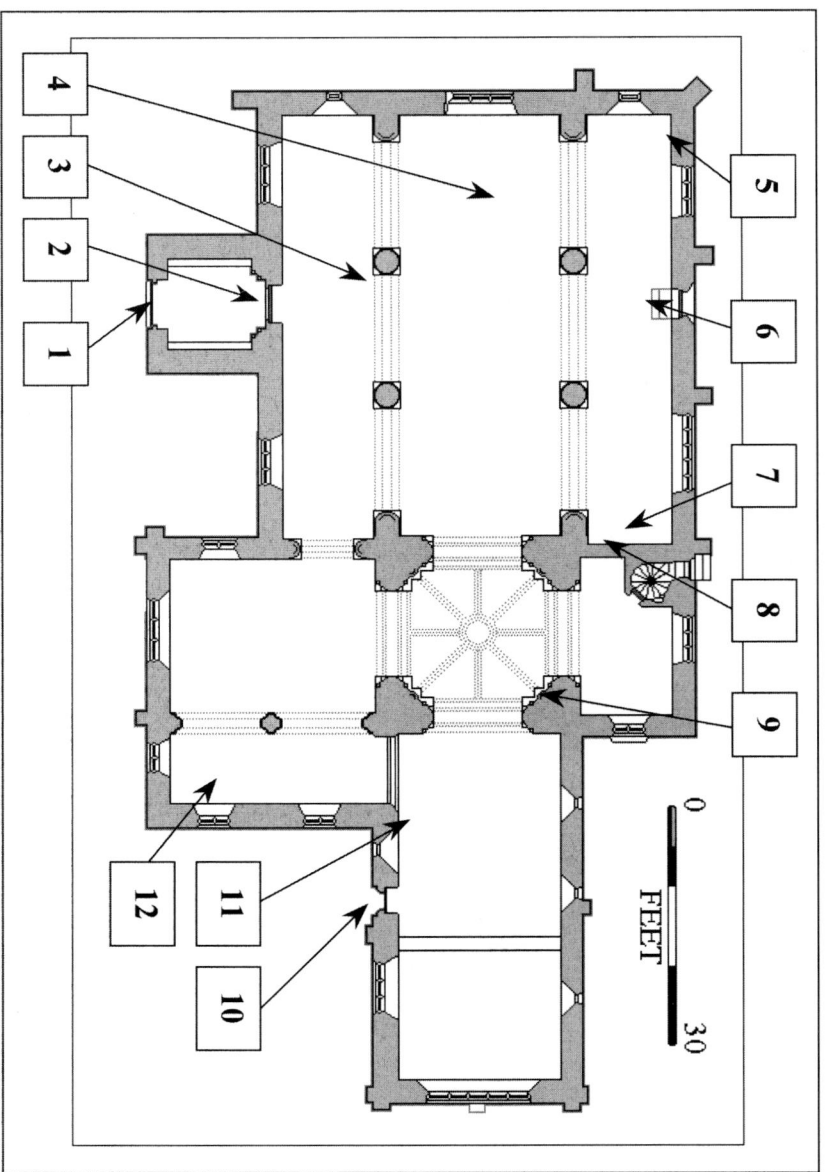

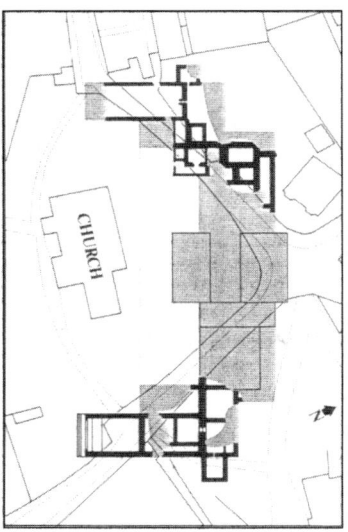

A reconstruction of the great roman building showing the probable outline (grey toned area).

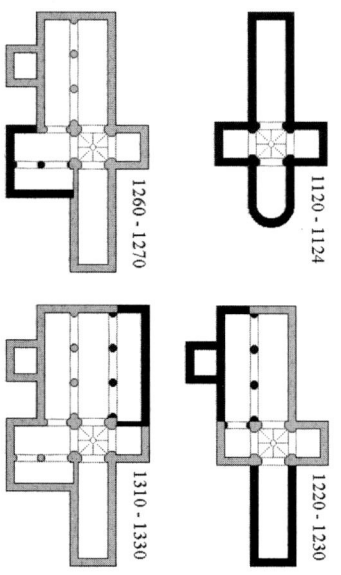

CHURCH

0 ___ 30
FEET

1120 - 1124

1260 - 1270

1220 - 1230

1310 - 1330

The development of the church. Some of the Saxon church can be seen incorporated into the Norman church. The Priest's room above the North Transept was added between 1310 and 1320, and the Spire was added to the tower in 1350.

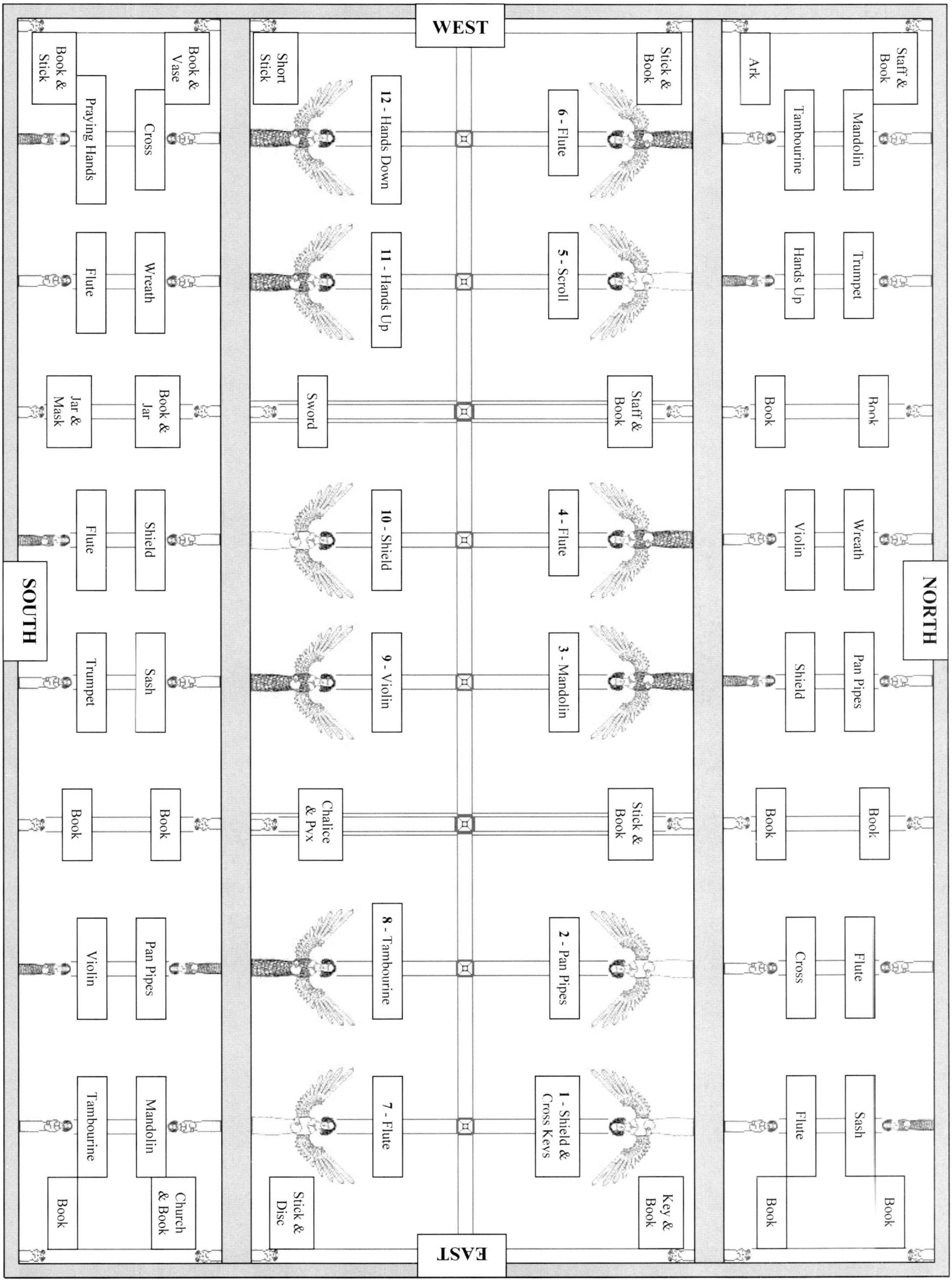

NORTH

SOUTH

Staff & Book

Ark

Tambourine

Mandolin

Hands Up

Trumpet

Book

Rook

Violin

Wreath

Shield

Pan Pipes

Book

Book

Cross

Flute

Flute

Sash

Book

Book

Stick & Book

6 - Flute

5 - Scroll

Staff & Book

4 - Flute

3 - Mandolin

Stick & Book

2 - Pan Pipes

1 - Shield & Cross Keys

Key & Book

Short Stick

12 - Hands Down

11 - Hands Up

Sword

10 - Shield

9 - Violin

Chalice & Pyx

8 - Tambourine

7 - Flute

Stick & Disc

Book & Stick

Book & Vase

Cross

Praying Hands

Wreath

Flute

Jar & Mask

Book & Jar

Shield

Flute

Sash

Trumpet

Book

Book

Pan Pipes

Violin

Mandolin

Tambourine

Church & Book

Book

83

Fig 6ff. Tony Evans (Tower Captain fourth from left in tie) with the Castor Bell-ringers after the Baptism of the new bells at the Patronal Mass 1999.

Fig 6gg. View of Castor Church interior painted in 1800 looking from the South transept across into the North transept.

Chapter 7

The Buildings of Castor

Castor is a village of considerable charm with many fine and interesting buildings. At the present time, there are around 85 buildings, as well as barns and other outbuildings, that date from before 1900 [1]. The location and appearance of these older properties reflect Castor's recent history as an agricultural community and give the village its historic feel. Since 1950, following the move away from agriculture, nearly three times as many homes have been added, extending over previously open land and filling in the gaps between the older buildings.

Pre-1900: Old Castor

The map (*Fig 7a*) shows the location of the older properties in the modern village. They follow the curve of Peterborough Road, the main road running roughly East to West through the village. Situated in an elevated position on the North side of the road in the centre of the village, is the Church of St Kyneburgha. Further older buildings are grouped to the East above the Church in High Street and to the West along Church Hill down to the area around The Green. Most are built in local limestone with roofs of Collyweston tiles, thatch or Welsh slate.

The variety of these buildings is typical of a flourishing, self-sufficient agricultural village with a church, several farms, public houses and other businesses, chapel and schools. The rest are mainly a range of small domestic dwellings with a few more substantial houses. Apart from the Church, they date from around 1600 although some show evidence of earlier builds and most have parts added or altered at later dates.

A great deal is known about these buildings, both from local knowledge and previous surveys of Castor such as those carried out by The Peterborough Society [2] and the Royal Commission for Historic Monuments [3]. A remarkably high proportion of the buildings has been accorded Listed status by the RCHM: for their historical or architectural significance, or even for being part of a group [4]. A list of these, together with brief descriptions, can be found in *Appendix 20*. In this chapter we have drawn mainly on information from these surveys and lists, as well as from local residents [5], to describe those buildings which, by their style and own particular story, illustrate the variety and interest of the buildings in the village.

The Church of St Kyneburgha

Previously described in some detail, this Norman church is the oldest building in Castor. It is the only Grade I listed building in the village.

The Farms and their Associated Buildings

There have been many farms in Castor although some of their farmhouses have been lost or incorporated into larger properties, including the Old Rectory and The Cedars. At the present time there is only one working farm in the village, The Hollies, but there were nine as late as the first half of the 20th century [6]. These farms, by virtue of their farmhouses, barns, stables and field walls, have a significant impact on the village today. All but one of these, Home Farm, belonged to the Milton Estate or the Church Commissioners and were occupied by tenant farmers. Most of the farmhouses have now passed into private hands. A few of their barns and stables remain empty but many have been sold separately and converted to modern dwellings.

Village Farm (formerly West Farm and sometimes referred to as Village Manor Farm) is considered to be the oldest building in Castor after the Church. Now partially obscured by mature trees, this stone house is set back from the Peterborough Road at the Western end of the village. It faces South-east with open land to the South and West. The building dates from the 15th century, with 16th/17th century alterations and further changes during the 19th and 20th centuries. Since the last surveys, two wings have been added; one to the Western end and one in the centre at the rear (see *Fig 7b*).

This is a very interesting building. It was originally H-shaped in plan and is a good example of a typical late-mediaeval farmhouse layout although very few original details remain today. Features of architectural merit remaining include its Tudor square brick chimneys, a gabled kneeler and apex stone on the South-west gable, original stone doorways and

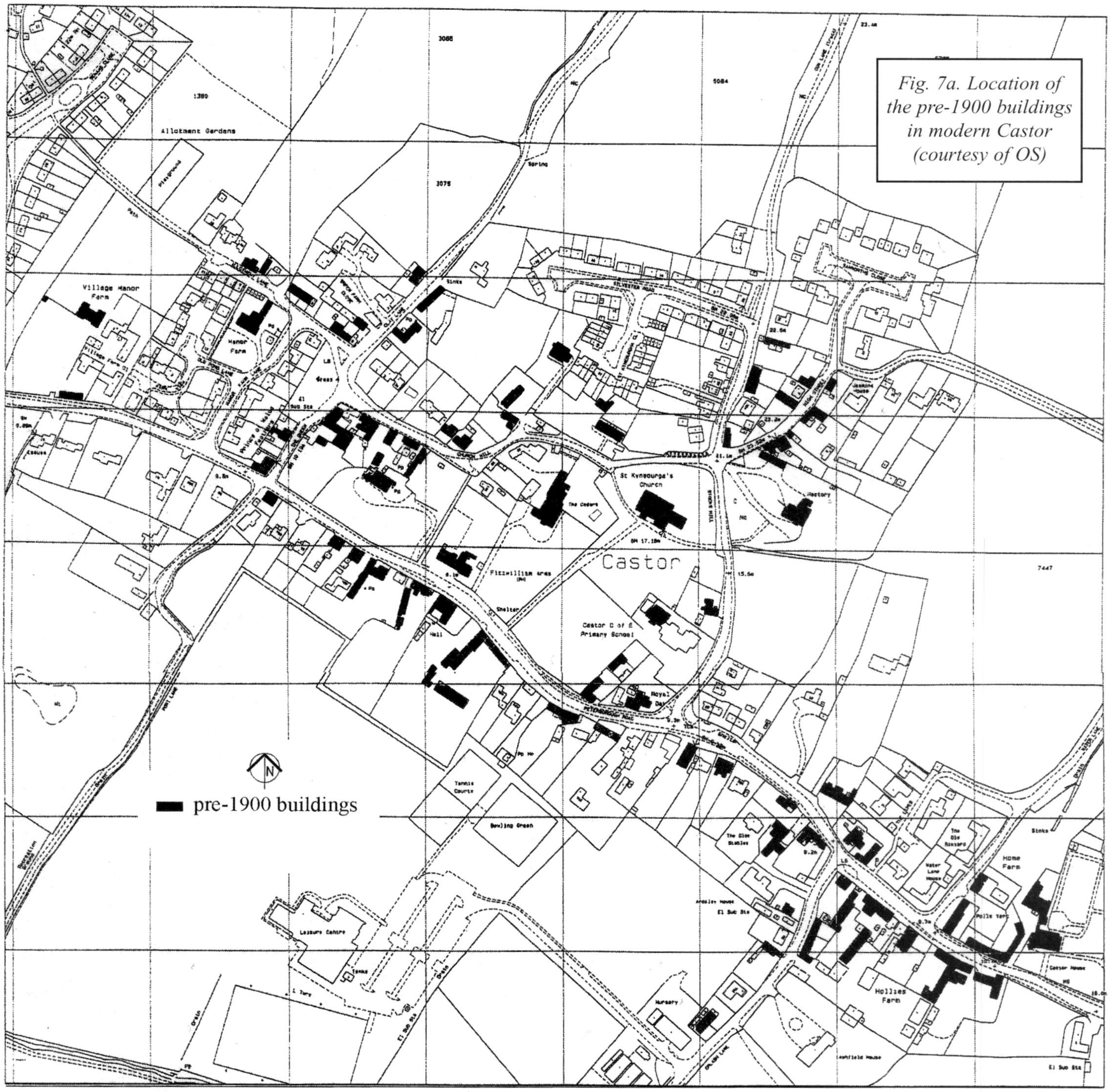

Fig. 7a. Location of
the pre-1900 buildings
in modern Castor
(courtesy of OS)

pre-1900 buildings

16th century beams in the Eastern ground-floor room. Most of the Farm's outbuildings have now gone but there is a charming 18th century stone-built dovecote to the West with a modern roof. The Wade family ran the farm from 1928 until their grandson, Theo Hensman, left in the early 1970s.

To the East in Manor Farm Lane is **Manor Farm** which is now almost completely enveloped by modern housing. It is a large 17th century L-shaped building with 19th century roof and windows. The house faces North-east and the main range is now made up of three rooms with fireplaces. The wing at the rear has an open fireplace. There were until the 1950s, two long 16th/17th century barns arranged end to end at the rear of The Green. The main outbuilding left now is used as a garage/store attached to the North-west end of the house. Peter and Rebecca Winfrey currently live there.

The remaining farmhouses show a very wide variety of size and style. There were two in Clay Lane. **Green Farm** (3 Clay Lane) is attached to 1 Clay Lane. It was last farmed by Rowland Longfoot who retired in 1979, and part of the land has been used for the Green Farm Close development and some for the bypass. The farmhouse is now considerably altered but is considered to have been originally similar in style to 1 Clay Lane and other early 17th century thatched houses, with one storey and attics. The house has since been raised and its thatch replaced although much of the ground floor remains, together with recent additions.

Opposite is **Top Farm,** also known as Major's Farm, (4 Clay Lane). It is a drastically altered L-shaped stone house. It probably dates from the late 17th/early 18th century but now has a section built on the front and a modern steeply pitched tiled roof, which was previously thatched. A medieval piscina thought to have come from the old Chapel-of-ease in Main Street, Ailsworth, forms an internal windowsill in one room, where an earlier fireplace has been uncovered by the present owners, the Davies family. Previous farmers here include Henry Colbert, William Carter and George Speechley until around 1932. After being rented out as a domestic residence for many years, the house passed into private hands from the Church Commissioners in 1960, with extra land bought in 1961 to form a garden to the rear. There is a large barn to the North under separate ownership. This has several triangular ventilation slits and wooden doors on the second storey and has been heightened in modern brick.

Several farmhouses are to be found towards the Eastern end of the Village. On the North side of Peterborough Road is **Limes Farm** (6a Peterborough Road) which was farmed by Dick and Len Longfoot until the 1950s. The house is probably early 19th century with two converted 18th century barns alongside (Old Bakehouse). At the rear is The Limes development built in 1986 on the site of the stables. On the other side of Water Lane is **Home Farm** with its many attractively converted barns making up Polls Yard [7]. Across the main road is **The Hollies** (5 Peterborough Road) which has been farmed by Mr Jim Wood since 1963. This smart early 19th century farmhouse sits at right angles to the road with a wing to the South. It is built of dressed stone with banding between the storeys and has a Welsh slate roof. There is an impressive collection of early/mid 19th century barns around the farmyard to the East of the house. The one along the roadside has several attractive features including vertical ventilation slits, double doors and a loft window in the West gable (see *Fig 7c*).

Mill Farmhouse (17 and 17a Peterborough Road) is now much altered. It is considered to be early 18th century and some original grey and brown brickwork can be seen on the gable at the Eastern end where the house joins the neighbouring properties. The house probably originally had the typical central door with stairs straight up ahead of it – rather like number 23 nearby. The Western end was rebuilt at the end of 19th century. A barn behind, possibly early 17th century, has a steeply pitched Collyweston roof with an interesting brick gable with a tumbled parape. (see *Fig 7d*).

Further along, opposite the school field, is the house now known as **Church View** (41 Peterborough Road). A hand-drawn map of Castor, tentatively dated between 1798-1826 [8], shows the premises of a wheelwright and carpenter (called Darby) next to the buildings where Church View is now. The date of the present house is uncertain but

*Fig 7b. View of the front of Village Farm, Castor, 2004.
(Photo: Kath Henderson)*

*Fig 7c. Castor barns: one of the derelict Darby's barns (top); one of the working barns of The Hollies (middle); Tithe Barn, a modern barn-conversion at Poll's Yard (bottom).
(Photo: Tracey Blackmore)*

Fig 7d. Mill Farm and barn, Castor. (Photo: Tracey Blackmore)

Fig 7e. The Old Smithy, Castor. (Photo: Tracey Blackmore)

possibly replaced or combined two dwellings in the early 19th century. It is stone-built with Collyweston roof and end chimneys. There is banding between the storeys and a central front door with a glazed oblong fanlight.

John Thomas Darby was tenant farmer and wheelwright here from about 1890 when this was all owned by the Milton Estate. The Darby family continued to farm here until the early 1970s. Theo Hensman took it over until 1978 when Monica Pollard (granddaughter of John Thomas) and her husband, Jim, bought the house and rear garden. It is now the home of the Chillcott family who have recently built across and joined the adjacent wheelwright's building to Church View. Some of the Darby barns still stand on Milton land, to the West near the Village Hall.

The **Old Smithy** (47 Peterborough Road) opposite The Elms became the farmhouse of the Harris farm from 1895 until around 1933. The house possibly takes its name from the fact that there was a forge where No 49 now stands. This very interesting L-shaped 17th century building is probably of two builds with the dressed stone gabled West-end dated 1676. There is a staircase in both parts and the early map of Castor does show this to be two houses [8]. It is built of coursed stone and has one storey with attics. The roof is mainly thatched although there is a single-story room to the left of the front door with a Collyweston-style roof. There is a central brick chimney serving two back-to-back fireplaces that still retain large timber bressumers (see *Fig 7e*).

Since 1933 this house has been at various times a Post Office and Antiques shop. Around 1969 it became the private residence of Rupert and Mary Speechley and now, Mary lives there with their daughter, Julie and her husband and son, the Taylor family. There is a beautiful garden to the rear. The barns adjoining the rear of the house were renovated in the early 1990s using the original stone to virtually rebuild the one furthest from the house. An old well was uncovered at this time and maybe relates to a pump shown on the map referred to earlier. There is a garage/storeroom on the roadside to the East of the entrance to the garden which is built of newly quarried local stone. Internally, the original kitchen has been opened up to incorporate a previously windowless 'room' at the Eastern end of the building. As late as 1990 there was only one bathroom in the property, downstairs to the front of the kitchen. Now four have been added upstairs reflecting the property's current use as a family home and guesthouse.

Large Houses

There are several substantial pre-1900 houses in Castor. These are all Grade II Listed buildings and have a certain amount of impact via their grounds, size and architectural style. They have also been the homes of professional or successful business people who have, over the years, contributed a great deal to the life of the village.

Castor House is one of the most important of the larger houses and is one of only two Grade II* listed buildings in the village. It is set back on the North side Peterborough Road in its own grounds at the foot of Love's Hill. Details of the house and its history are described in chapter eight.

The Old Rectory, situated on the corner of High Street and Stocks Hill, became the village's Rectory in 1861. This was at the time of the severance from the See of Peterborough when the Rector, the Rev George Andrews at that time, first began to live in Castor. It is now called the Old Rectory for, in 1977, the Rector, the Rev Adrian Davies removed to the present Rectory (5 Church Hill) and it was sold to the Cook family who still live there today.

Built of coursed dressed local stone with stone mullioned windows and a steeply pitched Collyweston roof this is a fine looking residence. It sits in an elevated position in its own grounds enclosed by a 19th century wall. This wall and the grounds to the front are of particular archaeological interest as they incorporate examples of the Roman herringbone walls and parts of the Roman Palace described in an earlier chapter.

This South-facing building was originally the Glebe Farmhouse owned by the Church and built in the late 17th century. Typically it had a central door with a heated room to each side of the hall. There were stairs to the upstairs leading straight ahead from the door, although the present stairs are now to the rear at the

Fig 7f. The Old Rectory, Castor. (Photo: Tracey Blackmore)

Eastern end of the house. A wing was added to the rear in the late 18th century but there is also some speculation that this may have originally been an outside building incorporated into the house. At the time of becoming the Rectory, the front was refashioned with a large room added on the Western end and a porch built over the door. There has been a small 20th century addition behind this large room and, at the time of writing, further additions are being built to the rear of the house (see *Fig 7f*).

The Old Rectory has played a significant role in the life of our villages. It often hosted the annual Church Fete and the room on the Western end, locally known as the Parish Room, was used variously for the Sunday school and Parish meetings. To the Eastern end of the grounds was a lawn tennis court that, in the days of Canon Carleton in the 1930s and 40s, was a very popular venue in the village. Later, during the time of the Rev Tom Adler, this area was also used by many as a cricket pitch.

The Cedars is a very substantial house located South West of the Church. It sits well back from the road and is not easily visible, being concealed by large hedges and magnificent Cedar of Lebanon trees from which it takes its name. The site extends from Peterborough Road through to Church Hill.

It is comprised of two storeys with attics and cellar, and was constructed in three sections of varying ages; the oldest section being a barn and coach house dating from the 1600s. The middle section, believed to be a 17th century two-room farm set at right angles to the road, was added to in the early 18th century. The main house has two rooms at the front with a central staircase and one room at the back. This adjoins the farmhouse to form a square and is serviced by a smaller staircase. It is made mainly from coursed stone with rusticated quoins and a Collyweston roof with flat roofed dormers.

Mr Robert Wright remodelled the stuccoed South front in 1799. It has three bays, the centre being advanced with fielded panel double doors and rectangular fanlight, flanked by a Greek Doric porch. All sash windows have glazing bars, and the centre window on the first floor has an eared architrave. (see *Fig 7g*) A rear barn was also added at this time with the date stone in the North gable end. A mounting block reading EB over 1708 stands by the back door though it is unclear where this came from.

In 1903, the house was rented to the fiction writer William Le Queux. The Hon Mrs and Major Pelham came to the Cedars after Lady Buxton, who left in 1918 and they added the single storey entrance hall to the West. The Pelhams continued to live there for over 40 years and were very much involved with village life.

Fig 7g. The Cedars, Castor. (Photo: Tracey Blackmore)

Major Pelham was Church-warden from 1923-45. Mrs Pelham was the founder president of the WI in 1931 and they were Chairman and Secretary of the Silver Jubilee celebration in 1935. She was also Treasurer for the 1937 Coronation celebrations. The ARP and First Aid station operated from the Cedars in the 1940s. Records from the *Fitzwilliam School Logs* show the cellars were used as shelters when the sirens sounded during school time.

The Hon Mrs Pelham, OBE, outlived her husband and died in 1961. She was the great granddaughter of the first Duke of Wellington and the Chapel of St Kyneswitha in the Church is consecrated in her memory. Dr and Mrs Dudgeon bought the Cedars over forty years ago and Mrs Dudgeon still lives there. Few changes have been made to the property during this period. Part of the land was sold in 1999 to build The Cedar Centre next to the Church.

Fig 7h. The Elms, Castor. (Photo: Tracey Blackmore)

The Elms is a large, impressive, mainly 18th century house set back but not obscured, on the North side of Peterborough Road, between Durobrivae House and The Fitzwilliam Arms. It is a two-storey building with attics and there is also evidence of a cellar but this appears to have been filled in. It is built of two parallel ranges, the South range being the longer. Collyweston tiles cover the steeply pitched double-span roof with two flat roof dormers to the front and rear. Chimneystacks are random rubble and ashlar. Like some other large houses in the village the South front is faced in ashlar, in this case concealing the changes in build on this elevation (see *Fig 7h*).

The section to the West of the central front door is believed to represent the original house. Two windows sit each side of the central glazed door with five windows on the first floor, all are sashes with glazing bars and stepped keystones. The timber cornice-mould below the parapet is a 19th century addition. A date stone reading 1769 with initials WWF appears on the Eastern end of the South range. The initials are believed to refer to William, the 4th Earl Fitzwilliam. By contrast the shorter North range is made from coursed stone with the few windows there being added at various stages. Two back bedrooms still retain ceiling cornices of 1769. A brick single-storey extension to the East of the North wing is a 19th century addition.

At one time The Elms' land went from Peterborough Road through to Church Hill and there were a number of outbuildings and stables. The *Deeds* from 1938 show the property complete with one acre and one road being sold to a Mr George Amies for £2200. Land, stables and outbuildings to the East were sold to Mr and Mrs Griffin in 1983, the road referred to in the *Deeds* runs from North to South through their land. There was also a bungalow on this land, known as 14 Church Hill, that has since been demolished. For a brief period The Elms offered bed and breakfast accommodation but is now a family home occupied by Mr and Mrs S Grys and their four daughters.

Durobrivae (also known as Duro Lodge) is the second Grade II* building in Castor. Views of it are not easy to come by. As well as many mature trees in the garden, it is set back from Peterborough Road next to The Elms behind high boundary walls and abuts directly onto the property behind in Church Hill. A glimpse through the narrow gate at the front shows a square, compact house in an intimate setting.

Although there is evidence of some earlier building, the main part of the house dates from the early 18th century. It has a double-span Collyweston stone roof with two storeys in the Southern front part and an additional storey, partly in the roof, in the Northern part. There is a single-storey kitchen wing to the North-west with an old pump encased in wood and lead against the South wall. It has an inscription with the initials S over W G (or C) and the date 1772.

Fig 7i. Durobrivae, Castor. (Photo: Tracey Blackmore)

The house has a very fine front (see *Fig 7i*). It is faced with ashlar and has a crowning cornice and end pilasters. The front door is left of centre with a rectangular traceried fanlight. The range of four uncommonly large sashed windows on the front have rusticated architraves and keystones. The rooms inside the Southern part still retain their plain 18th century panelling and chimney pieces and there is an 18th century dogleg staircase with square newel posts. The rest of the house is built in coursed rubble with mostly wooden-framed windows. Outside there is a two-stall horse box and double garage in the yard which has some interesting cobbling, as well as a small courtyard at the rear.

Mr and Mrs Carter (previously farmers from Ailsworth and then Top Farm, Castor) retired here in the 1930s. During the 40s and 50s it was occupied by the dentist, Mr Mann, and his wife who founded The Trefoil Guild for village girls who had left the Guides.

Castor Mill is a much-altered early 19th century corn water mill and miller's house. It straddles the Castor Lynch Backwater at the end of Mill Lane. Set in extensive walled grounds, there is the Mill Pool at the Southern side of the house and the front faces open farmland to the East with water meadows to the West. There is evidence of at least one earlier mill on this site.

The present building is made of coursed stone rubble with a hipped Collyweston stone roof. A half-hipped gabled wing has been added to the front of the mill part at the South end. There are two storeys with attics and a range of large modern windows. The mill played an important part in the life of many of the farms and small-holdings in the area and ceased working during the 1920s when the miller, Alfred Loweth retired. It was bought in 1929 by the late Mr William Brown and converted into an elegant private residence. None of the original machinery remains apart from some millstones in the extensively re-modelled formal gardens. There are exposed original beams inside and some of the oak from the mill was used to rebuild the main staircase. Sold again in 1981 it is now a conference centre.

Castor Windmill is nearby. This is a derelict three-storey tower mill built of red-brick dating from the early 19th century.

Cottages and other houses

These smaller properties include a wide range of domestic dwellings together with commercial and tradesman's premises. Most of them have undergone several changes both in usage and structure, since they were first built. Castor is fortunate to have a wealth of 17th and early 18th century cottages and buildings; some built originally of simple one-storey with attic design, typical of the period. We have chosen to show examples of various styles, as they are too numerous to include them all. Many of the properties mentioned are Grade II listed.

One of the earliest and smallest, **11 High Street** is unique in the village, being the only surviving cottage originally built on a single-room plan. The cottage is made from coursed stone, with a hipped angled thatched roof and gabled dormer. The lower hipped roof and boarded walls of the adjoining outbuilding make this a particularly attractive cottage. A second room was added in the 18th century, wooden lintels are chamfered and there is a simple plank door in the front elevation (see *Fig 7j*).

Most of these early houses were built on a two-room plan and immediately opposite, now sitting with its back to the road is **16 High Street**. Again, stone and thatched, the original front entrance to this cottage is still visible with the lintel and outline of the door in line with the original chimney stack. This cottage has undergone considerable changes, with the addition of a second chimney, upper floor, two dormer windows and an entrance door on the South East elevation. A single-storey extension was added to the South in 2003.

Fig 7j. 11 High Street, Castor: a simple, 17th century cottage originally built in a one-room, one-storey with attic style. (Photo: Tracey Blackmore)

Fig 7k. High Street, Castor. (Photo: Elaine O'Boyle)

Fig 7l. Vine House, Castor. (Courtesy of Joan Marriott)

Fig 7m. 1 Stocks Hill, Castor. (Photo: Tracey Blackmore)

Set at a right angle on the same side is **12 High Street**. This 18th century cottage, now with a concrete tiled roof, also has features of note, mainly its central stone chimney stack and stone mullioned three light ovolo window. A date stone showing 1724 can be seen in the gable fronting the road (see *Fig 7k*).

Other small stone and thatched cottages in similar style are dotted throughout the village. These include **1 Clay Lane, 12 Allotment Lane, 4 Splash Lane** with its date stone in the chimney stack with the inscription 1652 MR and **11 Church Hill,** which retains its door in the end wall, beside what would have been the only fireplace.

Some properties have undergone drastic changes in their structure and layout. **Hanover House** (17 Church Hill) is one such property. This house is very different in style to the previous cottages. It is a house of two storeys and attics built on a two-room plan but to a larger scale. The front is faced with ashlar with banding between the storeys. It has a three window range with flat wooden lintels, a plain doorway and rectangular fanlight. A date stone in the Southwest gable end reads TC 1748. The single-storey, coursed stone extension at the North-east end is believed to be a later addition.

In 1938 this property was listed as two cottages with a thatch and pantile roof [9]. By 1969 it was returned to a single dwelling with Collyweston roof and two attic dormers [3]. Reputed to have a friendly ghost, this attractive house was once the home of Edmund Artis, the Victorian surveyor.

To the East of Hanover House and North of the church is **Vine House**. For many years known as the Old Rectory because, prior to 1861, local and visiting clergy would lodge there. This was also built on a two-room plan in the early 17th century but later in the same century it was extended to the West to form a range of four rooms. In 1954 it was listed as three cottages [2]. After standing empty for many years the property was converted into a single dwelling. Extensive work in 1995 resulted in the building we have today. It has two storeys and a steeply-pitched Collyweston roof with coped gable ends, two gabled dormers and brick and stone ridge stacks. The front elevation has a five window range with leaded panes. One original ovolo moulded mullion window remains on the rear elevation (see *Fig 7l*).

16 Stocks Hill is not Listed but is a good example of how properties change. The present house was originally built as two cottages. The date stone reading IW over 1817 is believed to be the date of the original build. The South roof slope and wall were subsequently raised and the two cottages joined to make a much larger single dwelling.

Although most of the domestic dwellings have undergone changes and additions, luckily many have retained their frontage and character. **1 Stocks Hill** is a nice example. Modernised by Milton Estates in 1993, this pretty two-storey house made from stone rubble with Collyweston roof and brick stacks sits at right angles on the West side of Stocks Hill. The date stone reading 1803 can be seen in the East gable end. It has a three window range with wooden lintels and a plain central doorway. A lovely cottage-style garden at the front adds to the charm of this house. The sloping extension and garage at the rear were also part of the modernisation (see *Fig 7m*).

In contrast to this is **The Grove**. This secluded property with its sloping garden and long drive leading North from Church Hill makes quite an impact. Dated early 19th century the stuccoed front elevation with moulded cornices, regimented centre piece with volutes and corner dies is a façade fronting what is believed to be an older, more modest building. Evidence of this can be seen at the rear with the single-height stone work and sloping roof. There are full-length ground floor windows and round-headed niches flank the two outside first-floor windows. The central one is longer and all three have a moulded cornice supported on consoles that add to the grandeur of the two-storey front elevation (see *Fig 7n*).

Various businesses have operated from some of the dwellings. **Three Chimneys** (8 Peterborough Road), a very attractive thatched cottage, was once a range of small 17th century cottages, with a general store in what is now the garage. Moving West, immediately after The Royal Oak, we find **26 Peterborough Road**. During its time, this stone and thatch 17th century cottage has been a wheelwright's shop and also a post office. The entrance door is still visible in the South elevation fronting the road. Three tenement cottages added in the 18th century now form the rear wing of this L-shaped building.

Dragon House, the first property on the South side at the bottom of Love's Hill as you enter the village from Peterborough, was once the George and Dragon Inn. In 1847 the landlord was Robert Shelstone [10]. Rumour has it that its closure in 1929 was due to two people being killed in their horse and cart after leaving the premises. The last serving landlord was Stanley Glover. Bought then by Sir Richard Winfrey for his chauffeur George Newton, the property has since remained a domestic dwelling. Evidence of its past history is still present in the cellar with the indentation of beer barrels clearly visible. Now occupied by the Parr family this stone and thatched house is of several builds. A stone believed to have come from one of the chimney stacks, inscribed CIC 1703, is set into the lounge wall (see *Fig 7o*).

Castor has supported four public houses at various times. The remaining three all run parallel to the North side of Peterborough Road. The **Fitzwilliam Arms**, situated West of the Cedars, is understood to be the only one that was actually built as a coaching inn. Although retaining little of its internal structure, the stone, thatch and dormer windows convey all the charm and character of this 17th century building. A small wing at the rear of the property is now a kitchen. The rear garden stretches through to Church Hill. In the late 1930s and early 1940s people were regularly entertained by the Castor and Ailsworth Brass Band on the lawns. The building is currently an Italian restaurant (see *Fig 7p*).

The prominent position of the **Royal Oak** public house on the corner of Stocks Hill, adds very much to the overall appearance of the village. This building has evolved over several centuries. Built of coursed stone and thatch with the Western advanced range partly rendered. The date stone in the gabled cross wing reads LB over 1727. A plain doorway faces East on this wing. An 18th century canted bay window and plain doorway with simple wooden porch make up the East wing. Remaining ground floor casements are of two and three lights with glazing bars. Four gabled dormers and three brick end stacks complete the picture.

Fig 7n. The Grove, Castor. (Photo: Colin Humphries)

Fig 7o. Dragon House, Castor. (Photo: Tracey Blackmore)

The last of the three remaining public houses brings us into the 19th century. The **Prince of Wales Feathers** set at the corner of The Green and Peterborough Road is very different in style. It is basically two buildings that are now combined and much altered. The Westerly part facing Peterborough Road is considered to have been originally a single-storey 17th/18th century cottage. Built in stone rubble it has a steep pantile roof and two wedge-shaped dormers. The other part faces The Green and dates from the early 19th century. This is a larger stone, square shaped house with ashlar front and slate roof with gable ends. The arched central doorway with keyblock has a blind fanlight and modern door. The chimney stacks have brick tops.

A nice example of a late 19th century house is **9 Church Hill**, built in 1887 by the Fitzwilliam Estate for George Holmes, the Headmaster of the Fitzwilliam School. This house has all the qualities befitting the station of its intended occupant. Solidly built, with the emphasis on quality; the coursed stone is of regular size and the doors and windows are large with a uniform alignment. The roof is of Welsh slate with stone chimney stacks. Its elevated position on the bend of Church Hill adds to its feeling of importance in the community. Outbuildings once contained the coal house, privy and wash room. The original cooking range and copper are still present. The overall impression is of a smart and orderly property (see *Fig 7q*).

There are very few pre-1900 brick-built properties in the village. Examples include **51, 53 and 57 (Swan Cottage) Peterborough Road** opposite The Elms which were built in the late 19th century. Swan Cottage features two colours of brick with attractive banding between. Further back along the road, **11 and 15** are built of pale bricks.

The Congregational Chapel

This Independent Chapel near The Green in Church Hill was erected in 1848 under the superintendence of the Home Missionary Station at Nassington [11]. It is built of coursed stone with a slate roof. The gabled North end faces the street and has a central doorway with round-arched windows on each side. There was a single-storey extension to the West. The Rev George Amos, the minister at Nassington, was the preacher at the Castor Chapel in 1851 when the congregation numbered around 60 [12]. By the late 1850s the Chapel had become an outstation of Westgate Congregational Church in Peterborough and later transferred to the guardianship of Trinity Congregational Church in 1861 (see *Fig 7r*).

Fig 7p. Castor's Hostelries: The Fitzwilliam Arms (top), The Royal Oak (middle), The Prince of Wales Feathers (bottom).
(Photo: Tracey Blackmore)

The local tailor, Mr Alfred Ernest Parker, was a lay preacher there and one of five sisters from Ailsworth, Miss Christiana Sharpe, was organist and Sunday school teacher for many years. The Chapel did not have a Minister resident in the village but continued with a small and faithful congregation until its closure in 1975. The building has been used for various things since then including a period as an Antiques Centre. It was eventually completely refurbished in 1991 and is now the offices of Bothamley and Ellington, Civil Engineering Consultants.

The Village Hall

The current Village Hall opposite the Fitzwilliam Arms on Peterborough Road, was originally the Fitzwilliam National School. It was built in 1829 and originally consisted of only the room along the roadside. The second room, at right angles to the first was added in 1881[13] (see *Fig 30c*). When the school closed in 1956 it was offered to the Village for use as a Hall and, after refurbishment, eventually replaced the Old Village Hall (where 25A Peterborough Road is now) [14]. The interior was modernized and washrooms, a kitchen and a new upstairs added. Today this is a much used and popular venue for many of the Castor and Ailsworth Groups as well as outside events.

Castor School

The present CE Primary School was developed from the earlier Castor Infants School founded in 1861. Towards the Western end of the modern school can be seen the original Infants School Building, now the Hall of the present school [15] (see *Fig 30n*). The rest of the building dates from 1956 when the modern school began.

Post-1900: The Modern Era

Fig 7q. 9 Church Hill, Castor: The Schoolmaster's House. (Photo: Tracey Blackmore)

Fig 7r. Church Hill, Castor: View towards the Green with a glimpse of the Chapel near the end. (Photo: Tracey Blackmore)

Nearly 260 dwellings were built in Castor after 1900 and this has had an enormous impact on the nature and appearance of the village. Around 240 of these were built after 1950 with the move away from agriculture and expansion of Peterborough [1]. Land previously owned by the Church Commissioners or Milton Estate has now passed into private hands. As well as a Sports/Conference Complex, another hall and expansion of the School, there are barn conversions, replacements, infills as well as estate developments. These are mainly of small family houses and bungalows together with several more substantial houses. A few, especially the infills and conversions, are built in modern artificial stone with the rest being predominantly brick-built with modern roof tiles. Most are of pale-coloured bricks and many of the individual or smaller developments are set behind old field walls.

In 1936, the first two houses on Love's Hill, Hill House and Kentmere, were completed. The rest of these very substantial houses were built in the 1960s or later and they exhibit a wide range of styles. Rather like others, such as Evergreen and The Meadows set back on the North side of Peterborough Road, they are similar in impact to the larger older houses previously described. Other large houses have followed along the South side of Peterborough Road to the West which have also served to extend the built-up part of the village.

In addition to modern housing there are two new public venues in Castor. One is **Woodlands**, a large brick-built building with a bright red roof, built on Nene Valley Trust land in 1991 on the Southern outskirts of the village. It comprises a Gymnasium, Squash and Badminton Courts as well as Bars and Conference facilities. There are several playing fields and a Bowling Green. It is owned by AMP (previously Pearl) and at the time of writing it is closing and its future is uncertain.

The second new venue is the **Cedar Centre** built next to the Church on land bought from the Cedars. This Church Hall was built in 1999 to mark the Millennium with monies from a National Lottery Grant and public subscription. It is a very attractive, single-storey building with a high, vaulted hall as well as a kitchen and offices and is now used for the Sunday school and a wide variety of Parish meetings and other events. The centre has become an integral part of village life (see *Fig 7s*).

In conclusion

The buildings of Castor show a remarkable variation in size, style and purpose that generally combine well to give our attractive modern village. It has been interesting to discover how most of the older buildings have been added to or altered from a very early stage, reflecting the changing needs of the residents and the village. This continues today with many more families now living in the village and new businesses developing. There is a strong sense of pride of place within the community and so, hopefully, as Castor continues to evolve, care will be taken to conserve what we have as well as build modern properties that enhance the village.

Fig 7s. The Cedar Centre, Castor. (Photo: Tracey Blackmore)

Kath Henderson

Kath and her husband, David, came to live in Castor from the North-east in 1998. She has two step-daughters, Debbie and Pamela. A scientist by profession, and with a long-standing interest in history, Kath has found being involved in this Local History project very rewarding. In the course of writing this chapter she has enjoyed meeting a great many people and has learnt a tremendous amount about the village.

Elaine O'Boyle

I have lived along with my family in Castor since 1991. Old properties have always fascinated me with their sense of continuity and the history of the people that have gone before.

Notes

1. The Castor Built Environment Audit carried out by Castor and Ailsworth residents in conjunction with Peterborough Environment City Trust in 2002/3. (at Press)
2. Harry B Paten el al., Survey of Castor Village. *The Peterborough Society: 2nd Annual Report.* 1954 pp11-21.
3. Royal Commission on Historic Monuments (England*). Peterborough New Town: A Survey of the Antiquities in the Area of Development* HMSO London. 1969. pp45-49, 63-69.
4. *29th List of Buildings of Special Architectural or Historic Interest* compiled under Section 54 of the Town and Country Planning Act. 1971. Dept of the Environment Statutory List. 1974.
5. Including Rev William Burke, Mr Martin Chillcott, Mrs Jackie Cook, Mrs Kerry Davies, Mrs Rebecca Dudgeon, Mr Brian Goode, Mr Alan Gray, Mrs Val Grys, Mrs Joan Marriott, Mrs Maxine Parr, Mrs Monica Pollard, Mrs Margaret Sharpe and Mrs Julie Taylor.
6. Details of many of these farms, their land and agricultural practices, are described in *Chapters 20 and 21.*
7. Home Farm has a close association with Castor House and is described in greater detail in *Chapter 8.*
8. In 1798, the Rev White commissioned Leonard Bell to carry out a survey of Castor. This hand-drawn map showing the principal dwellings and occupants of Castor is considered to be part of the notes associated with this survey and is dated between 1798-1826.
9. Harry B Paten, Survey of Castor Village. *The Peterborough Society:* 1938/39.
10. *Post Office Directory of Berkshire, Northamptonshire, Oxfordshire with Bedfordshire, Buckinghamshire and Huntingdonshire.* W K Kelly and Co. London 1847 pp2059-60.
11. Thomas Coleman, *Memorials of the Independent Churches in Northamptonshire* 1853. John Snow. London. p376-7.
12. *Census Return* for Castor. 1851.
13. Further details of Village Hall in *Chapter 30: Castor Schools.*
14. This Hall was a focal point of village life from 1920 - 1956 as can be seen in *Chapter 32.*
15. Further details of original Infants School in *Chapter 30.*

Chapter 8
The Castor House Estate

Reconciling folklore with fact

> 'Castor has two fine old houses. One is the manor built for the Bishops of Peterborough. For over 200 years the bishops were also rectors of Castor, and lived here, and it is due to their love of gardens that the grounds of the manor house have so many fine trees – great cedars, a silver elm, a Judas tree and in the kitchen garden a cordon apple tree 15 yards long and still producing a huge crop of apples. We found living in this old home of the bishops the stout hearted non-conformist Sir Richard Winfrey.'

So wrote Arthur Mee in 1945 [1].

Six years earlier Gotch [2] wrote:
> 'The Manor of Castor belonged to the Dean and Chapter of Peterborough, and was let to a number of tenants. Castor House was almost certainly built by one of the tenants, possibly by Sir Thomas Alleyne or Dr. Giles Alleyne.'

Much earlier, in 1800, Gibson [3] wrote:
> 'Bishop White Kennett of Peterborough or his predecessor built Castor House, in about 1700. For many years the home of the Bishops of Peterborough who were also Rectors of Castor.'

There is no consensus from these accounts as to when, and for whom Castor House was built. It also raises the questions of whether or not the house was a manor house, what evidence there is of the Bishops of Peterborough having had a residence there, and if so, for how long.

Dating the building of Castor House and the adjacent Home Farm

The present Home Farm with its central chimneystack fireplaces and octagonal Jacobean dovecote is typical of around 1650 [4]. The rear portion of Castor House also appears to date from about the same time. It would originally have been a two-storey, single pile building, with just one fireplace in the West end and a gatehouse or stable, with lodgings above, in the East end. This date was further confirmed when, during recent renovations, a clay pipe dating from between 1660 – 1680 was found, in sand, under the stone floor in the West end of the house [5].

It appears that two single pile houses, of equal size, were built at about the same time in the mid 17th century. The two buildings appear to have been deliberately sited to avoid one house overlooking the other. This arrangement is sometimes found from the late 16th century to early 18th century when two members of the same family jointly farmed but wanted to live as two distinct households [6]. The earliest building, which has been formally dated, is the large barn on the corner of Water Lane and Peterborough Road. This was built in around 1600 [7]. Such a substantial barn implies the presence of a farmstead nearby. Interestingly, the footings and quoins of Home Farm and those at the rear of Castor House contain a large amount of Barnack rag stone. Barnack rag stone stopped being quarried around 1600. Its presence in such quantity

Fig 8a. Sir Richard Winfrey outside Castor House circa 1935, taken from his headed writing paper.

Fig 8b. Aerial view of Castor House and surrounding farm buildings circa 1970.

suggests that there may well have been earlier buildings on the site. It is likely that these were related to the Water Lane barn.

Circa 1700 Castor House was remodelled into a substantial three-storey, double pile house. The wine cellar with its barrel vaulted fine ashlar ceiling is also of around that period.

Was Castor House a Manor House?

We know that Abbot Alexander of Holderness (1222-1226) [8] built a hall for his manor at Castor. The location of this manor is not known. In 1541, the lordships of the two manors at Castor, and most of the Abbot's lands in Castor were given to the newly created Dean and Chapter. Home Farm and Castor House do not appear to be listed as part of the Manor of the Dean and Chapter survey in 1649, so it is unlikely that the manor was at Castor House at that time.

Did the Bishops of Peterborough own Castor House and Home Farm?

The Bishop, as successor to the Abbot, was granted some land in 1541 for his own personal use in Castor. Being only recently established, the Bishopric of Peterborough was very poor. The new Bishop was granted lands in Castor *'in demesne'* to try to reduce the shortfall of the income generated from his holdings in Peterborough [9]. We know that Bishop Howland was living in Castor in 1599 and *'died at his house in Castor in 1600'* [10].

Local lore claims that Home Farm is monastic in origin and had a room where the priests could celebrate mass in secret. Indeed, until 30 years ago, there was a strangely widened corridor, with just one small roof light and a door at each end, which would certainly have been large enough for such a purpose. During recent renovations a whitewashed roof space with a small door into it was revealed above this part – could it have been a 'priests' hole'?

The house of a dignitary, such as a bishop's was often known as a 'Mansion House' if it was not a manor house. A survey of the Castor House estate in 1798 refers to Castor House as the 'Mansion House' [11]. This is the first clear suggestion of a link between Castor House and the Bishops of Peterborough. When the Estate was sold in 1796 the 'Church' was the vendor. As we know that the Dean and Chapter did not own the Estate, it suggests that it was sold by the Bishop.

It appears likely that there were earlier buildings on the Home Farm site. It is therefore possible that this was the land granted in 1541 to the newly established Bishopric, and was the site of Bishop Howland's home.

Who commissioned the building of Castor House?

There is no documented evidence to show who commissioned the building works of 1650 or those of 1700. There were, however, two Bishops with similar names about this time and both were also Rectors of Castor. Bishop Thomas White became Rector of Castor in 1685 [12] and resigned as Bishop of Peterborough in 1691. Secondly, Bishop White Kennet became Bishop and also Rector of Castor in 1718 [13]. So, if a Bishop White commissioned the building of Castor House it would seem likely from the dates that it was Bishop Thomas White, between 1685 and 1691. Coincidentally, yet another White bought the estate from the Church.

The Whites

In 1796, Rev Dr Stephen White, son of Judge Taylor White of Chester, Treasurer of the Foundling Hospital, and Rector of Conington, came into a fortune and purchased the Castor Estate [14]. His son, William Archibald White of Lincolns Inn inherited it in 1824, which in turn went to his son, Stephen Prescott White in 1847.

Prescott White spent a considerable sum of money on Castor House until his death in 1866. He built the boundary stone wall and the gate piers at the front of the house, the kitchen garden wall, and the brew house built onto Home Farm. The garden boundary was altered at about that time to give Home Farm its own private rear garden. Prescott White started a book of the garden in 1857. He notes that there were already many 'old trees' and lists those that he intends to plant. Outside was the *'original stone-faced fishpond of the Bishops of Peterborough'* [15]. This pond was already built by 1828 and can be clearly seen on ET Artis' map drawn at that time [16]. The large pond had square corners, and would have been fed from the spring in Water Lane.

It would appear that Prescott White also substantially remodelled the inside of Castor House whilst retaining the front hall stone floor. The staircase is thought to be early 18th century, but the newel post has Victorian putty which gives the appearance of 'fine carving' on it. The canvas walls of the sitting room have been formally

8c. Castor House and gates circa 1960.

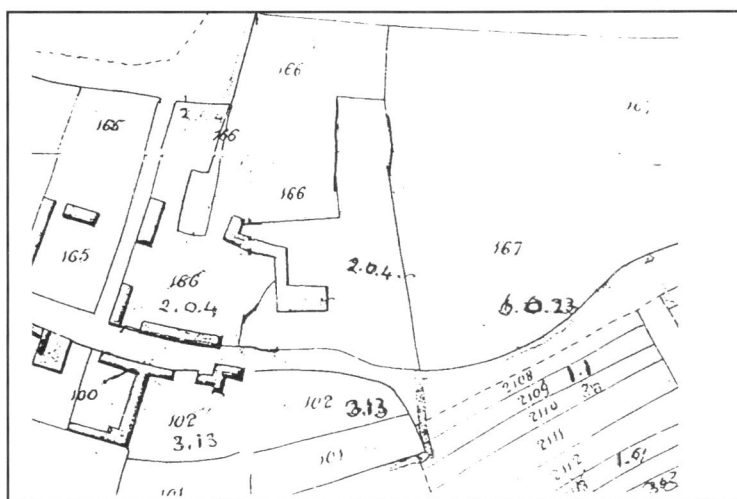

Fig 8d. Extract from Tithe map 1847 showing gardens surrounding Castor House, and the yard of Home Farm.

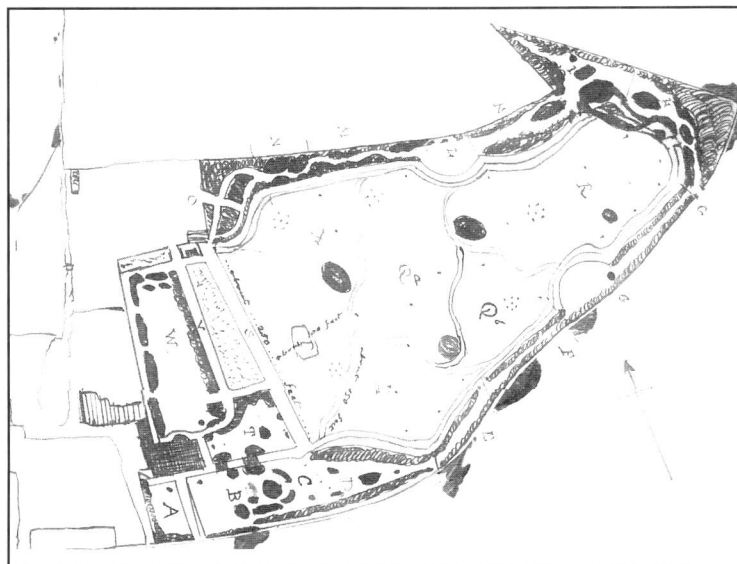

Fig 8e. Map drawn by Stephen Prescott White in 1860 showing that Home Farm now has a garden and that the front boundary wall and gate piers have not yet been built.

dated to no later than 1850. As the wood panelling surrounding the canvas walls flows uninterrupted through into the drawing room and front hall, it seems likely that that this was all part of these works. The front shutter door also appears to be part of this work, dating the front door with its wide expanse of glass to the mid 19th century.

Stephen Prescott White did not marry, and on the death of his younger brother Charles in 1859, adopted all Charles' children. The sixth child, Frank Armstrong, was born in 1850 and inherited the estate in 1866 on the death of his uncle. Descriptions of life at Castor House at that time are only thinly disguised in 'Loves Illusion', one of the novels by JD Berresford, whose father was Rector of Castor from 1864-1897.

In 1910, Colonel Frank White retired to Henley and let Castor House to a Mr Hinchcliffe, a businessman retiring from South Africa [17]. On Frank Armstrong's death, and that of his wife, in 1912 the estate was left to their four daughters, who divided it up for sale.

Gustave Bonner and Castor House

Gustave Ferdinand Bonner, who had changed his name from Bunheimer at the beginning of the First World War, bought Castor House and 15 acres of the estate in 1915. Bonner also wrote in the garden book that had been started by Prescott White nearly sixty years earlier.

'These records have been interrupted between 1860 and 1915. The rockery was laid down by Mr Hinchcliffe, who also built the fruit store at the end of the Tennis lawn and planted the wall fruit trees in the kitchen garden and opened out the 19 beds in the top garden.'

While Bonner was at Castor House, the gardener met with an accident:

'Tuesday, November 24 1917, Mr John Thomas Stranger the gardener at Castor House died in Peterborough Royal Infirmary as the result of injuries received by a branch of a tree, which he was felling, falling on him. At the inquest it was noted that he was employed as a gardener at Castor House by Mr Bonner, and that his wages were about 23s a week'. [18].

Bonner continues:

'Without a gardener from November 1917 to July 1918, when Isaac Bouy was engaged.

In 1918 owing to labour scarcity during the war, the spring bedding in both the top garden and Dutch garden consisted of forget-me-nots only, in all beds. In June 1918, the stone steps between the tennis lawn and Dutch Garden, in line with Sundial were added. In October 1918, 18 beds in the top garden were sown with grass seeds, leaving only a pampas grass (planted last year) in no. 2 bed. The roses were taken out of no. 1 bed and parrot tulips planted. The beds in the Dutch garden were filled in the autumn with alternately forget-me-nots and primulas.'

Bonner suffered ill feeling towards him because of his German descent. One day the front gates and piers were attacked by the locals and one of the eagles, which then topped the piers, was pushed off. As a result he decided to sell the house [19].

Fig 8f. The Dutch Garden at Castor House 1920s. The large green house and adjoining vine house can also be seen. The Dutch garden was changed to a small rose garden by Pat Winfrey and is now lawn.

The Winfreys

Sir Richard Winfrey

On 17 June 1919, Sir Richard Winfrey bought Castor House from Bonner for £2,500. A 21st birthday party for his daughter, Ellen, was held as a housewarming party [20]. In the sale documents Castor House is referred to as 'formally known as Clarke's farm'. Sir Richard was by then Mayor of Peterborough, as well as MP for South-West Norfolk. His first career had been as a chemist, with a keen interest in politics. At that time newspapers were a necessary part of becoming a politician, so in 1886 he bought his first newspaper, the Spalding Guardian, for a nominal £100. It was still to be printed under contract in Boston by the vendor, Joseph Cooke. Richard's staff consisted of him, one senior and an office boy. He had his own column in which he attacked the opposition Spalding Free Press for unbalanced reporting and castigated his political opponents. Richard's next purchase was the Lynn News; he also started the North Cambs Echo over the following six years.

Richard Winfrey's advice on a man going into politics was '*to get hold of the right sort of wife*'. This had not proved to be an easy task. He and his friend, Harry Millhouse, had both fallen for the same girl, Annie Pattinson. On the toss of a coin it was decided that Harry would court her and later Richard was best man at their wedding. When six years later Harry died the still single Richard was at last able to court and marry Annie.

Fig 8g. Sir Richard Winfrey speaking for the farmers' Red Cross effort circa 1935.

In 1893, Richard was surprised to receive an invitation to stand for parliament in the Southwest division of Norfolk. In this campaign he rode for a month around the vast rural constituency with literature showing that he had the support of over 1,000 Lincolnshire men. He had earned this support as a result of his tireless and successful campaigning to get smallholdings which could then be rented by farm labourers and thus give them some independence from the few large landowners.

He continued to champion smallholders, and in 1899 formed the 'Norfolk Small Holdings Association' to give the smallholders some financial independence so that they would not be dependent on the Poor Law guardians at the end of their lives. Richard was also instrumental in establishing the 'South Lincolnshire Small Holdings Association'. The two associations soon merged to become the 'Lincolnshire and Norfolk Small Holdings Association'. He was finally elected to parliament for South-West Norfolk in 1906, aged 48, and remained in office for 18 years. In parliament, Richard continued his efforts to help settle men on the land. This led to the Small Holdings and Allotments Acts of 1907 and 1908 under which, if the counties did not provide smallholdings, they would be provided over their heads. On buying a controlling share in the Peterborough Advertiser, Richard came to live in Peterborough.

From 1906 – 1923, Richard was the MP for South-West Norfolk. He was instrumental in drawing up the Corn Production Act of 1917, which by 1918 had already added nearly 3 million acres to the national total. Corn prices were thus guaranteed to farmers. Richard also championed Agricultural Wages Boards, which were set up to ensure minimum wages for the first time. After the war he piloted the Small Holding Colonies Bill, and saw it become reality through overseeing the allocation of 10-acre holdings of land released by the Crown in Norfolk, to returning servicemen. By 1924, 16,000 ex-Servicemen were settled on holdings, bringing the number of statutory smallholdings to 30,000. Later Richard offered a personal gift of £25,000 to help provide smallholdings for the unemployed and lived to see the tenants of these smallholdings play their part in the production of food during World War II.

In both 1907 and 1912 there had been talk of Richard being chosen as Mayor. He agreed to the idea on condition that the Tories supported his claim to be an alderman as well. This was not accepted so he left the meeting and went out hunting instead. On meeting the ex-mayor that afternoon whilst out riding he heard that Tory votes, with Liberals abstaining, had put him in the chair in his absence - a procedure never before heard of. Richard asked his solicitor '*to get me out of this*' but was advised that there was no escape. He accepted the situation but confined himself strictly to municipal engagements because of the claims of parliament and South-West Norfolk. In 1914, he was awarded a knighthood. After war was declared anti-German feeling in Peterborough led to crowds smashing shop windows and flinging about the streets meat belonging to Frederick Frank and Frederick Metz, both respected citizens of long standing. As Mayor, Sir Richard was asked to come and read the Riot Act so that, if necessary, the police could call on the Yeomanry who were then billeted in the city and camping in Milton Park. Sir Richard cycled into town and tried reasoning with the crowd who showered him with stones. In return he quickly read the Riot Act and cycled rapidly home. The police and troopers made several arrests and on the following Monday Sir Richard swore in a hundred more specials and asked the citizens to be indoors by nine o'clock. It is thought that this is the last time that the Riot Act was read in this country.

Sir Richard travelled widely. In 1929 and 1936 he spent time with General Smuts in South Africa. They exchanged acorns from their respective oaks. Sir Richard's acorn successfully grew into a tree in the wood at Castor House. In 1923 Sir Richard bought the adjoining Campions Close for £170.00 from the Ecclesiastical Commissioners for England.

In 1932 being grateful for 74 happy and successful years, Sir Richard decided to build four homes for retired employees. A small tablet can be seen on each of the two pairs of bungalows bearing the words 'In Gratitude'. The stone used was taken from a demolished pigeon house, on WT Cooke's land, in Splash Lane. Sir Richard had bought it from the Ecclesiastical Commissioners for £10 in 1925 [21]. It was the largest in the district, 30' x 24' with 1,760 nests.

In 1933 Sir Richard celebrated his 75th birthday by inviting two hundred employees to Castor House for a party, which included inter-office sports in the grounds and lunch in the village hall.
Arthur Mees' *'stout hearted non-conformist Sir Richard Winfrey'* said towards the end of his life *"If you have a clear conscience that what you do is from a deep sense of duty to your fellow creatures – that is enough. In public life a clear conscience and a thick skin will carry you through"*. Sir Richard died at Castor House on April 18 1944.

Richard 'Pat' Winfrey
During the Second World War the newspaper business had struggled and Castor House was heavily mortgaged to help keep the company afloat. In 1947 Sir Richard's son, Richard Pattinson Winfrey, by then chairman, formally grouped the newspapers in Eastern England to form the East Midlands Allied Press (EMAP). Under Pat's control the company expanded and paved the way for the third generation to carry on in the person of his sons, Richard and Charles Winfrey, which helped to make EMAP one of the top FTSE 100 companies in the UK.

Following Lady Winfrey's death in 1951 Pat Winfrey moved into Castor House and comments in a letter to his bank that the house is full of both dry rot and woodworm. *'I suspected that part of the house was bad because some while ago the floor in my mother's bedroom gave way and the legs of the bed in which she was lying went through the floor'.*

8h. Staff party at Castor House 1952.

Fig 8i. The accident involving an ambulance on Love's Hill. Peterborough Standard January 3rd 1958.

They were living in one downstairs living room with an electric cooker because the kitchen ceiling had collapsed. Pat Winfrey carried out the much needed repairs to the house. Pat continued the tradition of holding staff parties at Castor House and lived there until his death in 1985.

Love's Hill has been the scene of many accidents while the road was the main route from Peterborough to Leicester. Wet weather was thought to be the cause of the accident on 26th December 1958 when an ambulance crashed into the South side wall. The driver was almost completely uninjured but the accompanying ambulance man, Alec Broughton, died. At the inquest, John Fuery said he had lived in a cottage on Castor Hill for 3 years, and in that time had attended 17 accidents on the hill [22].

In the 1960s the Highways Commission widened the road after first demolishing part of the Castor House boundary wall at the lower end of Love's Hill. In recompense for land lost, the small piece of land between the wall, (which now sticks out strangely into Campions Close) and the road was given in exchange. The newly constructed wall was badly built and almost immediately began to crack. Pat Winfrey tried unsuccessfully for many years to get the Highways Commission to rebuild it.

Richard Ian Winfrey

Pat Winfrey's eldest grandson, Ian Winfrey, inherited the house in 1985. By then the house was again in a poor state of repair. Ian had the house re-roofed, rewired and re-plumbed. In 2000 he had the, by then dangerous, boundary wall rebuilt by local builders, Maffit Construction. Ian also planted up Campions Close with native tree species in 1991. He still lives at Castor House with his family.

Home Farm

The Polls

In 1918, Frederick Poll, who had been a farm manager at Holywell near Stamford, bought

Fig 8j. The Polls by the pond at Home Farm.

Home Farm. This was to be the only owner-farm in the area. The farm was then just less than 200 acres [23].

After Frederick Poll died in 1921, ownership of Home Farm went to his deaf mute son, Bob. Bob let the farm to his brother-in-law, Walter Longfoot, for whom he then worked as a farm labourer. Walter Longfoot with his wife and Bob Poll then lived at Home Farm [24].

The Winfreys

Later when Walter Longfoot died in 1960 Pat Winfrey bought the Home Farm. The bulk of the Farm's land was sold to Milton Estates. The Home Farm farmyard was developed by Charles Winfrey, one of Pat's sons, in the 1990s and is now four homes. Home Farm is now part of Castor House.

Fig 8k. Ian and Claire Winfrey with their children James, Rosalind and Duncan and dog Susie on the steps in the garden at the East end of Castor House.

Claire Winfrey

Claire married Ian Winfrey in 1988. They have a family of three children. She worked as a doctor in both General Practice and Palliative Care and then started a wholesaling business from home. For five years Claire was chairman of Castor Parish Council

Notes

1. Arthur Mee, *Northamptonshire*, 1945, p 70.
2. J. Alfred Gotch, *Squires' Homes and other old buildings of Northamptonshire*, 1939, p 1.
3. Rev Kennett Gibson, *The Parochial History of Castor*, written circa 1770, published 1800.
4. Harry Paten et al, *Survey of Castor village*, 1954 Peterborough Society.
5. Adrian Oswald *Clay Pipes for the Archaeologist*, 1975.
6. Pamela Cunnington, *How old is your house?* 1980.
7. Harry Paten et al, *Survey of Castor village*, 1954, Peterborough Society.
8. Rev Kennett Gibson, *The Parochial History of Castor*, written circa 1770, published 1800.
9. NCRO Document Hatton-Finch Papers 3130A
10. Symon Gunton, *History of the Church in Peterborough,*1686, Ed J Higham 1990, p 81.
11. *Survey of the Estate of the Rev. Stephen White*, 1798. Northampton Records Office.
12. See Appendix Two.
13. Ibid.
14. Sir Richard Winfrey, *'The garden book'* a notebook detailing changes in the gardens and notable local events, kept by the successive owners of Castor House from 1850.
15. Harry Paten et al, *Survey of Castor village*, 1954, Peterborough Society.
16. E.Tyrell Artis, *Durobrivae*, 1823.
17. Gustave Bonner, *'The garden book'.*
18. *The Citizen*, 27th November 1917.
19. Sir Richard Winfrey, *'The garden book'.*
20. David Newton, *Men of Mark*, 1977. This book has been the source of nearly all the material on both Sir Richard and Pat Winfrey.
21. Sir Richard Winfrey, *'The garden book'.*
22. *Peterborough Standard*, January 3rd 1958.
23. *Deeds of Home Farm.*
24. William Burke, *Notes on Michael and Ruth Longfoot*, 2002.

Chapter 9
Ailsworth Village

Early History

Ailsworth has evolved over the years from a small farming community to a modern village where agriculture is no longer the focus of village life. Aerial and field surveys have revealed evidence of prehistoric and Roman settlements in the surrounding area. The Roman market town of Durobrivae, to the South of the River Nene, was a thriving market and industrial area. Rich villas, farmsteads and pottery kilns were scattered along the Nene Valley and it is assumed that Ailsworth developed from one of these farmsteads. This was a time of change in the countryside; the Romans brought new crops and farming methods and organisation to the land. Ermine Street and King Street, which both run through the parish, were built as part of the network of military roads leading out of London. After the retreat of the Romans, the prosperity of the area declined and the villas and farmsteads were neglected, the land reverting to heath and scrub.

The Roman roads remained in use long after the collapse of the Empire and were used as parish boundaries. The Saxons did not settle along the old roads but built their homes half a mile or so away. During the 7th century Ailsworth was part of the Kingdom of Mercia that was ruled by the last pagan king, Penda. He was killed in 654 and succeeded by Peada, brother of Kyneburgha. The first recorded reference to Ailsworth can be traced to a Saxon charter of 948 when it was referred to as Aegelswurth. In another Saxon charter reference is made to an exchange of land that took place between Aithelwold, Bishop of Winchester, and Wulfstan Ucca. The Bishop gave Wulfstan land at Washington, Sussex and Wulfstan gave him land at Yaxley and Ailsworth. The estate at Ailsworth had been taken from a widow and her son because they were found to have stuck

Fig 9a. Main Street with Sharpe's baker's cart 1900.

Fig 9b. Lower end Main Street with horse drawn binder 1910.

Fig 9c. Ailsworth Green looking North along Main Street 1915.

Fig 9d. Peterborough Road looking East: Wheatsheaf pub on the right.

iron pins into an effigy of Wulfstan's father, Aelsfige. The woman was drowned at London Bridge, while her son escaped to become an outlaw. It is likely that the bridge referred to was nearby on the Nene and not in London, as London Bridge was not built until 1176. (This early history is covered more fully in preceding chapters in this book).

The entry in the *Domesday Book* in 1086 referred to the village as Eglesworde, an enclosure of a man called Agel [1]. A record of 1253 noted that the Torpel family owned land in Ailsworth. In the following years most of Ailsworth was held by Peterborough Abbey and in 1541 it was granted to the Dean and Chapter. After 1601, the Poor Law passed all the responsibilities of village affairs to the church, which became responsible for the administration of the village. Today Ailsworth is in the ecclesiastical parish of Castor and until recent times the Church Commissioners owned most of the land in Ailsworth.

At the end of the 19th century villages throughout the country underwent changes due to more modern agricultural methods and people moving into the towns. For example, in 1801, Ailsworth had a population of 154 and by 1851 the number had risen to 381. However by 1891 the number had fallen to 286 and by 1901 the village had only 251 inhabitants [2]. The village was becoming less self-sufficient and fewer people relied on farming for work.

Snippets of village life taken from Parish Record Books 1888-1964

In 1888, the Local Government Act was passed, and the County Councils, Rural District and Parish Councils were formed. This was the beginning of real change in the administration of the village. The running of the village was handed back from the church to the people of the village. Ailsworth Parish *Meeting Record Books* are a rich source of information about the village and document the concerns of the local people and the gradual development of the small village into a thriving rural community.

In 1894, the Overseers of the Parish, Mr W Briggs, a wheelwright and Mr H Sharpe, a farmer, called a meeting to decide whether or not the village should have a Parish Meeting or a Parish Council. Mr Carter of Manor Farm was Chairman of the meeting. Messrs Coulson, Hill, Hornsby, Pell, Sharpe, Sismey and Taylor, names still familiar today, were among the twenty parishioners present. They agreed to continue with a Parish Meeting. Mr Carter was Surveyor of the Highways and Mr Darby was collector of the Highway rates.

Parish land

The Parish Meeting was usually held in the Methodist Chapel Schoolroom, on the nearest suitable day to 'Lady Day' (25th March) and to 'Michaelmas' (29th September), to collect the allotment rents and to attend to the needs of the village. The provision and improvement of amenities for the village was a major concern. In 1897, the Board of Agriculture gave consent for the final draft of the enclosure of the open fields of Ailsworth. Twenty-two acres of land was allocated for allotments and a recreation ground in the parish [3]. An Allotment Committee was formed and Mr Holmes was appointed to survey and set out the allotments, and it was agreed to charge four shillings per rood. The allotments were to be kept free of weeds and well manured. In 1899, Mr

Fig 9e. Peterborough Road looking West. Barley Mow pub on the left.

Fig 9f. Taylor's Transport lorries and drivers, 1948.

Tebbutt of Upton donated £1 to be used for prize-money in the allotment competition. There were to be prizes of ten shillings, five shillings, three shillings and two shillings. In 1901, the County Council was asked to provide some gardening lessons for the allotment holders. Rents were collected at the meetings and the allotments were highly sought after. In 1940, there was a large increase in the number of vacant allotments and by 1946, when there were no prospective tenants, the allotments were advertised for the first time. By 1963, the number of allotment holders had fallen to seven.

Ailsworth Heath

In 1898, 110 acres of land on Ailsworth Heath, in the North of the Parish, was rented out at eight shillings per head for horses and four shillings for beasts, from May Day to Martinmas. No one could put stock on the Heath without a common right and unauthorised stock were impounded by the Pinder, Mr Sam Garfield, who was paid £1 a year plus fees. In 1940, Lieutenant Feeny, farmer at Manor Farm, complained that the path through the Little Moffat (as recorded in the *Minute Book*) was overgrown. He said that it was harbouring rabbits, which in turn were eating his crops. The Parish Meeting did not think that they were responsible for the poor state of the path, as the thorns had grown from the farmer's own neglected hedge.

Fig 9g. Sharpe's shop and Yard, 1960.

In 1948, the Air Ministry asked to use Ailsworth Heath for bombing practice. The Parish Meeting was against such use and sent a letter of protest to the Air Ministry. In October 1957, there were still concerns about Ailsworth Heath and the Maffit. The Meeting thought that because the land belonged to the village, they had an interest in its use as a bombing range. They were also concerned about the amount of timber that was being removed from the woods. In 1971, the Nature Conservancy asked for permission to graze stock on the Heath. Permission was given and they continue to manage the land.

Recreation and leisure facilities

From 1898 to1982, the Recreation Ground in Station Road was rented out for grazing. The land was let for herbage or eatage, with the parishioners retaining their rights to recreation under the Enclosure Award.

In January 1898, the herbage was let to Harry Sharpe. It was agreed that he could graze only sheep and that the rent was £1 a year. Tendering for the field was competitive and this was reflected in the varied payments. The last parishioner to rent the grazing rights on the field was Brian Sharpe. Over the years there has been a variety of play equipment on the Recreation Ground. Swings were first put there in 1902. They were taken down on the first of November and put back on the first of February. The swings were for the use of Ailsworth children and they were locked on Saturday nights and opened on Monday mornings. Later an 18 feet long seesaw was built, as well as four seats and a '*giant stride*'. The large trees around the Recreation Ground were planted in 1904. Vandalism was a problem in these early days and the swings were in constant need of repair. In 1930, Mr Parker, licensee of The Barley Mow pub, asked for the replacement of the trapeze with two swings and that the seesaw be removed. He suggested that the plank of the seesaw be made into a seat. It was agreed to lock up the swings on August Bank Holiday '*as strangers do more damage that day than village children do in the whole year*'. (Don't forget they were for use by Ailsworth children only). In 1935, new swings were bought costing £14 10s and the old framework was sold for 15 shillings. (Cliff Bass remembers part of the frame being in his father's shed). In March of the following year, the Recreation ground seats were beyond repair and new ones were purchased with money raised at a whist drive. The swings were finally removed from the Recreation Ground in 1961 due to their neglected state.

In 1939, it was agreed to ban all games on the Recreation Ground on Sundays. This was not changed until 1962, when Mr Charles Winfrey wrote on behalf of the football club asking for permission to play on Sundays. At the same meeting a Youth Club was planned for the Recreation Ground as part of a ten year development plan. No record was made of why this was not carried out. The provision of better leisure facilities was and still is a top priority. In 1952, Mr P Winfrey prepared a scheme for a joint playing field and village hall on the allotments in Allotment Lane, Castor. The proposed site for a new school was on land where Holme Close is now built. At a meeting in May 1952, Ailsworth agreed to support the scheme and asked that Castor and Ailsworth should have equal representation in any further consultation. There is no mention in the records why the scheme was never completed. In October 1974, a joint meeting of both Parish Councils under the Chairmanship of Earl Fitzwilliam met in Ailsworth Chapel Schoolroom to discuss the leisure facilities in the villages. Castor cricket field (Rushlees) was thought to be an ideal site for any such development.

Fig 9h. Manor Farm, 1960s.

Improving facilities

Lighting

The provision of houses, better roads and footpaths were major concerns for the members of the Parish Meeting. Lighting the village streets was one of the first jobs to be undertaken. In 1895, twelve oil lamps were bought costing £22 7s 9d. Mr Fox was paid £8 per year to light the lamps. (Until recently a few of the old lamp brackets were still on the walls of houses in the village). In 1931, Peterborough Electricity Department offered to supply electric lights at a cost of £4 per lamp. The Meeting agreed to ask for five lamps and to negotiate a cheaper price. After investigations the Meeting agreed that because the rates were already high, new electric lights would place too high a burden on the ratepayers. A vote was taken and twenty-six people voted against the proposal and only one person voted for the new lights. The Meeting eventually asked the RDC for twelve electric streetlights in 1938.

Roads and paths

The general feeling of the village according to the records was that the roads were badly maintained. In

Fig 9i. Aerial view of Manor Farm before the outbuildings were demolished 1960s.

1897, concerns were raised about the drainage of Splash Dyke, Peterborough Road and the state of the road near the pond. (The pond was on the Green near the bus shelter). Front Street was often said to be in a poor condition and there are many references to the state of the Willow Road (Station Road) and Church Walk. In 1913, the rates paid for work included: one shilling for working four hours to level a path, seven shillings and sixpence for fencing work over three days and one shilling and sixpence for lad, a horse and cart working for six hours. In 1937, repairs were needed on the Allotment Road and its drains. It was agreed to find an unemployed man to do the work and pay six shillings per day plus insurance. Mr Lattimore, the mole catcher, was paid ten shillings a year for killing moles on the allotments. At the

same time Mr A Cooke was asked to repair the broken stile in Church Walk, and because of the shortage of materials due to the war, he was told '*to do the best he could*'. In 1941, Castor Parish Council asked Ailsworth to pay half the costs towards clearing a four feet way through Gypsy Lane. This footpath formed the boundary between the two parishes. It was agreed to do the work. At about the same time, the Hon Mrs Pelham, of The Cedars in Castor, asked for the removal of the stile on the Parish boundary, for the benefit of the older members of the community. This was done.

Fig 9j. Barn in Main Street, 1970s.

Fig 9k. The barn (see fig 9j) after conversion.

Sanitation, refuse collection and water

During these early years night-soil was deposited on New Close, a field belonging to Ailsworth Parish, at the back of Castor's allotments. In 1934, it was agreed that night-soil should not be collected before 9pm in the summer months, that the charge for emptying should be £2 a week and £2 10s if emptied three times per fortnight. The RDC paid the Parish Meeting £10 a year to use the field. The Meeting continued to rent out the field for herbage while it was used as the dump for night-soil and in March 1938, a tender for £2 5s was received from Mr W Bass for the herbage in New Close. A collection of refuse was organised in 1920. Three dust boxes were placed around the village for refuse (not garden rubbish). Old tins and bottles were taken to the pits on Ailsworth Heath at this time. In 1938, when the RDC began a systematic refuse collection, the three old bins were sold for 10s 6d to Mr S B Sharpe. In 1934, protests were sent to the RDC about the proposed water scheme for the parish. It was felt that there was no need for the scheme. There was no water shortage in the village and local water was considered to be the best in the district; also the parishioners could not afford the extra costs. In September 1934, the Meeting agreed to support the Parochial Church Council in their bid to extend the churchyard by adding to it part of the Infant school playground.

Housing

In 1921, as a result of the Housing Act, the RDC proposed to build twelve houses in Ailsworth, although the majority of the village was against the scheme. In 1924, the RDC were told that no houses were needed. In March 1930, Mr Taylor told the Meeting that his two sons required council houses in Ailsworth. A survey of housing needs was carried out in November 1930. It showed that six people were in need of houses and that they were willing to pay rent of five shillings a week plus rates. Two of them had no homes at all and the other four lived in accommodation unsuitable for families, some of the children having to sleep on the floor. It was agreed to ask for six non-parlour type houses. Three pairs of houses were built in Main Street, two pairs in Peterborough Road and two pairs in Helpston Road.

Purchases for village use

Over the years a variety of things have been purchased for village use. In 1901, Ailsworth joined with Castor to buy a fire-engine. The money was raised by a compulsory rate. An invalid chair was bought for use in the Parish and was stored in the Chapel Schoolroom. (The rent for storage was four shillings a year). The chair was used until 1943, when it was deemed past repair and sold to Mr Ball for £1 1s. A seat costing £3 8s 6d was built round the horse chestnut tree on the village green in 1920. In July 1952, a special meeting was called to discuss the building of a bus shelter with money from the Victory Fund. The bus shelter is also the village War Memorial. Over the years Miss C Sharpe, Mrs E Taylor and Mr A Wing have looked after it.

Fig 9l. Council House, Main Street, 1930s.

Village celebrations

The village has always celebrated special occasions. In December 1897, it was agreed to send a donation of £5 0s 4½d to Peterborough Infirmary. This was the balance from the celebration held in honour of Queen Victoria's Diamond Jubilee. Mr Fitzwilliam was asked to plant two trees to commemorate the Diamond Jubilee. In March 1935, Ailsworth decided to celebrate alone and not join Castor in the Jubilee Celebrations. A budget of £5 was allocated for the celebrations. The festivities were held in the barn on Main Street. In February 1937, it was agreed to commemorate the Coronation of George VI, along the same lines as the Jubilee celebrations, the money to be raised by holding whist drives and a house-to-house collection. In October 1952, considerable discussion took place about the forthcoming Coronation of Queen Elizabeth. It was finally agreed to join Castor in their celebrations. A donation of £10 was given to the fund. Celebrations have continued to be joint ventures with Castor.

War years

There are few references to the First and Second World Wars in the minutes. The First World War was not mentioned in the records until August 15th 1919, when it was agreed to try to buy an army hut that could be used as a Reading or Parish Room. In 1938, forty-two people attended a Special Parish Meeting to hear a lecture

Fig 9m. Modern bungalow Andrew Close, 1960s.

given by PC Beales about Air Raid Precautions. Fourteen people volunteered to take an ARP course. In September 1941, a payment of 8s 9d was made as a contribution to War Damage, a further payment of 8s 9d was paid to the Collector of Taxes for War Damage in 1945.

Changes

After the war things changed at a quicker pace. A telephone box was installed on the Village Green, the bus shelter was built opposite the Wheatsheaf pub and Castor Station was closed for passenger traffic. In March 1956, Earl Fitzwilliam gave the Fitzwilliam School in Castor to both villages for use as a village hall. The nominated trustees were Mr Pell, Mr Maclean and Mr C Sharpe. In 1958, plans were received for a new development of bungalows between Helpston Road and Thorolds Way on the field where Singerfire Road, Casworth Way and Andrew Close are today. It was agreed to write and suggest that '*the proposed houses should be in keeping with the surrounding district*'. Concerns were also raised about the safety of Mr Harrison-Smith's barn in Main Street, which had recently burned down. (The houses near the surgery are now built on this site). In March 1963, the County Council was asked to make an order forming Ailsworth Parish Council. Mr Frank Taylor resigned as chairman due to ill health and Mr George Sharpe was then elected as Chairman.

Snippets from Ailsworth Parish Council Minutes 1964-2000

The first meeting of Ailsworth Parish Council was held in the Chapel Schoolroom on 28th May 1964. Ailsworth was still spelt Ailesworth. (The spelling seems to have altered gradually around this time). Mr George Sharpe was Chairman. The councillors were Mr W S Pickett, Mr M Gibbs, Mr H Lockwood, Mr J Taylor, and Mrs L Fisher. Items on the agenda included the ownership of the land in front of Singerfire Road, the state of repair of the bus shelter, street lighting, the proposed Castor playing field area, the burnt-out barn in Main Street, parking and poor footpaths.

A site for the township

The future of the village was thrown into turmoil in 1966 when the Hancock Report was published. This outlined the plans for the expansion of Peterborough. The Peterborough Development Corporation was set up in 1968 and its job was to double the size of Peterborough. Ailsworth and Castor were designated as a site for a new township. Both villages were against the development and an Action Committee was set up to fight the proposal. The Peterborough Development Corporation asked the Council if they would sell the Recreation Ground and the Field Allotments in Station Road. The Council declined to sell the land. A meeting was held with the Development Corporation which outlined its proposals for the village. This included 150 acres for recreation, spread throughout the new Castor Township. In May 1975, sixty-two members of the public were present at a meeting when Mr David Bath, Chief Planning Officer for the Peterborough Development Corporation, outlined the proposals for the new Township. Ailsworth and Castor were designated as Conservation villages and it was planned to build 10,000 houses in the new Township. In 1979, these proposals were thrown out by the Secretary of State for the Environment. The expansion of Peterborough was on the agenda again in 1987 and an Action Committee was set up to preserve the Nene Valley from expansion. In November 1987, a Public Inquiry into the expansion was held in Ely. A good case against the

Fig 9n. 109 Peterborough Road no longer has its top storey.

development was put forward. In August, the Council received the good news that Nicholas Ridley MP had decreed that the new Township for Peterborough should be built at the brick pits instead of at Castor and Ailsworth. The Council and Action Committee had worked tirelessly to oppose the expansion of the village, with good results.

Other local concerns
Other local concerns included speeding through the village, a proposed airfield at Sibson, the poor bus service to Peterborough, road hazards in Maffit Road, parking in Main Street, dogs fouling footpaths and fly-tipping. In 1968, the local road sweeper left the village and there was difficulty in finding anyone else to take on the position. The village was also hit by water and electricity cuts. During the fuel crisis of January 1974, the Council Meeting was cancelled as there was no heating in the Chapel Schoolroom. At the meeting on 6th March 1969, it was reported that the changing rooms and toilet on the Recreation Ground were in a dilapidated state. Complaints were received about the litter left after the weekly visit of the Fish and Chip van. In January 1975, planning permission was given for a Telephone Exchange in Helpston Road. £50 was given to the Chapel towards the costs for roof repairs, £10 was given to the recently formed Playgroup and £10 to Castor Church for the upkeep of the churchyard.

In 1976, Mr Arthur Chilvers retired as Clerk after 23 years of service to the Council and Mr Ernest Hudson succeeded him. Mr Albert Burgess was elected Chairman, replacing George Sharpe who had given forty years service to the village. Other members of the Council were Arthur Wing, Brian Sharpe, Jack Bailey, Judith Lytollis, Keith Salter and Jim Webb. Negotiations were started to acquire the Donkey Paddock in Main Street for the village and it was legally transferred into village ownership in 1980. The Firemen's strike in 1977 prompted a parishioner to inquire about contingency plans for the village in the event of a fire. In 1981, the village sign commemorating the Golden Jubilee of the local Women's Institute was erected on the boundary of the two villages. In May the Chapel Schoolroom was used for the distribution of butter, from the '*butter mountain*', to the Senior Citizens of the village.

In 1989, it was announced that work on the proposed bypass would begin in 1990. A bottle bank for the use of both villages was sited on Singerfire Green. At the end of 1989, Mr Ernest Hudson resigned as Clerk. Mr Clifford Richardson stood down as Chairman at the Annual General Meeting and Mr Michael Hinton replaced him.

Combined Councils?
Over the years there have been many attempts to combine the parish councils of Castor and Ailsworth. In July 1931, a meeting was called to consider the amalgamation of Ailsworth and Castor. Mr Holvey thought that this would be a good thing and he proposed the motion, but no one would second it. The Meeting voted unanimously against the amalgamation. The feeling of the meeting was that Ailsworth should remain Ailsworth. In October 1962, a letter was circulated to Ailsworth residents about the joining of Ailsworth and Castor Parish Councils. At an extraordinary meeting on Monday 26th November, it was agreed that Ailsworth did not want to amalgamate with Castor Parish Council. In May 1974, the merging of the two councils was proposed again; no councillor would support the proposal. Since then several attempts to merge have been unsuccessful but work together on projects carries on.

Forty years on

Although the population of the village has increased since the 1960s, the number of shops and local facilities has declined. We have lost Miss Sharpe's shop, Mr Quesne's electrical shop, the hairdresser's, the coal office and the post office. The cobbler, the blacksmith, the garage, the garage shop, the lending library inside Mrs Bass's Post Office all ceased trading. The home delivery of bread and meat stopped in the nineties. The Wheatsheaf and Barley Mow pubs have closed as has the Post Office and the Garage but Ailsworth Methodist Chapel survives and the Schoolroom continues to be a venue for meetings. The working farms, the movement of sheep and cattle on foot through the village streets, the smell of the pigs, the mud on the roads, the majestic tree on the Green, the annual visit of the circus are all now memories. Today, the horses that are kept in the old farm stables are for riding rather than farm work.

Fig 9o. Mr Albert Burgess aged 94. Ailsworth's oldest resident.

Forgotten are the old names of places that still exist such as Tree Piece, Top Doles, Gypsy Lane, Rushlees, Chapel Walk, Pond Terrace. The people who lovingly tended the land are gone but not forgotten. Today, the village is a busy community. Traffic calming measures have addressed some of the road problems and the bypass has taken away the heavy lorries. The concerns villagers faced in past times are still reflected in those of the present day but Ailsworth is set to take advantage of what the future has to offer.

Carole Humphries, Joan Pickett.

Carole Humphries - I came to live in Ailsworth in 1967, when Colin and I married. I feel fortunate that both our children, now married, live locally and enjoy village life. I hope that my work for Parish Council helps to improve the amenities in the village.

Joan Pickett – I came to the village when I married in 1961. I enjoy singing in the church choir, helping the children in school, where I was a governor and clerk for several years. I am also a member of both the Church and Parish Councils. I have three grown up children, the youngest, James, still lives in the village.

Notes

1. *Domesday Book*
2. Population – see Appendix Fifteen and census returns
3. Enclosures Act 1897

The information for this chapter is taken from the *Minute Books of Ailsworth Parish Meeting* and the *Ailsworth Parish Council Minute Books*.

Fig 9p. George and Margaret Speechley host a shoot at Manor Farm Ailsworth, 1920s.

Fig 9q. Gibbons' machines at Manor Farm, Ailsworth (Bill Feeney's) harvest, 1940.

Fig 9r. 18th Century milestone on the North side of the road approaching Ailsworth. Milestones such as this were ordered to be placed as a result of the 'Turnpike Acts' of 1744 and 1773. The Wansford-Peterborough road became a 'turnpike road' in the 18th century.

Chapter 10
The Buildings of Ailsworth

Introduction

Today, old and new houses, large and small, stand side by side, the result of the natural growth of the village of Ailsworth. It is now difficult to imagine what the village used to be like. Until the late 1940s there was a definite feel that Ailsworth and Castor were completely separate, each a village in its own right. There were no bungalows in Ailsworth and the houses in Thorolds Way, Castor had not been built. Fields divided the villages; only footpaths and the main road joined them together.

The variety of the housing styles we see today adds to the friendly feel of the village. No particular house or style of house dominates the village. There was no influence of an important estate on the design of the cottages. The larger farmhouses were built within the village, bigger and detached, alongside employees' houses. People needed to live near to their places of work. **The Stationmaster's house** in Station Road was the only house in the parish built away from the heart of the village. This was demolished in 1965. The oldest properties were situated in Main Street, Helpston Road, Peterborough Road and Maffit Road - the core of the old village.

The cottages were built close together, often directly onto the road or footpath and mostly of local stone. Roofs were thatched, clad with clay tiles, Collyweston or Welsh slate. Many of the cottages were built in long terraces and usually had small gardens, often detached from the houses. They had a range of outbuildings for the toilet, the wash house, fuel store and animal shelters. Life was very neighbourly in these conditions!

The largest buildings were the two public houses on Peterborough Road, the Chapel in Main Street and farm buildings. The pubs were important meeting places for the locals to socialise and air their views, and also for the passing trade. **The Methodist Chapel** was built in 1863, in the centre of the village. Today it nestles between an old stone cottage and a modern house.

Fig 10a. 111 & 111a Peterborough Road.

Peterborough Road

Peterborough Road is the major road running through the village. Here the **Paper Shop** and the **Village Butcher's shop** continue to be the hub of village trade and chit-chat. The old houses are all on the South side of this road. These all have direct access to the pavement, the variety of styles denoting the different ages of the properties. Some of these properties housed the old village shops. **115 Peterborough Road** was **The Barley Mow Pub** that closed in the 1950s. After the pub was closed one of the ground floor rooms was used as an office for the local coal merchant. Now the old pub has been converted into flats.

111 & 111a Peterborough Road, are a pair of

Fig 10b. The Wheatsheaf Pub.

Fig 10c. 15 Main Street.

Fig 10d. Walnut House.

Fig 10e. Straw Cottage.

three-storey houses, built of stone in the early 19th century. There was a butcher's shop in the right hand lower room until the early 1970s, and then it was a ladies hairdresser's until the 1990s. The houses have been recently refurbished. The former **Wheatsheaf Pub,** which was built in the early 19th century but closed in the 1990s also had a butcher's shop in the single storey extension. There are now three new houses built on the old car park. The two newer shops and former **Post Office and Garage** were built in the 1950s. The Garage buildings have recently been demolished to make way for two new houses. The smallest building in the village is the brick bus shelter with a shingle roof, built in 1952 as a war memorial.

Main Street

Many of the older houses have been pulled down; in the 1960s a lot of cottages were condemned and then demolished, and replaced with new homes. It is now difficult to imagine that there was a row of cottages between numbers 19 and 33 Main Street. Many people will still remember the other old cottages in Main Street. Ailsworth today is a far cry from the village of yesteryear. Cottages hugged the sides of the road, the majority having one room downstairs and one upstairs. Indoor toilets and bathrooms came much later. Most of the old properties had outside wash houses and outside toilets, some were for individual use, others more friendly *'two holers'*.

Part of number **10 Main Street** was for some years the village Fish and Chip shop and it also had been the home of Harry Haynes and family. **15 Main Street** was for many years the Sharpe family home. There used to be a shed in the garden that was the cobbler's and the barber's. **Walnut House** in Main Street dates back to the 17th century. In the 1970s the huge walnut tree in the garden was cut down and 2a Maffit Road was built on the site.

The Methodist Chapel was built in what was then the heart of the village. The houses to the North of the Chapel in Main Street are built on the site of old buildings belonging to **Manor Farm**, old cottages and a haulage depot which later became an agricultural depot for Brown & Butlins. Ruddle and Wilkinson Architects planned the present houses and they were designed to look like a group of old village houses. At the time the scheme won an architectural award. Across the road, **Barn Cottages** and the two bungalows in Maffit Road were built on Mr Bass's old farmyard which had since become the coal depot. Four houses were built within the curtilage of **Manor Farm** in the

1970s; high stone walls enclose these houses. Stone walls of varying heights are a feature of the village scene, some are remnants of the old farm walls. Four detached bungalows were built at **Kings Acre**, Main Street in the 1990s, on the site of a pair of semi-detached council houses, for the needs of the senior citizens.

41 Main Street is now called **The Old Brewery** but is still remembered by some as Miss Sharpe's shop. (The brewery used to be in the outbuildings in front of the house along with the bakery). The general shop closed in 1971, when the decimalisation of money was introduced. String and brown paper hung from the ceiling to wrap the bacon, ham and cheese. Boxes of goods were stacked from floor to ceiling filling the shop with nostalgic smells. Village people used to take their Sunday joints to be cooked in the baker's oven. The house is dated EWB 1758 on the East gable wall. It is part of a stone terrace, running through to Maffit Road. Two of the other cottages in the row have thatched roofs; the third has a clay pantile roof.

44 Main Street is a 17th century thatched cottage, its gable-end faces Main Street and its North elevation faces onto Cross Street. For many years this cottage was owned by **Manor Farm**. Afterwards it was bought by the Nature Conservancy and became the home of the Warden for Castor Hanglands. John Robinson and Roy Harris were two of the last Wardens to live there. It is now a private house.

55 Main Street was built in the 17th century. It is a large thatched house that was extensively updated in the 1960s. It has also been known as **Jasmine Cottage** and **Rose Cottage**.

Most old cottages have been altered and extended and show little resemblance to the original. In recent times old farm buildings have been incorporated into new homes, fields and farmyards have become sites for new developments and the old pubs, stables and barns have been converted into residential accommodation. Old barns and stables in the former farmyard at the top of Main Street have been converted into houses. The dovecote in this yard is now a garage. **50 and 52 Main Street**, the oldest parts of which were built in the 17th century, were formerly known as **Manor House Farm**. **50 Main Street** is now a dental surgery. **59 Main Street** is built on **Drakes Farm** once farmed by Mr Sharpe.

Fig 10f. Kings Acre.

Fig 10g. 44 Main Street.

Fig 10h. 50 & 52 Main Street.

Fig 10i. Thatchcroft.

Fig 10j. Southview.

Fig 10k. Manor House.

Maffit Road

There was evidence of an old dwelling along the track leading from the top of Maffit Road to the bypass. This was known as **Frog Hall**. The last remaining link with this 'house', a group of fruit trees, was removed in the early 1990s.

At the beginning of the fifties there were only three properties in Maffit Road, or Back Lane as it was sometimes called. **Numbers 2, 4** (now joined) and **15** all belonged to the Popple family. **15 Maffit Road**, the **Maltings**, is the only red brick property in the village. **Number 6**, at the top of the Jitty between Maffit Road and Main Street, was for many years a farm cottage for Manor Farm. The first new house to be built in the road was **Number 1**, the home of Len and Lorna Fisher. More houses with an individual style were soon built on the old small field-garden plots.

Helpston Road

In Helpston Road there are houses dating from the 17th or early 18th century that sit amongst newer houses. **Thatchcroft** (number 28) was for many years the home of the Pell family. **Southview** directly to the rear was the Jinks family home. These two cottages abut the side of Helpston Road.

The former council houses, built in the 1920s were highly sought after. They had spacious accommodation and large gardens, everything the old cottages did not have.

Old farmhouses include **The Manor House**, in Helpston Road, which acquired the name Manor House in relatively recent years. **The Limes**, also in Helpston Road, was built at the end of the 19th century. The last farmer to live there was Mr Fletcher. There used to be a smithy at the rear of this house where numbers **3a and 3b** are now built. The chalet bungalows to the North of this on Helpston Road were built on part of Manor House Farm in the early 1960s.

Larger new developments

In the late 1950s Shelton's builders built new bungalows along Helpston Road leading into a new estate - Singerfire Road, Casworth Way and Andrew Close. The houses in Holme Close were built in the early 1970s. The footpath leading from Holme Close to Helpston Road is part of the old path formerly known as Church Walk, and sometimes now called Chapel Walk. The name used obviously depended on where you were going.

Notes

The information about these buildings is taken from the *Listed buildings of Peterborough City Council*
See appendix nineteen and *The Royal Commission on Historical Monuments, Peterborough New Town.*

Fig 10l. 1960s 'new development'.

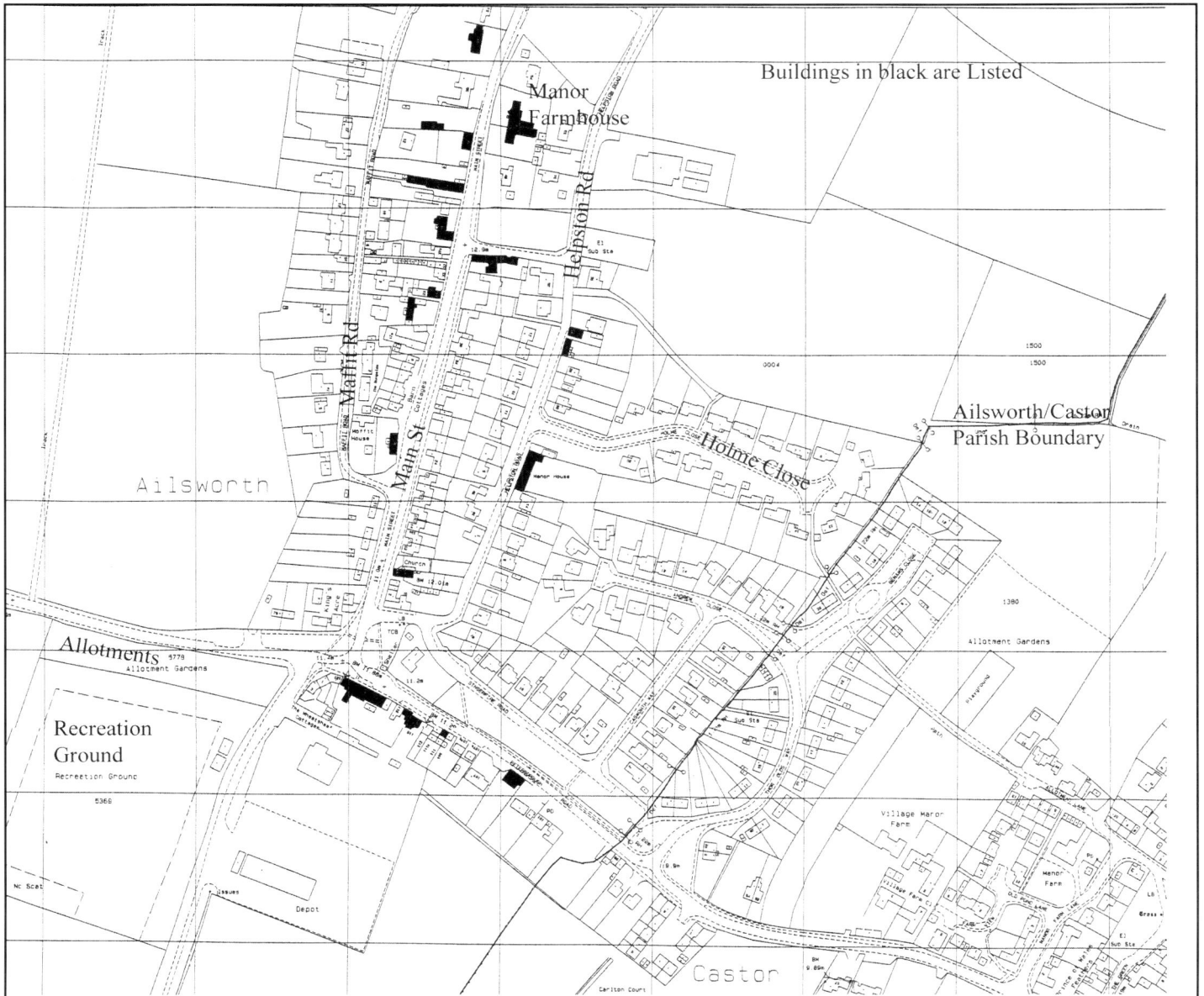

Fig 10m. Map of Ailsworth showing Parish boundary with Castor. Listed buildings marked.
Reproduced from Ordnance Survey mapping on behalf of The Controller of Her Majesty's Stationery Office
© *Crown Copyright 100042620 2004*

A Gibbons' Robey steam engine threshing at Manor Farm Sutton (Fred Holmes') May 1916: back to camera Mr Matchet (gamekeeper), Billy Brown with wheels on right, Charlie Clark on drum, Bob Gilbert (with fork) and Fred Gibbons beside it.

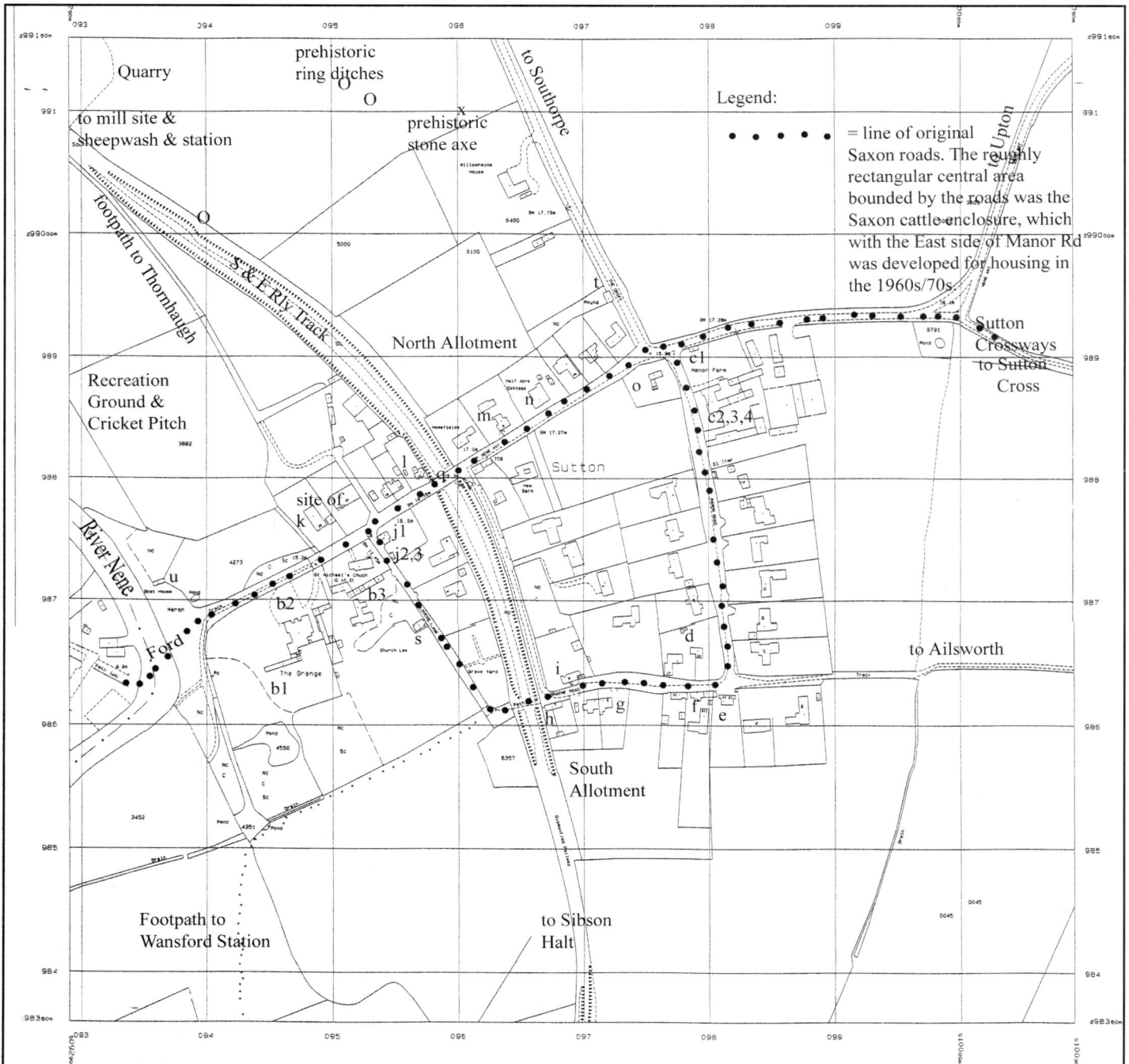

Map of Sutton, listed building noted by letter. Reproduced from Ordnance Survey mapping on behalf of The Controller of Her Majesty's Stationery Office © Crown Copyright 100042620 2004

Chapter 11
History of Sutton

Introduction

In compiling a history of the village from historical records one is in danger of ending up with an impression that villagers of former times would not recognize. For a thousand years Sutton was an agricultural community with lives dominated by the unrecorded continuity of seed time and harvest, storm and flood and the thrice-yearly fairs at Milton or Castor. These were not fairs of swings and roundabouts, but where a man would sell his labour for the coming year and where cooking pots and cloth, tools and trinkets would be purchased; the things that could not be produced by an otherwise virtually self-sufficient village economy. Of course, recorded events – hearth tax, poll tax, the Dissolution of the Abbey - were important but nonetheless transitory events in the continuing life of the community. And community spirit would be strong, fostered by the interdependence of villagers, where the four oxen needed to form a plough team could be owned by four different villagers, whose cooperation was essential to get their strips in the open fields ploughed and harvested. This strong sense of community lasted well into the 1800s, when only the poor and needy born in the parish would be eligible for parish relief. Incomers were sent back to their parish of origin. Records of such proceedings by the Overseers of the Poor still exist for the benefice:

John Stavely 5 Feb 1800
John Stavely of Alesworth, labourer. Born at Alesworth, aged 68. When he was about 19 he let himself for 1 year to William Hopkinson of Sutton, farmer from Michaelmas to Michaelmas and he stayed the whole year. When he was aged about 29, after returning from being a soldier, he let himself to Stephen Pauling of Castor, farmer, for 11 months from 1 month after Michaelmas to the following Michaelmas. He did not leave Stephen Pauling's service until 4 or 5 weeks after Michaelmas because he could not get his wages. He is married, his wife's name is Jane. He has gained no legal settlement elsewhere.
Signed by JPs, Chris Hodgson (rector), John Weddred, clerk. John Stavely made his mark.

Sutton as an almost exclusively agricultural community carried on for a thousand years, and it was not until the industrial revolution, or more specifically the coming of the railways, were there opportunities for alternative employment. The Lord of the Manor, in his evidence to a parliamentary select committee on enclosures 1 May 1901 said, *"There was a family of the name of Bew, who were old cottagers; the father and mother died leaving three sons. One, I found out has a good trade as a carpenter, another is a shopkeeper and another is a foreman in the Great Northern Works at Peterborough"* [1]. After 1871 the trades of stationmaster, porter, platelayer and railway labourer start appearing on the Sutton Census Returns [2] and there were twenty two baptisms of children of railway employees between 1868 and 1904 [3]. Even in 1964, the Peterborough Standard reported [4] *'Sutton really is an agricultural village where apart from about six people who work outside the village nearly everyone is employed on farms or in gardens... In 1811 there were 20 houses and a population of 103, and today with about the same number of houses the population has almost halved'.*

Roads
The Anglo-Saxons laid out their village to the usual plan of four roads enclosing a rectangular stockade where cattle would be safer from predators, both human and animal. The main house – the Grange – and the chapel were on one corner, in this case on the main road leading to the ford, access to which it would control. The presence of a fordable place across the river is probably why Sutton was sited here in the first place. This Anglo-Saxon road pattern still exists in Nene Way (formerly Main or Top Street), Graeme Road East (Back Lane or Bottom Street), Manor Road (Gaw Lane) and Lovers Lane (Church or Chapel Lane). All the buildings would originally have been on Main Street with crofts running down to Back Lane, on which houses were built later, possibly in the 17th century redevelopment of the village. Graeme Road South (New Road) alongside the railway cutting was added in 1867 after the Southern end of the village was effectively cut off by the railway. The old names lasted until the 1970s when the roads were renamed. I can understand the residents in expensive houses not wanting an address in Bottom Street or even Gaw Lane, but it does seem a pity to have renamed the attractive rural Church Lane as Lovers Lane – reflecting the activity with which this quiet lane had now become associated. Jefferies' map of 1791 (Fig 11a.) shows the road to the ford branching left at the ford and linking up with the extension of Bottom Street in what is now part of Footpath No 2. The Drift used to continue to Southorpe across what is now the A47, crossing the Upton road near Sutton Wood (Fig11a.). This is marked as common land on the 1843 Tithe Map and has only recently been ploughed up. Another occupation road used to run

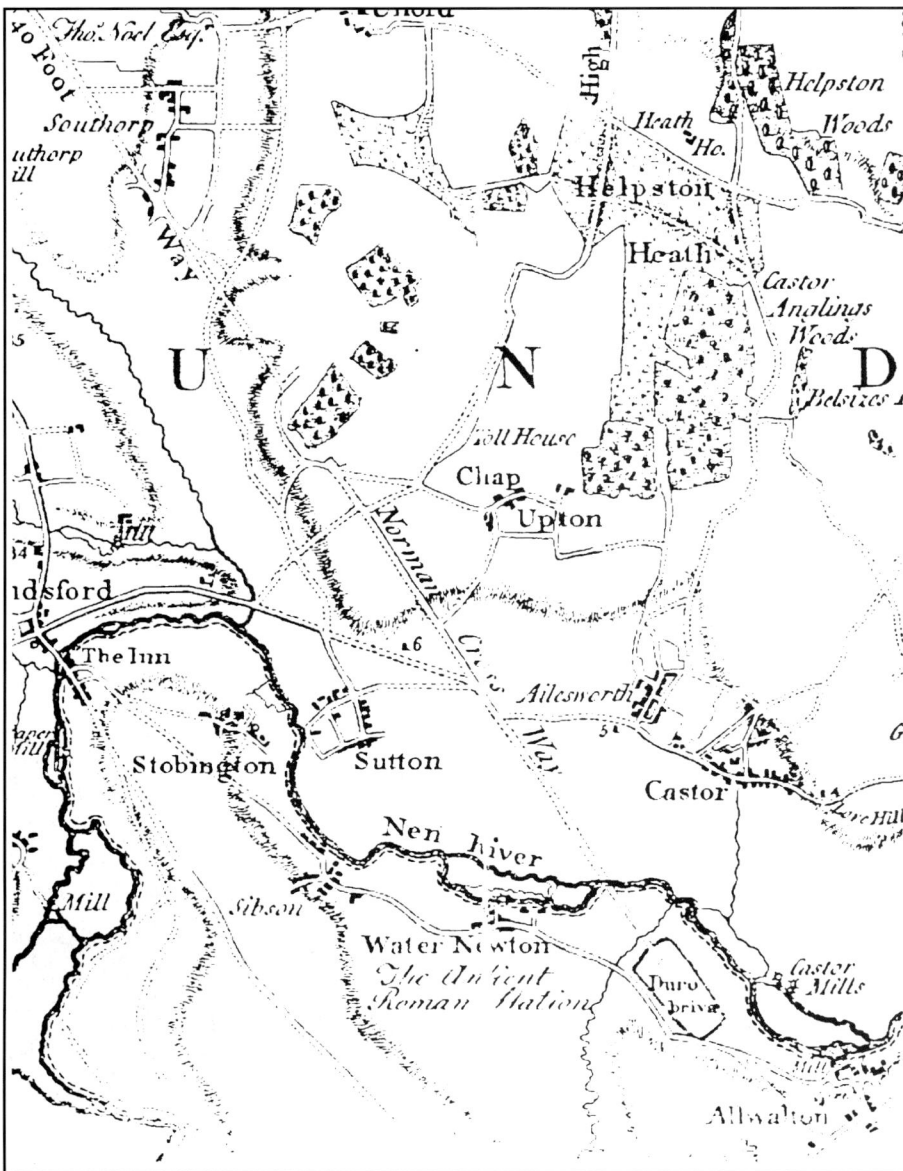

Fig 11a. Old roads in Sutton: detail from Eyre/Jefferies' map of Northants 1791.
Note turnpike milestone 6 North East of Sutton.

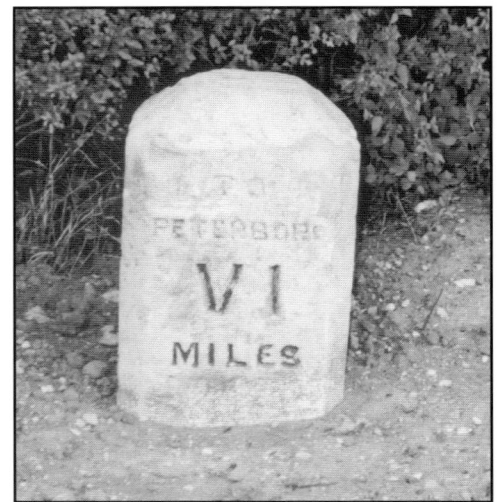

Fig 11b. Turnpike Milestone.

from opposite the church to the stone pits, up a ramp into the field behind and then alongside a stone wall to the A47. The stone wall was removed and the land ploughed up some 15 or 20 years ago, but one of the old gateposts to the A47 and one at the quarry exit are still in situ.

Until the passing of the act for the Peterborough to Leicester Turnpike in1753, having two major roads, Ermine Street (North/South) and the present A47 (East/West), in the parish must have been a great burden for the parishioners who were responsible for maintenance of all roads in the parish. When the turnpike was established milestones were erected (Fig 11b) and a toll house was erected at the Sutton/Wansford parish boundary. The adjacent field is still known as Toll Bar. The Toll House was demolished c 1866 when the road bridge over the new railway was built, and rebuilt at the top of the rise by the Southorpe Road junction. It was demolished in the 1950s when the A47 was widened, but its site is still marked by the presence of fruit trees and daffodils.

Prior to the enclosures Sutton's cottagers used to have summer grazing in Borough Fen (now Newborough) and a distress warrant was levied on the village in 1700 for non-maintenance of the road to the Fen – 'the Chayce'. Lord Fitzwilliam said in a letter his steward [5] 'I must defend those two townes (Castor & Sutton) where my estate lies from being oppresst…they ought not to pay to the repair of a road they never make use off'. One other former major road that now exists only as a bridleway is Sutton Crossways, which would have been the main road to Castor, the mother church and the thrice yearly fairs. Sutton's Anglo-Saxon Cross lies at the junction of Crossways with Ermine Street.

Boundaries
The village of Sutton lies at the South end of the parish. The parish boundaries would have been set in Anglo-Saxon times probably in the time of Abbot Adulf (AD 972-992) and included riverside water meadows, arable land on the higher ground and wooded uplands for forestry and hunting. The River Nene forms the Southern and South Western boundary, the Southorpe Brook or Wash Dyke and the old mill leat (of which more later) forming the Western boundary. The Northern boundary with Southorpe runs from the Southorpe Brook to Sutton Wood in a dogleg fashion. There are five ancient boundary stones around the irregular boundary of Sutton Wood all having the letter 'S' incised over a cloverleaf (see colour plate section). Ben Robinson of Peterborough Museum thinks these may be assart stones

which marked a 'thus far and no farther' point when woods were being cleared for arable land. Records show that Sutton Wood was a valuable resource for the Abbey. From Sutton Wood the boundary runs along Ermine Street which provides a curious anomaly whereby 220 yards of Ermine Street are in Upton whereas the land on both sides is in Sutton. From this point it doglegs West, South and East before rejoining Ermine Street at Hells Corner and running to Sutton Cross where again it doglegs in a generally Southerly direction to the Nene River. The 'doglegs' almost certainly relate to Anglo-Saxon or Romano-British field boundaries existing at the time. The Eastern boundary lies along the estate boundary of an Anglo-Saxon thegn of Ailsworth. The area in the North of the parish would have been inhabited in Romano-British and Medieval times. Sutton Wood was managed for timber and probably had a sawmill (the stream running from Sutton Wood to the Southorpe Brook is called Woodmills Dyke) and there is extensive ridge and furrow (Fig 11c) and an old boundary ditch (Fig 11d) on the North side of Sutton Heath adjoining Woodmills Dyke. Also there are remains of a Romano-British building (farmhouse?) (Fig 11h) near Sutton Wood where 3rd and 4th century Castor ware pottery has been found. Only last year a rare piece of 1st century Samian ware depicting a fallen gladiator submitting, with a potter's mark xxiii showing it was fired in Gaul, was picked up whilst field-walking.

Fig 11c. Ridge and furrow - Sutton Heath.

Fig 11d. Old field boundaries – Sutton Heath.

The Mill

An important part of any self-sufficient village's agricultural economy would be its mill. Sutton had a mill from its earliest days. It was sited where the Southorpe Brook (or Washdyke) flows under the present A47 near the old station and was known as Briggmilne or Bridgemill. Indeed an adjacent field was shown as 'Bridge Mills' on the Sacrewell estate map of 1729 and is still so known. That it already existed when the parish boundaries were drawn is evidenced by the fact that the head leat of the mill on the Wansford side of Southorpe Brook forms the parish boundary. The mill could well have been founded in Romano-British times, for a quantity of 3rd and 4th century Castor ware pottery shards have been picked up in the field known as Bridgemill Close. The Victoria County History notes [6] '*Royal Grants of Richard 1 and Henry III confirm the chapel of Sutton adjacent to the church at Castor together with the village of Sutton and the mill which Thorold Fitz Antekill gave to the monastery.*' A charter of King John dated 25 Dec 1199 [7] refers to '*a mill called Briggmilne, Thorold of Sutton's gift*' and Hugh Candidus [8] reports that Abbot William de Waterville (1145-1175) '*acquired wholly a certain mill at Sutton which pays fifty shillings a year and he granted and assigned this to the fee of the Infirmarium*'. It was subsequently passed to the Almoner and in 1379 the infirmarium notes a receipt [9] '*Et de lxvjs de Elemensario pro firma del Parkyrke et 1 molendini aqua apud Sutton*' (and 66 shillings from the almoner for a farm at Peakirk and a water mill at Sutton). An extract from Henry of Pytchley's Book of Fees [10] reads '*be it also remembered...John de St Mark or Medard granted to us a certain place adjoining our millpond of Brygmylne for 18 pence a year...*'. John Medard died in 1334.

In 1445 during the time as Almoner of William Morton the mill was completely rebuilt. He recorded the details in his medieval filofax which fortunately has survived and is in the British Museum [11]. He records the carriage by road of ten wagonloads of freestone, from the quarry (almost certainly Barnack) to the mill site and names each of the waggoners who were performing a '*luff boone*' to their feudal lord. He also records a site meeting with the mason and the bailiff.

'Meeting about the building of walls at Brygmylle. Noted on the 24th day of April Willelmus Morton almoner in charge, in the presence of Johannus Eyr bailiff and collector for Sutton, Robertus Conquest tenant of the same, Johannus Coldewell servant of the said almoner and others. Brother Willelmus Morton almoner called the meeting with Willelmus Schepey mason by which said mason is to build stone walls, width (to the Western boundary under the walls) nearly 12 feet, height from the footings 10 feet, in length 39 feet, thickness of two gables in the same place 2 feet as standard. Likewise the thickness of the other walls there 2 ½ feet standard with 3 buttresses at the Water Gate on the South side and 1 buttress in the other part 3 feet thick at the front as standard. 23s.4d.'

The newly built mill was allegedly used for other purposes, for in a visitation by the Bishop of Lincoln some of the monks accused Richard Ashton, Abbott till 1471, of gross maladministration and incontinence with three named women whose husbands received favours of the Abbott. Liaisons with one of the women allegedly took place at Bridgemill. The allegations were not necessarily true as monks were required to report rumour and hearsay, and at the time there were two violently opposed factions in the Abbey, one led by the Abbott and one by the Treasurer. This was presumably the Treasurer's faction getting their retaliation in first!

On the dissolution of the Abbey in 1535, the King's Value [21] records *'one water mill in Sutton belonging to the Almoner's Office - £2.0s.0d'*. It was evidently transferred to the Dean and Chapter for in 1547/8 arrears of rent were due to the Dean and Chapter: *'de firmario molendini vocate Bryggemilne xxs.'* (from the mill farm known as Bridgemill – 20 shillings). On the 5th April 1591 the Dean and Chapter instituted proceedings against one Thomas Griffin, for not having his corn ground at his lord's mill as was customary [25] WT Mellows notes in a footnote that this was the last occasion on which 'Mill suit' was brought, as by then the Dean and Chapter's mills were in such a state of dilapidation that Mill suit could not be enforced.

In the 1649 Parliamentary Survey of the Manor of Sutton the Commissioners for the sale of the Bishop's lands notes [12] *'one house formerly made a mill but now decayde called by the name of Bridge Mill consisting of two bayes with a little close adjoining called Millholme containing by estimation 1 acre 3 roods 0 perches. Annual value £2.0s.0d'*.

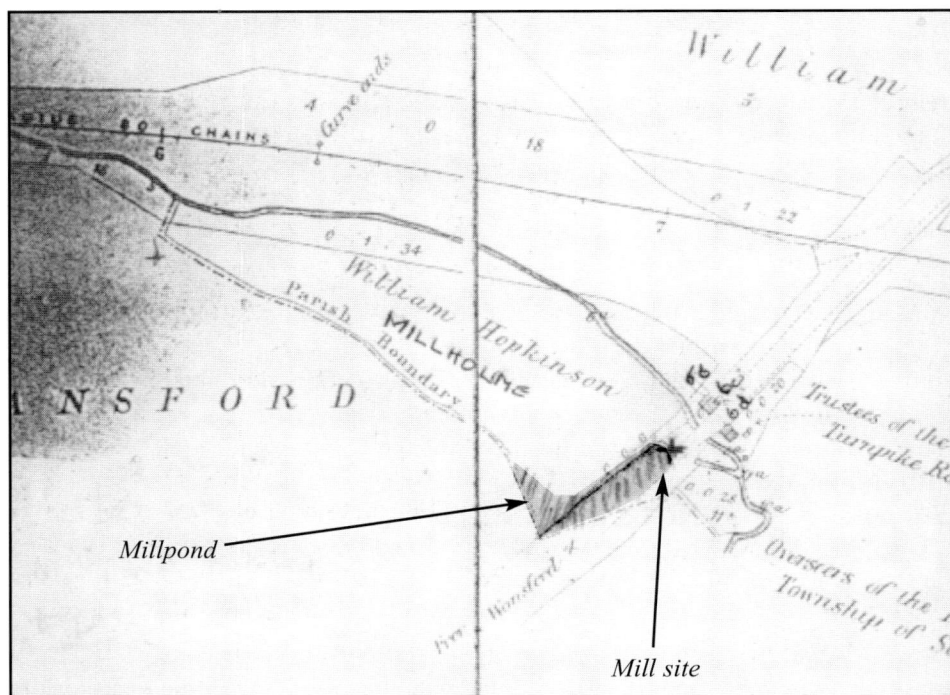

Fig 11e. Railway surveyors plan of Mill area c 1865. On the accompanying key 6b is sheepwash, 6c is house and 6d is toll house and garden, both belonging to the trustees of the Wansford district of Leicester-Peterborough turnpike.

And that is the last reference I can find to Bridgemill. But what happened to William Morton's ten cartloads of freestone? I believe William Hopkinson used the stone from the *'decayde mill'* to build his sheepwash nearby (Figs 13w.1&2) in 1844, for it is built of superior stone far removed from the rough stone expected of such a utilitarian structure. Certainly all evidence of the mill had gone by 1865 when a surveyor for the new railway drew his map showing of the mill's tail leat and overflow channel. (Fig 11e) There are still a few bits of building stone lying around and the silted up mill pond still fills up in times of flood. However auguring has not located any foundations of the mill house which may well be under the earthwork rampart of the new (in 1867) road bridge.

The Quarry or Stone Pits

Sutton used to have a quarry of *'excellent stone'* (Kelly's Directory 1854). It is fairly easy to establish when working ceased from a memorandum dated 7th December 1897 of the Peterborough Chapter Estates which reads: *'The Commissioners are also owners of 4a 2r 33p the site of a stone pit worked out many years since, which has yielded no rent for about 40 years'*.

It is less easy to establish when it started. The most likely time is in the late 17th century, when the Dean and Chapter would be looking for a local stone source to replace the worked out quarries at Barnack. Certainly the quarry was not

Fig 11f. Old working face Sutton quarry.

Fig 11g. River access Sutton quarry.

working at the dissolution for it is not mentioned in the King's Value in 1535 [21], nor for that matter in the 1649 Parliamentary Survey [12]. The village appears to have been extensively rebuilt in the 17th century by Bishop Dove or his family. The initials 'JD 1700' are on the North Bay of Manor Farm and the RCHM [13] lists seven houses or cottages in Sutton built in the 17th century and one 19th century house with reused 17th century windows. Perhaps the quarry was opened for this purpose and its river side-site made it possible to move the stone easily further afield. The remains of a gravel and timber wharf may be seen when the river is low, and it is recorded [14] that Elton Rectory was partly built of Sutton Stone, and the Dean and Chapter's lessees of the quarry for many years were Thompsons, a firm of Peterborough Church builders and repairers (Figs 11f & 11g).

Population

Sutton's populations seems to have been remarkably steady over 700 years, based on taxation returns, rent rolls and censuses, though it did fall to about half its present size post-war in the 1950s and 1960s before recovering to today's figure.

Poll tax 1381 [15] A tax on heads or polls was first raised in 1377 and again in 1379 and 1381. Sutton's record is from 1381 and was for all those over 16. Twenty three people paid sums between 8d and 4s.4d. with a total of 49s.10d and an average of 2s.2d. Using a multiple of 4.3 gives a population of about 100 people.

William Morton – Rent Roll 1451 [16] He records rents for twenty three messuages or cottages again giving a population of about 100.

Hearth Tax – 1669 [17] Each hearth was taxed at 2s.0d per year payable in two instalments at Lady Day and Michaelmas. Those too poor to be rated were exempt. Thirty householders are recorded, of which thirteen hearths were certified as exempt. One person had seven hearths, and five had three hearths. A total of the thirty three were liable for tax. Population about 120.

Compton Census 1676 (a religious survey) 80 conformists. No papists or non conformists. 23 families.

Mr Landen of Milton's survey 27th June 1768. Six farms, eight cottages, one house, three tenements. Total 18 premises, population about 90.

1811 Census quoted in Peterborough Standard [4] 20 houses, population 103.

Census 1841. 24 houses, population 121.

Census 1901. 23 houses, population 98.

Census 1961 and Peterborough Standard 1964 [4] 20 houses, population 58.

Electoral Register 2003. 50 houses, 101 electors.

Some other events in Sutton's history

Ice Age
Some of the oldest mammal bones in Peterborough Museum are of Wolstonian age and were found near Sutton Cross [18].

Prehistoric
RCHM [19] lists 7 Ring Ditches, 2 double ring ditches, 2 enclosures and a pit alignment in the parish – a prehistoric metropolis!

Roman
Edmund Artis undertook considerable excavations in the parish and discovered the remains of a Roman villa on Sutton Heath and several potteries and iron furnaces (Fig 11h).

Norman
Sutton is not mentioned in the Domesday Book but it should be remembered that it was essentially a tax return and Sutton was wholly owned by the Abbey, which was exempt from many taxes under Anglo-Saxon charters confirmed by William I in 1070.

1294 Full Hundred Court of Nassaburgh at Sutton [20]
'John de la Planche had withheld Suit of the Sacrist's court at Southorpe. An inqisition was made at the full Hundred Court of Nassaburgh at Sutton and found he was bound to perform the said Suit. The same paid for Sherrif's Aid 18d a year, for frank pledge 6d; for suit of court 8d.' (ie fined 24 pence with eight pence costs)

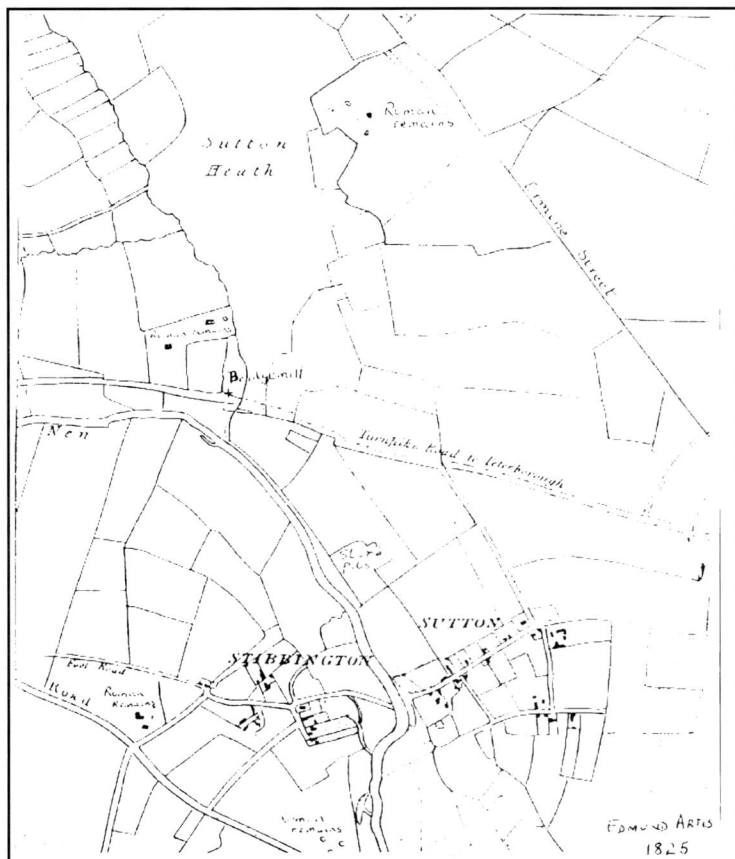

Fig 11h. Artis' map 1825.

1535 The King's Value [21]
At the dissolution of the Abbey, Sutton was valued as follows:

Sutton village	£14	12	0	½
Sutton Wood	£1	15	2	½
21 acres 20 perches price the acre 1s 8d				
Bridgemill	£2	0	0	
	£18	7	3	
Deductions:-				
Richard Robinson bailiff of the said Almoner's land at Sutton		13	4	
	£17	13	11	per annum

1536 Nassaburgh Musters
Sutton to provide 2 archers, 3 bylmen, horse and harness for a man

1548/9 Book of Robert Pearson general receiver for the Dean and Chapter [22]
'The first halfe yere anno secundo et tercio Edwardi Sext

Sutton of the balyf there sexto Aprilis	*iiij l*	*xv s*	—
Of the farmer there xviij Aprilis		*xl s*	—
Of Stacy there xiij June for his mylne		*xx s*	
Item for his coppye			*xiiij d.*

1650 Commonwealth [6]
'Manor of Sutton with all that messuage now or late in tenure of William Gardener in the town of Sutton and commonly called the manor house was sold by the Commissioner for sale of Bishop's lands to Thomas Matthews and Thomas Allen, citizens and grocers of London.' The sale was rescinded at the Restoration in 1660 (VCH).

1684 Great Fire of Sutton [23]

To relieve distress following the fire collections were taken in churches. Amongst these were:

1 Mar 1684 Elton – *'for a fire at Sutton in Caster parish Northampton, 11s. 5 ½ d'*

10 Feb 1684 Lamport – *'collected for John Ryleys brief of Sutton in ye parish of Castor, 10s. 6d'*

22 Feb 1684 Ormsby – *'for ye burning at Sutton in Caster Northampt, 2s. 0d'*

14 Sep 1684 Dallington – *'for a fire at Sutton in ye parish of Castor in ye countie of Northampton, 3s. 6d'*.

1762 Militia List

This lists all males aged between 18 and 45 and shows two farmers, a shepherd, a cordwainer (leather worker), a cooper (barrel maker), a butcher, three labourers, and three servants. The shepherd and a labourer had three children and would have been exempt as the maintenance of their children would otherwise fall on the parish, and the cooper was lame.

1797 Token

This was found during the building of Church Lees. The Curator of Archaeology at Peterborough Museum writes: *'This item would have been used as a farm token about 200 years ago. The worker would be paid with these tokens which could only be used for produce on that particular farm. The token would have been stamped by the farm. It was originally a bronze heavy penny from the reign of George III, 1797'*. The token had been used on seven occasions. At the time, Grange Farm was leased by William Hopkinson (1755-1821) from the Dean and Chapter.

1901 Enclosure of the Open Fields and Heath

The enclosure of 477 acres of the open fields aroused no opposition as by then there was only one cottager with any common rights remaining and he was farm bailiff to Rev W Hopkinson, Lord of the Manor and proposer of the scheme; in any case the open fields had for all practical purposes been enclosed - see Artis' map (Fig 11h) – by agreement of the occupants of the Grange and Manor Farm. However the proposal to enclose 133 acres of heath, which many regarded as a common, did arouse considerable controversy and was opposed by the City of Peterborough. The bill was carried in Parliament by the very narrow majority of seven votes – 151 for and 144 against [24].

The Village Today

The character of the village changed dramatically in the late 1960s and early 1970s. Increasing mechanization on the farm required fewer labourers. Their cottages, with their large gardens allowing ample scope for extensions, were sold

Fig 11i. Sutton and Upton Home Guard c1943. Back Row (l-r): Phillip Fox, Wilf Hornsby, Charlie Favell, John Fox, Harry Fox, Walter Fox; Middle Row: Harold Gathercole, Arthur Mason, Harry Ward, Steve Britten, Arthur Harris, Charlie Harris, George Ransome; Front Row: Allen Herbert (2ic), Jack Button (CO), Ernest Britten (Sgt).

Fig 11j. Sutton and Upton Cricket team c1950. Back Row (l-r) unknown, Geoffrey Fox, Phil Fox, unknown, Walter Fox, Tom Hornsby; Front Row: John Gathercole, Michael Skells, John Fox, Arthur Mason, Dick Smith.

Fig 11l. Sutton and Upton Coronation celebrations 1953: children and helpers on a horse drawn wagon, handled by Geoffrey and John Fox Front row (l-r) Graham Fox, Audrey Fox, Beverley Favell, Ruth Fox, Peter Mason, Rosalie Britten, Mrs Chambers, Nellie Britten.

Fig 11k. Sutton and Upton Coronation celebrations 1953: childrens' race – Graham Fox first, Linda Ward (lived at Old Station), second.

to professional people as they became vacant. Jack Button of Manor Farm, who had bought virtually all the Grange farmland from the Rev W Hopkinson's daughter Mrs Graeme, developed Manor Road by selling quarter-acre plots for approx £1000 with covenants to build a house on the plot costing not less than £10,000 – seemingly amazingly cheap now but at the time more than twice the price of a house on the executive development then taking place at Netherton. These houses tended to be bought by middle-aged established executives commuting daily to local towns, and for many years the village had few children, resulting in disuse of both allotments and recreation ground, which were then let for grazing. In all this time the little Victorian corrugated iron Reading Room remained the village's social centre, as indeed it does today with monthly coffee mornings, PC and PCC meetings, elections and the odd social occasion. Some years ago there was a proposal to replace it with a modern building but the proposal foundered in some acrimony because of disagreement on the scale of the rebuilding, where it should be sited and the cost. The issue will have to be addressed again in the near future though, as the Reading Room will not last for ever. Happily the adult population, whose numbers dropped to the fifties after the war, is again in excess of a hundred. The increasing number of children has resulted in current action to resuscitate the recreation ground by providing play-ground equipment, goalposts and seating. The recent Jubilee celebrations, including restoration of Sutton Cross, were enjoyed by all, and with continuing support for village institutions, such as the harvest festival and carol service, augur well for this growing community in its ancient setting.

Keith Garrett

Keith Garrett was a Canberra Navigator at RAF Wittering in the mid-50s. He bought the former station master's house in 1965, which makes him the second oldest resident, and the oldest incomer.

Acknowledgements

David Powell for advice on the Mill and Brian Walsh of Bourne for help in translating Latin texts, Richard Hillier Peterborough Library, Ben Robinson Peterborough Museum, villagers past and present or their descendants for anecdotes and photographs.

Notes

1. Minutes of Evidence Parliamentary Select Committee into Enclosure of Sutton, 2 May 1901.
2. Censuses Sutton Township 1841-1901.
3. Register of Baptisms Sutton Chapelry/Parish.
4. Peterborough Standard, 24 Jan 1964.
5. Letters Lord Fitzwilliam to his steward, p86, NRS 1990.
6. VCH Northants, p481.
7. Stenton ed, NRS Vol IV, p46.
8. Peterborough Chronicle of Hugh Candidus, p71.
9. Joan Greatex ed, *Account Rolls of the Obedientaries of Peterborough,* NRS, 1983, p45.
10. WT Mellows ed, *Henry Pytchley's Book of Fees*, NRS, 1927.
11. WT Mellows ed, *Book of William Morton*, NRS, pp70-105.
12. Parliamentary Survey of Manor of Sutton 1649, NCRO,
13. RCHM, *Survey of Peterborough New Town Antiquities*, HMSO, 1969, pp75-76.
14. Rev RF Whistler, *History of Elton*, 1900.
15. Poll Tax 1381, NCRO.
16. WT Mellows ed, *Book of William Morton*, NRS, p48.
17. Hearth Tax 1669, NCRO, E179.
18. Langford, *Cool Peterborough*, p20.
19. RCHM, *Survey of Peterborough New Town Antiquities*, HMSO, 1969,
20. WT Mellows ed, *Henry Pytchley's Book of Fees*, NRS, 1927, p62.
21. WT Mellows ed, *Last days of Peterborough Monastery*, NRS, 1947, pp6-8.
22. Ibid, p93.
23. Northants Notes & Queries 1884/5, p33.
24. Peterborough & Hunts Standard 24 May 1901.
25. WT Mellows ed, *Elizabethan Peterborough*, NRS, 1956, p51.

Chapter 12
Sutton Church

A Compilation and Updating of Original Documents

Introduction

For such a small and simple church there is much to fascinate, but any visitor to Sutton's ancient church would be well advised to leave his Pevsner [1] behind. Pevsner, normally so reliable, has got Sutton wrong, very wrong. The bellcote is not 13th century - the present single bellcote is c 1930 and replaced the original double bellcote seen in Figure 12b. The *'fine Norman chancel arch'* regrettably is not Norman – it dates from the 1867 rebuild, and, according to the Victoria County History [2], replaced *a 'plastered partition standing on a wooden beam'*. Pevsner also records a *'recumbent lion, Norman. The back shows this carried a shaft originally. It was thus probably connected with a portal of the type of the Prior's Door at Ely'*. However, Wright's directory of Northants published in 1884 states *'along the wall of the South aisle is a stone bench terminating in the figure of a lion, with a monster on its back'*. Certainly the four holes in the lion's body have been cut to take horizontal and not vertical shafts, and the lion (fig 12c) resembles the *Frith* (Sanctuary) Stool at Sprotborough church, Yorks. I must also take issue with Pevsner's *'little of interest externally'* and prefer Arthur Mee [3] who writes of *'a little Norman church with tall lime trees lining a narrow lane on one side, and the low walls and dark stone roofs of a farm bordering the churchyard on the other. Two terrifying gargoyles on the church wall have been looking Northwards for centuries, and many heads keep them company on the mouldings of the windows'* (Figs 12d & 12m). Mind you, he also suggests the lion may have been the side post of a flight of steps. I personally favour Wright.

Fig 12a. Sutton Church today.

Fig 12b. Sutton Church with its twin bellcote c 1900.

Fig 12c. Norman carving of recumbent lion. Is it a bench end (Wright 1884), sidepost of a flight of steps (Mee 1945) or part of a portal? (Pevsner 1968)

Fig 12d. Two terrifying gargoyles on the church wall.

Also of external interest is the Saxon carved stone, possibly originally the shaft of a churchyard cross, built into the dovecote which forms part of the South wall of the churchyard; and also the two scratch dials on the South East wall of the chapel (Fig 12n).

Description of the Building

The small church of St Michael and All Angels, Sutton, was built in the 12th century, probably between 1120 and 1130 as a chapelry in Castor Parish. It remained a chapel-of-ease to Castor until 1851, when it became an independent parish. In 1903, the parish was united with that of Upton. It again now shares its parish priest with Castor. The right of patronage is shared between Sir Philip Naylor-Leyland Bt of Milton, and Mrs Verity Gunnery, a descendant of the Rev William Hopkinson, a former Lord of the Manor and incumbent of Sutton.

Fig 12e. Carved bracket corbel and 13th century trefoil arch piscina.

Fig 12f. Carvings on the chancel arch capitals – almost certainly by the same hand as those at Castor.

Fig 12g. The base of the chancel arch columns – similar carvings are on the base of columns at Castor.

The Chancel

The only surviving features from the 12th century are the responds and columns of the chancel arch. In the 13th century the chancel was enlarged and a South chapel added. These were largely rebuilt in 1867-8; A Sykes was the architect. The East window above the altar dates from this restoration. In the North wall of the chancel is a small single-light 14th century window, and an internally rebated 15th century two-light window with transom. In the South wall of the chancel there is a 13th century *piscina* under a trefoil arch (Fig 12e), and higher in the wall, an arch, possibly late 13th century, was cut straight through the wall opening into the South chapel. This is similar in date and style to the arch cut in the South wall of the chancel in Castor Church. There is a further arch, semi-circular, with octagonal responds, cut in the wall to the West of the first arch, this providing access to the South chapel. The Norman-style chancel arch dates from the 1867 restoration [4], but the original Norman responds and shafts remain. The capitals and footings of the columns, consisting of interlacing scrollwork and 'elephants' feet', are carved in a style similar to those of Castor chancel columns (figs 12f & 12g). In the East wall of the chancel are two stone corbel-style carved brackets with human heads. These probably at one stage supported figures of Our Lady and St Michael or St Giles, for in the 14th century, every church was ordered to place a figure of Mary and one of the parish patron saint either side of the high altar. There was formerly a low stone screen at the entrance to the chancel, this was removed in 1867.

The South Chapel

The South chapel has a Victorian lancet window in the East wall, and two double-lancet windows, early English albeit restored. The arch leading into the South aisle is Victorian. There is a *piscina*, (not too dissimilar to the one now in 4 Clay Lane Castor) in the South wall of the chapel (fig12h). The South chapel, originally a chantry chapel, is now a vestry.

The Nave

The nave is only 34ft 6 ins by 15ft 3ins. The North doorway dates from the first half of the 13th century. In the latter part of the 15th century, the nave walls were raised, and the roof pitch heightened; the clerestory windows on the nave South wall and the three windows in the North wall date from this time, as do the external diagonal buttresses at the West end. The West wall was at some early stage rebuilt and thickened to support a bellcote, but the West window is Victorian. The corbels in the nave must date from the raising of the nave walls in the 15th century. The pews date from the Victorian restoration.

The South Aisle

A South aisle was created at the end of the 12th century by piercing an arcade of two bays with round-top arches with square *abaci* and plain circular bell capitals and shafts. The aisle is shorter than the nave. In its East bay is a square-headed South window, with ogee-headed lights, and in its West bay a square-headed South doorway with zigzag and pellet moulding. To the East of this doorway is the late 12th century recumbent lion sculpture referred to earlier. The aisle West window is Victorian. Exterior corbels suggest that the aisle was originally longer, with the West end being rebuilt in the restoration of 1867.

Font

The octagonal panelled bowl, perhaps 14th century, is supported on a central octagonal shaft and eight smaller shafts with capitals and bases. The panels may be a later addition (Fig 12i).

Fig 12h. Piscina in South chapel.

The Bells and Bellcote

In 1552 the Inventory of church goods noted (as recorded in North's *Church Bells of Northants* 1878) [5]:

'ffurst in o steple ij smale belles.
Itm in the same a sanct bell.
Itm ij hand bells.'

In 1878 *'the weight of the present single bell (there is a double bellcot) is 1cwt 2qrs 22lb and which at 1s 5d per lb cost £13 13 2'*. It is inscribed: *'J Warner & Sons London 1867 (Royal Arms) Patent (Diam 20 ins)'....*

'At the Death-knell three tolls are given for a man, two for a woman, one for a child before the knell. Until recently the age of the deceased was tolled out. Until the restoration of the church in 1867, it was customary on the first Sunday when Banns of Marriage were published for some young man of the congregation to rush to the bell-rope at the close of the service and jingle the bell.' [5]

Fig 12i. The font.

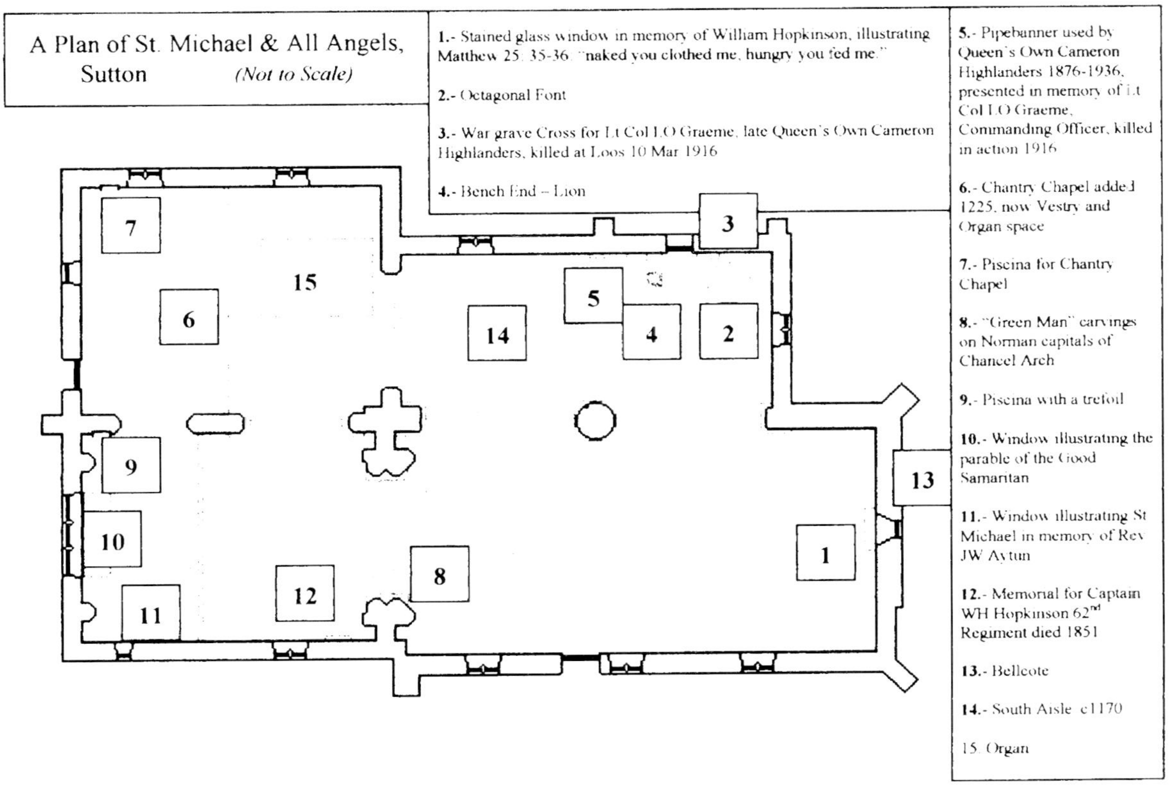

A Plan of St. Michael & All Angels, Sutton *(Not to Scale)*

1.- Stained glass window in memory of William Hopkinson, illustrating Matthew 25, 35-36 "naked you clothed me, hungry you fed me."

2.- Octagonal Font

3.- War grave Cross for Lt Col LO Graeme, late Queen's Own Cameron Highlanders, killed at Loos 10 Mar 1916

4.- Bench End – Lion

5.- Pipebanner used by Queen's Own Cameron Highlanders 1876-1936, presented in memory of Lt Col LO Graeme, Commanding Officer, killed in action 1916

6.- Chantry Chapel added 1225, now Vestry and Organ space

7.- Piscina for Chantry Chapel

8.- "Green Man" carvings on Norman capitals of Chancel Arch

9.- Piscina with a trefoil

10.- Window illustrating the parable of the Good Samaritan

11.- Window illustrating St Michael in memory of Rev JW Aytun

12.- Memorial for Captain WH Hopkinson 62nd Regiment died 1851

13.- Bellcote

14.- South Aisle c1170

15. Organ

Fig 12j. Church plan.

Kelly's Directory of 1914 records *'a Western turret containing two bells; a new bell was added in 1914 from the proceeds of a bequest by Mrs Murton, widow of a former vicar'*. This bell, (the present bell) was cast by Taylors of Loughborough. However, by 1931 Kelly's Directory was recording a single bell, and it appears the present bellcote was rebuilt about this time.

Stained Glass, Monuments and Heraldry

Chancel East window and glass: 1869 the 'Good Samaritan' in memory of William Hopkinson and his daughter.
Chancel North window and glass: a small ogee-headed 14th century light with early 20th century glass of St Michael by Kemp in memory of JW Aytoun 1918.
Nave West window and glass: 19th century stained glass, 1869, illustrating Matthew Ch 25.
South Chapel: a small lancet in the East wall with stained glass in memory of Charles Palmer 1857.
Stained glass in 1791 is described by Bridges [6] as follows:
North window: *'1745 the arms of see of Peterborough, the colours different; the field Az and the charge Or'*.
South Window: *'A. a chevron Or, surmounted of three piles in point G'*.

North Wall
Wall Tablet: William Henry Hopkinson, late Capt 62nd Regt, only son of William Landon Hopkinson, MD d 1851.
Wall Tablet: Elizabeth, wife of William Landon Hopkinson, died 1836; William Landon Hopkinson, died 1876.

South Wall:
Wall Tablet: William Hopkinson, died 1788; wife Elizabeth died 1795. William Hopkinson was born at Upton in 1727, and died in Peterborough. His only son John Hopkinson, BD was Vicar of Morton, Lincs.

South Aisle
Wall Tablet: partially glass fronted: Lieutenant Colonel LO Graeme, CMG, killed at Loos 1916; behind the glass a pipe banner with the regimental emblazon of the 1st Battalion The Queen's Own Cameron Highlanders.

The heraldic arms of the Hopkinsons appear on some of the memorials viz: *'Azure, on a chevron argent, between three estoiles or, three lozenges gules, within a bordure or; Crest: a demy lion rampant sable, incensed gules, first granted to Hopkinson of Alford Lincs, temp Elizabeth I'* [7].

Floor Memorials (from Bridges *History of Northamptonshire* 1796) [6]:
George Bunning, sen died 17 July 1727, aged 47
George Bunning, jun died 23 Jan 1736, aged 29
Anne, relict of George Bunning, and late wife of William Hopkinson died 16 Jan 1763
Elizabeth, wife of William Dewberry, died 10 Sept 1782, aged 67
George David Wales died 10 May 1782 aged 35

The reredos behind the altar is in memory of those who fell in the First World War.

Church Plate

From Markham's *Church Plate of Northants* 1894 [8]:
Silver Cup. Weight 4:3. Height 3 ¾ Diam of top 3, of foot 2 ½ Date circa 1650. No marks
This is a perfectly plain little beaker, of rough workmanship. It is almost cylindrical, with slightly hollowed sides; below it has three horizontal mouldings. There is only one other beaker in this County, and that is at the adjoining hamlet of Upton. It is therefore possible that this was made by a local silversmith in the same form as that at Upton.
Silver Plated Flagon. Height 8. diam. Of centre 3 ½. This is plain and uninteresting.
Pewter Plate. Diam 8 ¼. marks: (1) Between two pillars perhaps hare supporting a garb 'Samuel' above – below: (2) Between two pillars a rose crowned, "Made in London"; (3) Snow Hill London in oblong; (4) In four small shields: Lion's head erased; leopard's head crowned; Britannia; SS for Samuel Smith.
Pewter Plate. Diam 9 ½. Marks: (1) Rose crowned in shaped outline; (2) Eliz Royd in oblong; (3) lion sejant in circle 70 on the dexter side Eliz. (4) In four small shields: Leopard's head; lion rampant to sinister; black-letter E; black-letter R; (5) RB.

The Organ

The organ was made by J Walker in 1855. It was from Waldingfield Church, Suffolk, and was installed at Sutton by Rev William Hopkinson in 1888, and restored in 1961 by the generosity of his daughter, Mrs LO Graeme. Arthur

Mason, who now lives at Castor, used to pump the organ by hand prior to the restoration. He recalls that: *'Provided you kept the barrel full it was not too hard – the trick was to keep the indicator, a lead weight on a string, above head height'*. Nonetheless he does recall looking forward to the sermon! He remembers the restoration when the organ was completely dismantled and laid all over the pews and church floor. There were no services during this work which took about a fortnight. An unusual feature is the early Victorian barrel organ still intact, and of which there are very few examples in existence (Fig 12k).

Fig 12k. Barrel organ.

The Registers
Prior to 1758, all records were kept in Castor registers. One book contains marriages from 1758 to 1807, burials from 1763 to 1812, and baptisms from 1770 to 1812. Subsequent registers are:

Baptisms	1813 – current
Marriages	1813 – 1837
Marriages	1837 – current
Burials	1821 – 1830
Burials	1830 – current
Banns	1824 – current

Non-current registers have been lodged at the Northampton County Records Office.

Episcopal Visitation 1570
Bishop Edmund Scamler made an Episcopal Visitation in 1570 [9]. Such visitations reported not only on the condition of the church fabric and conduct of the priest, but also the behaviour of parishioners as well.
Helpston. *'Ther church is out of repare.'*
Peakirk cum Glinton. *'The parsonage is fallen in decae by the faut of Mr Wynwyrt.'*
Ufford. *'They had but on sermon this tow yere.'*
Stamford St Martin's. *'Edward Bele and Wilson be comon drunkerds and blasphemous of God's Word.'*
Thornhaugh. *'Thomas Baker and his wife dyd not comunicate at Ester last.'*
Werrington. *'Dor Toone impregnata est a quo ignoratur sed illa cum John Hewson vulgariter consociatur.'*
(Dor Toone is pregnant, by whom nobody is sure but rumour has it that John Hewson is responsible – sexual pecadillos were invariably reported in Latin!)
However at:
Upton cum Sutton. *'All is well.'*

Bequests
Recorded by J Fysher 1545 and reported in the Archaeological Journal 1913 [10]:
Sutton St Giles (chapel to Castre) to the sepulchre light - xii d. (twelve pence)
Maintenance to the chapel of Saint Giles in Sutton - iij l iij s iiij d. (three pounds three shillings and fourpence)
+Thomas Mosse of Upton d.1528   *iij s iiij d.* (three shillings and fourpence)
To Sutton Chappell -   *a seme of barle* (a measure of barley)

Recorded 1734. Robert Wright gave town lands to Sutton chapelry producing £9. 15s. 0d. for the poor.

Parish Meeting Minutes [11]:
1898 *'Mrs Mary Elizabeth Tobin, late of Weston-super-Mare, widow deceased, bequeathed a sum of £50 in 2¾% consols to the Rector, Incumbent, Churchwardens and Overseers for the time being of the parish upon trust to apply the dividends of income thereof in maintaining the tomb of her late father and mother, the surplus of such dividends to be distributed in their discretion amongst such of the poor of the parish of Sutton and in such manner as they should think fit.'*

1904. Hopkinson's charity. £200 in India 2½ % estimated to realize £6 p.a. to be used for relief of agricultural workers or their widows resident in the parish.

Restoration of the Chancel, South Chapel and South Aisle

The Vestry Book of 1865 records a decision to restore the church at a cost of £500. Measures were taken to raise a mortgage on the rates for ten years of £125. About the same time the Stamford and Essendine Railway Company, following upon a bill passed by Parliament on 25th July 1861, held a meeting of all parties entitled to commonable rights. The railway company paid £404 15s 0d for the extinction of all common and other rights for the railway to pass through Sutton. This money was used for the restoration of the church. Further contributions were as follows:

Lords of the Manor   £139 18s 0d
Rev W Murton (Curate for 40 years)   £20 0s 0d
Sale of work   £57 2s 4d
Collection from the opening service   £47 7s 3d

With other unrecorded contributions a total of £821 3s 4d was collected. The cost of the restoration was £820 18s 9 ½ d. Note – to make good the chancel roof only, in 1990, cost £13000! The restoration was carried out under the direction of Mr Sykes of Melton. The chancel and South Chapel were in great measure rebuilt, some of the old features being reused.

Church Life in the 1950s

The church played an important part in the life of Sexton, Charlie Favell. He was also in the choir, along with eight or so others, including Steve Britten, Rosalie Britten and Sheila Crane, Charlie's daughter. The men wore surplices. Mrs Graeme played the organ. The vicar was also the vicar of Upton, so they had alternate services with Upton: one week a morning service at Sutton and the next week an evening service at Sutton. The morning service was Mattins, followed by Holy Communion for those who wanted to stay for it. The evening service was Prayer Book Evensong. If some-one was not present for church, Mrs Graeme would send for them, and the service would not start until the missing person had arrived.

Every year on Good Friday the choir would walk to Sutton Wood, near the Southorpe Road, to pick primroses to decorate the church. At Christmas they would go carol singing round the village, and would call at the Grange, where

Fig 12l. St Michael's Church, Sutton c 1902 - only the lighting and heating have changed.

they went in to sing for Mrs Graeme. There would be choir outings, for example to Cheddar Gorge, or Matlock - long journeys but they always returned the same day. The trip was free for members of the choir. Other people in the village could also go if they paid for their fare.

The priests at that time were Mr Hasler, then Mr Beeny, Mr Matthews who rode to church on a bicycle, Canon Turner, Adrian Davies (also Rector of Castor and Marholm,) and then Mr Herbert, who was also an industrial chaplain. They all lived in the Vicarage at Upton (apart from Adrian Davies) – now known as Glebe House. Charlie Favell never went on holiday, never stayed out of the village. He loved the church and his garden. On New Year's Eve, he would go up to the church, and toll out

Fig 12m. ... 'low walls and dark stone roofs of a farm bordering the churchyard',
(A Mee)

the Old Year and ring in the New Year, and then call in at Church Cottage for a whisky. He would light the coke fire in church at Saturday tea-time, and then, at midnight, go up to the church to stoke the fire so it was ready for Sunday. He had a beautiful singing voice. His wife used to clean the church on Friday afternoons. If a lay-reader came to take a service, Charlie would always ask him in for tea. He died 11th April 1984 aged 79. His daughter, Sheila, born in the village, is the last of the original villagers in Sutton.

The Dedication – St Michaels or St Giles?

And finally the dedication - curiously the Victoria County History gives the dedication as St Giles based on a will in Northampton Record Office in which Thomas Mosse of Upton left 3s 4d to the chapel of St Giles in Sutton in 1528. The diocesan archivist has no record of a dedication other than St Michael, and points out that to change a church dedication requires an act of parliament. I have been unable to discover any such act.

I offer two hypotheses.
Firstly the main church may always have been dedicated to St Michael. However the South (chantry) Chapel may have been dedicated to St Giles, the patron saint of lepers and cripples. Prior to the surrender of the Abbey to Henry V111 on 30th November 1539 the manor of Sutton was administered and farmed by the Abbey Almoner who was responsible for such unfortunates and may have used the healthier as estate workers who would worship at, if not in the church. The VCH also mentions one of the church windows having internal rebates for a frame. These could originally have held shutters so the sacrament could be passed out to those not permitted to enter the church.

My second hypothesis is that on the dissolution of the Abbey and transfer of the chapel to the Dean and Chapter of the new Cathedral, the new authorities may have felt they wished to make a clean break with its former association with the Almoner, and chose what they felt to be a more appropriate Saint as patron. In the middle ages St Michael was one of the most popular saints and many parish churches were dedicated to him. He is regarded as the protector of all Christian causes and is often portrayed as overcoming the dragon (the symbol of evil) as depicted in our modern patronal banner and as described in the Book of Revelation.

Keith Garrett

Fig 12n. Scratch dial on the South wall of chantry chapel.

Notes

1.   N Pevsner *Buildings of England Series, Bedfordshire, Huntingdon and Peterborough*, Penguin 1968, p350.
2.   *Victoria County History, Northamptonshire,* 1901.
3.   Arthur Mee, *King's England, Northamptonshire,* Hodder & Stoughton, 1945, p321.
4.   *Royal Commission for Historic Monuments* 1969.
5.   North's *Church Bells of Northampton,* 1878.
6.   Bridges, *History of Northamptonshire,* 1796.
7.   WT Collins, *Heraldry Survey of Sutton Church* Heraldry Society, 2000.
8.   Markham's *Church Plate of Northamptonshire* 1894.
9.   An Episcopal Visitation *Northants Notes and Queries, Vol* II, 1907-9.
10. *Archaeological Journal,* 1913.
11. *Parish Meeting minute book.*

Acknowledgements

N Warnes, *Guide to Sutton Church .*
Sheila Crane.

Fig 12o. Rev William Hopkinson MA JP, Vicar of Sutton 1891, first Vicar of Sutton cum Upton 1903-1909; born 1840 died 1929.

Fig 12p. Anglo-Saxon carved stone – possibly former cross shaft on East wall of the dovecote on the South side of the churchyard.

Fig12q. Bracket, possibly a former corbel, now by the altar in the chancel.

Chapter 13
The Buildings of Sutton

The initial proposals for Peterborough New Town included a Castor township that would have extended from Ailsworth Westward both sides of the A47 to the Southorpe Road junction. Accordingly a survey of antiquities was carried out by the Royal Commission for Historic Monuments (RCHM) and published in 1969. (Some of the older village residents may remember the SOS – Save Our Sutton – campaign). All those buildings listed by the RCHM have been included in this chapter. The letter alongside indicates its map location. In addition buildings that lay outside the designated area, for example the station and the sheepwash have also been included. Details of St Michael's Church are in Chapter 12.

Buildings Listed by the RCHM

The Cross, consisting of the base and socket only, is at the junction of Sutton Crossways and Ermine Street, a rectangular stone 29ins by 33ins. To commemorate the Queen's Golden Jubilee, in 2001, the area surrounding the cross was restored, and an old stone inserted in the socket. The original cross shaft has long gone, for there was only a water filled socket at the time of the Black Death (1348). **a**

The Grange is a two storey house with stone walls and a stone-slated roof. It was built in the late 17th century on an H-shaped plan, incorporating some older walling in the South end of the West wing. Considerable additions have been made since the middle of the 19th century. The front was remodelled in 1880 – the datestone is inscribed 'WH 1880' – incorporating a 13th century double lancet window which may be from the church chancel, rebuilt with a new East window in 1867. The windows have stone mullions and transoms, but all are restored except in the South end of the East wing, where the jambs are original. The interior has been entirely refitted. The Granary, North East of the house and the Dovecote, South of the church, are initialled and dated 'WH 1786' and 'WH 1803' respectively. WH refers to William Hopkinson, whose family bought the manor of Sutton including the Grange off the Church. **b**

Manor Farm is a two storey house with stone walls and a stone-slated roof. It was built in the late 17th century on an H-shaped plan. The North cross-wing was extended in the 19th century and some reconstruction is commemorated in a datestone of 1900 with the intials 'WH'. The windows have ovolo-moulded stone mullions. The original staircase survives as do many old beams and a 17th century fireplace. **c**

Fig13a. Sutton Cross: Base of Saxon Cross at the junction of Ermine Street and the old A47.

Fig13b.1. The Grange: North front datestone 'WH 1880' showing reused 13th century window.

Fig13b.2. The Grange Granary: datestone 'WH 1786'.

Fig13b.3. The Grange Dovecote: datestone 'WH 1803'.

Fig13c.1. Manor Farm: datestones 'JD 1700' (J Dove) on North Bay; 'WH 1900' on South Bay.

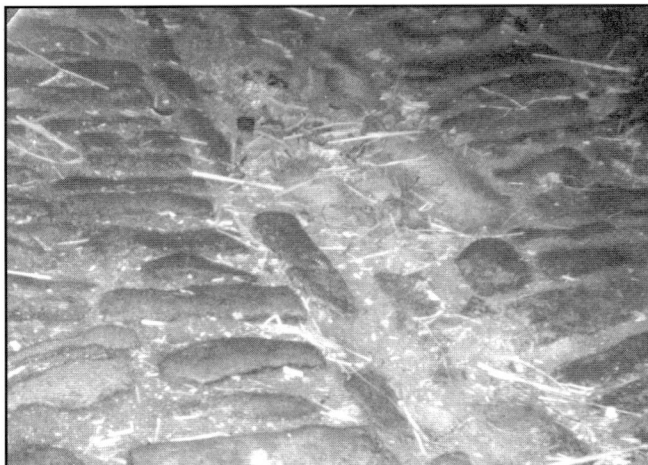

Fig13c.3. Manor Farm Barn 1845: floor detail; Pendle laid edge side up with central gutter.

Fig13c.2. Manor Farm Barn.

Fig13c.4. Manor Farm Barn: king post roof trusses 'WG. WF. IF 1845'.

House built in the late 17th century on a two-room plan with central chimneystack, was enlarged by the addition of a West wing probably early in the 19th century. The windows have ovolo-moulded stone mullions and straight ogee-moulded labels. **d**

Pair of Cottages, now a single dwelling, built in the mid 19th century. Windows had cast-iron casements divided into small hexagonal and diamond panes, but they have now been replaced. **e**

House mid 19th century has reused 17th century windows in the North wall. A single-storey outbuilding to the East is dated 'IC 1737'. Isaac Cant appears on the 1762 Militia List as a labourer. **f**

Houses built as a pair of cottages each of one room on plan, probably in the 18th century, have been much enlarged. The original chimneystacks are of yellow brick. **g**

Fig13d. 19 Graeme Road.

Fig13e. 12 Graeme Road.

House, 17th century, built on hall-and-parlour plan, had been converted into two dwellings, but now a single dwelling again. It contains a large oven built into the West wall and is now known as the Old Bakehouse. **h**

House, now Graeme House, built on hall-and-parlour plan c1700, had a third room added to the West in the 18th century; it was extended to the North in the mid 19th century. The 19th century porch in the Gothic style was added after the house became a vicarage when Sutton became a separate parish in 1851. **i**

Church Cottage, now 1 Lovers' Lane, 17th century, was built on a two-room plan with one end chimney; a second, central, chimney with a brick stack was inserted later in the 17th century. The bressummer to the central open fireplace is carried on a reused 12th century carved stone with chevron ornament. Its outhouse still contains an original earth closet and copper. A Victorian post-box is built into the West wall. **j**

Barns, three, including one, to the East, of the late 18th century with a roof of clasped-purlin construction and two, to the South West and North West, of the mid 19th century now demolished. These occupied the present sites of 20 and 22 Nene Way which reused the stone. Indeed No 22 is known as 'Barnstock'. **k**

Fig13f and g. Numbers 10, 6 and 4 Graeme Road: left outbuilding dated 1738; centre 19th century house with reused 17th century window; right pair of cottages.

Fig13h. Old Bakehouse.

Fig13j.1. Church Cottage: 1 Lovers' Lane with Victorian letter box and outhouse.

Fig13i. Old Vicarage: now Graeme House.

Fig13j.3. Church Cottage: outhouse copper.

Fig13j.2. Church Cottage: outhouse privy

Cottages, one detached and a terrace of three, were built in the mid 19th century with walls of rock-faced ashlar. Windows have cast-iron casements with small hexagonal and diamond panes. The terrace of three has been converted to two dwellings and the cast iron casements replaced with timber. The single cottage retains its original cast iron casements. **l**

House, mid 19th century has been much altered and enlarged; the original plan comprised a central entrance and stair-hall with flanking rooms. **m**

Cottage, built in the 17th century on a single room plan, retains some original stone-mullioned windows. **n**

Cottage, formerly the Cross Keys Public House, was built on a hall-and-parlour plan probably in the 18th century; the upper storey has a datestone inscribed 'WH 1888' when a second storey was added. **o**

Fig13l.1. Numbers 18, 14, 12 Nene Way.

Fig13l.2. On bicycle Leonard Brown (b 1878) In doorway William David Brown (b 1873) and Ada Mary Brown (b 1868). Now 12 Nene Way.

Fig13m. The Laurels.

Fig13o. The Old Cross Keys pub: now a private house.

Fig13n. Half Acre Cottage.

Other Buildings of Interest (Not Listed by the RCHM)

Fig13p.1. Sutton Station c 1886. Picture supplied by Mrs Anna Macdonald whose great-grandfather, Joseph Stevenson, was a foreman platelayer and would be one of those on the platform.

Fig13p.2. Station weighbridge cabin built 1867.

Fig13p.3. Former Stationmaster's house built 1867.

Fig13q. The Bridge taking Nene Way across the old railway track in the village as it may have looked prior to closure in 1929. Photo reconstruction by Ian Long. The lady in the picture is Ian's wife Mary.

Fig13r. The Footbridge to Wansford Station by foot path no2 as it was in 1896 (Peterborough Museum Society).

Fig13t. The Village Pound: re-sited here c1866 from its former site where Nene Way Road Bridge crosses the old railway track. The Vestry Book in 1858 reads 'All cows sent to graze on the green baulks to be led by halters and the pounder to impound all found without. A charge to be made to recover animals from the pound'.

Fig13s. The Reading Room: built before 1894, when records show the first parish meeting was held here.

Fig13u. The Old Boathouse: It is shown on a tithe map of 1843 and was burnt down in the 1960s.

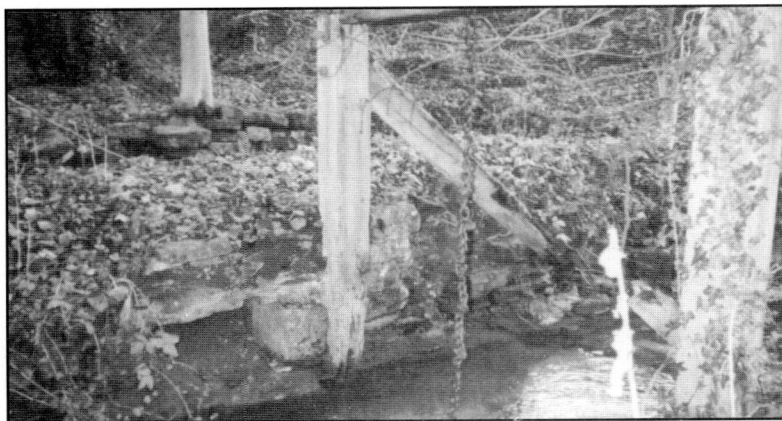

Fig13w.1. The Sheepwash: datestone 'WH 1844'. A shutter would be lowered by a capstan thus damming the stream and diverting water through the adit at the bottom of the lefthand post.

Fig13w.2. The Sheepwash: When the sheepwash was filled, (the water-exit (top right just in front of the arch) would be dammed. The sheep would be pushed in over a wooden ledge at the top where the ivy is now and make their way against the current to climb out along the ramp (bottom centre). Men with dunking poles would stand on the walls either side to make sure the sheep were thoroughly immersed.

Keith Garrett

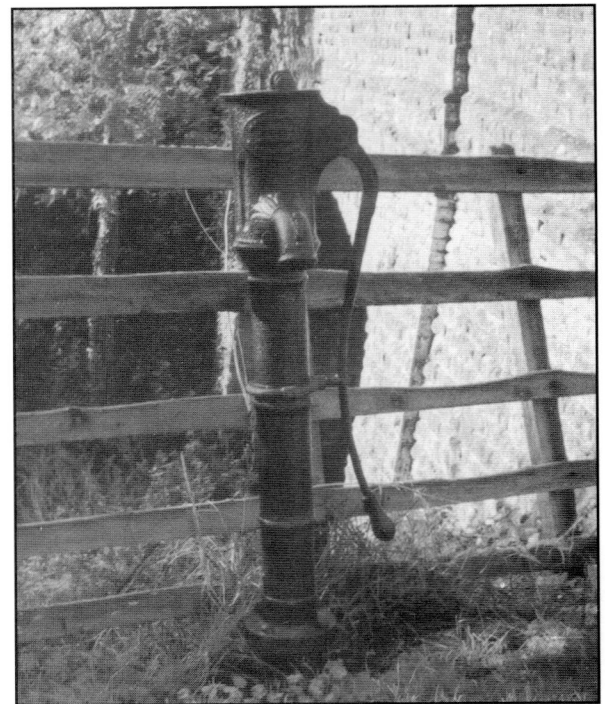

Fig13v. The Parish Pump: Mains water did not come to the village until after the war and mains sewerage not until 1989.

The Drift is an interesting old road name and indicates that cattle used to be driven up this road. One can imagine cattle from South of the river crossing the ford and being driven through the village to the 18th century Cross Keys Inn, where the drovers could rest and refresh themselves before continuing along the Drift to Stamford Market via Southorpe. There was a small walled enclosure opposite the Cross Keys shown on the tithe map, which might have been used as a cattle-pen while the drovers rested – there is no evidence of a house having been on the site.

Chapter 14
Upton History and Buildings

There has been a settlement at Upton since at least the Roman period and possibly earlier. The general RCHM archaeological survey of 1968 identifies three enclosures in the parish of Upton. One is marked by well-defined and wide ditches that enclose a rectangular area of 1.5 acres at the point Ermine Street joins with the Roman road to Wansford. It is only visible from the air. There is a second enclosure of two acres immediately to the North West of the first.

North East of the Roman enclosures is a larger undated enclosure of 2.25 acres that could indicate earlier occupation. It is apparently divided into two equal parts by an internal ditch and there appear to be traces of a smaller enclosure to its North West. There is also an enclosure complex that crosses the boundary with Ailsworth parish.

A Roman villa was surveyed in the Autumn of 2002, prior to which, coins dating from AD330, and a 1st century bronze brooch were found [1]. The villa consists of a main block measuring 35 metres by 18 metres on NNE-SSW orientation. A large number of tesserae, hypocaust and roof tiles found at the site all suggest a large residential building. A few years ago parts of columns were found, and a Roman coffin was discovered on Model Farm land. It is now used for cultivating wall-flowers. A Saxon gilt brooch was also discovered at Upton, reported in *Anglo-Saxon Cambridgeshire.*

In addition to Roman enclosures there is evidence of extensive Medieval ridge and furrow cultivation to the North of Top Lodge where three interlocked furlongs meet along the course of a small stream. The open fields of the parish were enclosed in 1843.

The most historical buildings in the village are certainly the Manor Farm House and the church. West of the church there is a small thatched cottage, built in the 16th century and rebuilt from dereliction in the 1950s. An inscription on a dedication stone on the front of the cottage reads:

'This Elizabeth I cottage then derelict restored 1957 by Harry Paten Chairman of The Peterborough Society with the generous collaboration from The 10th Earl Fitzwilliam President of the Society.'

At the West end of Upton stands Model Farm, which dates from 1685. It has a hipped roof, oblong moulded chimney shafts and symmetrically placed mullion windows [2]. Other buildings include Glebe House, the thatched Keeper's Cottage, and some 19th century houses, as well as newer council houses built in the early 1960s.

The manor represents, in effect, the early history of Upton other than the church. In essence the manor is defined by its geographical area, the fact that there was a Lord of the Manor, and that it

Fig 14a. Model Farm House built 1685. (Photo: J Tovey)

Fig 14b. Model Farm barns: the old barns were extended in the 19th century by the addition of barns that look like engine sheds. (Photo: J Tovey)

Fig 14c. Top Lodge Farmhouse 1920s: presumably the people are the Harris family's predecessors.

Fig 14d. Top Lodge Farm in 1950s: before the old barns were demolished.

Fig 14e. Manor Farm in 1930s: note the gable end extension on the right.

had a Manorial Court. Upton Manor appears in the charter of Wulfhere of Peterborough in 664, but not in the Domesday Book. However, it could have been included in the Ailsworth/Castor entry.

In the 12th century it was held by Godwin of Upton, then by the Wattervilles of Marholm. The Holding of Hugh de Waterville was confirmed to Peterborough Abbey by Richard I and Henry III in 1146 [3]. However, the Wattervilles lost the manor for a time. In 1176 it was taken from Ralph de Waterville and handed to Robert de Neville in punishment for de Waterville's participation in the 1174 rebellion against Henry II.

The manor then passed by marriage to the de Dive family. Asceline de Waterville recovered the manor from Ralph de Nevill in 1190. One of her two daughters, Maud, married William de Dive. Hugh de Dive was holding land in Upton as late as the reign of Edward I (1272-1307). The second daughter of Asceline de Waterville, also named Asceline, married one of the Torpel family and took the manor at Upton as her dowry. It then passed by the marriage of her daughter to Ralph Camoys.

The demesne consisted of five virgates [4] and a quarter of arable land, with six acres of meadow, and eight and three quarters virgates worked by labourers [5].

Ralph Camoys' son John then sold the manor illegally to Eleanor of Castille, Queen of Edward I, which led to the King granting custody of the lands to Peterborough Abbey at rent of £100 in 1290. In 1308 the manor was granted to Piers Gaveston by Edward II, who two years later, exchanged the manor and other lands for the county of Cornwall. Upton then passed to Edward's nephew John Earl of Surrey and then on to other relations and members of the royal family including the Earls of Kent, and the wife of Edward the Black Prince, mother of Richard II, and Edward IV (1461-1470 & 1471-1483). Edward then granted the lands to his mother.

In 1492 Upton was granted to Elizabeth wife of Henry VII (1485-1509) and during

Fig 14f. Air photograph of Manor Farm in late 1950s.

the reign of Henry VIII (1509-1547) formed part of the dower of four of his queens. The lands at Upton were afterwards granted to Sir Richard Wingfield in 1543-4 who built the manor house.

There was a second manor at Upton which never became a full manor there being no record of a manorial court. It was an amalgamation of two holdings, one of a manor at Southorpe and the other of land held by a Geoffrey of Upton. It was sold by John Stidolf to Robert Wingfield in 1562, thus uniting all Upton Manor.

There is not a lot left of the original manor building. What remains is a short length of the house with flat pointed mullion windows on the ground floor and square headed on the first floor. It is described thus in Bridges' *History of Northamptonshire* published in 1796:

'In the hall windows are the Wingfield's, and other escutcheons of arms [6]. *At the end are bow windows projecting very high, with balconies and stone work over them; and to the West is an embattled turret with small windows, but the house has been*

Fig 14g. Manor Farm 2004: All that is left of Upton Manor House; this house started as the Manor House for the Wingfields, was then bought by the Dove family, all but the kitchen range demolished after 1750, the gable wing on the East side demolished more recently, and the outbuildings replaced in the 1980s.
(Photo: J Tovey)

Fig 14h. Elizabethan Cottage. (Photo: J Tovey)

Fig 14i. Keeper's Cottage. (Photo: J Tovey)

Fig 14j. Model Cottages: Victorian farm workers' cottages. (Photo: J Tovey)

pulled down many years except the meaner offices, which now serve for a farm house.'

Following a renewal of the grant between Robert Wingfield and James I in 1613-14, the manor was sold to Sir William Dove in 1625. The Doves continued to hold the lands until 1750 – when it was sold to Lord Fitzwilliam – but borrowed on the property over the years. For example, an act of Parliament was passed in 1719 to allow Thomas Dove to raise £2000 on his estates at Upton, Sutton, Ailsworth and Castor for settlement of debts [7].

Since 1750 the manor has been owned by Milton estates and variously farmed by tenants up to the present day. The Tebbutt family were the longest-serving Milton tenant farmers, occupying Manor Farm, Upton for most of the 18th and 19th centuries. Two other major buildings, Model Farm and Top Lodge, are also farms, worked by the Longfoots and the Harrises respectively. As such a rural hamlet, Upton has always had a small population. In the Compton Census of 1676 there were 58 Conformists listed in Upton. This figure has fluctuated but has not grown appreciably. Census figures from 1981 put the population at 80.

Despite this, Upton provided three bill men and a constable with the residue of the town providing a harness for a man, according to the muster rolls of Nassaburgh Hundreds in 1536. The militia lists of 1762 show five men between the ages of 18 and 45, and the constable, John Sharman. These men were either servants or labourers.

The importance of farming to the rural community cannot be over emphasised. Perhaps one small illustration of this was reported in the Annals of Castor, a diary kept by John Hales, and published in the *Peterborough Citizen* in 1922. He reported that on 2nd October 1842: *'John Culpin of Upton cut his throat with a razor but not so as to kill himself. He was removed to Peterborough on suspicion of stealing three sacks of wheat from Mr J Tebbutt's [Manor Farm]. It was found in his garden, and he was sentenced to 15 years' transportation.'*

Fig 14k. Glebe House, the former vicarage built in 1912. (Photo: J Tovey)

Apart from the Manor and farms, and the 16th century cottage, the other most significant building in Upton is Glebe House, which was built as a vicarage in 1912. Around the same time the village hall was constructed, consisting of a small green painted corrugated iron hut that still exists today.

The building has had various uses including youth clubs and a drill hall for the Upton and Sutton Home Guard, which included Upton men such as Ralph Hornsby and Arthur and Charlie Harris of Top Lodge Farm.

A number of council houses were built on Church Walk, Upton in the late 1950s and early 1960s between Glebe House and the 'model cottages'. Some of these were built behind a row of three stone cottages which were then demolished. This marked the last development in the village, which remains an isolated rural hamlet.

John Howard

John Howard was born and brought up in Castor the son of Jack and Kate McNaughton. He grew up with his brothers Walter and Sam in what is now Vine House on Church Hill. Educated at Castor School, King's Peterborough and the University of Leicester, where he read English Literature, John earns a crust as a writer and journalist. After living in Canada and Spain for a time John now lives in Castor with wife Marta and son Charlie and daughter Alba.

Fig 14l. Village Hall. (Photo: J Tovey)

Notes

1. Paul Middleton, *Top Lodge Farm, Upton; Interim Report on Pre-excavation Survey,* January 2003.
2. N Pevsner, *Churches,* 1968, p.359.
3. Hugh Candidus, *The Peterborough Chronicle,* ed W T Mellows, 1997, p5.
4. A virgate is a measurement of land – usually 30 acres according to the *Oxford English Reference Dictionary.*
5. Bridges, *History of Northamptonshire,* 1796, p507.
6. A list of the arms and escutheons can be found in K Gibson's *Antonine Itinerary,* 1800, pp210-211.
7. Georgii C.6 (1719).

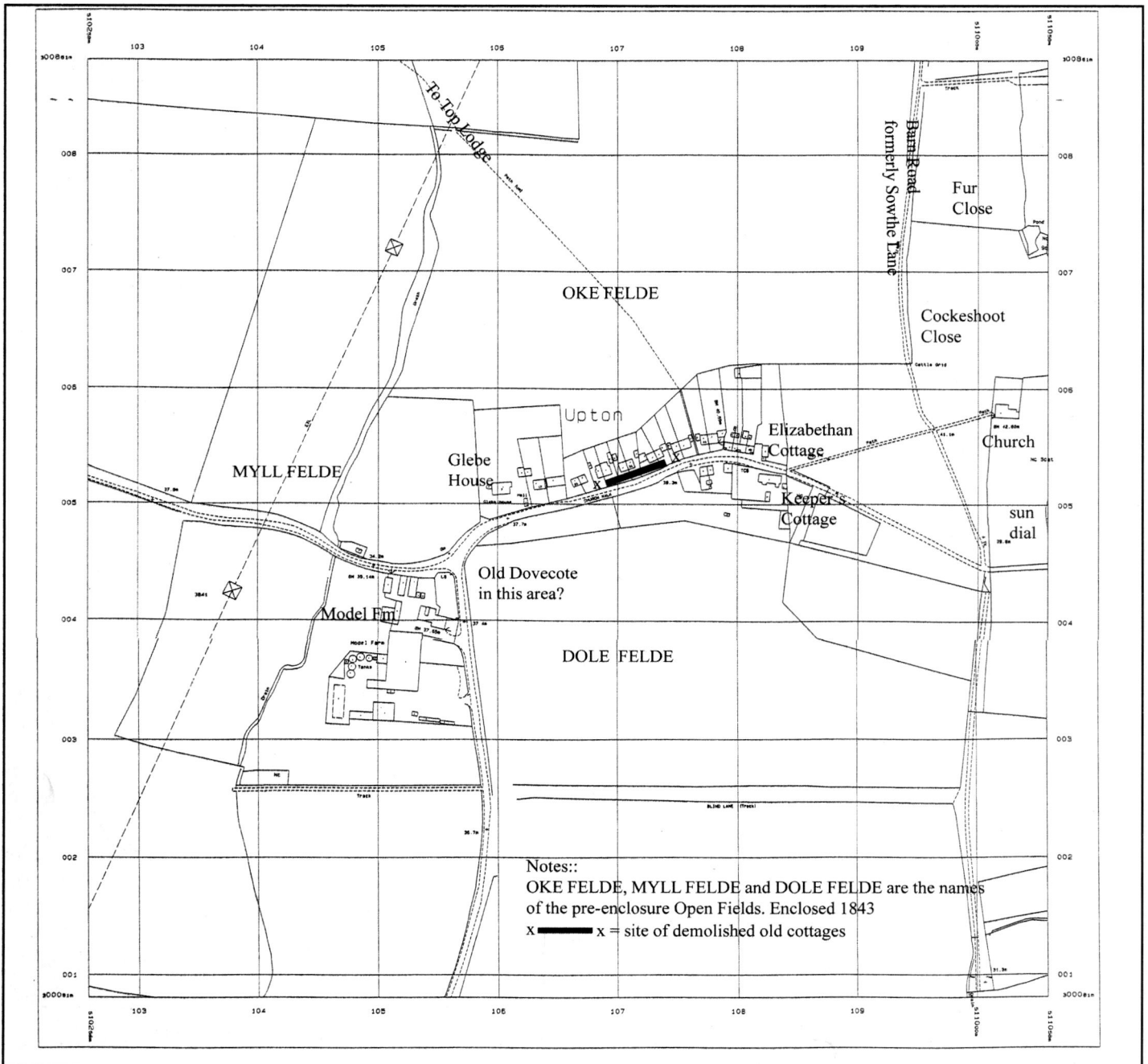

Map of Upton. Reproduced from Ordnance Survey mapping on behalf of The Controller of Her Majesty's Stationery Office © Crown Copyright 100042620 2004

Fig 14n. The only known photograph (taken c 1912) of the cottages. Until they were demolished in 1959, there was only ever one tap with running water which they all shared. It was on the roadside, in front of the central cottage. The drain is still in the road.

Fig 14m. Sketch of the row of three thatched stone cottages as remembered by Lyn Bell nee Hornsby. These cottages, with front walls on the kerb-side, were demolished in about 1959, after the council houses had been built behind them. When Lyn Bell was a child, Allen and Joyce Herbert lived in the left hand cottage, Lyn with her parents Wilf and Laura Hornsby in the centre cottage, and her uncle and aunt, Fred and Annie Hornsby, lived in the right hand one.

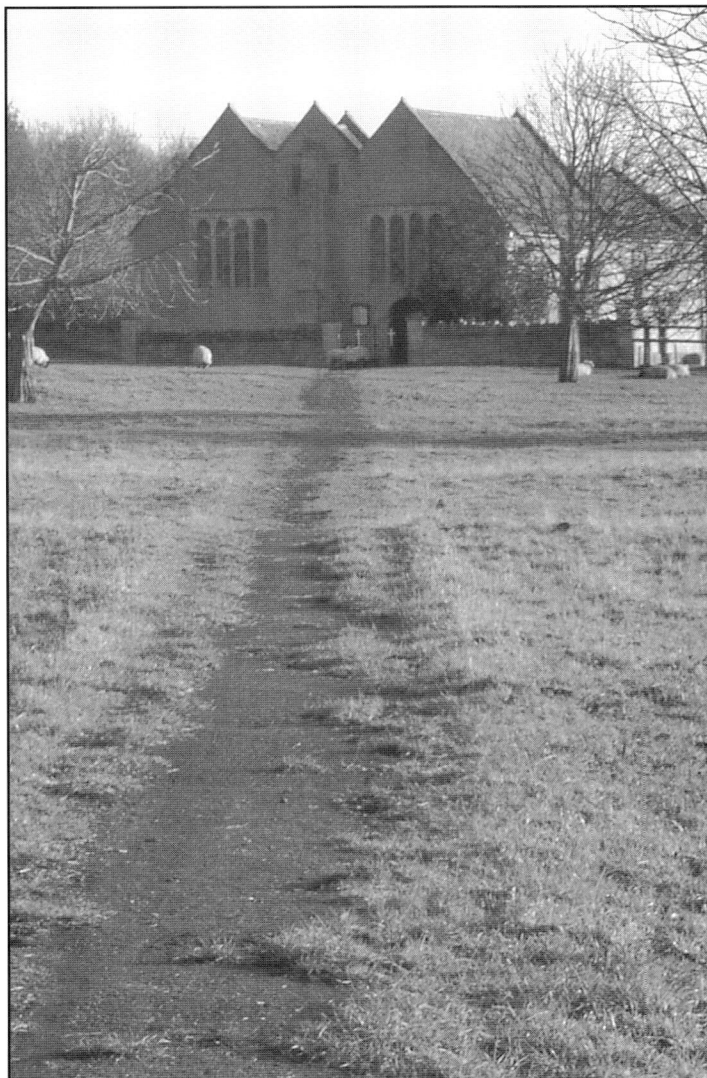

Fig 14n. The path across Church (Chapel) Close from the village of Upton to the church.

Fig14o. David Longfoot (in cab) loading fertilizer with Sam Jeffery in the yard at Model Farm Upton 2004 (Michael Longfoot behind the cab).

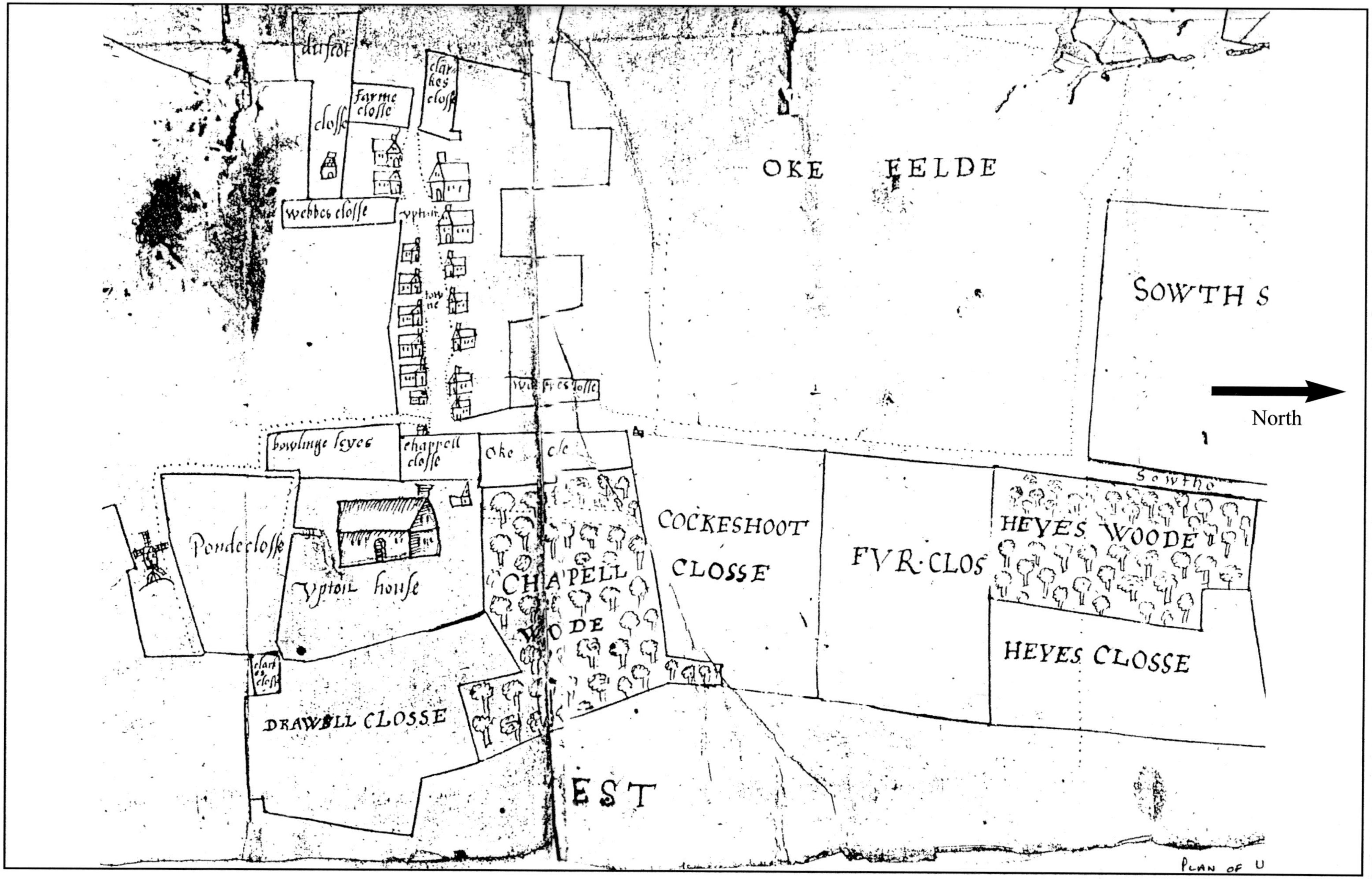

Fig 14o. Map of Upton 1582, drawn by Toby Houghton. North is to the right of the map. Note the dovecot ('dufcot') at the top and the windmill on the left. 'Chapel Wode' is now called Upton Wood, but its dimensions and boundaries have not changed over 420 years (compare with the 1:50000 map). 'Heyes Wode' is now called Hayeswood Spinney. The track running from left to right (North-South) in front of 'Chapel Wode' and 'Heyes Wode' is now called Barn Road, but was known then as 'Sowthe Lane'. The Roman road, King's Street or the Long Ditch (Langdyke) runs along the bottom (Eastern) edge of 'Cockeshoot Closse', 'Fur Clos' and 'Heyes Closse'. Note the names of the pre-enclosure Open Fields. (Courtesy Fitzwilliam Archives NCRO)

150

Chapter 15

Upton Church

The Church of St John the Baptist is remote and its history is closely linked with that of Castor Church. It occupies a field to the East of the hamlet of Upton, close to woods. It was built in AD 1120 during the reign of Henry I as a Chapel-of-ease to Castor Church. Upton became a separate parish in 1851, and in 1903 was united with Sutton. It is now part of the Benefice of Castor with Sutton and Upton, and Marholm, retaining close historical links with Castor Church.

The right of recommending a member of the clergy for a vacant benefice or making the appointment, the advowson, for the chapel of Upton in connection with Castor was confirmed to Peterborough Abbey by Richard I and Henry III, but the chief right to it was held by the lords of the manor. According to Hugh Candidus, author of *The Peterborough Chronicle,* who lived during the reigns of Henry I, Stephen and Henry II and was *'...at one time sub-prior of the Abbey, under Abbot Martin and then Abbot William de Waterville...',* a Papal Bull of Pope Eugenius III confirmed Castor and therefore Upton, to the Abbey of Peterborough, including *'whatsoever goods and possessions...Castor with the church and the chapels adjoining the same church with the mills and all its appurtenances'* [1]. This was during the time of Abbot Martin on 17th December AD 1146. Upton is specified as *'These estates which are held in fee from the same monastery...; the fee of Ascelin de Waterville: Thorp(Achurch), Marholm, and Upton, with all their appurtenances...'* [2].

Upton Church appears to have two dedications. In 1521 a John Strete of Upton left his body to be buried at Castor, but made a bequest to the 'Chapel of St Helen of Upton.' [3] Either the dedication of the church was changed about the end of the 16th century, or within the Church at Upton there was a side-chapel dedicated to St Helen, the mother of Emperor Constantine the Great, the first Christian Roman Emperor. Constantine was born in York, and there is a legend that his mother Helen was British. It seems likely that the North Aisle was a chantry chapel dedicated to St Helen, hence the confusion.

Fig 15a. The Church of St John the Baptist, Upton. (Photo: J Tovey)

Fig 15b. Bell Cote

Fig 15c. Chancel Arch - the shafts with their cushion capitals are not later than 1120.

Fig 15d. Pulpit: early 17th century semi-octagonal drum style, elaborately carved with vine leaves, grapes and flowers.

The twin-gabled church building consists of a nave and an aisle of equal width. A bell cote is situated behind a smaller central gable. It houses a single bell, weight 4cwt 3qrs, inscribed *'X T Hulman CW cast 1989'*. T Hulman is thought to have been a Church Warden at Upton. This bell replaced two smaller bells and one hand bell that were recorded in 1552.

The aisle was added towards the end of the 12th century, and the capitals and responds of the arcade from that date still remain. The South and West walls of the nave were rebuilt in the 17th and 18th centuries, while the chancel was rebuilt in its entirety in 1842. The chancel arch as described in the *Northamptonshire VCH* has: *'twin half-round shafts on the jambs with cushion capitals, and on the West face a small nookshaft with a similar capital on the North side, the corresponding shaft on the South having been cut away to make room for the pulpit'*.

The sanctuary is furnished in the Laudian style – although the furnishing pre-dates Archbishop Laud, who was executed by Parliament in 1645. The altar and altar rails are arranged for Prayer Book Worship of the Jacobean period. The octagonal pulpit is early Jacobean with carved arched panels, probably one of the finest remaining in the country. It is in such good condition due to the isolation of the church itself.

The Font, as it is now, is 17th century. The Altar table dates from c1620, and the altar rails are probably earlier. Behind the rails there are also two Jacobean oak chairs. The church plate consists of a beaker, possibly German c1610, and a paten c1680 bearing the Dove crest, the gift of Ann, widow of Thomas Dove, and a cup dated 1769.

The North Aisle was widened in the 1627 to include the stone steps, piers and balustrading to make space for the Dove family tomb, initiated by Sir William Dove, son of Thomas Dove, Bishop of Peterborough (1601-1630), and nicknamed by Elizabeth I as her 'silver dove' [4].

The tomb is built of Barnack stone with a canopy supported by four Ionic style pillars. On each side is a dove with an olive branch in its beak, the Dove family badge. Under the canopy is the armoured figure of Sir William Dove (died 1633), between his two wives. His first wife, Frances Downhall lies on his right; his second, Dorothy Neville, lies on his left. The tomb and effigies are thought to be the work of Nicholas Stone, Master Mason to James I and Charles I.

There are three sets of arms in the panels on the tomb chest. The West side is the Dove family arms *'of azure, a cross formy between four doves argent'* [5]. On the East side the arms are a combination of Dove and Downhall. The quartered arms are *'azure, a cross formy between four doves argent, impaling quarterly one and four, gules, a bend dancetty sable, and Downhall quarterly in two a fesse between six fishes haurient argent and in three a gryphon segreant sable'*.
The South side join the arms of Dove and Neville, forming *'azure a cross formy between four doves argent, impaling quarterly one and four a saltire ermine; two and three, gules, fretty or, on a canton per pale ermine and or, a lymphad with three masts sails furled sable'* [6]. The ship is included because the Nevilles trace their ancestry from William the Conqueror's admiral Neville. On the West wall of the North aisle there is also a wall monument to Mary, wife of Henry Dove, died 2nd

152

Fig 15e. Paten; engraved 'The Guift of Ann ye widdow of Thomas Dove Esqr of Upton 1683'. (Photo: NADFAS)

Fig 15f. Two Handled Cup: engraved with the sacred chi-rho monogram, assayed Newcastle 1769. 'Donated to the church by William Andrew, priest of Upton. On the tenth anniversary of his ordination in 1869'. (Photo: NADFAS)

Feb 1749, and her daughter Grenvill (sic), widow of Wright Serjeant of Castor, died 15th Nov 1814, with the Dove family crest.

The Wingfields, Lords of the Manor of Upton, also had a tomb in the church. According to Strype in his *Life of Whitgift*, Robert Wingfield was granted a licence to build a private family monument with a vault at Upton Church on 9 January 1601. The vault was made on the North side of the chancel. However, the vault was later taken down, or excluded by Sir William Dove. No trace now remains of a monument to any Wingfields in the church.

Fig 15g. Chalice Beaker, dated 1610-1620, possibly of German or Netherlands origin with three medallions of profile heads. (Photo: NADFAS)

Despite the fact that Upton Church is a small and isolated building, it has by far the oldest and most historically interesting wooden furnishings in the benefice. Indeed this may be due to its isolation, as it was by-passed by the Victorian fashion for replacing older fittings. In addition to the fittings already described, the Parish Chest is 17th century oak with iron straps. It is possible that the choir stalls were those shown in an old photograph in Castor Church chancel and moved to Upton in the 1890s. There are, in the church, some fine old brass and wrought iron candelabra brackets. The organ was made by Norman and Beard of Lewes Sussex in 1908. The lectern, serving as the Village War Memorial, was made in the 1920s.

Fig 15h. The Dove Monument: the North aisle was elevated and rebuilt to accommodate the memorial. There are 14 lead coffins in the vault below.

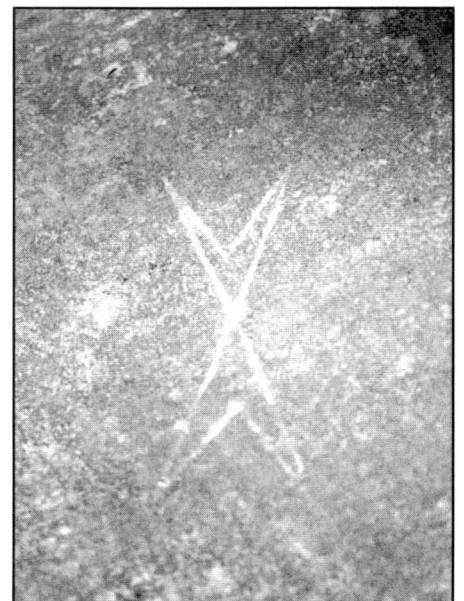

Fig 15i. Masons' Marks: these marks can be found in a number of places, including the balustrade, and appear to be associated with 17th century work in the North aisle. (Photo: NADFAS)

Fig 15j. Altar Table: dark oak, dated 1620, it includes the classic bulbous legs with cups carved with acanthus leaves.

Fig 15k. Chair: dark oak 17th century joined chair, with carved initials 'JD', incorporating older wood carvings.(JD is presumably John Dove).

Fig 15l. Chair: dark oak, engraved 'Joane Browne A WANT NOT D 1700'; joined chair again incorporating older wooden panel.

Outside, there is an intricately carved sundial in the field South of the church – which formed part of an Elizabethan garden linking the church and the Manor – dating from the time of Charles I.

It is a pedestal with regular plinths and base mouldings. It is designed to show the hour of the day as the sun shadows each compartment during its course, but there was no gnomon on the top of the dial. The West elevation was believed to have given the hour seven times from the seven planes contained in the main compartment [7].

A local legend attached to the church suggests the presence of a tunnel linking the church with the manor house. The legend has it that the church was once a cell of the Abbey of Burgh, and that Benedictine Brethren accumulated treasure there, which was never accounted for when they left. According to the tale, a local farm worker who was sinking a post hole close to the church came across a stone slab, which when raised revealed a paved tunnel. One end was said to lead to a secret exit from the church and the other end was found to be blocked by a fall of stone. Could there still be hidden treasure in Upton? Who knows?

More recently a banner was sewn by Rosie (Mimi) Goodacre to celebrate the Millennium. The present Church Wardens, Michael Longfoot of Model Farm and Peter Harris of Top Lodge Farm, were both born in the parish. It is likely that Upton Church, in the near future, will revert to the status of its first 700 years, that of a Chapel-of-ease in Castor parish.

John Howard

Fig 15m. Lectern:1920s, in memory of PO AJ Pendred, Royal Navy, and Pte HW Hornsby, Suffolk Regt, with roundels carved on the column symbolising the four evangelists.

Notes

1. Hugh Candidus, *The Peterborough Chronicle*, Ed by WT Mellows, reprint 1997, published by Peterborough Museum Society, p51.
2. Ibid p53.
3. Wills in Northamptonshire Probate registry, Bk B fol 142. Noted in Northamptonshire VCH, p485.
4. Arthur Mee, *King's England*, 1945, p338.
5. Arms of Dove, Sir Bernard Burke, *The General Armoury of England, Scotland, Ireland and Wales*, London 1878, p296.
6. W Ryland Bedford, *The Blazon of Episcopy*, London 1858, p89.
7. Rev Kenneth Gibson, *Antonine Itinerary* 1800, pp228-229 from a description given by John Carter FAS who drew several illustrations of the dial.

Fig 15n. Sundial: intricately carved sundial in the field South of the church dating from the time of Charles I. (As published by Bridges, 1796)

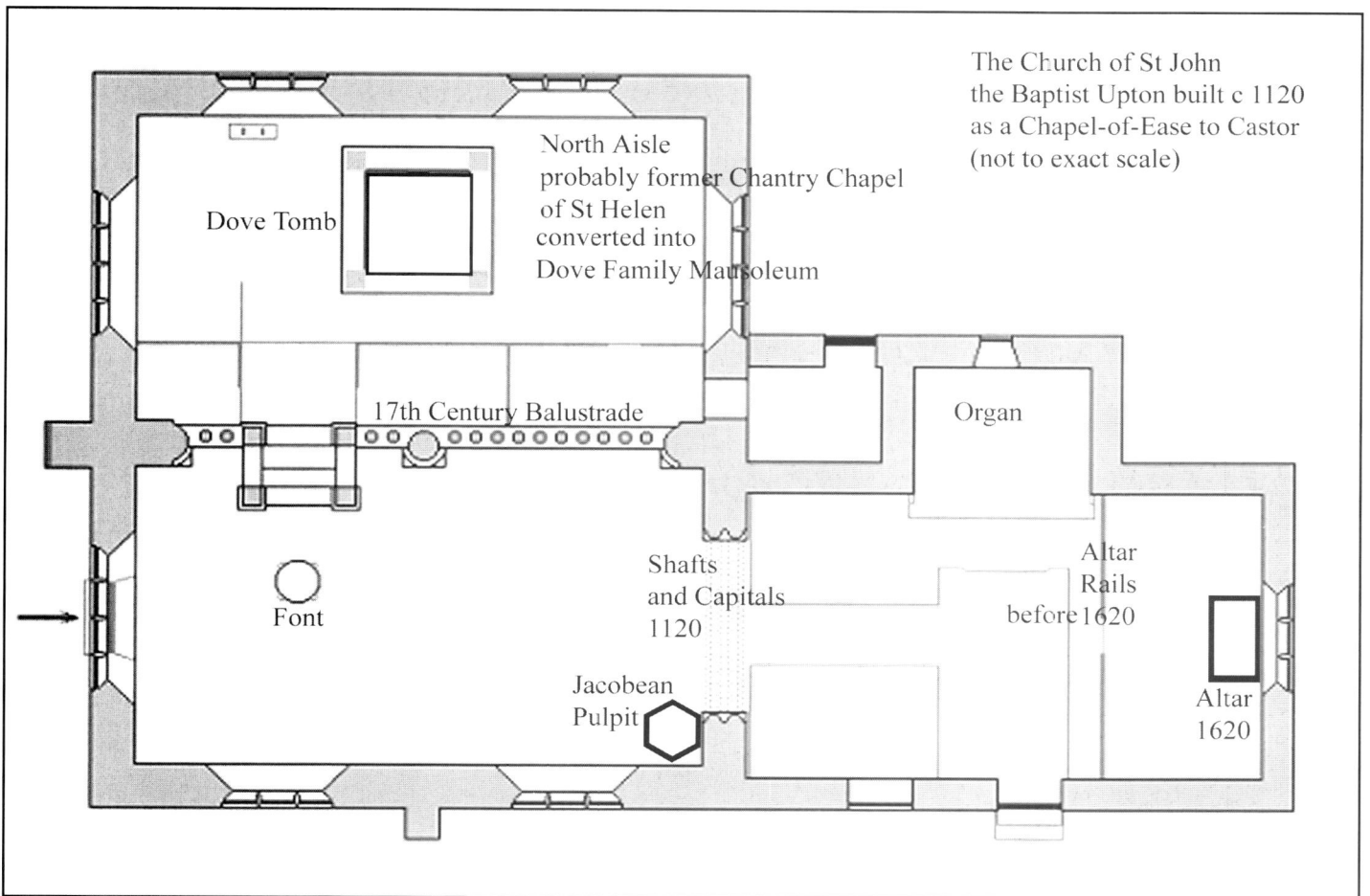

North Aisle
probably former Chantry Chapel
of St Helen
converted into
Dove Family Mausoleum

Dove Tomb

The Church of St John
the Baptist Upton built c 1120
as a Chapel-of-Ease to Castor
(not to exact scale)

17th Century Balustrade

Organ

Shafts
and Capitals
1120

Altar
Rails
before 1620

Font

Jacobean
Pulpit

Altar
1620

Fig 15o. Plan of Upton Church.

Fig 15p. Some Upton Church people 2004 (l-r)
Back: Peter Harris (churchwarden and farmer), Mark Blackmore, Claire Harris,
Corinna Blackmore, Michael Longfoot (churchwarden and farmer); Front: left Basil Dean
(organist), Keith Garrett, Chris Harrison-Smith (retired farmer), Anne Harrison-Smith,
Allen Herbert (retired farmer).

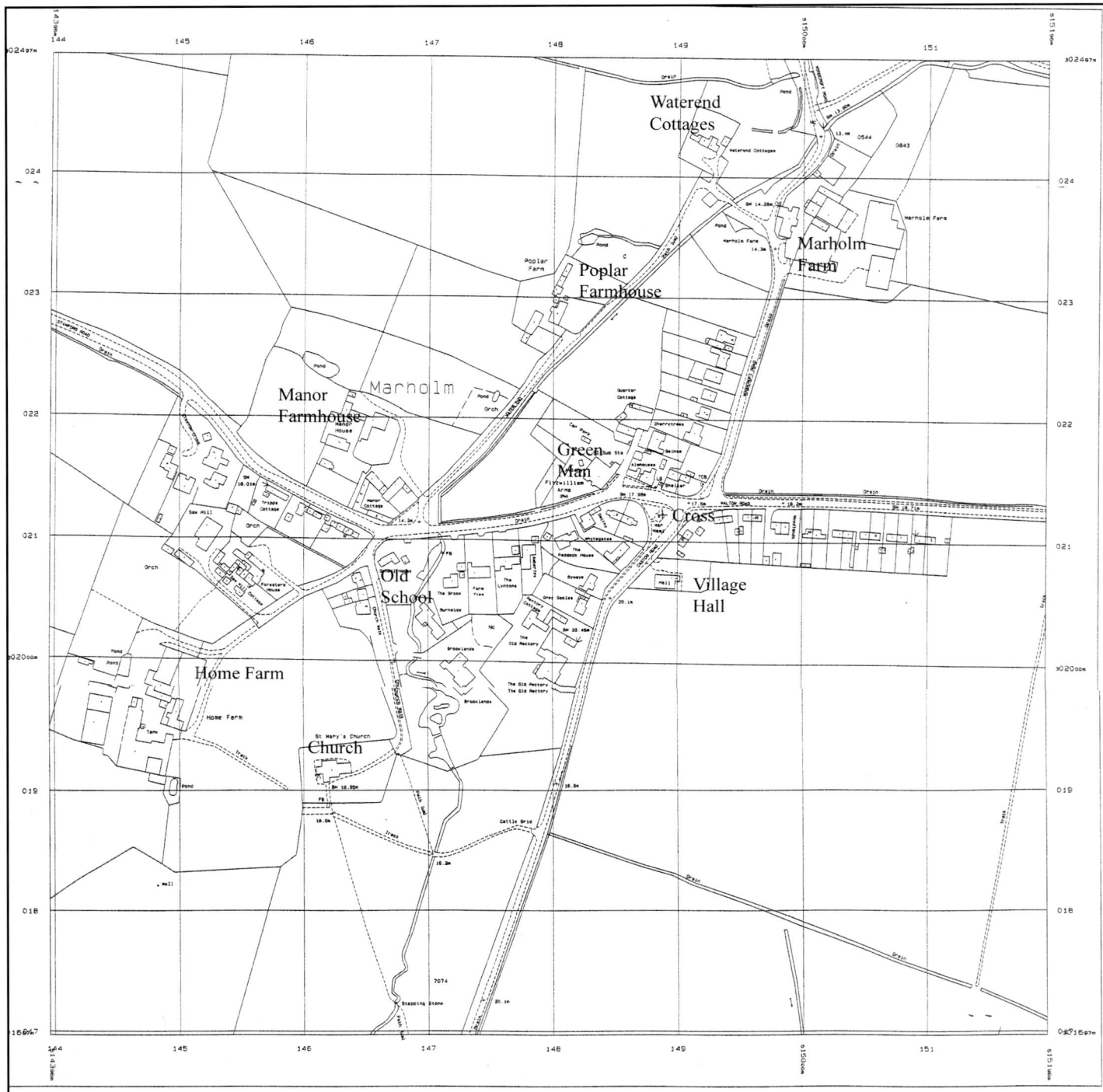

Map of Marholm. Reproduced from Ordnance Survey mapping on behalf of The Controller of Her Majesty's Stationery Office © Crown Copyright 100042620 2004

Chapter 16
Marholm Village and Buildings

History of the Village

Marholm village lies approximately four miles West of Peterborough and one mile from the seat of the Fitzwilliam family at Milton Hall. The parish covers some fourteen hundred acres, with the village positioned roughly in the centre. Today it remains a peaceful, largely agricultural community of some two hundred people. Although during the past fifty years the domination of agriculture has diminished, the village retains a rural feel, and in many ways is unchanged from its earlier history, despite the modern development, and proximity to a burgeoning city. To a large extent, this tranquillity has been preserved by the protection derived from Milton Estate, which has retained ownership of much of the property in the village. In addition, the Estate has curtailed further encroachment from the city beyond Mucklands Wood to the East, which delineates the border of Milton's sales, in the 1960s, of land to the Peterborough Development Corporation for the expansion of the city.

The name of the village most probably derives from 'mere', meaning pool, and 'ham', or settlement, and may refer to the pools by the Manor House. During the Middle Ages, the name was alternatively Marham, Marreham, Marrenham, Mareham, Morham and Marhome. By the 18th century it was commonly referred to as Marham and later known by the present spelling, Marholm [1].

Early History
The early history of the village is obscure, with few known archaeological sites. Not surprisingly, however, in view of its proximity to the flourishing Roman settlement in Castor, there is some evidence of their presence in the area now embraced by Marholm. The Royal Commission for Historic Monuments (RCHM) survey of 1969 recorded enclosure and linear features South-east of Burmer Wood, notably a small sub-rectangular enclosure of two acres. No interior features are visible, but there is a gap entrance near the middle of the South-eastern side leading to a track-way some 28m wide, bounded by ditches. In 1958, during ploughing some 350m North-west of the Manor House, the whole area was found to be covered with pottery, mainly Nene Valley ware. There were also large blocks of stone, some dressed. Similarly, traces of a Roman settlement, with pottery and a pillar were revealed some 150m East of Marholm Farm. This pottery is now in Peterborough Museum.

In the Saxon records of 664, the 'vill' of Marholm appears to have been confirmed to the Abbot of Peterborough by Wulfhere, although part of the land there was held before the Conquest by the Abbot of Ramsey. Marholm was famous for its quarries, reputedly supplying stone towards the building of Ramsey Abbey [2]. In about 1053, Ramsey exchanged with Peterborough his entitlement to *certain land in Marham ——- situated in the midst of beautiful woods* for land in Loddington [3]. Curiously, the village is not mentioned in the Domesday Book, nor does there appear to be a satisfactory explanation for this omission. Perhaps at the time Marholm was simply part of Milton (which does appear) with Marholm Church as Chapel-of-ease to Castor. The village is mentioned in 1145, in a Papal Bull of Eugenius III listing the possessions of the abbey. [4]

The advowson has always belonged to the Lord of the Manor, and has consequently passed through the families of Waterville during the 12th and 13th centuries, and then Thorpe. In 1384, William of Thorpe acquired through tortuous descent the whole manor, and on his death in 1391, he left to his kinsman, John Wittlebury, the manors of Longthorp, Milton and Marholm, thus uniting Marholm with Milton. From this date the descent of the manor followed that of Milton in Castor, with ownership passed to the Fitzwilliam family through purchase from the Wittlebury family in 1502 [5], where it continues to this day. Although Milton is in the parish of Castor, the family has invariably worshipped at St. Mary the Virgin, Marholm, which accounts for the many beautiful monuments to the Fitzwilliams in the church. The last Earl Fitzwilliam, the tenth in line, died in September 1979. He is buried in the churchyard, as is his Countess, who died in 1995. The present representative of the family living at Milton Hall is Sir Philip Naylor-Leyland, Bt.

Occupations and Growth of the Village
Since records began, the predominant occupation in Marholm has been farming, and this remains true today, albeit with a much smaller work force. Within the parish today are the ancient woodlands of Mucklands Wood, Pocock's Wood and

Burmer Wood, largely semi-natural woodland dominated by ash and oak. In wetter areas, sedges, tall herbs and grasses abound. As the village developed the woodlands gave way to accommodate feudal farming. The soil is light and sandy, mixed with limestone, and suited to mixed farming. Very little evidence remains of feudal farming methods, and there appears to be no correlation with modern field systems as set out in a map of 1886 in Noel Darby's possession. According to the RCHM study in 1969, nothing is known of the enclosure of the open fields of the parish, although extensive areas of ridge and furrow exist, as can be seen on aerial photographs around the village. These, quite unrelated to the existing fields, are arranged in end-on and interlocked furlongs, some with reversed-S curves, and have well-marked headlands up to 75cm high and some 14m wide [6].

Fig 16a. Marholm Farm: date stone 1633. (Photo: T Blackmore)

Fig 16b. Manor Farm (Photo: A Bone)

Fig 16c. Manor Farm: the brick built Tudor barn.
(Photo: T Blackmore)

The Farms at Marholm

Marholm and Manor Farms

The manor farm for the village is Marholm Farm - The Thatched House. The date 1633 is carved on a stone below the roof, but traces of the original building, particularly the deep recessed windows, suggest a much earlier origin. The farm has been occupied since 1912 by the Darby family, one of the oldest tenants on the Fitzwilliam estate, traceable on the Castor register for nearly 400 years. Thomas Rowe Darby, (1874-1935) father of the present tenant Noel Darby, took on the tenancy from his father John Thomas in 1928, at a rent of one pound an acre! After his death the tenancy passed to his redoubtable wife Eleanor, who was Churchwarden for some fifty years, and died ten days after celebrating her centenary on Christmas Day 1995.

Farming at Marholm and Manor Farms

During Eleanor's tenancy she was helped by Noel and his wife Joan, who moved to Manor Farm in 1969 and ran both farms as one mixed farm. The Darbys used to have a dairy herd which they gave up in 1968 because the land at Bretton was taken for development. The pigs went in 1960, and the hens in 1970; the poultry was run by Betty Andrews, who came to Marholm as a young Land Army volunteer during the Second War and never left! The farm is now entirely arable and whereas in the 1940s three hundred acres employed six men and a student, today on seven hundred acres, Noel needs only two [7] .

Until 1950, most of the work was still done by horses, as tractors were not easy to acquire during the war. They bought a Ford tractor in 1942, after which horses were used only for harrowing, pulling carts, muck-carting and rolling. By the end of the war they had four to six horses. It was a hard life for both man and beast. A single furrow was nine inches wide and six deep. It took three horses to pull a two-furrow plough, and two for a single. At one stage they hired steam ploughs, towed by a wire rope, from contractors who lived in caravans during the work. The biggest problem was carting the water and coal to the steam ploughs. Men sometimes had to carry sacks weighing two hundredweight for storage or transfer. Noel's father was six feet six inches tall and weighed eighteen stones, and would take part in a race from Castor to Marholm carrying a sack of barley, or in the tug-of-war.

Most of the produce from the farms was despatched by rail. Wagons pulled by horses carted the stuff to Helpston Station to be loaded up into trucks that had been ordered by telephone the previous day, and returned with fertilizers and coal.

Home Farm

Farming at Home Farm

Home Farm was most probably originally run to meet the domestic needs of Milton, rather than primarily for income. For many years now it has been run first as a mixed farm, including a dairy, by members of another Marholm dynasty, the Jarvis brothers, Toby, Stanley and Peter, and their wives, Mary, Fay and Vi [8]. As the brothers reached retirement during the 1990s, and with no family successors, dairy production finally ceased in 1998. This brought to a close a remarkable era that began just after the First

Fig 16d. Thomas Rowe Darby.

Fig 16e. Eleanor Darby.

Fig 16f. Noel Darby.

Fig 16g. Joan Darby.

Fig 16h. Home Farm. (Photo: T Blackmore)

Fig 16i. Home Farm Barn: Stan Jarvis in the yard. (Photo: T Blackmore)

World War, when the brothers' grandfather, George Jarvis, took on the tenancy of the adjacent Belsize Farm, then later Home Farm and the Fruit Farm (now Milton woodyard). His son Arthur took over the tenancy of Home Farm in 1947 and farmed cereals, sugar beet, potatoes, sheep and chickens.

The wheat was harvested before it was ripe, bound and built into stooks, and left in the field for about a fortnight before threshing in the stackyard. After harvest, villagers like old Mrs. Sharpe would go gleaning, or chickens were put in the fields to pick up the last

Fig 16j. Arthur Jarvis 'lambing' on North side of Home Farm.

ears of corn. The final task in the year was the sugar beet, harvested from September until January. The work was physical, unrelenting and hard.

Arthur also had a milk round in Peterborough, which was only mechanized in the 1940s. Iris Newton's father, Philip Winterton, rose at four in the morning to deliver the milk from large churns, in the pre-war days before bottling. He would also collect the newspapers and parcels for the villagers. He had Saturday and Sunday afternoons off, but his daughter never remembers him having a holiday.

Fig 16k. Philip Winterton with the Jarvis milk cart at Home Farm.

Grandad George Jarvis would go off to market every week in a pony and trap: fortunately the pony knew its way home as they all went off to the pub after market! By the late 1950s the horses had all gone, even Turpin, the big Suffolk Punch. Unbelievably, however, the cattle were still walked to their summer grazing at Whittlesey Wash through Peterborough, along the Lincoln Road!

Belsize Farm

Although Belsize is in both ecclesiastical and civil terms within the parish of Castor, it is considered locally to be part of Marholm. Belseys or Bellasis Grange is situated near Belsize Wood, immediately West of Milton, and between Castor and Marholm. The Grange was originally founded by Abbot Robert of Lindsey in 1214, in order to provide for the enlargement of an existing monastery farm there. By the 15th century, it consisted of some one hundred tenants, and was run at a profit by the Cellerar of the monastery. For practical purposes Belsize was a separate manor, but without a Manor House. After the Dissolution, Belsize went to the Dean and Chapter, was then stolen from the Church by Cromwell in 1650, then back to the Dean and Chapter at the Restoration, and thereafter to the Ecclesiastical Commissioners in 1836, who rented it to the Fitzwilliam family. No doubt this pattern was repeated in many parishes throughout the land during that time.

The attractive Medieval buildings at Belsize testify to its long history, which also includes the remains of carp ponds, old cobbling under the turf, and a bank known as Roman Bank suggesting even earlier settlement.

Farming at Belsize Farm

When George Jarvis came to Belsize after the Great War, he took on 230 acres, rent-free for the first two years. Times were very hard during the post-war agricultural Depression, and when in due course he

Fig 16l. Belsize Farm: a medieval grange farm in origin.
(Photo: T Blackmore)

was unable to make it pay, Lord Fitzwilliam simply told him to work the land until it did. He had beef cattle and a dairy, and ten working horses. In 1947, George retired, and his son Jack took on the tenancy, phasing out the horses in 1961. His son Dick followed him in 1962, when the dairy herd was sold, and the workforce reduced from seven men to four. He retired in 1996, and his son Trevor now runs an arable farm with his wife Jane, but with no additional help [9].

Life in the Village

The rhythm of life over the centuries in Marholm must closely have followed the pattern of many similar farming communities throughout England, governed by the ebb and flow of the seasons, and the demands of a

Fig 16m. Belsize Barn: this is the magnificent medieval grange barn adapted for more recent use. (Photo: T Blackmore)

major Estate. Until the last two centuries, when Peterborough began to develop as an engineering centre, the land was the sole employer, and this continued to be reflected in the daily life of Marholm until remarkably recently, when farming was revolutionized by mechanization and employment levels plummeted. John Hill lives in the house in the village where he took his bride Gina in 1960. The Estate had built two new houses on the site of the thatched cottages where John was born, alongside the Stamford Road. John's father Tom was the Horseman at Manor Farm.

Against this slow-moving and ordered backdrop, however, there were echoes of the outside world, and more turbulent times. Sir John Wittlebury, Lord of the Manor under Henry IV, was a personal servant to Henry V at the battle of Agincourt. His effigy, encased in his battle armour, lies above his tomb in Marholm church. The Muster Rolls for the Nassaburgh Hundred of 1536 [10] indicate how Henry VIII began to organize his army; residents were assessed to provide arms according to their wealth, and general musters were held at intervals, and as such were the forerunners of the later Militia Lists. The quota for Marholm was for four 'bilmen,' Thomas Idell, John Gyles, Nicholas Wylkynson and John Slater, *'and the residue of the towne to finde horse and harness for a man'*. Sir William Fitzwilliam, grandson of the first to hold the Manor, was Viceroy of Ireland for Elizabeth I, and saved her army there from annihilation. He was later Governor of Fotheringhay Castle and thus warden there during the imprisonment of Mary, Queen of Scots until her execution in 1584 [11].

The Civil War did not leave Marholm unscathed. Perhaps strangely, considering that Cromwell was from East Anglia, and his widow is buried in nearby Northborough, some three miles North of Marholm, the area remained strongly Royalist. The Reverend Michael Hudson, rector of Uffington as well as Chaplain to Charles I, met a particularly gruesome end as the War drew to a close. In 1648, a troop of Cromwellian horses passed through Marholm on their way to nearby Woodcroft Castle, where the Chaplain had taken refuge. Michael Hudson and his companions fought bravely from the ground floor to the roof, only at last to be overpowered. The survivors, including Hudson, were hurled from the battlements, but he managed to cling to a parapet as he fell. An Ironside sword at once severed his wrists, and he plunged into the moat, finally to be dispatched by a musket butt to the head [12].

After the Restoration in 1660, life seems to have settled back much as before the Civil War. In 1676 the Compton Census recorded sixty one Conformists and only two Nonconformists in the village [13]. But the development of the national infrastructure of a modern state swept relentlessly on - the old musters had been streamlined into Militia Lists, and in 1762 Marholm's constable, Benj Bull, recorded fourteen eligible males, including the village publican, Robert Collinge, despite having *'remarkable crooked legs'*. An analysis of the lists shows that most of the men, however, were employed within the agricultural community [14].

Charities

Like many small parishes, the local dignitaries founded charities for the poor, largely organised through the church. In 1533, Sir William Fitzwilliam left a bequest to the Merchant Taylors Company, of which he was a member, for payments for the upkeep of four almshouses, for the benefit of one priest and four poor men. The income for 1549 amounted to £17 18s 4d with the priest, Adam Potts, receiving seven pounds, and the balance divided four ways. The almshouses were rebuilt by a later Fitzwilliam, and five pounds deducted by him as rent for the buildings. In 1638 William Budd bequeathed ten pounds for the poor, with the interest of 5s 8p spent on coal at Christmas.

The Reverend Christopher Hodgson's charity, founded in 1849, consisting of £54 12s 6d in Consolidated stock, left funds for the upkeep of a tombstone with the balance to the poor. However, it was held to be illegal to set aside funds for the tombstone, and the entire amount went to the poor at Christmas. Lady Dorothy Fitzwilliam in 1878 established a trust of £300 in Canada bonds and £59 12s 6d Consols, for educational purposes in Marholm.

In 2003 it was decided by the Parish Council to wind up these charities, which had been ravaged by inflation, and were no longer appropriate, and the resulting sum of £2730 was divided three ways amongst Marholm Church, the Village Hall and the Parish Council.

Fig 16n. Marholm School: now converted into a private house.

Fig 16o. Marholm School: the Class of 1928. Teachers:
Mrs Oldfield and Miss B Saunders.
Children: back (l-r) Doris Jinks, Rene Crumpler, Rene Phillips, Edna Wagstaff, Elsie Jinks, Violet Stapleton, Vera Wagstaff, Marjorie Sharpe, Edna Johnson, Elsie Johnson, Daisy Law, Phyliss Clipston; middle: Ray Neal, Eric Torbell, Ken Handland, Jack Law, Eddie Law, Jack Phillips, Bill Stapleton, Grenville Sutton, Jack Winterton, Alec Clipston, Ernie Rollinson; front: Bob Law, Ted Crumpler, Roy Darby, Peter Johnson, Mary Stapleton, Elsie Wagstaff, Isla Sutton, Edith Blythe, Ivy Phillips, Nadine Johnson, Betty Darby, Dorothy Stapleton, Ernie Law, Ronnie Clipston, Herbie Rollinson.

Recent Times

The population of the village was recorded in 1801 at 109, and by the 1901 census, stood at 146. The developments of the 19th century reflected some of the social changes in the country. The village school was founded and financed by the Fitzwilliam family in 1864. After 1870, control of the school came under the Local School Board, and in 1903 passed to the Local Education Authority. It was a handsome building, consisting of one large room heated in winter by a huge stove in the middle [15].

In the 1920s, the villagers recall that the younger children were separated from the older by a curtain that was pulled across when the daily hymn singing had ended. Two 'formidable' ladies taught them reading, writing and arithmetic.

Enid Johnson's family came to live in the village in 1956, when her parents took on the village shop, and Enid joined the school. She describes how in the 1950s the children were still 'banked up' by age, with the little ones at the front, and there was only one teacher. Enid has stayed in the village with her family, and works tirelessly for the Church, where she is Churchwarden.

When it came to picking the late potatoes at the end of September after Harvest, the children would have a further fortnight off, even as late as the 1950s, to help out. The children were paid, and Arthur Jarvis at Home Farm always gave them a cup of hot cocoa made with milk in a big churn. They would have grown six or seven acres of potatoes in the Dryside Field, just opposite the cattle grid entrance to the church field.

The school closed in 1959. Almost a century after it opened, the building was bought by a doctor, John Murphy, who with his wife Audrey remodelled it into a comfortable home to bring up their three sons. John now lies in the churchyard, and Audrey still lives in the family home.

Apart from the dreadful toll of young life recorded on the War Memorial, the First World War left the village relatively undisturbed, but in the Second War the Royal Corps of Signals set up Headquarters in the village and life was transformed. Noel Darby recalls the hustle and bustle of those times, and the aftermath. The population swelled by some forty or fifty persons, and an anti-aircraft gun appeared in the Woodcroft Road.

The Rectory, empty since 1935, was occupied by the army and modified to accommodate many people, with multi-use baths and toilets! The entire six acres of land was covered in Nissen and army huts. George Read, whose father bought the rectory from the Church Commissioners in 1951, remembers that many of the huts were still occupied after the war ended, and turned into poultry and pig sheds as they became vacant. Roy and Di Armitage moved into the village in 1969. They have devoted much of their time and energy to the Church, Roy as Churchwarden in the 1990's. Beneath their smooth lawns is a concrete base, all that remains of an army hut.

Fig 16p. Marholm Home Guard.
Top Line l/r: F Wilson, N Darby, W Lambert, S Neal, J Waterworth, Sidney Glover, G Neal, C Bailey, unknown
Borrom Line l/r: R Stapleton, P Hill, T Oldfield, P Powdrell, Mr Squires, S Glover, W Stapleton, J Coles

Gradually most of the land around the Old Rectory was sold off for building, and bungalows appeared alongside the Stamford Road. Jim Baldwin spearheaded this development with his home by the stream that runs through the village. He was for many years the mainstay of the Church, as Churchwarden with Mrs. Darby.

Inevitably, life in the village changed considerably after such exposure, reflecting the social developments in the wider world. The idyllic, introspective rural pace described with great nostalgia between the Wars, centred closely around the farms, gave way to more frenetic times. Mains water arrived in 1926, and electricity just before the Second War. But roads were still rough, with granite chippings, and no kerb stones. Transport was by cycle, or a lift hitched on a milk float to Walton to take the train or tram into town. Entertainment centred around the church, or on the bowling green behind the almshouses, or in the local hostelry, The Fitzwilliam Arms, known far and wide as the 'Green Man' because of the topiary figure welcoming all-comers with outstretched arms.

The car in the 1920s was a curious rarity exciting the village children, such as the times when Mrs Adams' nephew drew up in his three-wheeled Morgan. Mrs Adams lived in one of the almshouses originally founded by the Fitzwilliam family for retired estate workers. She was an old lady who still wore black down to her ankles. Now the four cottages have been converted into two, on leases from the Estate. In one lives Freda Shimmin, whose family has a long taproot in Peterborough. She moved into the village in 1967, when she was a maternity nurse, and has always been active in church affairs. In the other, live Margaret and Al Gdaniec. Al fought alongside the British in the Second War and did not return to his native Poland. He worked in Peterborough, and is active in Parish affairs. He organised the Royal Jubilee celebrations, and the oak planted to commemorate the Millennium. Marholm is part of the Green Wheel Millennium Project, a network of safe cycleways, footpaths and bridleways around Peterborough.

The impact of the car has probably changed rural life in Marholm, and elsewhere, almost more than any other modern development, breaking up communities and greatly speeding up the pace of life. This has combined with the explosive growth of Greater Peterborough, now on the very doorstep of the village through the new township at nearby Bretton, virtually to demolish in one generation a way of life that had existed for hundreds of years. The beautiful Millennium sign on the green, designed for the village by Betty Andrews, the Land Girl who stayed on, commemorates the historic role of the village, with the Fitzwilliam crest over the church, the war memorial on the green, the fabled Green Man, and a tractor. Marholm in the early days of the 21st century remains a peaceful retreat, but the old farming families are making way for a different way of life. Hawkins the Clockmaker in Noel Darby's old barn is one way forward, but incomers tend to be employed in the new industries outside the village boundaries, often in the Capital, and the march of history suggests a very different future for this lovely oasis.

Fig 16q. Marholm Lodges. (Photo: A Bone)

Fig 16r. The Old Rectory: built by the Revd Christopher Hodgson to replace the Old Parsonage, Marholm and the original rectory at Castor (in which he lived as Castor's curate). (Photo: A Bone)

The Buildings of Marholm
The following buildings are those listed by Peterborough City Council Environmental Services as being of special Architectural or Historic interest.

The village is approached from Milton Hall along the Castor Road. The first buildings encountered, on the right, are a pair of 19th century semi-detached cottages, known as **Marholm Lodges.**

On entering the village you will then find, on the left hand side, the splendid **Old Rectory**. This was built in 1846, and a wing added in the 1860's.

A little further on the right is the **Village Hall**, recently rebuilt by public subscription to replace the old hall that was out of date and inadequate for modern needs. The wall shielding it from the road was a gift from the Earl and Countess Fitzwilliam to commemorate the Silver Jubilee in 1977 of HM Queen Elizabeth 11.

At the junction of Castor road and Stamford Road is the **War**

Memorial. This stone cross was erected in 1920 to commemorate the villagers who fell in World War I. It stands on a modern stepped base which itself supports an octagonal stone base which is all that remains of the original medieval cross. Since then the name of the sole victim of World War II has been added. In the 1960's the Memorial was moved from the junction of Woodcroft Road and Stamford Road to the present site. In 2000, Betty Andrews' sign to celebrate the Millennium was placed next to the War Memorial.

Opposite the memorial is the early 19th century **Blacksmith's Cottage,** recently renovated by Milton into a retirement cottage for the Estate, and next to this are the old 18th century **Almshouses** which have now been converted into two cottages.

After joining the Stamford Road the old **Blacksmith's Workshop** is the on the left. This was built probably in the early 19th century and has now been converted into a very picturesque cottage.

Fig 16s. The War Memorial and Village Sign. (Photo: T Blackmore)

Shortly afterwards is the only pub in the village, **The Fitzwilliam Arms,** but more commonly known as '**The Green Man**' due to the topiary box tree figure in the front. This originates from 17th and 18th centuries, but the building has recently undergone extensive alterations resulting in the premises becoming rather more of a restaurant than a village pub.

Still on the right hand side you will then find **Manor Farmhouse**, dating from the 17th and 18th centuries, and the home of Noel and Joan Darby.

In front of the Manor House is an unmade road leading down to the 17th and 18th centuries **Poplar Farmhouse**.

Fig 16t. The Almshouses. (Photo: A Bone)

On the opposite side of the road is Church Walk, where there are several houses of interest.
On the right is **The Old Parsonage,** a 17th century building that predates the Old Rectory. The date of 1626 is shown on some reused stone on the South side.

At the end of the Walk there is a road which leads to two semi-detached 19th century cottages known as **Foresters Lodge** and **Sawmill Cottage.**

Following this road to its end you arrive at **Home Farm,** where Stan and Fay Jarvis live. The building originates from the 16th and 17th centuries. The two barns and stables forming the courtyard date from the 18th century.

Fig 16u. The Fitzwilliam Arms: note the 'Green Man' topiary. (Photo: A Bone)

Returning to the main part of the village, after passing the Blacksmith's cottage on the left you come to Woodcroft Road. On the right you soon come to **Marholm Farmhouse,** dated 1633, and where Eleanor Darby lived. Attached to the farmhouse is **Hurn House** which is of mid 19th century construction. Before Noel and Joan Darby moved in after their marriage in 1947, the house consisted of a dairy downstairs and a single room upstairs, where originally an informal school was held before the Estate built Marholm Schoolhouse.

On the opposite side of the road are **Water End Cottages**.

Fig 16v. Poplar Farmhouse. (Photo: A Bone)

Fig 16w. The Old Parsonage. (Photo: T Blackmore)

*Fig 16x. Sawmill Cottage and Foresters Lodge.
(Photo: A Bone)*

Fig 16y. Water End Cottages. (Photo: A Bone)

They originally consisted of four dwellings from the 17th century, with 19th century additions. In 1945 the cottages were partially destroyed by fire, and rebuilt as two.

Between the Wars, the council built homes along the Walton Road, many of which have been bought by the tenants. After the Second War, the village expanded with bungalows along the Woodcroft Road and Stamford Road, and fine semi-detached homes for the Estate employees, now lived in by Bob Law and Don Hill.

Towards the end of the 20th century, the development was more in sympathy with the history of the village, with restoration of some of the older properties carried out by the Fitzwilliam family. Outbuildings on Manor Farm were transformed into retirement cottages for the Estate workers. The blacksmith's cottage and workshop were imaginatively renovated, and Poplar Farm was restored for the assistant Agent, William Craven and his family. The Fitzwilliam Arms yielded some of its identity as a village pub in favour of modernisation, and a private estate of four large stone-built family properties arose at the outer reaches of the village, towards Stamford. The village was declared a conservation area in 1990; nevertheless, all those who live here await with trepidation the early 21st century threats of compulsory purchase from Whitehall with the relentless expansion of village 'envelopes'.

Fig 16z. War Memorial before it was moved from the Woodcroft Road junction to its present location. The man first left is Ron Hudson, sixth from the left is Percy Smith, priest Rev Tom Adler. The photo must be pre-1957, as Percy Smith died that year.

Fig 16aa. Post-retirement visit by Revd Tom Adler for a Lunch Party at Manor Farmhouse with some ladies he married: (l-r) Joan Darby, Rene Foster, Gladys Chilvers, unknown, Tom Adler, Mary Jarvis, Elsie Sismey, Joan Marriott, Monica Swain, Ruth Longfoot.

Hazel Yates and Andrea Bone

Hazel Yates came to Marholm with her husband Rodney and son Ben in 1987, and they live at the Old Rectory. Rodney was Churchwarden from 1990 to 2000.

Andrea Bone moved to the village in 1984 and lives at Sawmill Cottage with her husband Peter and daughter Alice. Peter is a Forester at Milton, and in 2003 received a medal for twenty five years' service to the Estate.

We should like to thank everyone in the village for their help in contributing to this chapter.

Notes

1. *Place names of Northamptonshire.*
2. Rev. K Gibson *Antonine Itinerary,* 1769, p203.
3. Chronicle of Ramsey (Rolls Ser.) p169.
4. Rev WD Sweeting *Parish Churches in and around Peterborough* 1868, p1.
5. *The Victorian County History of Northampton,* Vol 2, 1906, p500.
6. *Royal Air Force Vertical Air Photographs,* F22/58 RAF/5164.
7. Notes on Noel & Joan Darby by the Rev. William Burke, Rector of Marholm 2002.
8. Notes on Stanley & Fay Jarvis by the Rev. William Burke, Rector of Marholm 2002.
9. Notes on Trevor & Jane Jarvis by the Rev. William Burke, Rector of Marholm 2002.
10. See Appendix Eight.
11. John W Richards *Cambridgeshire, Huntingdon & Peteborough Life,* February, 1970.
12. *ibid.*
13. See Appendix Seven.
14. See Appendix Eleven.
15. *Victorian County History of Northampton,* Vol 2, 1906, p502.

Fig 16bb. Cows going out to pasture after morning milking, Marholm early 1960s.

Chapter 17
The Church of St Mary the Virgin in Marholm

Marholm Church sits in a field on the Southern fringes of the village, and is shaded by massive Cedars of Lebanon that date from the 18th century. Around the churchyard is a most attractive Ha-Ha, to keep out intrusive cattle. The Church may be reached on foot from Church Walk or by car from Castor Road, across the cattle grid and along the track leading to Home Farm.

Fig 17a. Marholm Church with the Cedars of Lebanon

It is a small cellular linear church with a massive squat Norman tower capped by a small pyramid spire. The short Early English nave has an early perpendicular clerestory and Victorian North and South aisles. The whole Church is dominated, however, by the grand late perpendicular chancel built by Sir William Fitzwilliam in 1534. The tower and chancel are faced with ashlar, whilst the nave and clerestory are built of rubble masonry with ashlar dressings. The flat nave and chancel roofs are leaded with stone parapets, and those of the tower and chancel are embattled. The aisle roofs are covered with Collyweston slates [1].

Early History
The Church was founded in 1140, and dedicated to St Mary the Virgin [2]. A chantry in the church founded in 1367 by the Lord of the Manor, Sir William of Thorpe, was dedicated to St Guthlac. This has sometimes led to confusion over the name, perpetuated in a Church inventory even as late as the 20th century. A list of Rectors exists from 1217. (See Appendix Three). The advowson has always been with the Lord of the Manor and has consequently passed through the families of Waterville, Thorpe, Wittlebury and, from 1503, Fitzwilliam.

The history of the church describes a cycle of decay and renewal, with major rebuilding or refurbishment in the late 13th century, after a serious fire, in 1534, when Sir William Fitzwilliam built the beautiful chancel, and in 1868 with the extensive restoration by the Fitzwilliam family in memory of the fifth Earl.

The Tower
The West tower is reputed to be the oldest part of the church, built between 1180-90. It is low, with clasping buttresses on each side and arched slit windows, deeply splayed, which reveal the thickness of the walls [3]. The beams of the belfry have been well restored, with one 34 inch bell set in oak frame. It is inscribed:

Fig 17b. The West Tower

'TOBY NORRIS CAST ME 1673'
An inventory of the goods taken 23rd September 1552 states that at that time there were '*ij bells and a sctus bell yn ye steple*' [4].

The tower arch into the nave is a mixture of old and modern masonry. The arch itself was restored in 1868 and consists of two square cut rows of masonry. The half round pillars with crocket capitals supporting the arch are from about the 13th century [5]. Above the curtains screening the tower arch is a length of medieval wood carved with roses that is Tudor, or possibly earlier, and probably all that remains of the medieval Rood Screen.

Fig 17c. The Font and Rood Screen Carving

Further up the West wall in the nave is a curious stone figure carved as the top half of a man with his right hand raised, and a book in his left hand. The Victorian County History of Northampton of 1906 suggests that this may be a roof corbel as the top of the figure is on the same plane as the top of the chancel arch, and both could have supported the timbers of the pre-clerestory pitched roof. On the South side of the nave at both ends and level with the tops of the arches is part of a ledge which marks the top of the old nave walls, and on which the roof would have rested [6].

The Font
The 14th century octagonal stone font is based on the style of a Norman table font, on a short central stem with four smaller shafts. In the 17th century the bowl was decorated on each side with a rosette and leaf design [7].

The Nave
During the 13th century the nave was built with arcades of three bays. At the end of the century the whole church, except for the tower, was destroyed by fire, and subsequently rebuilt with a chancel, nave and two aisles. The pillars in the nave, resembling clusters of four columns with relatively simple moulded capitals on which the pointed arches are set, date from that time [8]. Most of the nave masonry is ancient, but part of the chancel arch was restored in 1868. At the side of the chancel arch against the half-pillars are the marks showing where a screen was at one time attached.

Fig 17d. The Nave and Clerestory

The clerestory dates from the 15th century and provides a window over each arch of the nave arcade. The windows on the South side are considerably longer than those on the North, reaching down almost to the points of the arches. Each window consists of three cinquefoiled lights fewer than four centred heads [9]. The roof is quite modern, probably from the late Victorian refurbishment.

The Aisles
The North and South aisles we see today, together

with the South porch, are Victorian, and were built during the restoration of 1868. The original aisles were burnt and the outer walls pulled down sometime in the 16th century. This probably followed the dissolution of the chantries in 1545. The nave arches were then blocked up and windows from the destroyed aisles were built into the blocking. The old South porch removed in 1868 was said to be Elizabethan, but poor. An Episcopal Visitation of 1570 recorded the sorry state of the church :

'*Marham. The glasse windows is in decay. The churchyard in ruyn. The last quarter sermon not discharged'*.

The only surviving window from the original 13th century aisles is in the East wall of the South aisle and is reputed to have been used as the pattern for all the other aisle windows [10]. It is a small window of two narrow pointed arched lights with a quatrefoil in the top between the points of the lights. The middle window in the North aisle is stained glass, which a small plaque identifies as dating from 1894.

Fig 17e. The Lady Chapel, showing the original 13th century window

The Organ

In 1895, by public subscription, the organ was built by Binns of Leeds. It comprises one manual and a straight pedal board. Although relatively small with only six ranks of pipes it has a very good tone and suits the building well. Set into the West wall of the North aisle, by the organ, is a 13th century piscina [11].

Fig 17f. The Chancel and East Window

The Chancel

The chancel is built on a much larger scale than the rest of the church. It was started in 1534, in the grand perpendicular style, by the first Sir William Fitzwilliam and contains his family vault under the raised floor on which the altar stands [12]. It is believed that the other members of the family also occupy the vault. The chancel has been described as a magnificent light, airy structure, and disproportionately large, perhaps because it was built to serve as the pantheon of his posterity [13]. Sir William died in 1534, one year before the Reformation began, after which church building in England virtually ceased for one hundred years. It seems quite possible that, but for the uncertainties of the times, he intended to rebuild the entire church in a similar grand style.

The chancel has a large East window of five cinque-foiled lights with tracery under a four centred head, and a wealth of Fitzwilliam heraldic glass. Two four-light windows on the North wall and two on the South are of similar design and detail, with fragments in their borders of old painted glass, possibly from the 16th century [14]. One of the windows on the South side displays the rebus of Abbot Robert Kirkton (a church standing on a yellow tun, or barrel, embellished with a capital R) [15]. He was Abbot of Peterborough, 1496-1528.

Between the windows on the South side is a small, modern doorway with a four centred head. The buttresses to the chancel are placed diagonally against the corners where the North and South walls meet the East wall. One buttress bears graffiti dated from 1717 to 1785. The drain pipes on the East wall are dated 1713.

The 1868 restoration, costing £2000, is recorded on a plaque on the North wall, above the choir stalls in the chancel, and reads: '*In remembrance of Charles William, 5th Earl Fitzwilliam born May 4th 1786, died Oct 4th 1857, this church was restored in 1868 by the surviving members of his family.*'

Fig 17g. Tomb of Sir John Wittlebury

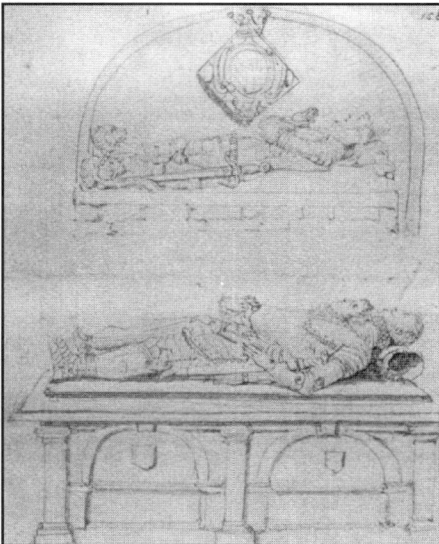
Fig 17h. Engraving of Effigy of Sir John Wittlebury in recessed arch

Fig 17i. Tomb of Sir William Fitzwilliam

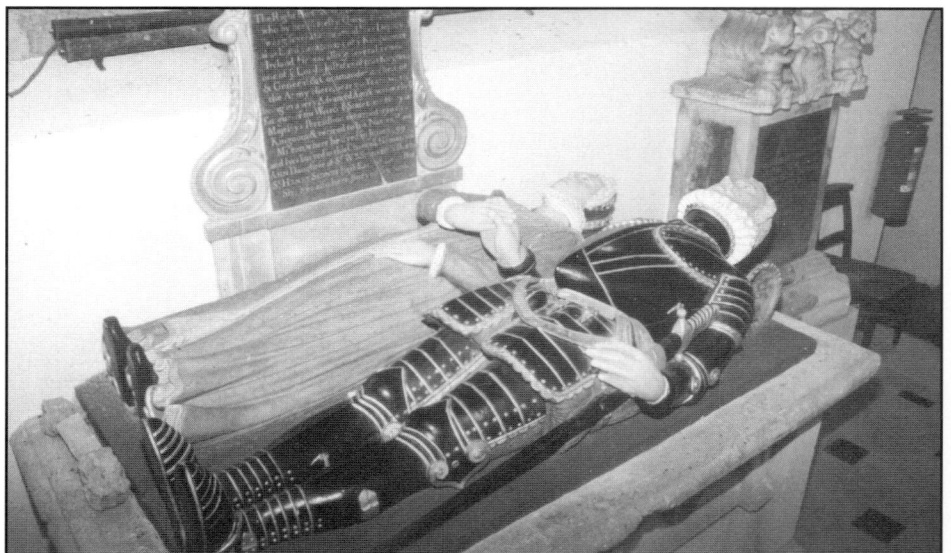
Fig 17j. Tomb of Sir William Fitzwilliam and Lady Anne

Effigies

At the East end of the South aisle is the effigy of a Knight in full armour with his head resting on a tilting helmet and his feet on a lion. It is believed to be the effigy of Sir John Wittlebury, Lord of the Manor during the reign of Henry IV, and the Knight who fought at Agincourt. The effigy is thought to date from 1410. The tomb was restored in 1868, and the effigy mounted on an altar tomb with an attractive carved frieze of little animals. Prior to that, the effigy rested in an arched recess, with the early 18th century coat of arms of Sir William Fitzwilliam, the first Earl of Southampton, above it, but the style and armour of the effigy is clearly three hundred years earlier [16].

John Bridges recorded in 1791 that around the edge of an old stone in the church-yard, moved out of the chancel, was the following inscription:-
'*Hic jacet* Johannes *Wiyttylbyr*i *qui obit viii die Maii, Ao. Dni Millmo. CCCC cujus aie ppicietur Deus. Amen*'
From Bridges' comment it seems likely that the effigy and memorial stone were removed from the old chancel when it was rebuilt as the mausoleum of the Fitzwilliam family [17].

As the chancel was built towards the end of the pre-Reformation period, there are few medieval remains. The earliest monument, in the North-East corner, is to the builder, Sir William Fitzwilliam, and his wife, dated 1534. Sir William was an Alderman of London and Treasurer to Cardinal Wolsey. The canopied marble altar tomb is typical of its kind in the late 15th and early 16th centuries, and may also have served as an Easter Sepulchre. At the back, below the canopy, are the kneeling brass figures of Sir William and his wife. The inscription on the tomb reads:
'*Syr Wylliam Fitzwyllyams knight decessed the ix day of August in the xxvi yere of Or Soverayn Lorde Kyng Henry the VIII in Amo Dni M cccccxxxiiii, and lyeth beuried under thys tombe*'.
It was damaged, possibly during the Civil War, and bears a brass plate recording its repair in 1674.

In the South-East corner of the chancel is a fine monument to commemorate his grandson, also Sir William, who died in 1599, and his wife Anne, the daughter of Sir William Sydney. Sir William is represented in armour, and holds his wife's hand.

Next to them is a monument to Edward Hunter, alias Perry, a son of Lady Fitzwilliam, who died in 1646. The white marble portrait bust is surmounted by

a tall black obelisk, with the inscription:
'*Grassante bello civili.*
To the courteous souldier.
Noe Crucifix you see, noe Frighjtful Brand
Of sup'tition's here. Pray let me stand'.

Between the two windows on the North wall is a magnificent memorial to William, Third Earl Fitzwilliam and his wife, dated 1719.The sculptor was James Fisher of Camberwell. It was made at a cost of £900. As the tomb stands today, only the central portion with the main figures survives. It is clear, however, not only from Bridges' text description in 1791, but also from a description in 1810 by Britton and Brayley, and again in a reference by the Reverend Sweeting published in 1868, that the tomb was originally much larger, with two side panels, as in the engraving. Most probably the side sections were removed in the restoration in 1868.

The panels of the reredos are covered by a decorative green cloth. Jim Baldwin - former churchwarden and organist, and devoted member of the church for many years - recounts that this is to protect the cracking wood and some very old inscriptions of the Lord's Prayer and the Ten Commandments, dating possibly from Elizabethan times. The pews and pulpit are all modern, and there is no trace of the medieval arrangements [18].

Sweeting records that in 1860 there was a decaying fresco on the West wall of the nave which extended over the ancient blocking of the tower arch. This depicted St Catherine, St Andrew and one other unknown woman, and also showed clearly the line of the old pre-clerestory pitched roof. Unfortunately this did not survive the 1868 restoration [19].

The Church and the Village

Marholm has always been a small village set in a rural parish - there were only 15 houses in 1791. The parishioners did not have the wealth to emulate many nearby parishes and raise a spire on the tower. The effort expended to raise the funds needed to improve the lighting by building the clerestory must have been considerable. The medieval peasant was illiterate. His knowledge of doctrine was often gained from images in the church and the somewhat lurid wall pictures that stressed the horrors and anguish of Purgatory and Hell. This was set against the mediation and compassion of the Virgin and the Saints. This type of learning as opposed to intellectual understanding meant that much of their faith, which was very real to them, was based on their emotions. These emotions were important in persuading many villagers to be generous to their village church [20].

Was it only fear that encouraged so many parishioners to give to their church? There was certainly considerable anxiety regarding the fate of their souls, but also a measure of communal identity which encouraged them to present their community in the best possible light before their near neighbours. Purgatory, the place and state of souls between death and final judgement, was a very real and fearful place to them. Thomas Aquinas expounded that the guilt of venial sin is expiated immediately after death by an act of perfect charity. Suffering must still be undergone, but would be eased by the prayers of the faithful [21]. The concept of Purgatory was responsible for considerable excesses and abuses of doctrine in the Middle Ages, but it was also an incentive for the beautifying and equipping of parish churches such as Marholm.

Church building counted as a charitable work. The wealthy built chantries and endowed them with income plus the commitment to say prayers for their soul. Marholm had two chantries – one, as mentioned, to St Guthlac, founded by Sir William Thorpe and Dame Anne in 1367, and the other by the Sir William Fitzwilliam who rebuilt the chancel [22].

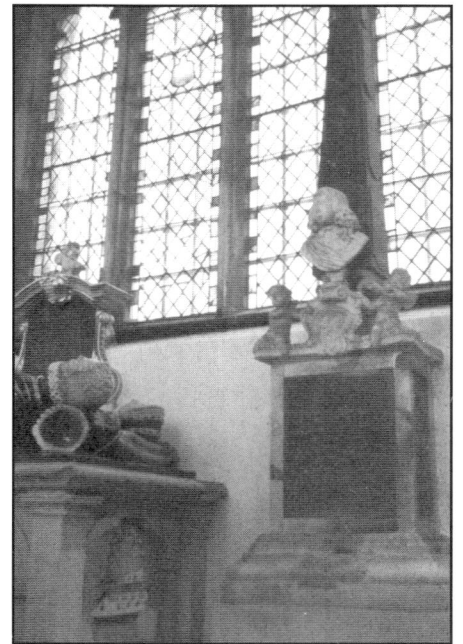
Fig 17k. Tomb of Edward Hunter

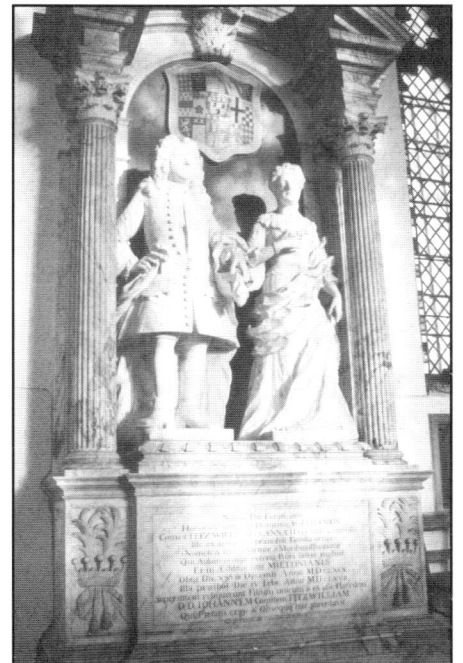
Fig 17l. Tomb of 3rd Earl Fitzwilliam by Fisher

Fig 17m. Engraving of original Fisher Sculpture

From the poorer people, considerable income was probably raised by parish celebrations such as plays, and collections or gifts in kind. [23] Unfortunately, Marholm churchwarden records have not survived from the medieval period.

Bequests were especially important. A gift to the church in which you had been baptised was customary. [24] Some of the bequests to Marholm in the early 16th century include:-

Robert Wyttylbury 1506 –   *'I will that incontynente after the deth of my wif the church of Marholm have vj bokes, that is to saye a masse boke, an antyfoner, a manuell, a processionary, an ordinall & a Legenda Sanctorum to remayne in the said church of Marham.'*

Alyes Bucchere 1513 –   *'I bequeth to saynt Gutlace a tawell" I bequeth my best coverlet to Marham chyrch and a flaxon schette.'*

Richard Wildbor 1522 –   *'To ye rode light & sepulchre light a sem (of) barley'*
'To ye torchys a sem (of) barley.' [25]

Recent Times

The Church in Marholm today continues to play a vibrant role in the community, and not only through the inevitable cycle of birth, marriage and death. There is a continuous need for preservation and refurbishment to which the parishioners have responded. In the spring of 1996, at an Ecumenical Festal Evensong, the renovated Lady Chapel was dedicated by the Archdeacon of Oakham, Bernard Fernyhough, assisted by the Rector William Burke and Father Peter Rollings, the Roman Catholic priest at The Church of the Holy Spirit, Bretton. The altar was presented by Noel Darby of Manor Farm in memory of his mother Eleanor Darby, who was Church Warden for some fifty years. The Gift Book and Stand were given by his wife Joan in memory of infant Noelle. The Votive Tray for candles was given by Fay Jarvis of Home Farm. The blue hanging lamp was a gift from Father Rollings and the Roman Catholic congregation of the Holy Spirit parish at Bretton. Sir Stephen Hastings, husband of the Hon. Lady Hastings, presented a 17th century Italian picture of Our Lady and Child, which had belonged to his family for some years.

Following the untimely death in 1997 of Lady Hastings, the daughter of the last Countess Fitzwilliam, her husband placed a plaque in her memory on the South wall of the chancel, and above the High Altar, an 18th century Venetian silver sanctuary light. Although Lady Hastings was Roman Catholic, she regularly worshipped in Marholm Church.

Fig 17n. The Hon. Lady Hastings' Memorial Plaque

The kneelers in the Church have been given by many of the parishioners in memory of friends and family. The nine wrought-iron candelabra were given by John and Gina Hill in celebration of their Ruby wedding anniversary. The green brocade curtains screening the tower arch were given in memory of Leonard Brown by his family. The Processional Cross carved by Glyn Mould was presented by Mary Jarvis in memory of her husband Toby.

The Church continues to inspire the community. The ladies' sewing circle made beautiful silk banners and pulpit cloths. An appeal for the reroofing of the church raised £15,000 from all kinds of sources, small and large - coffee mornings and tombola were held in private homes and the village hall, and bring and buy sales swelled the coffers. In September 2001 there was huge support for a wonderful Flower Festival, when professional and amateur enthusiasts gave their services to decorate the church. Over the centuries, the church must have witnessed many celebrations, but it is difficult to imagine that it could ever have looked more glorious than on that day. The work on the roof was completed in 2002.

Hazel Yates and Andrea Bone

We have drawn heavily in this chapter on a detailed history of our church written in 1995 by Mr R S Edwards, of Bretton We are most grateful to him for allowing us to use his work.

Fig 17o. Church Laity. l-r: Fay Jarvis (cross), Dora Hooper (server), William Craven (churchwarden), Roy Armitage (former churchwarden), Sir Stephen Hastings (former patron), Rodney Yates (former churchwarden), Enid Johnson (churchwarden), Gina Hill (verger).

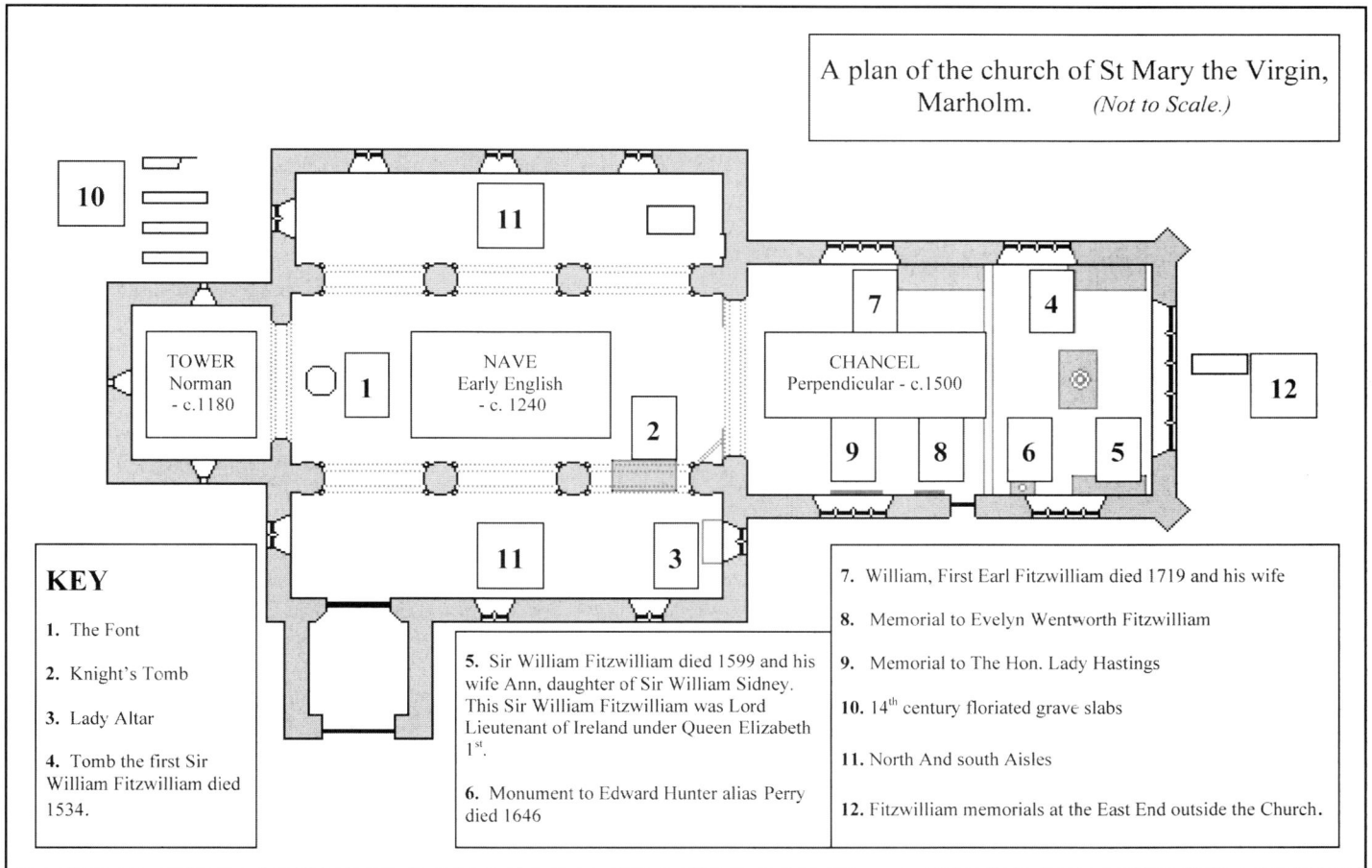

A plan of the church of St Mary the Virgin, Marholm. *(Not to Scale.)*

TOWER
Norman
- c.1180

NAVE
Early English
- c. 1240

CHANCEL
Perpendicular - c.1500

KEY

1. The Font

2. Knight's Tomb

3. Lady Altar

4. Tomb the first Sir William Fitzwilliam died 1534.

5. Sir William Fitzwilliam died 1599 and his wife Ann, daughter of Sir William Sidney. This Sir William Fitzwilliam was Lord Lieutenant of Ireland under Queen Elizabeth 1st.

6. Monument to Edward Hunter alias Perry died 1646

7. William, First Earl Fitzwilliam died 1719 and his wife

8. Memorial to Evelyn Wentworth Fitzwilliam

9. Memorial to The Hon. Lady Hastings

10. 14th century floriated grave slabs

11. North And south Aisles

12. Fitzwilliam memorials at the East End outside the Church.

Fig 17p. Medieval grave slabs North of the tower in Marholm churchyard. These are typical of the North Cambridgeshire region. Most of such stones at Castor have been re-used to cap the churchyard wall. The ones at Marholm are excellent 13th century examples of this art form.

Fig 17q. Marholm churchyard has a fine collection of 18th century chest (or table) tombs.

Notes

1   *The Victorian County History of Northampton*, Vol 2, 1906, p 500.
2   Colin Platt, *The Parish Churches of Medieval England*, 1981, p 8.
3   Leaflet prepared by Robert Walker for the visit of the Cambridgeshire Historic Churches Trust in 1990.
4   Rev. WD Sweeting *Parish Churches in and around Peterborough*, 1860, pp 3 and 8.
5   *The Victorian County History of Northampton*, Vol 2, 1906, p 501.
6   *ibid.*
7   *ibid.*
8   Rev WD Sweeting, *Parish Churches in and around Peterborough*, 1860, p 5.
9   Leaflet prepared by Robert Walker for the visit of the Cambridgeshire Historic Churches Trust in 1990.
10 *ibid.*
11 *The Victorian County History of Northampton*, Vol 2, 1906, p 500.
12 *ibid.*
13 The Correspondence of Lord Fitzwilliam and Francis Guybon his Steward 1697-1709, 1990, p 18.
14 *The Victorian County History of Northampton*, Vol 2, 1906, p501.
15 John Bridges, *The History of Northamptonshire*, 1791, Vol 2, p 518mbgh.
16 *The Victorian County History of Northampton*, Vol 2, 190,6 p 501.
17 John Bridges, *The History of Northamptonshire*, 1791, Vol 2, p 516.
18 *The Victorian County History of Northampton*, Vol 2, 1906, p501.
19 Rev. WD Sweeting, *Parish Churches in and around Peterborough*, 1860, p 7.
20 Hughes & Hatcher, *Medieval England - Rural Society and Economic Change* 1086-1348, 1978, pp 108-9.
21 Richard Morris, *Churches in the Landscape*, 1989, pp 360-1.
22 Rev. WD Sweeting, *Parish Churches in and around Peterborough*, 1860, p 1.
23 RN Swanson, *The Church and Society in Late Medieval England*, 1993, p 28.
24 Richard Morri,s *Churches in the Landscape*, 1989, p 356.
25 *The Parish Churches and Religious Houses of Northampton*, pp 145-6.

Chapter 18
Farming and the Villages

Although the practice of agriculture has evolved steadily over the centuries, there has been a fundamental change in the methods of farming over the last 50 years which has altered the lives of people in rural communities forever. Our villages all grew up around agriculture and until the last quarter of the 20th century nearly all employment derived from farming or from jobs allied to it. In the 1881 census the population of Castor and Ailsworth was over 1000 people [1]. Nearly all the men were employed in agriculture. At the beginning of the 21st century, in the whole benefice only 15 men are directly involved in farming. Continued improved mechanisation has been a most important factor that has helped improve efficiency but the consequence has been a reduction in the number of holdings due to amalgamations and far fewer people working on the land. A 500 acre farm that would have employed 15 to 20 men and used 20 to 25 shire horses before the Second World War could well be run by one man with appropriate machinery today.

Fig 18a. Village Farm Castor: 1934 Theo Hensman on Gilliva.

In the case of Castor and Ailsworth, the only time when other industries were as important as agriculture was during the Roman occupation when the area round Normangate Field was a mass of pottery kilns, surrounded by prestigious villas.

Evidence of Early Farmers
The earliest farmers have still left their mark in and around our villages. The large number of ring ditches and enclosures revealed by air photography [2]. were, in Iron Age and Roman times, the sites of small farmsteads and enclosures for stock. In 1975, a Roman farm was excavated in Castor along the Northern edge of Normangate Field [3]. It consisted of a farmyard and barn (40 feet by 20 feet), with ditches, stout fences and a palisade, pens and water tanks, probably for stock, dating from before AD150 to AD200. (See Fig 18c). Among other Saxon farms, the convent founded by St Kyneburgha in the 7th century would certainly have included a farm (probably worked by lay-brothers) to provide their food. The location and age of Village Farm in Castor suggests the possibility that it goes back to those days. If so, it would have been a church farm for nearly 1300 years, until it was sold by the Church Commissioners in 1985.

The Domesday Book
In the time of the Domesday Book [4]. 1086, the feudal lord of all the land in our villages was the Abbey at Peterborough. Castor consisted of two manors, Ailsworth of one manor, and Milton of another, all in the parish of Castor which consisted of 14 hides under the plough (a hide was 120 acres), 30 acres of meadowland, 54 ploughs and three mills. A full transcript of the Domesday Book entries is at Appendix 1. A total of 1680 acres was under the plough in 1086; at the time of the enclosure in 1898 this had risen to 3700 acres. Castor cum Ailsworth and Sutton were the last open-field parishes in Northamptonshire. WE Tate writes that *'the eventual enclosure of Castor Parish, completed in 1898, came about because of the death of a highly respected*

Fig 18b. Village Farm Castor 1930s: South view

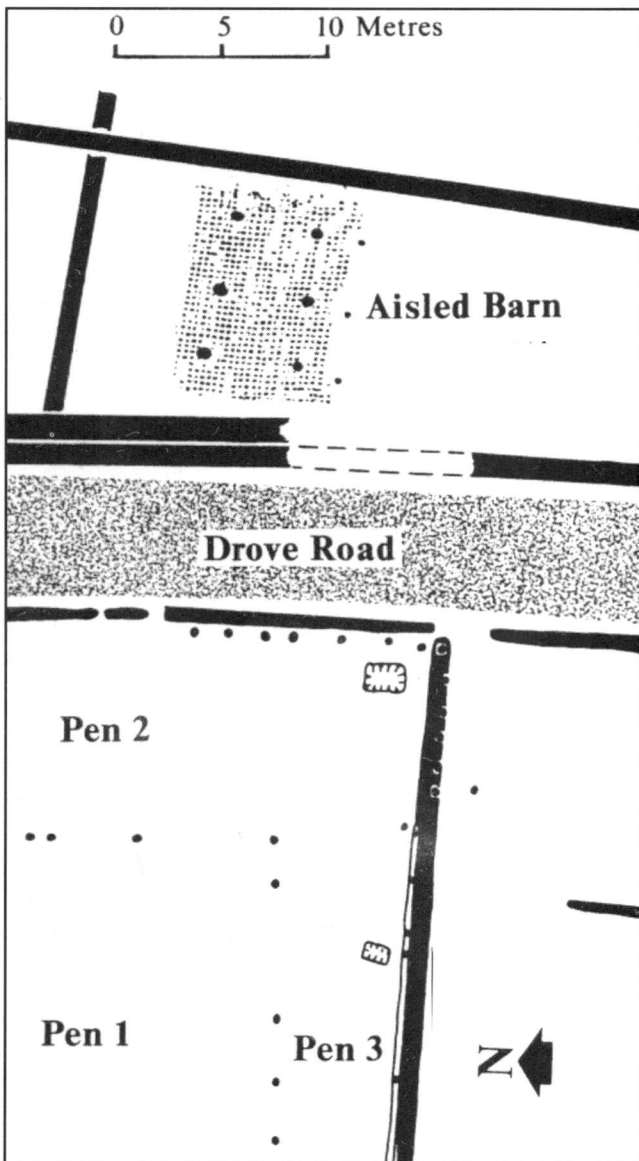

Fig 18c. Roman farm plan: excavated in 1973
Normangate Field Castor

Fig 18d. Castor Church: carving 1120 ox grazing. The
oldest pictures of farming in the villages are the carvings
in St Kyneburgha's Church. (Photo: J Tovey)

farmer who arbitrated when there were problems, exacerbated
by the appointment of a new agent by the Ecclesiastical
Commissioners who could neither understand, not had any
patience with the peculiarities of open field farming' [5].

Early Farming and the Beginning of the Villages

In lowland areas such as ours, medieval farmsteads were
grouped together in clusters (the start of villages as we know
them). The surrounding land was farmed in common, under a
system known as Open Field farming. The land was divided
into separate plough-strips, meadowland and common grazing
–the Three Field system. Oldfield, to the North of Castor and
Ailsworth, was, for centuries, common pasturage for the
villagers. The large arable Open Fields were divided into
unfenced strips about a furlong (220 yards) long and 10-20
yards wide called selions. Farmers had several strips,
intermingled among those of his neighbours. The good and the
poor lands were thus shared out. Common land, such as Sutton
Heath, was set aside for grazing.

The land was in effect owned by the Lord of the Manor. This
was a Saxon system that survived the Norman Conquest, and
in our case survived until the late 19th century. The names of
the large open fields in Castor were Thorn Field (the high
ground between the main road and the river East of Castor),
Milton Field (behind and to the North and East of Castor), Mill
Field (South of Castor between the river and the village), and
Normangate. In Ailsworth there were five open fields; Upton,
(North of the village on the way to Upton) Wood, Dales, Little
and Nether Fields (South West of Ailsworth) [6]. The fact that
the Open Field system continued so late in these parishes made
negotiations for the building of the Peterborough to Wansford
railway very complicated. In 1842 the L&BR Company had to
negotiate the purchase of 50 strips in Sutton, 103 in Ailsworth
and 273 in Castor from different farmers [7].

The typical 'ridge and furrow', wave-like undulations in curved
'S' shapes are thought to result from medieval ploughing
methods. 'Ridge and furrow comes naturally from driving an
asymmetrical mouldboard plough, drawn by eight oxen, within
the narrow limits of a half-acre strip' [8]. Cultivation remains
of the Open-Fields can be seen in the fields round the parishes;
in Thorn Field, for example, are traces of 'ridge and furrow
arranged end-on and interlocked furlongs, of ten with the
typical reversed-S curves' [9]. Cattle have always been
important for meat and milk, and oxen as draught animals in
the villages. There are two carvings of oxen on capitals of
Castor Church Tower (c 1120), and in c1240 Abbot Walter de
St Edmundo built a new cattle market at Castor [10].

Many former farmsteads still exist in our villages, but have
been converted into private houses, such as the Old Smithy, The
Cedars, Clay Cottage and The Limes, all in Castor, as also have
Poplar Farmhouse and the Forester's Lodge (formerly Fruit
Farm) in Marholm. The Old Smithy was farmed in the 19th

century by two families still living in the villages, the Dickens family and then the Harris family. The North wall of the barn in The Cedars at Castor has a date stone of 1709. By 1800, the smart South front was built by the Wrights, and it ceased to be a farm. Dispersed farmsteads in isolated locations were unusual. An isolated medieval farm generally indicated either a deserted village or a grange farm (a farm that belonged to a monastery) resulting from a grant of an assart. An assart was a pocket of farmland cleared from woodland, scrub or wasteland. Belsize Farm, on the border between Castor and Marholm is a classic example of this,

Fig 18e. Top Lodge Farm Upton: South view winter 1981-82

permission to assart having been granted cAD1214 [11]. Top Lodge Farm Upton, another isolated farm, may also have been a result of an assart, because it dates from well before the Enclosures in our benefice, or, as its name might indicate, some form of hunting lodge. Lower Lodge Farm Upton is now run as stables.

Land-use, ownership and grants to farm it, were the major preoccupation of the manor courts, and some farming families have a long history in our villages. For example, in 1351, William and Alice Sharp were granted an acre and a half of arable land in the fields of Castor [12]. There are still Sharpes holding land in the village today – Brian Sharpe was a tenant in 2001, and his son Paul, still holds land here. Only after the Enclosure of the parish open fields (in our case the late 19th and early 20th century) did dispersed farms become more common in Lowland England and we only have three: Top Lodge and Lower Lodge in Upton, Belsize and Scotsman's Lodge on Helpston Heath on the edge of the benefice.

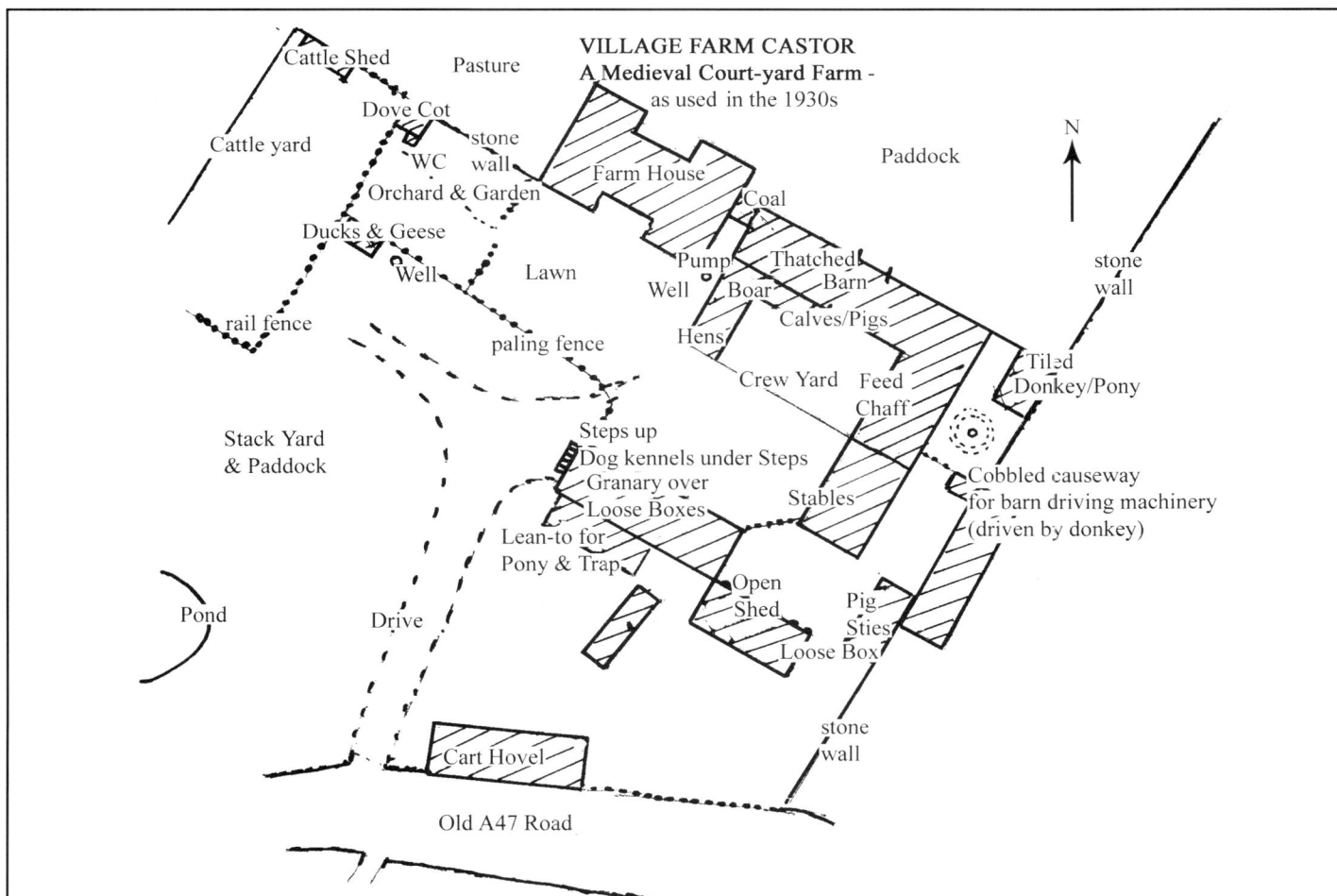

Fig 18f. Old Courtyard Farm: Village Farm Castor in the 1930s.

Fig 18g. Castor Church: carving 1120 - man feeding ox.
(Photo J Tovey)

Courtyard farms were common in the medieval period, of which Village Farm Castor (probably the oldest existing farmstead in the area) was a good example until its outbuildings were demolished in 1985. Home Farm Marholm still retains its ancient court yard and buildings. Such farmsteads continued to the 20th century, with a farmhouse for the family, a barn with access for carts, stabling, and byres for wintering the breeding stock, (most cattle were slaughtered on or about Martinmas - 11 November - until the 18th century). After the enclosures, dispersed farms became common. With land farmed in compact blocks, it became practical for owners to build new farms outside the village centres, in their newly allocated holdings. In the case of our villages the landlords (in nearly all cases either the Milton Estate or the Dean and Chapter or Ecclesiastical Commissioners) enclosed the land and did away with the Open Field system very late on.

The enclosure of land in Castor and Ailsworth was not completed until 1898. It is said that the Bishop and the then Earl Fitzwilliam stood at Salter's Tree, just off the Marholm Road and agreed that Milton Estate would take everything to the right, that is the North and East, and the Church would take everything to the left, that is the South and West. How true that is, is a matter of speculation, but certainly the church owned much of the land in Castor, all the land in Ailsworth and Sutton, and Milton owned the land in the East of the parish of Castor, all of Marholm, and all of Upton (which they had bought off the Dove family in the late 18th century). Sutton was not enclosed until 1903, once the Hopkinson family had bought the Manor of Sutton from the Dean and Chapter. It seems that historically all the farms in our villages have always been farmed by tenants (and still are for the most part). There were no owner-occupier farms in all these years in our benefice, with the exception of Home Farm Castor and then only for a period of 40 years from 1919 when Castor House and its Home Farm were sold off separately. The farm was bought by the Polls (Michael Longfoot's mother's family), until this too was sold in 1961, most of the land going to Milton, and the farmstead rejoined to Castor House.

The biggest barns in a farmstead were often used for threshing. They had large double doors, to allow access for the stacked carts. During the threshing of the grain by big hand flails, the doors were opened, to allow the wind to blow away the chaff. The bar across the floor of the door, to keep the wheat grain in the barn, is the origin of the word 'threshold'. Many of these barns have been pulled down (such as the one at Manor Farm Castor), or converted into housing, such as Home Farm Castor. The only such barns still in use are the magnificent barn at Belsize Farm, the barn at the Hollies and the smaller one at Home Farm Marholm.

Farming

For thousands of years farming has been about growing cereals and care of stock. What has changed has been the technology for doing this more efficiently. On the capitals of Castor Church (1120AD) there are carvings of oxen being fed. Oxen were still used in some areas for ploughing in the 18th century. The widespread use of large draught horses pulling ploughs, most people's idea of traditional farming, is relatively recent. Sickles were used for harvesting until the 20th century. Horses were still used for ploughing in the lifetime of our present farmers. Michael Longfoot of Upton, remembers the last time this was the case at Model Farm Upton in 1948.

Farming was hard work requiring intensive manpower. Threshing machines were introduced

Fig 18h. Village Farm Castor 1930s: stacking the wheat, Sid Hensman on top with pitchfork.

in the late 19th century, driven by steam. The contractors used by most farmers in this area were the Gibbons family, whose yard was in Castor beside the Village Hall. The first crop to be harvested was the grass used for hay (for feeding animals in the winter). The wheat was left in the fields after harvest to dry in stooks, and then brought into the stackyard, and 'stouked' – put into a stack which was then thatched on top to keep it dry. Often it would not be threshed until it was needed for sale.

It seems very likely that vine-growing took place until the Middle Ages in our villages. The Romans used to grow vines on the North bank of the River Nene. The carvings on the capitals at Castor Church (AD1120) include a man harvesting grapes and putting them in a basket, and we know the Abbey had vine-yards in Castor. Fishing rights were also important, and there seems for example to have been a medieval fish-pond for use of the monks at Belsize Farm. Dovecots, very much a feature of villages, especially in the yards of manor houses and farms were common. There are still dovecots at Village Farm and Castor House, and there was one beside Castor Churchyard until the 1950s.

Historically, the higher land above the river valley, such as Top Lodge Upton, being rather thin and 'brashy' has been used as pasture, and only the advent of stronger ploughs and modern fertilizers has allowed it to make successful arable land. Even so, farmers today would be doing well to get three tons of wheat per acre off this land, whereas in the Fen, in a good year, yields of four tons per acre are not unusual. This may explain why in 1762, more shepherds were recorded at Castor and its hamlets than in any other parish in the Nassaburgh Hundred– seven shepherds in all – *'confirmation that sheep had a prominent place in the agricultural economy of Castor during the eighteenth century'*. John Morton (1712) observed that in the Nassaburgh Hundred, heathland *'yields a sweet and cleanly Herbage, which feeds a Breed of small Sheep, whose flesh is usually much commended and esteem'd'* [13].

In 1849, there were 30 farmers and graziers in the villages (16 in Castor, four in Ailsworth, four in Upton, two in Sutton and six in Marholm), all tenants, employing hundreds of people. In 1874, there were 24 farmers and graziers, of which surprisingly six were women as the listed tenants. There are still eight working farms in the villages, most of the farming being arable. Some land is now farmed by people who live elsewhere. There are no dairies left, (the last dairyman being Stanley Jarvis of Home Farm Marholm, who stopped milking in 1998) but sheep and beef cattle are still kept. In 1949, the Longfoots of Home Farm Castor were delivering

Fig 18i. Motive Power – horses - Village Farm Castor 1930: George Wade, carrying granddaughter Mary Hensman, on a binder, being pulled by Pearl and Major.

Fig 18j. Motive Power – early tractor - Village Farm Castor 1940s: the same binder now being towed by the first tractor at the farm, George Wade on the tractor, his grandson Theo Hensman on the binder.

Fig 18k. Motive Power – today Peter Harris with a modern tractor, trailer and combine near Dead Man's Hollow Upton.

Fig 18l. Castor Church: carving 1120 - man picking grapes. (Photo: J Tovey)

milk to 208 houses every day. The milk was taken round in delivery buckets, (not bottles) by pony and trap, and ladled out into jugs which residents left on their doorsteps. This system carried on until the 1950s, when the Longfoots sold their business to Horrells. Until the 1950s every other house in Marholm still had a pigsty, and George Jarvis would butcher the pigs for the owners in the autumn.

Until recently agriculture was a family tradition. A man would farm, sometimes with his brothers, until he was ready to retire, then perhaps move into a cottage on the holding and his son would take over. Fewer sons now follow their fathers, although four have in our benefice – Andrew Harrison-Smith, Stewart Wood, Trevor Jarvis and David Longfoot. Farmers have traditionally contributed enormously to the community life of our villages (and still do). Three of our eight churchwardens, for example, are farmers, and many others like Jim Wood, Michael Longfoot, Theo Hensman and Noel Darby have also served for years on parish councils. They also provide great support to community activities with manpower and equipment. The continuing decline in numbers of people engaged in agriculture will undoubtedly affect the character of village life.

Fig 18m. Old Dovecot: This was demolished in the 1950s. Until the mid 18th century, dovecots provided an important source of protein in the winter.

Fig 18o. Home Farm Castor: 1920s duck pond with barns and haystacks behind.

Fig 18n. Brian Sharpe shearing sheep 1960s.

Fig 18p. The Gibbons threshing at Reg Cooke's farm, The Hollies in the 1950s. Bob Gibbons on drum, Ernie on trailer, Jim weighing sacks, Bill Coles on the stack.

Farming Today And Some Farming Families

Top Lodge Upton and the Harris family

Top Lodge Farm Upton, owned by Milton Estate, is farmed by Peter Harris (who lives there with his wife Claire) and his brother Brian. The Harris family have certainly lived locally since 1749, the days of John Harris. His great-grandson John lived at the Ferry Lodge and was Clerk-of-works at Milton. His son John William Harris was given £20 by his mother, to start farming on Lady Day 1880, and he took on the farm now known as The Old Smithy, in Castor. In the mid-19th century, this was farmed by the ancestors of Robert Dickens (of Evergeen Hill). The tenant in 1847 was Ann Dickens, who was still farming in 1874. JW Harris's farm at Castor included much of the land now farmed by Jim Wood at Hollies Farm, such as the meadows down Mill Road. The farm was mixed arable, sheep, a dairy and a milk round. He was also a keen horseman, and bought and bred some serious horseflesh. We read in his account book:

'Bought brown mare on 16 Mar 1895 for £30-19s-6d at Lutton from Mr J Brawn'.

His sons Arthur and Charlie worked with him, and Arthur spent much of his time breaking horses. John William Harris stopped farming at Castor in 1933 when they took on Lower Lodge Farm Upton. Arthur lived at Primrose Cottage, Church Walk Upton (where Dave and Elli Burton live now).

Fig 18q. A Harris farm in 1920s: John William Harris (mounted) with his horseman Ted Woodward in the courtyard of the farmstead that is now 47 Peterborough Road Castor the Old Smithy.

Farming at Top Lodge Farm Upton

Eventually, in 1940, the brothers went their separate ways and Arthur Harris (Peter and Brian's father) took on Top Lodge Farm (rent free for the first three years). The farmhouse at Top Lodge is very old, the Northern end probably being Elizabethan. At Top Lodge, farming was mixed and included arable, sheep, pigs, hens, beef cattle, cows and a dairy. The milk all went to Horrells, and had to be delivered to the roundabout on the now A47 (along with the milk from Manor Farm Upton) by 8am every day, never mind frost or snow – sometimes using a tractor and snowplough if necessary.

Peter Harris, Arthur's son, remembers three or four Shire Horses, including two greys and a bay. Arthur was very mechanically minded; he had a tractor in the war – it was an American Allis Chalmers Caterpillar Tractor; the 'War Ag' lent him £1000 to buy this in 1943. They finished with working horses before 1950, although the dairy ceased in 1968. Horrells used delivery drays for their milk rounds until the 1960s.

They bought their first combine in 1955, an Allis Chalmers American combine towed by a tractor. Before that they still used a binder, cut the corn, bundled it into sheaves; picked up the sheaves two-at-a-time by hand, and put them into stooks. They were manually loaded into a cart, and taken into the stack-yard. Gibbons' men would come up from Castor with their threshing machines and thresh in the yard. Loose straw was collected up, put into a stack and used as bedding. Threshing took place at

Fig 18r. Arthur Harris at Top Lodge Farm Upton using four legs to get about before the days of 4-wheel drive.

harvest or as soon as possible after. The grain was put into sacks from the threshing machines and the sacks carried up into a loft on a man's back. A sack of grain weighed 18 stone and beans 19 stone.

Peter took over the tenancy of Top Lodge in 1973, although he had worked there since the '60s. The land was very wet, and in recent years much of it has been drained, and ploughed up, turning it into arable. He has also taken over 100 acres from the Nene Park Trust since Theo Hensman retired (land which his grandfather had farmed in the past). He now farms 560 acres, mostly beef cattle, sugar beet, arable, sheep and suckler cows (home-bred) since the 1980s. Mains water arrived at the farm after the war, but mains electricity only became available in 1957.

Model Farm, Upton and the Longfoot Family

Model Farm Upton, owned by Milton Estate, is occupied by Michael Longfoot with his son David. Michael's great-grandfather, Richard Longfoot is buried in Castor Churchyard. He had two sons, Matthew and George (Michael's grandfather). George Longfoot farmed Green Farm Castor, but his son Walter (Wally) became an engineer at Brotherhoods, and so Green Farm was then farmed by George's nephew Harry Longfoot, and then Harry's son Roly Longfoot. Meanwhile Dick and Len Longfoot (sons of Matthew) farmed The Limes

Fig 18s. Top Lodge Farm Upton: Peter Harris and John Healey shearing in the 1980s.

Farm Castor. This is now a private house (Justin and Tracey Blackmore) as is Green Farm (Ron and Ros Pearson). Walter Longfoot reverted to farming when he married Kathleen Poll the daughter of Frederick Poll of Home Farm attached to Castor House. This was part of the White's estate.

Castor House and the attached Home Farm were sold by the White family in 1914. It was split up and sold again in 1919. Frederick Poll bought Home Farm and this was the only owner-occupier farm in the area. It was about 190 acres. All the other farmers were tenants of either Milton Estate or the Church Commissioners. Sir Richard Winfrey MP

Fig 18t. Home Farm Castor: Mrs Poll (Michael Longfoot's grandmother) with a sow and piglets in 1920s. The Poll and Longfoot families farmed here from 1920-1960.

bought Castor House and its grounds at the same time. After Frederick Poll died, the ownership of Home Farm went to his son Bob, but was farmed by his son-in-law Walter Longfoot, with the new owner, Bob Poll, working on the farm for Walter Longfoot.

In 1934, Walter Longfoot took on the additional tenancy of Model Farm Upton from Milton Estate; he farmed the land but let the house until 1955, the year his son married Ruth Watts. Michael and Ruth moved into Model Farm and farmed it in partnership with his father. Michael now farms it in partnership with their son David. Previous tenants had been Fred Allen, and before him Wilfred Holmes, who also farmed Lower Lodge Farm Upton. Meanwhile, Home Farm Castor was auctioned by the Polls in 1961. At the same time Michael Longfoot bought the meadows by the river.

For many years the family farmed Home Farm Castor and Model Farm Upton simultaneously.

Farming at Model Farm

The last field to be ploughed by a horse-drawn plough was the field behind the former council houses in Upton in 1948. The plough had one furrow and could work about an acre a day with the horse. The ploughman was Fred Hornsby, uncle of Lynn Bell. Three of the horses were sold in 1949 for a total of £60. The Longfoots still kept four horses for pulling muck-carts etc. Their names were Flower and Beauty (Percherons) and Sharper and Jewel (Shires). Fred Hornsby would come into the yard at 6am to feed the horses and get them ready for work in the fields by 7am. The last working horses went in 1960, the year Walter Longfoot died.

Farming at Model farm included arable, beef, sheep and pigs. Ruth also kept poultry, which at their peak included 800 - 900 hens. They also reared turkeys for Christmas, but stopped the hens c1970. They supplied eggs to the Means' shop in Castor. At one stage the Longfoots employed 12 men; they now only have two, Sam Jefferies and Mick Hill, although Tony Ladds (apart from National Service) spent all his working life on Manor and Model Farm Upton until he retired. The really big change was of course the advent of modern machinery.

Michael can recall in the early days when the barn at Poll's Yard (Home Farm) would be filled with barley and then Gibbons' men would come in with their threshing machines. The Longfoots bought their first combine harvester in 1950. It was a red, petrol-driven Massey Harris and cost £1000. The change-over was gradual; they still had binders for making sheaves, and haymaking; sugar beet was still picked by hand, knocked and laid in 1960s. Taylor's lorries (Taylor's Transport of Ailsworth) would take away seven or eight tons having taken five or six hours to load a lorry. Now a 28-ton lorry is loaded in 10-15 minutes. Without doubt the generation that has seen the real change would be that of Ruth Longfoot's mother, (a farmer's wife) who died in 1990 aged 95.

Manor Farm Upton and the Herbert Family

Manor Farm is owned by Milton Estate, having previously been owned by the Dove family until the 18th century. Allen Herbert took over Manor Farm Upton from his father, Thomas William Herbert, and farmed it until 1978. Allen and Joyce now live at 17 Peterborough Road Castor. George

Fig 18u. Walter Longfoot with a bull at Home Farm Castor 1940s.

Fig 18v. Home Farm Castor 1920s: Bob Poll milking.

Fig 18w. Model Farm Upton 1950s: Michael Longfoot (left) and Richard Green (right) with early Allis U tractor.

Fig 18x. The Longfoots' first combine working near Castor Heights in the 1950s.

Herbert, Allen's grandfather, farmed Glebe Farm Godmanchester, and was also at one time the Mayor of Godmanchester. He started work driving a coach and four horses, and eventually retired as a farmer. Thomas William Herbert, Allen's father, took over the tenancy of Manor Farm Upton in 1933 when Allen was 15. A family friend knew George Fitzwilliam of Milton, who asked him to take it on. It was considered a privilege to farm on the Fitzwilliam estate.

Farming at Manor Farm Upton:

When Thomas William Herbert took Manor Farm Upton, it was a mixed farm. The tenancy agreement shows the following details: Date of Agreement 27 April 1932; size, 245 acres, three roods and 17 poles. The previous tenant was JR Horrell. The terms of the agreement included the requirement to walk a foxhound puppy every year, and to deliver 12 tons of wheat straw for thatching every year. The Herberts later took on a further 42 acres, and when Allen retired they had 300 acres. Thomas William Herbert died 18 October 1959 age 68 years.

Allen, at first farmed separately from his father, with seven acres plus 60 odd acres by Top Lodge Farm. He took over the tenancy of Manor Farm Upton and moved into Manor Farm House in 1959. At that stage it included a dairy, sheep, and arable. They used to deliver one churn of milk around the village of Upton, the rest was delivered to the main road (Peterborough-Wansford) for collection.

They had six working horses before the war, French Percherons and Suffolk Punches, and a couple of ponies. One horse was Smiler, a cross-bred shire, almost a pet, but they bred from her. She was the mother of the horses they used to work. The last horses worked in 1946.

They also had an old Ford tractor, brought second-hand, then a grey Massey Ferguson, as well as a Crawler (Caterpillar). Their land was eight fields in Allen's time; the same area is now only two enclosures. Their busiest time was during lambing. At one stage the Ministry of Agriculture told them what to grow by the acreage, and they planted sugar beet, wheat, barley, oats and for the last two years only, also rape.

Fig 18y. Manor Farm Upton 1920s: note that the wing on the East side has since been demolished.

During the war, Allen Herbert commanded the Upton and Sutton Home Guard. Other members included Mr Gathercoal, George Ransome (Elsie Ransome's husband of Sutton), Arthur Mason (now of Benam's Close Castor), John Fox, Mr Ward, Charlie Favell (of Sutton, Sheila Crane's father – Sheila still lives in Sutton), Steve Britten (brother of Ernie Britten), Ernie Britten the platoon sergeant, Arthur Harris, Mr Fox, Charlie Harris, Arthur Fox, and John William Herbert. Thomas William Herbert of Manor Farm was the official Air Raid Warden. Whenever there was an air-raid warning, he would run out of Manor Farm into the field to Church Walk Upton shouting "Air-raid". Allen and his father used to shoot on the Milton Tenant Shoots.

If Allen went to a dance, and arrived home after 4am in his dinner jacket, his father would meet him and say "we're milking", and follow him out to the dairy, where he would milk in his dinner jacket and 'wellies' (which they wore to dances and changed there).

Allen handed the tenancy back to Milton Estate in October 1978; the estate wished to farm land itself, using Manor Farm Upton as the base for the operation. At this stage the estate pulled down some of the old farm buildings and built general purpose buildings and grain stores. The house is now occupied by Nick Vergette, with his wife Bridget. He farms much of the land that went with Manor Farm, in addition to his farm at Ufford.

Fig 18z. Brian Sharpe on hay cart 1950s.

The Hollies Farm Castor and the Wood Family

Jim, Patsy and Stewart Wood farm at The Hollies Farm, Castor, which is owned by Milton Estate.
The first member of Jim's recent family to be in farming was his grandfather, James Wood, who started life as a stone-mason working on cathedrals and churches. He eventually bought a dairy farm, Lower Bodmisken Farm at Blackborough near Cullompton, Devon, which is still farmed by the family.

George Wood left school at the age of 12, and left Devon at 16 to go coalmining in Tonypandy, Wales. By the time he was 26, he had qualified as a Blaster. He married Daisy Garrod and they ran hotels and public houses, starting with a pub in Tonypandy. He returned to farming running Welsh Lane Farm at Stowe, Buckinghamshire where Jim, the youngest of eight was born. George Wood then took on Manor Farm Yaxley throughout the second World War years prior to buying Brooke Farm, Polebrook, near Oundle. In 1946, George bought Rough's Farm in Sawtry. George died in 1953 leaving the farm to Jim (16 yrs) and two of his brothers.

Farming at the Hollies Farm, Castor

In 1963 Jim, Patsy and daughter Vanessa moved to the Hollies Farm (which his father had previously looked at and rejected years before), but still remained in partnership with his brothers Toby and Don at Sawtry until 1976 when the farm was sold to Tom Darby. Through the years many people from the village have worked at the Hollies. They include, George Magan, Ernie Reynolds, Don Ireland, Mick Lampard and Andy Smith.

Jim started at the Hollies with 250 acres of arable land. He began keeping sheep only after taking on the grassland at Castor Mill following Mrs Brown's retirement. Jim employed Julian Uff (Colin Longfoot's cousin) as shepherd. Later on Jim kept pigs. Over the years, Hollies Farm gradually expanded as more land became available and they now farm approximately 1100 acres with the help of Gladdy Craythorne.

Jim and Stewart have been partners in the Hollies since 1991, although both have independent interests. Jim has owned the butcher's shop since 1976; this has just recently been re-furbished and is now known as the Country Butchers. Stewart purchased the Prince of Wales Feathers in 1998, and after major renovations has leased it to Martin and Jane Rutter.

Village Farm Castor, the Wade and Hensman Family

Theo Hensman, with his wife Meena, ran Village Farm Castor, which was owned by the Church Commisioners. The family gave up the actual farm-house in 1978. The first member of Theo's family to be farming in the village was his grandfather George Wade. Theo's paternal grandfather, George Hensman, lived in Thornhaugh, where he kept the Post Office, bakers and a milk round. They kept cows for the milk round, and if the weather was bad the milk was carried round the village in pails on a yoke, for the pony could not get up the hill if it was icy. The cows were kept in a paddock near the house. Theo's maternal grandfather, George Wade, farmed at Sacrewell Farm, which was then owned by William Abbott, brother of Wyman Abbott the solicitor. George Wade came from Black Ham, Holme Fen.

Farming at Village Farm Castor

In 1928 the Wade family, Theo's grandfather George and his wife Mary, moved to Village Farm Castor. It came about this way. They used to go from Sacrewell to Peterborough Market to shop. If they could not get a lift on a carrier's cart they would walk the whole way. The route took them through Castor. One day when passing, Grannie (Mary) Wade noticed that Village Farm seemed to be derelict, so she inquired of the Church Commissioners to see if it was vacant, for they felt they were at the beck and call of William Abbott at Sacrewell and decided to branch out on their own as tenants. It turned out that Village Farm had been empty for ten years, so they took on the lease. To start with there were 80 acres, mixed and arable, with the grass round the house and in The Empties (the fields opposite the farm across the Peterborough Road.) Their livestock included at first long-horn style red cattle, quite vicious in temperament. In those days a bullock had to be three years old before it could be slaughtered. As a result of discussion with a Mr Burke, the Church Commissioners' agent, they took on a further 50 acres of arable land by Station Road, near the railway line.

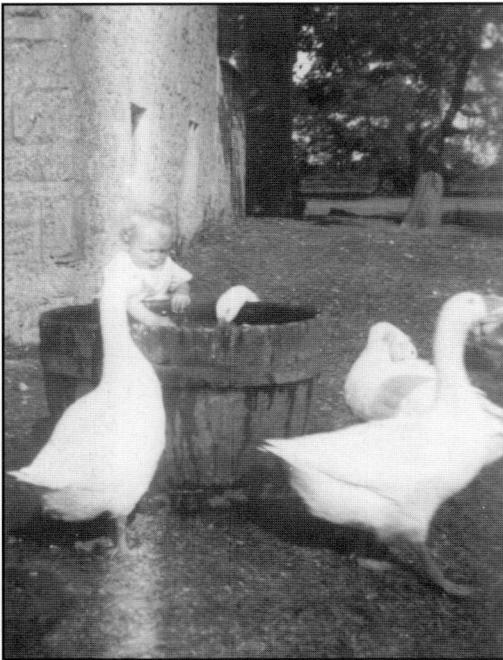

Fig 18aa. Village Farm Castor 1930s: North side, Theo Hensman playing with geese tub.

One day George Wade told Mr George Fitzwilliam that if he had any more land they would take it up at Village Farm. Within a few weeks he was sent for and biked up to the Hall, and was told *"there is more land for you Wade, between Duckpaddles, Oldfield Pond and White's Pond."* Mr Wade replied, *"I can't take that on, for it is farmed by a widow woman (Mrs Sharpe)".* *"Take it or leave it"* replied Mr Fitzwilliam *"for it is all you will have from me."* Mr Wade took it; this was a further 180 acres. He was given it rent-free for the first three years, then for ten shillings an acre thereafter, but of course this was not written down.

Fig 18bb. Village Farm Castor 1945: George and Mary Wade in trap, the pony is Polly.

They had no dairy at Village Farm; the cows were used for suckling calves, milk for the house and any excess used to feed young pigs. They had five horses that Theo remembers; Pearl was a lovely chestnut, Gilliva a dapple-grey, and Gypsy a chestnut. Pearl was struck by lightning during a thunderstorm in the Empties, and died in the field. Mr Wade bought a horse called Major, a dapple-grey, from Mr Jarvis. Mr Wade did everything; he was his own horseman. He would get up at 4 or 5am, feed the horses, have breakfast, and then go out to the fields at 6 or 7am. He would come back home at about 3pm, have dinner and sleep in a chair. He wore a large, long coat (which smelt of horse sweat and binder string), with deep pockets.

Grandpa Wade died in 1948 age 67. Grannie Wade remained, until her 80th year, at Village Farm, although it was too big for an elderly lady, so Theo in his teens moved back into it, and did it up a bit, and then Alf Wade and Doris also moved into it. Theo's father Sid Hensman also worked on the farm, having married George Wade's daughter Catherine. Sid moved in and worked for his keep, with no wages when he was just 21. All Catherine and Sid's children were born at Village Farm. Theo gave up the

Fig 18cc. Village Farm Castor late 1930s: Theo Hensman on Gypsy, behind Pearl (left) and Major (right).

farmhouse at Village Farm in 1978, but kept on the farm. He and Meena moved to 2 Splash Lane (a tied cottage for the Limes Farm) when Jack Longfoot moved out, then to Maffit Road (where Gladdy Craythorne now lives), then to Church View (41 Peterborough Road, a Milton house), then finally to 5 Andrews Close Ailsworth which they bought from Miss Goodyer.

Manor Farm Ailsworth, the Speechley Family and the Harrison-Smiths

Manor Farm was owned by the Church Commisioners. It has been recently farmed by two families still connected with the village, the Speechley family and the Harrison-Smiths. Julie Taylor (nee Speechley) and her husband John 'JT' now live at the Old Smithy Peterborough Road Castor with their son Charles and Julie's mother, Mary, Speechley. Julie Taylor's grandfather George Speechley farmed Manor Farm, Ailsworth as a tenant of the Church Commissioners.

Fig 18dd. Village Farm Castor 1930s: granary and crewyard, Lorna Sheppardson nee Wade with geese, left Robina Gibbons, right Mary Hensman.

George and Margaret Speechley, after their marriage in 1911, moved to Ailsworth where they took on Manor Farm. In the 1920s George's brother-in-law Harry Hines decided to try his hand at farming and took on Village Farm Castor, as tenants of the Church Commissioners. In the 1920s there was a Speechley farming in Ailsworth, a brother-in-law farming in Castor and another Speechley (Oswald) living at Three Chimneys, Castor.

George Speechley stopped farming in a big way, because of the agricultural depression in 1929, and he and his family moved into Clay Cottage, Clay Lane Castor, a house then owned by the Church. He took some animals with him, including a cow called Whitey, who was still around in the 1940s, and a hack named Polly, and two cart-horses, one called Turpin. (When Rupert Speechley married Mary in 1941 these animals were still around). George grazed these animals on the verges in Clay Lane, and sometimes tethered them on the verges of Helpston Road or the Heath. Martha, Margaret Speechley's maid when they married, accompanied them to Clay Cottage. Throughout this time George Speechley was a churchman, being Rector's Churchwarden at St Kyneburgha's for many years.

Extract of a reminiscence by Mary Speechley made in May 2002.
'Twenty five or thirty years ago I often met Rene Foster's husband who would stop and tell me, many times, about Rupert's father George Speechley who farmed at Ailsworth Manor Farm and for whom Mr Foster worked. Those years would be the earlier part of the 20th century. He was of course a young man and was so delighted that he was taught to drive the first tractor in the village – something he never forgot. The farm in those years was going strong and shooting and tennis parties were part of village life. George Speechley bought his first car from Gwen Heighton's father – a 'Lanchester'. The great and wonderful occasion of the birth of their son Rupert (father of Julie Taylor) in April 1920 after nearly ten years of married life caused them to send £350 toward the building of the Memorial Hospital on Midland Road Peterborough. The bells rang out too for his baptism as George was Rector's warden at St Kyneburgha's and his wife a devout church-goer. Sadly ten years later in 1931 Farmer George gave up farming– it was a reflection of those times in the depression years.'

The Harrison-Smith Family
In April 1945, Fred Harrison-Smith took on the tenancy of Manor Farm Ailsworth from the Church Commissioners. This consisted of 500 acres, the farm house and nine cottages and two yards for £952 per year. The previous tenant was a Mr Feeney, and before that Mr Colbert. They started

Fig 18ee. George and Margaret Speechley in trap 1910 - the year they arrived at Manor Farm Ailsworth.

Fig 18ff. Len and Cecil Sharpe hoeing beet 1950s.

with nine working horses, 120 cattle, 20 pigs, and a labour force of nine men and three women. When Fred Harrison-Smith farmed, '*never did his men work on a Sunday*'. He handed on the tenancy to his son Chris Harrison-Smith, and although the farm house is now privately owned, the land is still farmed by Andrew Harrison-Smith. Chris, and his wife Anne, retired to Midstone House, Southorpe and are active supporters of Upton Church.

God Speed the Plough

Chris Harrison-Smith writes of ploughing:

'*My family moved to Manor Farm Ailsworth in 1945. They brought with them six horses and a horse-man called Jim Barlow. He was a grumpy old man, who did not like us children around. "Mind, or them ther osses'll kick yer" he would say in a gruff voice, so we would hide round the corner till he had gone, and then we would give "them ther osses" a carrot – they never did kick us! Early in January we celebrated Plough Sunday, when the priest asked God's blessing for the plough and the ploughman… The importance of the harvest to the rural community cannot be over-emphasised.*

Ploughing nowadays is a mechanical, high-tech, high speed job, with one man in a tractor able to complete ten or 15 hectares in a day, that's 20 or 30 acres in English. What a contrast to those early days of ploughing; the ploughman would probably start the day by feeding stock or milking cows. By the time these tasks were complete and the team made ready in the field it would be likely 9.30am, then three hours walking up and down the furrows would follow, before a much needed rest and refreshment for man and horses. A further three hours in the afternoon would complete the day's ploughing. The horses would then have their feet washed and their hooves picked out.

In a day's ploughing, man and beast would probably walk over 12 miles. This is on the assumption they were using a single furrow plough at a furrow width of eight inches, and probably to a depth of six or seven inches. This would vary on the heaviness of the land, some land being called 'one horse' and some 'two horse' land, to differentiate clay land from gravel or loam. It was usual to use two horses side by side, the old horse would be in the furrow, whilst the younger animal was allowed to walk on top of the stubble or unploughed soil. This way the youngster learned what was expected of him or her, and to take commands or expletives of the plough-man.'

Fig 18gg. Carlo Hill ploughing at the top of Castor Hill, working for Colberts 1930s.

190

Ploughman's Song
Turn under plough, my trouble
Turn under griefs, this stubble.
Turn mouse's nest, gnawing years,
Old roots up, for new love tears,
Turn plough the clods, for new thunder
Turn under plough, turn asunder.

'So it is that January was, and it still is, the appropriate month for us all to say…GOD SPEED THE PLOUGH'.

Farming in Marholm

Farming life in Marholm is described in Chapter 16, but a brief summary of the farms and their families is included here for completeness. All the farms are owned by Milton Estate. **Manor Farm** and **Marholm Farm** are worked as one by Noel and Joan Darby who live at Manor Farmhouse. Noel's grandfather, John Thomas Darby, who died in 1912, farmed in Castor, living at the farmhouse there now known as **Church View**. He handed over this farm to his eldest son Jack Darby, and took the tenancy of Marholm Farm. From 1912-1928 John Thomas Darby's son, Laurie Darby, farmed Marholm Farm. The Waterworths had Manor Farm before Noel. In addition, in 1926, they took over **Poplar Farm** (at one stage lived in by Joan Law's father, Charles Barratt). In 1969, Noel took up Charlie Neal's land at **Gatehouse Farm**, which had previously been farmed by the Law family.

Belsize Farm and **Home Farm** are both held by descendants of George Jarvis who came to **Belsize Farm** in the 1920s. The Pike family had been the previous tenants. In 1928, George then took on **Home Farm** Marholm and the **Fruit Farm** (now Milton Woodyard). This had been farmed by William Law (Bob Law's father). George moved into Fruit Farm Cottage, leaving son Jack at Belsize and his son Arthur at Home Farm. Iris Newton (nee Winterton) also lived at Belsize as a child when her father worked for the Jarvis family. Graham Longfoot farmed **Ramshill**, (its disused barn is on the sharp corner on the Stamford Road), but this is now lived in by Wilf Hutchinson, the retired Milton gamekeeper, and his wife Mollie.

William Burke

Fig 18hh. Nick Vergette (right) of Manor Farm Upton with Carl Spears with 'Millie' the dog and a sprayer, 2004.

Fig 18ii. Jane and Trevor Jarvis in the ancient yard at Belsize Farm, 2004. Like many younger farmers they have now 'diversified' and they include livery horses in their work.

Fig 18jj. Michael (front) and David Longfoot feeding their bullocks at Model Farm Upton, 2004.

Acknowledgments

Will Craven
Noel and Joan Darby
Brian Goode
Peter and Claire Harris
Chris and Anne Harrison-Smith
Allen and Joyce Herbert
Theo and Meena Hensman
Bob and Joan Law
Dick, Jean, Trevor and Jane Jarvis
Stan and Fay Jarvis
Michael and David Longfoot
Iris Newton
Mary Speechley and 'JT' and Julie Taylor
Jim, Patsy and Stewart Wood
Nick and Bridget Vergette

Notes

1. 1881 *Census* OPCS – see Appx Twenty One.
2. RCHM *Survey, Peterborough New Town* 1969 pp15, 16, 21-23, air photography.
3. A Roman Farm at Castor, 1975. JP Wild. *Durobrivae Vol 4*, Nene Valley Research Committee, 1976, p26.
4. The Domesday Book – see Appendix 1.
5. Enclosures. WE Tate, *Northants Past and Present*, 1957, vol 2 p31-33, background to Enclosure of Castor etc.
6. Open Fields RCHM *Survey, Peterborough New Town*, 1969, pp18, 27, 28.
7. 1842 the L&BR *'A local railway plan for the time shows that land in that part of the Nene Valley was still being cultivated on the medieval strip system. When in 1842 surveyors acting for the L&BR were gathering information as to land ownership along the proposed branch line they probably faced their greatest challenge in the 2 mile strip between Wansford and Alwalton. According to the plan presented to Parliament, it could potentially cross 400 strips. 50 strips in Sutton, 103 in Ailsworth and 273 in Castor of strips, with 15 strips crossing the potential track bed in one mile length. The task was eased by many of the strips being owned by two landowners. The Dean & Chapter sold 64, Earl Fitzwilliam 43, and the White's 18, the Bishop 8 strips, and Mr Wright and William Bate one each.'*
   Castor Station - Peterborough's First Railway. PJ Wazakk & John W Ginn, *Nene Railway Magazine,* May 2002, DBR T/R 1006.
8. O Rackham, *The History of the Countryside*, Phoenix, 1986, p167.
   'A selion's length of about 220 yards is...as far as the ox can pull before he needs a rest...difficult to plough in straight lines, better to begin the turn well before the headland..'
9. Thorn Field, RCHM *Survey- Peterborough New Town, 1969* p27.
10. Symon Gunton, *History of the Church in Peterborough,*1686, Ed J Higham 1990, p302.
    – in the time of Abbot Walter de St Edmundo c1240... *"he made a new Bovaria at Castre."* A *bovaria* was a cattle-shed, or in this case more likely a cattle market.
11. Belsize Farm. Abbot Robert of Lindsay (1214-1222) founded a grange in the manor of Castor, which he granted to the Cellary comprising *'all our new assarts in Nassaburgh, that is to say Belsize with all its dependencies...'* He built houses at Belsize, and planted hedges and drained the land around it...*The fields around Belsize are small with many turns and returns. Large amounts of woodland still remain in irregularly shaped patches to remind us that in the Thirteenth century this was an area of colonization from the forest. The name indicates that already men had begun to appreciate the beauties of landscape. 'Belsize' means beautiful spot or site. Perhaps it seemed to the monks a pleasant spot by comparison with the flat and featureless fen to the North and East',* *Northants Landscape* p108 DBR H 1034.
12. Grant by William Warin to *'William and Alice Sharp of an acre and a half in the fields of Castre lying in Le Haam and in Wodefeld abutting on Brodewodesgates and Smalewodesgatis'.* Milton MSs no 404 NCRO.
13. *'In 1762, more shepherds were recorded at Castor and its hamlets than in any other parish in Nassaburgh – 7 in all. "Castor lies between Morton's heathland and the River Nene and contains much pasturage, including river meadow". John Stimson, maternal grandfather of John Clare, the poet, was a shepherd in Castor, and his name appears in the Castor Militia List. Clare referred to him as having been a "town shepherd as they are called, who has care of all the flocks of the village...", confirmation that sheep had a prominent place in the agricultural economy of Castor during the Eighteenth century'.* John Morton (1712) observed that in the Nassaburgh Hundred Northants heathland *'yields a sweet and cleanly Herbage, which feeds a Breed of small Sheep, whose flesh is usually much commended and esteem'd.'* William Cobbett in *'Rural Rides'* more than a hundred years later says of Nassaburgh Hundred *'Here as all over the country (sic) everlasting fine sheep.'*
    Notes from *'A Northamptonshire Miscellany'* ed Edmund White, 1983, p117; DBR: H 1044 and P1028.

Chapter 19
Occupations and Businesses

There are many primary sources of information to examine to get a sense of the range of occupations carried on in the villages throughout the centuries. A good source is the Parish Registers. From 1678 the lists of burials noted in the register had to give the occupation of the surviving next of kin. This was following the Act of Burying in Woollen. Ostensibly to protect the wool trade in England it was decided to forbid by statute the use of linen for burial shrouds by passing *'An Act for Burying in Woollen Onely. For the encouragement of the Woollen Manufacturers of this Kingdome and Prevention of the Exportation of the moneys thereof for the buying and importing of Linnen.'* The Act was passed in 1667 but largely ignored and was reinforced in 1678. It required relatives of the deceased to swear affidavits that the law had been satisfied. Failure to do so rendered them subject to a fine of £5. On the statute books until the 19th century the Law proved ineffective as the rich were not deterred from using linen by such a small fine, while the poor who could not afford linen had to use woollen cloth in any case.

In 1678 in the Castor Parish Registers we find William Briggs - labourer, John Neetham - labourer, Elias Wilson - joiner, George Blyth - victualler, Edward Wyman - shepherd, Thomas Power - blacksmith, and John Lambert - husbandman. In 1679, the register listed 11 labourers, two shoemakers, three yeomen, a butcher and a curate. The entries for 1680 reveal 12 labourers, three farmers, a husbandman, a tailor, a butcher, a mason and a victualler. Other occupations listed include wheelwrights, millers, and carpenters. It is clear that, in the 17th century at least, the economy of the villages was chiefly rural, reliant on agriculture and self-supporting in a population of 342, according to the Compton census of 1676.

There was little change in the rural economy of the parishes until the middle of the 19th century, when it is possible to see a broader range of occupations and trades emerging, as a trawl through the various directories indicates. Kelly's Directory for 1847 lists nine farmers, one postmaster, one surgeon, six shoemakers, one saddle and harness maker, one miller, two blacksmiths, two National School teachers, one carpenter, one wheelwright, three tailors, one agricultural machinist, three publicans, one mason, three shopkeepers, two butchers, one gamekeeper, and two bakers. All these served the communities of Castor and Ailsworth, which had a combined population of 1,079 in 1841. The Northamptonshire Gazette for 1849 lists 20 farmers and graziers, agreeing similar numbers to 1847 in the other occupations. Kelly's Directory for 1894 still includes village trades and occupations such as blacksmiths, publicans, miller, baker, shoemakers, undertaker, wheelwrights, grocers and shopkeepers. This self suffiency continued into the 20th century, when the pattern of work and employment, and the nature of the businesses began to change.

The Census of England and Wales 1901 also provides a good source of examples of other occupations in the villages. Charles Wright, who lived in The Cedars on Peterborough Road in 1901, had seven servants. These included a ladies maid, cook, three house maids, a footman and a hall boy. Police Constable John Robert Perkins lived on Peterborough Road with his wife Sarah. Durobrivae Lodge was occupied by James Markham, who was a watchmaker and jeweller. A Joseph Woodthorpe is listed on the Census as a chimney sweep, working on his own account. School House on Church Hill was occupied by George Holmes, a certificated school master. There were also two railway plate layers and a railway carriage repair man. However, the majority of occupations still related to agriculture and the countryside. Farm labourers, yardmen, farmers, and shepherds predominate. At Rose Villa on Peterborough Road there was also a market gardener, Thomas Hill, and a newsagent, Charles Hill.

Kelly's Directory for 1903 lists, among others, three shopkeepers, four publicans, two joiners, one wheelwright, one miller, bakers, shoemakers and masons. These occupations later disappear to be replaced by new ones, such as insurance agents and bankers. The focus begins to move away from self-sufficiency, but agriculture still dominates. In 1931 the population of Castor was 547 and that of Ailsworth was 241. Castor still boasted a blacksmith, wheelwright, tailor, shoemaker, grocer, stonemason, carpenter and undertaker, three publicans, a sexton, a rector, a curate, five teachers and a policeman. Ailsworth had a wheelwright, blacksmith, shoemaker, two butchers, two publicans and two bakers. But reflecting growth in industry, the village also had rail, transport and road workers. Both villages had also seen an increase in white collar occupations outside the hub of the village.

The Mills

One of the most important industries carried out in a self supporting rural economy was that of the miller. There are two mills in Castor. One is a tower mill, now derelict save for the shell, the other a large watermill which is now a private residence.

According to an entry of a burial in the Parish registers, the miller in 1681 was Thomas Coulton. Later in 1744, an entry in the local court records detailing an indenture for a pauper apprentice, shows a Francis Proctor being apprenticed to the then miller Athanasius Goodwin. Just over 100 years later the 1847 Kelly's Directory

Fig 19a. Castor Water Mill 1920s.

lists John Thomas Callow as operating both Castor mills. According to Trevor Wainwright in *'Windmills of Northamptonshire and the Soke of Peterborough'*, Callow died in 1850. Certainly by 1869 Richard Freeman is operating the mills. His name appears in the Northampton Post Office Directory for that year. He is known to have operated the mills until they were taken over by Alfred Robert Loweth who took over as a tenant of the Ecclesiastical Commissioners in 1888. By 1894 he had stopped operating the windmill and worked only the watermill, which he continued to do until 1924. After that the Old Mill became a private residence.

From 1894 onwards the tower mill fell into disuse and its superstructure was eventually dismantled leaving only the tower and a few floor beams. In 1919 a dispute between Loweth and George C W Fitzwilliam relating to the dismantling of the tower mill for the sum of £75 was heard at the Peterborough County Court [1]. This shows that the tower mill was not dismantled until 1918. Loweth had leased some additional land at the mill from Milton which was made a Michaelmas Tenancy. Loweth received notice to quit but remained in possession of the holding until July 1918 from which time he began to remove machinery from the tower mill on which he alleged a claim of right. He asserted the claim because he said he paid the Milton Land Agent, a Mr Norton, £20 for the machinery at the mill when he stopped using it in 1894. In 1918 the revolving top and first floor of the mill were still there but Loweth removed them and cut through the floor beams to remove the gear, making the structure unsafe. Milton was claiming costs to put the roof back on.

Fig 19b. Castor Windmill before 1914; only the shell of the tower is left today.

Machinery Hire and Haulage

Mills were an indication of the increasing mechanisation of agriculture. The introduction of agricultural machinery on farms as the industry improved from the late 19th century led to a change in occupations. Many farmers could not justify the purchase cost of the equipment, leading to the development of machinery hire companies. The need to transport the crops produced on the farms in the parishes also led to the development of heavy haulage.

Fig 19c. Traction engine pictured in Gibbons' Yard on Peterborough Road, opposite the Fitzwilliam Arms.

Harry Gibbons & Sons Agricultural Machinery Hire was operated from 'Gibbons Yard' next to what is now the village hall since at least 1847, when Thomas Gibbons is listed in Kelly's Directory as a machinist. However, the business is thought to have been established as early as 1840. At its height Gibbons had 40 traction engines, as well as various threshing machines and bailers. In the yard there were engineering workshops, a smithy, machine shop and carpentry workshops, all necessary to keep the machinery operational.

The business was still operating in the 1950s but eventually the yard fell into disuse and the buildings into disrepair. The property was sold in 1994.

Taylor's Road Haulage was the first major road haulage company in the area, and became an important local employer. In the late 1920s Frank Taylor began deliveries on a bicycle, then using a horse and trolley, and finally with a Brooke Bond Tea van.

In 1932, Frank and his brothers Walter, William and Stanley bought a 30 cwt six wheel Chevrolet lorry. After adding another lorry in the mid 1930s the Taylors bought a used Bedford, along with two new ones – registrations EG1029, and EG2763. Three further Bedford vehicles were added later, and by 1939 Taylors had built up a fleet of 20 lorries. In 1934, Taylor's had a contract with J Farrow's Pea Factory. It also had contracts with Slaters Corn Merchants of North Street, Peterborough and Curtis' of Oundle. Other heavy haulage contracts included Peter Brotherhoods, Baker Perkins and

Fig 19d. Cecil Taylor with his first lorry pictured in 1933.

ig 19e. Taylor's fleet drivers in 1948 in Main Street Ailsworth : (l-r) John Taylor, Frank Taylor, Cecil Taylor, Harry Cooper, Stan Hill, Graham Taylor, Joe Burfoot, Reg Hill, David Hill, Ernie Garfield, Frank Sheppardson.

Peterborough Diesel. The business was originally run from a garage on Main Street, Ailsworth but moved in the 1950s to Station Road, shortly after it was nationalised (1948). The company was run by British Road Services (BRS), which also ran public transport. BRS paid a retainer to Taylors to run the business as its contractor. In 1954 the fleet was increased to 40 vehicles when Taylors was able to re-purchase four Bedfords from BRS.

In 1967 Frank Taylor Transport amalgamated with John Taylor to become J W Taylor, still based at Station Road. The company also ran a coal business, which it sold off to an Oundle firm in February 1968 to concentrate on long distance haulage. The fact that a hauliers was present meant that other businesses grew up to service it. Most notably, Frank and Grace Taylor used a large wooden shed that was in front of their council house as a Transport Café.

Hutchinson's Heavy Haulage took over Taylor's site and now has a large fleet of trucks in a distinctive green livery.

In 1964, David Hill started D W Hill transport in the old blacksmith's yard, Peterborough Road, Castor. He bought a Ford Trader lorry and carted sand, gravel and stone for local quarries. In 1966, his brother Reg, who had previously worked at Taylors as a driver and mechanic joined him, and later that year his other brother Stan also joined the firm, resigning in 1970. As the business expanded they moved to larger premises at Stibbington, finally returning to Station Road, Ailsworth (where Stylaprint business is now located) until David and Reg retired in 1987.

Public Houses, Ale Shops and Beer Houses

The public houses and beer retailers were, and perhaps are still some of the most conspicuous businesses in the villages. Their names are traditional, reflecting historical events (George & Dragon, Royal Oak), local nobility or royalty (Fitzwilliam Arms, Prince of Wales) or village economy (Barley Mow, Wheatsheaf). At one time there were six public houses and several other beer sellers. The annual licensing session of the Peterborough Petty Sessions reported in the Peterborough Advertiser of 12 September 1863 lists one public house and two beer houses in Ailsworth and four public houses in Castor. The Northamptonshire Post Office Directory of 1869 lists three pubs and a beer retailer [possibly the Prince of Wales] in Castor, and a further three beer retailers – including one Robert Sharpe, and one pub, making a total of nine local watering holes. Some not listed as pubs were run via other businesses such as a grocers shop and a bakers shop in the case of Sharpe, which was in addition to their main business. The number of pubs in Castor and Ailesworth has gradually reduced to just two, in addition to a licensed restaurant and an 'off-licence' shop.

The George & Dragon, a thatched building, now known as Dragon House, is at the foot of Loves Hill. It was built in 1703 and operated as a Public House until the 1920s. In 1847 Robert Shelston was the licensee. By 1869 the pub was in the hands of local farmer, William Berridge. He was fortunate to have had a pub to take over. It caught fire in 1863, but the fire was prevented from spreading from the lath and plaster on the side of the chimney due to the thickness of the mortar.

On October 15th 1872, the pub was auctioned by Berridge through Messrs Jakes and Son of Cross Street, Peterborough. The advertisement for the auction lists among the items being disposed of 'six cane seated chairs, sofa in leather, 18 Windsor chairs, four arm ditto... fender and fire irons'. The Pub was bought by John Upchurch whose wife, Ann, was licensee up until 1903, when a Thomas Burdett is listed in Kelly's Directory as the landlord. By 1906 however, Joseph George Hammond had taken over. In 1914, William Pell was landlord and remained until the pub was closed sometime between 1928 and 1931.

The Royal Oak Inn was built in 1727 according to a dated stone in the fabric of the building and the RCHM Survey, but there is a stone in the gable end of the pub dated 1651, the date Cromwell defeated the Scots at the Battle of Worcester, ending Stuart hopes to retain rule. For almost 100 years the pub was run by the same family. Kelly's Directory shows the following licensees: 1847 – Mrs Elizabeth Smith; 1869 – Charles and Letitia Smith; 1894 – Thomas Hill Smith; 1914 – Elizabeth Smith; 1920 – Miss Edith Smith; 1931 – Mrs Gertrude Smith. By 1940 Charles Henry Evans had taken the pub on. In November 1967 The Peterborough Standard reports that James Webb, an oil engineer, and his wife took over the licence for a time.

Over the last fifteen years the landlords of 'The Oak' have been Walter and Jean Heslop, Clive and Pat Raine, Les and Sandra Hill, and current 'gaffers' Rob and Jaquie Sykes. The pub retains some unique features. In the quarry tiled back bar, a game of 'Ring the Bull' still exists. A careful look around will also show up numbers on some of the doors allowing unlicensed parts of the pub to be identified. The pub has long been the home of community organisations including the Helping Hands Club run by Elizabeth Smith, and bar maid Eva Gibbons. The Foresters also held their quarterly and annual meetings in the pub. For many years an Ind Coope-tied pub, the Oak is now part of the Pub Company.

The Fitzwilliam Arms was built around the same time as the 'Oak' and the 'George & Dragon,' in the 17th century. According to the Tithe Register for 1844, William Thurstone Smith paid on the 'Fitz Arms Pub, garden and orchard Tithe 5s.9d.' In 1847, at the time Robert Shelstone had the

Fig 19f. The George and Dragon before World War I.

Fig 19g. The Royal Oak.

Fig 19h. The Fitzwilliam Arms, 1920s.

'George and Dragon', and Elizabeth Smith was running the 'Oak,' the Fitzwilliam Arms was run by Mrs. Elizabeth Glitheroe. She was the widow of Thomas Glitheroe, landlord of the Fitzwilliam Arms, who reportedly *died from a fit while tunning his beer,'* on 22 December 1816, according to John Hales' diary. By 1869 the Popple family had the pub, the landlord being Samuel Popple.

Events at the pub often found their way into the local papers. From a report in The Peterborough Advertiser of 18 June 1862:

'On Tuesday afternoon, about 2.30pm, a singular occurrence took place at Mr. Samuel Poppel's [sic] at the Fitzwilliam Arms. Mrs Poppel [sic] and her servant were in the lower room....when they were startled by what appeared to be a loud explosion in the upper part of the house, which caused the doors to slam and the house to vibrate as though it would fall. They found in one [bedroom] that a large piece of the ceiling about a foot square had been smashed as though a heavy body had fallen upon it, a greater part of the remainder being left in a cracked state. There has been nothing to clear up the mystery.'

It must have been a slow news day. In the 19th century the pub was also the venue for the local Coroner's inquests, which had to be held locally, in a public place. In the absence of an official Coroner's Court a public house was deemed the most suitable location. In the 1860s the Coroner, a Mr. Hopkinson, the Deputy Coroner, John Torkington, and local surgeon Joseph Bodman, carried out inquests into a number of deaths in the villages including the suicide of a Castor stonemason, Thomas Robinson, who was unable to continue working due to illness, and those of Martha Turner, grocer, and her daughter, who were *'found dead in bed together from the effects of laudanum,'* again according to Hales' diary.

Sometime between 1884 and 1894, the pub was taken over by Henry Sarjeant Fitzjohn. According to the Census of 1901, his occupation was a farmer and brewers agent living in Clay Lane. By 1903, the landlord was Thurston Smith, a relative of the same Smith family that kept the Royal Oak, and he remained so until at least 1928. In 1931 Arthur Cole was landlord, and then William 'Bill' Smith. Many others followed, including, in the 1960s, Arthur Crawford and then R. Taylor, who took over the licence in November 1967. One of the last landlords to hold the licence was Roy Plews, who attempted to turn the 'Fitz' into a more traditional local pub in the 1990s. In the 1930s, the pub served Lyon's teas on the lawns at the rear of the pub and offered access to its own bowling green. The 'Fitz' has been a public house for most of its history but more recently has been converted into a restaurant. In the mid-90s it became a steak and fish restaurant with an oyster bar. Lately it has become an Italian restaurant, part of the Fratelli's group.

The Prince of Wales' Feathers, built in the early part of the 19th century, has always been a 'locals' pub. It was originally run as a 'beer house,' retail store, and off-licence. The landlord did not have a licence to serve spirits, and could only sell beer. James Wilson is listed as keeping an unnamed beer house in Castor in Northants Post Office Directory of 1874. By 1884, the beer house had been taken over by Edward Panter, local shoemaker, and was named the Prince of Wales. The pub was tied to Norwich-based Morgans Brewery Company which controlled 600 pubs by 1904. Morgans was acquired by Watney Mann in 1964, and the pub was tied to it until it became a free house. It stands on the corner of Peterborough Road and the Green, which became known as Panter's Corner.

The Prince of Wales remained with the Panter family until it was taken on by Bill Kingston. In the '30s the pub was tied briefly to the famous Wrexham-based brewery, Soames. Following his death his wife kept the pub until 1950 when it was taken on by Percy 'Wackey' Sismey, who was responsible for getting a license to sell spirits on the premises. Wackey Sismey kept the pub until 1967. Edgar and Madge Parker kept the Prince from October 1967 until the late 1970s, when John and Jean Anker took it on. The pub changed hands a number of times throughout the 1980s and 1990s. Recently the pub was acquired by local farmers Jim and Stuart Wood. They continued a modernisation of the bar started by Edgar Parker, who had joined the separate lounge and smoke room together. The pub was extended

Fig 19i. The Prince of Wales. At this time it was a Soames' pub.

into what was the old shop – subsequently a kitchen. The pub has for many years been the meeting point for village sports teams. Both football and cricket clubs use it, and motorcycle grass track and speedway enthusiasts used the pub in the past, when it had separate saloon and smoke room bars. The signs are still painted on the frosted leaded windows fronting the Green.

The Barley Mow, another beer house, was a Public House in Ailsworth from the early 19th century until about 1947, when it was closed for good and later converted into flats. The pub was tied to Grantham-based Mowbrays Brewers, now defunct. A three storey brick building, it was purpose built and had a long function room on the first floor. In 1849 the Northamptonshire Gazetteer lists George Hobbs as a beer retailer in Ailsworth. He is listed in the same publication of 1874 as the landlord of the Barley Mow. The pub remained in the hands of Elizabeth Hobbs up until at least 1924, when John Hobbs took the licence. The pub passed from the Hobbs family to a Mr Parker around 1928. The original frame for the pub sign can still be seen over the door.

The Wheatsheaf Inn was another later addition to the list of Castor and Ailsworth pubs, and was also built in the early 19th century. In 1849 it was in the hands of the Smith family, the victualler being William Smith. Thomas Hill Smith had the pub in 1869. By 1894, it was run by James Warr, who was also a local butcher. These publicans reflected the trend of publicans carrying out more than one trade. In The Peterborough Advertiser of 1 June 1854 the following advertisement appears:

'William Smith, Wheatsheaf Inn, Ailsworth Nr.Peterborough, Castrator and Spayer of Animals, returns thanks for the kind support he has received for 22 years, and begs to state that he regularly attends the Peterborough Saturday market. Orders also received at the Crown, Westgate, and Cross Keys, Narrow Street.'

By 1914, the pub was being run by James Fox who kept it until he died in his 80s. In the 1970s the landlord was Garth Foster of Castor and Ailsworth FC fame. He left the village to take the Island Queen pub in Islington, North London. The pub passed through three more changes of hands, John Crow, Tony and Friea Moore, and Colin and Val Roberts, until finally closing in the early 1990s. It is now a private residence, and three more small houses have been built on what was the pub car park. Like the Prince, the Wheatsheaf was tied to Watney-Mann brewery.

Retailing

Retailing businesses were also numerous and conspicuous in the villages. However, the number of shops and stores in the Parishes has also reduced over the years as occupations and employment have moved out of the villages.

General Stores
Wootton's Grocery and Drapery Stores was established in 1845 by William Wootton. The shop, located on the corner of the Green and Church Hill, was originally a small stone built thatched structure and remained unchanged until at least 1903. It was demolished and rebuilt by the Woottons in around 1915. Thomas Wootton was still running the store in 1924, but by 1928 the Woottons had retired and sold out to Mrs Christinas Fox, who had the shop into the 1940s. The shop has changed hands several times since it was sold by Woottons. After Mrs Fox, the shop was taken over by J R Smith, who had moved down from a shop on Church Hill, which became a hairdressers, and is now Griffin's Coal Merchants. In 1968 Mr Smith sold the business to Beryl Turner, who ran what was then the Spar Shop with her husband Gordon until the late 1970s. The 'corner shop' was then owned and run by the Trinders, the Jacksons, Rex and Dee Gates, and Gurmit Singh, before closing for good and being converted into flats now owned by Chapman Associates.

Sharpe's Store was end on to Main Street in Ailsworth. It is in Sharpe's yard, just beyond what was the bakers. The 1847 Kelly's Directory lists Charles Sharpe as baker and grocer. In the 1849 Northants Gazetteer, Chas. Sharpe is also listed as baker and retailer. The store was passed on to Robert Sharpe who is listed as a baker, beer retailer and grocer in the 1869 Post Office Directory. This accounts for at least one of the other beer houses/off-licences counting towards the village's large number of pubs. The shop remained in Robert Sharpe's hands until at least 1894 when Charles Sharpe is listed in Kelly's Directory as a draper and grocer. The shop remained open and in the ownership of the Sharpe family until decimalisation in 1970, when Miss Sharpe closed up for the last time. It is now a private residence.

Post Office
In 1847 the Post Office Receiver in Castor was one William Gates Horden. The entry in the Kelly's Directory of that year reads:

Fig 19j. Wootton's Shop 1890. Note the stump of the old village cross; it was used as a mounting block. It has since been repositioned on the Green.

'*Letters are received here from 8am till 5pm and forwarded through the Peterborough office by a messenger despatched for that purpose from thence in the morning who delivers all the letters free of charge beyond the postage and returns with the bags to Peterborough in the afternoon.*'

Sir Rowland Hill had introduced the penny post seven years earlier in 1840 with the first adhesive postage stamps, the Penny Black and the Twopenny Blue. In 1869 Horden was still the Receiver but letters were brought from Peterborough on a mail cart at 4.45am and despatched at 8am. The mail box for posting was open between 7am and 5pm, while money orders could only be sent or received at Peterborough.

By 1894 the Castor Post Office was also a money order office, and an Annuity and Insurance Office with Mr William Darby as sub-postmaster. He is also listed on the 1901 Census as a general shopkeeper. The Shop and Post Office was located in the thatched house next door to the Royal Oak Public House. Now, letters were carried from Peterborough to Castor Station (station master John Green) by the 6.33am train on the London and North West line which

Fig 19k. Mr Darby outside the Post Office in Castor c 1894

opened in 1845, and despatched at 5.25 pm and 8.55 pm. Ailsworth was served by a wall box which was cleared 8.55pm weekdays and 8.45pm on Sundays. From messenger, to horse and cart, to train, to post van, mail delivery typifies some of the changes to the rural economy. By 1920, Ailsworth had its own post office, with Arthur Cooke acting as the sub postmaster. In 1924, George Sellers was postmaster, and the villages were then served by a single office. By 1940, the post office and attached shop were run by John Hedley Cooper. The post office moved several times and was at one stage part of the shop on the corner of Helpston Road and Main Street in Ailsworth run by Mrs Eileen Bass. Mary Neal delivered the mail. When Mrs Bass retired, the Post Office moved again and was taken on by the Means Family of Peterborough Road. It remained on the site of Gordon Means' petrol station until it closed in 2003, but Jonathon Means still delivers the mail by bike for most of the village.

Butchers

Down the centuries the villages have had many butchers, operating from various premises too numerous to detail. Suffice to say many old village names have been connected with the trade including Thomas Sismey (1847); Martin Setchell (1849), George Mann (1849), Thomas Samworth (1869-1874), and James Warr (1894-1931). The current butcher's shop is owned by Jim Wood. Prior to becoming the butcher's shop the building, purpose-built as a shop had been an electrical retailers called Quesney's.

Garage

There has been a garage business in the villages since the car became commercially available. In the 1920s there was a garage owned by Tommy Wadd on Peterborough Road, between the Wheatsheaf and Barley Mow pubs. It started out as a cycle repair business and it can still be seen. Most recently Gordon Means Ltd operated until shortly after the by-pass opened. First it was a National Petroleum franchise and then became a British Petroleum filling station, until it was closed.

Newsagents

The Paper Shop is currently owned and run by Lila Khunti and is the only general store, off-licence and news agents left in the village. There has been a newsagents in the same building since the late 1960s run by Keith and Doris Goodwin. For a large part of the 1970s and early 1980s, the paper shop was run by DK Cooke (Farms) Ltd. Prior to that, newspapers either came via the Post Office, or could be purchased in the other stores

Fig 19l. Tommy Wadd outside his cycle repair shop and garage circa 1920.

Fig 19m. Hay carts waiting for loading 1920s.

Fig 19n. The Paper Shop is owned by Lila Khunti, who has faithfully provided an important service for the villages, despite frequent robberies and break-ins. The concrete blocks are to deter ram-raiders, an only too frequent occurrence at village shops by people from nearby towns. (l-r): Lila Khunti, her son Nikul, Barbara Osborne (nee Sharpe) (a former Castor School secretary and village post-lady) 2000.

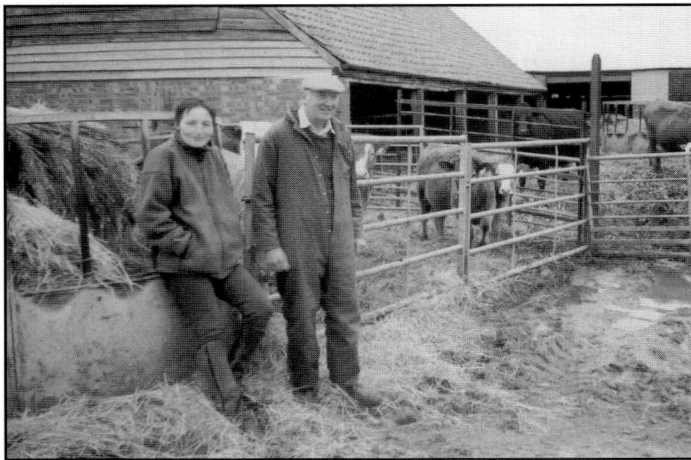

Fig 19o. Peter and Claire Harris with suckler cows at Top Lodge Farm Upton 2004.

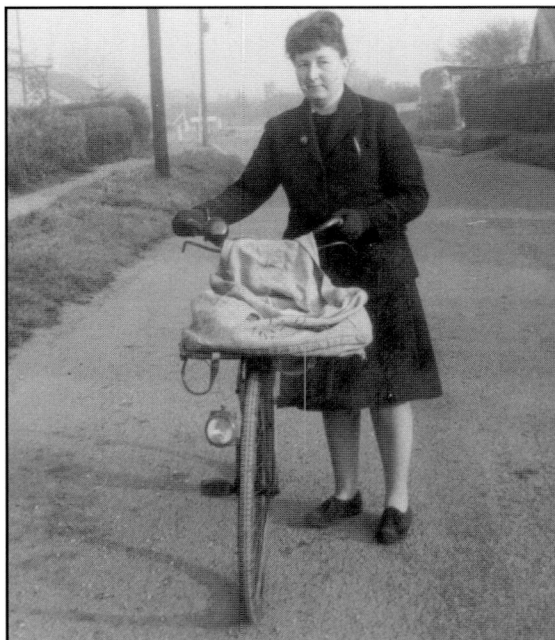

Fig 19p. Flora Smith nee Sutton, post lady on her rounds in Stocks Hill 1970s.

in the villages, or read in the Reading Room – which was run by Thomas Wootton in 1906 – or in the pubs.

In the Silver Jubilee year of 1977 the population of Castor was 700 and that of Ailsworth 425. Castor had three publicans, farmers, a shopkeeper, a hairdresser and a coal merchant based in the village. All other occupations now took place outside the village. The same was true in Ailsworth with one publican, three shopkeepers, a garage owner, hairdresser and post mistress. In 2004, the occupations based in the villages have changed again. Castor has two publicans and a coal merchant, while Ailsworth has a butcher, a shopkeeper and a vehicle dealership. Farming is no longer the mainstay of the community and employment takes place elsewhere with a majority in white collar and professional occupations.

The opening of the Castor bypass in the 1990s, the development of supermarkets, the popularity of the car, increased affluence, and the shift away from an agrarian economy, and the information technology revolution of the 1980s onwards, have all meant that rural retail occupations have declined and the villages are no longer economically self supporting. There is little passing trade and village residents use the independence the car offers to travel further to supermarkets and retail parks to do the shopping. Nor are the bulk of occupations of those living in the villages indigenous. Many of them are white collar professional occupations, including company directors, doctors, journalists and editors, publishers, managers, solicitors, IT professionals, all of whom either work in Peterborough or further afield.

John Howard

Note

1.   See Peterborough Advertiser 18 January 1919, p5.

Fig 19q. Butcher's Shop. The 'Country Butchers' is owned by farmer Jim Wood of the Hollies Farm. l-r: Jim Wood, Nancy Douglas (assistant), Eric Freeman (butcher), behind Tony Evans (former Tower Captain at Castor and now on the Diocesan Guild of Ringers.)

HARRY GIBBONS & SONS

Telegrams : CASTOR
Station : (1 Mile) Castor, L.M. & S.
ESTABLISHED 1840

*Agricultural Machinists
and Engineers*

CASTOR

PETERBOROUGH

Fig 19r. Advertisement for Gibbons' Threshing machine Contractors. The Gibbons family, with their yard beside the Village Hall Castor, worked not only for the farmers of our parishes but for farmers from a wide area around Peterborough from 1840 for over 100 years.

Fig 19s. A Gibbon's machine threshing at Herbert Dickens' farm at Castor 1898. Harry Gibbons is behind the water-boy.

Fig 19t. Scene in Gibbons' Yard Castor 1922, adjacent Village Hall.

Fig 19u. Machinery today - Spraying machine at Manor Farm Upton, left Carl Spears, right Nick Vergette (farmer).

Chapter 20

Leisure, Recreation and Village Organisations: Snapshots through history

Most of the organisations and institutions present in the villages today have their origins in the 19th century. A microcosm of British social history over the last 200 years, it is possible to trace the development of these pastimes and preoccupations in a rural context from sports, charity, friendly societies and entertainment.

Many of these organisations sprang up as a result of the industrialisation and mechanisation of agriculture that developed in the late 18th century onwards. As life became more organised on a national level, so Castor and Ailsworth formed football, cricket and tennis clubs, brass bands, friendly societies and self help groups. Some of these were a natural progression from pre-existing organisations, others were completely new. Some, like the Foresters, the Excelsior Brass Band and the Fire Brigade are now defunct. Others, such as the football and cricket clubs, the WI, and the Mothers' Union have gone from strength to strength. What follows is a brief history of village organisations and institutions.

Fig 20a. WI Drama Group circa 1955 (l-r): Mary Coulson, Alice Smith, Lily Thompson, Hazel Marsh, Jeanette Yates, Stella Mossendew, Florence Jackson.

Women's Institute

The first Women's Institute was founded at Stoney Creek, Ontario in 1897 by Adelaide Hoodless and Erland Lee. Following the outbreak of the First World War in 1914, a conference was called in London by the Agricultural and Horticultural Union to discuss the need for co-operation between industry and agriculture. As a result, the first WI meeting in the UK was held on 16 June 1915, in Llanfairpwll Wales [1].

The Castor and Ailesworth WI held its first meeting in 1931. It was organised by the Hon Mrs Georgina Pelham of the 'Cedars'. She was elected President with Mrs Annie Cooke as her Secretary. Until her retirement, Mrs Cooke had been Headmistress of Castor Infants' School and village correspondent for three local papers. They remained in office together until 1947, during which time they established the organisation and laid down the rules and regulations for the future. Since then there have been 13 presidents each giving their all to ensure the continuity of the group still enjoyed today. These have included Chris Sharpe who was President in 1952, Mrs E Taylor in 1977, and Lorna Gamlyn in 2003. The current President is Mrs Wendy Eagle. Living in South Bretton, she is the first non-resident to be President.

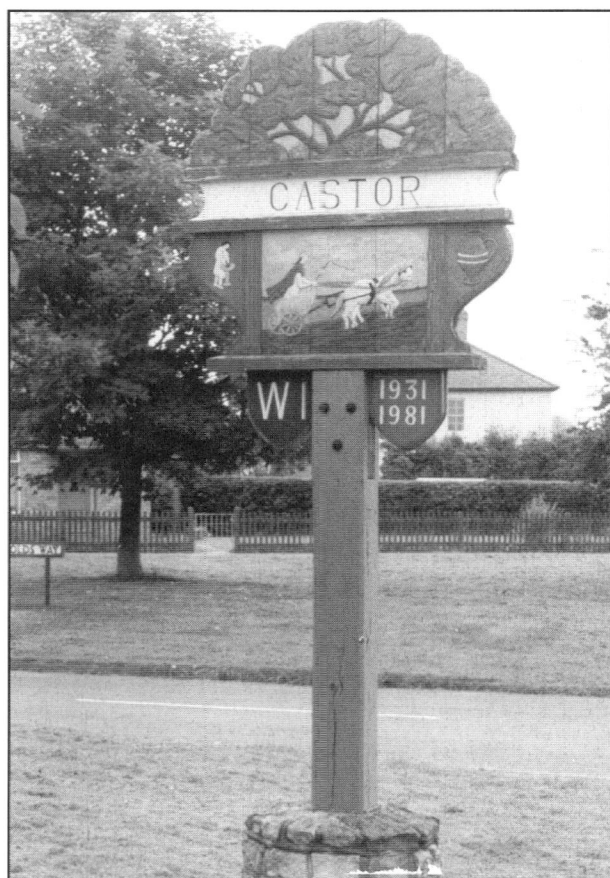

Fig 20b. WI Castor and Ailsworth Village Sign – 50th Anniversary 1981.

Fig 20c. Village Banner – 60th Anniversary 1991.

Fig 2d. WI Millennium Banner (l-r): Doris Barley, Lorna Gamlyn, Margaret Sharpe.

As an organisation, members have taken an active part in every kind of community event within the village such as supporting fund raising efforts for church and chapel, and assisting the Parish Council with many projects including keeping footpaths open by walking them weekly and organising rubbish collections.

Concerts and comedy plays by the Drama Group were performed for over 40 years, until it disbanded in the 1990s. In 1934 the Castor and Ailesworth WI achieved 78% in the Northamptonshire Federation of Women's Institutes Area Drama Festival, and was awarded a third class certificate. In 1953 a new group won first place in the Novice Class of the same event and tied for third place in the Open Class. The following year it took first place in the Open Class. Subsequently the drama group was second in 1957 and again in 1963. It set a record in 2001 when Castor and Ailesworth won the County Trophy for the fourth time.

The WI has made many gifts to the villages over the years. There are wrought iron pedestals in church and chapel, and it has planted trees on the village greens. It has supplied crockery for the village hall and a story sack for the Playgroup. To commemorate the WI's Golden Jubilee, Castor and Ailesworth raised £400 to provide a carved village sign and for the Diamond Jubilee members designed and made a collage wall hanging of a pictorial map of the two villages. It is on display in the church throughout the summer and in the Ailesworth Chapel Schoolroom during the winter. To mark the Millennium, a processional banner was made in cream and gold material, embroidered with gold thread. It hangs in St Kyneburgha's Church. The WI has been finding it increasingly difficult to fill vacant committee places, and membership ebbs and flows. But those who remain members have formed a strong loyalty to the organisation and continue to value craft meetings, social events and fellowship.

Football Club

Association football in its present form began in 1848 and the English Football League kicked off in 1888. Largely the preserve of the public schools and their alumni, the game started to take off following the introduction of the Saturday half-holiday following legislation passed in 1874 which completed the process of Saturday reduction begun in 1847. The resulting increase in leisure time combined with an increase in real wages meant that by the 1890s football had developed into a popular sporting culture [2]. Castor and Ailsworth FC has been in existence since at least 1894. A team photograph from that year shows members of the team including J Winsworth, J Sismey, W Coulson, H Coulson, E Griffin and J Mossendew. A later picture of the team taken around 1900 includes names such as W Bell, J Gibbons, L Longfoot, W Popple, AP Cooke and H Pell.

Throughout the 1920s and 1930s the club enjoyed continuity, running both junior and senior sides. Players from the juniors often graduated to play for the seniors. The junior side of 1925/26 included Bob Poll, Joe Hench, E Wyldbore, and Jack Coulson, who later turned out for the senior team in the 1930s.

Bob Doubleday was the Captain and Secretary of the Castor Saturday side in 1967-1968 season [3]. The club also ran an under 18 side established by Roger Parker. Fund raising at the club included whist drives held at the Village Hall. At the same time fund raising for the Sunday League side was organised by L Pell and J Wood. In the '67 - '68 season

Castor lost two of its players to rivals. Peter Smith went to Kings Cliffe, and Alan White went to play for Yaxley British Legion.

In 1977, the club put out two sides one in the Mid-Anglia Sunday Morning League Division 1, [4] the other in the Peterborough and District Sunday League Division 2 [5]. The club was run by G Foster (Chairman), G Boyall (Vice Chairman), and C Bass (Secretary/Treasurer).

Garth Foster started the team with Roy Harker because the then existing team comprised non-village players from the Peterborough Development Corporation – which had a tree nursery on land on Splash Lane employing a large number of people, many of whom did not live in the villages. This PDC arrangement kept young village players out of the team and they took little interest in the club. According to contemporary player, Mark Smith, Garth was surprised when mostly young players turned up for the first game: *Roy Harker said 'there are plenty of young old boys in the village who want to play football but can't get a game in the village side.'* Garth was from Nottinghamshire, where a young 'old boy' meant a fit old man and was confused by young and old being used in the same sentence to describe the village lads.

The core of the team included Mark Smith, Garth Foster, Roger Brisbourne, Paul Winsworth, Kevin Conkey, Simon Clark and Johnny Neal and was run strictly for village/parish players. According to Mark Smith the Sunday morning team was not particularly good, playing by the motto: *'If you can't get the ball, get the player.'* This 'physicality' would often lead to altercations with the opposition including a stand up 'punch-up' with Belmore FC in which David Whitby suffered a broken jaw.

The club folded for a while after Garth Foster left the village to take on a pub in Islington. It was resurrected in the 1980s and was run mainly by Simon Clark and later by Michael Savage, Nigel Hill, David Hill, Phil Moore and Steve Henson. Lack of support and decent playing and changing facilities meant a difficult time for the club and it was wound up again until the mid-1990s. The current set up was reformed in August 1996.

Between the '96 - '97 and '99-2000 seasons the Peterborough Sunday Afternoon League side played at Station Road, Ailsworth but moved

Fig 20e. Castor and Ailesworth Football Team in 1894. Pictured are W Cooke, W Fox, J Winsworth, A Cooke, Revd Collins, C Chapman, J Sismey, W Coulson, W Kingston, J Mossercew, E Griffin (with ball), H Coulson and T Oliver.

Fig 20f. CAFC in 1934. Back row (l-r): B Po'l, F. Sismey, T Hornsby, E Hammond, J Coulson, T Sismey, S Coles. Front row (l-r): E Wyldbore, L Goode, J Hinch, T Hancock, F Bossom.

Fig 20g. CAFC 1978/1979 pictured at the Station Road recreation ground; Back row (l-r): Mark Smith (on a 28 day suspension for fighting), Kevin Conkey, Russell Tooley, Garth Foster, Unknown, Robert Whitby, Nigel Dytham, Greg Boyall. Front row; T Cunningian, Chris Beecher, Simon Clark, Gladdy Craythorne, Cliff Bass.

Fig 20h. CAFC 1998/1999 Harris Cup Runners up; Back row (l-r): Phil Moore, Matt Wordsall, Richard Craythorne, Stefan Coenan, Paul Gough, Ian Cooper, Kevin Henson, Graham Snart, Kevin Conkey. Front row (l-r): Paul Smith, Jason Magan, Darren Burton, David Hill, Steve Henson, Dave Foster, Jason Reeves.

Cricket Club

Cricket was popularised by the Victorians and there has been a cricket team in the village since 1869. In 1935 the President of Castor Cricket Club was Major C Pelham, team Captain was J Coulson and Club Secretary was F E Griffin.

Later, in the season 1953/54 the cricket team was runner up in the Stamford Shield played at Burghley Park. Bert Woodward, W Sylvester, Alex Jakes, Ralph Jackson, Joe Woodward, Brian Sharpe, Gordon Glover, Herbert Jackson, Claude Sharpe, Jack Kingston and Alan Jakes were in the team.

The existing pavilion at the Cricket Club was completed in 1967. At the 1968 AGM held at the Fitzwilliam Arms it was reported that it was built from club funds at a cost of £250 by Neaversons of Peakirk, with no need for a grant. In the late '50s and early 1960s the club house was an old Nissen Hut with no door. Club funds stood at £61 2s 6d. The season had been a success and saw them win the Stamford Shield. Jack Barlow was the club's highest runs scorer and Cliff Goode was the best bowler with a total wickets haul of 47 for the season. There were 28 members present including Rev TP Adler (President), Mr L Pell (Chairman), Mr A Jakes (Secretary), and Mr R Coulson (Treasurer). All these were involved with the club over many seasons.

In 1977 the club officials were FC Winfrey (President), LC Pell (Chairman), and AN Jakes (Secretary). The '77 season had been a successful season for the club with the team winning the Stamford Shield, the Stamford Spastics Cup, the Peterborough League Jubilee Shield, and finishing as runners-up in the League.

Fig 20i. Castor and Ailsworth Cricket Club circa 1953/54, runners up in the Stamford Shield played at Burghley Park, Stamford. Back row (l-r): Bert Ward, W Sylvester, Alex Jakes, Ralph Jackson, Joe Woodward, Brian Sharpe. Front row (l-r): Albert Berridge, Gordon Glover, Herbert Jackson, Claude Sharpe, Jack Kingston, Alan Jakes. The names of the umpires are unknown. There is a match played between the Royal Oak and The Prince of Wales Feathers in memory of Brian Sharpe, played in a spirit of fun with teams regularly numbering up to 20 a-side.

Castor Cricket Club has enjoyed celebrity visits in the course of its history. England and Sussex Captain, Arthur E R Gilligan, visited in 1934 in the company of the then famous

from there to Woodlands the following season. Its best league position was fifth in Division 1 in 1999-2000. The team also won the Palazzo Cup in 2002-2003 season. In August 2000 CAFC entered the Peterborough Saturday League Division 6 but had to move to a base at Ringwood in Bretton because the Station Road facility was not good enough. The team has consistently performed in the Saturday league rising to first place in Division 4 in 2002-03, and finishing as runners up in the PFA Cup in its first two seasons in the league.

Until 2001-2002 the village teams were limited to three non-village players in each. Now there is no restriction on the number of non-village players but there are still five or six players from the village and the surrounding parishes.

cartoonist F H Cumberworth, to feature that day's match for the News Chronicle. In the late '80s the club entertained the then recently formed First Class Durham County Cricket Club which included such luminaries as former England all-Rounder Ian Botham, Dean Jones (Australian Test Star) and Wayne Larkins (ex-Northants and England). John Moulds hit a fifty for the cricket club. In 1989 Castor won the South Lincs First Division without losing a match. The side included star batsmen Dave Rager and Bruce Pell, who is Vice Chairman and has scored the most runs for the club.

Castor has a tradition of producing good left-arm bowlers including the late Alex Jakes (1950's), Terry Moon (1970s and 1980s) and John Mann (1980s and 1990s). All three performed with distinction for the club. John Mann even had trials for Gloucestershire.

Castor has always had a policy of playing both local villagers and players from outside the village. There are at least thirty plus villagers currently actively supporting the club either by helping the social committee or by playing for any one of the teams. In the '50s and '60s the club was able to field a team full of local villagers but always struggled at harvest time.

The most successful season in the Clubs History was in the year 2000 when the 1st XI won The Jaidka Cup, Rutland Division One, and the John Wilcox Cup. The 2nd XI won the Rutland League Reserve Division One.

In 2001 the 1st XI were within one wicket of winning the Cambs & Hunts Premier League having seven overs at the oppositions last pair before ending up runners-up that year. In 2001 the 1st XI also won the John Wilcox Cup again, and the 2nd team won the Rutland League Reserve Division One (which they have now won four years in succession).

The club bar is currently run by Colin and Val Roberts. Since the 1980's there has been a succession of volunteer groundsmen including; Colin Longfoot, the late Dave Mitchell, John Jarvis and Bryan Dellar. The current club President is Jim Wood who took over from Charles Winfrey in the mid 1980s.

Other Games

During the 19th century other traditional rural games became more organised. Ailsworth put a regular team in a local Quoits league. Two matches with scores were reported in the Peterborough Advertiser of August 28, 1880. It is not recorded where the games were played but Ailsworth won both convincingly. Played in two innings between teams of 10, the total score against Wansford was 203 to 130, and against Stamford 218 to 152. The team included the likes of local butcher and landlord of the Wheatsheaf James Warr, and farmer Joseph Popple. Castor also had a quoits team that played from its base in the George and Dragon pub.

Brownies/Cubs/Guides

In 1935 the Guides had around thirty members organised in four troops – Red Rose, Forget-me-nots, Nightingales and Robins. The Captain was Miss Joan Strong of Stamford. Apart from working for various badges, the group was mainly involved in producing Christmas hampers for poor East End families shortlisted by voluntary social workers. Hampers included food as well as items of clothing handmade by each Guide.

Fig 20j. 1st Castor and Sutton Girl Guides c 1936: Country dancing team at Church Fete. Back (l-r): Delsia Burton, Mary Cooke, unknown, Rose Taylor, Irene Baker, unknown, Margery Barton; Front: Peggy Garfield, Winnie Ward, Betty Catmull, unknown, unknown, unknown.

Fig 20k. Castor and Ailsworth Brownies and Guides c1956.

Following that there had been a change because, according to Mrs E Wing, the 1st Castor Guides were registered as a company in April 1959[6]. Prior to that, the company had been run jointly with Glinton and Longthorpe. The Guides celebrated its Silver Jubilee in 1960. To mark the occasion, the Castor Guides presented a water tap for the churchyard.

In the Silver Jubilee year of 1977 the Brownies were run by Mrs C Berridge (Brownie Guider), and Mrs C Boyall (Assistant Brownie Guider). The Guides were overseen by Mrs E Wing (Guider).

In 1935 Frank Sismey was Scoutmaster [7]. He was also Captain of the Bell Ringers for many years. More recently, in the late 1980s, the cubs were run by Peter Huckle.

Tennis Club

There has been a Tennis Club in the villages for many years, at least since the 1920s. It has often had a few problems attracting members. In 1968 the club abolished the visitors' fees in a bid to attract new members.

In 1977 Colin Humphreys (President) and Colin Brown (Treasurer) ran the Tennis Club. The club was thriving throughout the 70s. In 1969/70 it had around 21 members who played on two grass courts now located just off Holmes Close in Ailsworth. Members at that time included Kevin Conkey, David Banks, Simon Clark, Paul Winsworth, Julie Winsworth, Margeret Hill and Helen Clark.

Fig 20l. Tennis on the court behind the Fitzwilliam Arms Pub around 1930. Frank Sismey is on the right of the picture. The white cottage is now York Cottage. The tennis court no longer exists.

Fig 20m. Castor and Ailsworth Tennis Club 1969/70. Pictured are back row (l-r): Kevin Conkey, David Banks, John Neal, Ms Turner, Ged O'Callaghan, Julie Winsworth, Gareth Thomas, Colin Humphries, John Conkey, Bev Agness, Colin Brown, Lindsay Agness, Keith Oliver, Freda Brown, Margeret Hill. Front row (l-r): Ms Thomas, Cathy Neal, Helen Clark, Kate Humphries, Tessa Thomas, Simon Clark, Paul Winsworth.

The Tennis club was not always located on the Holme Close site. In the 1920s there was a court behind the Fitzwilliam Arms pub.

Castor Bell-ringers

The bells of St. Kyneburgha's Church, Castor were cast in 1700. As well as ringing for regular services the bells were used to mark times of historical importance. An entry in John Hales diary marked the funeral of the Duke of Wellington on November 18, 1852:

'The Duke of Wellington was buried in St Paul's Cathedral. It was a public funeral. All members of both the Houses, barons and judges and law officers, as well as soldiers from every regiment, attended, besides the different Companies and Orders of Garters etc....A minute bell was tolled at Castor from 7 in the morning until 4pm.'

Rules and regulations of the Castor Ringers dated 4th March 1879 and signed by Rev John J Beresford [8], father of the novelist J G Beresford, were stringent. Any ringer bringing ale or causing ale to be brought to the tower would be fined 1s per offence. Swearing and the use of improper language also attracted fines, as did lateness and unexcused

Fig 20n. Bell-ringers: Centre back: Frank Sismey, Jack Coulson; next row: Michael Longfoot, Rev T Adler, George Sumner; Walter Longfoot; middle row: Len Sharpe, Bert Ball, Brian Sharpe, J Plumber, unknown,unknown, Front: Win Sumner, W Vann, Margaret Bell (Sharpe), George Hankins, Sheila Ball (Roffe), J Mountfield.

Fig 20o. Bell-ringers in tower c1950 from (l-r): Jack Coulson, Len Sharpe, John Plummer, Frank Sismey, Michael Longfoot, and George Hankins.

Fig 20p. Bell-ringers 2004 (l-r): Delia Caskey, Jonathan Ardron, Edward Baxter, Maggie Noble, Anna Reed, Bev Rigby, Trevor Vercoe, Ginnie Sheldon; seated; Stuart Weston (ringing master), Steve Reed (tower captain), William Baxter (steeple keeper).

Fig 20q. The new bells being positioned for their Baptism July 1999. (l-r): Edward Baxter, William Baxter, Theo Hensman.

Fig 20r. Hand Bell-ringers at Christmas Party 2003, (l-r) Back: Alison Brown, Jackie Elliott (with blonde wig), Bev Rigby, Ginnie Sheldon, Sue Sansom; Front: Alison Gibson, Maggie Noble (captain, with ginger wig).

absence. Ringing was a male preserve until the 1914-1918 war when women were admitted to bell towers as ringers for the first time. However, the Tower Captains have been predominantly men. Tower Captain in 1952 was Mr Longfoot, who was succeeded in 1953 by Frank Sismey who remained Captain until the early 1980s.

Under the leadership of the Tower Captain Tony Evans in 1999, two more bells were cast, baptised at the Patronal Mass in honour of St Kyneburgha and St Kyneswitha and then dedicated after being hung, at a special solemn Evensong by the Archdeacon Bernard Fernyhough.

Since 1700 the bells have been rung regularly except in the winter of 1962 due to deep snow which prevented the ringers getting to the tower. The bells were also quiet between the years 1926-1947. This was due in part to believed structural weakness of the tower and the Second World War when the bells could only be tolled in the event of invasion.

The bell-ringers include the Hand Bell-ringers, run presently by Maggie Noble. In addition to church services, they play at the Royal Oak around Christmastide and elsewhere.

The Excelsior Brass Band

The Castor Brass Band, formed in January 1856 under the leadership of Mr J Cooke, remained unchanged until at least 1868. It comprised ten self taught tradesmen, all from Castor, who practised one or two hours, three nights a week. The band was engaged to play at village events including the annual meeting of the Ancient Order of Foresters held at the Royal Oak in July 1858 [9].

WT Cooke was the bandmaster in 1897 and continued in the

post until at least 1935. The band headed each procession during the village's celebrations of Queen Victoria's Diamond Jubilee, played selections of music during the day, and played for dancing in the evening. The cost to the committee of hiring the band was £8 10s a portion of which (£1 14s 6d) was donated by Cooke himself [10]. As well as his duties as Bandmaster, Cooke was a Castor-based builder and Undertaker.

Cooke also led the band at other Diamond Jubilee celebrations around the area, including the Helpston Feast, along with many members of the Ancient Order of Foresters.

Fig 20s. Castor Excelsior Brass Band pictured in its full uniform circa 1900, back row (l-r): E Newborn, unknown, W Newborn sen, W Kingston, unknown, R Taylor. Front row (l-r): J Fox (with drum), J Mossendew, W Cooke, F Tomlin, A Mossendew, W Bell.

The band played a prominent part in the Silver Jubilee celebrations of George V in 1935. It was at the head of a procession held on Sunday May 12th made up of members of village organisations including Castor & Ailesworth Comrades, The Mothers' Union, the WI, the Guides, The Girls' Friendly Society, The Foresters and the Cricket, Football and Tennis clubs. The procession assembled on the Green and the Castor Reading Room at 10.30am and proceeded to Castor Church where a service of thanksgiving was held. The band also played during the sports that were held in the field behind the Village Hall, which belonged to Mrs Darby. The band's fees were on this occasion £3 [11].

It was not only at Jubilees that the band performed. When the Rev JJ Beresford returned to Castor following his Brighton wedding in 1865, the Castor Brass Band paraded the village and then played from the battlements of the church [12]. Rural entertainments were also to be had.

'On Thursday week a large number of inhabitants of this village availed themselves of the fineness of the weather to make a party. They therefore, with members of the Castor brass band, ... selected a most pleasant and open spot in the midst of the wood and unloaded from wagons a goodly number of baskets, hampers etc. Cloths were spread out upon the grass round which the guests assembled and dinner was served in the true gypsy style' [13].

After the meal the company; 'headed by the band repaired to an adjoining grass field where dancing and rural sports were carried on' [14]. After the party, the band led the people home through the villages playing 'several lively airs' before the National Anthem.

In the late '20s and the 1930s, band members also formed part of the Castor Amateur Minstrel Troupe. It also had a regular engagement playing on the lawn at the rear of the Fitzwilliam Arms pub on Sunday evenings during the summer. The band also practised in the 'Tea-room' there.

The Foresters

The Court Greenwood Foresters, No 1228, were formed in Castor in 1841 as part of the Ancient Order of Foresters, which started in 1834 in Leeds. It was a friendly society whose members assisted each other by paying into a common fund from which sick pay and funeral grants could be drawn.

The structure of the Order consisted of Courts which were responsible for their own funds and for relief of their own members, all decisions being made by democratic vote. The majority of Courts linked themselves into Districts for mutual support [15]. The society grew between 1834 and 1912, but following the beginning of the Welfare State in 1948 many Courts disbanded including Castor's.

Fig 20t. Foresters' Parade passing the Royal Oak during the Castor Club Feast July 1907. Note the banner with the motto 'Unity is Strength.'

Castor's Greenwood Foresters met quarterly at the Royal Oak where reports of its funds were made. According to the annual report of July 1858, the court had had receipts of £114 7s 11d and expenditure of £53 11s 4d, leaving a balance of £60 16s 7d. At that time there were 119 members out of a population of just over 700 [16]. In its first 17 years the court had received a total of £1324 13s 9d, paid out £900 8s 5d and kept a balance of £424 5s 4d. In December 1862 it had saved £30 during the quarter and £52 during the half year [17].

Other benevolent societies included the Band of Hope and the Coal Club/Medical Club, which provided mutual support to their members in a similar way to the AOF.

The Fire Brigade

There was a volunteer fire brigade based in a small station close to Castor village Green. It was in existence from at least 1912 until the early 1960s. The brigade's first documented action was at a fire which destroyed three cottages on Stocks Hill in October 1912, which was reported in the Peterborough and Hunts Advertiser.

The fire ignited a beam in the chimney of one of the cottages and spread rapidly across the thatched roofs. Mr & Mrs Parker, Mr & Mrs Bell and family, and Mr & Mrs Tomlin occupied the houses. Mr Bell was a member of the fire brigade, and Fire Captain Cooke lived close by and was on the scene quickly, pumping water onto the blaze using water from his well via 700ft of hose, and saving the house of the Culpin family. Members of the brigade present at the fire were Capt W Cooke, A Cooke, CW Darby, W Bell, J Mossendew, L Longfoot, R Longfoot, WT Smith, W Gibson, R Taylor, W Fox, and H Sharpe, with ex Captain Harris. Another former fireman and local grocer, Mr Wootton, inaugurated a fund on behalf of the victims of the fire, which at the time of the report had raised over £30.

The Brigade was called into action again 15 years later when a fire broke out in cottages on Church Hill in July 1928. According to a report in the Advertiser the fire was started by sunlight reflecting through the glass of an open casement window and igniting the thatch. Two properties belonging to Mr & Mrs S Pendred and Mr & Mrs CP Jolley were damaged. The Jolley's daughter was able to rescue some valuable war memorabilia from the blaze. Mrs Fox, who ran the corner shop, called the brigade, and Captain R Taylor, Lieutenant Bell and Firemen A Jakes and B Venters attended the incident.

A pair of horses pulled the old Fire Brigade pump. During WWII the fire brigade had the use of a Coventry Cummins pump, but it was never used and done away with in the 1950's when the fire brigade disbanded. Ironically, the farm building next to the Fire Engine Station caught fire a fortnight later.

Members of the Castor Auxilliary Fire Service also attended the scenes of accidents. Bill Agness of the AFS was at the scene of a fatal accident that occurred on December 26, 1957 after an ambulance attending a call out skidded out of control on Loves Hill and collided with the stone wall bounding the paddock behind Dragon House. The incident was reported in the *Peterborough Citizen & Advertiser* the following day. The driver, Sidney McCoombe, escaped uninjured but his mate, Alec Broughton, died of head injuries received when he was thrown from the vehicle.

Fig 20u. Castor Fire Brigade during 1939/45.
Those identified in the picture are Ernie Bell, Horace Winsworth, Jack Longfoot, Frank Hammond, Arthur Foster, Charlie Bell and John Sharpe.

Mothers' Union

The St Kyneburgha's Church branch of the Mothers' Union was established in 1897. In 1977, the Mothers' Union had as its president Miss R Stokes. She was assisted by Miss G Heighton (Secretary) and Mrs E Sismey (Enrolling Member). The organisations motto is 'For home and family.' It is now led by Jay Winfrey (President).

The branch celebrated its Centenary at a special service in 1997, at which a statue of Our Lady and Child, which they had presented to the church, was blessed. This is now in the Lady Chapel. The Mothers' Union actively supports the work of the church in a whole range of activities. The members make up over 100 posies every year for children to give their mothers on Mothering Sunday. They support the work of the Children's Society by making up over 150 Christingles for the annual Christingle service in December, and they look after the Lady Chapel at Castor Church. The Mothers' Union banner is carried at all festal services in the church, and they decorate the banners with posies of flowers, topknots and ribbons for the annual Patronal Festival in July.

Fig 20v. Mothers' Union members and other helpers preparing banners for Patronal Mass at Castor July 1999. (l-r): Millie Weston, Win Smith, Joyce Clarke (at altar) Vera Pell, Jay Winfrey, Susan Sykes, Jennifer Sykes, Jackie Cook, Diana Burke. The Sykes family carried the St Kyneburgha banner that year.

The Evergreen Club

Mrs Coulson (Chairman) and Mrs Garlick (Secretary) headed

the Evergreens in 1977. Now, Bridget Goode looks after the organisation. The annual membership subscription for the twice-monthly meetings was 50p, with a 6p subscription per meeting attended. Members now take part in social gatherings, bringing small prizes for Bingo, Whist and Raffle, and organised trips to places of interest.

There have been and still are many other clubs and societies in the villages over the years, The Art Group, Judo Club, Tai Kwan Do Club, Gardeners' Club and so on. There have also been village associations that have united the villages in joint activities

Fig 20w. An Evergreen Club trip to Hunstanton. (l-r): Millie Weston, Margaret Sharpe, Gwen Berridge, Winnie Bushell, Kay Llloyd, Mary Lunn, Vi Jarvis, Bridget Goode (president), Richard Wright (helper), Mary Jones, Charlie Jones; at table: Monica Pollard, Kath Henderson and David Henderson (helpers).

including the Castor and Ailsworth Village Association (CAVA), and CASPRA, which have organised Firework displays and the annual Santa Claus parade respectively. These organisations have also been responsible for running some very ambitious village events such as the Pageant held in 1974 to celebrate the foundation of St. Kyneburgha's Church.

John Howard

Notes

1. See *History of the Women's Institute* by Audrey Constance on www.womens-institute.co.uk
2. Dave Russell, *Football and the English*, A Social History of Association Football in England, 1997, pp13-15.
3. *Peteborough Standard*, 15 September 1967.
4. Team: T. Lee, T. Enness, T. Hall, W. Wilson, S. Clark, J. Neal, G. Bircham, R. Whitby, R. Brisbane, K. Conkey, C. Beecher. Sub: P. Winsworth.
5. Team: J. Garner, C. Bass, G. Foster, K. Oliver, G. Brown, J. Warters, G. Craythorne, C. Banks, N. Dytham, M. Garner, C. Beeches, G. Boyall. Sub: K. Conkey.
6. Mrs E. Wing in *The Castor & Ailsworth Book of Jubilee Celebrations,* 1977, pp55.
7. *Castor & Ailsworth Book of Jubilee Celebrations*, 1977, pp62.
8. Taken from a wooden notice displayed in the tower.
9. *Peterborough Advertiser*, July 31 1858.
10. Final accounts of Castor Queen's Diamond Jubilee Festivities, June 22nd , 1897.
11. Statement of Accounts, Castor Silver Jubilee Celebrations, May 6th 1935.
12. *Peterborough Advertiser*, Sat June 24 1865.
13. *Peterborough Weekly News and General Advertiser*, Sept 27, 1856.
14. *The Peterborough Weekly News and General Advertiser*, Sept 27, 1856.
15. Audrey Fisk, The Ancient Order of Foresters: Its Evolution, 2002 (www.foresters.ws)
16. The Census of 1851 put the population of Castor at 772.
17. *Peterborough Advertiser*, December 27 1862.

Fig 20x. Two members of the Mothers' Union being presented with 50 year membership certificates by rev Adrian Davies. (l-r): Mrs E Sismey, Mrs Bracey, Mrs E Goode, Mrs K Bell.

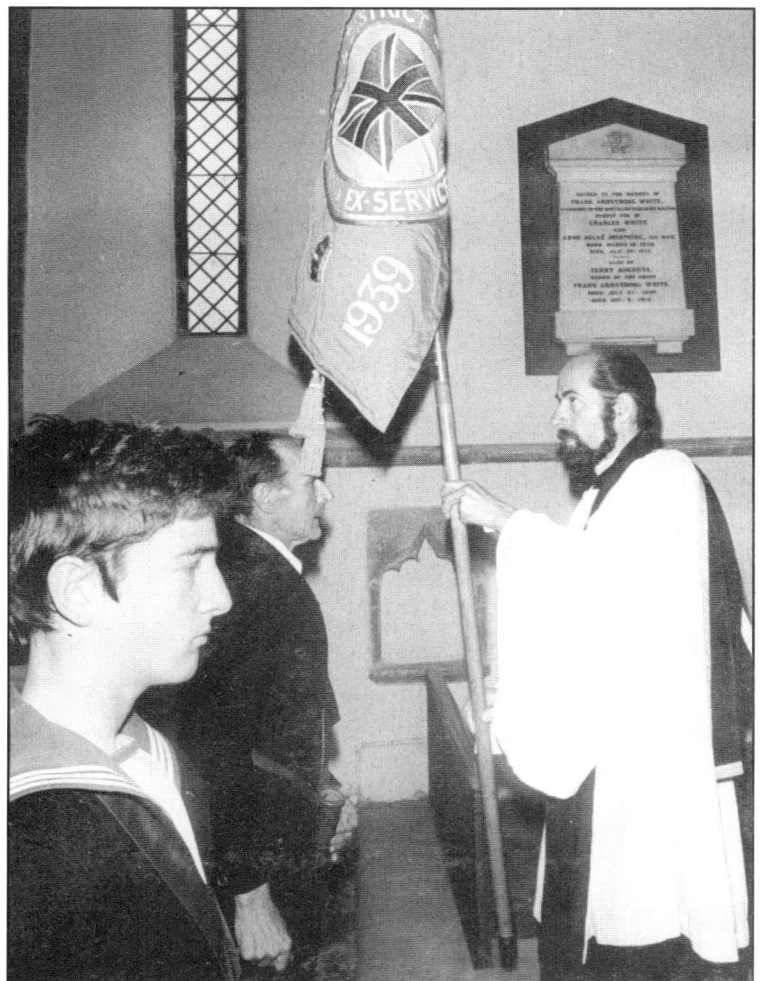

Fig 20y. The Ailsworth & District Ex-Servicemen's Association Banner is received by Rev Adrian Davies for Laying-up at Castor Church 1976.

Fig 20z. Members of the Mothers' Union preparing Mothering Sunday posies at Jay Winfrey's house. (clockwise) Lorna Sheppardson, Monica Pollard, Vera Pell, Joyce Clarke, Millie Weston (standing), Win Smith (standing), Rene Foster, Gwen Berridge, Joan Marriott, Grace Gibbs.

Fig 20aa. Members of the Mothers' Union 1950s.
Back (l-r): Rev T Adler, Mrs P Sismey, Mrs J Coulson, Mrs C Taylor, Mrs M Cade, Mrs C Bell, Mrs S Mossendew, Mrs V Pell, Mrs Ball, Mrs H Coulson, Mrs I Varnham (holding banner), Mrs L Goode, Mrs J Kingston, Mrs H Longfoot, Mrs K Longfoot. Front: Mrs Birch, Mrs B Pell, Mrs K Neal, Mrs G Dudley.

Fig 20bb. Evergreen trip to London 2003.

Chapter 21
Rural Pastimes

No book about village life would be complete if it did not tell of the people and some of the ways in which they prefer to spend their spare time. The next few pages are dedicated to villagers, past and present, whose love of the country way of life is their reason for their participation in what are now called 'country sports'.

In this country at present there is much emphasis on 'political correctness' and people who kill game tend to be regarded as cruel heathens. A person seen carrying a gun in the countryside is unlikely to be perceived as a sportsman. If you are new to village life this chapter may present a fresh perspective of what goes on around you.

Fig 21a. The oldest sporting image in the village; a wild boar hunt on capitals of Castor Church AD1120. (Photo: J Tovey)

Poaching

'*Stolen fruit is the sweetest*', they say. There are those who cannot accept that rabbits, pheasants, hare and deer, which wander freely from one man's land to another's could belong to anybody; after all, are they not called wild animals?

There are virtually no proper poachers nowadays as the advent of the supermarket and better wages has made the need to poach and risk the punishment almost non-existent. It was not so long ago that many families only had meat at Christmas times if they were given a couple of rabbits or a brace of pheasants by the local squire or farmer. Faced with this shortage, many men resorted to poaching to feed their families and also to supplement their low wages.

A good poacher had many tools for his trade. These would mostly be a silenced 410 shotgun, a few longnets, snares, purse nets and ferrets, and a running dog. The shotgun, nets and snares would all be well-hidden in case he had a visit from the local Gamekeeper. The poacher had to have an excellent knowledge of the Gamekeeper's movements, such as: When did he feed his coverts? Which pub did he drink in? Who were his closest friends? etc.

He also had to be in tune with nature. For instance, why are the crows and rooks turning away sharply at a certain part of their flight-line? Also, there might be the faint smell of tobacco smoke blown down on the wind which would mean there is somebody else in the vicinity.

The weather would also be a major factor. It would be no good setting a snare while there's snow on the ground as the footprints would give you away. But a windy damp night is perfect for poaching pheasants; the sound from the 410 will be slight if the wind is blowing away from the keeper's cottage. This is also the perfect weather to longnet rabbits at night. Providing you approach them from downwind the resulting catch will be worth the risk of capture by the keeper.

The poacher had to be as wise as an owl and as cunning as a fox. Many keepers had a grudging respect for the lone poacher who only took what he needed to feed his family. This respect did not extend to the organised gangs who came mostly from the cities to clear the pheasant coverts at night, and who would have no hesitation in setting about whoever tried to stop them.

In the old days, the penalties for poaching were quite severe and ranged from a £2 fine and a month in jail to transportation to the Colonies. Under a new law in 1816, a man could be transported for seven years if he was caught with rabbits or hares and equipment to poach. Many of the local squires and landowners were also magistrates, so the chances of being let off were pretty slim.

Colin and his mate 'Brooky' were two Peterborough men who used to poach the woods around Castor Parish in the 1950s and 60s. Colin said, "*We both used to wear leather jerkins over our jackets. We made a cut in the lining and we could get 26 pheasants in each jerkin, which was some weight. When we had done enough 'chopping out', as we called it, we would hide the birds and guns and pick them up later, that way we never had any game on us if we were caught coming out of a wood.*"

The days of the pheasant poacher are all but over, as the game dealers will only pay around 50p a brace. So you would need a lorry-load to make it pay, but I've no doubt there is still the odd person around who likes to take one for the pot. But we do get visits from the deer-poachers in our Parish. These people come from South Yorkshire in their Subarus with running dogs and have been known to take as many as 12 deer in a night. They are not pot hunters, but organised gangs who come in the early hours of the morning to poach for profit. I suppose the village poacher will go the same way as the village shop, post office and pub – confined to the history books. Another part of village life gone for good.

Longnetting

On a blustery night, when most people are thinking about switching the television off and going to bed, a small group of Castor men may be about to go into the fields to keep alive a traditional and, to most people, an unknown form of rabbit-control, the art of longnetting.

The longnet was widely used in Victorian times to catch large numbers of rabbits in a single sweep of a field. Rabbits caught by this method would command the very best prices at market as they were clean and unshot. The longnet was a favourite tool of the poacher. A good team of netters could set out 200 yards of net in under five minutes and maybe catch 40 or more rabbits if they were lucky. They would have set the nets at three or four different locations in a single night. Some sets may not have been successful but others may have yielded enough rabbits to make the night worthwhile. Two or three nights longnetting a week with good results would have boosted a poacher's income considerably. It was not uncommon for rival poaching gangs to be working the same area. When this happened it usually meant trouble. At worst a fight would break out but more often the nets would be stolen, putting one gang out of action for a while.

Longnets usually come in sizes of 25, 50 and 100 yards. A 25 yard net will have 50 yards of net, a 50 yard will have 100 yards and a 100 yard will have 200 yards of net. This extra net is known as the 'running kill' or 'the bag'. Basically what it's there for is to make sure the rabbit gets fully enmeshed when it runs into the net. If the net was taut like a tennis net, the rabbit would just bounce off.

Fig 21b. Mark Smith with a 100 yard 'quick-set' longnet, Mick Beeson with a 50 yard nylon net and plastic pegs, Kings Cliffe 2001.

In the old days, the nets were made from hemp. Today's nets are mostly made from nylon. There are two lines which the netting is threaded on to, known as the head-line and foot-line. At each end is an anchor pin. The net is held up by hazel pegs about 28 inches in length and positioned every five yards.

The object of longnetting is to approach your set down-wind of the feeding rabbits and set the net ten yards in front of the warren. This is only done at night. The best night for this is one which is dark and blustery with a little light rain. Moonlit nights are no good as the quarry will spot you and the net. The wind must be blowing towards the warren, so that the rabbits will not detect the human scent. Once everything is in place the netters move up the side of the field to a pre-determined spot, spread out across the field and then back towards the warren making enough noise so that the rabbits out feeding will instinctively run back towards the warren and into the net. That's the theory! It does not always go according to plan, sometimes the rabbits may not be out feeding at that particular time.

One of the most memorable nights for myself and the other members of the Castor netters was on the 8th August 1997 at a location close to Castor where we were asked to reduce the rabbit population. We were on the third set of the night, the first two only producing seven rabbits between them. We quietly set a 100 yard net in front of the warren. Once ready, and with voices at a whisper, we moved out into the field. Kevin and Steven Conkey moved up the left side, Mick Beeson and I went to the right. At about 400 yards we started to turn across and back towards the net. Spread out at 50 yard intervals we began to make a noise to force the rabbits home. As we approached we could hear the rabbits in the net. How many? Five, maybe six. As we moved along the net it was soon apparent that this was a good set. In the first 20 yards we had five, then six, seven, eight onwards 14, 15, 16, 17 in total. After removing them we decided that was enough for the night as it was about 3.15am.

We collected our push-bikes from the bushes where they were hidden and, with rabbits and equipment hanging from them, we made our way back to Castor. We slipped back into the village like a Commando raiding-party returning from a mission. With the streets void of man and machine there was a ghostly silence. We passed St Kyneburgha's Church, standing there in all her splendour like a wise old owl keeping watch over us all. I often wonder what stories she could tell from centuries past. Maybe the Cavaliers and Roundheads fought in the meadows; the sight of Kings and Queens passing this way, en-route to the Cathedral; the building of the railway and watching the men and women of the parish leaving from the station to fight in countless wars never to return. But, that night she was witness to the return of the longnetters.

Fig 21c. Mick Beeson removing a rabbit from a traditional hemp longnet 1998. (Photo: M Smith)

In four nights netting that August, we accounted for 92 rabbits. The warrens soon recovered and we've been back many times since. Longnetting was all but forgotten after myxomatosis was introduced into the wild rabbit population in the 1950s. This terrible disease killed 99% of the population.

Some people would say there is no place in the modern way of life for old traditions like longnetting, and it should be confined to the history books. Why do we do it? Because we enjoy it. We enjoy it in the same way that someone enjoys driving their classic car or renovating their old house. We are all helping to keep a small piece of history alive.

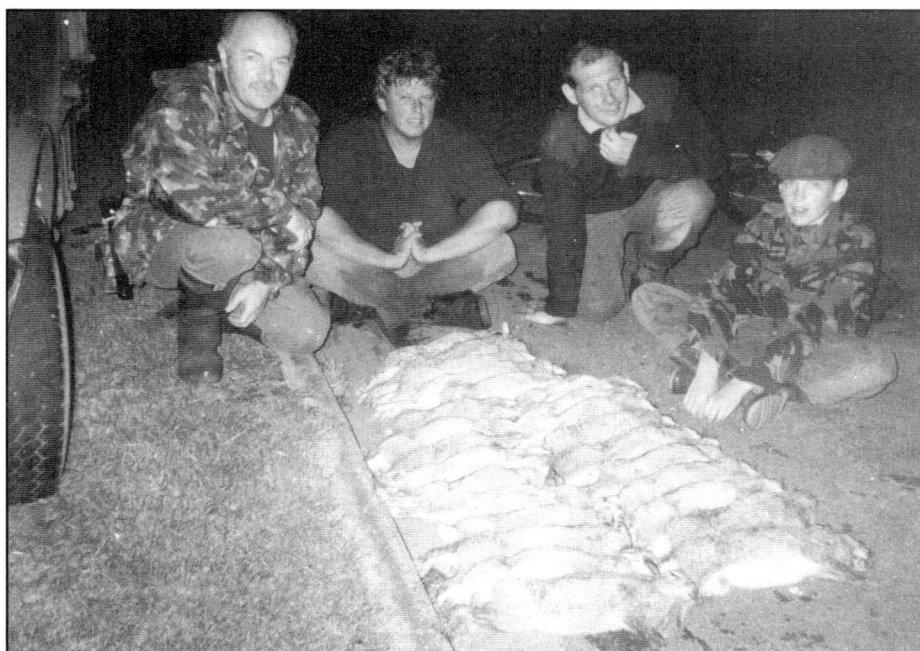

Fig 21d. After a night's Longnetting August 1997: Mark Smith, Mick Beeson, Kevin and Steven Conkey. (Photo: M Smith)

Ferreting

Many people keep ferrets but few actually use them to bolt rabbits from a warren. There's nothing quite like ferreting on a frosty winter's morning. It's also one of the best ways to reduce the rabbits if they are causing a problem.

Once you've arrived at your warren, and set your purse nets over the holes with the minimum of noise, the ferret is entered into a hole and then the wait begins. The ferret will pop its head out of different holes while it tracks the rabbits through the warren, then there will be a thumping underground so you know you're going to have some action pretty

Fig 21e. Mark Smith, Mick Beeson after a morning's ferreting Station Road, Ailsworth, December 2001. (Photo: M Smith)

soon. All of a sudden a rabbit bursts from a hole into a purse net. Quickly you gather up the net and rabbit, dispatch it, then place another net over the hole before untangling the dead rabbit from the net. Then the wait begins again. Once you're sure there are no more rabbits in the warren you move on to the next and repeat the process.

There are still a few people in the parish who enjoy ferreting, myself included. Mick Beeson has kept and worked ferrets for over 30 years. Steven Conkey and Carl Anker have recently started ferreting on a regular basis and spend most weekends in the winter working the warrens at a variety of locations around the parishes.

Game Shooting

It is estimated that there are some 10,000 Shoots in the UK, ranging from the small DIY Shoot to the more traditional country-estate Shoots which are steeped in history.

The Milton Estate Shoot has a link to one of the shooting fraternity's most famous and respected gamekeeping families, the Grass family. About 100 members of the family have been employed as keepers in the last 150 years all over the UK.

Fig 21f. Matthew Hill and Richard Anker wild-fowling at Whittlesey December 2000. (Photo: M Smith)

Jim Grass was Head-keeper at the Wentworth Estate in South Yorkshire which is the sister estate to Milton. Keith Dickinson from Upton was the last keeper to be employed by Jim Grass at Wentworth in 1967. He recalls, *"He was a real character and an old-style keeper but was lost on the modern methods of keepering. I remember at the end of one season he said to Harry Gail, 'Now who hasn't had any pheasants?' so I spoke up and said, 'Us underkeepers haven't had any', to which he replied 'Who said you were entitled to any?'"*

Fig 21g. Farmers' Shoot in Castor Hanglands c1910; John William Harris is 8th from the right standing.

Fig 21h. The legendary keeper: Jim Grass Wentworth Estate head-keeper age 75.

Fig 21i. Milton Keeper: Keith Dickinson near Sutton Wood Jan 2001. (Photo: M Smith)

Fig 21j. Keeper Wilf Hutchinson (rt) with Jack Meek at Cocker Spaniel Field Trial Meeting Milton Jan 1965.

"Another time we had decided to go rook shooting on the 12th May as we had far too many rooks. But after shooting just 20, Jim said, 'that's enough'. I couldn't believe it so after he had gone home I went back and shot 400 with my semi-auto rimfire."

"We used to come to Milton to load for the guns on the big two-day Shoots. We'd come on a Thursday and stay at the Angel in Priestgate, then spend Friday and Saturday shooting before returning back to Wentworth after breakfast on Sunday."

"It was while on one of these visits that I was asked to come and work at Milton. At the time, John Baldwin, Wilf

Fig 21k. Milton Keeper: Aubrey Weston walking his dogs by Milton Hall.

Fig 21l. Beaters and Keepers 1971: Aubrey Weston, Harry Taylor, Peter Hill, 'Hoss' Baker.

Fig 21m. Stan Cunnington of Upton, Milton Shoot beater and 'gamecartman', West end of Milton Hall. (Photo M Smith)

Fig 21n. Lifelong friends Kevin Conkey and Trevor Jarvis who have a combined total of 66 years beating on the Milton Shoot 2000. (Photo M Smith)

Hutchinson, Aubrey Weston and Les Keys were the keepers here. Sadly Les Keys died and Major Peacock came to me and said, 'Dickinson, Lord Fitzwilliam wants you to come and work here on the Upton beat.' So, I brought Sylvia my wife to Milton to have a look to see if she liked it. That was in 1970 and we've been here ever since."

"Two of the best shots I've seen at Milton were Nicholas Cobbold Jnr. and Lord John Manners, the brother of the Duke of Rutland and an ex-SAS man. He shot five partridge from the same covey while double gunning the Steepings Wood."

"I think my early years of keepering were the best; I used to love collecting up the wild pheasant eggs. Nowadays most shoots buy in the majority of the birds."

By the time Keith retired in 2001, he was the only keeper at Milton after Wilf Hutchinson retired and Aubrey Weston passed away. David Webster took over from him until 2003. The Shoot is at present let to a private syndicate who employ their own keeper, Jeff Cook. The Estate still retains a few days for family days, tenant farmer days and the end-of-season cock shoots.

The beaters and pickers up are the backbone of any shoot. A well drilled and experienced team can make the gamekeeper's day less stressful. There are a few long-serving beaters at Milton; Dick Jarvis from Marholm has been involved with the Shoot both as a gun and a beater for over 60 years, while John Hill and Peter Hill, also from Marholm, have done about 50 years each. Kevin Conkey and Trevor Jarvis started their beating days along with Tony Cunnington around 1971, which gives them 33 years each. The loyalty shown by these long-serving members of the beating team is a reflection on the quality and professionalism of the gamekeepers employed by Milton Estate, as few people would put up with being soaking wet, cold, muddy and tired, all for a small remuneration and a bottle of beer.

Game shooting is as much a part of life in these parishes as in any other country parish in the UK. A lot of private woodland was planted for shooting and is managed to provide the best habitat for the wildlife while also keeping control of the vermin. Should game shooting ever be banned then a lot of woodland would go unmanaged and probably be felled. The sad fact is that in our parishes the threat does not come from the anti-shooting campaigners but the city-planners as the threat of our five villages being swallowed up by a massive housing development has raised its ugly head again.

Fig 21o. Village boys camping at Milton Ferry c1918. Note the shotguns and the rabbits. The boy on the left is Arthur Harris.

Down by the Riverside

The river was used by the villagers for much more than fishing. There were two bathing places in Castor parish, one beyond the station, still used today, and another near the end of the track that continues from Splash Lane. There were a number of bathing huts there too, used for changing and for parties. Young people from the villages often camped down by the river-side, sailing their 'flatties' (small flat-bottomed sailing dinghies) or canoeing, as well as swimming.

The best way to end this chapter is with a quote made by King George VI: "*The wildlife of today is not ours to dispose of as we please. We have it in trust. We must account for it to those who come after.*"

Fig 21p. Butcher's Home Camp: people from the village camping in Ferry Meadow in the 1920s; note the 'flatty' and the barges.

Fig 21q. Canoes and punts on the river, Harris children and Alfie Mann on punt 1934.

Fig 21s. Charles Winfrey with a 24lb pike caught Boxing Day 1960.

Fig 21r. Harris children with friends and 'flatties' 1931.

Fig 21t. Jonathon Means with a pike caught at the 'Boot' Splash lane Castor, March 2002. (Photo: J Means)

Fig 21u. Milton hounds meet Castor Green Christmas Eve 2002 – in centre George Adams (Huntsman) with hounds. The stone wall behind is all that remains of the old Manor Farm threshing barn, now serving as a back garden wall for the houses in Manor Farm Lane.

Mark Smith

A descendant from Romany Gypsies, I was born in Castor and have lived in Castor and Ailesworth all my life. Married with two sons, my main interests are rabbiting and the photographic history of Castor and Ailesworth.

Chapter 22
Milton Park and the Fitzwilliam Family

Fig 22a. Milton Hall North Front.

Early Family History

In the 17th year of the reign of Henry VII in the year 1502, William Fitzwilliam of Gaynes Park Essex, purchased from Robert Whyttilbury for the sum of 1200 marks (£800) *'The manors of Milton Marham with their appurtenances in Milton, Marham, Caster, Etton, Maxsey, Norborough and Depyngate....and the wharfage and the profits of the wharf and water of Gunwade'* (now known as Milton Ferry).

The indenture or 'deeds' of the estate were handed over in the font of St Paul's Cathedral London as a sign of honesty and good faith in the transaction.

The Fitzwilliam family had long been established at Sprotborough in South Yorkshire until William Fitzwilliam (later the 1st Baronet) entered the City of London and made his fortune as a merchant and wool stapler. However he was also a courtier and became Treasurer and later High Chamberlain to Cardinal Wolsey who subsequently made him a member of Henry VIII's council *('for his wisdom gravity, port and eloquence and being a gentleman of comely stature'...)*

At the end of his life in 1531, Wolsey spent Easter at Peterborough Abbey on his way to York. Notwithstanding his fall from favour with Henry VIII, Fitzwilliam invited his old friend and patron to stay at Milton along with his entourage who camped in the park near the main house.

The story goes that when the king heard that Fitzwilliam had invited the disgraced Wolsey to stay, he was so angry that he ordered all the tops of the oak trees in the park to be cut off as a warning to the owner!

Fig 22b. Sir William Fitzwilliam, 3rd Baronet.

Fig 22c. Milton Hall South Front.

There is no doubt that a house existed at Milton before 1500 but the North front as we see it today is mainly late 16th century and the work of the third baronet. Sir William 3rd, a remarkable Elizabethan, was three times Lord Deputy of Ireland for Elizabeth I between 1560 and 1594 at which time *'being in a very advanced age and worn out by the fatigues of the war and the state there, he by Her Majesty's permission, returned to this kingdom and retired to his native place Milton where he died in 1599'*. He is buried alongside his wife on the South side of the chancel in Marholm church opposite his grandfather who occupies the canopied tomb on the North side.

In retirement Sir William 3rd was governor of Fotheringhay Castle and held this office at the time Mary Queen of Scots was incarcerated there. On the night before her execution, Mary gave the governor her seal and a portrait of her son James – later James I of England which still are at Milton to this day.

At the beginning of the 17th century, Sir William 5th was created 1st Baron Fitzwilliam in the Irish peerage and in turn his grandson was made 1st Earl Fitzwilliam again in the Irish peerage in 1716. It was this member of the family who employed William Talman to design the stable block and clock tower situated at the East end of Milton. As an architect, Talman had been responsible for works at Drayton, Burghley and Chatsworth. He had been Comptroller of the Kings Works since 1689 but he also worked closely with Christopher Wren who had married Lord Fitzwilliam's sister. It is thought that the reason Wren himself did not supervise the project at Milton is that he was too busy in London following the great fire of 1666. Bearing in mind that Wren was responsible for the design of nearly fifty City churches, not least of them a new St. Paul's Cathedral, the construction of which began in 1675, this may well be true.

The Eighteenth Century

The exterior of Milton Hall comprises three distinct styles of architecture. The Tudor and the Wren styles have already been noted but in the mid-18th century the main house was 'Georgianised' both inside and out. This work was carried out largely by Henry Flitcroft. The 18th century alterations came about following the marriage of the 3rd Earl Fitzwilliam to 2nd Marquess of Rockingham's elder sister and heiress Lady Anne Watson-Wentworth.

The union of the Rockingham and Fitzwilliam families was one of the most important milestones in the history of Milton. Thomas Watson-Wentworth, created 1st Marquess of Rockingham in 1746, inherited the Wentworth estate on the death of his father in 1723.

When he died four years later in 1750 he was succeeded by his fifth and only surviving son Charles, 2nd Marquess, who was twice Prime Minister between 1765 and 1782. His political influence and wealth was enormous but alas, the Prime Minster had no children of his own so his heiress was his elder sister Anne who had married the 3rd Earl Fitzwilliam of Milton. Anne, mother of William 4th Earl Fitzwilliam, died in 1769 and when Lord Rockingham died thirteen years later in 1782, William inherited estates in North and South Yorkshire, Northamptonshire and County Wicklow in Ireland. The additional net estate income is recorded as being over £30,000 per annum at the time of his inheritance.

Rockingham had engaged Henry Flitcroft to design the Palladian mansion of Wentworth Woodhouse so it is likely that this was the reason his brother in law (3rd Earl Fitzwilliam) chose the same architect for Milton even though differing schemes for Milton had been presented by James Gibbs (architect of the Radcliffe Library, Oxford and the Senate House, Cambridge) and M Brettingham (pupil of William Kent).

Much to the displeasure of Flitcroft, Lord Fitzwilliam refused to allow the demolition of the existing Tudor North front, so the new Georgian work had to be joined to the older part of the house which explains the unusual mansard roof stitching the old to the new.

The 3rd Earl died in 1756 at the early age of 38 and his son William became 4th Earl at the tender age of eight. Although most of the interior had been completed by the time of his father's death, it fell to the 4th Earl to complete the design of the Long Gallery and the adjacent Peterborough Rooms some fifteen years later following his return to England from the Grand Tour of Europe with his tutor Dr. Thomas Crofts. He employed Sir William Chambers to carry out this work in 1770 and 1771 and Chambers completed his commission at Milton by designing a temple which was given to the 4th Earl as a wedding present from his father-in-law Lord Bessborough. The temple stood on Temple Hill (close to the present Ferry Lodge site) until it became unsafe at the end of the 19th century and was taken down. A simplified version using the original pillars, bases and pediments saved carefully by the 10th Earl was rebuilt in 1986 in the woods at the West End of Milton Hall to commemorate the fiftieth anniversary of the creation of Milton (Peterborough) Estates Company.

The final phase of building work took place around 1800 when the 4th Earl instructed John Carr of York to convert a courtyard on the South side of the house into two libraries. As before with Henry Flitcroft, Carr had carried out major work at Wentworth, which is probably why he was chosen for the Milton scheme.

During the 19th century the Earls Fitzwilliam centered their lives at Wentworth and on the death of Charles 5th Earl in 1857 the lands were split. As a result of this division, the Yorkshire estates passed to the eldest son William (6th Earl) while Milton was inherited by his younger brother The Hon George Fitzwilliam who, followed by his son, George Charles Wentworth Fitzwilliam, continued to live in a more modest style. It is for this reason in all likelihood that Milton was never the subject of Victorian alterations and extensions.

The park at Milton was laid out in the early 1790s following a scheme designed by Humphrey Repton who had already landscaped the park at Wentworth. At both places he wrote and illustrated his suggestions in a leather bound 'Red Book' with colour washed overlays to explain his ideas and proposals. The Milton book is dated 1791. In order to improve the appearance of the park he even moved the line of the main road – a task from which lesser men today might shrink.

Fig 22d. William Fitzwilliam, 4th Earl.

Fig 22e. Mr George Wentworth-Fitzwilliam.

The Twentieth Century

The turn of the 20th century saw the end of Queen Victoria's long reign in 1901. Generally for English country estates this was a fairly settled time for those who had survived the agricultural recession of the late nineteenth century. The upheaval, turmoil and tragedy of the Great War was still some years away after which English estate life would never be quite the same again. For places such as Milton, the Edwardian era leading up to 1914 has been romantically described as 'a long summer day'. At Milton, George Fitzwilliam had taken up residence with his wife Evelyn and their children. George took a close personal interest in the running of the estate - the stables and kennels in particular. He supervised the ordering of fodder for the horses and the management in these areas. His knowledge of estate affairs was such that later in his life in the early 1930s when his Agent, Mr H Wilmot, was taken ill and unable to continue in office, George was able to run the estate himself for the best part of the year until a replacement agent in the form of Mr E W Mackie could be found.

Fig 22f. The Long Gallery in World War I.

For a time towards the end of the First World War, George and Evelyn moved out of Milton Hall as a wartime economy measure. They moved into Longthorpe House which later became the Agent's residence. Mr & Mrs Fitzwilliam made a significant personal contribution to the war effort by turning Milton Hall into a convalescent home for British Army Officers. Rooms such as the Pillared Hall, Smoking Room, Long Gallery and the Peterborough Rooms were all filled with rows of iron beds while the old masters remained in place on the walls.

Fig 22g. Ambulance and soldiers at Milton front door.

The hospital was run privately at George's expense and Mrs Rosie Reynolds, for many years housekeeper at Milton and whose father was coachman and later chauffeur to Mr George, can remember as a girl of four years old sitting on the hospital beds and talking to the soldiers.

It was at this time in 1917 that the late Daphne du Maurier made the first of several visits to Milton at the age of ten along with her mother and two sisters. It is quite clear from correspondence in later life between Miss du Maurier and the 10th Earl that the happiness and freedom experienced during these childhood visits made an enormous impact on the future writer which she never forgot. She told Lord Fitzwilliam that when she wrote Rebecca some twenty years later, the interior of Manderley was based on her recollection of the rooms and 'big house feel' of Milton in World War One.

Following the cessation of hostilities in 1918, the Fitzwilliams moved back into Milton but Evelyn died all too soon afterwards on Lady Day 1925 at the early age of 58. The fact that she was greatly mourned by her devoted husband is clear from the charming plaque which was placed in her memory behind the family pew in Marholm church. George continued on alone until his death in 1935 by which time the estate was in the depths of the severe agricultural depression which prevailed throughout the 1930s until the Second World War. Significant areas of land on the estate either lay idle or were let rent free for a couple of years rising to half a crown an acre if a tenant could establish a livelihood. The more fortunate farmers did survive in business and many of our tenanted farms are now still occupied by their sons and grandsons. The Jarvis, Morton, Darby, Longfoot, Harris and Garford families all began their Milton tenancies during these inter-war years.

Captain Tom Fitzwilliam (later 10th Earl) succeeded his father as master of Milton in 1935 and in order to preserve the estate holdings and to mitigate the effect of future death duties, much of the land and buildings was put into the ownership of a company and so in 1934 Milton (Peterborough) Estates Company was born.

At the outbreak of the Second World War the house and park were requisitioned in various stages by the Ministry of Works. Part of the house and the stable block were occupied by the Czech army and later Special Operations Executive who trained in the grounds and woods prior to being dropped by parachute behind enemy lines in France in the days leading up to the Normandy landings. An indoor pistol shooting range was built in the kitchen garden and recently when the stable clock tower was repaired we were amazed to note the number of bullet holes in the gold leaf ball at the base of the weather cock. Nissen huts were erected on the North front of Milton Hall and in dry times when the grass dies off, their concrete foundations still show through as a reminder of darker days. In one of the woods a large concrete arrow was set out in a clearing probably as a marker indicating the line of approach to Westwood aerodrome.

During the war, Captain Tom Fitzwilliam retained bachelor living accommodation at the Western end of Milton Hall for use when not on active service but he did not resume occupation of the main part of the house until his marriage to Joyce Fitzalan in 1956. At that time and in the meanwhile having inherited the title of 10th Earl, Lord and Lady Fitzwilliam supervised a major refurbishment of the house prior to moving back. Such was the quality of the work carried out that many of the rooms have not been redecorated or altered since then after nearly fifty years of use. Lord Fitzwilliam, a great countryman and supporter of many rural activities and societies, died in 1979 but his wife continued as chatelaine of Milton until her death in 1995 at the age of 97. She was succeeded by her daughter The Hon Lady Hastings who in turn was succeeded by her son Sir Philip Naylor-Leyland in 1997 following her untimely death due to cancer. Sir Philip and his wife Lady Isabella (nee Lambton) whom he married in 1980 continue to live in the hall today with their six children.

The Coming of the New Town

In the early 1960s, the concept of new towns was put back on the national political agenda by three forces; a surge of growth in the population, congestion and bad housing in the great cities and the idea that new towns could be 'growing points' for regions in economic decline.

Peterborough was earmarked as a town suitable for major expansion to alleviate the ever growing need for housing in the South East.

The gestation period of the new town of Peterborough was nearly ten years and fierce argument ensued throughout this time over the position of precise boundaries and how far the development should proceed to the West and North West of the town.

This is not the place to explain the complexities of the evolution and creation of Peterborough New Town, but suffice it to say that it is due in no small part to members of the Fitzwilliam family and their advisors that in 2004 Milton Hall remains a house in private occupation and Marholm and Castor are still rural villages. It is quite

Fig 22h. The Hon Lady Hastings, a much-loved High Sheriff of Cambridgeshire 1993.

clear that the original designers of the new town envisaged that Milton would become a Town Hall surrounded by a municipal park and Marholm and Castor would form an integral part of the new township much in the same way as Werrington and the Ortons do today.

In the end it was the creation of Bretton that had the greatest effect on Milton and in 1969 some 2,000 acres of estate land were acquired under threat of compulsory powers by Peterborough Development Corporation to provide the land on which to build the new township of Bretton.

Throughout the decade the issue of the new town must have been like a great ghost lurking in the background for those concerned with the control of the estate but it is remembered by those who lived here as a happy period administered by a benign triumvirate comprising Lord Fitzwilliam, his agent Samuel Egar and Major H M Peacock, a close friend of Lord Fitzwilliam who lived at the Ferry House, ran the shoot and was a highly respected authority on shooting and the breeding and training of gun dogs. Sam Egar had been assistant agent at Milton before the war and returned as Chief Agent to the Fitzwilliam Estates in 1960. Throughout the decade and before development opportunities arose following the creation of the new town, cash for estate buildings and improvements was in short supply. However this triumvirate of leaders is remembered with great respect and affection by all those who knew them.

Milton Today

Today Milton Hall stands proudly as the flagship of one of the great country estates of England. The park, some 500 acres in size comprising old pasture and oak trees originally laid out by Humphrey Repton is grazed by a flock of 1500 commercial breeding sheep – mainly North Country mules. In addition a small flock of pedigree Jacob ewes has existed at Milton for well over one hundred years. Every year nearly 3,000 lambs are reared and fattened off the grass for meat production.

A small suckler herd of twelve old English Longhorn cows are also usually to be found roaming the North park. The best heifer calves are retained for herd replacements and the remainder are either fattened or sold on to be finished elsewhere. The herd was started in 1980 with the purchase of 2 heifers from Leicestershire. At the time of their introduction to Milton, Longhorn cattle were a rare breed due to diminished numbers nationally. However with increased public awareness over food production, it is good to note that the qualities of the English Longhorn have once again been recognised and these cattle are now off the rare breed list.

The park is the only land on the estate today farmed in hand as a home farm and it is run by one extremely efficient shepherd, Les Hall with the help of his family and other part-time help as necessary at busy times of the year. The remainder of the farmland on the estate, the great part of which is arable, is let on agricultural tenancies to some fifty tenant farmers many of whom are now second or third generation occupiers of their holdings.

The woodlands on the estate were laid out primarily for shooting and hunting at various stages over the last two hundred years. In the main they are hard wood with oak and ash predominating and they are actively managed by a team of five foresters from the saw yard at Marholm. Our current Head Forester, Garry Atkinson, came down from Wentworth two years ago to succeed his namesake Michael Atkinson who retired after twenty-seven years in charge of the department at Milton. It says much for the team that this year all five of his staff, Mick Westlake, Mike Beeson, Peter Bone, Bob Latto and Kevin Conkey received long service awards with a combined estate service to date of 140 years.

The estate employs a total of thirty-nine full-time and eight part-time staff and sixteen retired staff continue to live in cottages in different areas of the estate. Heads of department all liaise closely with the chief agent and those in the estate office who consolidate and supervise the overall running of the estate with Sir Philip Naylor-Leyland.

The chief agent at Milton oversees the control of all the Fitzwilliam estates in Cambridgeshire and Yorkshire and more recently the Naylor-Leyland properties in North Wales. Samuel Egar held this position from 1960 to 1972 having succeeded Hubert Elliot who was Agent at Milton from 1938 to 1960. Later Mr Egar was succeeded by Michael Thompson who was Agent for twenty-three years until he retired in 1997.

His time in office saw major changes and expansion to the estate with the acquisition of farming land at Little Gidding, Sawtry, Upton, Sutton Heath and Ufford. Development was not limited to the agricultural part of the estate and in the newly enlarged City of Peterborough, where the Fitzwilliam family had traditionally held property, their commercial

Fig 22i. Milton Estate Staff 1988

MILTON ESTATE STAFF PHOTOGRAPH - JUNE 1988

Back Row: Terry Frampton(M.R.), Ross Bunkall(F.F.), Jason Stoessler(M.R.), Roy Coulson(M.R.), John Teufel(M.R.), John Rycraft(M.R.), Glen Adams(M.R.),
Left to Right: Mark Sharpin(M.R.), Edward Newell(M.R.), Bob Whitby(M.R.), George Elms(M.R.), Mike Beeson(Woods), Dennis Adams(M.R.), Pete Bone(Woods),
                   Kevin Conkey(Woods), Stephen Slater(Woods), Stephen Weston(S.H.G.), Tim Burgoin(Gardens), Bob Latto(Woods), Gordon Conkey(Woods),
                   Barry Sneddon(M.R.), David Harris(M.R.)

3rd Row: Giles Green(F.F.), Harry Allen(G.U.), Dick Dimmock(F.F.), Keith Gray(F.F.), Graham Crunkhorn(F.F.), Walter Youngs(M.R.),
Left to Right: Percy Mossendew(H.S.), Harold Osborne(H.S.), Ernie Bell(H.S.), Les Barber(M.R.), George Stapleton(H.S.), Miss Anne Trembath(H.S.)
                   Mrs. Kathleen Graves(H.S.), Mrs. Mary Harrold(H.S.), Cis Lunn(M.R.), Charlie Stapleton(H.S.), Miss Sarah Jackson(E.O.),
                   Miss Sarah Lawrance(E.O.), Bill Lemmon(Garders), Cliff Graves(Gardens), Miss Fiona Beaton(F.H.S.), Mrs. Rama Modhwadia(F.H.S.)

2nd Row: Mrs. Mandy Green(F.F.), Sid Coles(G.U.), Johnnie Bosworth(G.U.), Ian Doughty(G.U.), Chris Nattriss(G.U.), David Burton(F.F.),
Left to Right: Nick Baker(H.S.), Mrs. Evelyn Stapleton(H.S.), Miss Nichola Elms(H.S.), Mrs. Gwen Doubleday(H.S.), Mrs. Joy Baker(H.S.),
                   Mrs. Milly Weston(H.S.), Doug Neal(S.H.G.), Aubrey Weston(Game), Keith Dickinson(Game), Wilf Hutchinson(Game), Miss Jane Ayres(E.O.),
                   Mrs. Janet Wells(E.O.), Miss Katharine Kingston Jones(E.O.), Glen Westmorland(Kennels), Pete Maddison(Kennels), Paul Gardiner(Stables),
                   Mrs. Gill Wright(F.H.S.), Alan Brown(F.H.S.)

Front Row: Mick Westlake(Woods), Gordon Vincent(F.F.), Mrs. Ros Teufel(E.O.), Clem Bull(H.S.), Mrs. Phyllis Taylor(Stables), Miss Pam Scott(E.O.),
Left to Right: Michael Thompson(E.O.), Mrs. Fiona Thompson(E.O.), Sir Stephen Hastings, Lady Hastings, Lady Fitzwilliam, Sir Philip Naylor-Leyland,
                   Lady Isabella Naylor-Leyland, Henry Rayment(E.O.), Brian Richardson(M.R.), Mrs. Rosie Reynolds(H.S.), James Barclay(Kennels),
                   Mrs. Lucy Barclay(E.O.), George Adams(Kennels), John England(Stables)

M.R.   Maintenance and Repairs Department   H.S.   Milton Hall House Staff
F.F.   Fitzwilliam Farms   E.O.   Milton Estate Office
Woods   Forestry Department   F.H.S.   Ferry House Staff
S.H.G.   Stibbington House Gardens   Game   Game Department
Gardens   Milton Hall Gardens   Kennels   Fitzwilliam Hunt Kennels
G.U.   Gidding and Upton Farms   Stables   Fitzwilliam Hunt Stables

Staff unable to attend photograph

S.J. Beddows (E.O.)   M.H. Atkinson (Head Forester)   Mrs. M. Button (E.O.)   W. Turner (M.R.)
J. Gates (Gardens)   Miss June Wright (Stables)   S. Hobbis (Woods)   I. Holt (Stables)

interests were expanded and modernised too. Over the years the estate benefited enormously from his sound business acumen and also from his longstanding knowledge and experience of agriculture and the countryside.

As any landed estate comprises three elements of buildings, land and people, almost by definition it is a living organism and as such does not stand still for long. In order for an estate to consolidate and grow it requires not only efficient management but the vision and foresight of those at the helm to make the necessary decisions for the future brought about by ever changing government policy. All four agents mentioned above have been masters of their profession. Samuel Egar was President of

Fig 22j. Estate Office Staff 1938: l-r back: DW Matthews, Samuel Egar, E Mitchell, AJ Bond. Front: W Banham, Hubert Elliot, Miss C Bridgefoot

Fig 22k. Master Tom Naylor-Leyland's first shoot at Milton.
Michael Thompson, Master Tom, David Carrington, Lady Isabella,
Aubrey Weston, Roy Souter and William Craven

Midland Counties Agricultural Valuers Association the year he died in 1973 and Michael Thompson was President of the Land Agency and Agricultural Division of the Royal Institution of Chartered Surveyors in 1985 and Chairman of the Cambridgeshire branch of Country Landowners Association from 1994 to 1996. The present Chief Agent, Robert Dalgliesh continues in this tradition and he too will be President of Midland Counties Agricultural Valuers Association for a term of one year beginning later in 2004.

Sadly Michael Thompson's retirement coincided exactly with the premature death of Sir Philip's mother, the Hon Lady Hastings. Therefore 1997 became a particularly important milestone in the evolution of the estate with the appointment of a new Chief Agent and even more importantly a change of generation in the ownership of Milton.

Milton Hall, which for eighty years had only been occupied by husband and wife, now began to echo again to the sounds of a large young boisterous family.

Prior to Sir Philip and Lady Isabella taking up residence in 1999, part of the house was given a 'fifty year refit' which involved restoring rooms back into use at the far end of the house which had been empty since the First World War. This project, closely supervised by Sir Philip and his wife with a keen aesthetic eye and focused attention to authentic detail has resulted in a glorious transformation of those corners of the house that had been laid low but now lend themselves ideally to everyday family occupation.

Milton has entered the 21st century on a sound note. Despite what could have happened, it is not the Town Hall for Peterborough and the North Park does not form the basis of a municipal pleasure ground. Sir Philip having trained in Estate Management at the Royal Agricultural College Cirencester and having studied business management in New York, not only lives in Milton Hall with his family but takes a close personal and informed command of his estates supported by a staff nearly a third of which have served twenty years or more to date.

In order to mark the occasion of five hundred years of the family's ownership, a party was held last summer at Milton for staff, farm tenants and their families from Cambridgeshire, Yorkshire and Wales. By chance the anniversary coincided with Sir Philip's 50th birthday and Mr Tom Naylor-Leyland's 21st birthday. A splendid luncheon was served to some three hundred and fifty guests in a marquee on the North front and the day was much enjoyed by all present.

The estate has now entered its second quincentenary of ownership by the same family and there is much to be thankful for that we do so on such a positive note.

Fig 22l. Milton Pensioner's Party to celebrate Clem Bull's 90th Birthday at Poplar Farmhouse 2003. l-r backrow: Keith Dickinson, Molly Hutchinson, George Elms, Bella Craven, Ann Elms, 2nd row: Dorinda Richardson, Joy Baker, George Adams, Sue Adams, Sue Newton, Wilf Hutchinson, Brian Richardson, Phil Taylor, Elizabeth Craven, Millie Weston, Eileen Ladds, Sylvia Dickinson, Seated: Rosie Reynolds, Lady Isabella Naylor-Leyland, Clem Bull, Sir Philip Naylor-Leyland, Margaret Egar, on rug: Rector, William Craven, Pamela Dalgliesh.

Fox Hunting At Milton

Early days of British Foxhunting

It is an accepted statement in sporting circles that modern fox hunting began in the mid eighteenth century and from this time hunting the fox as opposed to the stag became a favourite sport of English country gentlemen. The early masters did not keep kennel books recording the pedigree of their hound breeding but by 1728 formal records were being kept by the Duke of Beaufort at Badminton in Gloucestershire. At Brocklesby in North Lincolnshire the kennel book goes back to 1746.

It is said that scientific hound breeding and hound management in the way we know it today goes back to Hugo Meynell who succeeded Thomas Boothby as the legendary master of the Quorn in about 1753.

The first recorded foxhound show was held at the Cleveland Society's Show at Redcar in 1859. Following a brief connection with the Yorkshire Agricultural Society it was moved to Peterborough in 1877 under the direction of Mr. Barford. It is now known as the Royal Peterborough Foxhound Society and the Fitzwilliam hounds were among the first big winners at these early hound shows in the days of Tom Sebright, George Carter and later in the days of Mr George Fitzwilliam and Will Barnard.

The tradition of fox hunting at Milton goes back to these formative years of the sport as the Fitzwilliam is one of the four great ancestral packs of England owned and maintained by the Fitzwilliam family ever since it was established by the 4th Earl in the 1760's.

The 4th Earl, founder of the pack, died in 1833 at the age of 85 and he was succeeded by his son the 5th Earl who died in 1857. At this point an important change took place as the Milton Estate and with it ownership of the hounds passed to the Earl's younger son The Hon George Wentworth Fitzwilliam. His elder brother who became the sixth Earl established a second pack in 1860 known as the Fitzwilliam (Wentworth) to hunt the Yorkshire country which hitherto had only been cub hunted by the Milton hounds which went to Yorkshire for several weeks in the Autumn each season.

The Golden Age

The Hon George Fitzwilliam was one of the finest huntsmen of his day and he continued in the Milton mastership until his premature death, the result of a bad fall at Moonshine Gap in 1874. The seventeen seasons during which he was master represent one of the high water marks in the history of the Fitzwilliam hunt. The partnership of The Hon George Fitzwilliam and his huntsman George Carter was said to be second to none. George was not only a horseman but a hound man as well and so devoted to his master was the huntsman Carter that when The Hon. George was dangerously ill following his fateful fall at Moonshine Gap, Carter was scarcely able to blow his horn! His son George Charles Wentworth Fitzwilliam who inherited the estate and the hounds was only 13 years old when his father died.

During the next few years the mastership was held successively by Mr Charles Fitzwilliam, The Marquess of Huntley, The Hon Thomas Fitzwilliam (at the time agent for the estate), Colonel Henry Wickham and Mr. Joshua Fielden. Finally in 1895 young Mr. George, having resigned his commission in the Household Cavalry, came to live permanently at Milton and thus began his great mastership which was to last for the next 40 years.

Meanwhile, the 7th Earl Fitzwilliam continued in his capacity as joint master until his death in 1943. He used to travel down from Wentworth and stayed either at Milton or at the Haycock Inn at Wansford which he had purchased for the purpose. The horses were all stabled at Milton with separate grooms for Lord Fitzwilliam's horses and those belonging to Mr George. On one side of the yard, Lord Fitzwilliam's staff wore a yellow uniform with yellow barrows and buckets, while Mr. George's on the other side of the yard wore green uniforms and pushed green barrows!

William Fitzwilliam (7th Earl) was one of the greatest figures in foxhunting history. He not only took over control of the Wentworth hounds but was inclined to take the bitch pack over to Coollattin, the estate in Ireland until in 1904 he established a new pack in that country. Several seasons later on the resignation of Lord Galway, he assumed command of the Grove country in Nottinghamshire which in those days was known as the Fitzwilliam Grove and so was in command of no less than four separate packs of hounds at the same time - three of them owned by himself and the Milton owned by his cousin Mr. George Fitzwilliam. There is no parallel for this in the whole of foxhunting history.

The Fitzwilliam (Milton) country was described in the early years of the twentieth century as follows: *'The famous Fitzwilliam country is naturally divided by the River Nene which meanders through the valleys of Stanwick, Thrapston*

Fig 22m. Loading up at Peterborough Station.

Fig 22n. 'Are we all on'?

Fig 22o. 'Tickets Please'.

and Oundle until it is lost to this country in the Fens of Peterborough which are agriculturally rich yet far too boggy for hunting. North of the River Nene is a fine woodland country in which young hounds revel in the early autumn and all hounds in the Spring; and South of the River Nene for nearly twenty miles right up to the Bedfordshire Ouse is one of the finest hunting countries in England. There are many natural woods, one of the largest near Huntingdon being Monks Wood which was the property of that fine sportsman the late Lord Chesham; and near that Southern end of the country there is much woodland about Abbotts Ripton and some attractive smaller woods between Monks Wood and one of the finest fox covers in England – Aversley Wood. Young sportsmen on long tailed blood horses may dream of quick bursts from gorse covers and very few have revelled in them more than myself; yet it is almost impossible to have a good pack of hounds, and consequent good sport without plenty of woodland. Then about fifteen miles from Huntingdon there is near Oundle the famous Barnwell Wold a big mother cover which always held plenty of foxes; and closer to Oundle, Ashton Wold; and also about Elton there are many good woods'.

This description of the Fitzwilliam country written by a well travelled fox hunter in 1908 is very typical of the period when the present day problems of motorways, urbanisation and electrified railways were yet to become thorns in the flesh of a master of foxhounds. Even when the late Tom Fitzwilliam (later 10th Earl) joined the mastership in the 1930s. Much of the land around Great Gidding was rough or even derelict due to the agricultural depression at the time. With the benefit of modern agricultural machinery and field drainage it is now considered the most productive arable land on the estate but in those days it was primarily a haven for foxes.

Indeed up until 1939 before the days of motorised hound transport, subsidiary kennels existed at Laurels Farm, Great Gidding where hounds were kept for three or four weeks cub hunting each Autumn. Another sight long gone is that of travelling to the meet by train. When hounds were due to meet in a far corner of the Country towards Higham Ferrers, the hunt horses, hounds and some mounted followers would hack down to Peterborough Station where a specially booked 'hunt special' would take them to Raunds where they would unbox and hack on to the meet. The whole procedure was then put into reverse at the end of the day.

Post War Hunting

Since the Second World War, the Fitzwilliam (Milton) hounds have continued to thrive. The continuity of family masters has been maintained by the late Earl Fitzwilliam, Sir Stephen and The Hon Lady Hastings and Sir Philip Naylor-Leyland ably supported over the years by joint masters such as the late Lord de Ramsey, Mr Michael Berry, Lord Kimball, Major Charles Deane, Major JA Warre, MC, Mrs Bridget Raby, Mr Rex Sly, Mr James Barclay, Mrs. Patricia Anderson and The Hon George Bowyer.

Hounds continue to meet most mornings in the Autumn hunting season and twice a week on Wednesdays and Saturdays from beginning of November until mid-March. George Adams continues in a long line of experienced professional huntsmen of this famous old pack of foxhounds and he is now in his twentieth season as huntsman.

Leaving aside the political issues with regard to field sports generally, the greatest difficulty that faces the hunt is that of reduced country due to the main London to Edinburgh East Coast railway, major roads such as the A1 and A14 and the rapid expansion of all the surrounding towns in recent years. The combined effect of all this has been to reduce the Fitzwilliam hounds to meeting twice a week during the main season as opposed to four days as was the case before the Second War.

William Craven

William Craven is a Chartered Surveyor and has been assistant agent at Milton since 1990. He is organist at Castor and Marholm and churchwarden at Marholm.

Fig 22p. Sir Philip Naylor-Leyland Bt MFH with George Adams (Huntsman) and the Fitzwilliam (Milton) Hounds.

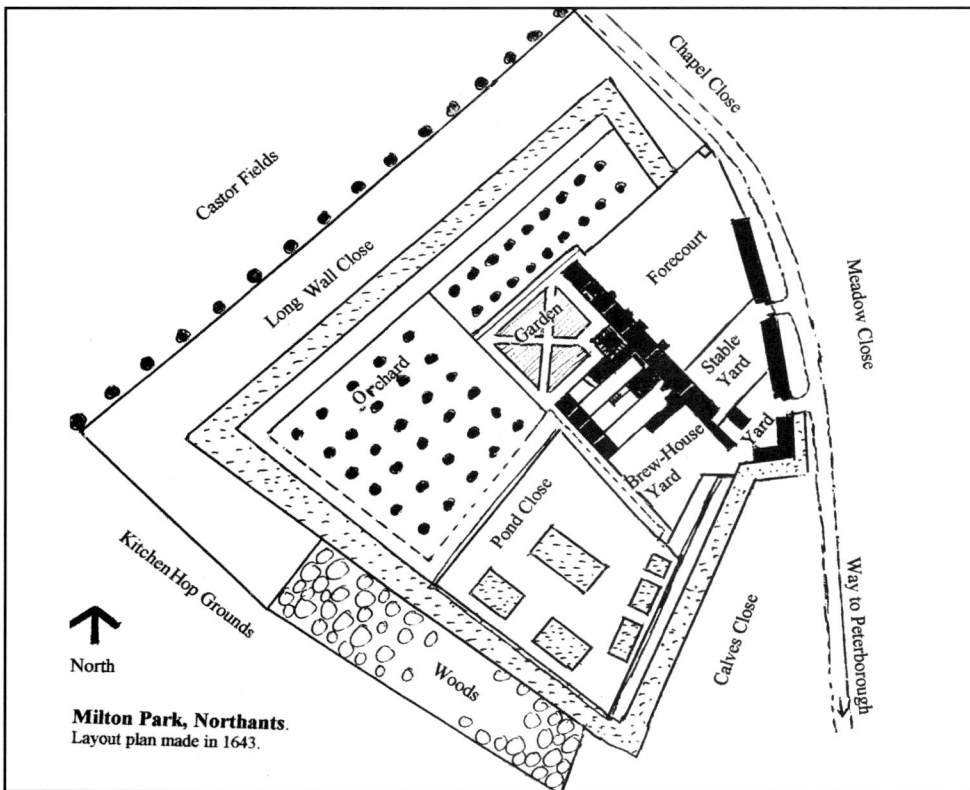

Fig 22q. Map of Milton Hall and Park drawn in 1643, before the addition of the Stable Range built in 1690.

Fig 22r. Fire at the Kennels Milton 1920s.

Fig 22s. Sir Stephen Hastings on 'Charlie' at the Fitzwilliam Point-to-point. This combination of horse and jockey were to go on to be three-times winner of the gruelling 4 and-a-half mile Harborough Cross Country Race.

Chapter 23
The Railways Through the Parishes

Part I: The London & Birmingham Railway

The first known reference to a railway in the Peterborough area was in 1825, when the poet John Clare encountered surveyors in woods at Helpston. They were preparing for a speculative London and Manchester railroad. Clare viewed them with disapproval and suspicion.

Plans for a Branch to Peterborough

On 17th September 1838, the London & Birmingham Railway Company opened its 112-mile main line, linking the country's two largest cities. It was engineered by George Stephenson's son, Robert. The journey took 5½ hours, at a stately average of 20mph – still twice the speed of a competing stagecoach. The final cost of the line was £5.5m, as against an estimate of £2.5m. Magnificent achievement as the L&BR was, it did not really benefit Northampton, since the line passed five miles to the West of the town. The first positive steps to put Northampton and the Nene valley in touch with the new mode of travel were taken in Autumn 1842, after local influential people approached the L&BR Board with plans for a branch railway from Blisworth to Peterborough. Traffic on the L&BR was healthy. On 16th January 1843, a meeting of shareholders was called at the Euston Hotel. They were told that the company had now done its own research and was able to recommend a line to Peterborough.

Fig 23a. Castor: Station Master's House.

There was some opposition from landed interests along the Nene valley. On 26th January 1843 at the White Hart Inn, Thrapston a meeting, chaired by Earl Fitzwilliam, expressed implacable opposition to the whole scheme on six main counts, from increased flooding to the danger of 26 road crossings, rather than bridges. The local papers carried many articles for and against the railway. The L&BR Board was equal to such opposition and answered the key objections. Arguments went on for about six months. The third and final reading of the Bill was on 26th June, after which it returned to the Commons for approval of some amendments. Finally, on 4th July 1843, Royal assent to the Bill was granted; an Act of Parliament had been created; construction could now proceed. A victory dinner took place on 27th July at the Angel Hotel, Northampton.

About this time an anonymous poem was written, entitled 'The wonderful effects of the

Fig 23b. Castor: Signal Box and Booking Office.

Peterborough and Northampton railway, or the pleasure of travelling by hot water'. Here are eight of its twelve verses:

"Now of all the great wonders that ever was known, And some wonderful things have occur'd in this town,
This great Peterborough railway will beat them all hollow, And whoever first thought of it was a wonderful fellow.
Oh! No my good friends when this railroad is finished, All coachmen and cattle will for ever be banished,
You will ride up to London in three hours and a quarter, With nothing to drive you but a kettle of hot water.
You can breakfast in Peterborough on tea, toast and butter, And need not put yourselves into a splutter,
You can travel to London and dine there at noon, And take tea in Peterborough the same afternoon.
What a beautiful sight it is for to see, A long string of carriages on the railway,
All loaded with passengers inside and out, And moved by what comes from a tea kettle spout.
What chance for the Cockneys who are fond of fish, They will have them of all kinds alive on the dish,
Fen geese and fat turkeys and all such cheer, There be more go in one day than now goes in a year.
And as to Innkeepers and Ostlers and all such riffraff, This railway will disperse them before it like chaff,
They must all list for soldiers or take on for marines, And curse the inventers of railroads and steam.
All great coach proprietors that have roll'd in their wealth, Are to ride upon donkeys for the good of their health,
And to keep up their spirits are to strike up a theme, Of the blessings of railroads and the virtues of steam.
So these are a few of the strange alterations, That this great Peterborough railroad will make in the nation,
But if the shareholders be not careful and mind what they are after, They may all get blown up by this boiler of hot water.

The Work Begins on the Peterborough Branch

Work began almost immediately. The L&BR appointed their Chief Engineer, Robert Stephenson, to take overall responsibility for the Peterborough branch. The 47-mile line was divided for contract purposes into three sections, the first two from Blisworth (junction with the main London & Birmingham line) to Oundle, being given to John Stephenson of Derby, son of an eminent Scottish engineer, and the third section from Oundle to Peterborough, to Mr Brogden of Manchester. Works on the line were generally light and easily tackled, a major part of the construction effort being occupied with sixteen bridges. The only larger undertaking was building the 616 yard ($\frac{1}{3}$ mile) Wansford Tunnel. Work on it began at the end of January 1844, the contractor being Mr Jones of Sheffield, but before work on the bore could start 136,000 cubic yards of earth had to be moved from the approaches. Three shafts were sunk on the line of the tunnel. A number of men working 20 ft down one of the shafts were nearly buried alive by a fall of earth. In March 1844 three local surgeons were retained at £70 pa to help those hurt.

Fig 23c. Castor Station: Looking West 1930.

Fig 23d. Castor Station: Looking East.

In general, with so little heavy work, progress was rapid; by January 1844 large quantities of rails, chairs and fishplates were being delivered to Wisbech by ship. Over the next few months more than a hundred vessels carried such cargo to Wisbech, where it was transferred to Nene river boats. The rails, bull-head type, were of wrought or malleable iron, in 15ft lengths; probably they all came from South Wales. Chairs were of cast iron. The wooden sleepers probably came from the Baltic. The L&BR main line originally had rails laid on stone blocks from the Pennines, but they had proved to be unsatisfactory, moving under heavy traffic. No doubt Robert Stephenson made them available to the Peterborough branch contractors; these blocks can still be seen in many of the bridges and each end of Wansford tunnel; some of these heavy stones reveal the cut out shapes and bolt holes for the rail chairs.

From the outset, the line was equipped with the new Electric Telegraph, only invented by Charles Wheatstone about 1840. The L&BR's Peterborough branch was one of the world's first railways to have this from its start. People were surprised to find, for instance, that time differed several minutes between Northampton and Peterborough. It was not until 1852 that railways in Britain agreed a standard time.

The Peterborough branch was built wide enough for a double track. However on opening it was all single track, except from Blisworth to Northampton and a passing loop at Thrapston. About a year later, with traffic increasing, the whole route was doubled. Also in 1846 the L&BR became part of the new LNWR, London & North Western Railway. LNWR was the largest UK railway company in Victorian times, with its main workshops at Crewe.

The final cost of the 47.4 mile line from Blisworth to Peterborough was £429,409; this was appreciably less than the original estimate of £500,000. Wansford tunnel was completed at the end of April 1845. Crowds flocked to see the 'stupendous work', together with what was said to be the tooth of a mastodon, and the bones of elephants, dug up near Sutton and Castor. Other archaeological finds occurred during construction of the Castor - Stibbington section; a small Roman statue (now at Woburn) was found at Wansford station; William Artis, Earl Fitzwilliam's agent and a keen archaeologist, was involved in finds where the railway crosses Ermine Street (just East of the site of Castor station).

In the field of railway construction, Navvy stories are legion. *'When the LNWR was being made about 45 years ago...the navvies and plate-layers used to choose their champions and fight on Sutton Heath for £10 a side on Sunday'*, reported Rev W Hopkinson in 1901. Most navvies were tough, very hard working, independent men, to whom we owe much. Railway steam shovels were not used in Britain on any scale until the 1890s, when the Great Central built its main line to London. Peterborough's seven rail routes were all hand made. Here is a downside tale. The writer of a letter to the Stamford Mercury in March 1845 described a visit he had recently made to the railway works at Wansford, and added the comment: *'The navvies and others, as they gradually withdrew from the works, leave bills unpaid in all the villages where they could obtain credit from trades-people or those who let lodgings; the losses sustained are in many cases very severe. And not only does the district suffer in a pecuniary view from the visit of these freebooters, but the fellows have taken many women from the neighbourhood, and in some instances the wives of decent men and the mothers of families, who have been induced to rob their husbands and abscond'*. Some of the navvies were good family men, who brought up their children as well as they could under their nomadic conditions, and saw that education was received where possible. Our parish registers contain records of the railway navvies and their families

The First Train into Peterborough

Peterborough's first railway opened for passengers on Monday 2 June 1845; it was a fine summer's day. From early in the morning, stage-coaches poured into Peterborough, bringing travellers and sightseers. It was estimated that the city's normal population of 7,000 had swollen to 10-12,000 by midday. The first train had left at 7am, with its six coaches full. The second left at 10.30am. At Thrapston this crossed with the first "Down" train from London, also crammed with people. At Wansford, 200 more people were waiting to board for the last leg into Peterborough, and many had to resort to riding on the carriage roofs! The train puffed its way into Peterborough (East) station, where it was greeted by a brass band and bell ringing.

Once the new railway had settled down, carrying cattle became a major proportion of the goods traffic revenue. A second substantial source of freight revenue by the mid 19th century came from the development of Northamptonshire's iron-industry. From the 1880s Peterborough's brick industry, aided by the Fletton loop line, created Westbound traffic. Coal, general merchandise, timber, agricultural produce and requirements were also regular goods.

As the 19th century progressed, the original L&BR/LNWR Peterborough branch from Blisworth became complicated by new routes and connections. In 1867 the Great Northern Railway's link line from Wansford to Stamford & Essendine opened (LNER after 1923). In 1879 an LNWR link from Seaton to Yarwell Junction opened, giving trains between Birmingham and Harwich an improved route - the Rugby line. Peterborough's Fletton loop line of 1883 enabled the GNR's Peterborough – Leicester service via Seaton. By the 1880s traffic on the Wansford – Peterborough section had at least doubled. The LNWR built their Woodston locomotive depot in 1885.

The Grouping into the Big Four

In 1923, after the World War One experience of close co-operation, Britain's railways were grouped; over a 100 companies were merged into a 'Big Four'. The once mighty LNWR became part of the London Midland & Scottish Railway, the LMS, which now owned and operated the Nene Valley line. In the 1920s, road transport really began to compete with the railways. The lightly loaded Peterborough – Leicester GNR service ceased in 1916 and was never re-instated. In 1929 passenger trains ceased on the Stamford – Wansford service; the line was taken up some two years later. Part of the LMS fight-back against the inroads of cheap and door-to-door road traffic was faster trains, but it was difficult to speed up cross-country routes like the Nene line. During World War Two, trains ran throughout the 24 hours; the build up to D-Day in 1944 was probably the peak.

Castor Station

Castor station opened in August 1853. At the height of its use some five trains in each direction stopped at Castor daily. In the 1887 timetable two additional trains stopped, if signalled! A single siding was added in 1897, off the line to Peterborough (in railway parlance the 'Down' line; in coaching days, travelling from London was in the 'Down' direction). I recall as a youngster in the 1940s that practically every day wagons of coal and farm products were unloaded and loaded at Castor. One day, during World War Two, I remember the excitement when a wagon with flames coming from an over-heated axle-box was hurriedly put into the Castor sidings, where no doubt a fire bucket of water was applied. In those days, some older wagons still had grease box lubrication, a system going back to the first railways. The station boasted a chocolate machine, and there were rudimentary toilets. Opposite the small station building was the Stationmaster's house. 'Up' line trains were little more than an arm's length from the dwelling. On the evening of 3rd January 1945 a German V1 'doodlebug' bomb exploded just West of Castor station, in a clump of trees close to the tracks; fortunately there was neither loss of life nor serious damage. Castor station closed to passengers on 1st July 1957 and to goods on 28th December 1964. Over the years Castor's station masters included Thomas Wright (1870s), John Green (1880s and in 1891), John Alfred Barnett (1890s), Lionel Green and Frank Abbot (1900s), Fredric Cowell (1910s) Albert Edward Brooms (1920s), in 1954 Mr Hankin was succeeded by Albert Spicer, who was also station master at Wansford. In the 1950s, Castor's main customer was J W Taylor who took several coal wagons a week; freight also included grain, seed potatoes and sugar beet. In 1854 the 5¼ miles to Peterborough took 12 minutes and cost 5d (1st), 4d (2nd), and 2d (3rd 'parliamentary'). In the 1950s it took nine minutes.

The Northampton – Peterborough passenger service ceased on 2nd May 1964. Likewise, the Rugby – Peterborough line

Fig 23e. Castor: Walter Taylor, Stationmaster 1957.

Fig 23f. Castor: Goods Siding 1950s.

ceased on 6th June 1966. For a few years after, passenger trains ran for Oundle public school each term. On the Rugby line, past Yarwell Junction, mineral trains served the Nassington iron ore quarries until the early 1970's. From 1845 until the 1960s, steam power prevailed; only in the twilight years were diesel trains used. Dr Richard Beeching deemed the Nene Railway uneconomic. The Birmingham to Harwich Continental night mail train ran until the 1966 closure. An irony of the Nene rail closure is that, in the 1960s, plans existed to expand Northampton, Peterborough and Wellingborough. Barbara Castle, Minister of Transport, said at the time that steps would be taken to preserve the route for future transport needs, but this never happened. In other parts of Europe, modernisation and electrification of such inter-urban routes was taking place. Sadly, here, it was not long before chickens roosted in Wansford signal-box. Soon all that remained of Castor station was its rusting wagon loading gauge.

The Nene Valley Railway

Peterborough Development Corporation (PDC), a government body, functioned from 1968 – 1988 to expand Peterborough by attracting people from London's boroughs; the New Town needed recreational provision. This was the setting for the rebirth of the Peterborough end of the Nene Railway. There were two other players: Dr Beeching had provided a fine length of abandoned rail route through the centre of the planned Nene Park; and the Rev. Richard Paten, local vicar and chartered engineer, in 1968, bought for civic display a former British Rail restorable steam locomotive. It was around this engine that a band of volunteers formed and put forward the NVR idea. Nine years on, in 1977, a leisure tourist train service from Wansford to a new station at Orton Mere began. It was operated by NVR, a charity company, under the Light Railway Act of 1896. PDC provided the capital, NVR the operating people. NVR acquired a Swedish engine built to the larger European Berne loading gauge. In consultation with HM Railway Inspectorate, certain modifications to the railway were undertaken.

Fig 23g. Castor: Loading Gauge 1986.

Within a few years a considerable collection of engines and carriages from across Europe came to the NVR. The combination of foreign trains, easy access from London, ready hotels, the river and Wansford tunnel have established NVR as a good location for the film industry. James Bond's Octopussy has been the greatest commercial success to date. In 1971 the late Rev Awdry OBE named a little blue engine 'Thomas' in Peterborough's sugar factory; the only 'Thomas' he ever named. Now it attracts visitors from across the world. Peterborough's independent Railworld, an exhibition centre and museum, began as an NVR working party in 1981. NVR's Santa Trains are amongst the best in Britain. Currently, Peterborough Cathedral and NVR both attract about 60,000 visitors per year. The late 20th century rail renaissance has many faces, including the enrichment of Britain by its heritage lines, not least the Nene Valley Railway.

Richard Paten

Born in 1932, the privileged son of a local business family that moved to Castor in 1937. After Marlborough School, National Service and a commission, he read Engineering at Cambridge, worked in Africa and in 1961 became a Chartered Engineer. Following ordination by the Church of England he did eight years parish work and 23 years as a chaplain for community and race relations. He is an originator and founder chairman of the Nene Valley Railway, Peterborough Interfaiths Council and Railworld. He is president of the Peterborough Civic Society. He married in 1975, was divorced in 2001, but is blessed with three children and one grandson.

Fig 23 h. Wansford Station: the Sutton train in the island platform c1900.

Part II: The Stamford & Essendine Railway

Sutton and Upton were served by the Stamford and Sibson branch of the Stamford and Essendine Railway, promoted by the Marquis of Exeter. It was to join the LNWR at Wansford, and so give access to Northampton. The 8¼ mile line was opened on the 8th August 1867, and the following day's Stamford and Rutland Mercury gave an account of the line and *'a magnificent dinner at the George Hotel given by Mr Jackson the contractor, who liberally invited about 100 persons to the entertainment'* and noted there are *'two intermediate stations for passengers, goods and coal, one at Wansford Road and the other at Barnack. At both places full arrangements are made for receiving and carrying the traffic of the district.'*

Fig 23i. Wansford Road Station c1930

Wansford Road Station (Fig 23i) is of course in the parish of Sutton, and the station was sited on the turnpike already served by carriers' carts and roughly equidistant from the three villages of Wansford, Sutton and Upton. The line opened late because the Railway Inspector was unhappy with the junction with LNWR. The junction was a source of friction years later when the S & E railway closed it and built a temporary terminus called 'Sibson' but actually in Sutton. S & E Railway claimed the LNWR was charging too large a rent for the traffic carried. Passengers had to alight and make their way across the fields and onto a bridge over the river (Fig 23j) to Wansford Station. This arrangement lasted from 1870 to 1877 before the junction was reconnected. This bridge had been erected by Sutton's Lord of the Manor for him to be driven by horse and trap from the Grange to the station. The present footpath No 2 dates from this time and gave him and villagers access to the station.

There were extensive cattle pens at Wansford Road Station, and sheep would be driven through the sheep wash before being loaded onto the train for Stamford market. Whilst there was no station in Sutton village, unofficial stops were made. Newspapers were dropped daily at the house by the level crossing occupied by a railway man. His wife would deliver them round the village. Also a small girl from Stamford would visit her aunt every Saturday, being dropped off at the level crossing by the 10.44am and collected later by the 4.35pm train. Arthur Mason recalls timing himself on the way to school by the 8.25am train. If he saw it he knew he wouldn't be late for school! He also remembers a Wansford butcher of ample proportions who used to go to Stamford every Monday morning and being assisted aboard through the narrow

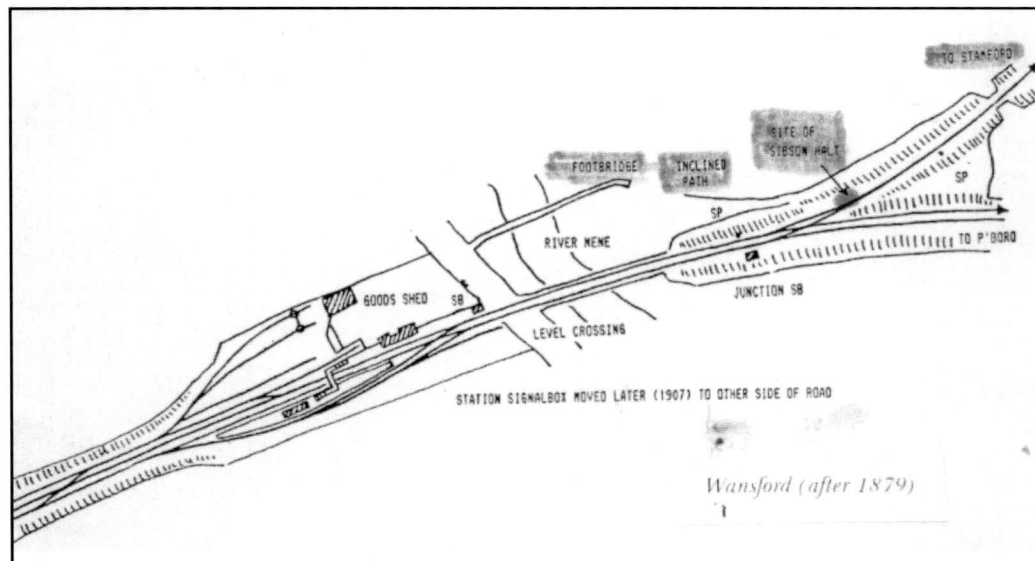

Fig 23j. Sibson halt Plan

carriage doors by the station staff. Laurence Tebbut, the former librarian at Stamford lived at Upton Manor Farm as a boy. He told me he used to be driven in a pony and trap to Wansford Road every morning to catch the 8.55am to attend Stamford School, returning in the evening by the 3.20pm or 5.45pm from Stamford and again being met by pony and trap.

The line was never a viable proposition and animal traffic to Stamford market always seemed to have exceeded passenger traffic. Indeed, whilst the line closed to passenger traffic in 1929 it remained open for goods traffic for a further two years. The station is now a private dwelling. (See also Figs 13p to 13r)

Keith Garrett

Acknowledgements

Much of this chapter is from John Rhodes, *The Nene Valley Railway,* Turntable Publications, 1983 (ISBN 902844 601), Mr Peter Waszak, NVR's Archivist, & author of *Rail Centres, Peterborough* by Ian Allen, and with John Ginns *Peterborough's First Railways: Yarwell to Peterborough,* NVR, 1995. (RW disc 12), and for Part II to DL Franks , *The Stamford and Essendine Railway*, Turntable Publications, 1971, and John Rhodes, *Great Northern Branch Lines to Stamford*, KMS Books Boston, 1985.

Fig 23k. 'End of the Line.' Wansford Road Station c 1945. Margaret White on the platform.

Milton Ferry Bridge, Lodge and gates beside the old A47 in the 1950s, before part of the Lodge was rebuilt up on the hill to make way for the by-pass.

The Ferry House on the morning of the fire 1 Jan 2003.

Chapter 24
The River Nene

The River Nene forms the Southern boundary of the parishes of Sutton, Ailsworth and Castor. The river, which is the focus of the Nene Park, which runs from the heart of Peterborough to Wansford, is a typically English river. It meanders gently between reed fringed banks, home to many kinds of wildfowl, where swans nest and herons stand motionless seeking their next meal, and it is the winter home for migratory geese. The Nene, which has one of its sources on the battlefield of Naseby,

Fig 24a. Residents of the River Nene - cygnets at Water Newton Mill.

is 145 km long and is the sixth longest river in the United Kingdom, although its gentle flow through the parishes is indicative of the fact that of all the major rivers in the UK, it has the lowest volume of discharge.

The peace and quiet of the river that is today enjoyed by walkers, anglers, leisure craft and the occasional swimmer belies the importance of the river to those who have lived and worked on its banks over the last two millennia. The river was for many years the main thoroughfare from Northampton to the sea, and has carried many cargoes that have been a key part of the economy of the area.

The Romans

At the time of the Roman occupation, the Nene at Castor was running on a very similar course to the one that we see today, as evidenced by the footings for the Roman bridge at the Ermine Street crossing which were discovered - and destroyed - by dredging operations in the present river in 1925. East of Peterborough the river flowed South through Whittlesey Mere to Floods Ferry then into the Great Ouse. Downstream from Peterborough *'so much has been done by man and by natural processes to alter and remodel the waterways of Fenland that not a single river now flows along the same bed and in the same direction as it did when the Conqueror invested Hereward .... on the island of Ely'* [1]. Given the nature of the Fens and their shifting rivers, the Roman settlement at Durobrivae was probably established at Castor as the most Easterly place where an all weather road between London and York could cross the river and not be subject to the regular flooding and changing river courses of the Fens.

Although Castor was the most Easterly crossing point of the river and the main Roman town in the area, there was plenty of Roman activity in the Fens. The Romans were probably the first to straighten and canalize some of the rivers in the Fens, both for navigation and for drainage. Archaeological evidence suggests that Car Dyke was built by the Romans to link the river Cam at Waterbeach to the Witham at Lincoln, a major Roman city with navigation links to York. Historians dispute whether the primary purpose of Car Dyke was drainage or navigation, but whatever the primary purpose, there is no doubt that it would have enabled the inhabitants of Durobrivae to trade extensively across a very wide area.

Fig 24b. The Nene at the site of the Roman bridge. The town of Durobrivae was behind the trees on the right, and potteries and ironworks located on the left bank.

The river was important for trade in a wide range of goods, and there is some evidence that there may have been a Roman wharf in Castor, close to where the railway crosses the river in the Southeast corner of the parish. Significantly, this site is downstream of the first set of rapids at Alwalton prior to the improvement of the rivers by Roman engineers. Raw materials were brought in to Durobrivae, including iron ore, clay and fuel for the iron works and pottery, and the finished products exported. Corn, hides and agricultural produce were also exported via the river. There were Roman quarries at Barnack and Wittering, and for heavy loads such as stone transport by water was the easiest option, so it is likely that a bystander on the Roman bridge would also have seen stone being taken down river to Car Dyke and beyond. It is also possible that the bystander would have seen cargoes of salt as one of the canalized sections of the Nene led into the fens and terminated a short distance from a Roman Saltern, where salt was extracted from the marshes.

The Church Builders

'No more enduring limestone has ever been quarried in England than that which came from the 'hills and holes' of Barnack .... Coarse textured and very shelly, it was particularly well suited to the robust character of both Saxon and Norman building in England' [2].

Barnack Rag was the mason's choice of building material for many of the ecclesiastical foundations in Eastern England. It was used in the seventh century for the building of the successive abbeys in Peterborough and, until about 1500, in the building of the great abbeys in the fens and surrounding areas. Transporting the stone from the quarry to the building site was a problem; some of the stones in the foundation of Peterborough Cathedral weighed up to three tonnes, and on land were moved on wooden sleds drawn by eight yoke of oxen. There is evidence of a dyke running towards the Cathedral from a point roughly where the Key Theatre is now situated, minimising the distance from the river to the building site, suggesting that the stone was transported by barge from Barnack. There is no firm evidence of where the stone was loaded into the barges for its trip downriver, although this probably took place near Wansford.

Taking a stone laden barge down river was no easy task. At the time there were no locks or staunches, so the river probably included a number of rapids that could only be negotiated with a heavily laden barge at times of high water. At times of low water when this was not possible, the barge was unloaded, the stones and sometimes the barge itself were dragged along the bank until there was enough water to re-float the barge and its cargo. Transporting stone was no pleasure trip, and sometimes took as many as ten days to complete the journey from Wansford to Peterborough.

Peterborough Abbey was one of the earliest owners of the quarrying rights at Barnack, but rights were granted by Peterborough to Ramsey Abbey during the reign of Edward the Confessor in return for the provision of *'4,000 eels for the Lenten fare of the brethren of Peterborough'* [3]. Other religious foundations were granted leases to use Barnack Rag, including Ely Cathedral and St Edmunds (Bury St Edmunds), Crowland, Ramsey, Sawtry, Spalding and Thorney

Abbeys. Although built largely from Caen stone, there are records of Norwich Cathedral purchasing stone from Barnack in 1301. All this stone would have been transported on the Nene and fenland waterways, but the passage of stone by the river was not always trouble free, and the Abbot of Peterborough was issued with a writ by William I forbidding him to interfere with the passage of stone from the quarry to the river.

For an annual rent of 6/- (30p) the Abbots of Peterborough and Bury St Edmunds were given the right to transport marble and any other stone by the river Nene between Alwalton and Peterborough. The abbey of Peterborough also had the right, granted by Pope Eugenius III in 1146, to take a toll from ships and boats carrying merchandise past Alwalton, 2d for a large ship, 1d for a smaller ship and ½d for a boat [4].

The document also refers to the carriage of a 'marble' on the river. This stone was quarried from the Alwalton Lynch [5] on the Eastern bank of the Nene between Castor and Alwalton, and possibly at smaller quarries in Castor and at Water Newton. The 'marble' is formed by the oyster beds that are laid down in the limestone, and it has been identified in a number of Cathedrals in the East of England. In Peterborough Cathedral the bowl of the font, the base of the pillar in the West porch and the effigy of Abbot Benedict on the North side of the choir are all of Alwalton 'marble', although the greatest quantity can be found in Lincoln Cathedral [6].

A quarry at Sutton also provided stone for local buildings, including the rectory at Elton, some five miles upriver. There is evidence in the fields North West of the village of the roadway down which the stone was dragged to the river, and at low water the remains of a timber and gravel wharf can still be seen. There is also a 'winding hole' and post in place. These were used to harness the flow of the river to turn a lighter ready for the return trip.

The Growth of Trade

There are no records of the use of the Nene for trade after the end of the stone trade in 1500 until a description of the state of the river in a pamphlet published in the 1650s, but it is probable that some trade continued. The pamphlet *'Some Considerations of the River Nine, running from Northampton to Peterborow, and so to the Sea; shewing the Feasibility and conveniency of making it Navigable'* signalled a greater interest in the use of the river for trade. At this time the head of navigation was at Alwalton, and large river craft and even some small sea going ships could bring goods some 30 miles inland from the Wash. At Alwalton the goods had to be transferred to smaller boats that could be portaged around obstructions such as shallows and mill dams. The writer of the pamphlet, whose identity is not known, estimated that the river could be made navigable for about £8,000 [7].

This proposal included 33 locks to take vessels of 8 to 10 tonnes, small enough to pass through the upstream bridges to Wellingborough, Thrapston, Oundle and elsewhere. The economic advantages of such a proposal were considerable, as

Fig 24c. The Nene at Water Newton.

at that time the cost of carriage alone of coal brought overland to Northampton was greater than the purchase price of the coal itself in Peterborough. This indicated that the Nene was being used for carriage of cargo well inland, at least as far as Alwalton, and that it made good commercial sense.

However, it was not until some 60 years later, in 1713, that any action was taken to improve the navigation above Peterborough. Small craft had been trading upriver before then; a record of 1648 shows a cargo of cheese being taken from Peterborough to the Michaelmas Fair at Higham Ferrers when the state of the roads in the wet season made overland carriage impractical. However, the boat had to be unloaded at sixteen mill dams, dragged over the dam and reloaded upstream [8]. In 1713 an Act of Parliament appointed commissioners to engage *'such Person or Persons to make the river navigable and passable'*. The Act allowed only for one person to make the whole river passable, but no one could be found to undertake the task. In 1724 a second Act was passed which allowed the task to be undertaken in as many stages as appropriate, and in September 1726 two people, Robert Wright and Thomas Squire, were contracted to make the section from Peterborough to Oundle navigable at their own expense, and recover the cost from tolls of 1s 6d (7.5p) charged on each tonne of goods carried. Thomas Squire agreed to improve the river from Oundle to Thrapston on the same terms, and this was completed in September 1737. The 'improved' Nene from Peterborough to Thrapston became known as the Eastern Division.

At the time that the Eastern Division was being developed further work was being undertaken to improve the navigation downstream, with a new channel being cut between Peterborough and Guyhirn, improving access to Wisbech. However, trade through Wisbech to the Wash was severely restricted by the state of the river below Wisbech. The main access to the Wash was still to the Great Ouse and Kings Lynn, so Peterborough became the hub of river traffic from both the Northern Fens and the inland route to Northampton.

Another Act of Parliament was required in order to ensure the development of the Western Division from Thrapston to Northampton. This Act, which received the Royal Assent in 1756, allowed the Commissioners to borrow money to undertake the work, which was completed in 1761. The completion of the task was a cause for great celebration in Northampton, as the price of coal in the town, where fuel had always been expensive and in short supply, dropped immediately to two thirds of the price it had been for decades before. The Universal Magazine reported: *'No less than 38 barges laden with coal and other merchandise and adorned with flags and streamers came up with the greatest of ease to the public wharf. ......The most general illuminations that were ever known, ringing of bells at all the churches, and every other demonstration of joy concluded the evening without the least rioting or other disturbance'* [9].

For a time the main route for bulk cargoes into and out of Northampton was the improved Nene, and tolls on the Western Division were generally healthy, covering the cost of maintaining the waterway and the salary of an inspector of works to supervise the maintenance of the river. However, proposals were put forward in 1792 to link Northampton with the Grand Junction Canal, and in 1793 an Act of Parliament authorised the construction of the link. This coincided with a reduction in income from tolls on the Nene, and the Commissioners were looking to the link with canal to be the salvation of the Western Division. For a while this proved to be the case, but records indicate that by 1827 almost 90% of the tolls were collected at Northampton, and only 10% elsewhere in the Western Division [10], and this had a knock-on effect on the through traffic on the Eastern Division.

The Decline of Trade and the Coming of the Railway

We now need to go back a few decades and consider the Eastern Division. The management of the division was originally in the hands of two families, the Wrights and the Squires, and in 1731 Wright sold his share of the tolls to the Squire family, who added total control of the Division to their other interests in Peterborough, which included lighters, inns, brewing and *'even a bank in Peterborough (but) the family seems to have extracted all possible profit from the Nene, without ploughing back enough of this to ensure satisfactory maintenance'* [11].

The Eastern Division included 14 locks and 8 staunches, whereas the Western Division contained 20 locks. This itself was an impediment to navigation as staunches, also known as flash locks, are not as easy to use as locks. A flash lock is effectively a weir with a single gate to allow navigation. Boats either had to navigate with or against the flow of water over the weir, or open the gate and wait until the water levels in the whole pounds on either side of the weir became equal, effectively dropping the water level in long stretches of the river. If the weir included a mill, this was very unpopular with the miller, as it deprived him of full power until the gate was closed and the water level rose again. An Ordnance Survey map of 1901 shows a staunch between Sutton and Wansford, and it is depicted in a watercolour in the vestry of Sutton church. (see colour plate section).

This, however, was not the only problem. A report prepared by Thomas Yeoman in 1759 had indicated that the navigation between Water Newton and Wansford was in a poor state, and commissioners seemed to have very little power to require the proprietors to take steps to improve the waterway. An Act of Parliament of 1794 gave the commissioners the power that they needed in

Fig 24d. Water Newton Mill, built in 1791 and converted for residential use after 200 years, in 1991.

order to ensure effective navigation, and the Act includes a clause stating that the river *'is in many Places grown up and decreased in depth, so that Boats and Lighters navigation thereon, for want of proper and sufficient Depth of Water, are frequently stopped'* [12]. The commissioners took some time to use their new powers and some improvements were made in 1802, but the effect of the link between Northampton and the Grand Junction Canal on trade in the Eastern Division was such that the tolls collected were insufficient to pay for the necessary repairs. By this time another threat to the viability of the navigation was not far over the horizon – the coming of the railway.

With most of the trade with Northampton coming through the Midlands, particularly with coal now coming from the Midlands coalfields rather than from the North East and upriver through Peterborough, the level of trade on the Eastern Division of the Nene never reached its former level, although in 1842 a document in the House of Lords Record Office records the passage of 4,772 tonnes of goods up and down the river between Northampton and Peterborough. Cargoes included iron, salt, oil cake, stone, slate, corn and timber, and the document also notes that this is probably a lower than average figure, on account of a dry summer and cold winter which would have made trade difficult. As each lighter carried approximately 10 tonnes of goods this volume of trade would have been carried in some 480 journeys, so a bystander on the bank at Castor would have probably seen two or three lighters pass in a day [13]. Wansford played a significant part in the river trade as a distribution point for goods coming up river and transferring to the roads for distribution throughout the East Midlands, from as far away as Leicester. Goods carried included timber, coal, grain and other agricultural produce. The wharf at Wansford was also used for the shipment of timber from the Burghley and Bedford estates, including the cut timbers for at least two men-o'-war which were shipped by river and canal to the shipbuilder's yard in London [14].

By this time the threat from the railways was coming closer, and the Commissioners of both the Eastern and Western Divisions agreed the proposals of the London and Birmingham Railway Company to build a line connecting Peterborough to Blisworth and their main London – Birmingham line. In 1843 an Act of Parliament gave approval for the construction of the line and for a while the river contributed to its own downfall through the profitable trade of carrying materials for the building of the railway. Records indicate that brick making machinery and other materials for the construction of the Yarwell tunnel were carried on the Nene, and a new cut created at Wansford to facilitate the shipping of quarried materials [15].

The coming of the railway marked a slow decline of river traffic above Peterborough, although trade carried on with some difficulty below Peterborough, particularly the import of timber via Wisbech. However, by the beginning of the 20th century the river was in a poor state *'The locks …. are in fair condition, although requiring a deal of handling in some cases, through their comparative disuse'* [16]. Bonthron, who was undertaking a pleasure cruise from Northampton to the Wash, reports that he had been warned about the state of the river, to the extent that it was impassable in places, and they would be unable to complete the journey. He was agreeably surprised to find *'a fine and attractive river'* and did complete his journey, although he did encounter weeds and rushes in some areas. However, it must be noted that he was travelling in a skiff, and bringing a laden lighter downriver will have been a very much harder, if not impossible, task.

However, by 1930 navigation was impossible, as a survey by the newly created River Nene Catchment Board made clear when it reported that in places the river was clogged with silt and vegetation, and that it was difficult to make out the channel in a *'series of shallow pools and rills that threaded their way uncertainly through a sort of morass'* [17].

Floods and Droughts

Drought and flood have been a regular feature of the Nene until the present day, and although improved management of the river in the 20th century has eliminated the worst effects of drought and ensured that the navigation is maintained, floods are still capable of causing chaos.

Fig 24e. The silting of the river. The silting of a backwater demonstrates how easily a slow flowing river can quickly become blocked.

The lack of water in the river was a regular hazard faced by lightermen, and it was reported in 1876 that there was a mere six inches of water at the Town Bridge in Peterborough, and that in order to enable the passage of boats, lighters were sunk across the river *'and they then put a tarpaulin in front; stuff it by the sides, put the deck boards here and there, and get two or three poor little boys, naked, to go into the river and stuff up the sides that the water may not escape'* [18]. By creating a temporary dam, the water level could be increased sufficiently for the passage of cargoes, although such measures took time and it was not unknown for a passage from Wisbech to Peterborough to take a month. By the 1930s a combination of silting and a dry summer meant that the river was so low at Sutton that people could walk across.

Other activity on the river contributed to the reduction in flow, as upstream of Peterborough millers put flash boards on their weirs to increase the depth of water behind their mills, and below Peterborough the depth was reduced from the middle of the 18th century by the railway companies extracting almost 900,000 gallons a day to meet the needs of their steam engines.

Floods were frequent and often extensive. In December 1848 a report described extensive flooding along the whole length of the river from Northampton to Peterborough, and in 1885 the Peterborough Advertiser reported: *'After a week's heavy rain with only slight intermissions of a few hours at a time, it was nothing more than was expected that the Nene should once more overflow its banks .... The staunches, the locks, the mills raised their slackers and opened their flood gates, but all attempts to keep within its natural channel were fruitless, and at the end of last week and the early part of this many thousands of acres of land were under water .... Above Peterborough the whole bed of the river was under water to the depth of several feet and as some of the highroads have to cross the valley, they became in many places impassable except for vehicles'* [19].

Floods are still a feature of the Nene, and although the fields adjacent to the river in the parishes of Castor, Ailsworth and Sutton have regularly flooded, the villages themselves have not been affected. The main events of the last century took place in 1912, 1947 and 1998. In August 1912 the water level at Peterborough's Town Bridge rose to 17' 8" above ordnance datum (the normal for summer being 8' – 9'), and many of the boatyards and riverside properties were flooded, with *'householders placing planks on top of barrels and using ladders to gain access at bedroom level'* [20]. Two of the most significant floods occurred in 1947 and 1998, although the Nene burst its banks on many other occasions. In 1947 heavy snowfall in early March had almost cut off Peterborough, many villages were isolated and over 1,000 lorries were stranded on the A1 between Wansford and Stamford. By 17th March a rapid thaw had set in and the flow of the river at Peterborough's Town Bridge was 200 million gallons an hour, compared with the normal winter flow of 12 million gallons per hour, and the river level peaked at 17' 9", some 8ft above normal levels. Between Castor station and Water Newton the river was quarter of a mile wide, although the worst flooding was avoided as the river levels had been lowered in anticipation of the thaw [21].

No such action was possible in 1998, when very high rainfall in a very short period did not allow the river levels to be reduced before the run-off from the ground already saturated by a wet winter entered the river. On this occasion the water level in Peterborough was slightly less than the record level set in 1947, but upriver of Wansford the floods set new records, partly because of the volume of water coming down from Northampton being held back by the Old London Road Bridge, which forms a significant barrier to floodwater [22]. From the Milton Ferry bridge, the view across to the sailing club on Lynch Lake in Ferry Meadows was of a continuous sheet of water, the course of the river being indistinguishable from the flooded water meadows and the lake itself. Again, although the river was almost at record levels, the villages of Castor, Ailsworth and Sutton were not flooded as they are set back from the river on slightly higher ground. (see colour plate section).

The Boats and the People

There is little hard evidence to give a picture of the type of craft that traded on the river in medieval times but an analysis of later boats – the fen punt and the fen lighter - provides clues as to the way boats carrying stone for the abbeys of the Fens might have looked. The clues suggest that the boats would have been double ended, tapering to a point at each end, as this would give greater rigidity than a boat with a flat, or transom, stern [23]. Evidence of the carrying capacity of these craft comes from Engine Farm in Whittlesey, where four blocks of Barnack ragstone lie in a field which once lay under Whittlesey Mere, the original route of the Nene. These stones, weighing eight tonnes in all, may have been lost when the boat carrying them foundered, possibly in a squall. The state of the rivers between Barnack and Peterborough, then on into the Fens, suggests that a draught of less than a metre would be needed, together with a broad beam to ensure stability. Putting all these factors together '... *the required vessel would have performed satisfactorily if constructed to a length of about nine metres, with a beam of just under three'* [24]. Over the centuries cargo-carrying craft in the Fens and the feeder rivers evolved into the fenland lighter, capable of carrying twenty tonnes, being thirteen metres long and with a beam of just over three metres.

The propulsion of commercial craft would have relied largely on muscle power, either human or horse. Quanting was one way of engaging human muscle power. Using a long pole, the lighterman dropped one end to the bottom of the river near the bow of the lighter, put the other end to his shoulder, and walked aft, taking his lighter forward. Using this method, the lightermen would have effectively pushed their craft every inch of the way! Hauling the craft from the bank, using either human or horse power was often made difficult by the state of the banks until the development of the river in the 18th century, when proper 'haling' ways were constructed, together with the locks. Using the wind was possible, and early prints show lighters using sails, although the very shallow draught of the lighters meant that this was practicable only when the wind was directly astern. However, probably the easiest method of propulsion was to 'go with the flow'. The building of the abbeys often took decades, or even hundreds of years, so the stone could be brought to the site at the leisurely natural pace of the river, requiring the use of human muscle only where rapids or other obstructions had to be negotiated.

The River Today

By the late 1920s the Nene was in a poor state, with very little trade on the river above Peterborough, although there was still some quarry trade to Wansford. It took a week for a small motor launch to travel from Peterborough to Northampton, and it had to be dragged overland in some places [25]. In 1930 the River Nene Catchment Board undertook a major programme of improvements, including the removal of the remaining staunches (including those at Sutton and Alwalton), the rebuilding of all the locks and the dredging of the river. This improvement is seen in the state of the river today, with the large guillotine locks, which were hard work compared with the hinged gates, but in recent years have been made easier with the installation of electric motors for raising the guillotine. The improvements encouraged the return of some trade, notably to the mills at Wellingborough, and Thames barges bringing grain to Cadge and Coleman's mill in Peterborough until the mid 1960s. Probably the last regular commercial use of the river above the port of Wisbech was made by the Nene Barge and Lighter Company which carried stone for the Catchment Board from Wansford to Sutton Bridge, near the mouth of the river, for the maintenance of the navigation at least until the mid 1970s.

Fig 24f. Milton Ferry Bridge, for many years an important crossing point of the Nene, now linking the parishes with Ferry Meadows Country Park.

It is ironic that the river is now maintained in a better state than it has been throughout almost two thousand years of known use for commercial purposes. The traffic has never been so light, and with the exception of the dredgers and other craft used for the maintenance of the waterway, all the traffic is for leisure. There are yacht clubs at Alwalton and near Orton Staunch, and regular boat trips are undertaken by the Key Ferry from its base by Peterborough's Town Bridge. The river also attracts walkers, anglers and families spending a day in the countryside, picnicking on the banks and taking the occasional swim on hot days, as has been the case since the 19th century. An Ordnance Survey map of 1901 shows a designated 'bathing place' at the end of Splash Lane, with an enclosure and small building, possibly a changing hut.

Although the use of the river for trade has never been easy, its effect on the economy of the towns and villages along its banks cannot be dismissed. For centuries, the only alternative to a lighter carrying up to ten tonnes of cargo was either a pack horse or horse and cart travelling on very rudimentary roads, and with a load many times less than that of a lighter. Much of the trade of the river simply passed through the villages of Castor, Ailsworth and Sutton, but the Nene certainly provided the means of getting local produce to market and until the coming of the railway was an economic lifeline, not only for the three riparian villages, but for all five parishes.

Nigel Blanchford

I have lived in Castor for 27 years, in Allotment Lane, Old Pond Lane and Samworths Close. I worked for the County and City Councils in a number of posts in the Education Department, and retired as Head of Community Education. Before coming to Castor I worked in maritime related jobs, and researching the history of our river has been an interesting variation on the maritime theme. I hope that you enjoyed the outcome.

Notes

1. Donovan Purcell, *Cambridge Stone,* Faber and Faber, 1967, p96.
2. *ibid.* p29.
3. *ibid.* p30.
4. The Precentor's Registers of Peterborough Northants Record Society, Vol XX, p 533, quoted in Donovan Purcell *Cambridge Stone* Faber and Faber 1967 p71.
5. A lynch is defined as a terrace or ledge, a stretch of flat land along a shore or river bank.
6. Donovan Purcell pp 72, 73.
7. John Boyes and Ronald Russell, *The Canals of Eastern England,* David and Charles, 1977, p196.
8. *ibid.* p197.
9. *ibid.* p200.
10. *ibid.* p208.
11. H.J.K.Jenkins, *Along the Nene,* Cambridgeshire Books, 1991, p31.
12. *op cit* John Boyes and Ronald Russell, *The Canals of Eastern England*, David and Charles,1977, p202.
13. Peter Waszak, *The effects of Railways on River Transport in Peterborough 1845 -1903,* Peterborough Local History Society, Vol. 24, Oct 2003.
14. *Peterborough Citizen,* 5th June 1928.
15. Peter Waszak *The effects of Railways on River Transport in Peterborough 1845 -1903,* Peterborough Local History Society, Vol. 24, Oct 2003.
16. P Bonthron, *My Holidays on Inland Waterways,* Thomas Murby, London, 1917.
17. H J K Jenkins, *Northamptonshire Past and Present,* Northamptonshire Record Society, Vol VIII, 1992, p 191.
18. *op cit* John Boyes and Ronald Russell, p216.
19. *Peterborough Advertiser,* 5th December, 1885, p6 col3.
20. Peter Waszak, *The Railway and Great Floods of the Past,* http://www.datum-line.co.uk/links_research/railway_floods.htm .
21. *ibid.*.
22. *ibid.*
23. H.J.K.Jenkins *Along the Nene,* Cambridgeshire Books, 1991, p15.
24. *ibid* p31
25. *op cit* John Boyes and Ronald Russell, p221.

Fig 24g. Water Newton Lock, built during the upgrading of the 1930s, now with a motorised guillotine gate.

Chapter 25
Natural History - Flora and Fauna of the Parishes

Introduction

In a legend of St Kyneburgha, the saint miraculously escapes three ruffians. She is able to run away along a path strewn with wildflowers, whilst they are caught up in scrub and brambles. In the church named after her, there is a fine banner, embroidered by the late Elsie Sismey. The flowery carpet at the saint's feet is clearly shown, as are a few bushes to thwart her assailant.

To our modern eyes, a carpet of wildflowers is rare and special. But in Kyneburgha's time, such displays would have been commonplace. The miracle was not the flowers that grew up in front of her, but the rough brambles that stopped her assailants. It is a measure of how the countryside has changed since Kyneburgha's days that we are surprised by the wildflowers.

The Benefice is a mixture of different wildlife habitats. To the South is the River Nene with its associated wet meadows. Rising above the valley is the drier land, with fields and pastures on clay or limestone, and then woodlands on the clay, often on the higher ground.

In this chapter we describe the natural history of the Benefice in relation to the historical landscape and particularly the landscape St Kyneburgha might have known. We give examples of the wildlife you can still see. As we can only scratch the surface, there are references to sources of further information at the end of the chapter.

Meadows and pastures

If you wanted to find somewhere with a 'flowery carpet' today, the meadows by the Nene would be a good place to start. There are records from *Domesday* of haymaking in the Nene Valley. We know that in 1086 there were 15 acres of meadows in Castor and 15 acres in Ailsworth too (Appendix 1). Saxon hay meadows would have been very different from most meadows we see now. The meadows were not uniform grass fields, but would have been filled with flowers that grow well in damp soil.

Fig 25a. St Kyneburgha Banner. This hangs at the foot of the tower in Castor Church and is taken in procession on feast days. (Photo: J Tovey)

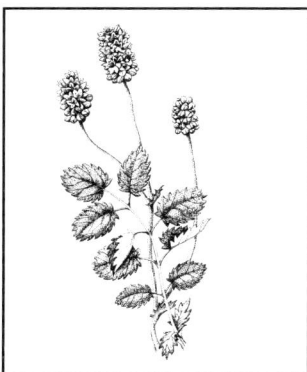

Fig 25b. Great burnet (Drawing: English Nature)

However, you can still see meadows with many of the plant species that were probably there in St Kyneburgha's day. Down by the Nene at Castor, and on the North side of the railway embankment, there are meadows that look different from the grassland around them. Look there in June and you will see dark crimson heads of great burnet, shocking pink shaggy flowers of ragged robin, fleshy pink spikes of marsh orchids and bright yellow buttercups. Look even closer and you will see that instead of plain rye grass, there are many different grasses, including creeping bent, meadow foxtail and crested dog's-tail. Later in the summer, the air is full of the scent of the creamy flowers of meadowsweet.

In 1985 Roger Banks, author and illustrator of *Living in a Wild Garden* [1] who has painted for the National Trust for Scotland and for many Wildlife Trusts, painted a watercolour he entitled *Waternewton Meadow*. This was actually of the Castor Flood Meadows and it is reproduced in the colour plate section. This picture captures the floristic richness of these remnants of the once-extensive grasslands that lay along the River Nene.

It would be very wrong to think that the meadows and fields which Kyneburgha knew were a wilderness. This was farming country even in Saxon days. The meadows were grazed by the villagers' beasts and cut for hay. The flowery carpet that Kyneburgha would have known was not the rare, special and unusual thing it now is: it would have been a normal pasture or meadow. Meadows like these did not survive by themselves: we can enjoy the sight only because of the way in which they have been farmed. Comparisons between Castor Enclosure maps (1898) and today show that only fragments of the flowery grassland now remain [2]. This loss has been due, by and large, to changes in agriculture, particularly in the mid-20th century, especially through the use of fertilisers and pesticides, and the drainage and conversion of pastures to arable land.

There are other sorts of fields where one could imagine a flowery carpet. These are just as rare now as the wetter flowery meadows, for much the same reasons. Climb up from the valley and you get onto the limestone. It is much drier and has a very different flora. At its best, the flowers you can find on the limestone around Peterborough have few rivals.

There is still flowery limestone grassland to the North of the old railway station at Sutton Heath, and also at Ailsworth Heath. The latter was common land which for several hundred years was grazed by sheep and cattle belonging to villagers from Ailsworth. This traditional management allowed numerous grasses and wildflowers to flourish, on ground that has never been chemically sprayed or re-seeded [3]. You can see yellow rock-rose, and purple milk-vetch. In some places, if you look closely, you can see the small green adder's tongue fern.

Go a little to the North into a neighbouring parish and you can see an even better example. At Barnack Hills and Holes National Nature Reserve, the grassland is a reminder of what the limestone grassland would have been like in St Kyneburgha's time. Over 300 different species of plants have been found there [4]. The most striking is the pasque flower, so-named because its rich purple flowers with their bright yellow centres open around Easter-tide. Castor Church was built of Barnack stone from those quarries, so the flower must have been familiar to the medieval inhabitants of the Benefice. Indeed, John Clare wrote of pasque flowers growing at *Swordy Well*, also called *Swaddiwell*, off King Street, just North of Ailsworth Heath.

Heathlands

*Fig 25c. Pasque flower
(Drawing: English Nature)*

One habitat that Kyneburgha, and indeed all our predecessors up to the early 20th century would have known well, has almost entirely disappeared from the Benefice, due to 19th century enclosures and 20th century agriculture. We have lost the extensive heathland described by John Morton in the early 18th century and later by John Clare [5]. These heaths stretched Eastwards from Wittering and had their own special plants. Indeed, they were noted for a special type of small sheep particularly associated with this district. All that remains is a solitary clump of heather and some patches of gorse and bracken at Castor Hanglands National Nature Reserve.

Woodlands

We must remember that the landscape around the villages is a working landscape. In some respects it was more of a working landscape in Kyneburgha's time than it is now. We heat our homes and cook with oil or gas or electricity: our predecessors used wood. Wood was used for tools, for building and for fuel. This wood came from actively-worked woodland. Woods were not the quiet refuges that we sometimes imagine. They were a busy and essential part of the village landscape. But they would not have looked as they do now. The woods would have been more open, with much more frequent coppicing. There would have been tall oaks and ashes, but probably many trees would have been *'stools'*, stumps from which grew the thin poles that the villagers needed for handles and for fuel. There are still thatched cottages in the villages. The thatching spars that hold down the thatch come from woods managed in much the same way as St Kyneburgha would have known. Indeed, as an active Abbess, running the monastery and its lands, perhaps it is not too far fetched to think that Kyneburgha would have had a good knowledge of woodland management. If you want to see pictures of medieval woodland, the charming Flemish book illustrations by Simon Bening, especially that entitled '*December*' (which is in the British Library), show what it must have looked like.

A study of land-use changes by R V Collier showed that, between 1919 and 1977, the distribution and area of woodland changed very little, although some broadleaved woodland had been replaced by conifers. The main reason for the lack of change was that most of the land of the Soke is crossed by the two large estates of Burghley and Milton. These estates have a long tradition of hunting and game shooting, with the result that the woodland has been retained [6]. The extent of 'ancient woodland' (that is, woods for which there is evidence that woodland has existed on the same land since 1600) has been estimated. The map in the colour plates section shows the woods still existing in the Benefice that are 'ancient'. You can reasonably infer that these areas were probably wooded at *Domesday* and even in St Kyneburgha's time. We know from *Domesday* that Castor had woodland six furlongs long by four furlongs wide and Ailsworth had woodland three furlongs long by two furlongs wide (Appendix 1).

Castor Hanglands

The most famous woodland in the Benefice is Castor Hanglands, which has been managed as a National Nature Reserve for 50 years. It is leased from the Milton Estate and the Forestry Commission, and managed by English Nature. It is one of only about 200 National Nature Reserves in England. It is the Benefice's wildlife 'jewel in the crown'. The Reserve includes the woods at Castor Hanglands and the grassland and scrub at Ailsworth Heath [7].

The woodland at Castor Hanglands is a relic of the historic hunting forest of Nassborough. Ancient woodland such as this is especially rich in plant and animal species. The ground flora holds many species indicative of an ancient

woodland including wood melick, yellow archangel and ramsons. Just over 50 years ago, before it became a National Nature Reserve, nearly all the large trees were felled for timber. In the Reserve, the native oak, ash, field maple and birch trees have been allowed to re-grow. Amongst them are rarer trees such as wild service, and shrubs like hazel, dogwood and spindle. In spring, the woodland flora includes a colourful mixture of bluebells, wood anemones, primroses, violets, wild strawberries and other plants. Large numbers of fallow deer may be seen in the wood. Browsing by the deer damages growth and kills new tree seedlings. Certain parts of the woodland are now enclosed by electric or plastic fencing, to keep the deer out and allow the shrubs and saplings to survive and form a dense understorey within the woodland. A leaflet giving a fuller description of Castor Hanglands National Nature Reserve is available from English Nature [8].

If you go to Castor Hanglands today, you can see oak, ash and maple, just as there would have been in St Kyneburgha's time. Indeed, the maple apparently gets its name from the use the Saxons made of it, to turn bowls or 'mazers'. There would probably have been fencing to protect the young coppice re-growth from deer and the villagers' stock. The fencing ('*pale*') would also have kept stock in, especially pigs, when they were put in the woodland to feed on acorns in the autumn. Much of the Hanglands survived until relatively recently: it was only in the 20th century that about half was cut down by the Forestry Commission and replaced with Scandinavian conifers. These conifers did not thrive and many are now being removed. New woodland and heathland is slowly returning.

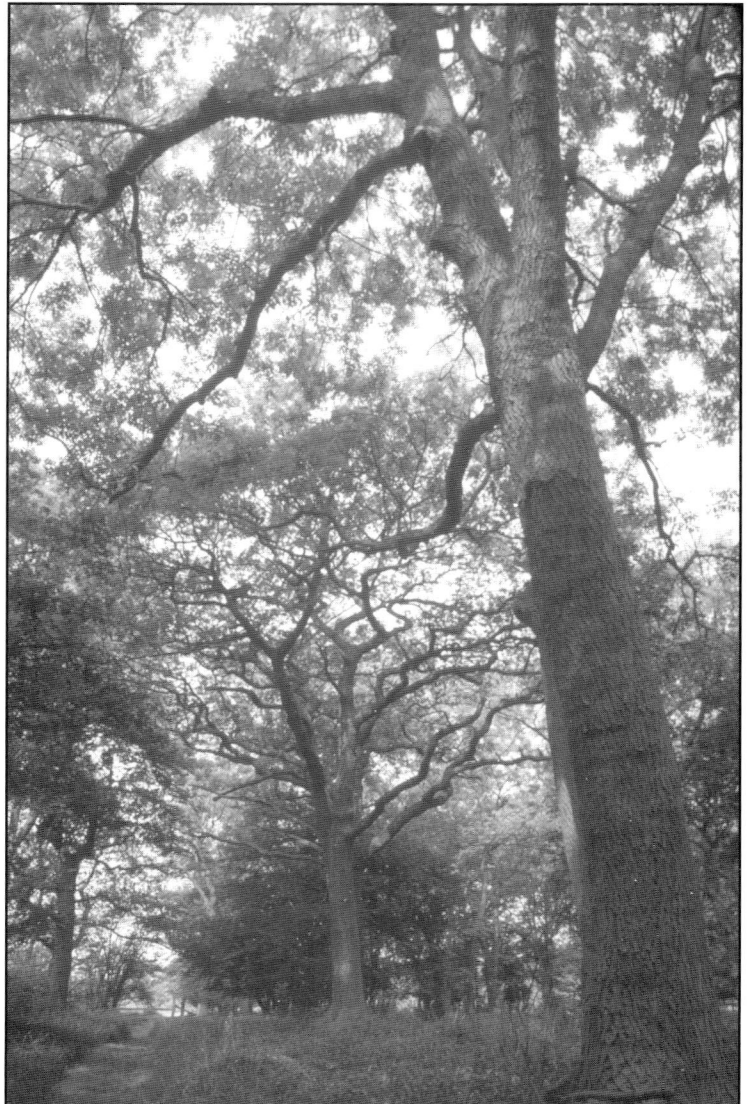

Fig 25d. Castor Hanglands NNR: oaks and bluebells along a woodland ride leading to Ailsworth Heath.
(Photo: Peter Wakely/English Nature)

On the St Kyneburgha banner there is a blue butterfly (perhaps a holly blue?). We can be pretty certain that there were more butterflies around in St Kyneburgha's day than today. The decline in butterflies in this area has been relatively recent. The Benefice has not been unique in this: it is a national phenomenon. What is perhaps more special is that the butterflies of Castor Hanglands were particularly studied [9]. It is one of the sites which has always been associated with rare butterflies, perhaps because it was close to the butterfly expert Charles Rothschild's estate at Ashton, near Oundle.

It is pleasing to be able to say that Castor Hanglands has been involved in recovery work for rare butterflies. The black hairstreak, a small dark butterfly with a prominent white spur on its hind-wings, is found in England only on the clayey, wooded ridges that run from Oxfordshire to Lincolnshire. It lives on blackthorn, but seems very fussy in its requirements. The adult butterfly is seen only occasionally on very warm days in June. The caterpillar feeds on blackthorn leaves, and the chrysalis, which is camouflaged to look like a small bird dropping, is hidden on the branches. Work done at Castor Hanglands National Nature Reserve has helped to develop better ways of conserving this species.

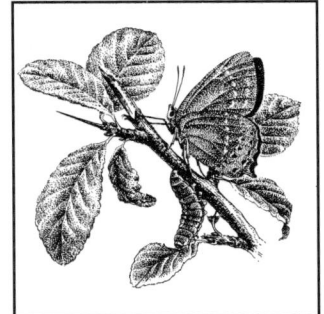

Fig 25e. Black hairstreak
(Drawing: English Nature)

The river, streams and ponds

The River Nene meanders across the floodplain, although it has been straightened in places to aid navigation. It marks the Southern boundary of the Benefice. There is an oxbow South of Castor that, until early in the 20th century, was part of the original course of the river. Yellow water-lilies grow there in profusion. Further upstream, Castor Backwater with its mass of reed beds provides a good feeding ground for many warblers and finches, as well as for coot, moorhen, mallard and tufted duck. Along the River Nene South of Castor and Ailsworth are many willow trees, including 'cricket bat' willows. Many of the willows are still pollarded. This is the traditional way of managing willows for the production of small poles used for stakes, baskets and hurdles [10] [11].

By the river you can see many plants that like wet conditions. Many are large and colourful, such as spires of purple loosestrife, golden marsh marigolds and pale pink lady's smock. There are of course, reeds, rushes and bulrushes, but also less obvious water-plants such as arrowhead, with leaves that live up to its name, and water crowfoots, with feathery submerged leaves and little white flowers that break the surface of the water. Perhaps the most noticeable insects are the blue damselflies, especially the common blue damselfly, the banded demoiselle, with big black spots on its wings, and sometimes the less common red-eyed damselfly.

The English farming landscape used to have far more ponds. These ponds were essential for watering cattle. There is a medieval pond at

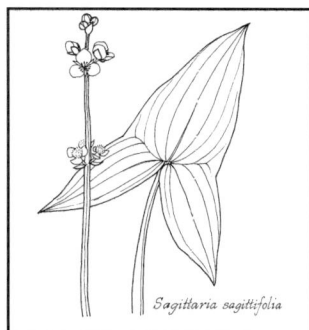

Fig 25g. Arrowhead.
(Drawing English Nature)

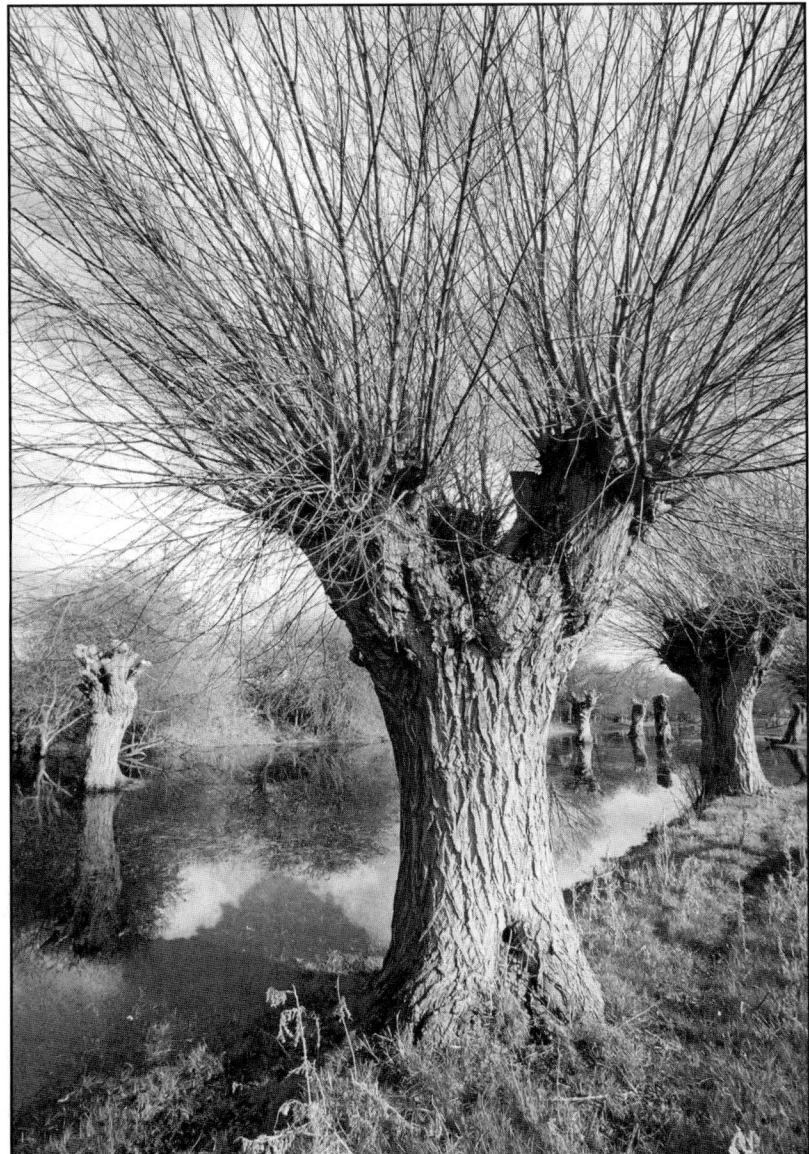

Fig 25f. Pollard willows: growing by Castor Level Crossing and pollarded regularly by the Nene Park Trust. (Photo: J Tovey)

Castor Hanglands and several other ponds have been dug on the Reserve over the years. These ponds provide an ideal habitat for many water-loving plants and insects. Eighteen species of dragonfly have been recorded on the Reserve. In early spring the main pond sees a gathering of several thousand common toads, in order to breed. This striking wildlife spectacle is made all the more remarkable by the way the toads then disperse and disappear, to return the next year.

The ponds at Castor Hanglands hold all three species of newt found in Britain - the smooth, the palmate and the rarer, and larger, great crested newt. The Soke of Peterborough is a stronghold for these rare amphibians, with England's largest colony of great crested newts to the South at Orton. They have also been found at Oldfield Pond, North of Castor.

Fig 25h. Common toad (Drawing: English Nature)

Hedges and arable fields

In this part of England, hedges are often not an ancient or medieval field boundary, but a much more recent division of the fields, although some hedges, particularly those along old tracks, are much older. Even though we lost so many big elms from the hedges in the last quarter of the 20th century, there are still elms surviving, but often as suckering shrubs rather than tall trunks: the young growth of the elm often escapes the effects of Dutch elm disease.

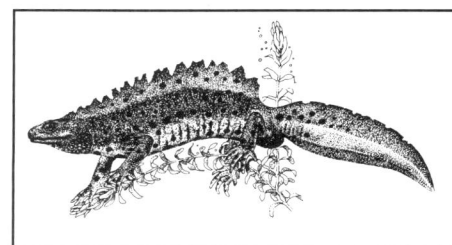

Fig 25i. Great crested newt (Drawing: English Nature)

What would the arable fields have looked like? They would have had weeds, but rather than simply poppies, wild oats and black grass as today, there would have been many more different flowers. Until very recently, you could see some examples of these rarer weeds in Normangate field, including round-leaved fluellen. More frequently seen is the field pansy. This species, when crossed with heartsease, is the ancestor of many of the original horticultural pansies [12]. The Benefice is not alone in losing its cornfield weeds: it has happened all over England. These colourful arable weeds thrived, partly because of the inability of our predecessors to sift seed as thoroughly as we do now, but much more so because they did not have the fertilisers and herbicides available to us today. We can produce more grain than St Kyneburgha's villagers would have thought possible, but the landscape is much less interesting as a result.

Fig 25j. 'The Dancing Ladies': This row of elms stood on the edge of Glebe Field running down to Peterborough Road, Castor. They were known as the 'Dancing Ladies' because their branches lightly touched each other and in the breeze appeared to be dancing together. It was a sad day indeed when in the 1980s they were felled, having fallen victim to Dutch elm disease. (Courtesy David Scott)

John Clare

The poet John Clare wrote lovingly accurate descriptions of the countryside around the Benefice. What is not so well known is that Clare was a very significant recorder of the wildlife around this area in the early 19th century. He made reference to 153 different plants in his writings [13] [14]. It might be assumed that Clare, the 'peasant poet', knew all these flowers from childhood and that they were part of the everyday vocabulary of farming folk. But we know that this was not actually so. Clare learnt to identify many flowers from Joseph Henderson, who was the head gardener at Milton Hall in the 1820s. In 1824, Clare writes of receiving a parcel of ferns and flowers from Henderson, including a hart's-tongue fern *growing in a well at Caistor'* (sic) [15].

In the Benefice, you can still see many of the flowers referred to in his poems:

Bluebells and field maple at Castor Hanglands:

'And snugly hiding 'neath the feather'd brake
Full many a Bluebell flower' (Clare, Village Minstrel 1821)

'The Maple with its tassel flowers of green
That turns to red a stag horn shaped seed' (Clare, The Maple Tree)

Lady's smock and yellow water-lilies by the River Nene:

'An wan-hued Lady-smocks that love to spring
'Side the swamp margin of some plashy pond' (Clare, Village Minstrel 1821)

'While Water-lilies in their glories come
And spread green isles beautifully round their home' (Clare, MS poems) [16].

However, Clare is perhaps better known for his laments over the loss of wild flowers and wild places caused by the Enclosures and agricultural developments. He wrote of the destruction of pasque flowers:

'I coud almost fancy that this blue anemone sprang from the blood or dust of the romans for it haunts the roman bank in this neighborhood and is found nowhere else it grows on the roman bank agen swordy well & did grow in great plenty but the plough that destroyer of wildflowers has rooted it out of its long inherited dwelling' [17].

It is not at all unlikely that it formerly grew on the 'roman banks' at Castor. The loss of the pasque flower could stand as a symbol for the impoverishment of our flora since Kyneburgha settled here.

Birds

On the St Kyneburgha banner there are no birds. We know that there are some birds that Kyneburgha would not have seen. In Upton you can see little owls perkily sitting on a willow. Little owls were only introduced into England in the 19th century. Indeed they were referred to as *'Lilford owls'*, after the estate further up the Nene valley, where they were introduced to England. However, we can be sure that there would have been many more species of birds to be seen in Kyneburgha's day, and indeed in the 19th century when Clare wrote about wildlife in and around the Benefice.

Fig 25k. Little owl (Drawing: English Nature)

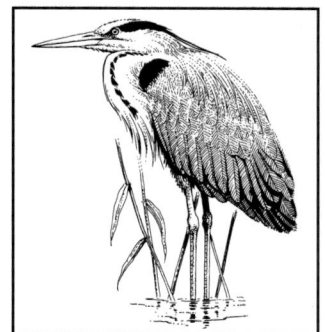

As an Anglo-Saxon princess, Kyneburgha would have known about falconry and probably owned hawks for hunting. Down by the river there would have been herons - no doubt abundant but probably also hunted using falconry. We still have grey herons - there is a large heronry on the Milton Estate and you can see these striking birds flapping slowly and powerfully over the villages. The Milton heronry was probably founded in 1819 and reportedly was once the largest in England [18].

In most years nightingale, whitethroat, garden warbler, grasshopper warbler, long-eared owls and many other bird species breed at Castor Hanglands. Our predecessors would have heard the sweet sounds of the nightingale and the skylark far more than we can do today. They would also even have heard the much less musical rasping of the corncrake. This bird is now extinct in England but hopefully will be re-introduced in Cambridgeshire. The churring of the nightjar was probably a familiar sound over Ailsworth Heath. We know that nightjars were still heard in Clare's day. He wrote that they were found on *'a wild heath, called Emmingsales* (Edmonds Sale, part of Castor Hanglands National Nature Reserve) *& I believe that is the only spot which they visit'*. He described their call as a *'novel and pleasing sound'* and then explained how to imitate it [19].

Clare also noted the fieldfares and redwings that still frequent the Peterborough area in winter. He described the fieldfares that *'come in large flocks and strip the awe* (hawthorn)

Fig 25l. Grey heron (Drawing: English Nature)

bushes as they proceed onward in their march...They are speckled like the thrush and make a busy chinnying as they flye'. In contrast the redwing is simply noted as *'smaller than the field fare and flyes silent'* [20].

The large and striking red kite would have been seen often, scavenging on carrion. In John Clare's day, the red kite appears not to have been infrequent. He writes:

'The old hen leads her flickering chicks abroad
Oft scuttling 'neath her wings to see the Kite
Hang wavering o'er them in the spring's blue light'

By the time Druce published his *Flora of Northamptonshire* in 1930 [21], he referred to the kite as *'one of our rarest birds'*, and thereafter it became extinct in England until its re-introduction by English Nature in the 1990s. One of the most encouraging things to record about the Benefice's natural history is that in 2003, a red kite was seen over Castor School by pupils and teachers. At a time when we see wild places under threat and even the commoner displays of roadside flowers, such as cow parsley, are being replaced by close-mown, suburban-style verges, the red kite is a sign that wildlife can recover.

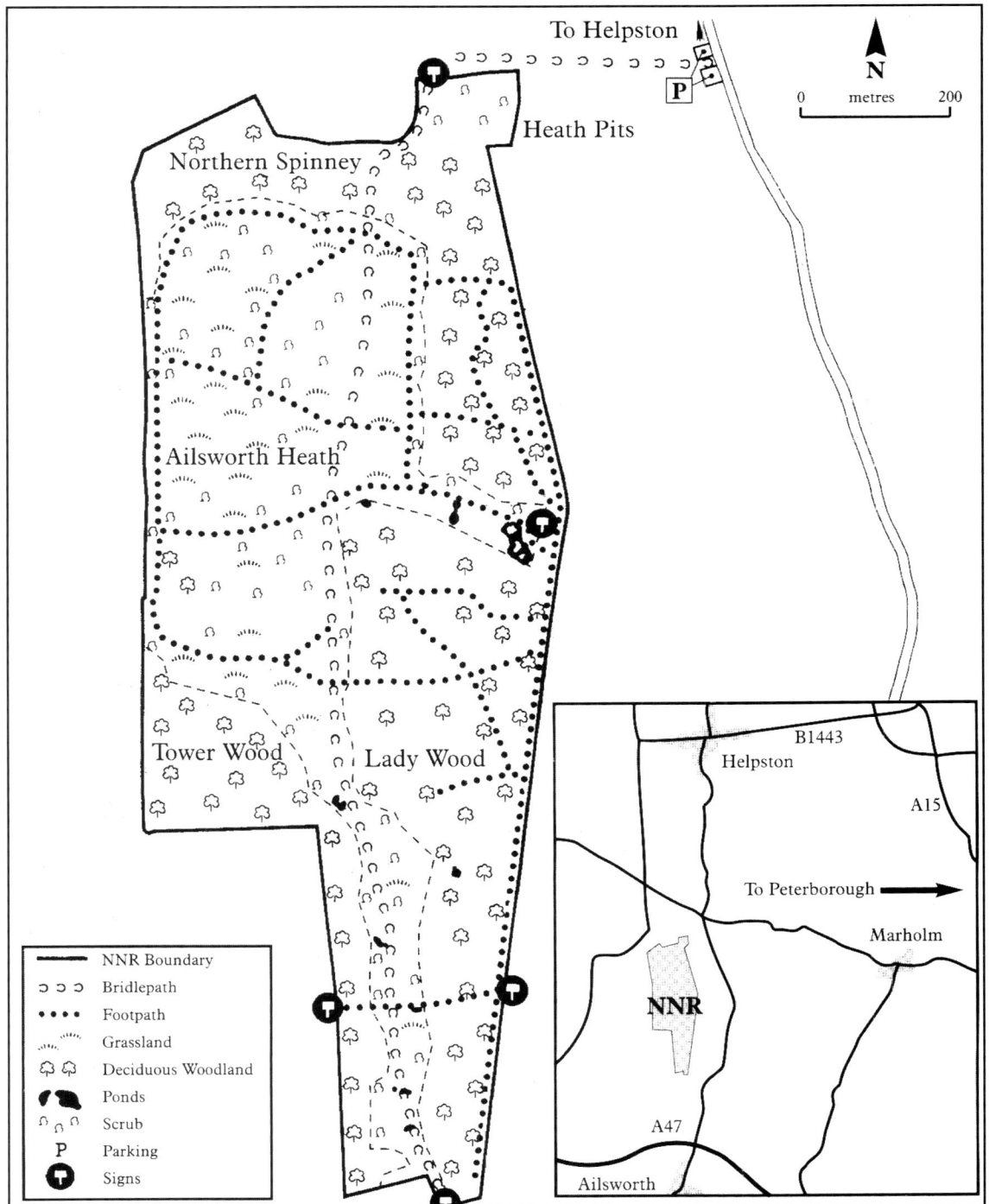

Fig 25m. Map of Castor Hanglands NNR. (Drawing English Nature)

More information

You can find out more about the wildlife around the Benefice by looking at the various recording schemes, many of which make information available on the Internet [22] [23]. Information on the special wildlife sites, including the three Sites of Special Scientific Interest (Castor Flood Meadows, Castor Hanglands and Sutton Heath & Bog) can be found on English Nature's Website [24].

You can visit Castor Hanglands: there is open public access to the National Nature Reserve.

Acknowledgements

Chris Gardiner, David Denman and Marc Turner of English Nature for help and expert advice.

Emily and John Finnie

Emily and John Finnie live in Castor with their son William. Emily first moved to the village in 1992 and John joined her when they married in 1996. Both have a long-standing interest in wildlife, especially wildflowers.

Notes

1. Roger Banks, *Living in a Wild Garden,* The Windmill Press, 1980.
2. R V Collier, *The Status and decline of butterflies on Castor Hanglands NNR,* Nature Conservancy Council CST Notes Number 8, 1978.
3. English Nature, *Castor Hanglands National Nature Reserve,* NNR leaflet.
4. English Nature, *Barnack Hills and Holes National Nature Reserve,* NNR leaflet.
5. G C Druce, *The Flora of Northamptonshire,* Arbroath: T Buncle and Co, 1930, p lxi.
6. R V Collier.
7. P Marren, *England's National Nature Reserves,* Poyser Natural History, 1994, p221.
8. English Nature, *Castor Hanglands National Nature Reserve.*
9. R V Collier.
10. Peterborough City Council Community Programme, *Country Walks Around Peterborough,* City Planning Department.
11. *Nene Way Guide,* Nene Park Peterborough.
12. R Mabey, *Flora Britannica,* Sinclair-Stevenson, 1996, p129.
13. G C Druce, p xci.
14. F H Perring, *John Clare and Northamptonshire Plant Records,* Arbroath, 1955.
15. M Grainger (Editor), *The Natural History Prose Writings of John Clare,* Clarendon Press, Oxford, 1983, p 207.
16. G C Druce, pp xcvii, xcix, c, cxiii.
17. M Grainger, p 61.
18. E M Nicholson, *British Birds,* 22:285.
19. M Grainger, p 33.
20. Ibid, p 134.
21. G C Druce, p xcii.
22. *The Postcode Plants Database,* www.nhm.ac.uk.
23. *National Biodiversity Network Website,* www.nbn.org.uk.
24. *English Nature Website,* www.english-nature.org.uk.

General Reference

A Colston and F H Perring, *The Nature of Northamptonshire,* Barracuda Books Limited, 1989.
A Colston, C Gerrard, M Jackson, L Moore and C Tero, *Northamptonshire's Red Data Book species to watch in the county,* The Wildlife Trust for Northamptonshire, 1996.
G Gent, R Wilson et al, *The Flora of Northamptonshire and the Soke of Peterborough,* Robert Wilson, 1995.

Chapter 26
People from the Parish Records

The Parish Registers

From 1537, by law, the established Church has been required to keep records of all baptisms, marriages and burials that take place within the parish boundaries of its churches. Technically, that included people of all denominations or of no faith at all. Dissenters and Roman Catholics tended to ignore the baptisms, and later kept their own records. In the case of marriages, at some stage, the only legal registrars were the Anglican parish priests, (Quakers and Jews were later granted an exemption). Therefore all legally valid marriages according to the law of the land at one time were conducted in Anglican parish churches. In effect, the civil state used the parochial clergy as unpaid civil servants, not just primarily to save money, but because the parish priest was often the only person who was literate. The use of the word 'parson' (the old pronunciation of 'person') dates back to well before 1537, to the times when even the aristocracy, as primarily soldiers, were often barely literate. The parish priest was a 'clerk-in-holy orders', hence the reason most of the old parish records are still in the care of the local church.

In 1837, Civil Registration of births, marriages and deaths, and marriage by civil ceremony became both possible and legal. Parish churches are still required to keep records of all baptisms, marriages and burials that take place on their premises. Although some of the older records have been deposited at Northampton County Record Office (NCRO) for safe custody, the legal records still exist as follows:

Castor: from 1538 – baptisms and marriages; from 1547 – burials.
Sutton: from 1758 – marriages: from 1763 – burials; from 1770 – baptisms.
Upton: from 1770 – baptisms and marriages; from 1855 – burials.
Note: In the case of Sutton and Upton prior to these dates all records were made and kept at Castor.
Marholm: from 1538 (The first 33 years having been re-written, the originals being lost).

Fig 26a. Thomas Dove Rector of Castor 1613.

However, the records kept by parishes are far more extensive than just those of baptisms, marriages and burials. The parish system was used to administer nearly all local matters including the making of Militia Lists and Muster Rolls, updating the Tithe Rolls and administering The Poor Law. The churchwardens were not just parish church officers, but also Bishops' officers in the parish and had additional civil, non-religious responsibilities. Other records include manorial court records; the church was Lord of the Manor in Castor, Ailsworth and Sutton for most of their history. Furthermore, all inscriptions about people, and therefore memorials in churches and on gravestones, can be seen as part of our parish records, as they all provide sources of information for historians.

Records of Baptisms, Marriages and Deaths
At first the details recorded were quite scant, merely a name and a date, and the event. For example:
in the reign of Queen Mary Tudor in 1556 'Robert Wyldbore was baptised on 16 October'. By the next century more detail is included. In 1613, we read that 'John Fitzwilliam son of William Fitzwilliam was baptized 24 February'. In 1677 'Dorothy the baseborn daughter of Susannah Wilson was baptised 31 March'. In 1744, we read of an historic marriage entry in Castor records which was to unite the Milton Fitzwilliams with the descendants of Thomas Wentworth, Lord Strafford, (Charles I's general who was impeached and executed by Parliament). It brought the name Wentworth into the Fitzwilliam family, as well as considerable estates in Yorkshire and ownership of the largest private house in Europe. 'The Right Honourable William Earl Fitzwilliam of the Kingdom of Ireland and Baron Fitzwilliam of Milton in the County of Northampton married the 22 day of June 1744 the Right Honourable the Lady Anne Wentworth, Eldest Daughter of Thomas, Earl of Malton'.

These records are signed on each page by the priest and churchwardens. For example in 1607 'Thomas Sryorhy Curate and Thomas Bate and Eusebius Catesbie, gent Churchwardens'. In addition the name of the monarch and the year of

Fig 26b. John Towers, Bishop of Peterborough and Rector of Castor, who was charged by Cromwell with High-Treason in 1646, and committed to the Tower London where he died 10th January 1648.

his reign are included on every page. *'30 January 1649. King Charles II begins his reign'.* So wrote the curate at Castor, although it was not actually the case. The 30th January 1649 was the day King Charles I was executed - the day England became a republic under Cromwell and his Parliament. The curate was showing his own political sympathies and continued to annotate records with the year of King Charles II's reign throughout the period of the republican Commonwealth. This showed some courage, especially when one recalls that the Rector of Castor, Bishop John Towers, had already been imprisoned under Cromwell's orders for High Treason and died in the Tower of London.

Later, more details are included, and records of marriages came to contain not just the name, age and condition of the bride and groom, but also their address, and the name and occupation of their fathers, as well as the names of the witnesses. Similarly, baptism records include not only the name of the child, but its parents' names, addresses and occupations.

In addition to the Registers, we also have extracts of the old manor court and abbey records covering the routine administration of the church and manors. For example, in 1295 a fine was levied on John de Assfortheby, the Rector of Castor, for taking hunting dogs into the royal forest without warrant [1]. We know from John Hales' lecture he was by no means the last hunting parson! In a letter of 1308, Abbot Godfrey wrote to John, Bishop of Lincoln, requesting him to institute William of Melton, chaplain, to the church of Castor, to which the Abbot had right of presentation [2]

Parish Officers' Local Records

In the year 1999, while clearing out the vestry at Castor, an old candle box was found, containing records primarily to do with the Poor Law, Resettlement Orders and Bastardy Orders, going back to 1714. These not only provide information for people researching family trees, but also a valuable social record of life in those days. They have been transcribed and indexed. The originals have been placed in the care of NCRO, but copies are kept in the Parish Archives.

Settlement Examinations
Settlement Examinations provide a great deal of information for historians and family tree researchers. Here is an extract from one example: *'On 17 July 1794 William Brown of Castor, cordwainer was examined. He was born at Castor. When he was about 13 years old his father let him to Thomas Bate of Castor, a farmer for 1 year. ...The next year he served Mr Pauling of Castor, farmer... after serving Tho Gibbins at Nunton in the parish of Maxey for one whole year, he went again to Eye... he was then bound apprentice to James Hanger, cordwainer in the parish of Castor...he has never gained any legal settlement since. He has a wife Elizabeth, a daughter Elizabeth aged 11, a son Samuel aged 9, a daughter Frances aged 4, and a daughter Rachel aged 1 year. Signed by JPs Rev Christopher Hodgson (Rector of Marholm and Curate of Castor), John Weddred Clerks, William Brown made his mark.'*

Bastardy Orders
It is quite clear that in agrarian societies bastardy was not so much a moral issue but an economic one. If an unmarried mother had a child, their upkeep became the responsibility of the parish. In order to reduce costs, the local court would attempt to establish the name of the father of the child based on an allegation by the mother. The alleged father was questioned on oath (and to be fair, it seems they readily came clean). A

Fig 26c. Sam Brown, born 1835 died 1925, farm bailiff and churchwarden at Sutton; what changes he must have seen.

court order would then be made for maintenance. These records can be useful for people researching their ancestry. Until recently it was not permitted to put the name of the father of an illegitimate child on birth or baptism records, even if he wished it. The Bastardy Orders can go some way towards remedying such a genealogical dead-end.

Footmen at Milton seem to be in court more frequently than some to answer such allegations (maybe it was their smart uniform that attracted the girls). But the records show that such activity was spread across all social classes, and before the respectable times of the late Victorian period, it was not a matter of shame so much as a

Fig 26d. Carlo Hill (father of Reg Hill) at rest while ploughing on Castor Heights c1935.

fact of life. For example, the Filliation Order made in the case of Anne Hallam (having admitted on examination the name of the father) 20 April 1822 reads as follows:

'Anne Hallam was delivered of a female bastard child at the house of William Hill in Castor on 15 Feb 1822, which child is living & chargeable on the parish of Castor. The JPs, the Rev William Strong & the Rev Christopher Hodgson (Rector of Marholm and Curate of Castor) adjudged John Gascoigne, a married man, servant man of Milton in the parish of Castor to be the father. They ordered him to pay 10s for the relief of the child up to the date of the order, 2s for the keeping of the said child as long as the child is chargeable to the parish, £2 to the Churchwardens and Overseers of the Poor of Castor for expenses incident to the birth, and 11s costs.'

The village doctor was just as human. 'On 12 July 1834, Susannah, wife of Thomas Barr, late Susannah Fitzjohn, was delivered of a male bastard child on 10 Jul 1819, chargeable to the parish'. The JPs adjudged 'Thomas Edward Baker, surgeon, to be the father'. He had to pay the Churchwardens 14s 6d for relief to date, 8s costs, and 2s a week for upkeep of the child'. The system dealt with people without fear or favour it seems; footmen, farmers, squires, labourers and doctors, clergy and churchwardens. The Abbot of Peterborough had previously to issue a public apology for the number of women he had entertained at his Brig-mill in Castor parish. On 26 February 1791, Thomas Bate (from a well-established farming family in the village, as were the Wrights and Serjeants) was 'bound over in the sum of £40, before William Walgrave, Churchwarden of Castor, and Robert Wright, Overseer of the Poor', after Mary Sewell claimed that Mr Bate was the father of her son. The court case did not seem to affect Mr Thomas Bate's standing in the community.

Other Local Court Records

One of the oldest court records found in the collection was a settlement certificate for 'William Jackson and his wife Florence of Alesworth' dated 18 Oct 1714. This was signed by 'Wm Tomson Churchwarden, Willm Setchell Overseer of the Poor and JPs W Fitzwilliam and T Fitzwilliam' – presumably of Milton. The records also include Indentures for Children as Pauper Apprentices. This was to ensure that orphans and paupers' children learnt a trade and were able to support themselves as adults. Here is an example from 30 November 1744:

'Francis Procter, a poor child of Castor apprenticed to Athanasius Goodwin, miller of Castor, to serve until full age of 21 years, instructing in trade and occupation of a miller.' This would have been at Castor Mill, which still exists. It not only tells us the name of the miller, but also those of other dignitaries in the parish. It was signed by William Bate and John Wright, Churchwardens of Castor, and also by JPs Henry Dove (a descendant of Thomas Dove of Upton, Bishop and Rector of Castor, whose son William was Lord of the Manor of Upton) and Wm Ash, with witnesses Danl Popplewell (Popple is an old Castor name) and John

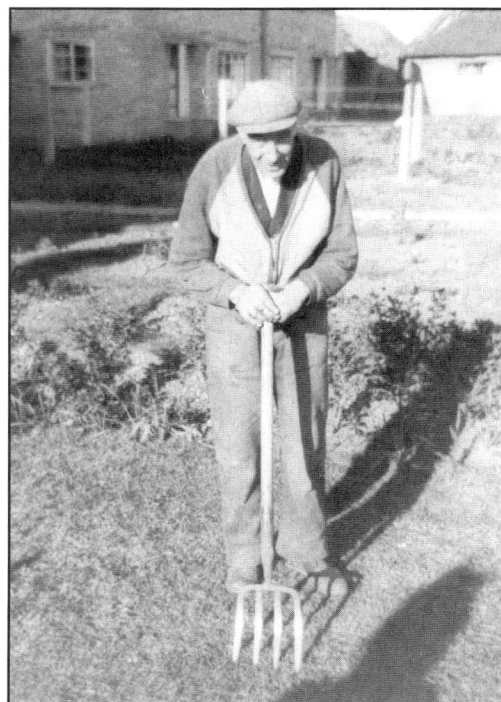

Fig 26e. Fred Hornsby, uncle of Lyn Bell, in his garden at Upton - the last man in our parishes to work a horse-drawn plough.

Fig 26f. 'A fine old gentleman' Len Sharpe, farmer and churchwarden, whose family have farmed here for centuries.

Fig 26g. Three winsome village girls outside 12 High Street Castor c1933: l-r Vera Gross née Hammond, Hazel Marsh nee Mann, Margaret Sharpe née Bell. The old lady second from the left is' Grannie' (Elizabeth) Bell who was born in the 1860s.

Fig 26h. Vic Griffin with a Taylor's Transport lorry, before he set up on his own. The Griffins are an old village family.

Dunston. On another indenture, the witness is a *John Wyldebore* as JP - one of the oldest Castor names. Betsy Wyldebore of Ailsworth who died in September 2003 was the widow of the last Wyldbore still living in the village.

Returns and Other Records

Population Returns and Censuses

The populations for Castor, Ailsworth, Sutton and Upton are at Appendix 14. The figures show us how the villages remained remarkably static over the years. For example, in 1672 Upton's population was 58. It was at its largest in 1831 at 122, and today is 67. Castor and Ailsworth achieved their largest population in 1851 (772 and 381); by 1951 they were down to 546 and 248, only starting to rise again with the building of new houses in the late 1960s. Throughout the 19th century, Sutton's population remained fairly static, being 122 in 1831, and approximately the same today (It was 125 in 1451!). In 1801 the Government ordered all parish clergy to provide a breakdown of the numbers of births, marriages and deaths in each parish by gender for the whole of the 18th century. There is still a copy of that return in the parish records. (Appendix 15). From 1841, the Government ordered a census of the whole population by parish, the names of every individual and their age, address and occupation. This has carried on at ten-yearly intervals ever since, the only gap being in 1941 because of the war. An analysis of the 1881 census for Castor and Ailsworth is at Appendix 21.

Muster Rolls and Militia Rolls

The Muster Rolls give us the names of able bodied men in a village, and the weapons available for call-up in an emergency. They were forerunners to the later Militia Lists. They give some indication of the wealth of a parish, as well as the names of some of the male inhabitants. In 1536, Castor had to provide *'two archers Robert Curtes and Thomas Marshall, and four bylmen'* (a bill-hook was a farm tool, basically a curved knife on a long pole), *'Henry Mosse, William Barnewell, John Wilson and Will Tyte, and to provide a horse and harness for one man'*. Upton only had to provide three 'bilmen', and a harness. The complete roll for 1536 is at Appendix 8.

The Militia Lists give us much more information than the Muster Rolls. They include the names and occupations of all able-bodied males between the ages of 18 and 45 in the villages, as well as the names of the Parish Constables, who were responsible for compiling the lists. They also include comments, such as marital status, number of dependant children, and sometimes personal details; for example, in the 1762 list for Marholm, John Pacey, a victualer, was noted as *'very full shouldered'* and John Read in the Sutton list as *'a cupper* (cooper), *lame'*. We also learn from this list that John Stimson, maternal grandfather of John Clare, the poet, was a town shepherd in Castor. (Clare's mother was born in Castor.) The complete lists for the villages are at Appendices 9-13.

Tithe Rolls

The Tithe Rolls give us the names of all those eligible to pay tithes. The 1844 roll lists about 120 householders in Castor and Ailsworth, many of whom still have descendants in the village today for example Boyall, Coulson, Darby, Gibbons, Hornsby, Harris, Jakes, Kingston, Longfoot, Mossendew, Newborn, Popple, Sismey, Sharpe, Wildbore, and Winsworth. The 1847 Tithe Register includes the names of householders, whether tenant or landlord, and a description of the property. Extracts are at Appendices 16 and 17.

Inscriptions

The oldest inscription is that of 17th April 1124, recording the dedication of the rebuilt church at Castor, but the oldest inscription referring to a specific person is the 13th century gravestone of Roger de la Hide at Marholm. This was originally inside the chancel but was later moved outside to the North of the tower. Other old memorials include those of the Fitzwilliam family at Marholm church, the Dove family at Upton and the Hopkinsons in Sutton. The oldest named internal memorial at Castor church is that of Guilfridus Hawkins, priest, died 1672. Grave-stone inscriptions and memorials were unusual for most people until the 18th century. One of the more curious early inscriptions is in the North West corner of the Lady Chapel at Castor which reads: *'Here lyeth the Body of William Newman whose days on earth was but a span. Upon ye 15 Day of May His Body ny ws laid in Clay. In the Year of Our Lord 1695. This you may read that are alive.'* Gravestones give not only dates and names of those commemorated, but often much other information about several generations of families and their relationships.

Fig 26i. Two Upton Teddy Boys, Tony Ladds and Barry Hornsby.

Other Published Works and the Parish Archives

Some published works contain valuable records about our villages: *Reminiscences of Mr John Hales* (1883); the Revd Kennet Gibson's History – *The Antonine Itinerary* (1769). Gibson was Rector of Marholm, and at the same time the parish priest for Castor, Sutton and Upton; The Revd W Sweeting's *History of Peterborough Churches* (1868); *The Victoria County History for Northamptonshire of 1901* (VCH); Arthur Mee's *The King's England – Northamptonshire* (1945); and more recently Pevsner's series on *The Buildings of England (Beds, Hunts and Peterborough)* (1968) and the Historic Buildings Listings. For those pursuing further historical research Gunton's *History of the Church in Peterborough*, (1686) and transcripts of ancient chronicles all give valuable information about our villages and their people. These include *The Peterborough Chronicle* by Hugh Candidus (12th century), *The White Book of Peterborough* (13th and early 14th century), and the Journals of the Northamptonshire Records Society. See also the 18th and 19th century Gazetteers and Trade Directories, as well as The Parliamentary Commissioners Survey of the Manor of Castor in 1649, and Mr Landen's Survey of 1765, both of which give detailed descriptions of manor properties in the villages, their inhabitants and land holdings, as do the Tithe Rolls. Copies of all these documents and references are in the Parish Archives, as are many others too, including recent interviews with farming families, reminiscences by those born or raised in the villages, and many records of World War II servicemen, as well as a record of all the men on the war memorial at Castor. The purpose of this chapter is merely to give an idea of the thousands of records kept in the parishes which refer to tens of thousands of people through the centuries.

Fig 26j. Mary Neal, who came here as a Land Army girl, worked at Home Farm Castor for the Longfoots and married into the Neal family of Marholm. She was the Castor and Ailsworth post-lady in the 1980s.

William Burke

Notes

1. *The White Book of Peterborough,* ed Sandra Raban, Northants Record Soc 2001, p 78
   (1295-6) '*Memorandum from the rolls of the Exchequer concerning a fine levied on John de Assfortheby for taking hunting dogs into the royal forest without warrant, which the abbot falsely claimed under terms of his own liberty…Et quia idem attornatus prius dixerat quod debitum predictum levari posset et idem Johannes clericus ets et beneficiates in ecclesia de Castr' et plura habet bona ecclesiastica ibidem de quibus debitum etc…'*
2. *The White Book of Peterborough,* ed Sandra Raban, Northants Record Soc 2001, p 228
   (1308) '*Letter from Abbot Godfrey and the convent to John, Bishop of Lincoln, requesting him to institute William of Melton, chaplain, to the church of Castor, to which the abbey has right of presentation and which is vacant de jure.*
   Presentatio domini Willemi de Melton' ad ecclesiam de Castre etc…'. Comment: This did not actually happen until 1314!

Fig 26k. The christening of Sam Burton at Upton Church 2003. Sam has both sets of grandparents and one set of great-grandparents all living in Upton within 100 yards of each other. l-r back: Stan and Ann Cunnington (great-grandparents), Mrs Burton (great-grandmother); middle: the four grandparents David and Ellie Burton and Sandra and Alan Marshal; front Robert Burton and Michelle Marshall (parents and Sam).

Fig 26n. John Truss, Bill Harris, Jim Harris, c1920.

Fig 26l. Banner Party Patronal Mass 2002; l-r: Amber Grys (candle), Linda Drury, Angela Hudson-Peacock, Chris Remnant, Joyce Clarke, Tasmin Brown (in front), Monica Pollard, Jenny Hammond, Adam Brown (candle), Grace Gibbs, Alison Brown, Audrey Boyman, Alice Castle (in front), Chris Brown, Eric Jinks (cross), Edmund Burke, Rector.

Fig 26o. In the 'Dickies' (paddock behind the Old Smithy) l-r: Flossie Coulson (daughter of farm foreman), Wilf Mossendew (son of stonemason), Jim Harris (farmer's son), Henry Gibbons (son of neighbour), Evelyn Mossendew (sister of Wilf) c1924/5.

Fig 26m. A parade in Castor during World War I.

Fig 26p. Shire and foal in field behind the Old Smithy 1920s.

Chapter 27
Military

Village People of Two World Wars – For King and Country

This chapter is about the people from Castor and Ailsworth who fought in the First and Second World Wars. It charts those who joined up and where possible their Regiments and any war decorations they received. The first part of the chapter concerns the men who served in the First World War, a list of their names, followed by information about all those remembered on the War Memorial. The second part includes many anecdotes and personal memories from ex-service men and women from both villages who served in the Second World War, followed by the names listed on the War Memorial and information about their service lives. The next part of the chapter is about the involvement of the Home Guard in protecting the villages during the Second World War and memories from some of those people who served in the Home Guard. In the final part reference is made to the Women's Land Army, the Ex-servicemen's club and about children evacuated to the villages.

The First World War

At the outbreak of World War I, on August 4th 1914, some men from Castor and Ailsworth were already regular servicemen and many more soon joined Kitchener's Army, looking on it as an adventure, which was to be over by Christmas. Most began their Army careers in the New Northamptonshire regiment, but were often transferred to other battalions. By September over 30 men had joined up and on the eve of their departure for Northampton, along with their parents, were entertained at a dinner in the Fitzwilliam School. Canon Hulbert held daily services of intercessions in the parish church and nursing classes were also set up. A Ladies' Committee was formed with weekly working parties being held at the Rectory, to produce garments, such as socks, which were sent out to the troops.

By September 1914 Private George Neville (1st Northamptonshire) had already been wounded and was invalided home for a short while after a bullet grazed his leg. He had been under fire for four days in the battle of Mons and was with his regiment in Louvain shortly before the town was entered and burnt by the Germans. He told of the many German atrocities but was *"anxious to get back to the front"*.

In November a recruiting meeting was held in Ailsworth Chapel, '*when practically the whole of the village was present. The Longthorpe Boy Scouts Bugle band marched through the villages to the Chapel. Many speeches were heard, Lady Buxton's was very well received as her husband was in the Navy. At the end of the meeting recruits were invited to come forward but none responded, however several men from Castor and Ailsworth had previously volunteered and been rejected because of slight physical disabilities.*'

By January 1915 at least 40 men from Castor and Ailsworth were serving in the forces, two were officers in the Navy, the remainder being non-commissioned officers and privates in the Army. In May 1915 Private J Hobbs (6th Enniskillen Dragoons) was invalided from the front suffering as a result of frostbite. He was among the first of the troops to go out and was in the trenches on and off for five months. The 2nd East Anglian Brigade was stationed in Castor and often held military concerts for the villagers in the grounds of the Rectory. The Red Cross Committee was busy raising funds, which were used to buy sheets, slippers and operating stockings for the Kensington War Hospital supply depot. From June to September 1915 2,280 eggs were collected in the villages for the National Egg Collection. Money was raised so that every soldier from the villages received a parcel valued at five shillings, which also contained a Christmas card from friends and mittens knitted by pupils from the school.

As the war continued many families had more than one son serving in the forces. By March 1916 Mr and Mrs John Jakes ('*a most respected and esteemed family*') had three sons at the front, Reginald (Queen's Royal West Surreys), Percy (6th Northamptonshire) and Arthur (2nd Northamptonshire). '*The family has set a splendid example to the rest of the village and neighbourhood.*' In July 1916 it was reported that '*Private Reginald Jakes had been severely wounded in the head and it is feared that he will lose the sight of both eyes. He is in hospital at Chelsea, London*'. The following poem appeared in the Peterborough Advertiser dated November 4th 1916, which is thought to be about Reginald Jakes.

Blind!

From Castor Hill, a youth went forth to fight
His country's battle o'er in Northern France,
Leaving home, his mother and his promised wife;
He saw the path of honour lying clear before him.
And so he went down to the Devil's caldron.

Through the battle of the Marne he came unscathed,
Ypres was passed with wondrous lack of wounds;
Then on the Somme, a fateful, bursting shell
Shattered his eyes, and left him poor indeed.
Two weary months in hospital, and then
The doctor's verdict cut all hope away;
Henceforth, for him, must be for-ever night.
And yet, the promised bride must have her say:

Nobly she played her part - the wedding bells must ring,
And she would be his light, his love, his day.
They wandered through sweet woodland glades together,
And nature, pitying, smiled upon him:
The flowers, the bees, the birds, and all the wild things
Called: 'Welcome! welcome! see, we dearly love you,
Because we know you're blind!'

A golden cord the maid wove round her boy,
And to the altar tenderly she led him,
Guiding his steps - a wife and mother blended:
Then, raising hands with heartfelt gratitude,
She thanked the God Who spared her hero's life.

High on the hill stands the shrine of the mighty Nazarene,
Crucified near two thousand years ago,
He lives to-day; deathless, immortal.
The young bride, gazing on the sacred edifice,
Took her darling by the hand and led him to the light.
W.A.C.

In December 1916 Percy Jakes was promoted to Acting Quartermaster Sergeant of his regiment and received the Military Medal for '*bravery on the battlefield.*' Later his brothers Ernest (Queen's Royal West Surreys) and Alexander joined up.

Mrs and the late Mr Harry Gibbons had three sons who enlisted in the 6th Northamptonshire at the outbreak of war, Ernest, John and Albert. In 1916 all three brothers were wounded, but returned to the front. Before the war they helped their mother in her business as a threshing machinist. Albert received a parchment certificate from the Major-General Commander of the 18th Division, British Expeditionary Force in France for '*conspicuous bravery and devotion to duty while on active service*', a copy of which was sent to his wife. He received the Military Medal which is now in the Northants Regimental Museum.

Mr and Mrs J Hornsby's three sons enlisted, Harold was at the front almost from the outbreak of war, George was badly wounded during the retreat from Mons and Ernest served in the Near East. All three were to survive the war.

Lance Corporal A. F. Hill, son of Mr William Hill, was awarded the Military Medal in 1916. The following letter was received: '*I have read with great pleasure the report of your Regimental Commander and Brigade Commander regarding your gallant conduct and devotion to duty in the field on 26th and 27th September 1916, at the capture of Thiepval.*'

The following list contains all those men from Castor and Ailsworth who enlisted during the First World War. Through the passage of time some names will inevitably have been omitted.

Barnes Charles	Gibbons Ernest	Hornsby George	Sharpe Cecil
Bass Cecil	Gibbons Ernest William	Hornsby Harold	Sharpe George
Buxton Bernard	Gibbons John	Hornsby Walter	Smith Arthur
Carter Frank	Goulding Frank	Jakes Alexander	Smith Percy
Chapman John	Griffin John	Jakes Arthur	Sismey Albert
Cliffe Arthur	Hankins George	Jakes Ernest	Sismey Percy
Cooke Alec	Harman Bernard	Jakes George	Taylor Charles
Coulson	Harman George	Jakes John Chapman	Taylor Walter
Coulson Walter	Hill Albert	Jakes Percy	Tranter Albert
Cox James	Hill Arthur	Jakes Reginald	Wadd
Cox William	Hill Cardinal	Longfoot H	Ward Amos
Crane (Arthur) Daniel	Hill Frank	Mossendew Albert	Ward James
Crane David	Hill Fred	Neville George	Warr Horace
Darby Charles	Hill Frederick	Newborn Percy	Warr William
Dudley George	Hill Walter	Nix Herbert	Wilkinson William
Ellis William	Hilton Leonard	Pank Hack Walter	Wood Frank
Garfield Samuel	Hobbs J	Parker Robert	Woodward Alfred
Gibbons Albert	Hornsby Ernest	Pearson Sidney	

War Memorial – 1914-1918

The following information details the service records of those men who gave their lives during the Great War.

Fig 27a.1. William Cox died 8 November 1914

Fig 27a.2. Daniel (Arthur) Crane died 16 February 1916

Fig 27a.3. Percy George Newborn died 23 May 1916

Fig 27a.4. Albert Hill died 1 July 1916

1914
Private William Cox 12060
William, a native of Ailsworth was the first person from either village to be killed. He had two brothers who worked in Sutton and his father, a horse keeper, lived at Upton Lodge. William first worked for Mr Amos Brown, of York Cottage, Sutton, later getting a job in Thorney from where he enlisted. William was in the 2nd Battalion, Grenadier Guards and died on November 8th 1914, during the First Battle of Ypres, when a small British Expeditionary Force succeeded in securing the town, pushing the German forces back to the Passchendale Ridge. His name is listed on the Menin Gate Memorial at Ypres, Belgium.

1916
Private Daniel Crane 13899
Daniel (6th Battalion, Northamptonshire Regiment) was the first person from Castor to lose his life. He was the son of Mr and Mrs H Crane and was married with three children to whom he wrote almost daily. He worked for Mr Gordon Smith and was very well liked by all his workmates. Daniel was seriously wounded in the back while on active service in France, on January 28th. He was taken to the casualty clearing station, where he remained for nine days before being taken to the base hospital at Rouen where he died peacefully on February 16th 1916, aged 31. He was laid to rest, with full military honours, on February 17th in St. Ewen's cemetery, Rouen. The Chaplain spoke of *'Pte Crane's great courage and fortitude'* and said that *'he was a great favourite with his comrades at the Front.'*

Fig 27a.5. John W Chapman died 2 October 1916

Fig 27a 6. Arthur Jakes died 7 March 1917

Fig 27a.7. Samuel Garfield died 23 July 1917

Fig 27a.8. Ernest Stuart Jakes died 1 August 1917

Sergeant Percy George Newborn 679

Percy was the son of William and Eliza Newborn, of Castor. He joined the Mayor of Leeds' Battalion at the outbreak of war and served in Egypt for some time. He had been in France only a few weeks with the 15th Battalion, West Yorkshire Regiment and in charge of a machine gun section, when he was killed in action on May 23rd 1916, aged 31. He was buried in Gezaincourt Communal Cemetery Extension, in Somme.

Private Albert Hill 13202

Albert was the son of James and Elizabeth Hill of Castor and served in the 6th Battalion, Northamptonshire Regiment. *'He was always a very steady and promising young fellow and a great favourite with his brother soldiers.'* He was killed in France on July 1st 1916, aged 24. He was laid to rest in Dantzig Alley British Cemetery, Mametz, Somme. There is a memorial stone for him in Castor churchyard.

Private John W Chapman 6127

John was the only son of William and Mary Chapman and lived at the Ferry, Milton Park. He worked for many years in the stables at Milton and *'was a general favourite both with Mr and Mrs Fitzwilliam and his fellow workers. He was of a most bright and amiable disposition and always had a pleasant smile and cheery word for everyone.'* He served with the 23rd Battalion, London Regiment and was reported missing for some time before his parents received official confirmation that he had been killed in action on October 2nd 1916, aged 24. He was buried in Warlencourt British Cemetery, Pas de Calais, France and has a memorial stone in Castor churchyard.

1917

Private William Edward Warr 23532

William was the son of James and Elizabeth Warr of Ailsworth and served with the 2nd Battalion, Northamptonshire Regiment. His brother Horace joined the Royal Buckinghamshire Hussars, but was invalided home. William was anxious to take part in the Great War and one of his Officers spoke very highly of him. He was killed in action on March 4th 1917, aged 30, and his name appears on the Thiepval Memorial, Somme. A memorial service was held at St Kyneburgha's church on Sunday, March 18th, attended by a large number of friends. A memorial stone can be found in Castor churchyard.

Lance Corporal Arthur Jakes 16173

Arthur was one of five sons of John and Hannah Jakes of Church Hill, Castor, who joined up during the Great War. Before joining the army Arthur was a regular member of the Church choir, a communicant and attended the Rectory Bible class. He was a keen Scout and for many years worked hard training others. Arthur was in the 2nd Battalion, Northamptonshire Regiment and was seriously wounded in action on March 4th. He died in hospital in France on March 7th 1917, aged 22 and was laid to rest in Bray Military Cemetery, Somme. A memorial service for Arthur was held on Sunday, March 18th and a memorial stone for him can be found in Castor churchyard. On the War Memorial Arthur is listed as Corporal, but as Lance Corporal on information from the War Graves Commission.

Private Walter Leonard Hornsby 201715

Leonard was the son of Thomas and Sarah Hornsby of Castor. He was in the 1st/4th Battalion, Suffolk Regiment and was killed instantly while in France, on April 23rd 1917, aged 30. He was buried in the Cojeul British Cemetery, St. Martin-Sur-Cojeul and has a memorial stone in Castor churchyard.

Gunner Samuel Garfield 86585

Samuel was the second son of Mrs Jane Garfield and the late Samuel Garfield of Ailsworth and before the war was employed at the Elastic Factory in Peterborough. He served with the 190th Siege Battery, Royal Garrison Artillery and was killed in action in France, only a week after being discharged from hospital. He died on July 23rd 1917, aged 22 and was buried in the Achiet-le-Grand Communal Cemetery Extension, Pas de Calais. There is a stone in memory of Samuel in Castor churchyard where his age is given as 24.

Lance Corporal Ernest Stuart Jakes G/6907

Ernest was the youngest son of John and Hannah Jakes. '*He was a very quiet and amiable lad, and was very much liked by all who knew him.*' He belonged to the old Castor Scout troop and voluntarily joined the 11th Battalion, the Queen's (Royal West Surrey Regiment). He had been wounded some months before he was killed in action on the Somme, only 20 years old and just five months after his brother Arthur. His name appears on the Menin Gate memorial, Ypres. On his memorial stone in Castor churchyard his death is recorded as July 31st, but the Commonwealth War Graves Commission have the date as August 1st 1917.

Gunner Charles William Victor Taylor 146339

Charles joined the 112th Brigade, Royal Field Artillery and was the eldest son of Richard and Miriam Taylor of Malting House, Maffit Road, Ailsworth. After leaving school he was telegraph boy at Castor Post Office and was later promoted to Peterborough Post Office. He volunteered for the army on May 10th, 1916 and was stationed in the North of England and Scotland for part of that time. He was a staunch churchgoer, a member of Castor church choir and the Rectory Bible class. He also belonged to the Castor Scouts and was an agent for the Peterborough Standard for several years. He was killed on August 2nd 1917, aged 20 and was buried in the Menin Road South Cemetery, Ypres. A memorial service was held at Castor church where there is a stone in his memory in the churchyard.

1918

Rifleman William Ebden Wilkinson R/34448

William was the second son of Caroline and the late William Wilkinson of Allotment Lane, Castor, brother to Len, Charlotte, Mary and Edith. He was a member of Castor church choir and Brass Band, beginning his working life as a forester on the Fitzwilliam Estate. Later he became second forester to Lord Lansdowne, at Bowood House, Wiltshire and it was from here, in 1914, that he joined the 2nd Battalion King's Royal Rifle Corps. In June 1916 he was wounded at Ypres and took part in the Battle of the Dunes, when he had to swim a river to save his own life. He had been on active service in France for nearly two years before he was killed by a shell, which fell at his feet, while he was standing at the door of his dug-out on June 7th 1918. He was buried aged 36, on June 8th in the Cambrin Military Cemetery, Pas de Calais and there is a memorial stone in Castor churchyard.

Private Arthur Henry Cliffe 49531

Arthur, the eldest son of Jacob and Annie Cliffe of Splash Lane, Castor joined the 6th Battalion Northamptonshire Regiment. He had only been in France a few months before he was killed on August 6th 1918. His name appears on the Pozieres Memorial, Somme. The Commonwealth War Graves Commission gives his age as 18, but the local newspaper states that he was 19 years old.

Corporal Ernest William Gibbons 850888

Ernest was the youngest son of John and Emma Gibbons, 52 Peterborough Road, Castor and joined the Peterborough Battery at the start of the war. He was in the Royal Field Artillery drafted first to India and later to Mesopotamia. His

Fig 27a.9. Charles William Victor Taylor died 2 August 1917

Fig 27a.10. Ernest William Gibbons died 15 October 1918

Fig 27a.11. William Ellis died 22 January 1919

Fig 27a.12. Reginald Jakes died 2 July 1920

first job was as a footman at Milton Hall, later working in Chertsey, from where he joined up. His parents received a letter from his former employer expressing sympathy and saying *'what a good, faithful and trustworthy servant and friend she had lost.'* Ernest died of pneumonia, in Mesopotamia, on October 15th 1918, aged 29 and was buried in Basra War Cemetery, Iraq. A memorial service was held in Castor church and there is a memorial stone in the churchyard.

Private William Ellis 57239

William was the son of Charlotte and the late William Ellis of Ailsworth. He joined the 25th Balloon Section RAF in 1916 and was posted to France in 1917. He died suddenly on January 22nd 1919 aged 38 and is buried in St. Andre Communal Cemetery, Nord. There is a memorial stone in Castor churchyard. His mother received the following letter. *'Dear Mrs Ellis, I very much regret to confirm the sad news of the death of your son, No. 57239, Pte W. Ellis, RAF, 25th Kite Balloon Section. He was admitted two days ago suffering from heart affection. He was not complaining at all and seemed very well and comfortable. This afternoon he complained of a sharp pain at his heart. The Medical Officer saw him and ordered some remedies, but he grew rapidly worse and died quite suddenly at 6pm. He did not suffer long and died very peacefully. He left no message and spoke of no one at home. His personal effects will be sent to you later through the War Office. With very sincere sympathy, Yours truly, H.M. Ferguson. Sister.'*

Private Reginald Jakes

Reginald was the third son of John and Hannah Jakes to die as a result of the Great War. Before joining up he was a coachman for the Fitzwilliam family. He was in the Queen's Royal West Surrey Regiment and after being badly wounded in the head was sent back to a hospital in Chelsea. He never regained his sight and was invalided out of the army in 1917, going to St. Dunstans where he learned to read Braille. Later he married Mildred, but sadly died on July 2nd 1920, aged 36, having picked up an infection in his eye sockets and was laid to rest in Castor churchyard. Three months later their son, also Reginald, was born.

The Second World War

Ex-Servicemen from the village

Many are the experiences recalled by the village born ex-servicemen of Castor and Ailsworth who returned safely having served their country during the Second World War. Nineteen men who joined up have very clear memories of that period in their lives, fighting battles in far off places, most of which were known previously only as names on the school atlas.

Fig 27b.1. Jack Atkins   *Fig 27b.2. Ernest Gibbons*   *Fig 27b.3. Reg Burton*   *Fig 27b.4. Harold Burton*

Royal Air Force

Ted Hilton

Ted is the son of Len and Mary Rolfe-Hilton late of Main Street, Ailsworth. A year after joining up he was posted to India – sailing from Gourock, Scotland – on the troopship *Maloja*. Destination was Bombay – then on to St Thomas Mount, Madras, and later to Colombo, Ceylon. Here a unit of the RAF Regiment was formed – which Ted did not take to, so he promptly volunteered for aircrew. He was posted to Palestine for training to join his future crew, flying Wellington Bombers. His next destination was Italy, bombing enemy territory in the North, Austria and Yugoslavia. Leaving the Squadron in 1945 he was sent to Cornwall prior to being demobbed. Ted finished his Service as Flight Sergeant Air Gunner – with a total flying time of 344 hours. He comments on how much he enjoyed his time in the RAF and getting the opportunity to see places and people he would not have done otherwise.

Jack Smith

Jack, born 1920, is the son of Percy and Fanny Smith – formerly of Peterborough Road, Castor. After basic training he was attached to the RAF Police. His first posting was to Iceland, later returning to the UK having volunteered for aircrew. Flying Halifax Bombers, raids were made on major German cities, mine laying in the Oslo fiords, bombing Doodlebug sites along the French coast and the German held positions at Caen. After the D-Day landings, jerry cans filled with petrol were flown by the plane load, endless times, into Belgium. Jack was demobbed at Oxford in 1946. He married Kath in 1944 living on Martin's Farm at Haddon. She died in 1966 and 9 years later, he married Alice. They still live in the same house at Haddon and in the year 2000, celebrated their Silver Wedding.

Royal Navy

Reg Burton

Reg, second son of William and Maud Burton – late of Stocks Hill, Castor – was the only village born lad to serve in the Royal Navy. He joined at Chatham Barracks, took a trade test, and became an Engine Room Artificer. Three months later he boarded a troopship to Malta and joined HMS *Brixham* – a minesweeper. They carried out duties in the Mediterranean, notably clearing a minefield in the Straits of Boniface and took part in a landing operation close to Toulon. Eighteen months later Reg was transferred to a Cruiser – HMS *Delhi* – which was attacked in the harbour of Split, Yugoslavia by German E-boats. He also served on ships in the Far East – visiting Australia, New Zealand and Hong Kong. He remained with the *Delhi* until it returned to the UK, on the day peace was declared in 1945. Reg was finally demobbed in December 1946.

Army

Harold Burton

Harold, brother of Reg, served with the Irish Guards, stationed in the Home Counties, and witnessed intensive bombing raids in those areas. He was in the D-Day landings, wounded in heavy fighting at Caen, and sent home to a military hospital at Stoke-on-Trent where he met and married Nellie. Their home was in Ailsworth – later moving to the former home of his parents in Castor. They had two daughters – Dorothy and Rosalind.

Ernest Gibbons

Ernie – son of Jack and Ethel – of Peterborough Road Castor – now Carlton Court – was in the Reserves and called up in 1939 immediately war was declared – aged 20. He served with the Suffolk Regiment. His first posting was to Bury St. Edmunds, and later to Chipping Camden, where the battalion was merged with the Green Howards. Ernie was at Dunkirk on D-Day and after 48 hours leave, was refitted with equipment and uniform and sent to the Middle East. In June 1942 he was taken prisoner by Rommel and the Africa Corps, and sent to three different camps, finally arriving in Stalag 4F in Germany. Most of the time he worked in gangs relaying and repairing railways and similar jobs. He was demobbed in 1946 – working on Wade's Farm, Horrell's Dairies, and later Peterborough City Council until his retirement. In 1952 he married Phyllis (nee Cooper). They made their home in the City where they still live.

Harry Gibbons

Harry – son of Tom and Harriet Gibbons – late of High Street, Castor, joined up in 1940 and was posted to Special Z3 Radar Unit and later to 103 Infantry Brigade Workshops as Staff Sergeant. A week after D-Day the regiment landed in Normandy pushing on to Belgium and Holland helping to get the lads out of Arnhem. From here he was sent to Germany and based at barracks in Munster Lager, on the edge of Luneberg Heath, later moving to Berlin. Harry was demobbed in 1946 and rejoined his old firm of Rota-Electric, becoming Manager of a branch at Colchester and later, Company Director. He retired in 1979 to care for his wife (formerly Millie Oliver of Ailsworth) who later died. They had one son. Marrying again, he now lives in Torquay.

Fig 27b.5. Harry Gibbons	*Fig 27b.6. Arthur Gibbons*	*Fig 27b.7. Richard Griffin*	*Fig 27b.8. Percy Griffin*

Arthur Gibbons

Arthur was the son of Albert and Ellen Gibbons – late of Peterborough Road, Castor. He joined the Army in 1939 serving with the Royal Engineers. He was stationed at Dover when the Battle of Britain was at its height but later sent to join the Eighth Army in the desert of North Africa and onwards into Italy with his unit. After the D-Day landings in France the regiment stayed in France until peace was declared. Arthur was always thankful to have returned safely – relatively unscathed – having been in many different theatres of war, all of which were in the thick of military action. A widower, he cared for his elderly mother until she died, afterwards living alone. He was a regular churchgoer, a faithful member of the Ex-Servicemen's Club and a good friend to many.

Richard Griffin

Dick – son of Jack and Ethel Griffin, late of Main Street, Ailsworth – joined the Royal Suffolk Regiment in 1942. A year later he was posted to Turkey and then to North Africa. In March 1944 he was sent to Tunis and in the June to Algiers. At the end of the same month he was in Italy and then on to Naples, followed by a posting to Gibraltar. Here he was promoted to Lance Corporal, serving with the Military Police until demob in 1946. On joining up Dick married Joan (nee Spademan from Woodnewton) in St. Mary's Church there. After demob he returned to work with Milton Estates, living in a Milton cottage in Church Hill, Castor, later moving to Great Gidding as Estate Manager. Here they brought up a family of seven girls, losing one of them – Elizabeth – while still a schoolgirl. Dick died in 1984 aged 64 years.

Percy Griffin

Percy – brother of Dick – was called up in the Army and was posted to Bury St Edmunds with the 49th Division Royal Engineers. After intensive training the regiment moved all over the British Isles, bridge building, mine laying, etc. He was in the invasion of France with the Second Front landing at Arromanches on D-Day plus One, pushing on through Belgium and Holland into Germany. During this time he was wounded twice, spending long periods in hospital. When demobbed at Aldershot he returned to Ailsworth in 1947. Two years later he married Ella (nee Wingrove) from Wansford where they made their home. They had two children – Jill and David.

Reginald Hill

Reg was the second son of the late Cardinal and Hilda Hill, Main Street, Ailsworth. He was called up in 1942, sent for training to Kimmel Park, North Wales, serving with the Royal Artillery Driver Training Unit. First posting was to the Orkneys – via Aberdeen. Here he joined the 19th Light Ack-Ack Regiment with their Bofor guns on Scapa Flow. Three weeks later – on Christmas Day – he was posted to the Isle of Wight stationed on Osborne Beach. One specific duty there was to give gun protection to the nearby Sanders Row Mosquito Aircraft Factory. Leaving the IOW, Reg was sent to London where gun emplacements were set up on the top of Canada House, Hyde Park and Green Park, their HQ being in Deans Yard, Westminster Abbey. From London the regiment moved to Haltwhistle, Northumberland for a tough six week battle course. From there his next move was to Doddington Park followed by another to Holyhead – Dawlish in Devon – and on to firing camp at Aberaeron, South Wales, for battle training with guns, and then to Pembroke. The Regiment left here for Sudbury and later returned to Wales. Next posting was to the Isle of Grain – giving gun protection to the Shell fuel tanks and the airfield at Biggin Hill. In June 1944 Reg was in the second wave of the D-Day landings at Arromanches, then on to Caen. Crossing the Seine at Elbeuf, a lot of German prisoners were taken, and again at Rouen, before moving off to Dieppe and Cassel. On again to the Ardennes and the Battle of the Bulge and on to Mardic, near Dunkirk, where sadly Reg saw his best friend killed as they were laying telephone cables at Lune Plage. At the end of the War he was with the Army of Occupation in Schleswig Holstein, Eckenford, near the Danish border. His next job was transporting women and children refugees to Ludenscheid by road and later as guard on a boat taking them to Oslo. Demob was in 1947 and in 1948 Reg married Phyllis (nee Brawn) from Moulton, Northampton, having

Fig 27b.9. Ted Hilton

Fig 27b.10. Reg Hill

Fig 27b.11. Alec Jakes

Fig 27b.12. Pam Jakes

Fig 27b.13. Peggy Nugent

Fig 27b.14. Bill Pearson

Fig 27b.15. Geoff Sharpe

Fig 27b.16. Jack Smith

met her when she was working as a Land Girl for farmer Walter Longfoot. Their family home was Thorolds Way where Reg lived until his death in 2003. They had three children – Margaret, Colin and Wendy.

Edward Mortimer
Ted was the stepson of Alexander and son of Olivia Jakes – late of High Street, Castor. He joined the Grenadier Guards serving from 1939-1945. He was in the battle zone of North Apulco, Italy and Casino. After demob he worked as a charge hand on the railway. He later married a Castor girl – Adele (nee Longfoot) and lived in Peterborough. They had one daughter, Rachael.

Alexander Jakes
Alec was the son of Alexander and Olivia Jakes – formerly of High Street, Castor. He volunteered for the Army in 1942 and was called up in February 1943, aged 19, joining the Royal Marine Commandos. Following training at Lympstone in Devon he was posted to Malta, spending some time in hospital having contracted sandfly fever. On recovery Alec was sent to a gun site in Sicily before returning home for training in preparation for the D-Day landings. Stationed in France, Belgium and Holland, he volunteered to join an advanced Commando Course based in Scotland where he received his 'Green Beret', having acquired the necessary qualifications. From there he was sent to India with the 42nd Marine Commandos to prepare for the relief of Singapore. This was aborted with the dropping of the Atom Bomb and the unit sent, as part of the army of occupation, to Hong Kong instead. On demob in 1946 he married Pamela (nee Baker) and they had two daughters – Lynne and Anne. In 1953 they moved into one of the newly built council houses in Thorolds Way where Alec lived until he died in 2003. He was widowed in 1999.

Fig 27b.17. Ted Woodward

William Pearson
William is the son of the late Sidney and Charlotte Pearson formerly of Long Row, Peterborough Road, Castor. Bill joined the Northamptonshire Regiment in 1944 and after six weeks training at Britannia Barracks in Norwich was posted to the Old Barracks at Northampton. Later he received special training on mortar guns at Shrewsbury and also attended the Army Driving School, gaining experience on motor bikes, Bren gun carriers and tanks. After being posted in Sloane Square London for a time, the order was given for the unit to move to an aerodrome at Cambridge. Here they were crowded into converted Lancaster Bombers for a ten hour flight to the Middle East, finally arriving in Tripoli, North Africa. The next stop was Egypt being stationed near the Pyramids. On then to India, refuelling in Iraq and landing in Karachi on Bill's 21st Birthday. A train journey across India – involving ten days and nights travelling – took them to Fort St. George Barracks, Madras. He was later transferred to the Manchester Regiment, India Command, moving on to Poona and Bangaban. Intensive training was done on Vickers machine guns ready to attack the Japanese on the many islands they occupied. Thankfully for the troops, the Atom Bomb was dropped and ended the war. Bill's journey home began aboard the ship *Strathnavenda* leaving Bombay and sailing via the Suez Canal, the Mediterranean and the Bay of Biscay. After 16 days at sea they docked at Southampton. Bill was demobbed at Chester, arriving home in the early evening just in time to enjoy his mother's rabbit pie! In July 1947 he married Joan (nee Sismey) from Ailsworth at St Kyneburgha's Church. They had two sons – John and Richard. Sadly Richard died whilst still a schoolboy in 1969. In retirement they live in Silvester Road, Castor.

Geoffrey Sharpe
Geoff joined up in 1944 serving in the Royal Electrical and Mechanical, Engineers (REME). His first posting was to Fort St. George – second to Royal Arsenal, London, and third to Derby. Here he became a 3rd Class Armourer. His

fourth move was to Tunbridge Wells and later back to Derby as 2nd Class Armourer, a job which entailed inspecting Arms for the whole of Southern England. From here Geoff was posted to Portland as Armourer to the Royal Artillery and promoted Sergeant before being demobbed in 1947. In 1945 he married Nora (nee Pearson). They lived in Sharpe's Yard, Ailsworth before moving to Glinton where they still live today. Geoff and Nora had two children – Patrick and Mary Anne.

Edward Woodward

Ted was the son of Alfred and Louise Woodward, late of Stocks Hill, Castor. Ted enlisted in 1944 as Apprentice Fitter with the Kings Royal Rifle Corps and was stationed in York. In 1945 he was posted to Tripoli and Palestine, then with the British Army on the Rhine until June 1952, returning home in August of that year. Following a period of leave and on the expiration of his service with the KRRC of almost 9 years, he was sent to the Army Reserves at Exeter – serving 3 years making a total of 12 in all. After demob Ted drove for Frank Taylor's Transport at Ailsworth, Read's Removals, Peterborough, and later for John Taylor's Haulage. In 1971 he married Nancy living in Peterborough Road, Castor until his death in 1994 aged 67 years.

Auxiliary Territorial Service.

Pamela Jakes (nee Baker)

Pam was the daughter of Charlie Baker, late of High Street, Castor, who was groom to Major Pelham of 'The Cedars'. She joined up in 1942 – in the Royal Signals – stationed at Beverley Barracks in Yorkshire. She was demobbed in 1945 and married Alec Jakes in 1946. They had two daughters – Lynne and Anne. Pam died in April 1999.

Peggy Nugent (nee Garfield)

Peggy is the daughter of Grace and Ernest Garfield – late of Main Street, Ailsworth. She joined up in January 1940, enlisted at Durham and was finally posted to the Duke of Wellington Barracks at Halifax. At the end of 1940 the Regiment were moved to barracks at Barnard Castle. The ATS became Number 6 Training Centre for permanent staff to train 1000 conscripted girls for their initial training – kitting them out with uniforms, doing drill, gas lectures, PT and route marches. In 1943 the centre closed and Peggy was posted to an Ack-Ack battery at Chesterton and later to Cambridge. She took her discharge in 1944 for family reasons and said – although wartime was so terrible – she had truly enjoyed her life in the forces.

Behind these memories is a record of just how far the men of Castor and Ailsworth travelled during those war years. Until now – beyond their own families – and often not then, little was known as to where they actually went; the European Continent, North Africa, Gibraltar, India, Egypt, Hong Kong, all the many theatres of war – the daily hazards encountered on land, sea and in the air. In retrospect, reaching and returning from such far flung destinations seems nothing short of a miracle. One common denominator among them all stands out, the great comradeship and friendship forged between themselves and their fellow men – something treasured – never to be forgotten.

War Memorial – 1939-1945

The following information details the service records of those men and women who gave their lives during the Second World War.

Fig 27c.1. Frederick William Thompson died 29 April 1943

Fig 27c.2. Maisie Rachel Hill died 23 October 1943

Fig 27c.3. Anthony Arthur Whittome died 23 April 1944

Fig 27c.4. Cyril Kingston died 14 August 1944

1943

Corporal Frederick William Thompson 5889128

Frederick was the son of George and Isabella Thompson, from East Jarrow and was born on January 7th 1916. He was married to Elizabeth and lived in Maffit Road, Ailsworth. Before leaving Jarrow Frederick was employed by Bilton Nurseries Ltd, moving to Castor to work for Goodyer's. He joined up with the 5th Battalion Northamptonshire Regiment at the outbreak of war and was killed on April 28th 1943, aged 27. His son Raymond was just one year old. He was buried in Thibar Seminary War Cemetery in Tunisia.

Gunner Thomas William Gibson 914882.

Thomas was the son of Laura and the late Thomas Gibson and husband of Alison. He came to live in Castor when his widowed mother married Charles Baker, who was groom for Major Pelham. His mother was the district nurse in Castor and the family lived in High Street. Thomas served as a Gunner in the Royal Artillery and was later attached to the 18th Indian Division. He was posted to Singapore and taken prisoner by the Japanese, later working on the Burma-Thailand railway. He died while in Japanese hands on June 30th 1943, aged 29 and was buried in Kanchanaburi War Cemetery, Thailand. A memorial stone can be found in Castor churchyard.

Private Maisie Rachel Hill W/113748.

Maisie was the only daughter of Cardinal and Hilda Hill, 49, Main Street, Ailsworth, sister to Stanley, Reginald and David. On leaving school Maisie first worked at Elton Hall and then in the accounts department of the London Brick Company before joining the ATS at the age of 17. She worked in the accounts department at Chilwell Barracks, Nottingham. Maisie was killed on October 23rd 1943 while travelling home from Nottingham on unexpected leave, she was 19 years old. Maisie was given a lift in a jeep at Wittering, by a sergeant in the American army, two minutes later it struck a stationary lorry and Maisie was killed instantly. Her brother, Reg, who was in the army, was given compassionate leave. The funeral service took place on October 27th, local residents saying they had never seen the church so full. Her coffin was draped with the Union Jack and she was buried in Castor churchyard where there were seventy-four wreaths. In the ATS Maisie was shortly to receive her first stripe as Lance Corporal. Her commanding officer said *'She was a remarkably fine girl, not only physically, but in her general character. She was of an amiable disposition, possessing many sterling qualities and she made friends wherever she went.'*

1944

Flight Sergeant Anthony Arthur Whittome 1324622

Tony was the eldest son of Arthur and Hilda Whittome of Thorney, living with his wife Freda, at Three Chimneys, Castor. He was a keen rugby player winning his King's School colours and also playing for Peterborough Town. He was in the Royal Air Force Volunteer Reserve and spent a year in Canada training for his wings. He had been in the RAF for about two and a half years when he was killed, while on active service, on April 23rd 1944, aged 29. His funeral service took place at Thorney Abbey, where he is buried in the churchyard. His coffin was draped with the Union Jack and was carried by six members of the RAF. On his gravestone it states that he was killed by enemy action while on duty.

Private William Cyril Kingston 14601247

William, known as Cyril, was the second son of Ethel and the late William Kingston and was born in Church Hill, Castor. He had two brothers and five sisters and attended the Fitzwilliam School in Castor. Later he went to Peterborough Technical School, learning the trade of carpenter/joiner. He sang in the church choir and was a talented sportsman, playing football for Castor and Ailsworth and the Post Office Engineers and was also vice captain of Milton Park cricket club. During the Second World War he was first called up to help repair damage to airfields and then for active service on May 6th 1943. He was with the 2nd Battalion, Royal Warwickshire Regiment before he was killed on August 14th 1944, aged 36. He was buried in Bayeux War Cemetery, Calvados and there is a memorial stone in Castor churchyard. A memorial service was held at Castor church when a pair of standard oak candlesticks for the altar, given by his mother, were consecrated.

1945

Aircraftman Jack Atkins 1185673

Jack was the son of Irene Atkins and Bob Gibbons of Stocks Hill, Castor and was married with one daughter, Ann. Before their marriage his wife worked for Major Pelham and Jack was a driver for Taylor Brothers, starting work there in 1937. He served with the Royal Air Force Volunteer Reserve in North Africa, where he contracted severe dysentery. He was invalided out of the RAF in 1943 and died in Roehampton hospital on October 8th 1945, aged 25. He is buried in St Kyneburgha's churchyard, his headstone was erected by the War Graves Commission.

Fig 27c.5. Jack Atkins died 8 October 1945

Castor and Ailsworth Home Guard

Castor and Ailsworth Home Guard formed a company from the two villages, comprising 34 men. Those exempt from National Service, being in reserved occupations, were officially 'called up'. The remainder were volunteers, some above the age limit and others retired. Most of them took the job as a duty to be done, and others more seriously, becoming well trained in many aspects of Army life.

Castor and Ailsworth were officially a Platoon of the Old Soke of Peterborough – 2nd Battalion of the Northants. Regiment, the 1st Battalion was Peterborough City, whose Chief was Colonel Crowden. Officers in charge of Castor and Ailsworth were Colonel Mellows (Chief), Major Percival (Company Commander), Platoon Chief (Mr. Shorrocks) and his Deputy (Mr. John Cooper) who, with his wife, owned the Grocery Shop and Post Office at No. 12 Church Hill. Len Hilton – Ailsworth – was Sergeant Major – strict and very smart on parade! Sergeants were Sam Catmull – village blacksmith and Harry Brewin. The youngest in the Platoon was 16 year old William Pearson (Bill) who joined in 1941. His father had been a Sergeant in the regular Army and also in the Great War. Being very keen, Bill trained hard, and was soon promoted to Sergeant and so became the youngest in the Battalion as well as the Platoon.

The old Village Hall was used for twice weekly training when a regular Army Sergeant attended, giving advice on guns, drill etc. Occasionally, weekends were spent at Uffington Park, near Stamford, training with the Regulars. Once platoon sergeants were given a month's training in an army camp at Dorking in Surrey.

Every fourth night Castor and Ailsworth Platoon took a turn guarding the Bridge over the Nene at Wansford – considered a vital link for keeping lorry convoys moving along the A1. The men slept in a room at the Cross Key's pub in Wansford, changing guard every two hours through the night. One man was stationed at each end of the Bridge, his first duty being to inspect beneath the arches checking if explosives had been placed there during the day. Both men had to challenge any person approaching the bridge during the night. When their shift finished it was home and get ready for the day's work ahead.

Other members of the platoon would be on night time duty - according to the rota - stationed at the top of Loves Hill. Two would also be based in the garden of 'Thornfields' - the home at that time of the Paten family. It overlooked the whole of the Nene Valley from Castor Mill to Milton Ferry. An observation post was concerned with the possibility of German parachutists landing in the area, having followed the line of the river! Should this have happened, an instant alert was to be sent to the HQ in Peterborough heralding an imminent invasion. Following advice received from the Ministry of Defence, nationwide, all kinds of obstructions were to be placed at entrances and exits to every village in case of invasion by German tanks. Ancient farm carts, old tractors, ploughs etc, long past their sell-by date, stood in readiness – again on the brow of Loves Hill, Marholm Road Hill, Chapel Lane Hill, Ailsworth, Station Road and the A47 to Wansford.

Faced with the might of an enemy tank corps the 'push-over' would have been swift to say the least!

Several 'Dads' Army' anecdotes have become part of village folk law. One relates to 18 year old Reg Hill who reported late for duty one night when he should have been on 'parachute' parade on Loves Hill. Reg's day job was long distance lorry

Fig 27d. Castor and Ailsworth Home Guard 1943.

driving for Frank Taylor's Haulage at Ailsworth. Having been on the road to and from Glasgow (top speed 28 m.p.h.) for almost 2 ½ days he arrived home at midnight. Falling into a deep sleep he failed to hear his alarm – set for 2am – and the start of Home Guard shift. Rousing an hour later he noted the time with dismay. Flinging on his clothes he grabbed his bike and pedalled furiously to his post. Reporting to his Officer (forced to cover for him), before he could apologise, he was greeted by *"What time do you call this Hill?"* Short of sleep, tempers flared and Reg was put on a charge of insubordination. The court martial took place at the HQ in the Royal Oak yard before all the 'top brass' from Peterborough and resulted in a Dishonourable Discharge! On reflection, Reg thought he had come off lightly and quickly repaired to the Royal Oak bar for a pint and a peaceful game of dominoes! Later he received a demand to hand in all uniform and equipment at once, which was done with tongue in cheek, as he had only ever been issued with an armband! Three weeks later he was in the Royal Artillery, serving for five years, having been at Dunkirk, France and Germany.

Bill Pearson recalls a particular training night when the Platoon Officer ordered him to take some men down to Castor Mill with their rifles at the ready. The Home Guard was acting on a report received that six Italian prisoners had escaped and were making their way along the riverside. Instructions were to hide in the Mill House garden and endeavour to capture them unharmed. Hidden in the bushes – and not feeling too brave – the silence of the dark night was suddenly shattered by geese, shut up in a nearby shed, setting up an unholy racket, adding to the tension! At the same time the men were alerted by a group of men making their way along the path in their direction. Bill gave the order to jump as they moved nearer and they were quickly downed with some force! Immediately an officer spoke, shone a torch and said *"Well done lads"*. It was a set-up test – passed with flying colours. Luckily no one was 'trigger-happy' that night.

Tom Cooke, younger son of the late Alec Cooke, was 11 years old in 1939. He recalls a Home Guard incident. At the time manoeuvres, in and around the villages, were a source of much curiosity and amusement for the youngsters. They followed them everywhere possible! Lots of training practice took place in the area of the Winfrey's wood on the brow of Loves Hill. Tom remembers the local army cadets acting as the enemy there once and when the Home Guard arrived no cadets could be seen. They had earlier shinned up the overhanging trees and a bombardment took place, thunder flashes raining down from above as the men marched along! No doubt havoc ensued – good entertainment for the spectators – with the 'enemy' proclaiming victory.

In hindsight, the Home Guard did a very worthwhile job, giving a sense of security within the community. There were many young mothers and widows alone in their homes, with men-folk in the forces, and most of them abroad. The threat of invasion was very real at the time and although many people did not always take them seriously, the rules – as laid down by the Wartime Government – were carried out in a well regulated manner of which they could be justifiably proud.

(With acknowledgement to Tom Cook, Reg Hill and Bill Pearson for their help and factual details) Joan Marriott. June 2003.

The Castor and Ailsworth Home Guard Company

Officers:
Major Percival
(Company Commander)
Mr. Shorrocks
(Platoon Chief)
Mr John Cooper
(Second To Chief)
Sergeant Major: Len Hilton

Sergeants:
Sam Catmull
(Village Blacksmith)
Bill Pearson
Harry Brewin
(Builder)

Members:
Bill Ashton
(Gardener for Winfrey Family)
Bill Bailey
Harry Coulson
(Carpenter)
Bill Capon
Jack Darby
(Farmer)
George Darby
(Farmer)
Gilbert Gibbons
(Threshing Machinist)
Reg Hill
(Haulage Driver)
Stan Hill
(Farm Hand)
Arthur Hill
John Harker
Harry Hill
Herbert Jackson

Eric Kingston
Jock Mclish
Doug Oliver
(Dairyman)
Bert Pell
Jack Pell
Bob Peppercorn
Sid Sharpe
Cecil Taylor
(Haulage)
Ernie Venters
Alf Wade
(Farmer)
Tom Woods
Charlie Ward
Ernie Ward
(Tailor and Postman)
Albert Wyldbore
(Railway Man)

Women's Land Army.

During the Second World War many 'girls' came to Castor and Ailsworth to work on the farms replacing the men who were serving with the Armed Forces. They helped with the ploughing, harvesting and with milking the cows. Some of these girls married local men and made their homes here including, Phyllis Hill, Joyce Herbert, Ellen Longfoot, Mary Neal and Kathleen Oliver.

Ailsworth and District Ex-Servicemen's Club.

The idea of starting a club for ex-servicemen was first thought of in 1935 after the Armistice parade by S Pearson, A Woodward and T Smith. They had marched to church behind men who had never served in the Forces and being serving soldiers decided to do something about it. A meeting was held at the Barley Mow on February 8th 1936, which was very well attended. '*There were many heated discussions and a vote was taken. Eleven voted for the club, five voted against and many dare not vote at all.*' The first meeting was held on February 22nd 1936 when officers were elected. Chairman S Pearson, Vice Chairman A Jakes, Hon Secretary G Hudson, Association Secretary C Bass, Hon Treasurer G Sharpe. The Committee consisted of L Hilton, W Fitzjohn, A Woodward, G Dudley, F Goulding and G Wilkinson. The rules of the club were, '*Members going against the rules of the club be dismissed, all medals to be worn on parade and that any member being a teetotaller need not break his promise.*' Over the years annual dinners and concerts were held until the club was disbanded in 1976.

Evacuees.

At the beginning of the Second World War a group of children, from Islington, North London, along with two teachers, were evacuated to the villages. On arrival they went to the village hall where local residents took the children to live with them. Irene and Betty Mann along with Julia and Irene Foster went to live at the shop on Castor Green, with Mrs Fox and her daughter Hilda. Irene and Betty's brother, David, went to live with the village policeman, Mr Trundle. The evacuees went to school in the Reading Room, while village children went to the Fitzwilliam School. Irene (Woodward) and Betty (Want) were here for just over a year, but eventually came back and married local men, still living here today.

Joan Mary Marriott (née Nix)

Including myself, I am at least the fourth generation on both sides of my family to have been born in Castor and lived here all our lives. My parents were Herbert and Mabel Nix (nee Jakes). They lived in the East cottage of three, converted from Castor's first Rectory (built in 1631), where I was born in 1923. I was married in 1949 and in 1957 moved with my husband and two year old son Geoff, to Thorold's Way Castor and in July that year our daughter Julie was born. I was widowed in 1988 and am presently living at the same address.

Margaret Rachel Brown (née Hill)

The Hill family has lived in Castor and Ailsworth for many generations and I was born in Main Street Ailsworth. My mother (Phyllis) and father (Reg) were married in 1948 after my mother came to work in Castor in the Women's Land Army. I have been involved with the church choir, the Sunday School, the Brownies, Girl Guides, Tennis Club and Bellringers, being Tower Captain at one time. I teach in the Peterborough area and live in Castor with my husband, Colin, and our sons Simon and Christopher.

Acknowledgements

Commonwealth War Graves Commission
Lincoln, Rutland and Stamford Mercury
Peterborough Express
Peterborough and Hunts Advecrtiser
Peterborough Standard

Mr and Mrs Harry Coulson
Lorna Fisher
Elizabeth French
Ernie Gibbons
Brian Goode
Gwen Heighton
Reginald Hill
Ces and Wally Lunn
Raymond Thompson
Irene Woodward

Chapter 28
Reminiscences – People and Places

There was once a musical, later a film, called 'Brigadoon', about a mythical Scottish Highland village where its entire community awoke for one day every hundred years. Talking about this one day to Joan Marriott, we tried to imagine what it would be like if all those folk our generation knew, quite suddenly appeared. Those characters had helped to shape our lives and had played, in some cases, no small part in helping to make our friendly community what it is today.

Old Homes

Lottie Kent (97) and her sister Phyllis Sawyer aged (92) were two of eight children of George and Sarah Dudley. They well remember their early home in one of the cottages at the end of Splash Lane. Today these cottages are two dwellings; however my generation will remember them as four. How did they cope? Folk in those days were resourceful. Mr Dudley bought and erected a wooden hut on the opposite side of the lane for the boys to sleep in. At that time their father, George, was horse keeper for Mr Darby. Four out of five of the Dudley boys had worked on one or other of the local farms. Mrs Dudley with her two sisters, Mrs Kate Neal and Mrs Louie Woodward were members of the Pywell family who have lived in this community for many generations.

Sheila Crane (Favell) is now the only resident of Sutton to have been born there. Although she moved to her present home soon after she married Gordon, she was born at a house called 'Cross Keys', reputedly a pub, which stood at the junction of Manor Road and Nene Way. At that time, Sheila says, most of the village and the surrounding land belonged to Mrs Graeme of Sutton Grange who was quite a stern lady, being a daughter of Canon Hopkinson. Washing to be hung out on Mondays only and no bonfires to be lit the church side of the railway bridge! Incidentally, Canon Hopkinson gave St Kyneburgha's church their bier which was used for the first time at the funeral of the Rev Merton, a vicar of Sutton.

Fig 28a. Four cottages in Splash Lane, now converted to two. As well as Mr and Mrs Dudley bringing up their large family in one, Mr and Mrs Jack Cliffe raised their family in one of the small cottages. Jack was the local chimney sweep.

Margaret Brown (Hill) was born in a thatched cottage in Main Street, Ailesworth, opposite Maffit Road. That early home was demolished, and Margaret moved from there in 1953 when she was four. The cottage had no running water; therefore all water had to be carried from a tap in a neighbour's yard. The toilet, which was shared, was, as in most cases at the bottom of the garden. Eliza Ward, an elderly lady, lived in part of the cottage, and Margaret recalls, mulled her glass of shandy by putting a hot poker in it. On Monday, 29th September, 1958, a fire destroyed a barn next to Margaret's former home. Later the barn, the thatched cottages and four brick cottages next to the Chapel were demolished for redevelopment. Damage to the cottage, which was also part-occupied

Fig 28b. An X marks Margaret Brown's (Hill) first home in Main Street Ailesworth, the part nearer the barn was the home of Mr and Mrs Manning. Iris their eldest daughter still lives in the village.

by the Manning family, could have been much greater but for the efforts of Claude Sharpe (Margaret Sharpe's late husband) and Doug Parker, who used fire extinguishers to douse the thatch. Mrs Lily French (Thompson) was commended by the fire crew for closing the barn doors, thus cutting off the oxygen supply.

I live in the house in which I was born 69 years ago, 15 Stocks Hill, formerly 4 Cow Lane. My parents were the first to move into the new house on Good Friday, 1929; Mr and Mrs Frank Hammond moved into theirs on Easter Monday. Vera Gross (Hammond) was also one of the first children to live in the new houses at 1 Cow Lane. Her father, Frank was the goalkeeper for Castor and Ailesworth football club for many seasons. His trade was that of a crane driver at Baker Perkins. Vera too, worked there, in the offices. After the war she married Johnny who left his native Poland during the German occupation. They then moved as newly-weds to Thorolds Way soon after those houses were built.

At first there was no electricity or water in the new Cow Lane houses. I well remember the pump, near our front garden, which did on occasions run dry. This meant carrying buckets from Mr Salmon's pump at the bottom of Church Hill. Mr Harry Coulson whose parents, too, were the first occupants in the new houses remembers Joe Samworth, (who gave his name to Samworth Close) as being the only man he has seen using a pair of yokes on his shoulders to carry his buckets of water from the same pump. Joe lived where Peter and Norma White currently live.

At 6 Cow Lane, a Mr and Mrs Woodward and their family resided. Mrs Woodward was also a Pywell. I do remember that our back door house keys were interchangeable. Mr Alf Woodward and Mr Sid Pearson were the only veterans who were 'Old Contemptibles'. (The small expeditionary force in 1914-15 which held that thin red line at Mons was dubbed by the Kaiser '*That contemptible little army*'). Mr and Mrs Pearson and family were residents of the Long Row, a row of terraced cottages on Peterborough Road, Castor, which were demolished in 1976.

Peter Jarvis was born at Belsize Farm (Castor Parish) in 1936, the third and youngest son of William (Arthur) and Faith. Arthur, his father George, and his three brothers, all worked at Belsize. In 1947, Arthur took over the tenancy of Home Farm whilst brother Jack carried on working Belsize. The two other brothers left farming. On Arthur's death in 1967, Peter and his brothers, Toby and Stanley, took over the running of Home Farm. Belsize continues to be farmed by Jack's son, Dick, and grandson, Trevor.

Rene Foster (Goode) - my sister - was born in the Police House in Peterborough Road where Steve Walker and his family currently live. Our grandfather was the village policeman. In 1922 the Peterborough Road house was a very modern dwelling into which our grandparents had moved from the former Police House situated at the corner of Port Lane. In those days this corner house, presently owned by David Rager, was then two dwellings, the other being lived in by a Mr and Mrs Ted Kingston. Ted had a small nursery garden. Sadly, in the 1950s, Mrs Kingston died in a fire that destroyed part of the house. Later Rene moved to one of the cottages on Castor Green where Liz Freeman now lives.

Here again, this was two dwellings, where our sister Jean (Trundle) was born. The other cottage was lived in by Mr and Mrs Charlie George and Charlie's brother Arthur (Jessop). Rene's first home after her marriage to Arthur (Jim) Foster was part of Manor Farm House in Castor, the part nearest to the Green. The previous occupants had been two Italian prisoners of war. When our father was stripping off old wallpaper he came across old newspapers which had been used as lining paper, some dating from the late 1800s. The loo, down the garden, was a vault type which pre-dates the bucket. It had two adult seats and a child's. Almost everyone had an outside bucket privy, often at the bottom of the garden; the buckets were emptied weekly by a Mr Hill and Mr Gibbons. It was an unenviable task but a very necessary one. Later a Mr Baker took over. The purpose-built horse-drawn cart was called the night-soil cart. I have seen a photograph of one in Norfolk where it was called the Honey Pot.

Fig 28c. Mrs Lizzie Ward, with her sister Gertie Taylor cleaned the church, and for many years trimmed and filled 36 paraffin lamps until 1936, when the church was lit by electricity.

Peggy Stapleton (Lunn) was brought up by her grandparents who lived at the far end of Main Street, Ailesworth, opposite the link road to the Helpston Road. When Mr and Mrs Lunn first came to the area they lived in a cottage on Castor Green. Mr Lunn worked at the Limes Farm for Dick Longfoot, later working for Harry Longfoot at Green Farm. After leaving farm work Peggy's grandfather worked as a roadman. His beat was from Ailesworth to Wansford. At that time there were at least two roadmen for each village. Paths and gutters were swept every week, grass verges surrounding the villages were cut with scythes and the drains were cleared. George Ward and Charlie George were roadmen in Castor.

However when a funeral took place at which Mr Will Cooke was the undertaker, George was required to pump the church organ bellows, and Charlie would be a pall bearer.

Raynor Snart was born in a small stone cottage at the far end of Main Street, Ailesworth, the home of Mr and Mrs Wilf Dudley and their daughter Greta, who were friends of Raynor's parents. The cottage, now with its white walls, is next to Mrs Chanell's house; 69 years ago it was the last dwelling on that side of the street. Until he was four years old, Raynor lived near the Lunn's house which was at right angles to the road. This house was demolished forty or so years ago. The Snart family then moved to one of the newly-built Council houses in Helpston Road. At that time the area was the epicentre for schoolboys. As well as the Snarts there were the Winsworths, Browns and the Jinks boys, a formidable group indeed. Soon after Raynor and Sandra married, they moved to their present home in Benhams Close (now in their 32nd year there) after Mr and Mrs Bob Baxter moved from there to Wakefield. The Baxters had lived in Benhams Close for eighteen months or so; their previous home had been a cottage in the Long Row.

Martin Sharpe is the only Ailesworth resident over 65 years of age still to live in the house in which he was born. His house is the last in the row before Maffit Road. Martin was one of eleven children of Sid and Olive Sharpe; they too, in turn, were members of large families. After leaving Glinton Village College, Martin worked for Mr Harry Longfoot at Green Farm, later working as a trainee baker for Chapman's in Old Fletton, cycling there each day. At 18 he was called up for National Service, joining the Army Catering Corps, serving in Korea, and travelling to Japan, Hong Kong, Singapore, Aden, Suez, Gibraltar and Germany. On return to Civvy Street he joined the Co-op Dairy as a rounds-man staying for 32 years. Sid drove a steam roller working on roads and airfields mainly in the Lincoln area, cycling from there to Ailesworth on Friday afternoons after a week's work and returning on

Fig 28d. Will and Annie Cooke. At their house, 'The Lilac's', now Mick and Elaine O'Boyle's home. Will was the Undertaker, Carpenter, Castor Parish Clerk, Bandsman, Fireman and for almost 70 years church Organist at Waternewton. Mrs Cooke was Headmistress of the Castor Infants School for 41 years, Hon Secretary for the Castor PCC and for many years the local correspondent for the Peterborough Standard and the Peterborough Citizen and Advertiser. They both died in 1956. Will on 29th November aged 91 and Annie six days later at the age of 92.

Fig 28e. Mrs Hill with daughter Dawn, outside the little cottage which stood where the Gibson's house stands. Later Mr and Mrs Ernie Hill and Dawn moved to the Long Row.

Fig 28f. The same cottage in Peterborough Road. This was where Don, David and Frank King lived with their parents. Mr Sid King then worked for Mr Fletcher at Manor Farm Castor.

Fig 28g. Looking along Peterborough Road with 'Three Chimneys' in the background, at that time a Mr Baxter had a small general stores in the house. Mrs Kent and her sister Mrs Sawyer remember going there for groceries and also paraffin, for the lamps. The large tree to the left of the telegraph pole was a walnut owned by Dick Longfoot, on the site where Mr and Mrs Robert Dickens now have their home. I was with a group of London evacuees one evening when PC Maddocks 'apprehended' us scrumping walnuts.

Sunday evening. He also had a large collection of copper kettles which he had won in ploughing competitions. Mrs Sharpe did casual work on local farms, for example, potato picking, hoeing sugar beet, and harvest work.

Don and Frank King's first Castor home was a small thatched cottage which stood next door to the Police House on the site where Brian and Alison Gibson's house now stands, sharing the same building line as Ian Sheldon's house, and it possessed all the mod cons of the day - one cold water tap! Mr and Mrs King had moved there from Melton Mowbray. Sid was a farm labourer and came to work for Mr Stan Fletcher of Manor Farm, Castor. The Kings came to Castor with their three sons in 1949 when their youngest son Frank was aged one year old. He and his two brothers attended Castor Infants and the Fitzwilliam Schools before going on to Glinton Village College. Frank was aged about 14 when his father went to work for Mr Rowland Longfoot at Green Farm and moved the family into the cottage in Clay Lane next to the farmhouse. They lived there until the family moved to Silvester Road when Sid went to work for the Rural District Council. On leaving school, Don started his working career with Mr Harrison-Smith at Manor Farm, Ailesworth. David worked at the Co-op Bakery. Sadly he died aged 25, after what seemed a very minor accident on his motor cycle. Frank worked at Mr Elliott's poultry farm, opposite the Royal Oak, which was at that time a very thriving business. The brick buildings which made up the farm were once stables. More recently converted by Phil Brown, they are homes to his daughter Eugenie, son-in-law Walter and their sons Jack and Sam Howard, and his father-in-law, Douglas Gillam.

Fig 28h. The Old Smithy Castor, in the days when it was the farmhouse for the Harris family 1920s.

Anecdotes

At one time during my working life, I had the great pleasure of working with a wonderful chap by the name of Clem Barrett who came into the world in one of the thatched cottages in Church Walk at Upton. His mother sent Clem's dad, who was a gamekeeper for Mr George Fitzwilliam, to fetch the doctor from Wansford, when her time was due. Clem senior borrowed a horse for the journey and followed behind the good doctor on the return trip to Upton. However, in the darkness, the horse slipped and its rider was thrown off. Later, after young Clem was born, his father's nose was set at the kitchen table over a glass of beer.

I once asked Clem what form of transport was provided for the children from Upton and Sutton; he told me that Mr Sharpe the Baker gave them a lift in his horse-drawn cart. However, during those winters, when the snow was too deep for the horse to traverse the long climb to Upton village, the children would walk across the fields towards Ailesworth.

They would walk over the Maffit Road and down the little jetty to Main Street, here the Ailesworth gang would lie in wait, snowballs ready. Clem said, *"We had many a skirmish through the village and into Tween Towns, and on to the school; Mrs Cooke somehow managed to dry our coats around the stove."* Apparently Mr Sharpe managed to get to Sutton on most occasions unless the snow was extremely deep. Sometimes pupils from Upton and Sutton attending the Fitzwilliam School would often walk to and from school during the summer.

Clem would tell me that his childhood, and indeed beyond, was happy, living in Upton. There the boys had a club in their Village Hall which was affectionately known as the Tin Tabernacle. There the boys met for board games. The leader, whose name escapes me, also taught them to box. Forming them in a circle he would stand in the centre, close his eyes, and then throw a pair of gloves one way and the second pair in another direction. Whoever they hit had to box. All went well until a stranger came to the village. Very little was known about him. Even when he joined the club he merely sat and read his paper and said little. Boxing time came, one pair of gloves hit a particular chap and a second pair missed Clem who ducked out of the way; the gloves then hit the stranger. *"Now, I'll see what he's made of,"* thought Clem, who went on to say, *"He stood up held out his hands for someone to tie on his gloves,*

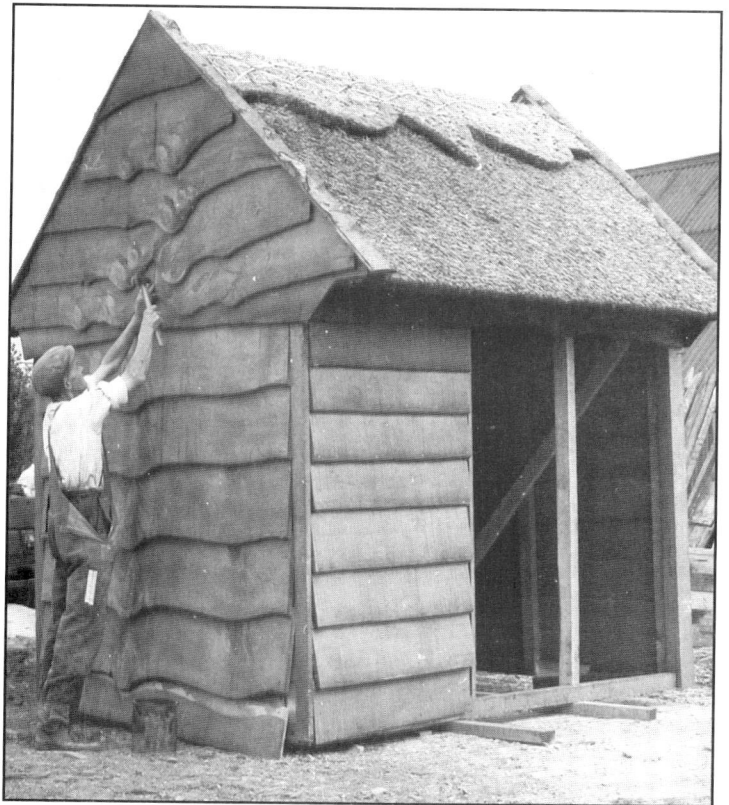

Fig 28i. My very good friend Clem Barrett. We spent so many happy hours working together at the Marholm Saw Mill. Clem would regard himself as a 'hedgerow carpenter'.

and as soon as he 'framed up' I knew this wasn't the first time he had put on a pair of boxing gloves. A short cross from the stranger sent his opponent hard against the wall with a clang." *"we all had a spar with him"* said Clem, *"but no-one landed a useful punch."* He then took off the gloves, sat down and continued to read his paper. He hadn't even removed his jacket.

As a young man and young husband and father, Clem found work at an Upton farm. It was threshing time. Clem was carrying 18-stone bags of grain to a barn. When lunch-time came, his wife, with their first child in her arms, brought his pack-up. Ernie Gibbons (threshing machinist) had Clem, his wife, plus baby son, stand on the scales that weighed the corn. The entire family did not weigh 18 stones. Years later, Clem applied for farm work in the Fens. The farmer, a huge man with a gravelly voice, barked, *"Can you carry corn?"*

"Yes," replied Clem, *"if you put it in two pound sugar bags!"*

At the time contractors were laying the sewer through our villages in the early 50s, I stopped to talk, and have a warm, at the night-watchman's brazier, at that time in Splash Lane. We were joined by Mr Dick Longfoot from the Limes Farm. As we chatted, four or five cars travelled along Peterborough Road. Dick remarked: *"When I was about 12 years old and at the Fitzwilliam School (now the Village Hall), Tom Gibbons and I were standing in the playground, when a shout went up, and all the school ran to the railings looking towards the Royal Oak. There, walking down the centre of the road was a man carrying a red flag, and several yards behind him was a chap in a motor car chugging along. That was the first car we had seen. Tom who had abundance of home spun wisdom said, 'Dick, in years to come, youngsters like us will run to these railings to see a horse and cart go by.'"*

Fig 28j. The Milton Estate's stand at the Peterborough Show at Eastfield. The photograph shows Brian Goode, Vic Winterton and Clem Barrett. The summerhouse was made at Marholm Sawmill, and thatched by Percy Pettifore, the Estate thatcher. Mr John Ward from Clare Cottage Helpston purchased it.

I was privileged to live next door to a part of the Gibbons family, Bob, his wife Rene, and their son Jim. Bob would walk down his garden path, and engage me in conversation for an hour or so at any given time, always so interesting. A lasting memory I have of Bob is prior to the loos being incorporated in the house.

On a warm sunny Sunday afternoon in July 1955, Reg and Joan Marriott took their baby son Geoff to St Kyneburgha's to be baptised. All their family and friends sat in the pews near the font. As time came and passed for the baptism and no priest materialised, Joan became a trifle concerned. After a couple of coughs and still no Rev. Adler, she looked into the vestry. There was no one there. After conferring with the family, she walked over to the Rectory (now the home of Jonathan and Jackie Cook). Joan knocked on the kitchen door. Still no response, she then walked into the garden and there was Tom, sound asleep in a hammock, his face covered by his newspaper (The People). Joan began in a soft voice, "Rector" and then louder, "Rector." At this point, the reverend gentleman lifted his head, the newspaper fell and he exclaimed, "Joan, the baptism! Come to the kitchen." There she was given a white enamel jug and instructions as to where she could find the water tap in the churchyard. Tom arrived at the church full of apologies, took the cover from the font, put the water in the brass ewer and Geoff was in due course baptised. Joan confided to me years later, "Until then I thought baptismal water came from the River Jordan."

Fig 28k. Mrs Lizzy Ward, her husband George and her sister Gertie. As well as the trio cleaning the church and lighting the stoves there, Mrs Ward cleaned the Infants school, the sisters 'hosted' the doctors' Friday surgery at their house, and delivered medicine. George, who was one of the village roadmen, also 'pumped' the church organ.

The Rev Thomas Adler was a very good cricketer and while at Selwyn, Cambridge, played for his college. Soon after arriving here in 1947, he captained the Castor and Ailesworth team. Playing away one Saturday afternoon he faced the bowling. The ball was delivered and the bowler appealed for lbw. "Not out," said umpire Mr George Jinks of Ailesworth, (Eric's father). During the tea break the Rector said, "That was a close call George." "I couldn't give you out Sir," said the umpire. "You hadn't made your 50!" (That story was related at Tom's funeral service.)

A few weeks after Mr Albert Berridge arrived in Castor as the new headmaster at the Fitzwilliam School, his cousin, Chris Fillingham, came as organist and choir master at the church. Mr Salmon, who had recently retired as headmaster, had been a disciplinarian in both school and church. Whilst Chris was very competent at his job, he was still only in the VI form at the King's School. The boys turned up for choir practice half an hour before the men and during one of these practices a certain Mrs Lizzie Ward and her sister Miss Gertie Taylor came into the church. I must explain here that Mrs Ward did not take prisoners. They approached the choir stalls, waited until we had finished the piece we were rehearsing, and then Mrs Ward said with great aplomb, "I would like you to take the mats from the nave into the churchyard so that we can beat them." Chris rather hastily said something to the effect of "We don't have the time to do that." Big mistake. Mrs Ward drew herself up to all of her five foot two and quickly replied, "Don't you be so bloody cheeky or I'll clip your ear!"

Fig 28l. Gertie carried on with the surgery in her home 51 Peterborough Road after George and her sister died, here she is with Dr John Caskey, I have no doubt she 'filled the doctor in' with the odd remedy that might have escaped him at medical school.

Needless to say, we had to drag those rather dusty mats outside. Sadly we learned last year that Chris had died. His wife sent us a painting of the church, which he had done as a young man. Mr and Mrs Ward and Gertie, lived in what is now 51 Peterborough Road. Every Friday afternoon, Dr Stein and later Dr John Caskey held a surgery there. Later the two sisters would collect any medicine that had been prescribed from the Peterborough surgery. One could collect it from their house, or for a small charge of three pence it would be delivered to your door the following morning.

During the early part of the 1940s, two families came to live in Castor - the Saunders and the extended family of Gus McNaughton. Harry

Saunders was a hairdresser at the Baker Perkins factory in Peterborough. The factory was involved with the war effort therefore it was difficult, when working certain shifts, to get a haircut, hence Harry's barber's shop. Mrs Saunders, who was Irish, was a very good amateur entertainer and was in great demand at concerts in the area. I can almost hear her singing *Paddy McGinty's Goat* and *Danny Boy* now. Their two eldest sons were in the services. Ron was in the Royal Navy and Richard in the Commandos. I think there were seven Saunders children in all. The house, now called Hanover House, had been the home of a Mr and Mrs Thompson. Then, suddenly, it was like a minor invasion when the Saunders moved in, they were a breath of fresh air!

At that time Hanover House was two dwellings. A smaller part at the far end was lived in by a Mr and Mrs Bill Hill. They had three children. One son, Frank had a son Geoff, who married Joyce Winsworth. Bill spoke rather abruptly and didn't use three words if two would do. The story goes that one night of the 31st December he turned to his wife Jane in bed and said, *"This is the last time I will speak to you this year. Goodnight Janey. Blow the candle out!"*

Gus and Lotti McNaughton had both been on the stage from an early age. After moving to the little white cottage in Church Hill (at that time almost derelict) Gus still played on the West End stage and also co-starred in films with George Formby. They were wonderful people. As children at school we would see Gus on his bike and pretend to shoot at him. In typical cowboy style he would clutch his chest and gasp, *"You've got me, you critter."* We thought it great to have our own film star in our midst. One afternoon, a whisper went around the school that there was a very large car outside the Church Hill cottage. I suppose a dozen or so boys went to investigate after school and were confronted by an ex-army Humber painted in a fawn colour. We gathered around it to get a closer look inside. At that point the owner came out and opened the doors for us. It was George Formby himself.

Gus and Lotti had two children. Betty was married to Eddie Childs. Their son, Ted, went on to be a head of a private school for boys, and daughter Mary, at one time, was a manageress at The George Hotel in Stamford. Eddie too was on the stage playing in summer shows and Dame in Pantomime. We did not meet their son Jack until after the war. Jack, who had been a POW in Japanese hands, was also to star in films. He married actress Kay Callard. Jack and Kay had three sons John, Walter and Sam Howard. Sam now lives in Canada - his mother's native country, Walter and John still live in Castor.

Where the school playing field is, there was once a thriving nursery garden owned by Mrs Eleanor Goodyer (whose husband had a bakery business in Ailesworth). With the help of her two daughters and casual help she grew salad crops, house plants and cut flowers, and made up wreaths and wedding bouquets. Her eldest daughter Win had a full time job as a cost accountant for Farrows, the canners, in Peterborough, later taken over by Colman's Mustard. This meant Win had to go to Carrow Road, Norwich, every other week to work on the accounts. However on Sunday mornings during

Fig 28m. Gus McNaughton and his grandson Ted Childs outside the white cottage on Church Hill. The whole family, who were all connected to the stage or screen were wonderful folk. Lotte, Gus's wife, would keep me enthralled for hours when she spoke about so many of the old Music Hall stars, Marie Lloyd, Rob Wilton, Sid Walker, Harry Champion and so on.

Fig 28n. The Goodyers greenhouses being demolished. The site is now the Primary school playing field.

Fig 280. Mr Dick Taylor, brother of Mrs Ward and Gertie. Dick was gardener for six Rectors, he also held various posts at the church, and was a member of the choir for over sixty years. One of his sons, Charles, was killed in the Great War.

the winter months it was Win's job to cycle from Ailesworth to the nursery to stoke up the boilers that heated the three large greenhouses. Early one snowy morning she 'saw' Mr Frederick Storey sweeping the snow from the front of his cottage (now called Spring Cottage). They exchanged pleasantries and Win went on her way. Later, whilst having her breakfast, her father came into the room and exclaimed, *"Another piece of sad news. Fred Storey has died." "When did he die?"* asked Win. *"Late last night",* Mr Goodyer replied.

The Storeys had a son, Leonard, who later became a professor of veterinary surgery in New Zealand. After his father's death Mrs Storey joined Len and his family there. She died there several years later; her cremated remains were interred in Fred's grave in Castor churchyard.

If Mr Dick Taylor had possessed a CV it might have read thus: bell-ringer, gravedigger, sexton, clock winder, choir man, bandsman, a former member of the Fire Brigade and gardener for six incumbents. At the time when Dick sang in the choir it was all male. Ron Hudson, another long standing member of the choir, told me how, at one Sunday Evensong, Canon Carlton (Rector 1922-1947) announced the psalm, walked across to Dick, had a few words with him and then left the church by the Priest's door. Choir and congregation carried on singing, but with two verses to sing Dick began to look agitated. With one to go and still no Rector he looked very worried. Then, as they began the Gloria, Canon Carlton re-emerged and returned to his place. After the service was over and the choir were back in the vestry, the Rector explained that he had had a sudden thought. He had not shut up his chickens for the night and he had heard that a fox was on the prowl. He had simply had to go and sort it out!

The Cooke family played a very important part in the life of our community. Will and Annie Cooke lived in The Lilacs, now the home of the O'Boyle's. Will was in partnership with his brother Alec. Being carpenters and undertakers, they did a great deal of work in the church. Alec and his wife Elgiva lived on Peterborough Road where the Sheldons now live; the workshop was at the end of the house. Will was organist at Water Newton church for almost 70 years, missing only three Sunday services, once through illness and twice when the meadows where flooded. At one time he was chief fireman for the local brigade, Clerk to Castor Parish Council, a bandsman and leader of a quartet dance band which was known locally as 'Will Cooke and his Thirsty Three'. Annie had been the headmistress at the Castor Infant School for 54 years. They died in 1954 within two weeks of each other.

Alec and his wife Elgiva had three children, Mary, Jack and Tom. Jack was also a carpenter, carrying on that trade on the railway and travelled on holidays extensively from Moscow, where he swam in the Volga, to St Lucia. He also took cruises on some of the famous liners. Tom - a whole chapter could be given over to Tom - was indeed a legend in his own lifetime. How could those of us who lived here during the war forget Tom's bit for the war effort? He cruised around the village collecting waste paper with a truck towed by his bike, nothing too unusual there. However Tom's bicycle had no handle bars but a very large steering wheel. Snow has always held a fascination for children. Once again Tom rose to the occasion. The Glebe field gate was left wide open and Tom's six seater toboggan was hauled up the hill, kids clambering in. Tom at the controls would come hurtling down the slope, clear the right hand gate post by a few inches enabling him to turn sharp left down Stocks Hill. (Don't try this at home - there was next to no traffic during the war years). Although I did not witness it, Tom told me his steering malfunctioned and he ploughed into Mr Mossendew's (Mick Westlake's) fence demolishing a couple of yards of paling which he had to repair. Our parents were unaware of the mortal danger we were in.

Tom sent me some of his memoirs. He was 11 years old in 1939 and remembers how it was impressed on them in school about the hardships that could be expected to come. He also comments on the rumour (rife at the time) about the non-bombing of Burghley House at any time throughout the War. It was said that Goering, Hitler's second in command, had impressed on his pilots that anyone bombing it would be court marshalled, as he intended Burghley to be his future residence. It was always understood this was the reason that no bombs were dropped in the Stamford area, in spite of RAF Wittering being a mere stone's throw away.

Another incident he recalls very clearly was a stick of eight bombs falling on a very large chicken coop beside the Upton-Sutton cross roads. Soon after dawn half the villagers set off to the bomb site to view the damage. (Needless to say the bombs were dropped in total darkness so none could anticipate the result). All that could be seen was a massive hole; not a feather or a scrap of wood could be found. The following day 'Lord Haw-Haw' was shouting over the airwaves about the total destruction of an aircraft hanger and a secret aeroplane housed in the said shed!

Fig 28p. Tom Cooke and Chris Wade at the Fitzwilliam school reunion. Who could forget Tom's bike with the lorry steering wheel, or the explosion which rocked the village and was thought by many to be the beginning of the Invasion? Chris, who originated from Village Farm, is also from farming, engineering stock, and now lives with his family at Kings Cliffe.

One day in 1942, a long convoy of American lorries was speeding through Castor towards Wansford. On the bend past the Royal Oak, two large bombs rolled off one of the vehicles and into the gutter with a loud crash. Fortunately they were not fused and posed no danger. Later a pickup truck was sent to collect the stray bombs!

Tom recalls some fisticuffs with American servicemen and a group of soldiers from the 51st Highland Division which took place outside the Royal Oak, a detrimental remark having been made about kilts. It all became very heated needing both British and American Military Police to smooth things over.

At the Fitzwilliam School reunion, one of the many recollections that were recounted was the time when, in Mr Salmon's absence from the class room, Tom climbed on the headmaster's stool and advanced the clock by 30 minutes. Mr Salmon returned to the class. At 12 noon (by the clock) there was a certain amount of shuffling of feet. Mr Salmon looked at the clock, then looked at his pocket watch and dismissed the school, all three classes. It was not until he arrived home, (where Mr and Mrs Bradshaw now live) rather too early for his lunch, that he realised he had been taken for a ride. Now why did Mr Salmon think it was Tom and admonish him? I wonder. I don't think Tom would object to me mentioning that he was born with a hair lip and cleft palate. There was not the expertise available when Tom was small to rectify this condition. It was only when Tom reached adulthood that he was able to get the attention he needed. He went through 36 operations before his doctors and Tom were satisfied with the final result.

Bar meals go back further than you may suppose. Like thousands of communities up and down the country, folk have had nick names for generations. One such man in these parts was Sixer Ward. His real name was Charlie. Reg Hill remembers how Sixer would walk every Sunday at mid-day from his house in Church Hill, the house where Mrs Lesley Rigby now lives, to the Wheatsheaf at Ailesworth for a pint, or maybe two. On this particular Sunday he was still in the Bar when his wife came in carrying his lunch on a tray, which she placed on the counter saying, *"If you can't come home to eat you may as well eat it here."* Charlie apparently, as placid as ever, took Lucy at her word, asked mine host Jim Fox for some cutlery, pepper and salt, and ate his Sunday roast there and then.

Fig 28q. Four comrades in arms. Dick Taylor, (Gardener) Charlie Wyldbore, (Golf Course Green keeper) George Ward (Roadman) and Alec Cooke (Carpenter and Undertaker). All four men were involved with the church.

Fig 28r. Mr Percy Sismey's daughter Joan has no idea how her father became known as Wacky, however that was the name he answered to. He was for many years a Kennel man for the Fitzwilliam foxhounds, a shepherd at Milton, and latterly he and his wife were licensees at the Prince of Wales at Castor. The photograph shows Wacky shearing a Jacobs's ram at Milton.

Fig 28s. Another wonderful character, Sam Catmull. He would talk, or quietly sing hymns as he fashioned a horseshoe on the anvil. It was a privilege to be in his forge and watch him work. He played bowls, and took his grandson to see the 'Posh' (Peterborough United) play.

Transport for away matches for the local football team was sometimes a problem until Mr Eustace Mountain, who worked for Smith's Crisps offered to take them in his van. One Saturday, when driving through Stamford, the brakes failed whilst going up hill and the van rolled back down. Eustace did well to keep control. In doing so he was forced to mount a pavement and the van came to rest against a shop front. Little or no damage was done. However, it was impossible to open the rear doors as a wooden partition divided the cab from the team. They had to rely on the mercy of the good people of Stamford to extricate them!

Another great character from Ailesworth was Tipler Rollins, a shepherd, who furthered numerous boys' education of my and quite possibly an older, generation. Tipler was badly disabled and walked with the aid of two walking sticks. He looked after the Fitzwilliam Jacobs flock which grazed the Milton golf course. (There were few players during the war years.) It was a treat to be invited by Tip to ride with him in his horse-drawn trap. He had two dogs; one ran by the side of the trap, whilst the second ran underneath it. It was the boy's job to open and close all gates, plus any other task that required a little running about. Education - he most certainly taught us about tupping, lambing, using his shepherd's crook, spitting and swearing. Tipler was never short of volunteers. I was one of many who assisted him; a little later Keith Sharpe almost became his apprentice. Keith's Uncle George, who was a brilliant cobbler but not such a brilliant barber (boys sixpence, men a shilling), lived and had his business at the stone house in Main Street just beyond Maffit Road. Sometimes Tipler would sit in Mr Sharp's workshop whilst George repaired shoes or boots or cut hair. This was a time to listen, when you were privy to all manner of information.

Another well known Ailesworth figure and shepherd was Percy (Wacky) Sismey who at one time had been kennel man for the Fitzwilliam Fox Hounds. Later he looked after Major Peacock's gun dogs at Ferry House. At the same time he and his wife Elsie were mine hosts of the Prince of Wales. Like his father, Percy held a licence to slaughter livestock; it was not uncommon to watch him kill a pig in its owner's back garden.

Sam Catmull was the local Blacksmith who had his forge - still there today - with its red pantile roof, in the yard at 49 Peterborough Road. Sam, too, was a delightful man. I loved to get there on a Saturday morning, pump his forge and watch him fashion a horse shoe from a straight piece of metal and smell the acrid smoke as the hot shoe came into contact with the horse's hoof. Sam was a veteran of the Great War and a sergeant in the Home Guard. He played bowls on the Green in what is now Holme Close and was a regular at church for Sunday Evensong. Sam was a widower who brought up two daughters. Later he married Mr Jack Bettles's widow and lived in the farmhouse where Jack had farmed, now the home of Mr and Mrs John Taylor, 'The Old Smithy'.

Mrs Lottie Kent whose mother Sarah Dudley was a member of the Pywell family, well remembers Butty Chambers from

Helpston bringing his Swing boats and Roundabout to Ailesworth Green each year. Lottie also recollects that the horse chestnut that graced the green for so many years until it became a victim of a storm, was planted as a sapling in Fred Tomlin's bowler hat. At one time the tree had a lovely hexagonal shaped seat built around it. Fred was also a member of the Castor and Ailesworth Excelsior Brass Band, and at one time played the harmonium at the Castor Congregational Chapel on Church Hill.

My father had a great friend in Stan Wilson, who lived at the corner of Splash Lane, now the home of Ted Fairchild. Stan's mother-in-law, Ethel Stanger took laundry for the Cathedral. Stan was a very keen angler, gardener and amateur wine maker, which prompted Stan and dad to make a batch of Elderberry wine in Ethel's copper, (the large receptacle she used for boiling the clothes). They were under the misapprehension that they had cleaned the copper out thoroughly after using it, but apparently not, for the following Monday morning when Ethel removed the clergy and choirs' white vestments, they came out a pretty shade of pink, and the air was blue, dark blue.

Some Incoming Warriors

Percy Dexter, late of the Green Howards, wounded both at Dunkirk and on D-Day, died at Castor 4th June 2000. His wife Doreen still lives in Castor.

Douglas Gillam, RAF Bomber Command, flew from RAF Wittering. Was shot down over occupied France in 1943, taken a POW to Stalag Luft IV as a Flt/Sgt, and later promoted to WO on the instructions of the RAF by the German Camp Commandant. Douglas lives in Castor.

Sir Stephen Hastings, MC, MFH, former MP, late Scots Guard, SAS, SOE and Foreign Office, came to live in Castor after marrying the Hon Lady Hastings of Milton Hall. He has written his autobiography 'The Drums of Memory'.

Wally Lunn, late Petty Officer in the Royal Navy, was twice torpedoed and plucked from the sea whilst serving on HMS Medway, and again on HMS Adamant, both submarine depot ships. His brother 'Ciss' Lunn late Northants Regt. saw the body of Cyril Kingston of Castor carried back through the lines on a stretcher. Wally's daughter Ros married Ron Pearson and lives at Green Farm Castor.

Arthur Griffiths, Air Vice Marshall, CB, AFC, WWII fighter pilot, at one time the youngest flying instructor in the RAF. Shot down twice in two weeks after D-Day in Northern France, and spent the last 9 months of the war as a POW. At one time he was stationed at RAF Wittering. Arthur died 13th February 2003. His wife Nancy still lives in Castor.

Jim Webb, Chief ERA, joined the Royal Navy as an apprentice in 1935; served on the old Ark Royal and later the destroyer HMS Vixen at Portland under the command of Lord Mountbatten. Jim then saw service on HMS Courageous on North and later South Atlantic patrols. Also on the Russian convoys, he was on the crew of the Hermes when it was sunk in 1942, later joining first HMS Battler and later Barunda on anti-submarine patrols in Japanese waters. Jim lives in Ailesworth.

John James, volunteered as a Territorial at the beginning of the war firstly joining the London Scottish, being posted first to Norway then to Scotland to train as a commando. He then transferred to the Kings Own Lancashire Regt. Commissioned at Sandhurst, he became a Captain Instructor in the Royal Armoured Corps. Towards the end of the war he applied for a permanent commission in the Royal Tank Regt. John left the Army as a DAA & QMG with the rank of Major. John lives in Ailesworth.

Eric Waterfield was 18 years old when he joined the Army in 1942 and served in the 2nd Battalion of the North Staffordshire Regt. He took part in the bridgehead landing at Anzio in Italy, from there he saw action in Palestine. Eric also lives in Ailesworth.

Arthur Wing, joined the Royal Navy in 1948 and served on the aircraft carrier HMS Perseus; this was the time when the Navy was experimenting 'catapulting' aircraft from the flight deck. He served on several other vessels before leaving the service in 1952 with the rank of Stoker Mechanic. Arthur lives in Ailesworth

Arthur Chilvers, joined the Manchester Regt in February 1942 before transferring to the Army Catering Corps in 1943. In November of that year he found himself at Milton where he was cooking for service personnel from numerous countries. During 1944 he was sent to Ware to cater for two Generals who made up a commissioning board. Arthur left the Army in 1946 as Corporal and lives in Ailesworth.

Wallace Giddings, served in the Fleet Air Arm from 1941 to 1946 and sailed on American-built escort carriers. There were five vessels that made up the escort each with the capability of flying 20 aircraft. Wallace gained the rank of Petty Officer Radar/Radio air crew/mechanic mainly on the *Fairey Swordfish*, a biplane (affectionately known as the String Bag because of its masses of bracing wires,) which was very effective against detecting and destroying U-boats. He saw action in the Atlantic, Mediterranean, and on the Russian convoys, also taking part at the D-Day landings and the liberation of Italy at Salerno. Wallace lives in Ailesworth.

Ernest Hudson was also in the Fleet Air Arm, entering the service in 1943, and was also a Radio Operator. He sailed to America on the *Queen Mary* (at that time used as a troop ship) to further his training. He served on the Light Fleet Carrier *HMS Glory* servicing radio equipment on various aircraft including the American built Vought Corsairs, seeing service in the Atlantic and later the Pacific. Ernest left the service in 1946 as a Petty Officer, he lives in Ailesworth.

Jim Thompson-Bell, Sqn Sgt Maj, MM joined the Lancashire Regt in 1940 and later also served with the Royal Armoured Corps where he was a Sgt Instructor on such tanks as the Churchill, Sherman and the Comet, the forerunner of the modern tank. He then served with the 1st and then 2nd Fife and Forfar Regts. He saw active service in France, Belgium, Holland and Germany where he was decorated for gallantry. Jim also lives in Ailesworth.

Leonard Danks, late Chief Petty Officer, served in the Royal Navy throughout the war as Supply and Secretariat. From 1940-1942 he served on *HMS Medway*, and was transferred from that ship one week before it was torpedoed and sunk in the Mediterranean on 30th June (see Wally Lunn). From 1943-1945 he was based at Chatham. Leonard lives in Ailesworth.

Fig 28t. The local Constabulary in Milton Park. Seated is PC W Goode, and standing on the right is PC, later Sgt A Trundle.

Charles Clarke joined the Royal Air Force in 1940 and trained as ground crew electrician. He later re-mustered, and retrained in South Africa as Air crew, Navigator / Air gunner, flying in the Wellington bombers and Liberators. After various postings in the British Isles, Charles also saw service in Egypt and India, he left the service in 1946, he now lives in Castor.

Ted Fairchild is our only Korean War veteran, having served there with the Norfolk Regt. Leaving at the end of his National Service as a Corporal, he joined the family building firm. He lives in Castor.

Fig 28u. PC W Jackson. It was Mr Jackson who called in at the old village hall to reassure us that the explosion that had 'rattled' the building during a concert that we were watching, was a V1 rocket, (Doodlebug) and it had exploded near the railway station.

Our Village Policemen

I can go back no further than my grandfather PC Walter Goode, who came here from Werrington. The Police house in those days was part of the cottage on the corner of Port Lane, now the home of Dave Rager. The family later moved to the new police house, now the home of Mr and Mrs Steve Walker on Peterborough Road. It then became the home of PC Steve Maddocks who worked his way up the promotion ladder to become Deputy Chief Constable of Peterborough.

PC Wilfred Jackson moved here from Glinton during the war. It was Mr Jackson, who came to the old Village Hall part way through a concert, to assure us that the explosion that had shaken the building, and frightened us out of our skins, was a German V1 rocket, which had exploded harmlessly, in Mr Wade's field near Castor station. The Jacksons were the first occupants of the new police house opposite Village Farm. Mrs Florence Jackson now lives in a Peterborough nursing home, aged 93.

Fig 28v. PC E Brawn. Mr Brawn was an ex-serviceman. When he came to Castor he had two sisters living here, Mrs Phyllis Hill and Mrs Kath Oliver, both former Land Army girls.

Fig 28w. The Newborn family on their 'Vinco' cycles which were manufactured at the Heighton's Works at Elton. The photograph was taken in 1912, (l-r) Edward, Percy, (Sgt killed on the Somme 1916) Florence, (Heighton, Gwen's mother) Frederick, Ernest, (Head Verger at Lincoln Cathedral) and William. Their father was a tailor, and the first organist at Castor church, before that he had played the harmonium there.

Fig 28x. Castor boys join up in 1915. At an early camp before they had their uniforms, including Ernie Gibbons (died in action 1917), Jack and Albert Gibbons, William Burton (father of Reg Burton, Delsia Bailey and Grace Gibbs), and two Jakes boys (both died in action 1917).

PC Ted Brawn followed; he had two sisters already living in the village, Mrs Phyllis Hill and Mrs Kath Oliver, both former Land Army girls. Ted was an ex-serviceman. PC Keith Boyce had a larger beat and was issued with a Police car. PC Allan Paul followed and was with us for several years, later moving to Peterborough. PC Richard Weaver came here not exactly a stranger to the area, for he had been a Fireman in the Royal Air Force at Wittering.

Fig 28y. Castor boys now issued with uniforms, 1915.

Fig 28z.. Great War veterans at a reunion in Prince of Wales, Castor. (l-r) Back: R Neal, E Hilton, S Pearson, G Sharpe, R Parker, E Kingston. Front: B Harman, E Taylor, P Sismey and G Dudley.

Brian Goode.

I still live in the house into which I was born 70 years ago. It has been a delight to write down just a few random memories I have of people and places. There is so much more that one could have included, but I hope this has given you a little insight of a community of which I am justly proud to be a part. I would like to acknowledge, John O'Mahony for his valuable advice. For photographic material, I wish to thank, David Scott, Gwen Heighton, Joan Sismey, Jane Steward, (Brawn) Betty Jones, (Taylor) Audrey Neal (Taylor) Florence Jackson, Beryl Turner, (Jackson) Peter Harris, and thanks to Harry Coulson for putting so many names to faces for me.

Chapter 29
Castor Parish Council

Introduction

Castor Parish Council came into being as a consequence of the Government's Parish Councils Act in 1894. Before this time, the responsibility for local administration was shared by the Church Wardens, the Overseers of the Poor and the Manor Court. The Church Wardens were (and still are) elected at the annual Vestry Meeting, while the Overseers of the Poor and the Manor Court were elected at an Annual General Meeting of the parish. These annual Parish Meetings continued to be held until the mid-1980s when they were superseded by an Annual General Meeting of the Parish Council, a session which is open to the public. The Manor Court was responsible for access issues and for the overseeing of local businesses and farming. This was particularly important as the farmland around Castor and Ailsworth was not enclosed until 1894, with crops being grown on scattered field-strips and livestock pastured on common land.

The Enclosures Act did, at least, make provision for recreation grounds for each village as well as field gardens or allotments of land. Castor was unusual in that it was the only parish to be granted its own riverside bathing place in addition. This was situated at the end of the Splash Lane footpath and was later furnished with a wooden changing hut by the Parish Council. A newspaper report, dated February 16th 1894, quotes the Commissioner for the Board of Agriculture, who, speaking at a public meeting in the Castor schoolroom, explained the allotments to his audience, saying *"the quantity to be set out would give a quarter of an acre to every cottage in the villages. This land would be vested in the Churchwardens and Overseers as trustees, who would be bound to let the land to the labouring poor at an agricultural rent"* [1]. These recreation grounds and allotments later became the responsibility of the newly-formed Parish Councils. Castor Parish Council still owns most of the land allocated then, although the old field names like Rush Lees, Oldfield and Ferryfield may not be familiar, and the village still benefits from the income generated from letting the land.

Fig 29a. George Fitzwilliam Esq., flanked by his two sons, Toby, on the left, and Thomas, on the right. George and Thomas, who later became Earl Fitzwilliam, served as Chairmen of the Castor Parish Council for 69 years between them.

The first Parish Council
On December 4th 1894, the first Parish Meeting to be held under the newly-passed Local Government Act took place at Castor Infant School [2]. It would seem that there was considerable interest in the village because it was recorded that 65 out of a total of 133 electors attended the meeting and 13 names were put forward for the seven seats on the Parish Council. Those elected were as follows: George Charles Wentworth Fitzwilliam, Esquire, of Milton Hall, George Edwin Holmes (Headmaster of Fitzwilliam School), Alfred Briggs (coal merchant), Alfred Sykes (architect), John Thomas Darby (farmer), Thomas Wootton (tailor, grocer, etc) and Lewis Winsworth (shepherd). Major Frank Armstrong White, later Colonel White, of Castor House, who had chaired the Parish Meeting, was unanimously elected as chairman, whilst Mr Holmes agreed to act as the unpaid parish clerk.

The early years
The new Parish Council worked diligently to maintain and where possible, improve the village and its environs. The early meetings were infrequent and the business was mostly about the maintenance of the footpaths and drainage ditches, the renting out of land owned by the Parish Council and the annual election of School Managers. The minutes of every meeting were, and still are, written up in a businesslike fashion by the clerks, briefly and to the point. There is never more than a hint of the sometimes heated discussions which must have taken place over the years and only on the

Fig 29b. Colonel White, Chairman of Castor Parish Council from its founding in 1894 until 1910. (Courtesy of Ian Balfour).

Fig 29c. Sir Richard Winfrey, Parish Councillor in the 1930s. (Courtesy of Claire Winfrey.

rarest occasions has any dissent been detailed. Only once, and that relatively recently, have matters come to such a pass that the councillors have had to resolve 'that all members address the chair and do not speak when others are doing so'.

On the whole, matters ran smoothly in those early years and there were few interruptions to the steady way of life of the village. There was one notable exception, however, and feelings ran very high, as evidenced by the number of column inches devoted to the case in the *Peterborough Standard*. Without warning, a footpath running beside what is now the Old Rectory, over to Water Lane, then across a field belonging to Colonel White, before reaching the Peterborough Road, was blocked off by a 'dead hedge' just inside the Colonel's field. The villagers were reported to have been 'much inconvenienced' and they were very angry. Mr G Holmes, agent to Colonel White, on the other hand, was reported to have remarked that he had 'never before heard such a storm not in a teacup but in a spoon'. At the next Parish Council meeting, the clerk, Mr G Holmes (yes, the same one), produced maps of the 'proposed' footpath diversion and asked the Council to sanction them. As Colonel White was chairman of the Parish Council, but absent, perhaps diplomatically, from this meeting, it was tactfully proposed that a committee should be formed to look at the path. In the meantime, at the dead of night, some enterprising person or persons chopped a neat hole through the hedge. Mysteriously, it was never discovered who was responsible for this act of vandalism, but the contented villagers immediately resumed using the old path. To be charitable, the villains of the piece were probably just being presumptuous, but the villagers refused to accept the 'fait accompli' and in the end a special meeting of the Parish Council was called and by true democratic process the old course of the footpath was restored.

The Second World War
The Council minutes from the period of the Second World War are, perhaps intentionally, not very informative, though much must have been discussed. It is interesting to note that already in January of 1939 the Council was debating the possible need for extra sanitation in the event of the Government Evacuation scheme coming into force. The Parish Council's Allotment Committee evidently took its work very seriously, and the members zealously inspected the allotments, chastising those tenants who were not putting their plot to full use. There was also some concern expressed when the Roman Bank (Ermine Street) in Normangate Field was ploughed over and it was agreed that this should not have been done. After the end of the war, the Parish Council asked the County Land Agent if the ploughing could stop and in early 1947, the War Agriculture Executive Committee eventually replied that this could happen 'as soon as the state of emergency no longer existed'.

The Fire Station and Reading Room
In an obituary for Mr G Holmes, published in the local newspaper in 1911, he was described as school headmaster, clerk of the Parish Council, churchwarden and 'Lieutenant of the Castor Fire Brigade', which he organised. The Parish Council had borrowed £100 in 1901 'to purchase the engine and appurtenances and for the erection of a suitable engine house'. Newspaper cuttings from the following year tell that the voluntary Fire Brigade had a Shand, Mason and Co. manual engine and that each member had been equipped with boots and a cap. The villagers felt that the men should be properly equipped with uniforms and that year, and on several other occasions, a concert was held in the schoolroom to raise funds. There are few reports of the Fire Brigade's work, though we do know that when lightning struck thatched cottages in Upton, the Castor Fire Brigade was called out. Later, in July 1928, it attended a fire at three

thatched cottages in Church Hill. There was not a lot that could be done to save the thatch, though the damage was limited to some extent by their efforts. They had been more successful at subduing a fire which broke out over the stables at The Elms in 1927 and were no doubt very satisfied that the Peterborough Voluntary Fire Brigade, which had also arrived on the scene, was not needed. In December 1927, a special Parish Meeting was held, presumably because so much concern had been expressed about the ineffectiveness of the old manually-pumped fire engine. A resolution was passed '*That this meeting approves the steps already taken for the purchase of a Motor Fire Engine for the Parish from Martins and Co. Ltd, Stamford*'.

Fig 29d. Members of Castor Fire Brigade c.1912. Left to right: Will Cooke (Captain), John Gibbons, Dick Taylor, Alec Cooke, Charles Goodyer.

Occasional notes appear in the minutes of the Parish Council meetings regarding the upkeep of the Fire Station and equipment and it was not until April 1939 that the Fire Brigade Act shifted the responsibility for the Fire Brigade to the Soke of Peterborough Rural District Council. The village's Fire Station and equipment were sold, but ironically, just over a year later, the Parish Council felt the need to request the allocation of six stirrup pumps in view of the danger of bombing.

The Fire Station was on Castor Village Green, along with the Reading Room. This was another important village amenity, for which the Parish Council became responsible in 1906. The Council noted with some satisfaction in 1933 that the Reading Room had made a profit of five (old) pence with receipts of £22 3s 6d and outgoings of £22 3s 1d, despite the fact that a sum had been paid for the laying on of electricity and installation of an electric light that year.

Other duties

It was also the Parish Council's responsibility to provide 'receptacles' and a night-soil cart (a wheelbarrow in the early days, but as the years went by, a cart with a tank on it was purchased) and it is sobering to realise that this was the situation until 1954, when a sewer pipe was laid. Even then, there appear to have been mixed feelings about this particular piece of progress. A note appears in the minutes for the meeting on October 24th 1954, to the effect that the Council wondered if the sewer pipe was adequate to serve the whole of Castor and Ailsworth and it was reported that '*since the sewer had been laid very offensive smells have been noted*'. Not all the properties were immediately converted to the wonderful new water closets and in 1962, the Parish Council noted that some cottages still had pail closets and resolved to ask the Peterborough Rural District Council to complete the work.

The maintenance of the recreation grounds has been an important job and the villagers have benefited much from the Parish Council's work. However, there have inevitably been a few occasions when it has proved impossible to please everybody. Initially, all the recreation grounds were rented out to local farmers for grazing, the rent providing useful income. In 1934, the Castor and Ailsworth Cricket Club sent a letter of complaint to the Parish Council about the state of the Rush Lees Recreation Ground, now more commonly known as the Castor

Fig 29e. Castor Fire Brigade in full uniform, early1900s. Standing, left to right: Rev A Bek (Curate), Mossendew, Unknown, Unknown, C Darby, R Taylor, G Holmes (Clerk to Castor Parish Council). Sitting, left to right: G Ward, AA Cooke, W Cooke (Captain), L Longfoot, Unknown.

Cricket Ground. The farmer who rented this field, a Mr Fletcher, obligingly agreed not to let his cows onto the field on the day of the match or the preceding day! In 1936, some swings were erected in the same recreation ground, as part of the Silver Jubilee celebrations for George VI and, when these were handed over to the Parish Council, it was decided that a caretaker should be provided and two locks and chains purchased to fasten up the swings every Saturday night until Monday morning. Attitudes slowly changed and in 1965, a children's playground was created on what had been part of the TweenTowns allotments, after a decision had been made to sell a small portion to raise funds. In 2003, the Parish Council again provided funds to completely redesign the playground and install new equipment to make an area which is colourful and challenging as well as safe for today's children.

Planning Issues

After the war, the Parish Council became progressively more involved in planning issues. Perhaps the first major one was the attempt to requisition Ailsworth Heath as a practice bombing range in 1948. Needless to say, the Parish Council resolved to *'write to the appropriate authority, protesting with the utmost vigour against the proposed requisitioning'* and the idea was thankfully dropped.

During the 1950s, demand for new housing grew and the quiet farming villages began to change. The Council tried to ensure that decisions were in the best interests of the village, but its influence was limited. In 1959, the Clerk procured a copy of the County Development Plan, which evidently caused some concern and prompted the Parish Council to ask the County Planning Officer to inform them if any large developments were planned. Again in early 1960, the Council minutes state that the Council *'decided to inform the County Planning Officer that the Council considered that the village had grown enough and that they would wish to be informed of any large-scale development proposed in the vicinity of the church or rectory and to hope that any development would be of a higher standard than that being carried out at Ailsworth.'* It was realised that the Council would need more strength and in 1963, Castor Parish Council was canvassing support from other parish councils in their request to be able to comment on plans for development in the village before the plans were approved. By 1965, the Parish Council was supporting a Private Member's Bill in Parliament which was intended to ensure that parish councils would receive notification of all planning applications for development in their area and would be given 14 days to give their comment.

In 1966, the infamous 'Hancock Report' was published, with its plan to extend Peterborough Westwards to include Castor, Ailsworth and Sutton. In April of that year, the Council held a special meeting, well-attended by parishioners, at which Mr Hancock himself explained his plan and answered questions. The fears of residents were not however allayed, and an ad hoc committee of the parishes of Castor, Ailsworth, Sutton and Upton was formed. Castor Parish Council wanted the committee to be an official committee, with fully delegated powers, under the Parish Councils, but Ailsworth Parish Council disagreed with the move and the committee worked on independently. Although opposition was not unanimous within the Council, a strong letter was sent to the Ministry of Housing and Local Government, voicing the Council's objections to the plans. The view was expressed that *'All village life in the rural community encompassed by the four villages of Castor, Ailsworth, Sutton and Upton would be eliminated'* should the plan be implemented and that *'The villages should be allowed to develop naturally.'* There is little further reference to the progress of this plan, which must have caused some heated debate, except that in December 1969, there is a note referring to the fact that Castor and Ailsworth would not be developed before 1980.

The idea of a major expansion of Peterborough did not however go away. In 1975, Peterborough Development Corporation invited the Parish Councils of Castor, Ailsworth and Sutton to the unveiling of plans for a Castor Township. Throughout 1975, the Parish Councils of Castor and Ailsworth worked together, producing comments on the plans.

The debate rumbled on and then in April 1978, an open meeting was held in the Village Hall to discuss the development plans. After much debate, the Parish Council voted at the council meeting afterwards by five votes to three in favour of the resolution *'that the Council are against the latest proposals of the Development Corporation on economic grounds and are prepared to make representations at all levels to stop the future development of the Western Sector* (of the proposed township)'. The provision of a bypass had been linked to the acceptance of the new development, but the Parish Council focussed its efforts on getting a bypass whatever the outcome. The campaign against the township was taken up by an informal committee. This committee, initiated over a cup of coffee by Mr and Mrs Reg Lambert, Mr and Mrs Arthur Freer and Mr and Mrs Ken Trevitt, was quickly joined by Mr Arthur Chilvers, Deputy Chairman of Castor Parish Council. Help was enlisted from Ailsworth, Sutton, Upton and Marholm and Sir Stephen and Lady Hastings of Milton also became involved. The committee and its allies worked hard, gathering information and lobbying the organisations concerned, until finally, after a change of government in 1979, the plans were once again shelved.

In 1986, Cambridgeshire County Council undertook the first five-yearly review of its Structure Plan and once again the idea of a township around Castor and Ailsworth was raised. This time, the villagers were better prepared (and probably more united!). The County Council sent out questionnaires to residents, to assess local opinion. The Parish Council for its part sent a letter to all parishioners stating that its members were unanimously opposed to the development and encouraging everyone to complete the questionnaires to show the strength of feeling against the township. Ailsworth Parish Council acted likewise.

In addition to the official channels being taken by the Parish Councils, an 'Action Group for the Preservation of the Nene Valley' was organised, which was well supported. The fund-raising event which was held in Harrison-Smith's barn in Ailsworth ought to be part of local folk history, as about 400 people attended and a substantial sum of money was raised for the cause. Once again, the plans were eventually shelved, in favour of developing the old brick pits to the South of Peterborough where Serpentine Green and the Hamptons are now emerging, but who knows what the next Structure Plan might propose?

The Bypass

Traffic problems were not new. In 1935, the Parish Council had asked the County Council to erect 30mph signs for the village, but received the reply that Peterborough Road was not deemed a built-up area. In 1960, a bypass was first mentioned, with the County Planning Officer promising to keep the Parish Council informed of any developments. Progress on this issue was slow and, in 1971, the Clerk reported to the Council that there would be no bypass until 1985. The minutes record that in May 1973, a petition was handed to the Minister for Transport, signed by Castor parishioners, requesting that the date of construction be brought forward. In 1976, the traffic through the village, particularly the increasing number of ever larger lorries, was causing damage to roads and stonework to such an extent that the Parish Council even attempted to get the A47 temporarily re-routed until the bypass was built. The re-routing proved impossible and a cycleway was suggested as an alternative way of avoiding the increasing numbers of accidents. This too came to nothing. In May1981, a letter was received from the Peterborough Development Corporation stating that *'one of the consequences of the Secretary of State's decision concerning*

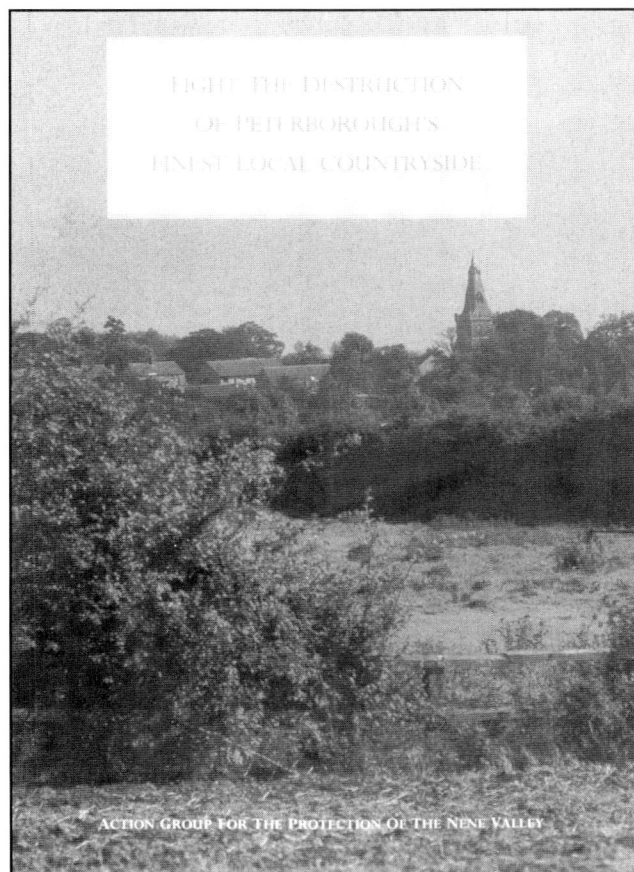

Fig 29f. Campaign Brochure published by the 'Action Group for the Protection of the Nene Valley'

Fig 29g. Devastation caused by a lorry which jack-knifed and demolished both the bar of the Royal Oak and a garage on the opposite side of the road. The garage had just been rebuilt following a similar accident.

Castor is that the Corporation no longer has any material interest in a Castor bypass. The matter now appeared to be for the Department of Transport in Consultation with Cambridgeshire County Council.' The villagers continued to suffer from the rumbling of laden lorries, the crashing sounds of empty lorries driven over bumps in the road, the vibrating of windows and doors (and sometimes everything else) and the alarmingly rapid decay of stone walls. Then in December 1981, the villagers heard on the national news, no doubt with mixed feelings, that 40 tonne lorries were to be allowed on the roads and the construction of bypasses was to be speeded up as a consequence. Two more accidents were recorded in the village within a fortnight. The Parish Council continued its lobbying, and by July1982, the Council minutes record that of the two routes proposed for the Castor Bypass, the Council was *'overwhelmingly in favour of the Southern route'*. This route would have passed just to the South of the Cricket Ground and villagers' opposition grew, such that in March 1983, the minutes record that after what was termed 'a healthy discussion' on the merits of both routes, a vote was taken and there were five in favour of the Northern route and four in favour of the Southern. The Secretary of State for Transport confirmed the Northern route and by October of 1984, the Council was informed that soil tests were to be undertaken, the first step towards the building of the new road. The villagers enthusiastically

Fig 29h. The handing over of a plaque to commemorate the completion of the bypass. Left to right: Michael Hinton (Chairman of Ailsworth Parish Council), a representative of the Roadworks Co Ltd, Charles Winfrey, Reg Lambert (Vice Chairman of Castor Parish council).

celebrated the eventual completion of the bypass. A fun run/walk/pushchair push took place along its length on the day before the new road was opened. The next day, despite the rain, other events were held to celebrate, including the tying of a white ribbon across Peterborough Road outside the Royal Oak to symbolise the closure to through traffic. The Chairman of the Parish Council was finally able to report to the Annual General Meeting in May 1992 that *'the much awaited bypass has changed the face of the village beyond all recognition and it is now a place of some tranquillity'*.

The Councillors

The Parish of Castor has been fortunate in that it has had many dedicated people, willing to spend much time and effort in the interests of the village. It is remarkable that in the first 85 years, the Parish Council had only three chairmen. Colonel Frank White and George Fitzwilliam, Esquire, served on the first Parish Council in 1894 as Chairman and Vice Chairman respectively. Then, in 1910, George Fitzwilliam took on the post of Chairman, serving until his death in 1936, when he was succeeded by his son, Thomas Fitzwilliam, later Earl Fitzwilliam, who in turn served for a grand total of 43 years until his death in 1979. Other names are noted in the Council minutes: Major Pelham, for instance, died in 1946, having been a member of the Parish Council since 1925 and in 1955 Mr W Cooke retired after 33 years. More recently Mr Reg Lambert served for 20 years; Mr Alec Jakes served for 32 years and Mr E J Wood for 37 years, all of them at a very significant period in Castor's development.

Castor Parish Council today

The Parish Council has changed with the times and nowadays councillors tend not to serve for such long periods. Today's councillors no doubt wish sometimes that life still went at the easy pace of a hundred years ago, when the only business at one Annual Parish Meeting concerned moles and resulted in a proposal *'that a voluntary association for the purposes of catching moles be hereby formed'*. It may be disputed as to whether Parish Councils have more power now than they used to, but they are at least consulted on issues affecting their areas. All applications for planning permission are passed to the Parish Councils for their approval or not and Councils make recommendations about such matters as roads, footpaths and lighting. It is good to know that the village has an official body to represent the interests of its residents and deal with all the intricacies of local government on our behalf.

Fig 29i. Charles Winfrey giving a speech, before symbolically tying a ribbon across the road to close it to through traffic, while his wife, Jay, prepares to open a celebratory bottle of champagne.

Fig 29j. The completion of the flood relief scheme, 1977. This much-needed scheme was championed by the Parish Councils of Castor and Ailsworth. To celebrate its completion, a seat was donated by Anglian Water. The ceremony was attended by Albert Burgess (far left)and Arthur Chilvers (third from left), the Chairmen of Ailsworth and Castor Parish Councils respectively, as well as John Sharpe (second from left)and Elizabeth Goode (far right), the oldest residents, at the time, of Ailsworth and Castor respectively.

Fig 29k. Jim Wood, Parish Councillor from 1965 to 2002

Fig 29l. View of the Glebe Field from Castor church. This is the field in which the row of elms known as the 'Dancing Ladies' used to grow (see Fig 25j.) The field was part of the Rectory grounds until it was compulsorily purchased by the Development Corporation. The field's presence, in the middle of Castor next to the school, helps preserve the 'open feel' of the village centre. The walls round the field, like many in Castor, lead one to speculate how many walls in Castor contain stonework that has been re-used since first being used in the Roman 'praetorium'.

Fig 29m. The Village Hall Castor, formerly the Fitzwilliam School. The Village Hall is run by a committee on behalf of the residents of Castor and Ailsworth, the Chairman of which is Ian Sheldon.

Fig 29n. Castor Green looking South in the 1950s. Note the socket and stump of the old village cross on the right underneath the tree.

Fig 29o. View of the old barn at Manor Farm Castor from Church Hill, 1950s.

Stephanie Bradshaw

Stephanie moved to the old Schoolmaster's House in Castor in 1990, but her interest in the geology and archaeology of the area dates from a decade earlier.

Notes

1. All quotes from newspapers in this chapter are based on a collection of newspaper cuttings, compiled by Joan Marriott, many of which were written by Annie Cooke. Headmistress of Castor Infants School from 1886 to 1927, Annie Cooke was also the local correspondent for the Peterborough Standard, the Peterborough Citizen and Advertiser and the Stamford Mercury for 40 years.
2. The minutes of the Annual Meetings of Castor Parish and the minutes of the meetings of Castor Parish Council have provided much of the material for this chapter.

Chapter 30
Castor Schools

There have been four main schools in Castor. The first began in the early 19th century and was held in the Vestry of St Kyneburgha's Church. The Fitzwilliam National School was then set up in 1829 in the building that is now the Village Hall and Castor Infants School was founded in 1861 on the site of the current Village School. These two schools closed in 1956 and the present Castor CE (VC) Primary School opened in their place.

The idea in this chapter is to tell a little of the story of these schools and, in particular, the Fitzwilliam and Infants Schools. Much of the interest of their story lies in the fact that it involves people, places and events within the memory of many of those still living in the villages. In addition, their story also gives a glimpse into the development of Elementary State Education in a typical rural setting.

Fig 30a. Selected milestones in education in England

1800s	Dames's schools, Day and Sunday Church schools.
1811	First National Schools.
1844	Factory Act releasing children for schooling.
1862	Increased Grants leading to 'payment by results'.
1880	Education compulsory to age of 10.
1891	Schooling 'free'.
1893	Leaving age raised to age of 11.
1899	Leaving age raised to age of 12.
1902	Local Education Authorities formed.
1907	Doctors and nurses allowed into schools.
	Free Grammar Schools places – the Scholarship
1922	Leaving age raised to age of 14.
1944	Leaving age raised to age of 15.
	Beginning of Secondary Education for all.
1966	Phasing out of the 11+.

The Vestry School

This day and Sunday school was typical of the early Church Schools that formed around the beginning of the 19th century when the move to educate working-class children was gathering pace [1] [2]. Most of what is known about the school comes from a lecture in 1883 by John Hales who went to this school in the early 1830s [3]. The school was there before 1829 but, although it is known that the Sunday school continued for many years, how long the day school remained open is still uncertain [4] [5].

The school was held in the aisle to the East of the South Transept that is now the Lady Chapel of St Kyneburgha's Church. There was an entrance door between the two windows on the Eastern wall which, although blocked up now, can be clearly located from the outside. Another doorway led into the Chancel. In those days education in this type of school was not free and Mr Hales refers to a '...*fee of 6d/week with books and fireing extra*.' Typically, several boys had their fees paid for them by the Rector (at that time the Bishop of Peterborough) and local charitably disposed ladies.

Who taught at the Vestry is unclear. Mr Hales mentions a schoolmaster but does not name him. A schoolmaster called William Horden has been associated with the school although it is known that he taught at the Fitzwilliam School later [6]. The curate apparently came to inspect the progress of the scholars as well as ringing the bell for the morning and afternoon sessions. Not much is known about the lessons but it was usually the case in this kind of school that the pupils received religious instruction and learnt their numbers and letters. Some copybooks with illustrated copies of the Psalms are the only details known [7].

The Fitzwilliam and Castor Infants Schools: Elementary State Education

With a few exceptions, these two schools between them provided Elementary State Education from 1829 to 1956 for most of the children of Castor, Ailsworth, Upton and Sutton, and occasionally Castor Mills and Milton Park [8] [9]. It has been possible to find out a great deal about the life in these schools using information contained in surviving school records like the *School Logs* [10] as well as recollections of former pupils and teachers [11].

Each school had its own Board of Managers comprising Government representatives together with the Rector and other local residents of some standing. The Fitzwilliam had the more robust regime, teaching children from seven and eventually up to fourteen, with an increasingly complex curriculum. The Infants School retained a gentler, although disciplined ambience and took in children up to seven years of age.

Fig 30b. Castor Infants School : Group III with the children in typical pose. Early 1900s. (Courtesy of Joan Marriott)

Despite these differences, the schools had several things in common. Each enjoyed a great deal of support in the form of funding, prizes and treats, from some of the residents of the 'big' houses and farms. These included those living at Castor House and the Cedars in Castor, the Tebbutts of Upton Manor, the Hopkinsons of Sutton Grange and the Carters of Ailsworth Manor Farm as well as the Fitzwilliam family of Milton.

In addition, a remarkable continuity was achieved within the villages through these schools. All the headteachers gave long service and, living in Castor, also played important roles within the Parish Council, the Churches and the organising committees of various groups and celebrations such as Jubilees and Coronations. There have also been many families, including the Pells, Jakes, Longfoots, Sismeys and Sharpes from which successive generations of children came to Castor. This sense of continuity and rhythm was further enhanced as both schools followed the same School Year, sharing the same holidays and special days.

The School Year

In 1880 the School Year began in January. It was marked by the transfer of the seven-year olds from the Infants School and the promotion of most children to the next Standard. In 1920 the start of the year was moved to April. It was not until the Education Act of 1944 that the Year in these schools started to run from September to July.

By 1880 the pattern of holidays and special days was well established. This was influenced a great deal by the Church Calendar and, in a rural parish such as ours, by harvests and village events. The main holiday or harvest holiday first ran from about 8 August to mid-September – sometimes brought forward or extended if the harvest was early or late. At first, the Easter break was only Good Friday and Easter Monday and there was Whit week that moved along with Whitsunday. There were always two weeks off at Christmas. Further regular holidays included a day's holiday at the beginning of May and August and half days given on Ash Wednesday and Ascension Thursday after a morning visit to Church. Later the Easter break was gradually lengthened and the Whit week fixed around the end of May. Half-term holidays in February and October did not come in until 1938.

Popular additional days were given for local events such as the Forresters' Feast and Church Restoration Fete in July and the Peterborough Bridge Fair in October. During this period there were many Royal events – weddings, coronations, jubilees, funerals – all of which warranted further holidays. Half days were often 'enjoyed' on Inspection Days or were granted by visiting dignitaries.

Fig 30c. Castor Fitzwilliam School built in 1829. The wing on the left was added in 1881. (Photo: David Henderson)

The Fitzwilliam National School: 1829 – 1956

An early map of the village shows that this school was built on part of a farmyard belonging to the Milton Estate [12]. Today it can be seen as occupying the NE corner of what was Darby's Farm on Peterborough Road opposite the Fitzwilliam Arms.

The School Building

The school was erected and paid for in 1829 by Charles William, the 5th Earl and began as just the main wing alongside the road. Built of stone with a slate roof it originally had two storeys. The upstairs room was removed towards the end of the 19th century to create a single high room (the present upstairs was added when the building became the Village Hall in 1957). How the upstairs room was used remains unclear but there was a schoolmistress called Martha Hales living in the 'Milton School' with her family in 1861 [13]. An extension was subsequently added to the rear at the Western end of the building to provide some storage and cloakroom space.

By 1865 there were ninety children present in the single big room. As they would be of various ages and Standards it is not surprising that a Government Report in 1865 stated '...a classroom is much wanted.' However it was not until 1881 that a second room, attached at right angles to the first, was added at the expense of William Thomas, the 6th Earl Fitzwilliam. With the use of a heavy plush curtain in the big room the school now had three classrooms.

Electricity, sewerage and running water did not come to Castor until the 1930s. Before this, conditions in the school were very primitive but similar to those that most children would have experienced at home. Thus any drinking water had to be brought in and the toilets were earth closets or (upgraded to!) buckets away from the main classrooms. Lighting was by daylight or lamps and there were open fires and then stoves for heating. Some remember it was often so cold first thing that the ink would be frozen. It was not until after 1945 that electric lights and chemical toilets were installed. The school had two gravelled playgrounds, the larger outer one for the boys and PE sessions, with the smaller inner one for the girls – 'not really big enough for our skipping' was often the girls' complaint (especially with a pile of fuel in the corner).

The Headmasters and their Assistants

Details about the first Headmasters are very sparse. Mr William Coates was in place by 1841 [14] and was succeeded by Mr William Horden for a short time between 1861 and 1864. The earliest available Log names Mr Henry Glasse as the Headmaster by 1864. He retired in 1885 and Mr George Holmes, who died in post in 1911, took his place. During this period these Masters implemented some very significant changes in legislation including the increasing complexity of funding and Grants, the establishment of compulsory education and the development of the curriculum.

Mr Thomas Salmon took over in 1911 and stayed for 33 years until his retirement in 1944, when Mr Albert Berridge was appointed. He remained until the school closed in 1956 but then became the Head of the new Primary School until his retirement in 1973 – 29 years service in total. These two Heads also faced many challenges including further expansion of the curriculum with the raising of the leaving age, development of extra-curricular activities and the introduction of the scholarship. In addition, there were also the war years to deal with as well as the development of medical services in schools.

For most of the time there were also Assistant Teachers – some training 'on the job' and taking annual examinations in Peterborough until qualified. One long-serving Assistant was Mr George Sellars who was there for 26 years from 1899. Often a pupil would become a Pupil Teacher and take groups of children for particular lessons. The Heads instructed these in the lessons they were to give and there are many references in the Logs to both excellent and botched presentations. Until the early 1900s there were also paid Monitors who were selected older children who could supervise or teach the younger children. The Rector of the day played a very important role within the school: teaching, taking prayers and testing the children. In addition, at various times, part-time teachers came in to teach subjects like Needlework and Cookery.

Funding

From the 1830s all Elementary Schools received an annual Government Grant. In this school this was generously supplemented by the Fitzwilliam family. By 1890 the Grant had risen to £108 14s 0d and was enhanced by the then Earl's contribution of £89 14s 0d [15]. The family also paid for some of the maintenance of the school building in exchange for a modest rent and had already paid for the building of a house

Fig 30d. Castor Fitzwilliam School: PE lessons in the Boys' playground. 1946. (Courtesy of Margaret Berridge and Graham Spence).

Fig 30e. Castor Fitzwilliam School with Mr George Holmes – Headmaster from 1885 – 1911. c1890. (Courtesy of Castor Primary School).

for the Headmaster at 9 Church Hill, Castor in 1887. At first, further income came from the pupils' weekly payments although many had their fees paid for them by local benefactors including the Earl, the Rector and the Rev Hopkinson of Sutton Grange. Records show that these payments were often linked to attendance or performance.

This relatively simple scenario quickly became more complicated after 1890 when a Fee Grant replaced the Pupils' Fees. The Arts and Science Grant came in around the turn of the century for the purchase of special items such as maps or extra staff as the curriculum expanded. Fund-raising also began around this time through renting out the Schoolroom and sale of needlework at the year's end.

In the Classroom

In its early years it is likely that the school admitted children from age five upwards but from 1861, when the Infants School opened, it took in children from around the age of seven. At first they were divided into two classes with each class containing at least two Standards, which probably roughly equated to year groups. There was a great deal of emphasis on Religion with morning Assembly as well as the Rector teaching and testing about prayers and the Scriptures. At the time there was also an intensive drive by the Government to check that the schools were spending their Grant effectively. This heavily influenced the curriculum in that there was an enormous amount of 'rote-learning' and mainly subjects that could be inspected easily were taught. Thus at first, there was a heavy emphasis on the three Rs, singing and recitation. The *Logs* record a large amount of testing by the Headmaster prior to the annual Inspection, for the Grant could be reduced if results were poor. The Inspection of the 'class' subjects involved written tests, an oral examination and examples of the children's work such as needlework samples.

In 1886, Geography and Drawing were added as 'class' subjects for the boys and Needlework for the girls. Geography and History for all and Science for the boys soon followed. Gardening for the older boys began in 1910 on a plot of

Fig 30f. Castor Fitzwilliam School: Gardening in Port Lane c 1920. The teacher is possibly Mr George Sellars who was Assistant Teacher 1899 – 1925. (Courtesy of Brian Goode).

land on what is now the present School Field and in that October half a ton of potatoes was harvested together with various other vegetables. In 1914, land in Port Lane was rented from Mr Harris, and gardening continued there until closure of the School. There were 14 plots worked and by all accounts these provided ample opportunities for mishaps and larks by the boys both in the garden and on their way there and back.

From 1914 various six-week courses in Housewifery were laid on for the older girls. At first these were in the Reading Room on Castor Green. After 1929 they transferred to the Old Village Hall on Peterborough Road where stoves were

Fig 30g. Castor Fitzwilliam School: Gymnastics with the older boys. 1946. (Courtesy of Margaret Berridge and Graham Spence).

installed together with cupboards for each girl's utensils including rolling pin and saucepans. During the early war years, the Methodist schoolroom in Ailsworth was used because the Village Hall was being used as a schoolroom for the London Evacuees. In the 1930s team sports were introduced with stoolball for the girls and cricket and football for the boys. Football matches against other schools began after the war although Castor never seemed to manage to beat Barnack.

After the leaving age was raised to 14 in 1922, the older children brought in Mail Order catalogues to practice making out orders, writing to firms as well as learning how to write applications for jobs. One very important development that began in the 1920s involved selected 11-year old pupils sitting the Scholarship to earn one of the free places in the Grammar Schools in Peterborough. At first only very few were entered – five in 1930 with one pass – and they went into Peterborough to sit the test. Later this was taken at school in Castor and eventually, after the war, was open to all as Secondary Education became available for pupils over the age of 11.

Special Events
The basic curriculum was enhanced from time to time by special events and trips out of school. Various people visited to entertain the children. Mr William le Queux from the Cedars, for example, gave various talks, including one in 1909, on his trip to Lapland and the Russian Tundra. The Rector or the Fitzwilliams with friends gave gramophone recitals or sang to the school. On special occasions informative talks were given on 'The Census' or, in 1914, 'Our Navy'. During the second World War, the Head addressed the school on the dangers of touching anything suspicious and types of bombs. There were often talks by visiting missionaries such as one in 1917 by the Rev Wallis on 'A street scene in China'. When the annual prize-giving and sale of needlework was in December it usually included carols and sketches. Later, the prize-giving was moved to the new year-end in July and then there was an annual Christmas Party in the Old Village Hall.

In 1925, the Hon Mrs Pelham of the Cedars presented a flag and flag-pole for the playground. It was flown for the first time on St George's Day that year and also used on Empire Day and Armistice Day from then on. Usually Mrs Pelham would attend and give out gifts of miniature flags for the children to wear or present the school with portraits of the king and queen. Occasionally members of the Royal Family stayed at Burghley House and, as in 1932, the children were lined up outside to watch them to pass.

As well as holidays given for various Sunday school or Village Treats, Choir Trips or Garden Fetes and such like, the children were also taken on trips out of school. One resident remembers a Christmas visit to Milton Park around 1914 with a mug of cocoa and a present, with dripping to take home. In 1925, a busload went to a Musical Competition in Peterborough and on several occasions there were film shows in the Village Hall or at the Infants School ranging on subjects like the Post-Office, the RSPCA and Cadburys! Later, buses allowed trips more regularly into Peterborough and, after the War, more ambitious away days to places such as London and York became annual events.

Rolls and Attendance

There are some indications that the school was to have 170 pupils [4] but such a high Roll was never recorded in the *Logs*. The early ones show numbers in excess of 100 but with widely fluctuating attendance of between 42-80%. Things improved a great deal once attendance became compulsory in 1880. Pupil numbers settled to 80-110 up to around 1935 with attendance gradually rising to over 90%.

Although attendance did not become compulsory until 1880 it was already being fairly closely monitored according to the earliest available *Log* of 1864. This reflected the increasing awareness of the need for an educated population as well as an attempt to make sure the schools were spending the Grant properly. At first there were regular inspections of the registers themselves to ensure that the Headmaster was filling them in every day, with lots of admonishments for incomplete returns. From 1880 there were also Attendance Officers who chased up absentees and '...*irregular...*' children. A cunning plan was also devised by which attendance became linked to the annual inspection tests. Those with poor attendance were not allowed to take the test and this in turn reduced the school's performance and on some occasions led to a reduction in the Grant.

Several factors affected attendance, and a great deal of effort was put into encouraging the children with annual prizes for good attendance donated by local residents. There was a long-running battle to get the Sutton and Upton children to school. Horse-drawn transport was arranged for the winter months from the early 1900s although this sometimes foundered in very bad weather. Attendance on the days following the harvest holidays were frequently down as well as during the potato-picking period in October, although during the Wars, boys over 11 were granted leave of absence for bona fide work on the land. When each village had its own Feast or Sunday school outing numbers were low. Wet or very cold weather was often given to explain away low attendance. There were also many times when outbreaks of influenza and mumps, for example, reduced the numbers and, on some occasions, led to closure of the School.

From 1940 the number on the Roll in the school dwindled to around 70. Although the leaving age was raised to 15 from 1944, the children over 14 went to school in Peterborough for their final year. Then, in 1949, those over 11 began attending the Arthur Mellows Secondary School in Glinton. This effectively left the Fitzwilliam as a Junior School with only 27 on the Roll. By 1956 the decision had been made to close the school and open a new Primary School together with the pupils from the Infants School.

Castor Infants School: 1861-1956

Castor Infants School opened in 1861 with the support of the Rector, the Rev George Andrews, and public subscription. It was built on the SE corner of a close called Church Close adjoining the churchyard. This land had belonged to the Church Commissioners but, according to a conveyance document, was transferred in 1861 from the Bishop of Peterborough '...*unto the Rector and Churchwardens of Castor cum Ailsworth.*' [16]. The document goes further and states that this land was '...*to be used as and for a School for the education of children... and for no other purpose*'. and '...*which said school shall always be conducted upon the principles of the United Church of England and Ireland.*'

Fig 30h. Castor Infants School: View of the School from the Church tower. Stocks Hill and Peterborough Road can been seen behind the Dovecote on the left. c 1920. (Courtesy of Joan Marriott).

The School Building

The school consisted of a single-storey brick building with a Collyweston roof. There was a small porch over the entrance at the Western end and a square brick-built cloakroom on the front. Inside was just one large room - which is now the Hall of the present Primary School. At an early stage a gallery was erected at the Eastern end of this room. Many former pupils remember it being used for the 'babies', the under-five's, until around 1935 and speak warmly of a rocking horse and large doll on the gallery for them to play with. The other children formed two classes in the main body of the room and from 1897 to the mid-

1930's a curtain was used to form two 'rooms'. There was a small playground, part gravel and part grass with outside toilets. Inside there were two open fires and then stoves. The children often took turns to sit near the fire and sometimes those coming from Sutton and Upton would arrive so wet that their coats would be draped over the fire-guard all day to dry. The only water was a pump for drinking water with two enamel mugs in the cloakroom.

The Headmistresses and their Assistants

At the present time little is known about the early Headmistresses other than their names - a Miss Johnson in 1877 [17] and, Miss Elizabeth Grenfell in 1884 [18]. Mrs Annie Cooke, who came to the School as Miss Jennings in 1886, remained for 41 years until her retirement in 1927. Miss Bessie Ambrose was appointed in her place and was still the Headmistress when the school closed in 1956. There were also Assistant Teachers, such as the long-serving Miss Muriel Hales. She arrived in 1912 and remained until her retirement, from the new Primary School in 1959. In addition there were also Pupil Teachers from time to time as well as older children from the Fitzwilliam who acted as Monitors when required. Remarkably, for a period of some 36 years, the task of teaching the infant children of the villages fell to just three teachers – Mrs Cooke and Miss Hales from 1920 to 1927 and then Miss Ambrose and Miss Hales from 1927 to 1956. These women taught the brothers and sisters of two, if not three, generations of the same families; children who are now our villages' elder residents.

Funding

This school also received annual Government and Fee Grants and, in 1890, these amounted to £66 6s 0d. [19]. However rather like the Vestry School, the Ecclesiastical Commissioners as well as several local residents also supported it. In that year, this came to a substantial £29 7s 0d The Voluntary School Aided Grant for special items was also introduced around this time and, in 1897, the *Log* records how this was used to buy curtains and a new cupboard. This period also saw the beginnings of fund-raising by hiring out the room for teas or meetings and there was the first school concert in 1896 which raised funds to buy fans, mirrors and musical equipment.

Fig 30i. Castor Infants School: Class II with the rocking horse and doll from the Babies' Gallery. 1911. (Courtesy of Joan Marriott).

In the Classroom

The school admitted children from aged five to seven, who were variously arranged into two or three classes covering three Standards. For most of the time there was also the under-five or Babies' section with occasionally children as young as three. In the early 1900s this section was allowed to reduce because of staff shortages. However, during the First World War it was reinstated to release some of the young mothers for war-related work.

The lessons were mainly a combination of Religious Instruction and the 3 Rs and remained so throughout. The children learnt their letters and numbers and were guided from writing in sand-trays through slates and chalks to paper and pencils. Recitation and singing played an important role and gradually drill, drawing and handicrafts were introduced. By 1900, just as in the Fitzwilliam School, a detailed prescribed syllabus was in place for each Standard. Often lessons would be taken outside in the

Fig 30j. Castor Infants School: Class I with Mrs Annie Cooke on the left – Headmistress from 1886 – 1927. Early 1900s. (Courtesy of Joan Marriott).

Fig 30k. Castor Infants School: Class with Miss Muriel Hales – Assistant teacher from 1912 – 1959. c1922. (Courtesy of Joan Marriott)

summer and, from 1913 a little gardening was tried. All this was also subject to regular scrutiny by the Rector and the Authorities although this regime is not recorded in the *Logs* as being as intensive as in the Fitzwilliam School.

Those pupils who had reached the required Standard, usually in their seventh year, were transferred to the Fitzwilliam School at the start of the School Year. One of the teachers, or an older pupil from the Fitzwilliam, would lead them by the hand from the Infants during the first or second week of the new term.

Special Events

These children also enjoyed the usual round of Fetes, Feasts, Sunday school and Choir outings as well as film shows in the school. Up until the First World War, there was also an annual treat given by the Rev Hopkinson at Sutton Grange. The children were taken in the farmers' wagons and, in August 1893, there are reports of '...*games in the large barn...*' and '...*sweets and nuts for all.*' [20]. Mr and Mrs Carter of Ailsworth also often laid on a Christmas tea for the children. Much later, when buses became more readily available, there were visits such as those to the Mobile Theatre during Peterborough Art Week after 1945 and to see 'A Queen is Crowned' at the Odeon in 1953.

Other trips out of school were not so enjoyable. From 1928 when the School Dental Service began, there were annual inspections at school and those children needing treatment were taken across to the Reading Room. Here, an older boy from the Fitzwilliam would work the treadle for drilling the teeth. Sometimes his concentration would waver resulting in a kind of quick-slow-quick effect – still very vivid in the memory today!

Rolls and Attendance

The earliest mention we have of the number on the Roll is in the *Log* of 1894 when 79 out of 86 children were present. The attendance then seems to have fluctuated quite widely throughout; affected by a combination of the parents' willingness to send the children, the weather and travel, and illness. These young children were often away with coughs and colds or if the weather was particularly nasty. If older brothers or sisters were absent from the Fitzwilliam, then the young ones also stayed away. Those from Sutton and Upton were frequently missing. If there were occasions when the parents were present, such as one of the annual treats, then an appeal would be made to them to send their children

Fig 30l. Castor Infants School: Class with Miss Ambrose – Headmistress from 1927-1956. c 1930. (Courtesy of Brian Goode)

regularly. In 1895 special prizes for regular attendance were introduced and at one point, money was offered to some of the Upton children to encourage them. At various times, transport in the winter months was provided including covered carts and Sharpe's Bread Van, and from 1942, a more regular service began with Mr Taylor's van.

Up to 1930, the *Logs* of both schools record cases of various illnesses. Children with scarlet fever, diphtheria, tuberculosis, scabies and ringworm were excluded. Epidemics of measles, mumps, chicken pox, influenza and whooping cough often decimated the attendance and sometimes led to school closure. Before 1910, a doctor only came into schools to confirm these cases and authorize any exclusion or closure. After 1910, regular medical inspections began, first with the School Doctor and then, from 1917, with the School Nurse as well. Thus began the monitoring of the children's general health – 'verminous' heads, undernourishment and skin complaints - as well as the gradual decline in the more serious illnesses.

The numbers on the Roll generally remained between 90-110 up to 1919. After this they fell to around 50 and below until the closure of the school in 1956.

Castor Church of England (VC) Primary School: founded 1956

The Countess Fitzwilliam with her husband William George Thomas, the 10th Earl, opened this school in July 1956. This Voluntary Controlled school replaced the two previous schools in Castor. Additional Church land to the East of the Infants School had been made available and so this school was founded on the same site and with the same principles as the earlier school.

The school developed from the Infants School building. After refurbishment it was transformed into an Assembly Hall/dining room with a kitchen built at the rear. Three modern classrooms were added to the Eastern end of the Hall and a further classroom was built to the West in 1958/9 [21]. A swimming pool was installed in the 1960s but was removed in 1998. A further classroom was erected in 1999 where the pool had been. Various small offices have been added from time to time along the length of the main classroom block, the latest being a Library area in 2000.

Fig 30m. Castor Primary School: Aerial view from the South showing the original Infants School with modern extensions to the East. 1958. (Courtesy of Margaret Berridge and Graham Spence)

The new school opened during a period of great change in the village. From 1949 none of the children over 11 went to school in Castor and from around the mid-1950s, there was an enormous influx of new families into the village. A measure of continuity from the earlier schools was achieved however as Assistant Teacher Miss Hales from the Infants School stayed on and Mr Berridge, from the Fitzwilliam School, was appointed Headteacher. He retired in 1973 and was succeeded by Mr George Stevenson. The present Headteacher, Mrs Cathie Marriage, followed upon his retirement in 1995. Just as before, these Heads have implemented several fundamental developments in education including the 11+ and its subsequent phasing out, changes in school-management practices as well as the introduction of School League Tables and the Ofsted Inspections.

This school began with 90 pupils, aged between five and eleven, arranged into three classes. Now there are five with a Roll of 130. It continues to admit children from our villages but with any surplus places available to others. There is now more staff including a Deputy Headteacher and Teaching Assistants as well as the Class teachers. At the present time, the school has an annual Budget in the region of £350 000.

Fig 30n. Castor Primary School: 1961 Centenary Celebrations with the children outside St Kyneburgha's Church. Mrs Berridge is on the right with Mrs Scott and Mrs Mossendew behind. On the left is Mr Albert Berridge – Headmaster of Castor Fitzwilliam School 1944-1956 and the Primary School 1956-1973. (Courtesy of Margaret Berridge and Graham Spence)

Fig 30o. The way we were. A class of Fitzwilliam schoolchildren with Assistant Teacher, Mr Sellars. Pre-1924.
(Courtesy of Peter Harris)

The curriculum has become more diverse, reflecting the tremendous changes there have been in contemporary life since the late 1950s as well as the explosion in information technology. Trips out have also become more sophisticated including residential visits as well a richer choice of Arts venues and Inter-school sporting and musical events. One of the major changes has been in the role of parents within schools generally. In the older Castor schools, the parents only came into the school on very few occasions such as prize-giving or medical inspections. Now they play a fundamental role in school - life: they are fund-raisers and Governors, and schools are now a great deal more accountable to them as well as to the State.

As well as these many changes there are some things that, in essence, have not changed. Government Funding is still complicated and fund-raising for extra things is a way of life. The diversity of the modern curriculum can only be admired although, with the current demands of accountability, the opportunities for extra-curricular events for the children still largely rest on the dedication of the teachers.

And finally
It has not been possible here to give anything other than a rather broad view of the present Castor Primary School. However this is not entirely inappropriate. There will come a time when it will be this school's turn to have its history written in greater detail. Rather then, it is better to pause for reflection at this moment in our own history. It is surely fair to say, that the quality of our village community-life today is, in part at least, a testament to the pupils and teachers of the Castor Fitzwilliam and Infants Schools.

Fig 30p. Castor Infants School: Class with Miss Hales around 1920. (back row) l to r: Stanley Glover, Stanley Pell, Ted Mortimer, Cecil Whybray. (third row) l to r: ? , Bertha Brown, Eva Taylor, David Britten, Wilf Mossendew, Arthur Cooke, Miss Hales. (second row) l to r: Len Storey, Floss Coulson, Nellie Taylor, Lizzie Afford, John Reed, Don Reed, Jack Cooke, Barbara Kingston, Billy Harris. (front row) l to r: Harry Coulson, ? , Jack Kingston, Mona Reed, Edna Hammond, Evelyn Mossendew. (courtesy of Joan Marriott)

Fig 30q. Castor Fitzwilliam School: Mr Albert Berridge (second from right) with Assistant teacher Mr Dyason and three Student Teachers. Late 1940s. (courtesy of Margaret Berridge and Graham Spence)

Fig 30r. Rather a smart turnout! Class of Castor Infants. Early 20th century. (courtesy of Castor Primary School)

Fig 30s. Castor Infants School: Class with Miss Hales around 1927. (back row) l to r: ? , Harry Gibbons, Doug Oliver, Gladys Smith, Edna Hammond, John Sharpe, Miss Hales. (third row) l to r: Alma Glover, Morrey Jakes, Joan Sharpe), ? , ? ? , Adele Longfoot. (second row) l to r: ? , Millie Oliver, Enid Longfoot, ? , Muriel Cliff, ? , Gladys Cliff. (front row) l to r: ? Pearl Garfield, Claude Sharpe, ? , Reg Hill, Stan Hill. (courtesy of Brian Goode)

Fig 30t. View of Primary School from the Church Tower. 1958. The original Infants School can be seen to the right with modern kitchens and classrooms to the left. (courtesy of David Scott)

Kath Henderson

Kath and her husband, David, came to live in Castor from the North-east in 1998. She has two step-daughters, Debbie and Pamela. A scientist by profession, and with a long-standing interest in history, Kath has found being involved in this Local History project very rewarding. In the course of writing this chapter she has enjoyed meeting a great many people and has learnt a tremendous amount about the villages.

She thanks Mrs Cathie Marriage, Headteacher of Castor Primary School, for granting such easy access to the old School Records. Kath is also indebted to Mrs Margaret Sharpe for her assistance with researching the old School Logs and former pupils' recollections.

Notes

1. According to *The Peterborough Society's 3rd Annual Report.* 1955. p13 there was also a school established by the clergyman in the cottage next to the Church in Sutton, at least between 1861-1880.
2. As well as these Church Schools there were also the Dames' Schools which provided this kind of early education. There were several in our villages although details remain sketchy.
3. Mr Hales was Sexton at St Kyneburghas for 60 years and extracts from his lecture are given in *Appendix 18.*
4. *Post Office Directory of Berkshire, Northamptonshire, Oxfordshire with Bedfordshire, Buckinghamshire and Huntingdonshire.* W K Kelly and Co, London. 1847. pp2059-60. Records only a Sunday School in Castor in addition to the Fitzwilliam School.
5. One or two Castor residents whose grandparents were of school-age in the 1850s believe they attended this Church School rather than Castor Fitzwilliam School.
6. *Slater's Royal National Commercial Directory and Topography: Northamptonshire.* Isaac Slater, Manchester and London. 1862. p67.
7. Notes made by Albert Berridge, Headmaster of Castor Fitzwilliam School from 1944, relate how he had spoken with Mr A A Cooke whose father had gone to the Vestry School (although it is not clear if this was the day School). He had shown him some of his father's copybooks with illustrated copies of Psalms.
8. Marholm had its own school until 1959.
9. Other exceptions included those in a position to attend fee-paying schools in nearby towns. Also, around 1894, some of the children from Sutton went to Thornhaugh and the *School Admissions Register* records pupils coming from private tuition in Dame's schools. As late as 1994 there are reports of some children being admitted who had never been to school before. In addition, not all pupils transferred to the Fitzwilliam from the Infants School. A few were in a position to take up a place in fee-paying schools, such as the Deacons School, in Peterborough.
10. These *Logs* were hand-written by the Headteacher in official hardbound books. Day to day events such as visitors, closures, attendance and classroom activities had to be recorded and Attendance Officer's and Inspector's Reports copied in. Although they vary in fullness and style they are a rich source of information about the schools.
11. Including Mrs Margaret Berridge, Mr Brian Goode, Mrs Jenny Hammond, Mr Alec Jakes, Mrs Lottie Kent, Mrs Cathie Marriage, Mrs Joan Marriott and Mr George Stevenson.
12. In 1798, the Rev White commissioned a survey of Castor. This hand-drawn map showing the principal dwellings and occupants of Castor is considered to be part of the notes associated with the survey and is dated 1798-26.
13. *Census Return* for Castor. 1861.
14. *Census Return* for Castor. 1841.
15. Castor Fitzwilliam *School Cash Book.* 1870-1901.
16. Extract from the *Public Registry* of the Lord Bishop of Peterborough. 31 May 1861.
17. *Post Office Directory of Northamptonshire.* Ed E R Kelly. Kelly and Co Ltd, London. 1877. pp272-3.
18. *Commercial and General Directory and Blue Book of Northamptonshire.* C N Wright. Abel and Sons, Northants. 1884. pp241-2.
19. Castor Infants *School Account.* 1890.
20. *Peterborough Standard.* August 1893.
21. Probably to accommodate children from Marholm whose school closed in 1959.

Chapter 31
Celebrations

As far back as the older residents can remember, we here as a community have always pulled out all the stops and celebrated, when the occasion arises. The first street party that I can remember in these parts was in 1995, when we celebrated the 50th anniversary of VE Day. Three people had travelled through Peterborough via Thorney, and until they arrived in Castor had seen little evidence of jollification. We invited them to stay, and stay they did.

The Diamond Jubilee of Queen Victoria - 1897

There had been two special services at St. Kyneburgha's in the morning and evening of Sunday 20th June, by Command of the Queen. The programme for the Tuesday 22nd began at 10.30am with a Procession through the village, meeting at the 'Stocks'. After a short service taken by the Rev Collins, the curate, lunch was served at 1pm. Men and women dined in the Large Booth, children in the Infants' School. At 2.30pm sports commenced in Mr Hunt's field. Boys' prizes were 1/6, 1/- and 6d respectively, and there was a 4th prize of 2 glasses and 2 spoons. Girls' 1st prize was 15 yards of calico, 2nd 8 yards and 5 yards for 3rd prize, the 4th prize was the same as that for all the races. The mens' prizes consisted of money; however the women were awarded 18 yards of calico for 1st prize, 12 yards for 2nd and 6 yards for 3rd prize. Mr George Fitzwilliam gave each child a Jubilee medal, and each received a Jubilee mug from Mr Sykes. Tea was served at 5pm in the same venues as lunch. The Peterborough Advertiser, on 26th June 1897 reported: *'At 10 o'clock (evening) all proceeded to the bonfire, from the top of Castor Hill upwards of 20 fires could be seen, including the reflections from Lincoln and Ely Cathedrals. The Castor Brass Band who headed the procession in the morning played a selection of music during the day and also for the evening dance'.* Mr Fitzwilliam gave trees to both parishes, as a lasting memorial.

Ailesworth had their own celebrations but very little was recorded other than a few vague memories that Mrs Nellie Longfoot recounted to Silas Harvey for the Jubilee Book in 1977. Here she says that 'A Tea' was held in the Jubilee Barn.

The earliest photograph of the Band available was taken in 1897 at Helpston Feast, members of the Ancient Order of Foresters are on the right of the photograph.

800th Anniversary of the Dedication the Church of St Kyneburgha 1924

The two local newspapers, The Peterborough Standard and The Peterborough Advertiser, each gave us two full-length columns in their broadsheets to report this very important date in our calendar. The service of Dedication on Wednesday April 30th was led by the Bishop of Peterborough, Dr Bardsley. As one reporter, possibly Mrs Annie Cooke, described it, *'On Wednesday afternoon all roads seemed to lead to Castor, and great multitudes travelled to the village by every conceivable means of locomotion. Long before the time for the service to commence, the church was full, and the churchwardens (the Hon Mrs Pelham and Mr F Chappel) then proceeded to wedge late comers into various nooks and corners.'* Both reports named all those present, also all 28 of the clergy. As well as this being a service of Dedication, it was also one of Thanksgiving at the completion of much refurbishment in the church. At this time the 8th century Saxon figure was discovered under the floor near the altar rail. The Bishop preached from the text, 1. Chronicles, 29: 3, *'I have set my affection to the house of my God'.* During his sermon he said, *"I am tempted to say a word about the ministry of women in the Church, as I think of Hilda on the Yorkshire coast, of Etheldreda, Kyneburgha, and many others of those days. I rejoice at the revival of the order of deaconesses in the Church today."*

Fig 31a. Castor and Ailesworth Band at Helpston Feast in 1897, quite possibly before they had purchased uniforms. Bandsmen. (l-r) unknown, unknown, Fred Tomlin, Bill Cooke, unknown, Dick Taylor, unknown. With them are members of the Ancient Order of Foresters.

After the service a large number of people stayed to tea in the Infants School and the Bishop, in a very brief address, referred

Fig 31b. Castor church spire undergoing repairs in 1920. Local men carried out the work (l-r): W Cooke, AA Cooke, R Coulson and A Jakes.

to the wonderful service they had experienced. He thanked all who had made the celebration a success, those who had carried out the work in the church, and also the congregation that had attended. The Rector, Canon Morse, in thanking the Bishop, said he regretted that illness had prevented Major Pelham (Churchwarden) from attending the service. Mrs W Carter entertained the bell ringers to tea later.

The Silver Jubilee of King George V and Queen Mary - 6th May, 1935

The Programme commenced at 2pm with sports in the field behind the Village Hall, kindly loaned by Mrs Darby. There were 22 assorted races with money as prizes, juniors 1s.6d, 1s and 9d. The prize for winning the Greasy Pole was a leg of mutton given by Mr Cole (licensee from the Fitzwilliam Arms). The prizes for the winners of the Tug of War were cigarettes, given by Mr Mackie, (Mr George Fitzwilliam's Agent). The sports concluded with a cricket match between the ladies and the men. At 4pm, tea for the school-children, and residents of 65 years and over was served. A presentation of Jubilee Souvenirs was made to the school-children at 4.45 pm with an interval at 5 pm. Castor Brass Band played during the races, and at 7 pm there was a 'Social' in the Village Hall when the King's Speech was relayed. From 9-12 pm there was dancing in the Village Hall, to the music of Mr Will Cooke's Dance Band. The day was financed by public subscription.

The Year of the Three Kings

At the Annual Church Meeting in January 1936, the Rector, Canon Cornelius Carlton, stated that 1935 had been a very eventful year. The Silver Jubilee of their Majesties King George V and Queen Mary had been celebrated in May. Now,

Fig 31c. The Castor and Ailesworth Band playing at the Silver Jubilee Celebrations of King George V and Queen Mary in 1935.

early in the New Year of 1936, they were mourning the loss of their late King. Of the following Annual Meeting in January 1937, Mrs Annie Cooke, the Hon Secretary, wrote that the Rector had opened the Meeting with a short review of the work of the past year; and had referred to the abdication of King Edward VIII, and the accession of King George VI and Queen Elizabeth.

The year 1936 had indeed been a momentous one. King George V died on 20th January 1936, King Edward VIII's accession was on the 20th January and his abdication on 11th December 1936, and King George VI acceded to the throne on 11th December 1936.

The Coronation of King George VI and Queen Elizabeth – 12th May, 1937

Two years on, an almost identical programme was used in the villages to celebrate the Coronation. Again there were sports. However on this occasion there was a Carnival Procession which assembled at Castor Green and arrived at Mrs Darby's field at 2.45 pm. The National Anthem was sung and then the sports began. Apart from the usual races, there were races for 'Football Dribbling', 'Skipping', and 'Thread the Needle'. This was followed by a race for men over 50 years and an 80 yards ladies' race. There were also 'Pillow Fights'. As before there were prizes of a leg of mutton and cigarettes, these having been given by the same donors as before. Children's tea was from 4.30 to 5 pm when there was a presentation of a souvenir. Teas for adults were served from 5 to 6 pm; those attending Tea were expected to bring their own crockery and cutlery. According to the receipts from Brown's the Butchers, the cost of 50lb of tongue, 50lb of ham and 80lb of pressed beef was £14 1s 8d. The Hon Mrs Pelham managed to get some discount from Fowler & Son, Bakers: for 30 large loaves and 24 dozen mixed cakes, the bill came to £2 6s 6d less 4s 6d. Mr Fox's account for sugar, salad cream, tomatoes, Eiffel Tower Lemonade, 15lbs of butter and yet more cakes, came to £3 13s 1d. This receipt was signed over a 2d postage stamp bearing the head of the former King, Edward VIII. The Castor Brass Band played during the afternoon, there then followed a concert in the Village Hall, followed by a dance to Will Cooke's Dance

Band. The previous Sunday there had been a special form of Divine Service, commended by the Archbishops of Canterbury and York, held in the church, at which members of Castor Parish Council, Ailesworth Parish Meeting, and all local organisations, headed by Castor Band, had been present. The procession assembled at the Reading Room. The people who attended remember the two days as something very special.

The Coronation of Queen Elizabeth II - 2nd June, 1953

On 4th November 1952, Mr Leeds, Clerk to Castor Parish Council, called a Public Meeting in the Village Hall to consider whether the two Parishes should combine for the Coronation Celebrations, and if so, what form these celebrations should take. Mr Berridge, the Headmaster, had written to Mr Tait, the Chief

Fig 31d. Arthur Foster on his decorated Combine at the Coronation Celebrations of Queen Elizabeth II in 1953.

Education Officer, requesting the names of firms producing suitable Coronation souvenirs. Mr Tait replied to the effect that he was awaiting confirmation from the Education Authority; as yet they had not decided what to give the children by way of a souvenir. Mr Berridge received a letter from the Ministry of Education dated 20th November that indicated the arrangements made by the Minister of Food for the supply of sweets additional to Ration Book allowance. Also, some souvenirs, flags, and bunting would be exempt tax for a period of one year from 1st October. The Care and Protection of Rural England wrote offering advice for any village commemoration, such as tree planting, improving village greens, or provision of new seats. At a Public Meeting on January 6th, Mr Len Sharpe proposed, seconded by Mr Walter Taylor that tea should be provided for all between the ages of 16 to 70 on payment of 1s per month for 5 months. Miss Win Goodyer said she would agree to this on the understanding that all children and old people should be given a free tea. This was carried and a group of residents from each village agreed to collect the money. £124 was collected by way of the collection, donations and a variety of functions. Earl Fitzwilliam mentioned that some of the people at Milton intended to join in the Castor Celebrations; it would be necessary for someone to collect in that district. He suggested that the secretary should ask Mr Philips and Mrs Peacock if they would undertake this.

A very full programme was arranged under the chairmanship of the Earl Fitzwilliam. On Friday May 29th, the presentation of Coronation souvenirs to all children took place on the lawn of Cedar House at 3.30pm. On Sunday May 31st a special form of Divine Service, issued by Command of the Queen, was used in Castor Church. It had been hoped that all inhabitants of Castor and Ailesworth would attend; it was, indeed, very well-attended.

On Monday June 1st prizes for the Best Decorated Houses were, 1st prize £1 10s 0d, 2nd prize £1, and 3rd prize 10s 0d. On Tuesday June 2nd the Church Bells were rung and Holy Communion was sung at 7.30am followed by a special children's service at 9am. (By midday the rain had begun, and by the time the Carnival Procession left Ailesworth at 2pm it was raining heavily.) There was an assortment of floats in the procession, plus one of Gibbons's traction engines, a combine harvester, and the old Fire Brigade pump. The procession arrived in Darby's field behind the Village Hall at 3.50pm. This was also the venue for the Sports. As far as I can recollect the rain had by now stopped and spectators began to peel off raincoats. The National Anthem was sung heartily in the field before the Children's Concert began in the Village Hall at 4pm. Tea was taken from 5 until 6.30pm. To accommodate the large crowds Mr George Amies from the Elms had organised a marquee from Snowdens, at a cost of £16. As in the past, all were expected to bring their own crockery and cutlery. Tea, supplied by Turnhills (meat tea at 3/- and 2/- for a carton tea for the children), which was served by the Mothers' Union. When all were fed and watered, the sports began. These were for girls and boys. There were races, too, for women and men from the age of 16 to 40 and over. The sports concluded with a 'Tug of War', this time not for cigarettes, but £2 for the winners and £1 for the runners-up. From 9 to 9.15pm the Queen's Speech was relayed from a radio hired from Johnson's of Peterborough. Mr Longfoot had tried to obtain a television for the day, but whether it materialised or not, I am not certain. After the speech, a Social and Dance took place, this time with music provided by Mr Litz's equipment which Mr Len Fisher of the Prince of Wales operated. The Castor Excelsior Brass Band also played during the festivities. At 11.30pm, a huge bonfire was lit by Mr WW Longfoot and Mr K Leeds. The Rev T Adler had contacted RAF Wittering who floodlit the church. This was a very fitting close to a most memorable day.

Fig 31e. Raynor Snart with a decorated Fordson Major tractor and Drill at the Coronation Celebrations in 1953. This photograph was taken in the field which is now 'Woodlands'.

Fig 31f. One of the Gibbon's Traction Engines at the Coronation Celebrations. The two man crew was Bob Gibbons and Bill Coles.

Fig 31g. The Old Contemptibles led by Mr Sid Pearson of Castor, their secretary, parade to the church where their Standard was 'Laid-up' on 9th July 1967.

Laying up of the Old Contemptibles Standard – 9th July 1967

As the Peterborough Branch of the Association became increasingly smaller, it was decided by them to lay-up their Standard in a place of worship. Mr Middleton, from Whittlesey, their secretary, who had been to our church on a number of occasions, asked if it might be laid-up here. And so, on the evening of Sunday 9th July 1967, in the presence of HRH the Duchess of Gloucester, 24 Old Contemptibles assembled with their loved ones, when their Standard was paraded for the last time, and then laid-up. The service was conducted by the Rev T Adler, their branch Padre, himself a former Army Chaplain, and the Bishop of Peterborough, Cyril Eastaugh MC, who gave the address. Mr Sid Pearson, the last surviving 'Old Contemptible' of our community, led the parade; sadly his 'chum' Mr Alf Woodward died 24 hours before the service. Mr Bill Middleton continued to attend our Remembrance Sunday service for several years. His only son was RAF aircrew, and was killed on a bombing raid.

850th Anniversary of the Dedication of the Church of St Kyneburgha 1974

The Celebrations began on Thursday 16th May with a Festal Evensong and Procession at which Bishop Douglas Feaver preached. On the following Wednesday evening, the choir of Peterborough Cathedral gave a recital of 'Music through the Ages', conducted by Stanley Vann, their Director of Music. Saturday 25th May was the first of three days when a Pageant was staged in the Glebe Field. The Pageant was a huge success. It eclipsed anything that MGM could produce. '*The Story of St Kyneburgha*' was written and produced by Kay McNaughton. We auditioned for parts, and all but the final dress rehearsal was held in her garden, at that time the old, old Rectory, now Vine House. I well remember that last rehearsal in the Glebe field opposite the School on Stocks Hill. Poor Kay threw the script on the ground and said something unprintable, but to the effect that it was a shambles.

The big day came. We changed into our costumes in the Rectory garden (now the Cook's home), Jim Wood allowed us to remove a section of fence to the field, and then to the strains of some rousing music through amplifiers in the trees, we made our entrance. There were no speaking parts; Jack, Kay's husband, was the narrator (hidden from view in some bushes) - a delightful man who called a spade, a spade. As we came into view of our audience at the bottom of the field, a breeze rustled the leaves, and from the corner of my eye I saw papers blowing about, and then those immortal words from Jack echoed loud and clear through the speakers, *"Oh, that bloody wind!"* Theo Hensman was as ingenious as ever, designing a mechanism with strips of tyre inner tube and metal pegs which allowed the Cross to rise as Kyneburgha 'built' her nunnery. We played to packed houses each time. Farmer Jim Wood had loaned us bales for seating. The weather was perfect and it was just good to be a part of those celebrations, and, yes, Kay was happy with it too.

I am certain that the Flower Festival held in the church was our first. Miss Dorothy Ward, sister to Mr Eddie Ward, one of the churchwardens, gave us expert guidance. Another first, I think was the photographic exhibition we held in the vestry. Joan Marriott and I collected dozens of old local photographs from numerous residents in both villages and beyond. On the evening of the 26th May we had a service of Hymns of Praise conducted by the Rev Adler.

The Silver Jubilee of Queen Elizabeth 11 – 4th June 1977

The Rev Lloyd-James, an Ailesworth resident, wrote A Jubilee Poem as a forward to the Souvenir Programme. A new word had appeared in our vocabulary - Disco - for on Saturday 4th June, there was a Disco and Dance in the Village Hall from 8pm until midnight with dancing to the Barry Jay-Disco Show. Chance of a lifetime for local girls: the selection of Miss Jubilee 1977! The girls were sponsored by various businesses. The winner was Jackie Woodward (now Elliott) sponsored by Anne and Garth of the Wheat-sheaf, Ailesworth. The day had really begun with a Jubilee peal of bells at 10am. The Castor and Ailesworth Bell-ringers attempted a quarter peal in honour of the Silver Jubilee of Queen Elizabeth II. The Bells were not rung at the Coronation of King George V, in 1935, because it was feared at the time that the Tower was unsafe. During the day, judging took place of decorated houses, and /or premises, and best garden. On Sunday 5th June, at 6.30pm, a Service of Thanksgiving was held in the church.

There were sports in the School playing fields on Monday 6th at 2pm. Events and activities had been arranged for children and adults under the watchful eye of Mr George Stevenson (Head teacher at the Primary School). At the conclusion of the Sports, tea was provided for the children, and Miss Jubilee 1977 presented Jubilee mugs and mports prizes. Refreshments were on sale for adults during the afternoon. An open air Barbeque and Dance, to Coda Five and Tony Ellis Disco, was held in Castor School forecourt, starting at 8pm to midnight (plus) with hot hogs on sale, and a licensed bar. Miss Jubilee was in attendance. Had it been wet, the Barbeque would have been in the Village Hall. With hindsight, I am so very relieved that it was a dry evening! During the afternoon of Thursday 9th June the Senior Citizens were given Afternoon Tea, and a sherry for the Royal Toast, which was served at The Prince of Wales, with the help of Edgar and Madge Parker. The young people of the two villages, through their Youth Club, provided this hospitality from the proceeds of a ten mile sponsored walk. The final event – brought to us in that 'Venerable Venue of Varieties' Castor Village Hall – was the Jubilee Music Hall. This was a superb show. Days later, I remember Dr Dudgeon asking me if I had enjoyed the show. He viewed it as being one of the best amateur shows he had seen. The Rector, Adrian Davies, Chairman of the Celebrations Committee, wrote at the end of the programme that it was hoped that our Jubilee Booklet would be on sale at the end of the year. It was, thanks to the stoic work of its editor, Silas Harvey.

Castor Fitzwilliam School Reunion – 14th August 1987

A quote from the Reunion programme (26th March 1987*): 'A cold, wet and windy evening. Inside 2B Thorolds Way, Joan arranged the furniture, adds a few extra chairs and gets out the cups and saucers. The doorbell rings. From the shadows of the porch four smiling faces appear from beneath dripping brollies – Lorna, Robin, Grace and Gladys arrive followed by Ron and Brian. Together we debate organising the first Castor Fitzwilliam School Reunion spanning 87 years, would it catch on? What if it proved to be a non-starter? We agreed to spread the word, note the reaction and proceed from there. The response amazed us! The attendance register rapidly passed the 100 mark.'* The evening was a huge success, So many old

Fig 31h. The Men's Breakfast float begins its journey from Ailesworth recreation ground at the V E Celebration in 1995.

girls and boys, the ladies wore badges bearing their maiden names, Tom Dudley at 83 was the oldest there, with Tom Brown, a close second at 82; I was very much in the infants' class at 53. The tables groaned under the weight of the food, the drink flowed, and so did those wonderful stories. Mr Albert Berridge, the school's last Headmaster 'caned' Alec Jakes, who was dressed as a 1930s schoolboy. Someone had made superb posters depicting: a cookery class, Mr Salmon (a former head) with a class of boys on their way to the school gardens, and the Hon Mrs Pelham, complete with those long ear rings, standing with a group of children saluting the union flag, with the caption: '*A Glorious Thing This British Empire.*'

Thirteen married couples who had attended the School were given wooden spoons. Beryl Banks, nee Dudley accompanied us at the piano as we sang those old folk songs we had learned in that very room. Several poems were written especially for the day, **Hygiene** - The last verse went: '*Then a girl, very bold asked outright and she was told, you shouldn't know that at your tender age so, very kindly, turn over the page*'. Another was **Cookery Class 1933,** beginning: '*Through frost, snow and winter sludge. Down the Village hall we trudge. There Miss Hollywood lays in wait, to catch the ones who crept in late*'. **The Gas Mask** concluded: '*When you see the mismatched window, I think you ought to know; that it wasn't Hitler's bombs to blame, it was David's lethal throw*'. (David Hill). Grace Gibbs, nee Burton, wrote the poem. **In Who Done It?** Tom Cooke was only too happy to recount his story, about tampering with Mr Salmon's clock. The third verse read: '*This lad shall be found if it is the last thing I do. Speak up now, who did it, just give me a clue*'? *His face was all red, he was waving his stick, I can tell you by now, and we were all feeling 'frit'.* It was truly a very special evening, so much to talk about, so little time, and, yes, there were a few friendly tears as we parted. A final quote, '*Time for Goodbyes, echoing and drifting away into the darkness, leaving behind never to be forgotten memories with those of us privileged to be there*'.

Fig 31i. The Fitzwilliam School reunion 14th August 1987. Back row (l-r): Brian Goode, Grace Gibbs (nee Burton), Ron Hudson, Robina Gibbons (nee Wade) Beryl Banks (nee Dudley) at the piano, Front row (l-r): Doreen Jones (nee Manning), Iris Butler (nee Manning) and Dawn Coleman (nee Hill).

Fig 31j. A cookery class at the Reading Room on Castor Green 1915, (Fire Station in the background) Back Row (l-r): Gladys Longfoot, Rose Todd, Cary Hill, Edie Hill, Annie Hill. unknown, Hornsby. Front Row (l-r): Alice Sismey, Barrett, unknown, Annie Maria Crane, unknown, Gladys Ward. unknown Two Belgian refugee's whose father worked for a Mr Baxter of Castor.

VE Thanksgiving Service – 7th May 1995

Douglas Gillam and the House group compiled the service in the absence of an incumbent, the Rev. Willett, who took part in the D Day landings, officiated.

VJ Thanksgiving Service – 20th August 1995

This service was incorporated within the Eucharist by the celebrant, the Revd Randall, a former RAF chaplain. Both of the above services were taken by visiting clergy during an interregnum.

Celebrating the Millennium – 10th June 2000

On the 31st December 1999, as the half-muffled bells, including our two new ones, rang out the Old Year and the Second Millennium, the candle-lit church at Castor was packed with people coming in to reflect or light candles, or just to be with other people. A large crowd gathered round the beacon in the churchyard, lit on the stroke of midnight; rockets were fired from the Old Rectory garden, courtesy of Jonathan Cook, and the un-muffled bells rang in the New Millennium. But the main Millennium Celebrations were planned for the Pentecost-Whitsun weekend in June.

The Millennium committee did us proud, with attractions going on right through the day. A

Cavalcade and Parade formed up at Ailesworth Recreation ground and slowly moved off to Woodlands. The Parade was led by the Peterborough Highland Pipe Band. Many residents from our villages took part, from the Brownies and Guides, to our Senior Citizens riding their scooters - possibly Mr Burgess was the most senior, at 91. The local horse riders looked magnificent, as did members of the Gardeners' Club, who were there in force - one looked not unlike Gay Search, and yet another was the image of the voluptuous Charlie Dimmock. Another look-alike was Alison Gibson's mother, who looks incredibly like our Queen. I imagine that a number of children who lined the route will long remember the day when they saw the Queen riding along the Peterborough Road in the back seat of Steve Walker's car. The Royal Oak had a float depicting Queens from the past, as did the WI float. A number of other village organisations and individuals added to the carnival atmosphere. Tables and chairs were put in place along the centre of the road, from the Fitzwilliam Arms to Church Walk. From 10.30am until early afternoon the Springfield Jazz Ensemble played near the entrance to the School Field. At 12 noon balloons were released, and by this time a small army of volunteers had formed a line from the refrigerated van and had passed down all manner of tempting food onto the tables (see colour plate section). We were entertained now by the Pipe Band. The wheelbarrow race was a great success, with just a tiny hint of danger! The prize-giving for this event was preceded by the Morris Dancers' display. Other attractions during the day included swing boats, steam organ, bouncy castle, and Keith Downs, the magician. The Village Hall hosted a Photographic Exhibition, and teas were served to the accompaniment of Leonard Danks at the piano. A first class Roman Exhibition was staged in the Cedar Centre.

The following day, Choir and Banners processed to the School Field for our Open-air Benefice Picnic Mass on Whit Sunday. The Salvation Army Band provided the music, ably assisted by Will Craven at the piano. The Revds Ron Amis and Barbara Howett assisted the Rector, William Burke, at the Altar. At the close, 50 Doves (symbolizing the fifty days between Easter and Pentecost) were released. A picnic on the School field was held after the service. The Banner near the church notice board read: **'Celebrate 2000 years of Christianity'!** I feel we did.

The earliest reference to bells in St Kyneburgha's appears in North's *Church Bells of Northamptonshire* 1878, where it was stated that in 1552 Castor possessed: *'Furst in o steple iiij grete bellys'*. These were replaced in 1700 by a new ring of six, cast and installed by Henry Bagley of Ecton. The

Fig 31k. The Street party on 3rd June 2002 to celebrate the Golden Jubilee of Queen Elizabeth II. The photograph was taken opposite the Village Hall.

Fig 31l. The Royal Oak float depicting Queen Elizabeth I, (Sylvia Sewell) Queen Victoria, as a young woman (Eleanor Hoggart) and Victoria in later years (Sharon Fitzjohn).

Millennium and the 300th anniversary of the birth of our bells fell in the same year. To mark this unique occasion, the ringers decided some twelve years ago to attempt to raise the money to augment the six to a full octave by the addition of two new trebles. During this period the ringers themselves raised over £7,000 by running various functions. To raise the required final cost it was decided to 'sell' family names which would be inscribed on the bells. William Baxter undertook this task which produced £8,500, but as yet there was still a short fall. However with grants from the Peterborough Diocesan Guild Bell Fund and the local Parish Councils, plus various other fund-raising events, they eventually made it. The new bells were cast by Taylor's of Loughborough, witnessed by the Rector, church wardens and a party of benefactors and ringers. The two new bells were duly baptised on 11th July 1999, and dedicated to St Kyneburgha, and her sister St. Kyneswitha on 17th October 1999 at a special service, by the Ven Bernard Fernyhough, Archdeacon Emeritus.

On 11th July 1999 new Vestments and Hangings were dedicated. The materials were generously donated by David Collison and Vanessa Edison-Giles, and a small army of ladies sewed and embroidered, an Altar Cloth, Altar Curtain, Aumbry Veil, a Legilium and Pulpit Fall, Chasuble and Stole. Each has a fish motif, this is because the Greek word for fish-IXTHUS-spells out in Greek the initial letters of the phrase 'Jesus Christ, Son of God, Saviour'.

The Golden Jubilee of Queen Elizabeth 11 – 3rd June 2002

The celebrations began on Saturday 1st June when a Jubilee Prom was staged on the School field. It was indeed a

Fig 31m. Jubilee Prom. Staged on the School field 1st June 2002.

wonderful spectacle, with so many people, some in evening dress, the picnic suppers, the candelabra, and the wonderful music. I am certain Castor has not seen the like before. The following day the same venue was used for an open-air Mass which was also well attended. His Worship the Mayor and the Mayoress of Peterborough joined us. During the service, Emily, the daughter of Katie and Stuart Bowen, was christened. In the afternoon on the following day, there was an Exhibition of old photographs and of the Parish Archives in the Cedar Centre. Monday, too, proved to be a wonderful occasion, indeed a memorable day, not least as the weather was so kind to us. At 10am the food was taken down to a refrigerated van on the school field in readiness for the Street Party at noon. Our village Policeman, Richard Weaver, at the request of the Castor Parish Council, had blocked off the road from The Royal Oak to Manor Farm

Fig 31n. Jubilee Street party on 3rd June 2002. Why were the customers looking towards Ailesworth?

Lane. At 10.30am the Parade of Floats left Ailesworth. The church bells rang for an hour from 11.45a.m. As soon as the Procession had travelled through Castor, the tables and chairs were placed down the centre of the road and the Street Party began. It was a most wonderful atmosphere; many residents from both villages sat down in relays. Folk who had possibly not even met before were happily chatting to one another. It was also good to see some expatriates return to the fold for the day. At 2pm one could try one's hand at carpet bowls in the Village Hall, while Lynette Blanchford played Golden Oldies on the piano during the afternoon there. Also at 2pm a Treasure Hunt was arranged. When darkness fell, Theo Hensman's beacon in the churchyard lit up the night sky; seconds after, John Ivans lit his, at Hill Farm, Chesterton. We were one of a vast chain of beacons that circled the country.

Brian Goode

Fig 31o. The Coronation celebrations of King George VI and Queen Elizabeth 12th May 1937. Those on the British Empire float include: Nora Pearson (nee Sharpe), Mary Cooke (nee Weire), Doris Ward (nee Truman), Hilda Fox (nee Sismey), Jean Goode (nee Trundle), Gladys Stone (nee Chilvers).

Fig 31p. Coronation float 1937, as it passes the old Tithe Barn at Castor Green. (The object hanging from the chain, is the 'slipper' the breaking system!) Children on the float were - Hazel Mann (nee Marsh), Margaret Bell (nee Sharpe), Vera Hammond (nee Gross), Olive Ward (nee Enness). Edna Pearson (nee Trasler), Joyce Goode (nee Harris), Jean Smith.

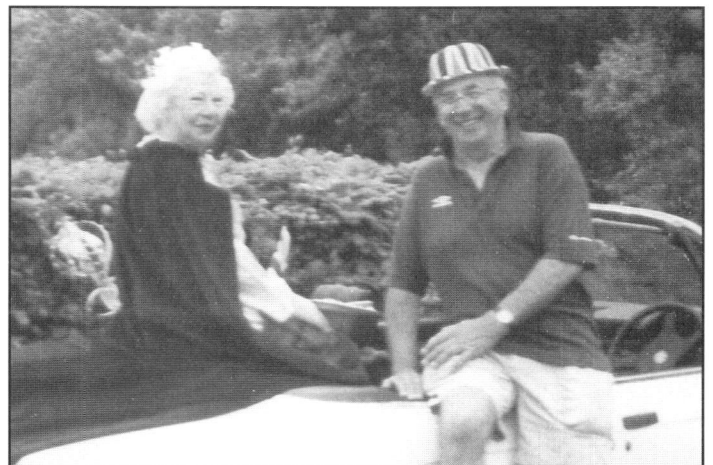

Fig 31q. The Queen and David. A rather 'matey' subject.

Fig 31r. Dedication of the wall in Church Walk, 1949, in memory of Major Pelham, churchwarden. The Hon Mrs Georgina Pelham unveiled a plaque in the wall. The Rev T Adler conducted the service.

Fig 31s. Dedication of the wall. The choir return to the church after the ceremony.

Fig 31t. Dedication of Vestments and Hangings on 11th July 1999. The photograph shows the chasuble and Altar cloth. The background material was green, for 'ordinary' time.

Fig 31u. Douglas and John Gillam at the Golden Jubilee celebrations, 3rd June 2002.

Fig 31v. Fitzwilliam School reunion, 14th August 1987. Lorna Wade (nee Sheppardson), David Hill, Hilda Bell (nee Summerskill), Joyce Maddison (nee Turner), Audrey Taylor (nee Neal), Rosemary Sharpe (nee Clarke), Robina Wade (nee Gibbons), Billy Want, Gracie Burton (nee Gibbs), Brian Goode.

Fig 31w. The Open Air Mass at the Millennium Celebrations. (l-r) the Revds William Burke, Barbara Howitt, Ron Amis and Dr Ian Baugh.

Fig 31x. What happened next? Theo Hensman (far left) prays that the webbing strap holds as the first of the two new bells are unloaded!

Fig 31y. A prayer answered: Tony Evans and Theo transfer the bell to Theo's pickup.

Fig 31z. Mrs Gladys Jeffries from Helpston, an expatriate from Castor, who at one time lived with her mother and brother in Allotment Lane. With her, taking a breather at the Jubilee Celebrations, is her granddaughter Denise Smith, Mark's wife.

Chapter 32
Flags and Bunting

The First Village Hall of Castor and Ailesworth

One Thursday evening, at the beginning of the 1920s, there was a well attended meeting of the ex-Servicemen from the villages of Castor and Ailsworth. The meeting, held in the Infants' School, was chaired by Sir Richard Winfrey, MP. Its purpose was to consider '*the desirability of an additional memorial to our fallen heroes and in memory of the victory achieved by our brave Servicemen in the 1914-18 war*'. Before the week had ended, another meeting was convened by Mr Fitzwilliam, Chairman of Castor Parish Council. This one was held in the Fitzwilliam School to consider what sort of further memorial should be adopted in the village. By a large majority it was decided to have a hut or building to use as a village facility.

A committee was formed comprising three members from Castor Parish Council, three members from Ailsworth Parish Council and six members of The Comrades. (The Comrades were soldiers who had fought together in the First World War).There were also six ladies from the village – Lady Winfrey, Mrs Carter, Mrs WT Cooke, Mrs Speechley, Mrs Harry Sharpe and Mrs Morse, as well as four gentlemen – Sir Richard Winfrey, MP, Mr Speechley, Mr Wootten and Mr Heighton. The future Village Hall was beginning to take shape.

The need for village clubs was becoming an issue of national importance. Newspapers from 1921 urged their readers of the need for village clubs citing;

> '*country living as being fairly tolerable in the summer but the winter dreary and unattractive with nothing in the way of social entertainment. This condition may satisfy the pre-war villager but the return of the ex-soldiers, bringing with them new ideas, are becoming a dynamic force within their respective localities. The towns and villages are becoming great magnets with ever increasing powers; the country people themselves must make their own entertainment.*' (Peterborough Advertiser, 1921).

The Village Clubs Association, started by the Agricultural Club in connection with Wages Board, had been formed to urge the pressing necessity to establish in each rural community a social centre where all people of the community could meet for common recreation. It was suggested that this would provide '*a social uplift that would bring the community together and inspire a free and compete circulation of ideas which would endow the people with the ties of community spirit*' (Peterborough Advertiser, 1921). In this way '*families would be bonded together and labour stabilised*'. The need for a Village Hall was further established.

The news of the new hut spread quickly around the village – there was no doubt that such a place was urgently required. The folks of Castor and Ailsworth had always enjoyed a good social life – the only drawback being the lack of a large hall where lots of people could meet together. Until this time the Infants' School had been used to accommodate the village whist drives, dances, concerts and such like, but it was far from satisfactory.

General enthusiasm for the Village Hall produced amazingly quick results. In just over twelve months from the initial idea the 'Comrades of the Great War' club was founded. The aim was to create a meeting place, for the ex-Servicemen from the villages of Castor, Ailsworth, Sutton and Upton, to meet and enjoy themselves together was underway. However, it was not all plain sailing. The proposal to create a meeting place **solely** for ex-soldiers was an

Fig 32a. Sir Richard Winfrey MP, first treasurer of the Village Hall Committee.

Fig 32b. Percy Heighton, first secretary of the Village Hall Committee.

unpopular choice which met with a good deal of opposition. After many meetings and much wrangling it was decided at a public meeting to fundraise throughout the villages to provide a hall which could be used by **both ex-Servicemen and parishioners**. So the Comrades agreed, threw in their funds and a public subscription list was opened.

Mr RP Heighton and Mr Mackman became secretaries whilst Sir Richard Winfrey, MP, took on the duties as Treasurer. He was able to use his influence discreetly - consequently the fund thrived tremendously under his enthusiastic guidance, aided by the Ecclesiastical Commissioners who also generously granted a lease for the site of the hut, and a donation for £50 as well!!! The site chosen was 25a Peterborough Road, Castor, a plot suitable to accommodate both proposed Village Hall and a bowling green round the back. Terms agreed were to lease the site for twenty one years at a '*nominal rent of one shilling per annum*'.

So well did the public respond to the appeal that by 29th June 1921 the committee was able to purchase the Hut from the YMCA. It was a spacious affair, made of wood, measuring 65 feet by 35 feet, previously used as a YMCA hostel at Luton.

The cost of the building was £100. The local newspaper enthusiastically described the new Hut as '*all that can be desired as a public hall. It is splendidly ventilated and lighted by windows and skylights in the daytime. In the evening three brilliant oil illuminations light the room, and by a little tact and good taste the interior has been beautifully transformed. The walls covered in two shades and bordered in stencil work*'. Figure 32d is the only known surviving photograph of the old Village Hall.

In December 1921 the fundraising was over and the Hut was opened by Mr George Fitzwilliam. There seemed to be some confusion as to the correct name for the hall for it was referred to as the 'Village Hall', 'The Victory Hall', 'The Red Triangle Hut', 'The Hut' and 'The Comrades Hall' and at the opening it was referred to as 'Castor's Town Hall'. In his opening speech Mr. GW Fitzwilliam gave special thanks to The Comrades who: '*throughout the summer had spent their evenings and Saturdays digging out and laying the foundations, and also undertaking the actual erection of the Hut itself*'. Mr GW Speechley was singled out for special praise for providing horses and vehicles for bringing bricks from Norman Cross and '*presenting and carting gravel, roofing and etc*'.

At the opening ceremony three hundred

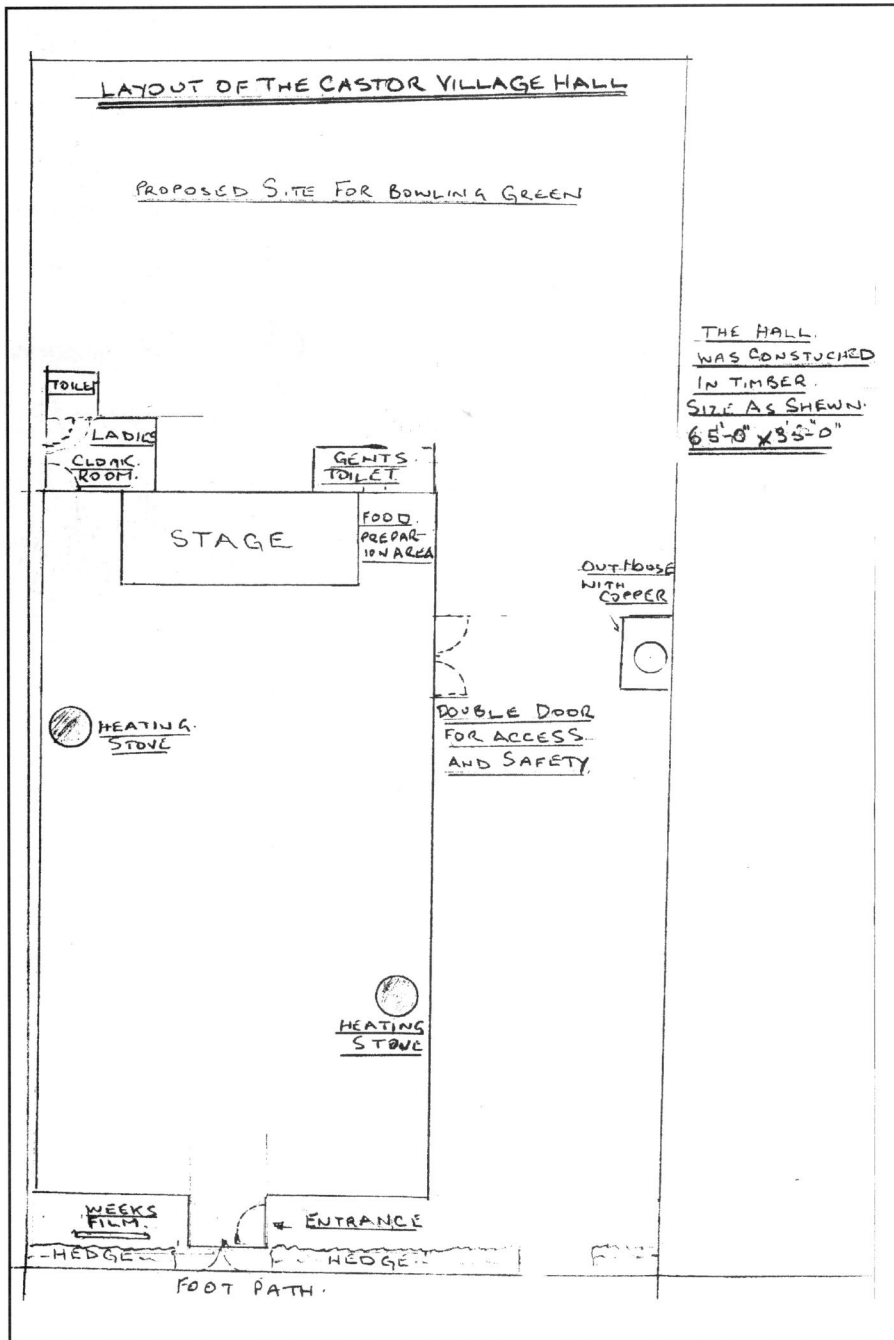

Fig 32c. Outline plan of the interior of hall.

people from the four villages sat down and tucked into a MEAT TEA followed by music, games and dancing. The sheer number of people made a numerical record for the largest tea party ever held in Castor up to that time. The Hall itself was bedecked with flags and bunting for this splendid occasion. Lady Winfrey led a team of 32 tea-makers and assistants for this grand affair. Mr WT Cooke presided at the opening tea supported by Mr G Fitzwilliam, Sir Richard Winfrey, Mr Heighton and Messrs Mackman. Mr Cooke told the assembled people about the development of the Hall. Whilst Mr Heighton, possibly overcome by the event, looked round the flag bedecked room and said "*he had come to the conclusion that Castor was one of the finest places in the country*". Next, Mr Reynolds from the YMCA Northampton enlightened the audience, informing them "*the Hut was an old acquaintance of his where he had trained lads for their more serious part overseas*" – for the Hut was previously used by the Army to train soldiers for hideous warfare in France. He spoke

Fig 32d. The only known surviving external photograph of the old village hall.

Fig 32e. Two members of the First Committee: George Speechley buying a car from Percy Heighton (driving) in front of Manor Farm, Ailsworth.

of the origins of the 'Red Triangle Huts' saying "*at the present time the YMCA has five hundred of their huts in the rural districts of England*". It was a momentous evening as the opening of the hall was a great success - a good omen for the future social life of the village.

By January 1922 the Hall opened its doors – the job was done and the fun could now start! The villagers had at last got their Village Hall and they intended to use it. The programme was both extensive and varied with events well attended. The Comrades enrolled 80 members on 1st April 1922 – no doubt the old soldiers felt themselves on familiar territory in the old army hut, talking about campaigns won and lost in which they had fought, as well as remembering their poor comrades who never came back.

Work continued to develop both amenities and entertainments. Sir Richard had mentioned in his opening speech "*now we have the hut we could do with a billiard table*" and by March 1922 a full sized table was purchased and fitted. Interestingly the opening match featured Peterborough's one armed billiard expert. The price for a game was 3d for half an hour.

The new Village Hall was used for an extensive range of purposes. There were Whist Drives where 132 people sat down to play cards, making 33 tables. In June 1922 the Hall was let out to Church Army Evangelists who slept overnight on their way to Blackpool. Ailsworth Methodist Church hired the facility for a splendid concert when a choir from Boroughbury entertained with duets, quartets and recitations. The enthusiasm of the villagers was tremendous -

supported by Sir Richard and Lady Winfrey, who were now busy organising events for the Hall Lighting Fund. One of their first functions on 21st December 1922 was '*two dramatic humorous Dickensian recitals*' given by Mr Laurie Toseland and his small son, Iain (aged nine years) to which they extended a hearty invitation to all the inhabitants of the villages. During the interval, delightful music was played on a piano and violin by Mrs V Read and Mrs P Scott. This was much appreciated by the audience which included prominent guests including Sir Leonard and Lady Brassey and Mr and Mrs George Fitzwilliam. At the end of the evening, mindful of his Treasurer's role, Sir Richard said "*to avoid entertainment tax there would be a silver collection instead of tickets*". The event raised £8 15s. **And so the pattern of varied entertainment for the village was set.**

In 1923, Mr E Hales wrote enthusiastically of a visit to Castor after a 30 years absence, highlighting '*cinematic entertainments held in the Village Hall one night a week*' although he noted that despite '*the now splendid road, the pedestrians have been neglected because there were no paths or very few, although it was possible to go to Peterborough by bus on three days a week*'. Intriguingly, Mr Shaw from Peterborough hired the Village Hall for the purpose of showing films. The safety conscious committee records that '*the apparatus to run the cinema would be in a fire proof cabinet. The electricity would be obtained from a motor lorry outside of the building*'. They gladly gave permission for Mr Shaw to fix up an advertising board outside the Village Hall. In March 1924, Castor even held a whist drive and dance for 'The Castor Nigger Troupe Fund'.

The Hall had many other uses apart from entertainment. The Education Authority approached the Village Hall Committee to hire the facility for six weeks from November to January to enable the older girl pupils from the Fitzwilliam School to attend Domestic Science lessons. The scheme was approved and the Hall let for this purpose for four shillings per day. Miss Hollywood was engaged to teach these invaluable skills returning like a migrating swallow for many, many years. She would arrive in the cold mornings on a large 'sit up and beg' bicycle, which she rode from Helpston, a distance of over five miles. The Hall would be made ready for her arrival – the combustion stoves, which provided the heat for the Village Hall, were removed and two large portable cooking stoves (which ran on solid fuel) were set in place. These stoves were temperamental things, especially difficult to light. They had a habit of belching out thick black smoke into the cookery class – the cooking utensils were ancient and became blackened by the smoke and heat. There was a very large steamer, big enough to steam a pudding in a cup for every member of the class. Pastry was also one of Miss Hollywood's fortes; the recipe would be chanted to make sure that it was never forgotten: "*Eight ounces of flour, four ounces of fat, pinch of salt, water to mix*".

By the end of 1924, Mrs WT Cooke and her lady helpers had raised £19 17s 7d for the Crockery Fund. With that money they purchased a storage cupboard, white crockery lettered 'Castor Memorial Hall' and teaspoons. The balance left after this major purchase was £1 1s 6d with which they planned to buy new tea towels. However, the billiard table had not proved a great success and was to be sold for a proposed price of £50.

The 'Roaring Twenties and Thirties' did not pass Castor and Ailsworth by. Popular dance bands were used time and time again - indeed, some bands were rebooked for a period of over 20 years. Favourites included The Castor String Band, The Castor Brass Band, Dick Handcock's Band, The Three Nibs, Excelsior Dance Band, The Wansford Jazz Band, Don Maycock's Band and the local trio – WT Cooke, G Handkins and R Taylor. By far the most favourite evenings were the Fancy Dress Dances. To give a taste, in January 1930, over forty children and adults wore fancy dress costumes, which were reported to be both '*exceedingly clever and original*' – obviously much thought and creativity was involved in the making of these splendid garments. For example, Peggy Garfield dressed as a candlestick, Cloris Gibbons bounced along as an airship, Don Harman went as a hot water bottle only to be outdone by Vera Hammond as a picnic closely followed by Alma Glover adorned as a Brussel sprout

Fig 32f. The Castor Minstrel Troupe.

whilst Burt Woodward purred his way in as a black cat. Nippies (Lyons Corner House waitresses) seemed to be a very popular and modern costume – for at one 'do' there were four of them as well as *'Charley Afford who came as a carrot!'* A few people carried life long legacies from these 'frolics' gaining permanent nicknames, the classic one being Alec Jakes, who went as that well known Indian leader and was for ever after known as 'Ghandi Jakes'.

As with the dances, so the Whist Drives were well supported. Players competed for a dazzling array of prizes including silk stockings, a pork pie, a ladies bag, bedspread, new bolster, table cloth, string bag or silver plated trinket box for the winning ladies, whilst the gentlemen might hope to win a case of pipes, a new safety razor or tobacco pouch.

But nothing is new, for even then there were disruptive elements whose anti-social behaviour had to be checked. On 3rd May 1929 police were informed of disorder in the Village Hall – the chief offender being a Mr Simpkins from Peterborough. Sir Richard proposed *"the committee should write to Mr Simpkins and request that he does not use the Hall again."* Again, on 2nd September 1929, Peterborough visitors who were attending Castor Dances were behaving badly and *'using disgraceful language'*. Consequently, Dances were banned for over six months only to resume *'subject to the policeman visiting the Village Hall sometime during the evening of dance'.*

By the early part of the 1930s physical culture had arrived in the village – so popular was this new venture that the Village Hall was booked for two evenings each week for the participation in **keeping fit**. Perhaps this was an antidote to the grim economic situation for many working people throughout the country. In April 1931, in the Peterborough area alone, 3,634 people were unemployed – a misfortune which seemed to dominate the whole of this decade. Surprisingly, the social life of the village did not appear to be badly affected. New societies continued to be formed including the Gardening Society, which proposed to hold an annual produce show. A popular joke enjoyed throughout the four villages originated from a Village Hall entertainment. It went something like this:

Elderly gent to modern mother, *"Your son has swallowed a tin soldier."*
Modern mother, *"I will buy him a new one."*

In March 1930, a survey was conducted in the two villages to ascertain if residents would *'accept electricity in their homes'*. The Village Hall Committee was keen to consider the benefits that this would bring such as *'lighting at the touch of a switch'*. However, there was a delay in supplying the whole village with this service. Investigations reported to the committee by Sir Richard Winfrey found that owing to *'connection difficulties with way - leaves and similar matters, electrical connection would be delayed for up to ten weeks'*. Social events carried on regardless. Peterborough and Fletton Football Club enjoyed a dance in the Village Hall. The Women's Institute had over 200 people attend a social where the Hon Mrs Pelham recited a poem about the motor car. Not to be outdone, Mrs Jakes performed her favourite *'I do like a good drop of milk in my tea'*. Community singing and dancing followed.

Despite the economic hardships, £2 4s 6d was raised in April 1930 to provide a complete 'first aid outfit including a stretcher' to be used in case of accidents by the residents of Castor and Ailsworth. Around Christmas time the annual Comrades' Tea was eagerly anticipated. This was the highlight of the year for the many children of the local ex-servicemen. In 1931, 130 children from the four villages came for a sumptuous feast, laid out in the Village Hall. There were sandwiches, cakes and jelly for tea. The boys would compete with one another to see who could eat the most sandwiches, of which there were always plenty. Then they would brag about how much they had eaten; sometimes the claims were quite staggering. The writer clearly recalls one boy, who shall be nameless, boasting he had scoffed 32 sandwiches alone. After tea there would be crackers, then games, followed by singing. Before leaving the Hall the children were given sweets and oranges. On the way home the boys would usually sing the same song:

A woman stood at the churchyard door, - ooh, ooh, ooh, ooh, aaah, aah, aah,aah,
She saw three corpses carried in - ooh, ooh, ooh, ooh, aaah, aah, aah, aah
The woman to the corpses said - Shall I be like you when I am dead - ooh, ooh, ooh, ooh, aaah, aah, aah, aa
The corpses to the woman said…..yaahhhh

At this point the boys would bellow the *yaaahhh* as loud as they could; so loud that the little girls would cry. Boys being boys, didn't care one little bit, and would go laughing off into the darkness.

After years of making their own entertainment in the villages, villagers found that rival events in Peterborough ensured a fair bit of competition. Tantalisingly, local papers advertised feature movies such as 'Damaged Lives'. This risqué movie was the talk of Castor. It was shown in the City Picture House in Peterborough; the most censored film which had broken all records in the film business attracting a record attendance of over 300,000 people. The new craze - roller skating- was also on offer in Peterborough at a price 3s for men and 1s 6d for ladies. If a Castor person wished to stay at home, radio programmes could be enjoyed; anything from 'Music Hall' to 'In Town Tonight'. Alternatively, you could do-it-yourself and provide your own musical entertainment with a piano from Claypole's Music Shop for £50.

On 1st July 1932, there was a momentous social occasion when the Duke and Duchess of York passed through Castor and Ailsworth en route to Burghley House after a visit to Peterborough Show. The village was gaily decorated with flags and bunting. Almost the whole population of the two villages lined the main street to wave and cheer this important couple who were destined to become our next king and queen. At one point in their visit they kindly stopped their car and stayed a while to acknowledge the crowds. It is easy to imagine the excited population talking about this important occasion over a nice cup of tea in the Village Hall.

Unemployment in the Peterborough District continued to rise. In 1934 over 3,000 people were without jobs and the local mayor instigated an unemployment fund. Nevertheless, this grim figure did not stop the local papers advertising a Hillman Minx car for £150, a new OK Supreme motor cycle for £35 and a man's new suit for £2 10s, whilst £3 19s 9d would purchase a brand new racer bike. No doubt the local youths would gaze longingly at the adverts which were every bit as tempting as they are today. But on the whole most girls and young men stayed put and did not venture further afield than Castor for their entertainment.

National events were celebrated with great enthusiasm – usually with community celebrations and parties in the Village Hall. 1935 brought the Silver Jubilee when every house in the village was decorated and the Village Hall was bedecked with flags – even the tables inside the hall were spread with bunting instead of table cloths. The sumptuous tea was provided free for children up to the age of 16 and village residents aged 65 and over. In 1937, around Castor and Ailsworth, meetings galore took place to plan the celebrations for the coronation of King George VI. Ailsworth held special meetings in the Wayside Café – a tea stop owned by Mr Frank Taylor situated in the last house on the right hand side of the road as you leave Ailsworth (78 Peterborough Road). A donation of £1 18s 1d had been received to start the ball rolling (26th February 1937).

Facilities at the Village Hall had been steadily improving although the planned bowling green had failed to materialise. Electricity was eventually installed and by March 1938 water was gushing from the solitary tap. What a relief this must have been for the users of the Village Hall for the following letter shows what a hard slog it had been to introduce water into the villages of Castor and Ailesworth.

THE WELLS OF CASTOR
BERKENHAMPSTEAD
April 12th 1935

TO THE EDITOR

Sir, - When I read the "Advertiser" I was surprised to see many villagers of Castor opposing the pure water scheme for the village. When I lived there, I can state my experiences about the wells of Castor. We drew our water from a dilapidated arrangement, with bucket and chain, and very often in the bucket found large, black snails, some fresh, some out of date. On examination you could see they were covered with tiny insects, no doubt living on the remains. I also drew up a kitten which had been missing for over a month, badly damaged by the descending buckets. Since then I have had no faith in wells.
I saw several opened, made only of loose stones, partly fallen in, with rat runs clearly seen round the outside. I also noticed that people were being buried in the low lying part of the Churchyard, only a few yards from the well supplying the Infants school. The drains, too, were just left open after leaving the cottages making the country lanes places to get off as quickly as possible. A learned doctor described it as the most unhealthy village he knew of; indeed, he used stronger language than that. I wonder if these items have anything to do with the curse of cancer, which so long has hung over the village. I once read Castor had a greater percentage of deaths from this cause than any other village or town in the district. Of recent years I hear of five deaths from this complaint, of persons living within a space of 100 yards from the village green.

You may publish this if it will help to convert one or two to your great cause. Enclosing my card, I beg to subscribe myself,

A LOVER OF THE OLD VILLAGE.
(Peterborough Advertiser, April 12th 1935)

Perhaps these new amenities were instrumental in raising the letting fees for the Village Hall on November 1st 1937. New charges were introduced namely: Village functions 17s 6d nightly; Non village functions £1 nightly.

The caretaker was Mr Johnnie Glover, a veteran of the 1914-1918 War, in which he had lost a leg. Industriously he also mended shoes in a little shed tucked away behind his house at 6 High Street, Castor. His caretaker's wages were 5s per week for the summer and 7s 6d for the winter. For this Mr Glover worked extremely hard for there was an enormous amount of work to do. He was responsible for lighting the stoves in the winter and filling and lighting the copper in the little wash house for the committee ladies to have hot water to wash the dishes. What a relief it must have been for him when the water was laid on to the Village Hall. He kept everywhere clean and spotless. The dance floor would be gleaming as round and round the floor he would go scattering a substance (which may have been soap flakes). This made the surface slippery – just right for dancing.

Fig 32g. Old Village Hall: Fancy Dress Party in 1930s; Alec Jakes at right standing (wearing a straw hat).

Castor folk particularly loved dancing and all would enthusiastically join in with a variety of steps. There would be village favourites, like 'The Lancers', 'The Pally Glide' (Palais Glide) and 'Spot Waltzes' with prizes, as well as the regular dances of the time: the Quickstep, Military Two Step and some even tried the Charleston. There was the 'Paul Jones' when men and ladies formed two circles – one within the other. When the music struck up the ladies walked in one direction and the men the other until the music stopped - whomever you were opposite was your partner until the music stopped again. In this way many new relationships were formed and the regular rhythm of village life continued.

The Women's Institute learnt how to make gloves. New crocks were purchased for the Village Hall and a dance was held to buy a new clock. Mr and Mrs Coles made afternoon tea for nine bus loads of people who were returning to Leicester after a holiday in Great Yarmouth and **THEN…….WAR**

The ARP held a special meeting in the Village Hall (on a Sunday evening of all nights) to make special arrangements to carry out effective services if needed. The Village Hall was adapted as a Clearing Station in the event of an emergency!! How the Old Comrades must have shuddered when 70 people attended a lecture in the Village Hall on the subject of air raid precautions and anti-gas know how. On 15th September 1939, 100 children from London arrived in the Village accompanied by their teachers and a Toc H helper. They were all homed within the villages. They seemed to be interested in the countryside, although somewhat perplexed. One child shouted to his friends, "Come over here and look at these ants". The ants were, in fact, chickens! Consequently, at the annual Comrades Tea Party, an additional 70 evacuee children were invited to join with the village children, making 180 children in all. The Village Hall was turned into a school for them but this did not last long for, by 14th February 1940, both village schools were temporarily closed through shortage of fuel. The winter weather was particularly severe and long icicles hung enticingly from the Village Hall roof. Children, starved of sweets and ice creams, broke off the icicles and sucked them like sweets.

Mr WJ Cooke was quick to organise alternative wartime uses of the Village Hall. The ARP and WRVS met there. The London County Council was charged 10 shillings a day for the use of lights, fire and cleaning for out of school activities for the evacuees. This may have resulted in surplus funds for the Village Hall because finances showed £85 in hand. This was to have been used for renovation work but because of the war, work was unable to start. May Day festivities were also cancelled because of the War. Village life was changing fast.

Raising money and aid towards the War Effort became the main priority for village functions. The Hon Mrs Pelham formed a Working Group and under her guidance Christmas parcels were sent to every Serviceman from the villages of Castor and Ailsworth. Each parcel contained hand knitted socks, mittens, helmets, caps, scarves and a box of sweets.

Fig 32h. Old Village Hall: The Longfoot Family (l-r)- Walter & Kathleen, Dick & Lucy, Jack, Harry & Nelly, Len & Gertie.

On 3rd May 1940, WI reports that a new resident, Mrs Saunders, had enrolled as a member. If there was ever a person to be in the right place at the right time it was Mrs Saunders.

Mrs Saunders was Irish and like most Irish people she was full of fun. She could sing, mostly comical Irish songs, **and** play the piano. Mrs Saunders quickly became a great favourite at all the 'Village Hall Dos' and soon everyone was singing one of her songs. The chorus, went something like this:

If you ever go to heaven,
You can bet your bottom dollar note,
That the angel with the whiskers on
Will be Paddy McGinty's goat.

Living almost next door to Mrs Saunders was the film actor, Gussie MacNaughton. He appeared in George Formby films. Gussie and Mrs Saunders did much to improve the village social life in the early Forties when everyone needed cheering up, ***and, as well,*** Gussie called all the ladies, "DARLING".

A different kind of social life was now emerging in the villages exclusively connected with the War Effort, although the Brass Band still played on the lawn at the Fitzwilliam Arms. The support among the villagers for any function to do with the War was overwhelming. People would regularly walk from Upton and back, often in the dark as there were no streetlights, to attend Village Hall functions. There were dances to support the Spitfire Fund, The Lifeboat Fund, The Air Raid Relief Fund, the ATS Comfort Fund, The Air Raid Victims Fund, Soldiers' Parcel Fund, The Lord Mayor's Air Raid Victim Relief Fund, The Hospital Relief Fund, The Nursing Fund and the St John's Ambulance Fund, as well as for overseas aid including Aid to Russia and Aid to China. On top of these £34 4s 2d was required to put together 42 Christmas Parcels for local Servicemen. The Village Hall also provided a useful venue for the services based around the District –the Milton ATS and RAF organised a splendid two night function featuring the Starlight Band on Friday night followed by the Star-Dusters on Saturday - tip top entertainment. It was also rumoured that Clarke Gable joined in the Village Hall fun one night whilst based at Polebrooke. As well as dances, regular Spitfire Whist Drives took place although the Knockout had to be abandoned because of an air raid warning in 1940. It is not surprising that the Garden Fetes were cancelled although donations could still be given to the Church Fund instead!

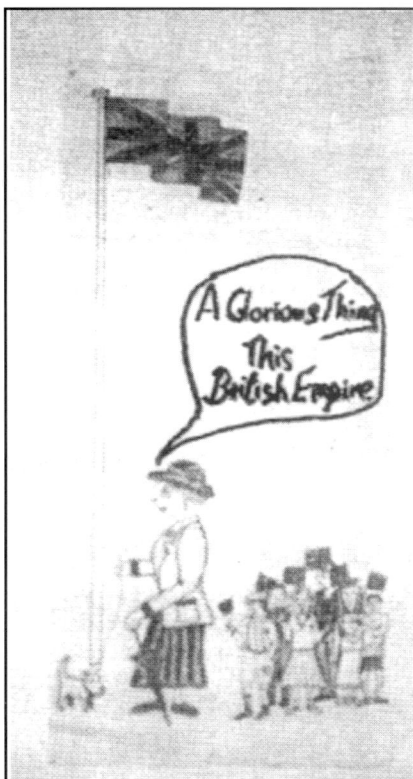

Fig 32i. The Hon Mrs Pelham.

The Hon Mrs Pelham, a prominent and influential village lady, proved an able leader in organising the village woman to make and send welfare to the Service men. They made, from their own materials, 193 knitted pairs of socks, caps and helmets, 46 pairs of mittens, 50 pairs of gloves, 120 pairs of mine sweeping gloves, 82 pairs of steering gloves, 29 pairs of seamen's waistcoats, 29 knitted quilts and 188 children's garments. In addition, Mrs Pelham sent fresh vegetables to the Minesweepers every other week. She understood that children of all ages could be useful especially when there was a War on; she organised this force to collect salvage and take it to an old stable in the grounds of her house (Cedar House) for recycling. Children went from house to house to collect old paper, toothpaste tubes and similar stuff; at other times they were sent out to forage for acorns and rosehips. Village life had altered but the strong social bond was still there. People worked together to support the Servicemen, to try to make them comfortable in their terribly dangerous lives.

The wartime village was a hive of activity; children dashing about collecting salvage, woman leaving their household chores to work in factories and on the land. The whole scene was changing. Men left their families to go to war in strange place overseas, whilst other men came here to assist our country in a time of great need. The Village Hall Social Committee worked hard to provide some sort of social life for the Service people who found themselves within reach of Castor. They came from all directions drawn by the magnet of entertainment in the Village Hall. They came on foot, by bike or by lorry from bases at Wittering, Kings Cliffe, Milton Park, and Sibson. The American Servicemen often came on extra large khaki bicycles and would arrive in a pack like cowboys in the movies. The Village Hall would be packed, heaving to the music of Glen Miller, Joe Loss and Harry Roy, played on the records of Dick Uff and his Radiogram. There was hardly ever any trouble, as all just wanted to enjoy themselves. One evening some French sailors jumped so high in the 'Pally Glide' that they went right through the floor. Mr Glover quickly covered the hole with some chairs and the dancing continued.

Half way through the evening, refreshments were served. Considering the rationing situation, the Ladies' Committee who served the food had a very difficult job to supply the eats. There were sandwiches made from egg and cress, tomato and cucumber, salmon and shrimp paste followed by a few cakes for the lucky ones. As soon as the refreshments were announced there was a virtual stampede as people jostled three deep just to get at the food. The ARP had its eye on the Village Hall though. The Village Hall Committee got into trouble because the black out curtains were too thin and showed light *'through and around the edges'. (Peterborough Advertiser,1941).*

Increase in hall bookings had its benefits. Village Hall funds had risen well enough for the Committee to invest £75 on War Saving Certificates during Wings for Victory Week 1943. To commemorate this week a daily programme of entertainment took place over six days. The success of this effort was rewarded with a certificate, which was framed and now hangs in the present Village Hall. A particularly successful 'Salute the Soldier' week took place in March 1944 involving a programme of activities including a keep fit display, old time dance as well as other fundraising events throughout the other villages. The aim to raise £2,000 was exceeded with a staggering total amount of £3,953 10s. In 1945, the Director of Education was once again in touch with Committee to discuss the use of the Village Hall, this time to serve school meals for the village children. This proposal was agreed. Meals were considered excellent costing 5d a day or 2s 1d a week. Food was prepared in Peterborough and fetched every day by Barbara Sharpe (now Osborne) in a large shooting brake.

However, as the Village Hall was approaching the end of its lease, it was necessary to review the situation. The Committee approached the Ecclesiastical Commissioners to renew the lease on the same terms and conditions as before. It was at this time, after a period of almost 25 years (during which time he was the instigator of much splendid entertainment on offer in the Village Hall, especially in the early days) that Sir Richard Winfrey declined to become a Trustee again.

By 3rd January 1945 people, on the whole, were feeling more relaxed. The War was going well; Allied Forces were now advancing rapidly towards Germany and the end of the War at least seemed to be in sight. In the Village Hall a concert was in full swing, playing to a packed audience when suddenly there was a most tremendous explosion. The roof and the walls of the Hall seemed to lift and expand in one fear-filled moment. The lights went out and a colossal feeling of fright swept the audience. A voice shouted, *"Keep in yer seats".* Everyone was aware of the activity of the people in charge. In the darkness someone played 'Land of Hope and Glory' on the piano and the policeman arrived. Pandemonium ceased and something like order was restored – even the lights came back on. Later, everyone, found out that the bang was caused by a Doodlebug flying bomb – a bit off course but near enough to the railway line at the bottom of the Station Road for one old resident to remark, *"Old Jerry knew what he were doing 'cos, make no mistake, that bomb was bound for Castor railway station."*

After the big Doodlebug scare things gradually started to improve. There were big parties and celebrations in the Village Hall as some of the Servicemen started to come home for good. There were flags everywhere – pretty well every house flew a flag. There were special church services of thanks and an air of relief swept the village.

New users took advantage of the Village Hall. The Anton's daughter and father started a tap and ballet class called the Antonians. On 27th March 1946, the Committee agreed that the Village Hall could be used for Infant Welfare. A place where babies, toddlers and expectant mothers could meet with a specially trained welfare nurse, to be weighed and get a free allocation of rose hip syrup, milk or orange juice powder. Sound Services, SW19, applied to show film entertainment. For a hire charge of £1 each night the residents could enjoy a modern film each Monday evening. By the early 1950's it became apparent that the dear old Village Hall, which had served everyone so well through many difficult years, was coming to the end of its life. A new Village Hall was discussed on 2nd August 1951. At this meeting Mr G Sharpe and Miss C Sharpe representing the Ailsworth Committee offered the following terms - £500 for a new

32j. The Rector: Revd Tom Adler.

Hall if Castor Committee would contribute the same. For this sum they would want equal representation on the Committee and a suitable site for a new building to be found between the two villages. The Revd Tom Adler, on behalf on the Committee, said that he would make enquiries for such a location. However this proved unnecessary when it was agreed that the old Fitzwilliam School would become the new Village Hall.

On October 1953, the old hall was valued by Fox and Vergette (Auctioneers) as £250, with the furniture etc worth an estimated £234 11s 4d. Interestingly, four years later, after the hall was sold, Mr Paten made a statement of the building account saying '*the sale of The Village Hall and the Reading Room together made a total value of £100 much less than they had hoped to get*'. By February 1956, the Committee came to the conclusion that it was no longer possible to maintain the Castor and Ailesworth War Memorial Hall after 30th June 1956.

On 21st November 1957 the new Village Hall opened its doors. At the opening ceremony, the Revd Tom Adler in his introductory speech, referred to the old hall and its place in village life, outlining previous plans to build a new hall on the new housing site. He explained that this had proved to be too expensive. Then the Fitzwilliam School had become vacant and a scheme to adapt this building was formulated after Earl Fitzwilliam had said "*he would be pleased to hand the building over to the village if it could be used to their benefit*". Mr Paten thanked the people of Castor and Ailesworth for raising the money for this venture. The Chairman then called on the Earl Fitzwilliam to open the new Hall. He said "*it was a real pleasure to be here on this occasion*" and recalled the fifth Earl who had originally provided the building as a school in 1829, and the dedication of the old hall in memory of the men who had fallen in the First World War. The new Village Hall was ready to receive future generations of the people of Castor and Ailsworth and a new chapter in their village social life was about to begin.

As for the old Village Hall it ended its days as chicken sheds in the Oak yard opposite the Royal Oak Pub.

Fred and Grace Gibbs

I, Grace, was born at Christmas time in Jasmine Cottage, Main Street, Ailsworth, the youngest member of the Burton family and grandchild of the Gibbons Thrashing Machine family. When I was six years old we moved to Cow Lane, now 18 Stocks Hill, Castor. Fred, who originates from an old fishing family in Great Yarmouth, and I were married at St Kyneburgha's Church on Easter Monday 1954. Although we have lived in many other places, we were always drawn back to Castor and Ailsworth. We now live in Ailsworth.

Fig 32k. Cartoon of cookery classes.

APPENDIX ONE

DOMESDAY BOOK RECORDS NORTHAMPTONSHIRE FOR THE HUNDRED OF UPTON

In 1066, Duke William of Normandy conquered England. He was crowned King, and most of the lands of the English (Anglo-Saxon) nobility were soon granted to his followers. The Domesday Book was complied 20 years later. The aim of the survey was to establish what or how much each landowner held in land and livestock, and to find out what it was worth. These extracts are copied from the Phillimore Edition published in 1979.

We know from the records of Ely Diocese the questions that the Commissioners asked as they went round the counties surveying them viz:

1. The name of the place. Who held it before 1066, and now?
2. How many hides? (*Note: a land unit reckoned as approx 120 acres.*)
3. How many villagers, cottagers and slaves, how many free men and Freemen?
4. How much woodland, meadow and pasture? How many mills and fishponds?
5. How much has been added or taken away? What the total value was and is?
6. How much each free man or Freeman had or has? All freehold before 1066, and when King William gave it, and now; and if more can be had than at present?

The Hundred of Upton included the following villages: **Ailesworth, Castor, Milton**, and stretched from Wothorpe and Burghley in the Northwest, to Glinton and Werrington, down to Peterborough and Castor (almost the same area of the Soke of Peterborough). A Hundred was an adminstrative division of a County, so called because it comprised a hundred hides of land. A Hide was a measure of land reckoned sufficient to support a free family with dependants. The meeting place for the The Hundred of Upton was for many years the Langdyke Bush.

Below are extracts from the Domesday Book that mention **Castor, Ailesworth and Milton**. Note that Sutton, Upton and Marholm are not mentioned in the Domesday Book, but probably their entries included with Ailsworth and Milton respectively.

CASTOR
(Domesday Refs: Map U4; Grid L12 98; Text Refs 6,4. 6a,1)
AILSWORTH
(Domesday Refs: Map U1; Grid L11 99; Text Refs 6,5. 6a,3)
MILTON(Castor)
(Domesday Refs: Map (U6); Grid 14 99; Text Refs 6a,2)

EXTRACT:

LAND OF PETERBOROUGH (ABBEY) in UPTON Hundred:
Castor.
3 hides. Land for 12 ploughs. In lordship 2, with 1 slave;
13 villagers and 2 smallholders with 3 ? ploughs.
A mill at 8s(shillings); meadow 15 acres;
woodland 6 furlongs long and 4 furlongs wide.
The value was 20s; now 50s.

Ailsworth.
6 hides. Land for 12 ploughs. In lordship 2 ploughs;
17 villagers, 2 smallholders and 8 freemen with 12 ploughs.
2 mill at 12s(shillings); meadow 15 acres;
woodland 3 furlongs long and 2 furlongs wide.
The value was 20s; now 70s.

LAND OF THIS CHURCH'S MEN in UPTON Hundred:
In CASTOR five men-at-arms hold 3 hides from the Abbot.
In lordship they have 5 ploughs; 9 villagers, 5 smallholders and 3 slaves with 2 ? ploughs.
The value was 10s; now 40s.

Roger holds **MILTON** from the Abbot. 2 hides. Land for 3 ploughs.
In lordship 2, with 1 slave;
5 villagers and 6 Freemen with 2 ploughs.
Woodland 3 furlongs long and 1 wide.
The value was 20s; now 40s

In AILSWORTH three of the Abbot's men-at-arms hold 3 hides;
They have 3 ploughs
Value £3."

APPENDIX TWO

We do know the names of some of the Parish Priests of Castor from before 1228 eg
Richard, Priest of Castor before 1133, who on becoming a Monk gifted Castor Church to Abbey.
Robert, Chaplain of Castor, succeeded Richard in 1133.

RECTORS OF CASTOR from 1228 AD
1228	Virgilius, d. buried at Castor. Note: Curate at Upton was Swein, Curate at Sutton was John
1240	Will de Burgo
	Pet de Augusta, d.
1287	Joh de Affordeby, d., formerly rect. of Polebrook
1314	Will de Melton, r. there was a vic.of Pightesley of this name 1306-10 and vic. of Wedon 1347-49
1316	Rog de Northburgh
1317	Rog de Nassington
1320	Joh de Aslakeby
1336	Hen de Edenford
1340	Alex de Ormesby, LLD
1345	Rob Swetman de Dodyngton
1355	Joh de Wilford
1355	Gervas Warde
	Rob de Austhorp
1372	Ric de Leycester
	Will Borstall
1378	Tho Hervey, buried at Castor
1383	Tho Pykwell
1385	Joh de Langford
	Ralph Repyngham, d. Preb. of Lichfield and Sarum, also dean of S.Adde, collegiate church Salop
1416	Will Kynwolmersh. Presented by abp. of Canterbury: he was dean of S. Martin's, London, and buried in the cloister there. In 1422 he was appointed 'Domini Regis Thesaurarius.' Bridges gives two successive rectors the same name.

1419	Tho Whiston, LLD
	Ric Raynhill, r. also Rect.of Stanwick and Paston.
1449	Will Witham, LLD, r.Archdn. of Stow, 1464, dn. of S.Mary, Leicester, 1462
1459	John Colynson, r.
	Tho Harby,d., buried at Castor
1460	Joh Sybely, d.
1466	Will Wytham, LLD, r.
1466	Tho Tanfield, STB, d., buried at Peterborough Abbey/Cathedral, also rect. of Harpole and Gayton.
1474	Tho Dalyson
1477	Tho Blencho
1477	Joh Palady, LLB, d.Rect. of Arthingworth, 1461, Holcot, 1496, Weston Favell,1470, Blisworth,1473, also warden of Wappenham, 1470-90, and there buried, 'nuper Gardianus hujus Ecclesie.'
1490	Hen Rudde, LLD, d. Rect. of Weston Coville, Camb, 1478, Cottingham, 1486, Pitchley, 1487, Downham, Camb.,1490. Also vic. gen.and comm. of Ely diocese. In his will he directs his body to be buried at Bury S. Edmunds 'before S. Christopher.' He left £50. to Peterborough monastery, and legacies for vestments to Castor.
1506	Joh Gayton, d.
	Joh Marys
1543	Augustine Dudley, d. Fuller mentions Dudley as a reputed martyr. 'yet on enquiry, his sufferings amounted not to loss of life.' There was but one martyr in the county, John Hurd, a shoemaker, of Byresham, burnt at Northampton, 1557
1544	Hug Rawlyns, AM.He assisted in drawing up articles against Ferrar, bp. of S. David's, ultimately burnt at Carmarthem, 1555.
1546	Joh ap Harry, LLD, d., buried at Castor, Princ. Of Broadgate Hall, Oxf., chancellor of Llandaff and Peterborough, and Archdn. of Northampton.
1549	Will Jeffrey, LLD. Archdn. of Northampton, chancellor of Sarum.
1561	Chr Hodgeson, AB, d. Preb. of Peterborough.
1600	Laur Stanton, STP, d. Dn. of Lincoln, and rect. of Uffington, Linc. Buried at Uffington, where is a monument to him in alabaster and marble.
1613	Tho Dove, AM, d. Bishop, buried at Peterborough Abbey/Cathedral, Archdn. of Northampton, preb. of Peterborough
1629	Warner Marshall, AM, d. Bishop, Preb. of Peterborough
1632	Will Peirse, STP, r. Bishop
1633	Augustine Lindsell , STP, r. Bishop
1634	Fr Dee, STP, d. Bishop, buried at Peterborough Abbey/Cathedral
1639	Joh Towers, STP, deprived. Bishop, buried at Peterborough Abbey/Cathedral
1646	Edm Spinkes, deprived. Also rect. of Orton Longueville. Ejected under the Act of Uniformity.
1660	Benj Laney, STP, r. Bishop
1663	Jos Henshaw, STP, d. Bishop
1679	Will Lloyd, STP, r. Bishop
1685	Tho White, STP, deprived. Bishop
1691	Ric Cumbreland, STP, d. Bishop, buried at Peterborough Abbey/Cathedral
1718	White Kennet, STP, d. Bishop, buried at Peterborough Abbey/Cathedral

1728	Rob Clavering, STP, d. Bishop, buried at Peterborough Abbey/Cathedral
1747	Joh Thomas, STP, r. Bishop
1757	Ric Terrick, STP, r. Bishop
1764	Rob Lamb, LLD, r. Bishop
1769	Joh Hinchcliffe, STP, d. Bishop, buried at Peterborough Abbey/Cathedral
1794	Spencer Madans, STP, d. Bishop, buried at Peterborough Abbey/Cathedral
1813	Joh Parsons, STP, d. Bishop
1819	Herb Marsh, STP, d. Bishop, buried at Peterborough Abbey/Cathedral
1839	Geo Davys, STP, r. Bishop, buried at Peterborough Abbey/Cathedral
1851	Geo Andrews, AM, d., buried at Castor
1864	Joh Jas Beresford, STB. Formerly fellow of S. John's, Camb., and precentor of Peterborough.
1897	L Leader Cooper
1911	Charles A Hulbert, Hon Canon
1918	Lloyd T Jones, Hon Canon
1920	Wallace R Morse, Hon Canon
1926	Cornelius Carleton, Hon Canon
1947	Thomas Payne Adler - also Rector of Marholm, ashes buried at Castor
1975	Adrian Paul Davies - also Rector of Marholm, Sutton and Upton
1982	John Anthony Harper – also Rector of Sutton and Upton
1995	Wm Spencer Dwerryhouse Burke - also Rector of Marholm, Sutton and Upton

KNOWN CURATES OF CASTOR

1230	Swein – Chaplain at Upton
1230	John – Chaplain at Sutton
1553	Edward Stokes
1606	Thomas ?Sryorhy
1610	Henrye Smith
1622	Thomas Booker
1667	George Gascoigne
1672	Geoffrey Hawkins
1673	S Wisher
1681	John Cooper
1685	John Coveney
1688	Thomas Abbot
1700	Oliver Pocklington
1706	George Baxter
1716	Henry Bedell
1750	Joscelyn Perry – also Rector of Marholm
1770	Kennet Gibson – also Rector of Marholm
1772	Thomas Layng – also Rector of Marholm
1796	Christopher Hodgson – also Rector of Marholm
1849	Jos W Harman, AM – also Rector of Marholm
1854	Constantine B Yeoman – also Rector of Marholm

APPENDIX THREE

RECTORS OF MARHOLM from 1217 AD

1217	Gilb de Preston
	Hugh de Waterville
1271	John de Schardelow
	John de Doscrile
1313	Adam de Suthwick

1317	Tho de Veer
1322	Tho de Tyrington
1341	David de Wollure
1342	Ric de Sandford
	W de Sandford
1361	W de Sandford jun
1382	Ric de Grymesby
1385	John Noppe jun
1409	Rob Kinge
1418	Ric Taillor
1440	John Bokvyle
	John Colvile
1483	Rob Wolmer
1511	Nich Messenger
1542	Ed Keble
1546	Tho Britefield
1565	Tho Sedgewicke (or Cheswick)
1577	W Hills
1602	W Linsdell
1613	Tho Whitfield, AM
1642	Sam Green, AM
1670	Purbeck Halles, AB
1675	Jeremiah Pendleton
1704	Paulin Phelips
1735	Joscelin Percy- also parish curate for Castor
1756	Kenneth Gibson, AB - also parish curate for Castor
1771	Tho Layng, AB - also parish curate for Castor
1791	Christopher Hodgson, LLB - also parish curate for Castor
1849	Jos W Harman, AM - also parish curate for Castor
1854	Constantine B Yeoman
1860	Rob Shapland C Blacker, AB -
1879	W Hopkinson -
1880	George Howard Bigg
1888	Edward Biscoe
1890	Robert Swann
1900	Percy Williams
1909	James Bryan Turner
1938	William N Westmore
1942	Vacant
1947	Thomas Payne Adler - also Rector of Castor
1975	Adrian Paul Davies - also Rector of Castor
1982	James Samuel Bell
1984	William L Knight
1990	Peter M Hawkins
1995	Wm Spencer Dwerryhouse Burke - also Rector of Castor

APPENDIX FOUR
ANTHEM FOR THE FEAST OF ST KYNEBURGHA with ST KYNESWITHA AND ST TIBBA

In the Middle Ages, when the anniversaries of local patron saints were to be celebrated, it was customary to read passages from their life story (Vita) and sing chants on the same topic, very often setting to music sentences from the Vita .This chant for The Feast Of St Kyneburgha with St Kyneswitha and St Tibba was of this type being transcribed from a medieval manuscript. St Kyneburgha and her sister St Kyneswitha were daughters of the fearsome king Penda of Mercia. They converted to Christianity, Kyneburgha founded the convent of Castor in Northamptonshire and was succeeded as abbess by her sister. With their kinswoman Tibba they were later buried at Peterborough. The Feast of the Translation of St Kyneburgha was celebrated on 7th March annually at the Abbey. Today it is still celebrated by the children of Castor School who lay flowers at her shrine in Castor Church.

SOURCE: The source for the background information above and the Latin and English texts of the chants comes from the literature accompanying a Compact Disc recording entitled "Chant in honour of Anglo Saxon saints". The singing was by a group called Magnificat, directed by Philip Cave and recorded in Durham Cathedral in 1995. (CD ref is CGCD4004). The CD was produced by a firm called Griffin of Church House, St Mary's Gate, Lancaster LA1 1TD. The music was transcribed from an original manuscript by David Hiley, who also wrote the foreword above. The text was translated by Davis Norwood. Philip Cave is a member of The Tallis Scholars and a layclerk at New College Oxford

Laudet dominum cum Petro sancto
Burgensis ecclesia in claris
lampadibus Kyneburgha et
Kyneswitha ac Tibba

In translatorem sanctarum
reliquiarum exorta est regis et populi
tempestas naufragosa sed mox
imperante domino facta est
tranquillitas magna. Nobis quoque
bene prosperetur trinitas benedicta
per nos, o beate Kyneburgha et
Kyneswitha ac Tibba.

Gloriosa dispensatione dei interfector
regis et martyris Oswaldi, Rex Penda,
protulit gemellas rosas Christo de sua
spina – Christianissimas filias Christo
suscipiente de pagano parente. Gloria
patri et filio et spiritui sancto.

Let the Burgensian church praise the Lord,
together with St Peter, and, with their
bright torches, let Kyneburgha and
Kyneswitha and Tibba do likewise.

Against the remover of the sacred relics
there arose a fierce storm from king and
people but, ere long, at the bidding of the
Lord, peace was fully restored. May we also
find good fortune, o blessed Kyneburgha,
Kyneswitha and Tibba, our blessed trinity.

By the wondrous contrivance of God
the slayer of Oswald, king and martyr, King
Penda, fathered two roses for Christ from
his own thorny stock and Christ received
these devotedly Christian daughters from
their pagan father. Glory be to the father
and to the son and to the holy spirit.

APPENDIX FIVE

THE CHURCH OF ST KYNEBURGHA OF CASTOR.
INVENTORY OF CHURCH FURNISHINGS 1558AD
(copied from Revd WD Sweeting's Book on the Parish Churches round Peterborough published in 1868, spelling modernised in some cases)

First: in the steeple four great bells. Also one Sanctus Bell and two handbells.
Two silver-gilt Chalices
One Chalice of silver- gilt
One cross with foot of copper and gilt.
One bras' holy water stock
Two small candlesticks of latten(brass compound)
One cope of black velvet. One cope of tawney velvet. One white cope of taffa damask bordered with tawney taffa. One other white cope of white fustian. One vestment of crimson velvet. Two dalmatics of old crimson velvet for the deacon and the sub-deacon. One vestment called the golden vestment. One whole suit (meaning a chasuble and dalmatic and tunicle) 0f white taffa damask. One god vestment of red and green silk . One old vestment of white taffa damask. Two vestments of green dornyx (Tournai cloth). One pall of coarse gold work. An altar hanging of red silk, with a fringe of white damask. A rare cloth of white silk. A fringe for an altar of red and purple velvet. A cross staff of copper and gilt which was delivered on to Doctor ap Harry (the previous Rector) and Sir Thomas Bolt is his executor. Two kerchiefs. A Bible and the Paraphrases. (Of Erasmus) Four corporals with two cloths. Three old red silk cushions. Three altar cloths of diap. Seven other of flaxen. Three diap cloths whereas Doctor ap Harry had one. Four plain bowls. Three flaxen sheets (Linen cloths for Holy Communion.) One old red fringe for an altar of red silk. A cross cloth of silk. A pyx of copper which Doctor ap Harry had. And Sir Thomas his executor. One censer of brass. Two lead cruets. Two great candlesticks of latten sold for 18(pounds/shillings?) which was put in the poor mens box.

APPENDIX SIX

THE CHURCH OF ST MARY THE VIRGIN AT MARHOLM
INVENTORY OF CHURCH FURNISHINGS 1558AD
(copied from Revd WD Sweeting's Book on the Parish Churches round Peterborough published in 1868, spelling modernised in some cases)

Two bells and a Sanctus Bell in the steeple.
One vestment of black velvet.
A Chalice of silver with a paten pcell-gilt
One cross of latten(brass compound)
Two altar cloths
Two surplices
A cloth of sey(or fey)
Two candlesticks of latten
One pair of censers of latten.
Two cruets of pewter.
One corporas case of gren velvet
One cope of black velvet and another of blue damask in the hands of My Lady Fitzwilliam

A vestment of crimson velvet and another of satin alrygs(?) within the hands of the said lady.
Two harnesses for deacons of the same blue damask within the hands of the said lady.

APPENDIX SEVEN

COMPTON CENSUS OF 1676
Province of Canterbury (Extract from page 340)

Decanatus Peterburgh (Peterborough Deanery)

	Conformists	Papists	Nonconformists
Bernack	370		1
Castor	340		2
Sutton	80		
Upton	58		
Collyweston	160		
Easton juxta Stamford	260		
Etton	54		
Helpston	300		6
Maxey	370		20
Marham	61		2
Norborough	180		4
Peakirk	220		1
Paston	480		
Peterburgh	1950	2	20
Siberton			
Stamford St Martins	400		7
Thornhoe	243		1
Ufford	300		
Whittering	110		1

APPENDIX EIGHT

MUSTER ROLLS 1536
Musters in Nassaburgh Hundred 1536
The early history of the army is found on the rolls of the Constables and of the Earl Marshall. They record the names and retinues of those who appeared at the rendezvous and proffered their service. There are also the Scruttage Rolls, and in the 15th century the Commissioners of Array, which force in each county. In the reign of Henry VIII, general musters of all the "fencible men" were held at intervals by virtue of commissions under the great seal, the residents being assessed to provide arms according to their wealth. The "press" was much abused. This led to an act for the "taking of musters." This is copied from Mellows Publications in the NRS. Below is one such muster roll taken in 1536, a forerunner to the later militia lists.

Castor
Robert Curtes	} archers
Thomas Marshall	}

This towne to finde horse and harnes for a man

Sutton

John More	} archers
Nicol Beyll	}

This towne to finde horse and harnes for a man

Upton

Henry Browne	}
Richard Broke	} bilmen
Henry Brewster	}

Marham

Thomas Idell	}
John Gyles	} bilmen
Nicholas Wylkynson	}
John Slater	}

Hen Mosse	}
Willm Barnewell	} bylmen
John Wilson	}
Will Tyte	}

John Rose	}
Will Nicholson	} bylmen
Will Wryght	}

Hugh Style constbl and all the residue of the sd towne to provide harnes for a man

and the residue of the towne to finde horse and harnes for a man

APPENDIX NINE

MILITIA LIST AILSWORTH 1762 Nassaburgh Hundred

It was part of the responsibility of the Parish Constable to compile the Militia Lists. In the case of Ailsworth the Parish Constable was William King, whose name appears at the end of the list. This is copied from Mellows Publications in the NRS.

AILSWORTH

Decm. 11 1762. A lest of the in habitants and sarvents of Alesworth from the aedge of 18ten to the aedge 45.

Willm Briggs, farmer
John Briggs, farmer
Danoll Baet, farmer
      r   *mason*
John Ganer <masner>
<Thos Searieant, carptner>laem
Willm Braken, labear
Thos Masan, woodman
<John Brown, shapard> por man,
      3 childrn
Thos Gunton, sarvant
    Gabriel Sapten
<Garboll> Sapten, sarvant
Thos Poap, sarvant
John Shalsten, carpenter
Clapol Cober, blacksmeth
<Robt Stapoll, meler> 6 chiln

Thos Pamer, meler
<Will Clapol, labear, poeerman,
    4 children>
<Willm satcholl, bucher>
    Turner
John <Toner>, bucher
Charls Smeth, gadner
Robt Scalet, labear
John Edwards, carptner
Wm Sutton, searvent
    Eaton
Wm <Etean>, seavent
Hanery Daws, searvent
Willm Gunell, wearver
Sam Bryan <h>aleceeper
    Jucob
<Juckobt> Gunsey, labear
Wm Lasbey, labear

        Willm King, cunstabell

APPENDIX TEN

MILITIA LIST CASTOR 1762

It was part of the responsibility of the Parish Constable to compile the Militia Lists. In the case of Castor the Parish Constable was Robert Wright, whose name appears at the end of the list. This is copied from Mellows Publications in the NRS

MILITIA LISTS– 1762 - Nassaburgh Hundred

CASTOR

A list of the inhabitance and servents in Castor wit Milton that is qualified to serve one the melishe for the parish above menched for Northamptonshire as folrith. December ye 3, 1762

1.	Mr Wright Serjent, ferm	
2.	Mr Wm Wright, surgon	
3.	Mr John Peeter, fermer	
4.	Mr Tho Bate, fermer	
5.	Mr Wm Wolgrave, fermer	
6.	Mr Rob Laxton, fermer	
7.	Mr Clem Tompson, fermer	
8.	Mr Knotton, gardner	*Number of children*
9.	Mr Crow, park keeper	*Each famleys*
10.	<Nat Guding, miller>	4 children
11.	<John Shelston, carpend>	8 dit
12.	<Tho Chapel, blmacks>	3 dit
13.	<Wm Shelston, bacor>	3 dit
14.	<Tho Brown, taler>	3 dit
15.	John Darby, juner, weelrigh	btc
16.	James Stanger, shumaker	btc
17.	Scmuren	
18.	John Rudkin, shewmacor	
19.	Edward Serjant, bacor	btc
20.	Mr Wm Serjant, farmer	
21.	John King, laber	2 dit
22.	<Wm Smith, taler>	3 dit
23.	Wm Suton, laber	1 dit
24.	Tho Dolby, shepard	2 dit
25.	<Wm Cope, laber>	5 dit
26.	<Tho Liming, shomaker>	4 dit

27. <Wm Hill, laber>   3 dit
28. <Wm Chamberling, butcher>   6 dit
29. <Tho Shelston, carpindr>   6 dit
30. <Tho Judsen, laber>   7 dit
31. <John Stimson, shepard>   5 dit
32. John Broten, laber   2 dit
33. Tho Serjeant, laber   2 dit
34. James Willkson, carpindr   wid
35. Mathe Boland, laber   2 dit
36. Tho Bate, backer   bct
37. Wm More, laber
38. Wm Edwards, laber
39. <Tho Dawkens, wever>   3 dit
40. <John Burbig, laber>   4 dit
41. <Wm Herson, laber>   4 dit
42. Tho Snel, laber   2 dit
43. Edward <Numon> *(Newman)*   1 dit
44. <Gorg Green, laber>   4 dit
45. John Hale, masner
46. John Dunston, laber
47. <Tho Tweltrees, laber> *(Twelvetrees)*
48. John Woddell, laber
49. Robt Cuper, serven
50. <Mr Brickwod, turpik>
51. John Parrish, serven
52. Robt Peper, dit
53. Robt Ex, shepard
54. Wm Sandfild, dit
55. Wm Rowell, dit
56. Robt Gregry, dit
57. Gabril Core, dit
58. John Traton, dit
59. Wm Quiner, dit *(Wilkinson)*
60. Mathey <y groom> dit
61. Ricgard Hudson, sheprd
62. Wm Lenton, dit
63. Tho Gilby, dit
64. Wm Cobley, laber   6 dit
65. Wm Dolby, sheprd
66. Wm Leading, servent

Robt Wright, custable

John Sweby, masonWillm Scotney, shepard
??????????????? John Hurd, farmerman

Notes and Comment:
(1) bct & btc = bachelor; 2 wid=widower
(2) Nos 54-60 and 62-3 have been counted as servants and not
as shepherds in Tables 2a and 3a. If nos 54-60 had been
shepherds, it would have been unnecessary for Robert Wright
the Constable, to indicate that no 61 was also a shepherd.
Moreover "Mathey <y groom>" is more likely to have come
into the category of servant rather than shepherd. Nos 62 and 63
are more difficult to place. If they were shepherds this would
mean that out of 66 listed men, seven (10.6%) were employed in
looking after sheep. This is an exceptionally high proportion
compared with other occupations, even at Castor where sheep
were numerous (p117). (One shepherd is also recorded ar each
of Castor's two hamlets, Ailsworth and Sutton). Moreover, it
will be seen from the table of "Number of children. Each
famleys" that Wright was quite unreliable in his use of the
abbreviation 'dit'(ditto).

APPENDIX ELEVEN

MILITIA LIST MARHOLM 1762 Nassaburgh Hundred
It was part of the responsibility of the Parish Constable to
compile the Militia Lists. In the case of Marholm the Parish
Constable was Benjamin Bull, whose name appears at the end
of the list. This is copied from Mellows Publications in the NRS

Decr 2d 1762. A list of all persons in the parish of Marholm
liable to serve in the militia for the County of Northampton.

Jos Chamberlin, grasiers and farmer
Aug Foster, cottager & labourer
<Adam Cook, labourer> 3 children
James Wright, do
Miles Stanyon, do
<Wm Sayles, junr., do> 3 childn
<Wm Griffin, do> 3 childn
Robt Collinge, victualer, remarkable crooked legs
<John Pacey, do, very full shouldered>
Saml Chapman, servt
Hen Baxter, do
Edwd Lincoln, shepheard
Wm Allen, shepheard
Richd Bell, do

                              Benj Bull, constable

APPENDIX TWELVE

MILITIA LIST SUTTON 1762 – Nassaburgh Hundred
It was part of the responsibility of the Parish Constable to
compile the Militia Lists. In the case of Sutton the Parish
Constable was Thomas King, whose name appears at the end of
the list. This is copied from Mellows Publications in the NRS

December 5 1762. A list of the inhaberts and servents between
the ages of eighteen and forty five years.

Mr William Hopkinson, farmer
Mr John Parkinson, farmer
John Dots, servant
William Avary, servant
William Hilliard, servant
William Hardey, cordwainer
            3 children
<John Read> cupper, lame
<Thamas Brawn> shapard, 3 child.
James Gardner, labour
Issaac Cant, labour
            Aislaby
John Rudkin, shewmacer

This is to give notice that thers names will be given in on
Saturday next eleventh day of December by nine of the clock in
the forenoon at William Elyer, Peterborough, and aney man may
appeal that day and no appeals will be afterwards.

                              Thomas King, constable

APPENDIX THIRTEEN

MILITIA LIST UPTON 1762 – Nassaburgh Hundred

It was part of the responsibility of the Parish Constable to compile the Militia Lists. In the case of Upton the Parish Constable was John Sharman, whose name appears at the end of the list. This is copied from Mellows Publications in the NRS.

December 11, 1762. Upton in the County of Northamptonshire. A trew list of the men from eighteen years and forty five.

John Patman, labour
Fransis Basbay, labour
    Sails
John <Salls> sarvant
John Colman, sarvant
William Sharman, farmar,

John Sharman, cunstable

APPENDIX FOURTEEN

POPULATION – CASTOR, AILSWORTH, SUTTON, UPTON

Year	Castor	Ailsworth	Sutton	Upton
115				
125				
120				
85				
1672(adults)	340+2	<incl	80	58
1801	475	154	110	76
1811	453	209	103	91
1821	494	249	113	103
1831	669	289	118	122
1841	716	363	121	113
1851	772	381	129	114
1861	745	366	112	100
1871	680	394	99	107
1881	661	333	92	72
1891	634	286	84	75
1901	639	251	98	85
1911	586	240	85	90
1921	576	227	78	93
1931	547	245	91	106
1941	-	-	-	-
1951	546	248	64	72
1961	627	315	58	100
1971	693	357	114	80
1981	740	450	120	80

Sources: Various

APPENDIX FIFTEEN

1801 POPULATION RETURN – CASTOR
FORM of ANSWERS by CLERGYMEN in ENGLAND,

To the Questions contained in the Schedule to an Act, intituled, *An Act for taking an Account of the Population of* Great Britain, *and of the Increase or Diminution thereof.*

County, &c
Hundred, &c
City, Town, &c
Parish, &c
Northamptonshire
Nassaburgh
Castor and Ailsworth

QUESTION 4th

	BAPTISMS		BURIALS			BAPTISMS		BURIALS	
Years	Males	Females	Males	Females	Years	Males	Females	Males	Females
1700	5	9	9	9	1787	8	13	9	4
1710	6	5	4	1	1788	9	6	13	15
1720	11	7	13	22	1789	14	6	4	5
1730	15	17	3	2	1790	12	9	13	7
1740	7	13	5	5	1791	7	9	9	3
1750	8	5	6	14	1792	8	13	7	3
1760	10	9	8	7	1793	8	14	6	4
1770	11	10	8	9	1794	13	5	10	4
1780	12	6	10	11	1795	14	7	10	10
1781	10	9	9	10	1796	4	9	3	6
1782	8	6	15	11	1797	9	18	10	11
1783	9	7	12	18	1798	8	12	8	13
1784	10	3	12	8	1799	12	14	11	7
1785	10	7	11	10	1800	12	9	12	5
1786	8	8	7	4					

QUESTION 5th

MARRIAGES

Years	No. of Marriages	Years	No. of Marriages	Years	No. of Marriages	Years	No. of Marriages
1754	3	1766	6	1778	4	1790	4
1755	2	1767	3	1779	7	1791	7
1756	6	1768	4	1780	7	1792	6
1757	3	1769	10	1781	6	1793	8
1758	1	1770	2	1782	1	1794	3
1759	1	1771	5	1783	3	1795	9
1760	5	1772	5	1784	3	1796	3
1761	4	1773	7	1785	6	1797	9
1762	8	1774	4	1786	5	1798	9
1763	5	1775	4	1787	5	1799	5
1764	0	1776	10	1788	4	1801	3
1765	1	1777	2	1789	5		

REMARKS (if any) in Explanation of the Matters stated in Answer to the 4th and 5th Questions

4th Question. The Parish of Castor includes the hamlet of Alesworth. The Inhabitants of the two small villages of Sutton and Upton bury at Castor, but their Baptisms are registered in their own parishes, by the Curate thereof.

5th Question.

CERTIFICATE OF THE CLERGYMAN.
I, Chris. Hodgson LLB (Curate) of the Parish of Castor in the
County of Northampton
Do certify, That the above Return contains, to the best of my
Knowledge and Belief, a full and true Answer to the 4th and 5th
Questions contained in the Schedule to an Act, intituled,
An Act for taking an Account of the Population of Great Britain,
and of the Increase orDiminution thereof. Chris Hodgson

Witness *Robt Wright* One of the substantial Householders of
the said Pariah, &c of *Castor* this *17th* Day of *April 1801*

Indorsement County, Riding or Division} Northamptonshire
Hundred, Rape &c } Liberty of Peterborough
Parish, Township } Ailsworth   Rector, Vicar Curate or
officiating Minister, to whom this Schedule was delivered Revd
Mr Hodgson
Signed by Hept Brachen High Constable

APPENDIX SIXTEEN

TITHE REGISTER FOR CASTOR – 1844 List of Owners and Tenants

Abbey	William
Aford	Henry
Artis	E.T
Aspittall	Matthew
Almond	Mary Ann
Andrew	Henry
Boyall	William
Banning	Thomas
Ball	Ann & Catherine
Bate	William
Briggs	Samuel
Briggs	William
Beeby	James
Burdett	Thomas
Bodman	James B
Beeham	Edward
Berridge	William
Bew	Richard
Borth	Sam
Close	Charles
Callow	John Thomas
Compton	Edward
Clarke	The Rev. H
Cook	John
Culpin	James
Carr	The Rev Chris
Carter	Eunice
Coulson	John
Christmas	Thomas
Christy	Alexander
Darby	John Thomas
Drake	Elizabeth
Dickens	Ann
Deacon	Bartholomew
Dean	Richard
Desborow	John
Ellis	William

Edis	Charles
Fairweather	John
Freer	Ann
French	Gabriel
Fitzjohn	Richard
Fenn	George
Fox	Mrs. Ann
Graham	John
Gibbons	Thomas
Goodyear	Charles and Sarah
Groom	Thomas
Gaches	Charles
Glitheroe	Thomas
Hopkinson	William
Hardwick	John
Hunt	John
Hobbs	Robert
Hewitt	James
Hodgson	The Rev. Chris
Hordern	William Gates
Hornsby	John
Hill	Thomas and Harry
Hazlitt	Ann
Howson	Francis
Hales	John
Harris	J.W.
Jakes	John and William
Judson	William
Knighton	Richard
Kingston	George
Longfoot	??
Locke	James
Munton	William
Mappison	John
Marriott	Richard
Merrishaw	James
Mossendew	John
Newborn	William
Neville	Thomas
Oliver	John
Palmer	Charles
Popple	Joseph (Wood Field)
Popple	Fanny
Paeker	Reuben
Pywell	George and Martin
Pell	John
Panter	Edward
Pearson	William
Read	Widow
Rudkin	Thomas
Sismey	William and Edward
Sewell	John
Sharpe	Charles
Stanger	John Thos and Frances
Sergeant	John
Setchell	Martin
Smith	Thomas
Stevenson	William
Smith	Sarah (Manor Farm with M Almond)
Smith	Wm Thurston Fitz Arms Pub, garden and orchard Tithe 5/9d
Shelston	Robert

Savage	James
Sturgess	John
Strong	Colonel
Sykes	Alfred
Southam	Mrs.
Tebitt	Alfred
Tomlin	John
Rebworth?	Alfred
Tailer	Robert
Upchurch	Anne
Woolton	Thomas
Watts	John
Wootten	Thomas
Wyman	George
Wildbore	Charles
Wimpers	John
Warr	James
Wood	Percy
White	A,A
Yarwood	Francis
Woodhead	George
Winsworth	??

APPENDIX SEVENTEEN

TITHE ROLL 1847
LIST OF OWNERS/OCCUPIERS AND LOCATIONS
CASTOR and AILSWORTH
SEARCH RESULTS at Northants County Record Office 2003
re Castor and Ailsworth

Notes
Bold heading = landowner
No = plot number for tithe apportionment
Name beside number = occupier
After dash - = description of property as given in roll
Address in brackets = attempt to identify present site of property
Task not completed due to illegibility of part of tithe map
Some obvious properties missing from this list; eg Castor House, Village Farm, The Elms,
Vast majority of all property in both villages owned by Dean and Chapter or Fitzwilliams

PROPERTIES BELONGING TO DEAN AND CHAPTER and latterly ECCLESIASTICALCOMMISSIONERS
No 36: Wm Bate –house, yard, dovecot, homestead and garden (Manor Farm Ailsworth),
No 156 Wm Butler (house now 16 High Street Castor)
No 87 Wm Bate – house and orchard (site now The Limes Ailsworth, where Gibson's lived/now Leeds)
No 15 Robert Drake – cottage, yard and garden (now where Hilary Pounsett lives)
No 14 Wm Freer – cottage, yard and garden (now where Hilary Pounsett lives)
No 36a Gabriel French – farm homestead, cottage, garden and close (now part of old Manor Farmhouse)
No 18 John Graham – cottage, yard and garden in Main Street Ailsworth
No 88 John Hales and the Widow Ward – Peterborough Road Castor (area c opp Winfrey homes)

No 89 George Key – cottage and garden– Peterborough Road Castor (area c opp Winfrey homes)
No 21 Wm Newborn – Main Street Ailsworth 'A' side.
No 83 Thomas Sismey – house, yard and garden, (immed East of house now called Church View)
No 13 Charles Sharpe – farm (top part of Main Street Ailsworth)
No 25 George Smith – farmhouse and homestead (L-shaped house, left bottom of Main Street Ailsworth)
No 91 Frances Stanger – cottage and garden (now where Ted Fairchild lives)
No 92 John As(f)ton – cottage and yard (little cottage in Splash Lane)
No 86 Harriet Chapple – (now site of Ian Sheldon's house)
No 75 John Mappison – (site West of Old Smithy Peterborough Road Castor)
No 97 John Serjeant – farm homestead (now Bramble Cottage site, Stuart Wood)
No 164 Thomas Smith – farmhouse homestead (now Three Chimneys)
No 1 Thomas Fen – cottager (site in area of King's Acre)
No 127 Richard Marriott – farmhouse and homestead (now Manor Farm Castor)
No 90 Richard Marriott – (site immed West of Ted Fairchild on P'boro Road Castor)
No 100 Wm Callow – farmhouse and homestead (now The Hollies)
No 165 Wm Callow – farm homestead (site of the barns for The Limes, P'boro Road Castor)
No 169 Wm Callow – Campion's Close
No 81 John Darby – cottage and garden (West of Church View nr Village Hall)
No 89 – on P'Boro Road Castor (c opp Winfrey homes)
No 166 Wm Berridge - farmhouse and homestead, Close

LANDOWNER RICHARD DEANE
No 117a Thomas Wright – cottage and yard (now R & L Wright's house, Main Street Ailsworth)

LANDOWNER ANN DICKENS
No 133 Wm Stanger – cottage, bar and garden (John Neal's house on The Green Castor)

LANDOWNER JOHN DICKENS
No 66 Matthew Aspital – cottage (site E of Village Sign Cottage, P'boro Road)
No 132 George Pywell – cottage and garden (East of the Cabin on Allotment Lane)

LANDOWNER ELIZABETH DRAKE
No 53 Elizabeth Drake – house and yard (next to old Wheatsheaf pub)

LANDOWNER RICHARD FITZJOHN
Nos 62,63,64 Richard Fitzjohn – cottage and yards (Main Street Ailsworth)

LANDOWNER Hon GEORGE FITZWILLIAM
No 126 Castor Pound on The Green
No 148 Ed Artis – house and garden (Now Hanover House Church Hill Castor)
No 520 Ailsworth Pound (top of Ailsworth, off Helpston Road)
No 79 School and House (Village Hall)
No 149 Mary Ann Almond – house (now The Grove Church Hill Castor)

No 113 James Beeby – house and garden (site now York Cottage Church Hill Castor)

No 29 Samuel Briggs – house, wheelwright, shop etc (area of Ailsworth Green junct)

No 31 Eunice Carter – farmhouse and homestead (now 10 Main Street Ailsworth nr Chapel)

No 47 Eunice Carter – yard, garden and close (Ailsworth, P'boro Road)

No 82 John Darby sen – house, yard and garden (now Church View P'boro Road Castor)

No 76 Ann Dickens – farmhouse, homestead and garden (now The Old Smithy, 47 P'boro Road)

No 80 – farm, homestead and Close (site now East of Village Hall)

No 152 Wm Dickens - cottage and garden (now 11 High Street Castor)

No 98 Richard Fitzjohn – homestead and close (now 17 P'boro Road Alan and Joyce Herbert)

No 30/48 Gabriel French – farm homestead (site of Old Chapel Church Hill Castor)

No 147 John Pell – cottage and garden (now 11 Church Hill Castor)

No 117 John Stanger and others – cottage and garden (area of 6 Church Hill Castor)

No 33 Martin Setchel – farm homestead and close (North of Limes, Helpston Road Ailsworth)

No 119 William Pearson– cottage and garden (area of 6 Church Hill Castor)

LANDOWNER EDWARD GIBBON

Edward Gibbon – house yard and garden (area of 6 Church Hill Castor)

No 137 – hovel and close (top left of Clay Lane)

No 120 Joseph Bodma(Bodman?) – house, building and garden (now Durobrivae Lodge Castor)

No 146 Will Yates Hordern – cottage and yard (now 7 Church Hill Castor)

No 145 Richard Marriott – farmhouse and homestead (now area of old barn, rt side of Clay Lane)

LANDOWNER RECTORIAL GLEBE

No 112a Wrights – field (school field, next to the Cedars, P'boro Road Castor)

No 128

LANDOWNER WHITE

N0 109 Elizabeth Holmes – close (school field)

APPENDIX EIGHTEEN

Extracts from a lecture delivered by Mr. John Hales Castor Infant school-room 28th April 1883 "Castor, past and present"

….I shall now endeavour to give a few of my recollections of this place during a little over fifty years, commencing with the church and its connection, show the difference of things then and now.

There have been four Rectors, two resident and two non-residents, the latter being Bishops of Peterborough, who were Rectors of the parish up to the year 1851.

I will now describe as well as I can the appearance of the interior of the church at about the time previously stated. In the first place, the North Door was used as well as the South, so you may fancy what a nice draught there was. There was then no inner door where the red door now is but on right hand side as you come in at the South Door the seat had a back to it about six feet high to keep the wind from the ears. The pulpit and reading desk were against the middle pillar, North side of middle aisle and from that to where the reading desk now stands were large high square pews about six feet high; again, where the pulpit stands, also on the greater part of the South Aisle and West End, and under the tower. The place now occupied by the organ was used as a place for a very large plough, also for a bier for carrying the dead and generally for a rubbish heap or place for decaying flags and hassocks; also to work and letter gravestones in. The bodies of strange persons drowned such as Watermen etc, were also deposited here; I have known three persons to be so deposited. I have also seen and heard an inquest held over one of them in the church; it was over a person found drowned in a fish pond opposite the Keeper's house at the Ferry; this was in April 1840 and the coroner stood in the old writing desk. Most of the windows were plastered up on the bottom part to the height of about two feet. The three circular lights in the top of window under the sundial were plastered up in the same way.

Where the present vestry now stands was held a day and Sunday school, at which I received a greater part of my earlier education. There was a door on the side near the chancel door for entrance from without and another on the inner side where the commandments now stand. These commandments were then placed in the school, between one of the arches. The schoolmaster used to enter the church by this door to ring the treble or smallest bell at nine o' clock, and at two, to call us scholars together. All the bells were then rung on the ground floor and were very dangerous. Our poor old clergyman once had an idea that he could ring one. There being a tenor raised for a funeral and the clerk being called away, he pulled it off and the consequence was it pulled his watch out of his pocket and smashed it on the slab floor and quite cured him of his ringing mania.

At the West End of the Nave was a large gallery used by the choir, in which I have seen and heard nearly every conceivable instrument except the big drum. I have also heard banns forbidden. Another thing which would seem strange and out of place now was giving notice from the clerk's desk of any rates there might be laid for the relief of the poor and for the necessary repairs of the highways, and of any meeting the ensuing week for the appointment of "Pinder" and "Mole catcher", such meeting to be held in the "Royal Oak" The next sentence would probably be "To sing to the Praise and Glory of God". The said clerk himself frequently forming the whole choir.

Another curious custom I must note, which I have seen practised within the last twenty years, that was for the women to curtsey to the pulpit and the men to stroke their hair straight down their forehead as they came into church. It was also a custom, if a person died at Upton, when they were brought here to be buried, to have all the bells chimed, and if a member belonging to a club died, it was customary for his surviving fellow members to follow him to the grave wearing hat bands and gloves. They were each entitled to a quantum of ale before starting, following which was often a scene better fancied than described. I also remember the first conformation being held in the church. I also very well remember and have rung the pancake bell at 12 o'clock on Shrove Tuesday, when the said pancakes were supposed to have been thrown out of the belfry windows. It must be borne in mind that there were no Chapels in the parish at that time; there was a preaching at a house in each parish at certain times.

Now for the changes and anecdotes and superstitions of the inhabitants. There is not, I believe, a single individual residing as the head of the family. I have known at least three heads of the Milton family, the same of the Stewards and the same at each inn. There is only one house in the two villages that I have not known death in. Now for the superstition. Up to the year 1834 there was living in the village a reputed witch. She died at the age of 82 years. So you may fancy her antiquated appearance; nose and chin nearly meeting and walking with a hooked stick. Whether she had the proverbial black cat I am not able to say but this I do know that we boys of that period treated her with very great respect when and wherever we met her. It was generally believed and currently reported that if certain of the farmers killed a pig and did not send her a fry, the pig would not take the sale; If a cow calved and she did not receive what was usual to send on such occasions, the calf would not do well, and when they brewed their ale and forgot to send her new beer the beer would not keep. (I often find mine will not keep now.)

Education was not so cheap in those days; nothing under sixpence per week at the church school, with books and fireing extra. There were only these, and Dames' schools, previous to 1829, when the late Lord Fitzwilliam built the present National Schools. Our clergyman and other charitably disposed ladies and gentlemen were in the habit of sending several boys to school and paying all fees, etc. The clergyman used to come at certain times to see what progress they were making and I well remember one word, he would insist upon them spelling, and that was ABEL. He would make them all spell it as follows, "A by the self A; B-E-L, BEL-ABEL". And if they were not getting on so well as he thought they ought to have done, he would put a high dunce's cap on them and set them on the top of the tomb, within the rails near the chancel door. Another custom which has not gone out of practice so very long, was with the cows that were about to be grazed on the Common during the Summer. The best jumpers were selected from each farm and at twelve o' clock on the Eve of Old May Day, were taken to the dyke or drain, at either the "Plash" or the "Brook" which ever field was to be grazed for that season, and a man had the halter, one to each cow on the opposite side of the dyke to the cows, another man stood with a large stick, and at the first stroke of twelve he struck and there was then quite as much excitement as there is at any of our great races, as the first cow over had the greatest prize, vis:- the "Garland", the second the "Poesy", and the third the "Whistle Spoon". On the next evening these several winners paraded the town with their honours on their horns but woe to the last; its honour was not on its horns but on its tail and was called the "Morkin or Dishclout" and was considered a disgrace for that season to the unfortunate lad who tended it. Again on the same evening it was customary to place bushes in

a conspicuous place at the greater part of the farm houses. I have seen them put down the chimney, the bushy part sticking out of the top. There were three grades of bushes; the first the white thorn, for the prettiest and cleanest damsel; second, the blackthorn for the slattern; the third, for one of loose morals; the division of these favours often causes a fight between the young men of the period. The last old custom was the observance of plough Monday; a bell rope was obtained and sticks knotted in it, and about a score lads with a primitive plough to Milton, where other parishes met them, and a trial of strength was indulged in, but the climax was about one o' clock when they returned, and Castor and Ailsworth met at the division of the two parishes, and hooked ploughs together to see which were the strongest, the women giving great aid in pulling; this generally wound up with a free fight.

As to modes of locomotion, postal accommodation and dress, I do not remember ever seeing the 'pillion' in use, although I have seen several pillions and can well understand that they were not comfortable as some of the more modern substitutes. I remember the time when nearly the first spring cart was set up, but not with such springs as are now used, but good strong ash springs which would shake you up and let you know they were there. Previous to 1835 the roads to Marholm and Helpston were simply impassable for any vehicles without two horses. Our means of getting to Stamford or Peterborough was either by coach, or what was called a sociable; the former running from Stamford to Wisbech, and the latter from Stamford to Thorney. They both changed horses at the Royal Oak, the other means were by carrier's cart, of which there was one 'Leatom' from Peterborough to Stamford and back on Fridays, and 'Nutt and Chapman' from Stamford to Peterborough on Saturday and 'Blackwells' from Nassington to Peterborough on a Saturday, the latter generally returning and arriving at Castor about nine o' clock on Saturday evening. If your business called you to London or the North, you must meet the coach at 'Kate's Cabin' or the 'blacksmith's Shop' at Water Newton. When I was twenty years of age, I had not been twelve miles from home. The chance of migration were very small and expensive, but after the railway was formed, things were very much altered for the better. I well remember when Earl Fitzwilliam removed at certain times from Milton to Wentworth, seeing the large waggons conveying the luggage, and a coach and six horses the servants.

Then the postal accommodation; the post office at Peterborough was upon my first recollection opposite the "Angel Hotel" in narrow street. We used to get a letter about twice per week, by the errand women at the cost of nine pence each; and if perchance we had one from Wansford it would cost one shilling; if we sent to Peterborough it was a great chance if we got them, they must come by the regular channel, the errand women. A great many poor people took their letters to Milton, and got them franked by Earl Fitzwilliam. It was quite an event at that time to write a letter, no envelope or stamp but sealing wax or water bound up your missive. But in 1840 the penny post came into operation and in 1846 a rural messenger came from Peterborough and set us to rights in this matter.

Now with regard to dress; there is quite as much alteration in this as in other matters. Fifty years ago you would not see one man in fifty wearing trousers, but small clothes (and most of them leather). No braces but a leather belt, and either gaiters, leggings, or top boots. I have seen more than one clergyman in the pulpit with boots and spurs. The dog hair hat was the principal hat. The ladies have kept quite a pace with us, as at that time the elder, and in many cases the younger women, wore the red or scarlet cloak as their principle or outer garment. The bonnets I can hardly describe better than by saying, the material was straw and the shape or fashion, the largest coal scope you could find. The boys, the veritable gaberdine or smock frock, and also by the man, a white one was considered a Sunday garment. The improvement in the buildings I think show themselves.

I would now say a few words on the sanitary state of the period. The drains were all open in the streets, and by the 'Prince of Wales' up to Mr. Sharp's was an open drain running from a butcher's shop; this was all right and proper. On the green in front of Mr. Wootton's was a large pond generally full of stagnant water but these things no notice were taken of, and people seemed to live as long in those days as now. I have heard it was because there were not so many doctors.....

APPENDIX NINETEEN

LISTED BUILDINGS - AILSWORTH
Helpston Rd
Manor House - C17 or C18 house
28(Thatchcroft) - C17/18 cottage
30(Southview) - C18 cottage

Main St
10 - C17 origin/C18 cottage
44 - C17 range of cottages
46(Punchbowl) – C18 cottage, restored
50 & 52 (The Cottage) – C17 house, remodelled in 1865
15 – C18 house
Walnut House – prob C17
19 – C17 cottages
39 - C18 house, with early 19C wing
41 – house dated 1758
43 – C18 cottage
45 – C18 cottage
47 - C18 cottage
49(Kek Cottage) – early C18 cottage
51 - C17 cottage
55 - C17 house

Peterborough Road
105(Spring Cottage) – 1811 AD
111 & 111A - C19 pair of houses
115 – C18 house
117 – early C19 cottage
Wheatsheaf – early C19 house

APPENDIX TWENTY

LISTED BUILDINGS - CASTOR
Allotment Lane
12 – C17/18 cottage
14(The Cabin) – C18 cottage with alterations

Castor Road
Belsize Farmhouse – C16/17 former grange of abbey
Belsize Barn – C16/17 long barn
Stamford Lodge – late C19 gate piers

Church Hill
4(Pine Beams) – cottage dated 1796
6 – C17/18 cottage, restored. S end dated 1649
11 – C17 cottage
17 – C18 house
The Grove – C19 stone house, stucco front
23(Vine House) – C17 house extended to W, former rectory
Outbuilding to Vine House C18

Clay Lane
1(the Little Cottage) – C17/18
5 – C17 or C18 cottage
4(Clay Cottage) – late 17 house, altered

Ferry Hill
Robin Hood and Little Standing Stones
Lodge to Milton Park – C18 Gothick

The Green
Prince of Wales Feathers – early C19 stone house
Base of village cross
3 – Mid C19 cottage
Durobrivae and pump – early C18 stone house with earlier origins
Outbuilding NW of Durobrivae – probably C18
Durobrivae garden wall - probably C18

High Street
1 (Stone Lea) – C18 coursed stone rubble cottage
11 and outbuilding – probably C18 and C17
12 – early C18 cottage (date stone 1724)
14 – C18 cottage
16 – C17 cottage

Love's Hill
Stone 260 yds E of Castor House – poss medieval cross shaft

Manor Farm Lane
Manor Farmhouse – C17, refashioned early C19

Mill Road
Castor Mill – early C19 water mill and house
Windmill 150 yds E of Mill – early-mid C19 brick tower mill

Milton Park
Milton Hall – from 1594
Stables – 1690
Stables and Smithy – 1720
Harness House – late C18
Old Laundry – c 1700 brew-house
Kitchen Garden Walls – late C18
The Dairy – C18/19, with Roman pavement from Castor
Orangery – c 1791
Kennels – prob 1767 – reused med material
Kennels House – early C19
Lodge – c 1791
The Ferry House – C17
Park Farm House – mid C19 cottage

Peterborough Road

Castor House – early C18 house
Castor House gates, piers and walls – late C17
Home Farmhouse – probably C17
Barn SW of Home Farm – probably C18
L-shape range, stables, barn, brewhouse (SE of No 6) – C17/C18
8(Three Chimneys) – C17 range of cottages
Royal Oak – 1727
26 – C17 cottages
St Kyneburgha Church – Saxo-Norman Church
Church Wall – C18, some medieval body stones as caps.
The Cedars – early C18 house, façade early C19
Mounting Block W of Cedars – 1708
Fitzwilliam Arms – C17 restored
36(The Elms) – 1769
Stables NE of 36 – early C19
Village Farmhouse – C15/16 origin
Village Farmhouse Dovecot - C18
3(Dragon House) – C17/18 house
5(Hollies Farmhouse) – early C19
Hollies Barn – early/mid C19
17/17a – probably early C18
Barn to S of 17 – C18 stone
Barn to SW of 17 – C18 stone
23 – early C18 house
37 – early C18 house
Village Hall – former school 1829
Barn S of Village Hall – C18 stone
43 and 45 – early C18 house
47(Old Smithy) – probably early C17

Ferry Meadows

Ferry Bridge – 1716

Splash Lane

2 – C18 cottage
4(Willow End) – date stone 1652, rest early C18

Stocks Hill

1 – 1803 stone house
2(The Old Rectory) – late C17, refashioned c 1860
The Old Rectory Garden Wall - two sections of Roman foundations in C19 wall

APPENDIX TWENTY ONE

Castor Census Analysis 1881

It is only in the 19th century, with the introduction of a ten-yearly census of the whole country, that we are first able to get a complete picture of who lived in the village, and what they did. This procedure has been going on for almost 200 years, but I have chosen just one year, as an example, to get an idea of what was happening here just over 120 years ago.

According to the 1881 Census there were 1,321 residents at the time of the Census, of whom 765 were born in the village. This total includes 36 men and 51 women who gave their age as over 65. Other adults, aged 21 and over, were more equally divided between men and women, 288 men and 292 women. When we look at the group of residents between the ages of 5 and 20, there are 248 boys and 205 girls, and the infants were equally divided, 100 boys and 101 girls.

When we try and follow what all these people did for a living, the most notable fact to emerge is the conclusion that the majority of residents gave their occupation as 'Agricultural Labourer.' This classification includes both men and women, as well as young boys who could have only just left school. What the women did who were so described is not clear, although many women gave as their occupation, such jobs as, charwoman, domestic servant or general servant.

Many of the other activities are very similar to what we have come to expect in our village in the twenty first century. We read about women who describe themselves as, Housekeeper, shopkeeper, needlewoman, nurse-maid, washer-woman, laundress, governess and seamstress. I was very impressed by the lady who described herself as 'Gentle woman.' There were various servants living at the same address.

The villages at the time of this Census must have been quite self sufficient. There was no need to dash off by train to Peterborough when something was needed. There was somebody in the village who could do all that was necessary. Here are some of the services available in the village:- florist, sewing mistress, shoemaker, tailor, nurse, boarding school mistress, slater, carpenter, wheelwright, bricklayer, blacksmith and stone-mason.

There must have been a good supply of shops. I can find Grocer, Butcher, Baker, together with several others who are simply described as 'Shopkeeper'. There was one entry which made me realise that some aspects of the village never change. There is an entry for a 'Letter Carrier (female).' There are others which we no longer need, such as Station-master, Porter, Plate-layer, Engine cleaner.

Other occupations listed inform us quite clearly the nature if the Parish in which we live. Very many of the residents give their occupations which tell us at once the substance of the economy of the village, and its reliance on the folk who work on the land. Over ninety residents give their occupation as 'agricultural labourer'. These include both men and women, and are people of all ages. Some have ages which indicate that, in modern times, they would still be at school. Others are still working at an age when more modern labourers would have already been classified as pensioners.

The reliance of the community on agricultural workers appears again when we find residents whose occupations are:- Huntsman, Food boiler, Whipper-in, Second huntsman and Groom. The corn milling industry seems to have been fairly active. I have found two people described as Millers, one as a Journeyman Miller and another is recorded as a Miller employing five men. It was a little surprising to find that the Census records, not only what job each man held, but also how many men he was able to employ.

This last information became most noticeable when we study the farming industry. The Census is not just a list of names and addresses. Every farmer has listed in his entry, how many acres of land he works and also how many workers he employs. The largest farm was 600 acres owned by Thomas Carter who employed 16 labourers and 6 boys. One of the Marholm farms was 320 acres and employed 11 men and 4 boys. The number of employees does not always relate to the acreage of the holding. A small farm in Castor, owned by a woman, was only 17 acres. She employed one man who was also a coal merchant.

The most notable difference between Castor of 1881 and the Castor of today comes to light when we find that there is listed a Rector of Castor, a Rector of Marholm, a C of E Clergyman in Sutton, and another listed as a 'Visitor'. Another difference between 'then and now' is in the matter of place of birth. In 1881 the majority of residents were born in the village. I wonder what the percentage is today.

Douglas Gillam
Douglas Gillam lives in Castor near his daughter, grandchildren and great-grandsons. A former head-master, he was a prisoner-of-war during the World War II, having been shot down over Germany.

APPENDIX TWENTY TWO

GAZETTEER 1849
CASTOR AILSWORTH SUTTON UPTON & EXTRACTS 1849 NASSABURGH HUNDRED.
From 'History, Gazetteer, and Directory of Northamptonshire etc' William Whelan & Co
Publ Whittaker & Co MDCCCXLIX (1849ad), p 696
Lord of the Manor is Earl Fitzwilliam under lease from Dean & Chapter Rectory living worth c£1000pa

PARISHES, &c.	Acres	Houses	POPULATION			Rateable
			Male	Female	Total	Value
Castor et al 1801AD					815	
Castor et al 1831AD					1198	
Castor et al 1841AD					1313	
Castor 1849AD }	7,020	135	380	336	716}	£6850
Ailesworth, *hamlet* }		76	178	185	363}	
Sutton, *chapelry* }		24	57	64	121}	
Upton, *chapelry* }		23	61	52	113}	

(440 Acres in common(land))

Householders in 1849
Marked 1 are at Ailesworth, 2 at Upton, and 3 at Sutton
Fitzwilliam, The Rt.Hon.Earl, Milton House
Milton, The Hon. Viscount, Milton House
Fitzwilliam, The Hon. Geo, Wentworth, Milton House
Almond Mr. John
Andrews Rev. Geo., curate
1 Ball John, joiner
Bodmin Jph., B., surgeon
Brown Rt., shoemaker
Burbidge Manton, harns mkr
Callow John Thos., miller
Coates Wm., schoolmaster
Chapel Saml., blacksmith
Cox Joseph, tailor
Cook William, joiner
2 Dickins Wm., beer retailer
Elmond Mrs. Mary Ann
1 Goodyer Sarah, shopkeeper
Hales John, stonemason
Hales Mrs. Sarah
Hordern Wm., schoolmaster
Henson John, whitesmith
1 Hobbs Rt., beer retailer
Horden Wm., letter receiver
Holmes Eliz., shopkeeper
Glithero Eliz., vict., Fitzwilliam Arms
Mapperson John, shopkeeper

Murton Rev. W., M.A., curate
1 Newborn John, blacksmith
O'Brian Alderman R., Esq,
Oliver John, shoemaker
Panter George, shoemaker
Pearson Wm., tailor
Setchell martin, butcher
Stanger Frs., shoemaker
Sharpe Chas., baker, &c.
Smart Ed., blacksmith
Smith Eliz., vict., Wheat Sheaf
1 Stokes William, butcher
Sullivan Caroline, schoolmrs.
Shelston R. vt. George & Dragon
Tebbutt Mr. Thomas
Turner Thomas, baker
Wright John, Esq.

Farmers & Graziers
2 Almond Harriet
Berridge William
Callow William
1 Carter Thomas
Dickins Peter
Fitzjohn Samuel
3 Hopkinson William
Mann Geo., (& butcher)
Marriott Richard
Marriott Richard, jun.
Nix Thos., Manor House
1 Popple Joseph
3 Palmer Charles
1 Sismey Edward
1 Smith John Thomas
Smith Sarah
Smith Thomas
2 Tebbutt Jospeh
2 Tebbutt John
2 Wright Rt., Lodge

MARHOLM EXTRACTS
From "History, Gazetteer, and Directory of Northamptonshire etc" William Whelan & Co
Publ Whittaker & Co MDCCCXLIX (1849ad), p 706

PARISHES, &c.	Acres	Houses	POPULATION			Rateable
			Male	Female	Total	Value
Marholm 1801 AD					109	
Marholm 1849 AD	1,790	34	103	94	197	2000
Glebe Land is 41 acres						

Directory in 1849
Rev Jas.W. Harman, M.A., rector
Mr Thos. Mann,
Rt. Allen, blacksmith
H. Boyer, woodranger
Thos. Gibbs, bailiff to the Earl Fitzwilliam,
Wm. Marston, vict., *Fitzwilliam Arms,*
Farmers:
Henry Lincoln,
Robert Mann,
Wm. Mann,
Jane Vergette,
John Wright,
James Wright.

APPENDIX TWENTY THREE

GAZETTEER 1874
CASTOR AILSWORTH SUTTON UPTON EXTRACTS
1874 NASSABURGH HUNDRED
From "History, Gazetteer, and Directory of Northamptonshire etc" Publ Whittaker & Co 1874ad, p652

PARISHES, &c.	Acres	Houses	POPULATION			Rateable
			Male	Female	Total	Value
Castor	4797				680	£5686
Ailsworth	1324	87			394	£1419
Sutton	888				99	
Upton	1180				107	£1507

Castor Directory - Householders
(Marked 1 reside at Ailesworth)
Fitzwilliam, The Hon Mrs G. Wentworth, Milton House
Almond Mr John
Andrew Rev. Wm. M.A. vicar of Upton & rural dean, The Elms
1 Ball Mrs Catherine, coal mer.
Beresford Rev John James, B.D., rector
Bodman Jospeh Baker, surgn.
1 Boyall William, cottager
1 Briggs William, wheelwright
Carter Geo. huntsman, Milton
Chappell Samuel, blacksmith
Christmas Thomas, shopkpr.
Cooke John, carpenter
1 Coulson John, cottager
Darby John Thos. wheelwright
Darby William, shopkeeper
1 Drake Mrs. Mary, cottager
1 Drake Robert, cottager
1 Ellis William, cottager
1 FitzJohn Thomas, shopkpr.
Fox James, tailor
Fox William, annuitant
Freeman Richard, miller
1 Gaskell Mr John Robert
Gibbons Thomas, machineman
Glass Henry, nationl. schoolmr.
Goodyer Mrs Emma, grocr.&bkr.
Hales John, stonem & builder
Hart John, carpenter
1 Hobbs George, beerh. Barley Mow
Horden Wm. Parish clerk & P.-O.
Hunt John, baker & shopkpr.
Jaques George, gamekeeper, Milton Ferry
Lee Geo, house steward, Milton
1 Newborn Wm. blacksmith
Oliver Mrs. Catherine, shoemkr.
Panter Edward, shoemaker
Panter Mrs Elizab. shoemaker
Popple Samuel, vict. Fitz-William Arms and baker
Samworth mrs Elizab. butcher
Sewell John, cottager
Sharpe Mrs jane. shopkpr. & bkr.
1 Sharpe Robt. Geo. grocr&bkr.
1 Smart Edward, blacksmith
Smith Charles & Letitia, vict. Royal Oak
Smith Mrs Sarah, The Grove
1 Smith Thos. Hill, vict. Wheat Sheaf, and contractor

Stanger James, shoemaker
Sykes Alf. Archtct. Milton Ferry
Upchurch John, vict. George & Dragon
Warwarr- , butcher
Warraker Jno. gardener, Milton
White F.A. Esq., Castor House
Wilson James, beerhouse
Wootton Wm. tailor & shopkpr.
Wright Mrs Mary, Church Close
Yeoman John, Esq. land agent, Milton Ferry

Farmers & Graziers
Berridge William
Callow William
1 Carter Thomas
Carter Thomas, jun.
Darby John Thomas
Dickins Mrs Ann
Fitzjohn Richard
Fitzjohn Richard, jun.
1 Howson Francis
Hunt Mrs Frances
Longfoot Richard
Marriott Jon. Ths. Bellsize Ldg.
Popple Joseph
1 Popple William
Sewell John
1 Sismey Edmund Hilsworth

Sutton And Upton Directory.
(Marked 1 reside at Upton)
1 Almond John, farmer, Upton Lodge
1 Dickens Mrs Sophia, shopkeeper
Hopkinson Mrs Mary Ann, Manor House
Murton Rev. Wm. M.A. vicar
Palmer Mrs Sarah, farmer
Pauley Samuel, shopkeeper
1 Tebbutt Mrs John (Mary Ann), farmer, Manor House
1 Tebbutt Mrs Wm. (Mary A.), farmer,

MARHOLM EXTRACTS GAZETTEER 1874
From "History, Gazetteer, and Directory of Northamptonshire etc" Publ Whittaker & Co 1874ad, p663

NASSABURGH HUNDRED.

PARISHES, &c.	Acres	Houses	POPULATION			Rateable
			Male	Female	Total	Value
Marholm	1368				147	£1774

Marholm Directory
Householders
Blacker Rev Robert Shapland Carew, M.A. rector
Boyer H. Wood, steward and farmer
Parish William, blacksmith
Stimson Mrs Mary, vict. *Fitzwilliam Arms*
Wright James, cottager.
Farmers:
Allott George, *Willows*
Mann George
Mann William (and auctionr)

Picture Gallery

The benefice is unusual in having a picture of most of the Rectors from 1613 to date. This is, of course in part because from 1613 until 1851 the Bishops of Peterborough were the Rectors, and thus sufficiently distinguished to have their portraits painted. Here is a selection of some the portraits; the rest may be seen in the vestry at Castor, having recently been refurbished in memory of John Gillam. Copies of portraits of the two of Bishop-Rectors, Thomas Dove and John Towers, are in Chapter 26.

Thomas White, Rector from 1685 until 1691, when out of loyalty to King James II, he resigned rather than take the oath of allegiance to William of Orange.

Frederick Dee, Rector from 1634 to 1639.

William Lloyd, Rector from 1679 to 1685.

John Hinchcliffe, Rector from 1769 to 1794.

Richard Terrick, Rector from 1757 to 1754.

John Parsons, Rector from 1813 to 1819. Note Peterborough Cathedral in the background.

Herbert Marsh, Rector from 1819 to 1839. Note that he is sitting in the same chair as John Parsons.

George Davys, the last Bishop-Rector, Rector from 1839 to 1851. He was also at one stage tutor to Queen Victoria.

George Andrews, who was originally the Curate, was the first Rector since 1613 not to be the Bishop of Peterborough simultaneously. He was Rector from 1851 to 1864 and was responsible for the foundation of Castor School and building the School Hall still used today by the school.

Some People and Places

Early Days of one Village Family

While many people were employed in farming or ancillary trades, others were employed in service, in the police force, and as landlords of public houses and so on. One such family was the Pell family. William Pell, with his wife Fanny, was the landlord of the George and Dragon at Castor before 1914. They still have descendants in the village today, Bruce Pell, and both Peter and Evelyn Chitty. One of William Pell's sons, Edgar joined the police force. He was to be the father of Len Pell, a churchwarden at Castor, and grandfather of Bruce Pell. One of William Pell's daughters, Emma (born 1889) married Alfred Gubbins, at one stage a foot man at Milton. Emma and Alfred's daughter is now Evelyn Chitty. This collection of photographs shows some aspects of the life of this family from the turn of the 20th century, until the Second World War.

William and Fanny Pell, landlords of the George and Dragon.

One of William Pell's daughters, Emma, married Alfred Gubbins, (left) born 1888, here shown as a footman in livery before 1914 at Milton Hall. The man in the centre is the butler Mr Pullen.

Edgar Pell, son of William Pell, in the Yeomanry during the First World War. Note the carbine in its saddle holster. He later joined the police.

Two of William Pell's daughters Gladys and Elsie in front of the George and Dragon before 1914.

Even house staff on big estates had to be prepared to turn their hand to any job when necessary, including in the stables and acting as loaders and beaters on shoots (pre-1914).

During the First World War the George and Dragon was also run by William and Fanny Pell ran as a convalescent home for wounded soldiers. This photograph is taken in the grounds of the pub; part of Castor House can be seen in the background.: (l-r) back, 1 Gladys Pell,3 Elvina ('Vina') Pell, 5 Alfred Gubbins husband of Emma Pell, 6 Edgar Pell, 7 Elsie Pell. Front William and Fanny Pell with convalescing soldiers.

Edgar Pell (grandfather of Bruce Pell) as a policeman.

Dora, Elsie and 'Vina' Pell outside their house in Ailsworth.

Shooting party at Milton: beaters and loaders; the man fifth from the right is Alfred Gubbins, husband of Emma Pell (pre-1914).

William Pell's daughters 'Vina' and Emma . They are dressed in the special clothes worn by workers in the munitions factory at Baker Perkins during the First World War. Vina later married farmer Jack Bettles.

Elsie, Vina and Gladys Pell.

Alma Glover and Evelyn Gubbins (now Chitty) at Hunstanton 1931; both their mothers were daughters of William and Fanny Pell.

School Photo: 1929: (l-r) back: Hilda Parker, ?, ?, ?, Alec Jakes, Evelyn Gubbins, Miss Ambrose; middle: Harry Hill, Peter Daley, next four unknown; front: Doris Ward, ?, ?, ?, Joan Nix, Joyce Fisher.

Scenes from the Summer Festival of St Kyneburgha of Castor.

This double celebration of both our Patron Saint, St Kyneburgha of Castor , and our village community takes places every summer in early July, consisting of a barbecue and dance on the Friday night, the Church Fete on the Saturday afternoon, and a Festival Mass, at which the church banners are decorated with flowers and ribbons, and carried in procession to the church. More photographs of the St Kyneburgha Summer Festival Weekend appear in the colour section.

Julie Taylor, who chairs the Church Social Committee and organizes much of the weekend, with farmer Jim Wood checks the hog-roast will be ready for the Friday Night barbecue and dance.

Kevin Daley, with his sculpture of the Lady who started it all St Kyneburgha- before it was placed in Castor Church for its dedication in July 2000.

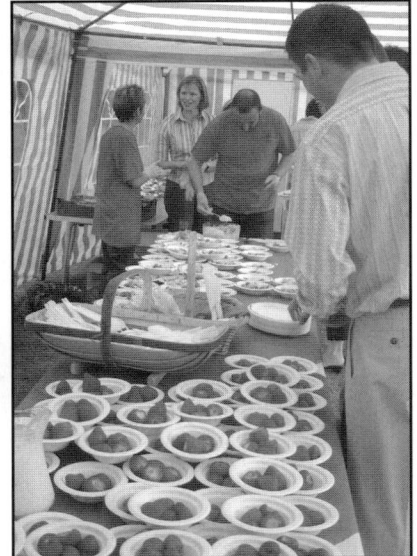

Alison Brown and Wendy Dominguez serving at the salad and pudding table on the Friday Night.

People gathering on the School Field Castor for the Friday Night, while the band warms up.

The weekend involves hard work by many people; two of the stalwarts are Ian Sheldon and Phillip Brown, with their presentations given to them in thanks for all they have done, AD2003.

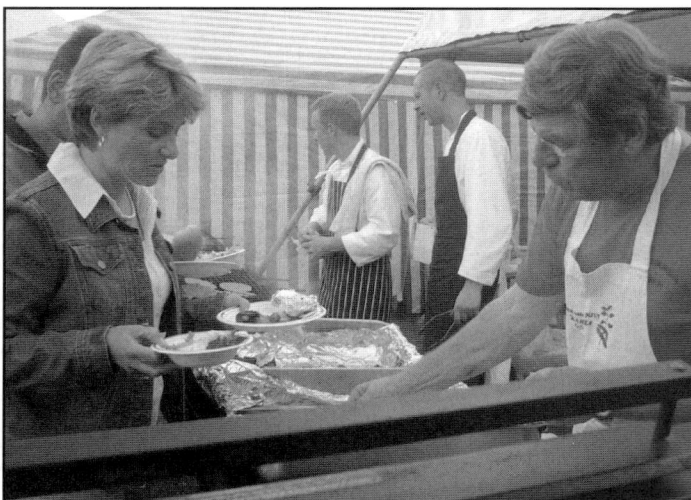

Helen Jarvis being served by 'JT' Taylor.

Some families picnic on the grass, others sit in the marquee for their supper: in the middle Sue Chambers, Anne Armstrong, Jack Armstrong, Robert Dickens, and Leslie Rigby.

358

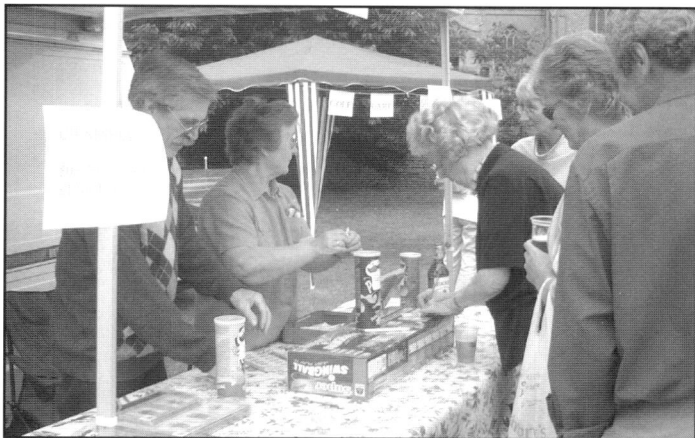
Brian and Bridget Goode at their stall on the Saturday Fete.

Afternoon tea in the marquee at the Saturday Afternoon Fete: sitting at the centre table are Jim and Patsy wood.

'JT' Taylor on duty again, now at the Fete; this time about to serve Steve Reed, the Tower Captain.

Judith Dickens serving at the barbecue.

Bruce Pell runs the raffle with his Aunts, Barbara Osborne nee Sharpe and Christine Sharpe.

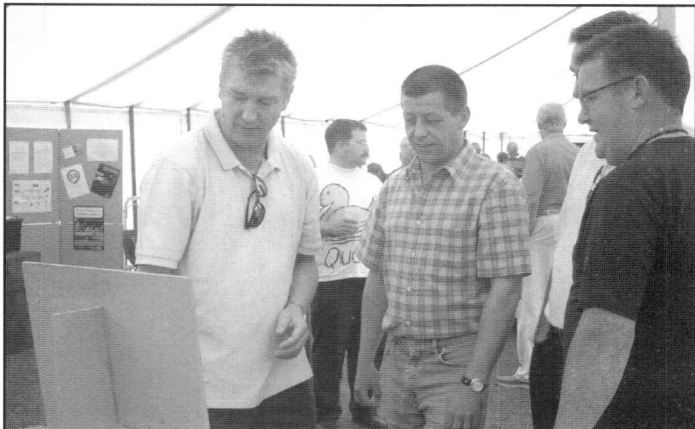
Steve Grys, Mick O'Boyle and John Elson at the Card Table.

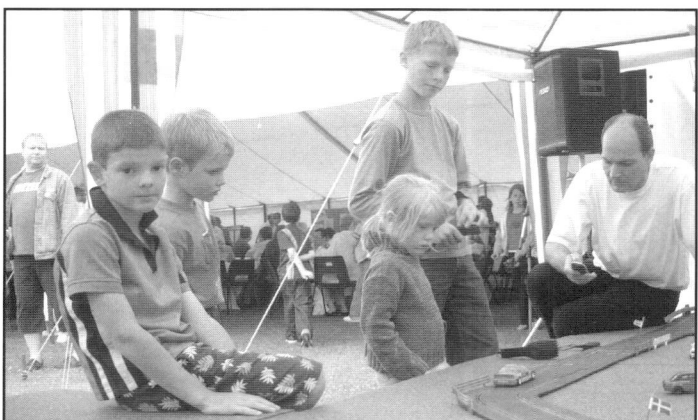
Gary Elliott running the Scalextrix stand; the children are Ross Elliott, Helena Brown and Adam Brown.

The Art Exhibition in the Cedar Centre on Sunday Afternoon.

Sutton Golden Jubilee Celebrations 3 June 2002

Celebrations for the Queen's Golden Jubilee took the form of a Street party and a Barn Dance in the evening.

The Barn Dance in the barn at Manor Farmhouse.

Street Party In Manor Road; Manor Farmhouse in background.

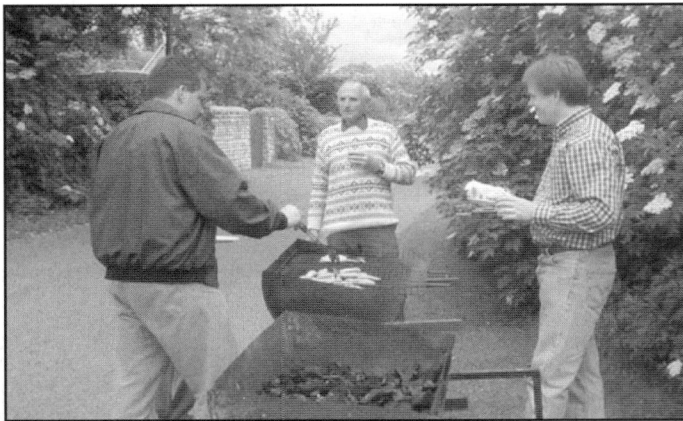

The Jubilee barbecue at Sutton

The Jubilee barbecue at Sutton

The beacon is lit.

The Barn Dance in the barn at Manor Farmhouse.

The band at the Barn Dance.

Games and Guys in the field.

Some Village People and Places Then and Now.

Augusta Stevenson, born 1871 in Ailsworth, died in Sutton 1934, daughter of Joseph Stevenson a plate-layer and later Lay Reader at Sutton Church.

Kenneth Stevenson born 1873 in Ailsworth, Augusta's brother, outside his house in Sutton.

War-time Wedding: First World War Castor Church: note officer on left saluting bride and groom.

B Squadron Northants Imperial Yeomanry camp at Milton 1906.

War-time Wedding: Second World War Marholm Church: (l-r): John Waterworth (Marholm farmer), Lt Bertrand (French officer, groom, later killed while flying his Spitfire in France), Kathleen Darby (bride), Noel Darby, Betty Darby.

Shooting Castor Hangland: 2nd from left A Drury, end right Frank Morton of Scotsmans Lodge Farm 1930s.

Post-war Wedding: Party at Ferry Lodge 1949, having married at Castor Church: (l-r) George Stannion, Rev Tom Adler, George Dunham (groom), Betty Sherborne (bride), George Sherborne, Iris Sherborne.

Wedding at Castor Church 1950s: Graham Taylor and Janet Harris.

Wedding at Castor Church 1999: (l-r) Jane Weaver, Paul Sharpe (groom), Mandy John (bride), Simon Clarke; front: Samantha Dunham, Sophie Clarke, Zoe Clarke, Molly Beale.

Evacuees at the Old Mill Castor during World War Two.

Catherine Hensman nee Wade with daughter Mary at Village Farm Castor.

Jack McNaughten, actor and resident of Castor.

Joe Dudley with plough horses at Home Farm Castor – Joe worked for the Poll family.

Castor boys in the yard of what is now the Old Smithy: Jim Harris, Jack Cook, Bill Harris 1920s.

Margaret and Jim White in February 1945. Margaret was born in Sutton.

Margaret and Jim White re-visit Heath House Sutton, where Margaret lived as a child.

Brownies 1959.

Ferry Lodge, beside the old A47, the day the bulldozers moved in. Part of the house was rebuilt on the hill above the new by-pass.

Milton Ferry, the route is cleared for the new A47 by-pass.

George Sharpe, a former chairman of Ailsworth Parish Council 1964.

The Norman stone cut with chevrons, used as a support for the bresummer at 1 Lover's Lane Sutton, was presumably taken out of the church during the Victorian restoration.

Graham Fox of Sutton at a ploughing competition at Baston.

Looking North under the old road bridge over the now disused railway line at Sutton; the village pump is on the right.

Robert Jarvis of Home Farm Marholm, with his Longhorn cow 'Maydencroft Angela' and Longhorn bull-calf 'Marholm Nero'; Champions at the East of England Show 1992.

'Gladdy' Craythorne, who works at the Hollies Farm, haymaking 2001.

The 'Ronnie Baker and Quentin Rigby' float during the Millennium parade Castor 2000.

Castor Village Hall is the setting for a wide range of social events: here it is the Burns' Night of 2001. The honorary Scotsman for the night 'addressing the haggis' is Bertie Fitzjohn, on his right his wife Sharon.

Fig 28. Michael Longfoot and Allen Herbert, both Upton farmers in their time, at tea in Lyn Bell's 'Open Garden' 2002.

Julie Taylor, who chairs the Castor Church Social Committee, also, with her team, provides support for other village events, on this occasion the Burns' Night.

Lyn Bell nee Hornsby of Upton opens her beautiful garden in aid of Upton Church.

Marholm Lodges, back view. The house on the left is the Keeper's Cottage.

Christingle at Castor: the nativity tableau, Annabel Martin as Mary 2002.

The old North side of Top Lodge Farm Upton, probably Elizabethan in origin; old maps show that there was a toll-gate here in the 18th century.

Thatchers working at 'Three Chimneys' Castor. This house was at one stage three cottages and more recently the home of Dr John Eades and his wife Ann.

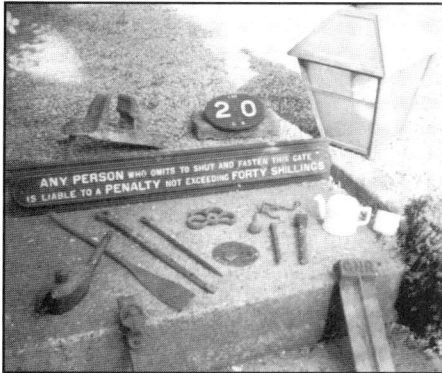

Items of railway memorabilia found by Keith Garrett around his house, the old Station-master's house at Sutton (Heath House).

Hoss' Baker of Marholm, captain of the 'Mighty men of Marholm' winners of the Evening Telegraph Tug-of-War competition.

The Walker family outside their house in AD 2000. (l-r): Sophie, Emily, Jo, Steve, Ben. This is one of a series of photographs taken of every household in the villages of Castor and Ailsworth outside their homes as a Millennium record (Photo: T Blackmore).

The outbuildings of 'The Elms' now converted by Vic and Sandra Griffin as part of their home and garden.

This isolated barn, its Collyweston roof gone, was the barn when Ramshill was a farm at Marholm.

The path to Sutton Church, with its lovely Spring flowers, was restored for the Millennium by Michael Rose of Sutton.

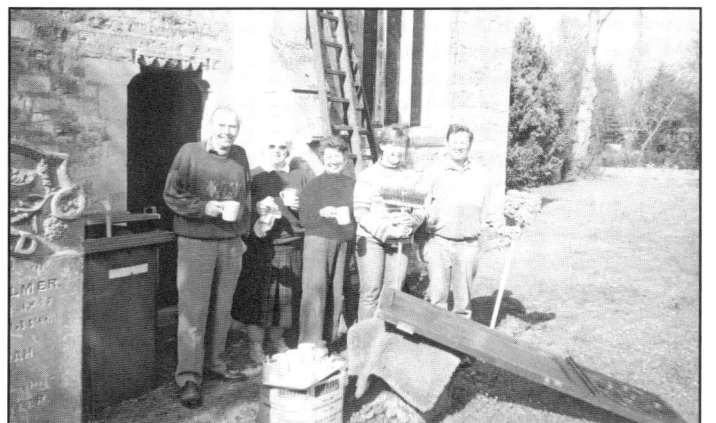

A cleaning day at Sutton Church. (l-r): Bob Cattrall (churchwarden), Susan Custance, Marilyn Gardner, Alison Maddigan, Clive Gardner (churchwarden) 2004.

The ancient meadows between Sutton and the River Nene.

Sutton Church from the South, a view not often seen. The section at the right (south-east) was possibly the Chantry Chapel of St Giles.

'Robin Hodd and Little John'. Two ancient marker stones in a field between the old A47 and the River Nene at Ferry Meadow.

Houses on Church Hill Castor; No 11, and behind it 'Hanover House' once the home of Edmund Artis.

Old byres beside the Village Hall Castor.

The gate in the wall of the 'Old Rectory' was probably inserted in 1851, when the Glebe Farm became the Rectory; note the section of old barn wall alongside the path.

The other side of the gate: Jackie Cook Chairman of the 'Friends' of Castor Church with her dog 'Whisky'.

A view of Vine House, the original rectory from certainly before 1634, taken from Castor churchyard.

Not often seen in photographs, the North side of Castor Church, including the North Aisle Chapel.

Castor Church West End. The central part was the nave of the original Norman Church. It shows three different styles of window: top middle Norman, right Early English, lower centre Decorated styles.

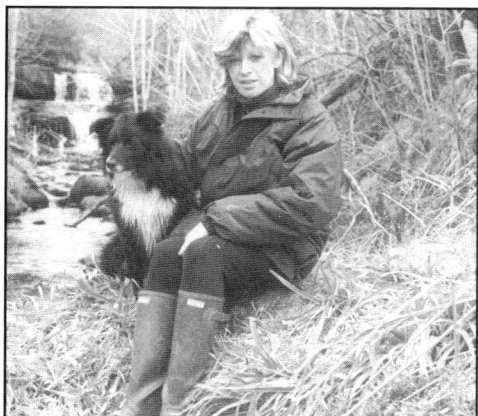

Jackie Elliott nee Woodward, born in Castor, breeds Border Collies.

View of Marholm Church across the meadow from the South, Home Farm can just be seen to the left.

Marholm People outside the Old Almshouses 1945: Michael Hill (brother of John Hill) in pram, David Bates in 'wellies'.

Marholm People outside the Old Almshouses 2004: (l-r) Jane Jarvis of Belsize Farm and daughter Isabelle, Freda Shimmin, John Hill from an old Marholm family.

Working beside the 'Old School House Marholm: Stephen Weston, born in the parish, with dogs Bran and Jet; behind is a section of the converted outbuildings of Manor Farm.

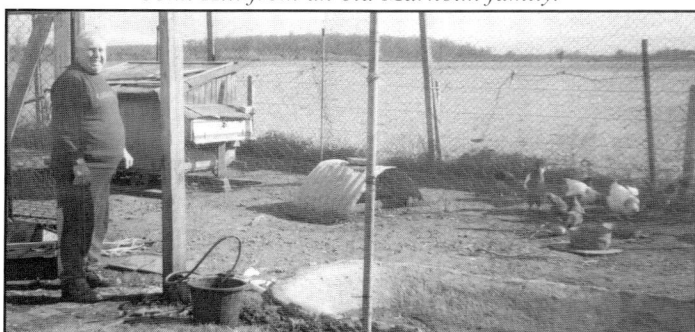

Colin 'Jagger' Jarvis from a Marholm farming family, with some of his many hens on his small-holding on Walton Road Marholm. Muckland Wood is on the horizon.

'Fergus' the bull of top Lodge Farm Upton with his owners Peter and Claire Harris.

Tony Evans as Tower Captain (back left) with his first band of ringers.

A medieval body-stone on the North side of Castor Church. Many other such stones have been for capping the churchyard wall.

Stewart Wood and Gladdy Craythorne shearing at the Hollies 1993.

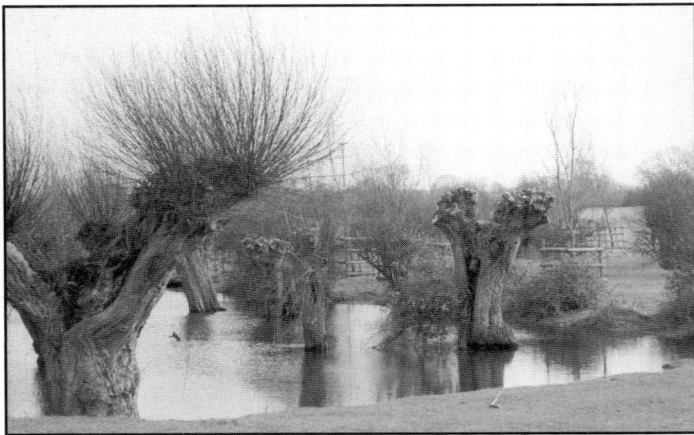

Pollarded willows in the meadows between the railway line and the River Nene.

An Upton view looking East towards Manor Farm

People at Noel Darby's farm sale: (l-r): Peter Jarvis, Robin Morton, Will Craven, Stan Jarvis, George Morton 2004.

End of an era. Noel Darby's farm sale in the field beside Marholm Farm 2004. The two men in the middle are Stewart Wood and Gladdy Craythorne.

Brown family group, wife and children of Sam Brown. (Farm bailiff at Sutton). Ada Mary 1868-1917, Leonard 1878-1959, Amos 1865-1938, Mary Ann nee Moyses (wife of Sam Brown) 1838-1918.
(Photos provided by Mrs Enid Williams, Sam Brown's great grand daughter).

Joseph Stevenson, born Castor 1834, died Sutton 1894, a foreman plate-layer, lay reader and churchwarden lived at 4 Nene Way Sutton.

Leonard Brown in RFC uniform, World War One.

John Harris at the Ferry, with his grandchildren. (l-r) Frank Harris, John Houghton; front: Arthur and Charlie Harris (in dresses).

Billy Want of Castor driving a steam engine from the Gibbons yard. Billy's step-father was Gilbert Gibbons, and he worked in the yard on leaving school.

Jarvis family of Marholm wedding group at Belsize. Front (l-r): third from left Faith Jarvis, 4th Charles Watts, 5th Laurie Annie Watts, 6th Caroline Rose Watts (bride), 7th Cyril John Jarvis (groom), 8th Emma Jarvis, 9th George Jarvis (with Ernie Jarvis on his knee). The girl in front is Margaret Watts. (1926)

Rogation Sunday Procession in Church Hill Castor beside Vic Griifinís shop 1992; Eric Jinks (crucifer), John Harper (rector), Rev Gordon Clarke is wearing a panama.

Three horsemen in the yard of the Harris farm in the 1920s (now the Old Smithy Castor).

South face of Water Newton Church tower. The zig-zag moulding above the bell louvres arch came originally from the Norman chancel of Castor Church, and was moved and re-used here when the chancel at Castor was rebuilt in 1220.

View of Manor Farm Upton from the South-east 1920s.

A pony and trap waiting outside the Fitzwilliam Arms Castor 1920s.

Jim Thompson-Bell MM beside his tank, North-west Europe 1944. Jim now lives in Ailsworth.

Charlie Harris and Sam Catmull the blacksmith (before World War Two).

George Adams, Huntsman of the Fitzwilliam (Milton) Hounds, with his hounds at Castor Church Summer Fete.

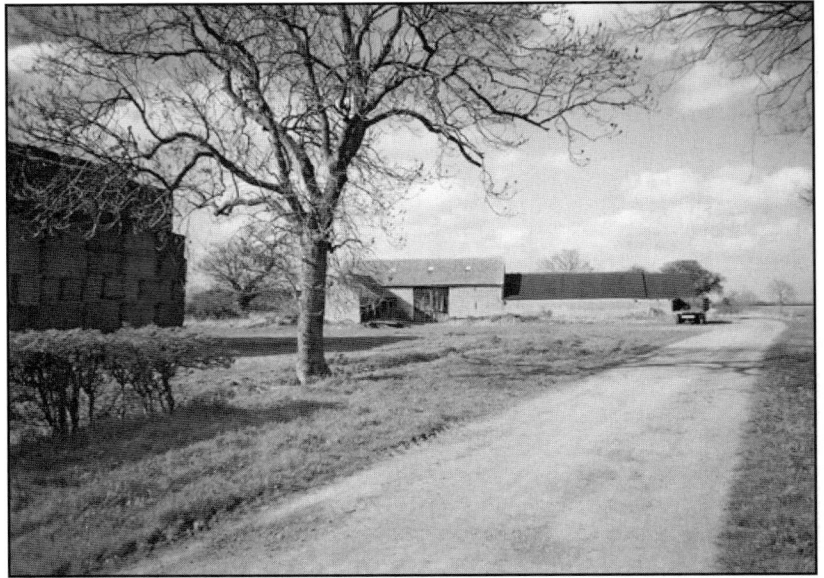

Tebbut's Barn, beside the Barn Road Upton. This track is shown on a 1582 map as 'Sowthe Lane'. The Tebbut family were tenants at Manor Farm Upton from the 18th century to the 20th century, being Milton's longest serving tenant farmers. The Barn Road clearly replaced the former Roman road King Street (a few hundred yards to the East) as the main thoroughfare early on, certainly before the 16th century.

Sheds at the isolated Tebbut's Barn Upton

The entrance to the converted yard at Manor Farm Marholm. The former outbuildings are now attractive cottages.

Friendly faces in the pasture beside Home Farm Marholm.

In 1536, the village constable in Upton was Hugh Style; in 1762, the village constable in Castor was Robert Wright. PC Richard Weaver, shown here, is our last village constable for the five parishes. In the last few years the police house has been sold, Richard is leaving and is not to be replaced. We now police ourselves.

The 'Gerbs': A new village band, this time a rock band called the "Gerbs", playing at a party in the Cedar Centre 2004.

St. Georges' Day dinner 2004, Sitting down for dinner.

St. Georges' Day dinner 2004, the Village Hall is prepared.

St. Georges' Day dinner 2004, The party's over - time to go home

A Web of Village Relationships

This shows the descendants of Charles Sharpe and other village family groups connected by marriage or descent. Those marked* still live in one of our villages.

Charles Sharpe=Sarah Savage

Robert Sharpe=Ellen Freer
1833-1892

Harry Sharpe=Mary Anne Fox
1869-1947

Joe* & Rene* Woodward
Jackie* & Gary Elliott*
Dan*, Steffi*, Alex* & Ross* Elliott

Betty* & Billy* Want

Harry = Nellie Longfoot Sharpe | Beatrice Sharpe | Cecil=Ethel Sharpe Mayes | Ethel = Charles Sharpe Woodward | Frances Sharpe Chappell | Leonard = Maud Chappell Sharpe | Christina Sharpe | Kathleen = George Sharpe Jarvis

Roland Longfoot | Claude = Margaret Sharpe Bell* | Vera = Len Sharpe Pell | Barbara = Harold Sharpe* Osborne | Brian = Christine Sharpe Freeman* | Paul = Mandy | John*

Colin* = Janet* Longfoot

Bruce Pell* | Jennifer = Clifford Osborne Goode | Paul = Mandy Sharpe* John* | Lisa Jarvis

Michael Longfoot*
David Longfoot*

Roy Coulson*
Harry Coulson*
Brian* & Bridget Goode*
Rene Foster*

Tom * Sharpe
Samantha Dunham

Keith and Heather Sharpe*

Peter & Evelyn Chitty*

Barry and Anna Hornsby*
Peter & Jenny Hammond*
Mick & Lyn Bell*
Adrian & Chris Bell*
Jim Marsh*

Dick & Jean Jarvis* Stan & Fay Jarvis* Peter & Vi Jarvis* Toby & Mary* Jarvis
Trevor & Jane Jarvis*
Melissa & Isabelle Jarvis*
Rachel Gimn*
Colin Jarvis*
John & Gina Hill*

Harry, Joe and Annie Jarvis*
Andrew & Helen Jarvis*

Eileen Ladds*, Marcus & Sarah Ladds & Charlie*
Martin & Helen Jarvis

Index

The Index refers to the chapter texts and does not include captions to pictures and the Appendices.